THE TWO-PARTY SYSTEM
IN THE UNITED STATES

VAN NOSTRAND POLITICAL SCIENCE SERIES

Editor

FRANKLIN L. BURDETTE
University of Maryland

LONDON, K.—*How Foreign Policy Is Made*

PLISCHKE, E.—*Conduct of American Diplomacy*

DIXON, R. G., JR., and PLISCHKE, ELMER—*American Government: Basic Documents and Materials*

SPROUT, HAROLD and MARGARET—*Foundations of National Power*, 2nd Ed.

LANCASTER, LANE W.—*Government in Rural America*, 2nd Ed.

JORRIN, M.—*Governments of Latin America*

TORPEY, WILLIAM G.—*Public Personnel Management*

PLISCHKE, ELMER—*International Relations: Basic Documents*

LINEBARGER, P. M. A., DJANG, C., and BURKS, A. W.—*Far Eastern Governments and Politics—China and Japan*, 2nd Ed.

GOODMAN, WILLIAM—*The Two-Party System in the United States*, 2nd Ed.

WATKINS, J. T., IV, and ROBINSON, J. W.—*General International Organization: A Source Book*

SWARTZ, WILLIS G.—*American Governmental Problems*

BAKER, BENJAMIN—*Urban Government*

DILLON, CONLEY H., LEIDEN, CARL, and STEWART, PAUL D.—*Introduction to Political Science*

ZINK, HAROLD, PENNIMAN, HOWARD R., and HATHORN, GUY B.—*American Government and Politics: National, State, and Local*

ZINK, HAROLD—*Modern Governments*

HENDEL, SAMUEL—*The Soviet Crucible: The Soviet System in Theory and Practice*

THE TWO-PARTY SYSTEM IN THE UNITED STATES

WILLIAM GOODMAN

Professor of Political Science
University of Tennessee

SECOND EDITION

D. VAN NOSTRAND COMPANY, INC.

PRINCETON, NEW JERSEY

TORONTO   LONDON

NEW YORK

D. VAN NOSTRAND COMPANY, INC.
120 Alexander St., Princeton, New Jersey (*Principal office*)
24 West 40 Street, New York 18, New York

D. VAN NOSTRAND COMPANY, LTD.
358, Kensington High Street, London, W.14, England

D. VAN NOSTRAND COMPANY (Canada), LTD.
25 Hollinger Road, Toronto 16, Canada

Published simultaneously in Canada by
D. VAN NOSTRAND COMPANY (Canada), LTD.

Library of Congress Catalogue Card No. 60–14393

PRINTED IN THE UNITED STATES OF AMERICA
BY LANCASTER PRESS, INC., LANCASTER, PA.

Preface to the Second Edition

Ideally, it can be hoped that the need for the second edition of this textbook is as apparent as the need, periodically, to review and reconsider the developments of the American party system. The author is entitled to hope. The judgment must be made by the readers.

Events in the last four years have permitted new evaluations and perspectives. The present revision attempts to present these to the extent it is possible to identify some and to extract others from the growing quantity of relevant publications.

A revision, incidentally, permits a reconsideration of emphases as well as rearrangements of material in the process of updating. The basic organization of the data has not been changed but the occasion has been used to improve the discussion in Section III by giving more-deserved attention to organized interest groups. Otherwise, the changes are designed to sharpen the presentation by addition of pictorial material, by extensive rewriting and by expanding the discussion of voting qualifications and nonvoting.

The one element common to both editions is that the errors of commission and omission remain solely those of the author.

W. G.

Knoxville,
June, 1960

Preface to The First Edition

The justification for adding another textbook in the field of political parties in the United States will, the author hopes, be found in three particular features of this volume.

First, the party system is treated as an entity and the sections of the book follow in a sequential order dictated by the interrelations of the phenomena which constitute the system. There can be endless disagreement about the accurate placing of individual pieces of data and about the exact perspective in which all of the data should be seen. The fact remains that the party process flows from the foundations of the system to the methods of internal control and order—called organization; to the bases for appealing to the electorate; to the synthesis of organization and bases in the continuity of elections and campaigning. One result of this treatment of the party process is to rearrange and even reverse some of the familiar sequences of topics. An explicit value of this presentation should be a more accurate following of the circuitous procession of events. The three great areas of the party system represented by Sections II to IV are in reality intermingled, not watertight compartments. In political operations there is an inseparability which not only defies exact description but also is partly lost by the location, identification, and examination of major components.

Second, this book is about two-party politics in the United States. One result of this emphasis is to place minor parties in a less crucial role than they are sometimes given and to cause them to make their appearance at various points throughout the book instead of discussing them *in toto* at only one point. Another result of this emphasis is to deal with what is done and with what does or can happen. If the discussion includes practices or attitudes considered to be immoral, the problem must be attacked elsewhere. This is not a book on morals or ethics. The analyses and descriptions may be attacked for being inaccurate or incomplete. To attack them for being immoral or insensitive to ethical standards is to miss the point. Censure, if it is to be directed toward sin, should be reserved for the sinners not for the reporters of sin. The censure in this case should fall upon followers as well as leaders, average citizens as well as public officials. If the system is sinful, everyone within the system is involved.

Third, the consideration of reforms in the party system, those with apparently far-reaching implications, is reserved for the final section. This method of organization is not dictated primarily by convenience in presenting the material, but largely for the reason the material is not an integral part of the description of the system itself. This discussion would be placed last for another reason. Virtually anyone can point out what he considers to be imperfect or indefensible in the party system. Proposals for making changes need not be based upon either information or understanding. Proposals can be sheer subjective, off-the-cuff pronouncements, since everyone is likely to have his own personal concept of heaven and to be willing to fashion a political and social structure out of the thin air of his own predilections. Presumably, proposals for reform of any basic element of the system will either directly or indirectly affect other elements, and in order that the maximum implications of the reforms can be appreciated, the logical place to discuss them is at the end. Incidentally, taking up reforms separately makes them more unified and comprehensible than would a piecemeal treatment of reforms in connection with each process or practice when it is first introduced.

This book has been an individual effort, but no one writes at any length on any subject without a profound dependence upon his contemporaries and upon those who have preceded him. I am indebted beyond my ability of expression to the many men and women who have turned their minds and energies to the study of government and political parties. Each contribution to the field of inquiry which has helped either to answer questions or to raise more penetrating questions is part of the body of literature to which every reappraisal must return and from which new appraisals must begin. When a writer is also a teacher, he has a special indebtedness to his students, for teachers learn while they are teaching. This book would not have been the same without the stimulation of the classroom.

Personally and directly, I owe much to the editor of this series of publications, Professor Franklin L. Burdette, whose cooperation has been gracious and whose help has been unique.

WILLIAM GOODMAN

Knoxville,
April, 1956

Contents

PREFACE v

THE BASIC ASSUMPTION xiii

CHAPTER   PAGE

SECTION I—FRAMEWORK

1. THE APPEARANCE OF PARTIES WITHIN THE NATION-STATE . . 3
What Is Meant by Party?, 4; The Genesis of Parties, 7;
The Process of Acceptance, 9

2. THE FUNCTIONS OF PARTIES 15
The Role of Parties in the Power Struggle, 15; Party Operation of the Electoral Process, 16; Parties and Ideological
Choices, 21; Party Operation of the Government, 22; Parties
and National Unification, 27

3. THE STATUS OF THE AMERICAN TWO-PARTY SYSTEM 29
Efficacy of the System, 29; Explanations of the System, 29;
Departures from the System, 40; Some Distinctive Character-
istics of the System, 44; Effects of the System upon the Power
Struggle, 51

SECTION II—ORGANIZATION

4. THE INVENTIONS OF THE MACHINERY 57
Forerunners of Organization, 57; Rise of Formal Nominating Systems, 63; Creation of Party Committees, 68; Organization: Local in Origin, Decentralized in Composition, 70

5. THE ELABORATION OF PARTY ORGANIZATION 73
Revival of Party Organization, 73; Rules and Usages of
the Party System, 74; Nature of Party Organization, 80; The
Impact of Leadership upon the Party, 85; Techniques for Controlling the Party Organization, 88

6. OPERATIONS THROUGH THE ORGANIZATION 99
Patronage, 99; The Advantages of Office, 111; The Changing Organization, 116

CHAPTER   PAGE

7. NOMINATING SYSTEMS 121
   The Convention System, 123; The Direct Primary System,
   130; The Blending Process in Nominating Systems, 146; The
   County Unit System, 150

8. THE EVOLUTION OF NATIONAL ORGANIZATION 153
   The Presidency and the Electoral-College System, 153;
   The Congressional Caucus, 157; Adoption of the National
   Convention, 166; Permanent Suprastate Committees, 169; The
   Presidency and the Executive Branch, 176

9. THE FORMAL OPERATIONS OF NATIONAL CONVENTIONS . . . 184
   Preconvention Procedures, 186; Sessions of the Convention, 203

10. CONVENTIONS AS THE OPERATION OF THE TOTAL ORGANIZATION 215
    The Groundwork of National Conventions, 217; Conven-
    tion Operations, 238

SECTION III—BASES OF BIPARTISANISM

11. HISTORICAL REVIEW OF THE ECONOMIC BASIS OF BIPARTISANISM 251
    Economics and Politics, 252; The Constitutional Period,
    255; The Federalist-Republican Period, 1789–1825, 257; The
    Democratic-Whig Period, 1825–1852, 262; The Republican-
    Democratic Period, 1854–, 265; The Margin Between the
    Parties, 275

12. THE INDIVIDUAL BASIS OF BIPARTISANISM 279
    Influences Tending to Produce Individual Similarities,
    279; Influences Tending to Produce Individual Differences,
    282

13. SECTIONAL AND CLASS BASES OF BIPARTISANISM 295
    Sections, 295; Classes, 300; Relation of Section and
    Class, 310

14. THE BIPARTISAN BASIS OF ORGANIZED INTEREST GROUPS—THEIR
    PLACE IN THE NATION 321
    Organized Groups with Political Significance, 321; Atti-
    tudes Toward Groups, 325; Membership and Organization,
    327; Types of Organizations, 330; Groups v. Parties, 339

15. ORGANIZED INTEREST GROUPS—ISSUES AND PARTISANSHIP . . . 344
    Issues Generated by Groups, 344; Agriculture, 346; Busi-
    ness, 349; Labor, 353; Veterans, 357; Government Bureaucracy,
    359; Nationality and Race, 362; The Special Case of the Ne-
    groes, 364; Religion, 368; Women, 371

CHAPTER PAGE

16. EVALUATIONS AND IMPLICATIONS OF ORGANIZED INTEREST GROUPS 375
Political Techniques, 375; Groups and the General Welfare, 381; Groups and Other Classifications, 388

17. THE MASS BASIS OF BIPARTISANISM 393
Cycles in Elections and Candidates, 393; Election Upheavals, 401; Limitations of the Mass-Basis Analyses, 410

SECTION IV—ELECTION CAMPAIGNS

18. SUFFRAGE AND VOTING 417
Suffrage and Politics, 417; Voting Requirements, 418; Systems of Voting, 436; Election Administration, 448

19. PUBLIC OPINION, PROPAGANDA AND CAMPAIGNS 458
Raw Materials—Public Opinion, 458; Techniques of Opinion Management—Propaganda, 478

20. CANDIDATES AND MANAGERS 485
Politics as a Way of Life, 485; The Management Function in Politics, 495; The Politician as Campaign Strategist, 501

21. LEADERS IN SEARCH OF FOLLOWERS 508
Initiation and Motive Power of Candidates, 508; Campaign Techniques, 512; Evaluation of Techniques, 537

22. FINANCING AND REGULATING CAMPAIGNS 542
Money in Politics, 542; The Control of Money, 550

SECTION V—REFORMS

23. CAN WE REDIRECT THE DYNAMICS? 567
Politics as Sin, 568; Nonvoting, 574; Reformed Representation, 585

24. SHOULD WE OVERHAUL THE MACHINERY? 594
Presidential Nominations, 594; Presidential Elections, 609

25. CAN AND SHOULD WE MAKE OVER THE PARTY SYSTEM? . . . 627
The Actual Status of Parties, 627; Possibility of the Reforms, 640; Desirability of the Reforms, 649

INDEX 661

THE POT CALLS THE KETTLE BLACK

The Basic Assumption

Underlying all discussions of government are certain assumptions, whether recognized or not; and in the course of considering political parties in the United States, there is usually a wealth of assumptions. The major assumption of this book is that political parties cannot be discussed outside of the confines of the operations of a free government, democratic in philosophy and representative in form.

Free government is conceived here as being marked by at least two characteristics. First, it is a system in which individuals' opinions are both openly recognized and sought for in the determination of public policy. Political forces are the product of individuals constantly forming and re-forming into heterogeneous groups in order to pursue their interests more effectively than they can individually. Individual opinions in this manner become institutionalized through organization of individuals with similar interests and are expressed through group leaders who devote their complete talents to the objectives of their respective groups. There is also a constant and huge volume of unorganized opinions being expressed; and when this expression becomes sufficiently cohesive and consistent to reflect a segment of the public—i.e., an *ad hoc* group—it is politically potent and commands respectful attention. The expressions of opinions (organized or unorganized) amount to evaluations both of proposed public policies and of the results of policies in force. The process of seeking solutions by discussion, compromise, and consensus is achieved openly, and the formation of decisions in an arena of clashing interests and perpetual conflict is proclaimed as the actual and the most desirable way to proceed.

Second, free government is a system wherein individuals have varying opportunities to rise to leadership. Individuals, being different, are not equal in their aptitude, desire or luck. Therefore, they do not all have the same opportunity, but they all have some opportunity in the sense that artificial or arbitrary impediments are not put in their way. The result is to achieve to the maximum extent, a "circulation of the elite," to use Pareto's famous phrase. Leaders come and go with the unceasing ebb and flow of political forces; the lowly may rise and the lofty may decline. There are classes and social strata, but there are no hard-and-fast laws which require any man to die in the caste to which he was born. The existence of many avenues to power and leadership is a concomitant of free government.

Political parties are incomprehensible if these two characteristics are not present, because parties, being the instruments through which governments are operated, dominate the attention of those who wish to influence government. Since the struggles to achieve public objectives are fought in and around parties, leadership in government depends upon leadership in political parties, and the leadership pattern of parties tends to be fluid to the extent that ambitious men can compete freely for the positions of influence and authority. Although stable organization cannot be maintained by constant upheavals and it is a mark of wisdom to operate within an organization so that it will not be destroyed in the process of capturing it, there are opportunities to exert varying degrees of leadership throughout the party organization and to become a member of its elite. Whenever a party leadership successfuly represses such a "circulation," the result is almost certain to be either atrophy of the organization or an explosion from the lower levels of the hierarchy.

To study the record of political parties is to study the essence of free government in action and in evolution.

Framework

Party divisions, whether on the whole operating for good or evil, are things inseparable
from free government.——*The Works of the
Right Honourable Edmund Burke,* I, p. 222.

CHAPTER ONE

The Appearance of Parties within the Nation-State

At the beginning of a discussion, it is logical to define the key terms upon which the discussion is based. Finding a definition for "political parties," the key term of this book, depends upon the concept of party to be defined. Perhaps the term "party" as applied to ancient Greece, for example, is simply a convenience; it is the best term available for designating a particular phenomenon. To make this point is to recognize the cause-and-effect relation between free government and the development of political parties. While some ancient governments are designated "democracies," their operations scarcely simulated the substance which is called "democracy" in the United States.[1] In the interests of clearer thinking and more exact terminology, the ancient phenomenon called "party" should not be confused with the modern phenomenon called "party." The antecedents of the modern phenomenon are found, rather, within the historical limits of the nation-state organization and of democratic philosophy. This lineage is now sufficiently long to give parties the dignity of an old tradition; but parties were a delayed development in democratic, nationalistic civilization. They evolved into the forms familiar to us much more recently than their present status would suggest.[2]

If the additional question should be raised, When did the modern party first appear? we would again be compelled to fall back on the first question, What is a party? Since the definition and the historical appearance are closely related, it is both reasonable and expedient to define today's party and then trace these characteristics backward in time to discover their antecedents. It is after all the present-day party and its development that concern us.

---

[1] "The ancient 'democracies' were still, even in form, class-states, and therefore the decisive changes of government were brought about by revolution rather than by party victories."——R. M. MacIver, *The Modern State* (London: Oxford University Press, 1926) p. 398.

[2] *Ibid.*, p. 400. Taking 240,000 years as the period of time that man has walked erect and taking the beginning of this period as the start of a day and the present as noon, "then at about twenty minutes before twelve there appeared the beginnings of Egyptian and Babylonian civilization. At about one and one quarter minutes before twelve, the printing press was invented. . . . About forty seconds before our noon man began to use the modern political party. . . ."——Dwight Whitney Morrow, "Introduction," p. xxxv, in A. D. Morse, *Parties and Party Leaders* (Boston: Marshall Jones Co., 1923). It is hardly likely that the intervening years since these words were written would require any recalculation of the time element.

3

WHAT IS MEANT BY PARTY?

There is a wealth of definitions of a "political party."[3] Some stress one characteristic and some another, but all attribute to a party certain characteristics which distinguish it from other kinds of groupings and organizations, both of the present and of the past. The characteristics of a party become, in extended form, the definition of a party.

(1) Political parties are *voluntary associations,* free groupings of individuals. If a party were composed of people under compulsion to play their parts, the results of their actions would be as unpredictable as the reasons for their compulsory association would be incomprehensible. To state this characteristic is to make it obvious. To fail to understand it would leave one as perplexed as the foreigner in the United States who attended his first dancing party, and after closely observing the human gyrations, asked his host if this sort of thing was compulsory or if it was possible to have the servants do it for them.

There are two corollaries of this free-association characteristic. One is the *extralegal status of parties.* They are not illegal, since they are not prohibited in constitutions and statutes, but they are not authorized, created, or otherwise sanctioned except indirectly by constitutions and statutes. They are outside the law, yet simultaneously the instruments through which government is conducted. They have come within the law in the United States only through statutes designed to regulate the conduct of elections and control campaign finances. Parties, like the common law, receive the attention of legislative bodies only when there is agitation to change the rules.

The second corollary is a *restricted membership.* A party actually is the group participating directly in the association itself, not those regular or vicarious supporters who participate only by casting ballots for party candidates. It is the active and more-or-less full-time members who constitute the party. This situation has been clouded by contradictory views which have come primarily from certain political philosophies of ideality and from the ingratiating assertions of the leaders of parties. The situation is confused in another sense when we try to determine just who is active enough to be considered part of the party. This question involves both the degree and the nature of participation.[4]

---

3 Peter H. Odegard and E. Allen Helms, *American Politics* (New York: Harper & Brothers, 1947, 2d ed.) pp. 1-3; E. E. Schattschneider, *Party Government* (New York: Farrar & Rinehart, 1942) pp. 35-37. J. C. Charlesworth, "Is Our Two-Party System 'Natural'?" *The Annals,* Vol. 259 (1948) pp. 1-3; Morse, *op. cit.,* pp. 10-11; C. J. Friedrich, *Constitutional Government and Democracy* (Boston: Ginn & Company, 1950, rev. ed.) p. 419.

4 Maurice Duverger, *Political Parties: Their Organization and Activity in the Modern State* (New York: John Wiley & Sons, Inc., 1954) pp. 90 ff. Frederick C. Engelmann, "Membership Participation in Policy-Making in the C.C.F.," *Canadian Journal of Economics and Political Science,* Vol. 22 (1956) pp. 161-173. It is not the average citizens who merely vote

(2) Parties are organizations in the sense that they are held together with a combination of *discipline and loyalty* existing in the relations among the members, those who professionally and openly belong. The members identify themselves individually with the party, its history, its struggles, its objectives. This basic attitude of loyalty toward the group is one of the most distinctive aspects of the modern party and the most satisfactory single explanation of its dynamics and permanence.[5]

(3) *Parties are organizations* in the sense that they are creations of elaborate and intricate machinery that functions on various geographic levels reaching from precincts to national committees or their equivalents. "The organization" becomes a specialized term of reference to committees, chairmen, caucuses, secretaries, managers, delegates, liaison men, arrangements, plus an infinite number of other concepts both concrete and ethereal. This characteristic of parties is the most easily identifiable, the most familiar in a superficial way, and yet the least understood in its detail and its grand design and operation. It is an engrossing preoccupation all by itself and, for many party members, a substitute for principles and policies and historical comprehension.

(4) Parties are distinguished by their *objective of winning elections* through their combined organization. The object of winning elections is to conduct the government, the institution which determines to an increasing extent the method of distribution of the good things of life—the granting of favors and the conferring of perquisites and privileges.

(5) Parties are characterized by existence in the plural. The modern version of totalitarian tyranny operates through the organization of a party, but it is a party without competitors. A party, as free men think of it, is a party *in competition with others,* seeking the objective of winning elections. The essential characteristic is a party system wherein one or more parties hold the positions of authority and one or more seek to oust them and install themselves.

(6) A final characteristic may not appear to be so universal as the previous five. Parties developing in the nation-state are associated with the loyalty of people to their homeland, i.e., nationalism. Parties by their nature are *patriotic organizations* whose leaders extol the virtues of their

---

but "the members of a party committee, and the partisans in public office, [who] constitute a group that does justify the exact application of the term 'party.' "——E. E. Robinson, *The Evolution of American Political Parties* (New York: Harcourt, Brace and Company, 1924) p. 4; Schattschneider, *op. cit.,* pp. 53-61. Charles A. Beard, *The American Party Battle* (New York: The Macmillan Company, 1928) pp. 14-16.

[5] "A party . . . is . . . united also by the possession of certain common interests, which will produce the same responses in men of similar dispositions and impulses, and, if their association is long continued, will be reenforced by the growth of habits of cooperation in politics and the establishment of traditions of struggle and achievement. . . ." ——A. N. Holcombe, *The Political Parties of To-Day* (New York: Harper & Brothers, 1924) p. 349.

nation in driving home the allegation that they are safe recipients of their nation's power. Parties vary in the degree to which they emphasize nationalism—some parties go to extremes of chauvinism—but this characteristic is so constantly reflected in their conduct and assertions that a party which eschews patriotism or attacks its own country is both rare and lacking in the full attributes of a party. In some European countries from time to time organizations have agitated for the detachment of some part of the country in order to incorporate it in an adjoining country. Such organizations, by definition, would fail to be genuine parties, and the term "party" may have been attached to them for want of any other name; in fact, their status as something apart has often been signified by calling them "separatist parties." It is for this same reason that so-called Communist Parties, outside the Soviet Union, are not parties in the sense the term is used throughout this book. They are not only unpatriotic in all of the usual senses but also attached by unyielding commitments of personal loyalty and organizational arrangements to a foreign power.

In conclusion, a definition of the political party of today can be stated as follows: *A political party is an organization whose members are sufficiently homogeneous to band together for the overt purpose of winning elections which entitles them to exercise governmental power, in order to enjoy the influence, perquisites, and advantages of authority.* Here, with some characteristics either stated or suggested, is a working definition of parties suitable for the purposes of this book.[6]

The Inevitability of Parties. There is something more to be added, a conception above and beyond definitions and memorizable characteristics. Properly understood, parties are an altogether unique development, but so inevitable that they appear very ordinary. More or less unconsciously and almost in spite of themselves, free people came to accept parties and in so doing came into possession of an instrument through which they could protect themselves while providing for their own regulation. Parties are both the result of freedom and the guarantor of freedom. They were a response to the challenge of finding alternatives to tyranny, and the alternative they provided was an opportunity for a more widespread control which would reflect more accurately the variety of interests and views. What other kind of instrument could have done this job? Apparently none, for

---

6 This classification of party characteristics is arbitrary rather than orthodox. Other writers arrive at different emphases: C. J. Friedrich extracted two—stable organization and pursuit of ideal benefits related to the ideas or principles of the whole population.—— *Op. cit.,* p. 421. Another view of the essential elements is: "a theory of government, a fairly stable and continuous organization, and a purpose to control administration by means of a majority in a representative assembly."——W. C. Abbott, "The Origin of English Political Parties," *American Historical Review,* Vol. 24 (1918-1919) p. 582. H. R. Penniman, *Sait's American Parties and Elections* (New York: Appleton-Century-Crofts, Inc., 1952, 5th ed.) pp. 151-2, presents two characteristics, one having to do with government policy and the other with personnel.

parties have consistently and universally been accepted as *the only tenable alternative, as a working system, to tyranny.* They are the only understandable and dependable alternative so far developed.[7]

THE GENESIS OF PARTIES

The United States party system traces its lineage back into the history of Great Britain, where the genesis of parties as we know them occurred. Since they were a spontaneous and natural development, they were obviously not created at one single stroke. In fact, they evolved so gradually that their earliest manifestations were almost unnoticed.

If all of the six characteristics of parties be considered, there was not much time lag between their appearance in England and in the United States. However, the mother country did precede and give direction to the colonial developments, so that the direct antecedents of our political organization existed beyond our shores. In the pursuit of these antecedents, the investigator quickly encounters the most delightful array of tenuous and imponderable data. Students of the question are in something of a quandary themselves or assign contradictory emphases to specific historical landmarks in English history, but this state of affairs is hardly surprising. With the various understandings and interpretations of the various characteristics, it would be a miracle if scholars achieved uniformity in discovery and analyses.

Indefinite Date of Origin in England. It is generally conceded that English parties were in existence from the time of the Restoration in 1660 or shortly thereafter, and it is equally well recognized that parties preceded the Restoration. In the struggles of the Cromwellian revolution there emerged groupings in Parliament reflecting various shades of opinion. The groupings were temporary and kaleidoscopic, but some of them at least coalesced long enough to be identifiable and are designated varyingly as groups, factions, and parties. Although they rose and declined with the turns of events, they represented sustained views on public policy and partook of some degree of internal organization if no more than the cohesion built around a trusted leader. We are told that February 8, 1641, is the "safest choice" of a date for the beginning of parties.[8] But the antecedents of the party struggles can be found in the preceding century and even further back, in the dichotomy of kings versus barons.[9]

---

[7] "Without the party-system, we may conclude, the *coup d'état,* the *putsch,* or revolution, are the only methods of securing a change of government."——MacIver, *op. cit.,* p. 399; Schattschneider, *op. cit.,* pp. 1-4. Elihu Root, *The Citizen's Part in Government* (New Haven: Yale University Press, 1920, 2d printing) pp. 51-52.

[8] S. D. Bailey (ed.), *Political Parties and the Party System in Britain* (New York: Frederick A. Praeger, 1952) p. 13.

[9] *Ibid.,* pp. 1-12.

One is now ready to agree that the task of discovering party origins "is a perplexing one. The gradual transition from one species of ideas and organization to another is easy to apprehend in the result; it is extraordinarily difficult to realize in process, much less to fix in formal phrase." [10] The comprehension of the problem is the major part of the battle. On the one hand, it is impossible to know when each and all of the paraphernalia of parties were first used or what constituted their initial use. On the other hand, it is quite possible to set either a date or, more likely, a general period as the point of appearance of certain characteristics. Those who want to follow the party history back to fundamental ruptures over public policies, e.g., the Reformation, can trace the antecedents of the Whig and Tory Parties (the progenitors of the modern parties) which undoubtedly were identifiable and functioning groups before the end of the seventeenth century.[11] We get different results depending on the emphasis—whether on issues or on organizational machinery. Once it is understood that the causes of division preceded the formation of opposing groups, we can appreciate the observation that "in one sense, the great party struggles were over before the party system emerged." [12]

Observable Evolution of English Parties. Given the existence of parties based upon fundamental divisions within Britain, it is easy enough to follow them as they finally took over the substance of governmental power. While the form and symbols of sovereignty were permitted to remain with the monarch, the party system gave life and spirit to the governmental machinery. Eventually the custom arose that "the king ought to choose all of his ministers from one of the two great parties. . . . The Whig administration of Sir Robert Walpole sets the precedent for party ministries and thenceforward, though there are occasional aberrations, the bonds of party are drawn tighter." By degrees the principle of the ministry's joint responsibility to Parliament was established; but the essence of this evolution lies in the ministers' representing a party primarily rather than the king and in the general political understanding that "a defeat of a minister would be a defeat of a party." In time, one of the ministers was accepted as the first or Prime Minister and the king was bound to choose his first minister in conformance with the will of the House of Commons and to act on the advice of his ministers.[13] The amazing fact about this entire process is its accomplishment outside statutory enactments or formal principles of law;

10 Abbott, *op. cit.*, p. 580.

11 *Ibid.*, pp. 583-584; also Bailey, *op. cit.*, pp. 14, 17-18. Leslie Lipson in his article "The Two-Party System in British Politics," *American Political Science Review*, Vol. 47 (1953) pp. 339-341, takes the position that "party" was as valid a term in the seventeenth and eighteenth centuries as at the time he was writing.

12 Bailey, *op. cit.*, p. 13.

13 F. W. Maitland, *The Constitutional History of England* (London: Cambridge University Press, 1913) pp. 395-397; Lipson, *op. cit.*, pp. 341-346.

it rests entirely upon usage, although it can be enforced, if necessary, by either the action or the inaction of the House of Commons.

THE PROCESS OF ACCEPTANCE

Attacks on Emergent Parties. This abbreviated view of British party development obscures the opposition which accompanied parties. It is possible to discover the approximate time of the parties' emergence into general political awareness by the appearance of criticism of parties, or rather, criticism of factions, as parties were originally designated. It is perfectly understandable that ingrained ways of thinking, conditioned by preparty methods, would be incompatible with the methods of a party system. Because a party was a grouping of a small number of men, it was denounced as an organization devoted to its own members' private and selfish ends—an odium similarly attached to pressure groups in the twentieth century. Since the leaders of factions were looked upon as enemies of national solidarity, it is not to be wondered that both the manifestations of parties and their leaders were attacked.

A quite different aspect appears in the attacks that came from those who apparently had something to gain by their opposition and whose indignation was directed at a particular party. Although Halifax's condemnation of parties as "some sort of conspiracy against the nation" [14] could hardly have been more sweeping, there is reason to suspect that he was motivated by something less than strict principle.[15] Jonathan Swift, however, in his *Advice to the October Club,* written around 1710, attacked the Whigs for becoming an "independent faction" in opposition to both the court and the country parties; [16] and Samuel Johnson assured Boswell that "The first Whig was the Devil." [17]

Difficulty of an Opposition Party. Especially indicative of the expedient attitude adopted toward parties was the growth of a court or king's party during the eighteenth century—a party composed of those whom the king could control through the distribution of royal favors and from whom he selected his ministers. At last a party or faction was accepted, but competition was not to be encouraged. Opposing groups were made to appear as treasonable conspiracies against the Crown. The fact that the minority party in the House of Commons is now called His (Her) Majesty's Loyal Opposition is extremely pertinent in view of the history of parties in Britain.

---

[14] Quoted in Odegard and Helms, *op. cit.,* p. 7.

[15] Bolingbroke is probably in the same category; Bailey, *op. cit.,* p. 20.

[16] F. E. Smith (ed.), *Toryism* (London: Harper & Brothers, 1903).

[17] Boswell, *Life of Johnson;* see also H. J. Ford, *The Rise and Growth of American Politics* (New York: The Macmillan Company, 1898) pp. 90-93.

Burke's Counterattack. It remained for Edmund Burke, writing his *Thoughts on the Cause of the Present Discontents* in 1770, to take up the challenge that had gone begging for nearly a century. As a point of departure for his defense of parties, he indicted the court faction which, he insisted, was subverting the House of Commons and destroying free government by its attack upon parties. The court party was developing the doctrine, he pointed out, "that all political connexions are in their nature factious, and as such ought to be dissipated and destroyed." This attempt, he insisted, was motivated simply by the desire to eliminate opposition. Yet Burke was much too good a pleader to deny outright all of the charges made against parties; he admitted, rather, that the behavior of many of them would make "persons of tender and scrupulous virtue somewhat out of humour with all sorts of connexion in politicks." Despite the "circumscribed and partial interest" of some party members,

> where duty renders a critical situation a necessary one, it is our business to keep free from the evils attendant upon it; and not to fly from the situation itself. . . . Every profession, not excepting the glorious one of a soldier, or the sacred one of a priest, is liable to its own particular vices; which, however, form no argument against those ways of life; nor are the vices themselves inevitable to every individual in those professions. Of such a nature are connexions in politicks; essentially necessary for the full performance of our publick duty, accidentally liable to degenerate into faction. Commonwealths are made of families, free commonwealths of parties also; and we may as well affirm, that our natural regards and ties of blood tend inevitably to make men bad citizens, as that the bonds of our party weaken those by which we are held to our country.[18]

Burke, by the logic of his position, defined party as "a body of men united, for promoting by their joint endeavours the national interest, upon some particular principle in which they are all agreed." [19] This definition has attained a classic status because Burke succeeded in expressing an ideal; many men find in his language a description of what they would like to think a party is. Yet neither before nor since Burke's time has this definition borne much relation to reality. As a contrived statement of something Burke was intent upon defending, it was meant to help win an argument. Only in this sense can the definition be understood. To take it literally is to get lost in a quagmire.

---

18 *The Works of the Right Honourable Edmund Burke* (Boston: Wells and Lilly, 1826) I, pp. 422-424. Even in 1770 the word "faction" had become so charged with unpleasant connotations that it would not do for Burke's purposes. Burke implied that "connexion" was an acceptable word, although he also used the word "party" indicating its more pleasant meaning as well as its birth sometime previously as an appropriate term to apply to political groupings.

19 *Ibid.*, p. 426.

Value of Parties: The Views of Madison and Washington. Burke failed to convince not only many of his contemporaries in Britain about the value of parties but also a representative assortment of his contemporaries on this side of the Atlantic Ocean. Two particularly representative examples of the adverse American view are found in James Madison and George Washington.

Madison went on record in the course of his collaborative labors with Hamilton and Jay to encourage ratification of the Constitution in New York. In the now famous tenth paper of *The Federalist,* Madison boldly announced in the first sentence that one of the most important advantages of "a well constructed Union" was "its tendency to break and control the violence of faction." [20] The "propensity of this dangerous vice" most alarmed the friends of popular governments who were complaining "that the public good is disregarded in the conflicts of rival parties." We sense the very epitome of the historical aversions to parties when Madison adds that he understood a faction to be "a number of citizens, whether amounting to a majority or minority of the whole, who are united and actuated by some common impulse of passion, or of interest, adverse to the rights of other citizens, or to the permanent and aggregate interests of the community." [21] The remainder of his discussion was directed toward methods for controlling the effects of faction since the only other method of control would be to destroy liberty itself.

George Washington in his "Farewell Address to the People of the United States" (which was not delivered by him but was printed in the *American Daily Advertiser* in Philadelphia on September 19, 1796) set out, first, to remove himself as a third-term candidate for the Presidency and, second, to offer to his countrymen "the disinterested warnings of a parting friend." Prominent among the "warnings" was the assertion that faction was the product of "combinations and associations" which destroyed the principle of individual obedience to established government and "put in the place of the delegated will of the Nation, the will of a party." Even if factions occasionally served "popular ends, they are likely, in the course of time and things, to become potent engines by which cunning, ambitious and unprincipled men will be enabled to subvert the Power of the People, & to usurp for themselves the reins of Government . . . ."

Washington's discussion plainly suggests that he was not so well equipped as Madison for analyzing a way around the problem presented by "the Spirit of Party." Madison would not impose prohibitions for fear

---

[20] *The Federalist* (Modern Library ed.) p. 53. In Number 9, Alexander Hamilton had opened up this general subject by attempting to show "the tendency of the Union to repress domestic faction and insurrection." (p. 51.)

[21] *Ibid.,* pp. 53, 54. As late as 1799, " 'Faction' and 'party' were . . . used interchangeably; and both words were terms of reproach."——A. J. Beveridge, *The Life of John Marshall* (Boston: Houghton Mifflin Company, 1929) Vol. 2, p. 410, note 2; also pp. 74-76.

of suppressing fundamental liberties, but would harness and checkmate the effects of factions by the free interplay of competition. Washington, on the contrary, would obstruct the growth of and discourage the tendencies toward faction in order to insure the continuance of fundamental liberties. He suggested as one kind of extremity of faction a tendency of the "disorders and miseries . . . gradually [to] incline the minds of men to seek security and repose in the absolute power of an Individual." Yet Washington had no antidote beyond exhortation and rigid public virtue. Madison reflected, both as a writer and as a politician, a shrewder understanding of the politics of his own and of future generations.

American Heritage of Antagonism. An antagonism to political divisions from the Patriot point of view in the 1770's and 1780's would be somewhat understandable. The Whig-Tory schism during the Revolutionary period and afterwards was hardly worthy of emulation. The implication of Tory opposition, as far as the Patriots could see, was unadulterated disloyalty and subversion. In addition, there was very likely a point of view that opposition to one's policies could not be sincere or valid. Thomas Jefferson, who had consciously and actively helped to organize the first genuine American party, took a nonparty tone in his First Inaugural Address, although one cannot be sure to what extent his words reflected a distaste for party spirit as such rather than the wiles of a politician seeking to allay the opposition's fears and bid for a wider support. The crowning blow to the prestige of opposition parties was delivered, ironically, by an extreme group among Washington's own Federalists when they carried their conflict of interests to the point of secession during the War of 1812 and conspired with the British to attach New England to Canada.[22]

Lack of Party Philosophy. It is evident in any case that the philosophical basis for parties followed, instead of preceding, the appearance

---

22 Daniel Webster, who is usually thought of as a good party man, concluded that parties were unavoidable "and if they are formed on constitutional questions, or in regard to great measures of public policy, and do not run to excessive lengths, it may be admitted that on the whole they do no great harm." James Russell Lowell insisted that, even if a "necessary expedient," government by party "is also a necessary evil" because it forces men "to postpone interests of prime import and consequence to secondary and ephemeral, often to personal interests," and "to confound one for the other."——Quoted in Charles E. Merriam, *American Political Ideas* (New York: The Macmillan Company, 1920) pp. 271-272, 280. Professor Holcombe, writing in 1933, was of the opinion that "In practice parties doubtless fall somewhere between the worst [i.e., unions for private interests without agreement upon any principle] and the best [i.e., Burke's definition], and must be accepted as unavoidable evils in modern states, or, taking a cheerier view, as imperfect but indispensable instruments of representative government."——Arthur N. Holcomb, *The New Party Politics* (New York: W. W. Norton & Company, Inc., 1933) p. 86.

and development of parties. Consequently, the theory has been largely a retroactive explanation and the justifications may have sounded like rationalizations. The task of defense was seldom pushed beyond the practical necessities of the moment. One result of this neglect has been to create the impression that since we have always had them around (like mountains, taxes, and comic strips) parties are accomplished facts of life. Another result has been a refusal fully to accept parties and largely for the same reasons expressed by Englishmen and Americans in the seventeenth and eighteenth centuries. Parties still strike us as dangerously divisive, and in the scale of values their status is low rather than high. When emergencies approach, we make a virtue of unity and denounce in the most scathing terms the specially destructive tactics of party operations. This drumbeat of condemnation can also be a sublimation of the taste of sour grapes in the mouths of defeated candidates.[23]

The modern party was conceived in revolution, gestated in turmoil and confusion, and born in the agony of fundamental historical changes. Like any unwanted offspring it was ignored when possible and insulted when it became obstreperous. The significance of its existence was not perceived but the implications of its growth were abhorred. Nevertheless this monster child of deformity finally captured the nation-state and became the instrument of a new age in politics.

Selected Bibliography

Bailey, Sydney D. (ed.), *Political Parties and the Party System in Britain.* New York: Frederick A. Praeger, 1952. The Hansard Society Series in Parliamentary Government, Vol. 5.

Bulmer-Thomas, Ivor, *The Party System in Great Britain.* London: Phoenix House, 1953, Chaps. 1–3.

Duverger, Maurice, *Political Parties: Their Organization and Activity in the Modern State.* New York: John Wiley & Sons, Inc., 1954, Introduction and Chap. 2.

The Federalist. New York: Modern Library, Inc., Numbers 9 and 10.

Friedrich, Carl J., *Constitutional Government and Democracy.* Boston: Ginn & Company, 1950.

Hexter, J. H., *The Reign of King Pym.* Cambridge: Harvard University Press, 1941. Especially Chaps. 2–4, 8, 9.

Macaulay, T. B., *The History of England from the Accession of James II.* New York: Harper & Brothers, 1856, Vol. 2, pp. 563 ff.

MacIver, Robert M., *The Modern State.* New York: Oxford University Press, 1926. Reprinted 1950.

---

[23] John Marshall, attributing his defeat for Congress in 1799 to the circulation of canards about him, wrote that it was "despicable in the extreme . . . Nothing I believe more debases or pollutes the human mind than faction."——Beveridge, *op. cit.,* Vol. 2, p. 410. Beveridge goes on to say that translated into modern language Marshall's sentiments would be: "Nothing, I believe, more debases or pollutes the human mind than partisan politics."

Merriam, Charles E., *American Political Ideas.* New York: The Macmillan Company, 1920. pp. 278-309.

Odegard, P. H., and E. A. Helms, *American Politics,* 2d ed. New York: Harper & Brothers, 1947.

Penniman, Howard R., *Sait's American Parties and Elections.* New York: Appleton-Century-Crofts, Inc., 1952, 5th ed., pp. 154-161.

Schattschneider, E. E., *Party Government.* New York: Farrar & Rinehart, Inc., 1942, Chap. 1.

CHAPTER TWO

The Functions of Parties

Although party systems vary from nation to nation, parties formed under the aegis of freedom and the nation-state have certain similarities. This result could hardly have been otherwise. Politics in a representative form of government, wherein liberty and individualism have a high value, has its own peculiar attributes and modes of operation. It is in the forwarding of the inherent requirements of this system that political parties fulfill the functions which justify their existence.

To discuss these functions comparatively raises the question of how much we know about various countries' political parties. The electoral functions, organization, and campaign techniques of parties abroad are better understood, for example, than are their roles in forming public policy. The void created by the neglect of comparative data on parties is increasingly recognized, and one of the most inviting frontiers of political investigation is the science of political parties—stasiology.[1] Within the very real limitations of knowledge, the present chapter compares parties in the United States, England, and France in some of their identifiable functions.

THE ROLE OF PARTIES IN THE POWER STRUGGLE

Whatever happens in politics happens because of people, not because of abstractions like political parties which represent people. Political parties are organizations operated by people in an environment of conflicting objectives. An objective in politics which can be achieved without effort and/or opposition is so rare as to be unknown; and if it occurs, the process of attaining it is outside the realm of politics per se. This clash of personal ambitions seeking contradictory objectives is often called the "power struggle."

How Parties Affect the Power Struggle. Parties do not create the power struggle nor do they either intensify it or make it more immoral. They simply mark out certain confines in the political sphere and direct the power struggle into distinctive channels. They impose rules in the game of seeking political objectives, and the participants acknowledge their willingness to operate within these limits as long as all competitors are similarly bound. The general public accepts the desirability of the system and is able, as a rule, to sense any attempts to subvert it. In this way the power struggle is regulated politically by the competition of leaders and by

---

[1] The term was used by Maurice Duverger, *Political Parties: Their Organization and Activities in the Modern State* (New York: John Wiley and Sons, Inc., 1954). See Frederick C. Engelmann, "A Critique of Recent Writings on Political Parties," *Journal of Politics,* Vol. 19 (1957) pp. 423-440.

the insistence of followers upon the observance of the ground rules by leaders. Within these rules the power struggle is controlled in the only possible way, inasmuch as ambition cannot be curbed by legal concepts predicated upon statutory or constitutional prohibitions. Political parties perform the inescapable function of any political society of regularizing and institutionalizing the power struggle and making it amenable to a practical and actual control. This function is performed with reasonable efficiency because there are comparatively few relapses into hypocrisy or adolescent denials of the necessity of such a function. The United States, for example, is extremely fortunate in having as early a heritage of candid portrayal of this basic activity of political life as that of James Madison, who formally stated it in 1788 in the tenth paper of *The Federalist*.[2]

In one sense, the channeling of the power struggle is *the* function of political parties. All other functions are, relatively, subservient or by-products. Certainly they are not carefully planned ahead of time or adopted in conformance with anyone's concept of altruism. They result from the inevitable requirements of the political system of a free society.

PARTY OPERATION OF THE ELECTORAL PROCESS

Acceptance of Elections. If political parties are to be the instrument for the operation of government, the rank and file requires a method for indicating its individual judgments collectively. Men have found no better method for achieving this end than having elections. How else can large numbers participate? At the same time we do not accept elections purely as excuses for public exuberance or for the exercising of civic reflexes. The technique of elections works when elections prove something, when they determine who will hold the offices and what the general direction of policy will be. This is not to say that elections serve only this purpose. They also offer an outlet for human energies released by the tradition of liberty. Periodically, men can vent their spleen, release their pent-up emotions, and relieve some of their frustrations. In this sense, elections are purgations, permitting us to get some of the dirt out of our systems. Having done so, we are satisfied—if not actually embarrassed—and are content to

---

2 That is, his solution for the dangers of seeking personal ends through public political means was a free competition of factions (parties). Although his apparent assumption of an emerging multiparty system proved to be wrong, his analysis is just as valid when applied to pressure groups operating around parties or to factions within parties struggling for control of its machinery in order to direct public policy. In either case, the problem for the many is how to control the ambition of the leaders among them. This dilemma, indigenous to organized human society, is constantly recognized; and Madison's solution is often reformulated, e.g., "If we must set a thief to catch a thief, so we must set a politician to watch another politician, a party to watch another political party."——Jack E. Holmes, Foreword, p. vi, in C. B. Judah, *The Republican Party in New Mexico* (Division of Research, Dept. of Government, University of New Mexico, 1949); also p. 19.

await the next election. By satiating ourselves during election campaigns, we substitute voting for insurrection and release tensions through expression instead of through explosions.[3]

Parties and Size of Electorate. A major function of parties is to operate an understandable and workable electoral process, and the crucial aspect of this function increases with the size of the electorate. A dozen voters can arrive at agreements among themselves by face-to-face discussion. They may ratify their conclusions and disagreements by a formally cast vote or by verbal understandings. Permanent divisions may appear among the twelve voters, but those with similar opinions on one or several questions would hardly be so asinine as to organize themselves into a party with all its trappings of officers and ceremonies. It is not susceptible of precise distinctions at what point in the growth of the size of the group party organization becomes feasible. Nor is there any profit in raising the ancient egg-or-chicken argument about which came first, parties or an electorate.[4] We can simply begin with the observable interdependence of the two elements. Party leaders in the United States, except for the Federalists, have proceeded on the assumption that in order to succeed they need more voters, and parties have been correspondingly strengthened and solidified as the number of voters increased.[5]

Supplying Candidates. The appearance of an electorate produces a most elementary justification for parties. If a substantial percentage of the total population is to participate in elections with any effectiveness and meaning, they need to be provided with a limited number of choices for any given office. Otherwise, their votes will be so dispersed among an unlimited number of candidates that the results of elections will be ludicrous. The existence of parties solves the problem of alternatives among candidates. This argument gets its point from the almost invariable practice in free societies of basing elections upon selection by the majority or by a plurality. Without organized presentation of candidates, to elect by a majority would necessitate an endless series of runoff elections to eliminate the less popular candidates. Viewed in terms of the electoral process, par-

---

[3] A. D. Morse, *Parties and Party Leaders* (Boston: Marshall Jones Co., 1923) pp. 5-9.

[4] This process can be argued from either direction. In the sense that parties appealed to and satisfied varying views existing within the public, parties were the result of such views and the voters created the parties. In the sense that leaders organized voters by suggesting where their interests lay and by urging policies in pursuit of those interests, parties created the electorate.

[5] E. E. Schattschneider, *Party Government* (New York: Farrar & Rinehart, Inc., 1942) pp. 48-49. It is remarkable that this function of parties is so seldom appreciated. From reading some of the literature, one can get the reverse impression, that party leaders are engaged in some kind of conspiracy to restrict the electorate.

ties are the organizations that make the operation meaningful, if not actually possible.[6]

The situation is equally well clarified for potential candidates. Those who wish to be elected must first be nominated, and nomination is made by parties. A man who is ambitious to hold office affiliates with a party organization in order to have an opportunity to be presented to the voters as a party nominee. A genuine party is so committed to the furnishing of a candidate for each office that if no party member can be found who seeks a particular office, the party leaders very often arbitrarily select one (if the convention method is used) or induce someone to file (if the direct-primary method is used).

Developing Issues. Since the normal objective of both the party and its candidates is to win each election as it occurs, they seek good reasons, i.e., issues, why they should win, and present these issues to the voters. It may be necessary to develop issues beforehand so that they will be available during the campaign, and this task requires considerable foresight and planning on the part of party leaders and hopeful nominees. On other occasions the issues are ready-made and at hand, and the problem is to work out an advantageous approach to them. Sometimes it is difficult to find any useful issues because the voters really are not very disturbed about anything. In sheer desperation, in this kind of situation, the candidates may talk about themselves and the altruistic aspirations of their constituents, the wickedness of being a candidate of the other party, and so on.

Quite frequently certain issues are embarrassing to one party, which tries to ignore or soft-pedal or explain them away, but competing parties will be sure to emphasize such issues. The voters have access to the arguments, explanations, and defenses of public policies and political conduct which are pertinent to each campaign. In two-party systems the major parties may simultaneously want to avoid a particular issue, but they probably will not succeed if it is a genuine question of concern to a substantial number of people. Whenever a party leadership is convinced that an issue cannot safely be put aside, the issue will be dealt with. The over-all result is that issues that can be related to voters' interests and aspirations will be developed and presented, and we have the basis for the frequent observation that parties provide a brokerage service in politics by supplying candidates for office and presenting in understandable terms the great issues which the people are called upon to decide.

Operating the Mechanics. Since the first function of parties is to provide a control mechanism for the power struggle, the participants in

---

[6] *Ibid.,* pp. 50-53; Elihu Root, *The Citizen's Part in Government* (New Haven: Yale University Press, 1920, 2d printing) pp. 40-44.

that struggle insist upon controlling the avenues to power by operating directly or indirectly the mechanics of elections. This undertaking includes the detailed administration of polling places and receiving boards, the counting and certifying of returns, the judicial or administrative interpretation of the statutory regulations. It may be a dangerous exaggeration to say that party leaders seek these tasks as a means of unfair or illegal advantage, but they perpetually evidence the keenest interest in the functioning of the process. If it should become possible to bring some completely disinterested robots down to earth from another planet to operate the mechanics of elections, plentiful objections of a caustic and explosive nature can be anticipated from many quarters having a stake in the outcome of the elections.[7]

Making the Process Concrete. One result of this method of operations is to make the process eminently concrete. Anyone who really wishes to do so can comprehend it. There is no magic, mystery, or baffling formulas to penetrate. What is done is done by people, and other people know them and observe them. It is an all-human process, and no one doubts it. The party system, then, has the gratifying result of bringing the electoral process down to a practical level so that all may know and understand it if they wish. This function is a classic example of limitations upon leadership resulting from competition among leaders.

Developing Intraparty Loyalty. While these functions are complete in and of themselves, they in turn have given rise to certain resultant functions. As so frequently is the case with organizations dedicated to certain objectives, a condition precedent to pursuing the objectives is dependability of the organization itself. It is usually challenging enough to compete in elections without having the base of operations, which is the organization, fail in its support. A political party is formed or inherited by a group of leaders who first must be assured that the party organization will hold together during its future battles. As a result, party leaders attempt most assiduously to inculcate a spirit of loyalty to the party as an institution and as the representative of an idea worth fighting for. Members on the lower reaches of the party hierarchy and the dependable party voters are constantly impressed with the need for being "regular" in their allegiance and for staying with the party in bad times as well as in good times. Legends are developed to reinforce individual determinations to be loyal. If a party has a history, it is always glorious when expounded under party supervision; its former leaders were the essence of everything that the society holds to be positive and good. The party may have a flag or insignia

---

[7] See Charles Hickman Titus, *The Processes of Leadership* (Dubuque, Iowa: William C. Brown Company, 1950) pp. 122-123.

or symbols to identify it both to the public and to the members themselves, as the Republicans and Democrats use the symbols of elephant and donkey. These devices are supposed to call up a signal response of partisan support. No technique can be overlooked in binding fellow partisans to the party organization and convincing them of the necessity to adhere to their allegiance.

Enforcing Party Regularity. Usually, it is easy to explain to people that elections are won by organization and that organization means unity and cohesiveness. In case some members doubt the truth of this admonition, they will be convinced by the practical demonstration of losing an election because not everyone put his shoulder to the wheel. Inasmuch as professional party members are not playing a game for fun alone, but for high stakes which involve their future careers, they cannot tolerate needless threats to their ambitions. In some party systems leaders have compulsory means to enforce party regularity. These disciplinary measures may be used sparingly, but are available as a means of last resort. In Great Britain, for instance, the final step in the disciplinary process is to put fractious members out of the party and forbid them the use of the party label thereafter. In the United States, where this extremity cannot be used, resort may be had to withholding the favors within the discretion of leaders. By the same token, regularity is rewarded by granting appointment to party or government positions, aid in seeking nominations, help in being elected. The "bolter" is the one person that loyal party members abhor, and whenever possible the bolter is subjected to the severest punishments.

The ultimate objective of all of these efforts is to protect the party's monopoly of the electoral function. Parties cannot exist unless they preempt the field in offering candidates; so-called independent candidates—those who run without party designation—are uniformly disparaged by all good party members. The philosophy of party monopoly is founded on the contention that everyone should belong to a party as he should belong to a church and should seek his political objectives through the party mechanism. In the liturgy of political parties, to run for office as an independent is tantamount to seeking the meaning of life and death as an atheist. Here we have the other side of the coin of the electoral function of parties. It is an essential function if the electoral system is to be manageable, concrete, and comprehensible; but the followers—i.e., the voters—get the candidates the parties offer or at least the candidates who are able to enter direct primaries of the parties. These are the choices the voters get, these and no others.[8]

---

[8] Parties may, and often have, performed services of a personal nature directly for citizens as a means of winning their gratitude and, at election times, their votes. This function is really an adjunct of the electoral, not a separate function by itself.

PARTIES AND IDEOLOGICAL CHOICES

Infinite Number of Ideologies. It stands to reason that if parties are to be of any practical use they will mirror and give expression to the ideological divisions within the public. Yet, as a practical matter, no party system can faithfully reflect all the myriad ideologies within the public or give expression to all the shades and subtle nuances of different views on public policy existing in the minds of citizens. What passes for agreement on public questions is probably a position nearest to many opinions, one which can be accepted by people although it is not the exact solution they would have liked. The politician deals with aggregates and approximations, not with exact reproductions.

Relation to the Number of Parties. Different party systems offer varying ranges of ideological choices to the electorate. Some societies require more parties than others because of more ideological differences to which leaders must appeal. It is inconceivable that there should be fewer than two parties in a free government. Beyond two the number can, conceivably, stretch to infinity although there is a point at which the number stops or the society suffers from the chaos of internal ideological division. Even in some multiparty systems there are really only a few large parties surrounded by a number of insignificantly small parties which have little more than nuisance value. However, there is a relation between the number of ideological choices presented to an electorate and the number of separate political parties. A party system discharges the function of providing ideological choices whether the range be wide or narrow.

Value Judgments Regarding Party Systems. As soon as the discussion of parties reaches the point of distinguishing between the two-party system and the multiparty system, it is inevitable that invidious comparisons will arise. Some observers will invariably argue the merits of the system they know and understand. Others will just as likely pine for a system being used elsewhere because of its reported advantages. Here is a case where the grass may appear greener on either side of the fence, depending upon one's conditioning or predispositions. Forming value judgments on the relative merits of these two systems is quite understandable, but such judgments are by their nature inconclusive and often invalid. For some strange reason, human beings tend to argue that if a given system works in Timbuctoo, it automatically will work in Podunk; what is worse, we may even go so far as to conclude that since the Timbuctoo system is very serviceable, the

Podunk system cannot be serviceable because it is different. This kind of thinking reflects an idealization of uniformity and standardization. It is courageous, to say the least, to maintain that a system which is a going concern in the practical field of political operations is worthless or inferior to some other system. Actually, either a two-party system or a multiparty system can satisfactorily discharge the function of presenting ideological choices. This is not a question susceptible of doctrinaire answers. In France, for instance, it would appear that there is greater interest in reflecting more precise ideological divisions within the public through the political parties than there is in the United States, where greater emphasis is placed upon a party's capturing the government.

The objective is to have the system that generally satisfies the people, one that they can understand and operate with reasonable efficiency. A system would be subject to a justifiable indictment if it were neither accepted nor understood by those who operate it, for it would almost surely fail. An indigenous system which is permitted to develop by natural stages is superior to a system either voluntarily borrowed or involuntarily imposed. A system implies the formulation of rules, whether legislated or customary, and rules make explicit the objectives of the system as well as set out the particular norms of action. The satisfactory operation of the rules of a political system depends upon acceptance of both the objectives and the means of attaining them. The fun of the game of baseball is winning within the rules of the game. Neither the players nor the fans would tolerate violations of the rules, for the game has meaning only in terms of them. They would have no value to those who do not understand the game. By the same token, foreigners in a country may ask the most extraordinary questions about its party system because they do not understand it and cannot avoid evaluating it in terms of the system they are familiar with.[9]

PARTY OPERATION OF THE GOVERNMENT

The ultimate objective of political party leaders and the capstone of the organization's functions is taking over the governmental machinery and operating it in conformance with the rules of the political system through the acquiescence of the nation, including those who unsuccessfully competed in the election campaign. The universal desire on the part of the politically ambitious to operate the government is so universally taken for granted that it would be needless in this discussion to go behind the phenomenon and ask why this should be the case. Certain it is that we cannot understand any other attitude than the familiar one of eagerness,

---

[9] Joseph G. La Palombara, "The Italian Elections and the Problem of Representation," *American Political Science Review*, Vol. 47 (1953) pp. 676-703, presents the thesis that the two-party system is inappropriate for Italy.

and the phenomenon is, if unexplainable, at least fortunate.[10] The simple fact of the matter is that in order to have government someone must operate it, and we are quite prepared to have prestige and perquisites attached to the authority of holding office if that is the way to get the offices filled and the work of governing accomplished. In the course of operating the government, parties perform at least two distinct services or subfunctions.

The Compromise Function. The first step in governing free men is getting them to agree on a sufficient number of fundamental questions so that regular and orderly procedures can be established and maintained. No point of agreement can be anything more than a departure for the next disagreement; at no time does the problem of differences of opinion and clashes of interest cease to exist. The function of a party is to reconcile those differences within it to the extent that the organization can proceed with a workable unity and with confidence.

The art of compromise has succeeded so well that we are inclined to doubt its pervasiveness. The genuine desire to reach agreements in the course of conducting free government is so strong and such a large number of compromises is reached quietly without fanfare or publicity that it is easy to forget that compromise is constantly going on. Equally it may be forgotten that compromises themselves are embedded in roots of agreement and consensus already existing. The potential differences among people's opinions are so vast that a breed of doctrinaires would eventually destroy themselves. Even in practice the differences are great enough to require constant preparation and invention of techniques to produce agreements. Even individuals with the maximum of common interests and outlook will reveal a discouraging number of inharmonious views. Medical doctors do not agree about the various problems of medicine on either the scientific or the administrative side. Teachers disagree about how and what to teach. Farmers disagree about techniques of farming. Industrialists disagree about industrial policies. Labor-union members disagree about the role of labor unions. Within any homogeneous group it is quite possible that certain questions should be avoided entirely if relations are to be peaceful.

Political parties are composed of individuals with diverse points of view. The wonder is not that the Republicans and the Democrats disagree among themselves, but that they have such genius for internal agreement. A political party may at one or another time in its history disagree in-

---

10 The implications if the situation were the reverse are incalculable. Assuming the objective were that of being the governed instead of the governors, perhaps public office would be imposed as a punishment by society for wrongdoing; and to operate the governmental machinery would be a hazardous and arduous task that all sane and self-respecting men would avoid. From time to time, officeholders complain of their burdens so fervently that they almost establish the accuracy of this reverse situation. However, no such complaint has been sufficiently eloquent to persuade either them or their competitors that the race is not worth the reward.

ternally on practically every subject except the desirability of winning the next election. In this sense, personal ambition in the pursuit of objectives can be a cohesive as well as a divisive force; even ambitious men must work together to get the things they want. When viewed as either a political or a social function, the process within a party of reconciling the differences of its own members as a means of advancing the interests of the whole is important in the highest degree. Any factional or segmental success in bringing agreement into men's lives contributes ultimately to the final synthesis of getting a nation to agree to a given policy in order to be governed. Parties, as major groupings within the total public, are of the greatest aid in forwarding national compromises by producing party compromises.

Comparisons of different party systems are instructive both in suggesting the various roles a party can play to reconcile disagreements and in demonstrating that no one system is necessarily right or wrong. If the system fulfills the function, that is all the citizens can expect; they can begin casting about for reforms when the parties fail to do what the system requires of them. Three distinct types of party systems reflect three alternatives both in the ways in which and in the extent to which this function is carried out.

In the first type, that of Great Britain, the system emphasizes party discipline. The process of reconciling differences within the party is carried to a very advanced stage, with the result that a party platform is a commitment of the party's members in the House of Commons. Of course there are public questions on which the party officially takes no position, and the members are free to vote as they please. But a party has a central program bearing upon major aspects of public policy and can be depended upon to implement its program if it operates the government. The initial and the decisive reconciliation of differences occurs on the party level in this system, is carried through to the government level, and becomes public policy when the party controls the House of Commons. The reconciliation is of a permanent and binding nature and occurs before the election.

A second type of system is found in France, where the multiparty system makes easier the reconciliation of differences within a party because each party is composed of more homogeneous points of view to begin with. Not only is a French party closely tied to a particular ideology within the electorate, but also, as a result, party leaders must represent their followers fairly accurately or be defeated for office. While identity of opinion will not be found and personal rivalries are just as prevalent as in other sys-- tems, a French party can succeed to a relatively high degree in presenting a united front on a program of public policies. The mark of the multiparty system, however, is the assumption that no party will elect a majority of

the members of the legislative body, in this case the French National
Assembly. In contrast to British practice, no one party's program will
become the official government program. Rather, the government is operated by a coalition of two or more parties whose leaders are required to
reconcile their differences on the government level in the process of governing. Since the electoral base of even a large French party is a minority
of the country, the process of reconciling differences within a party is no
more than a prelude to reconciling national differences in order to govern.
The crucial stage of compromise is reached after elections, both when governments are originally formed and subsequently when issues arise that
split the governing coalition and threaten its ability to continue to act in
concert.[11]

The third type of system is that in the United States, where a situation
between the British and French systems has developed. The American
party performs the function of reconciling its differences to the extent
that it can conduct a vigorous campaign for office, but it does not have
either the disciplinary power of a British party or the cohesive ideological
base of a French party. The American party to some extent glosses over
some of its internal disagreements or tries to ignore them; an issue on which
general agreement is impossible is avoided by party leaders, for it can
unhinge the party and consign it to defeat, as was the case with the issues
of prohibition and religion in the Democratic National Convention of
1924. As far as possible, compromise is achieved on the party level, but
there is always the frank recognition that some differences must be deferred
to the government level. Like a British party, but unlike the French, one
party in the United States will normally win a majority at an election and
will be entrusted with the operation of the full government machinery.
However, since even the party winning the majority was unable to reconcile all of its differences before the election, difficult problems will await
the solution of compromise after the party takes over the government. In
this sense the American system resembles the French, but not the British.
In the United States the compromise function of government is fulfilled
on both the party and the government level, in Britain on the party level,
and in France on the government level.

It is appropriate to note that even in tyrannies this function of reconciling differences must be performed and is done through the agency of
a party organization. It is a tribute to the party system developed under
free government that the concept of party is retained in twentieth-century
tyrannies, but the dynamics of the party system are perverted by the
prohibition of political competition through the one-party monopoly. The
elite in the modern tyranny is identical with the elite of the one party,

---

11 "As a rule, however, decisions are reached by ministers and Parliament, on lines
largely of their own devising, rather than by the people directly."——F. A. Ogg and Harold
Zink, *Modern Foreign Governments* (New York: The Macmillan Company, 1949) p. 549.

and the hierarchy of the party is in effect the hierarchy of the government. Because the perverseness of human nature overrides even the admonitions of tyrants, the one-party system makes provisions for reconciling the differences within the governing elite, and this function is normally carried out at the highest party levels, for example, in the Soviet Union at the level of the Presidium.

The Function of Responsibility. If the reconciling of differences is the first step, as well as a continuous process, in the function of operating the government, the final step or the summation of the party's function is to assume the responsibility for what happens while the party operates or shares in the operation of government.[12]

Once in office, no group of leaders remains on dead center. Certain policies are promoted or encouraged in conformance with the leaders' interests and concepts. From the point of view of the governed, the efficacy of public policies is too crucial to be ignored. They insist upon fixing responsibility somewhere for what happens, whether the leaders like it or dislike it. No party leaders will admit responsibility for unpopular policies if they can possibly extricate themselves, but all will be eager to the point of insistence to claim responsibility for popular policies. They may pose as champions of a policy while it is popular and scorn it with the finest invective if it should become unpopular. It is quite possible that the governed may be forced to its own conclusions about responsibility for what happens in spite of assurances to the contrary. A party's leaders may be assigned responsibility by the public without the leaders agreeing that they are responsible. In this operation the public may reason on a basis of responsibility by association or by propinquity. The man who was nearest to the crime may well be the first suspect. The party that is operating the government is the first to be accused when things are not going well. This party function of assuming responsibility is not always a function that the parties will agree to or accept, but it is a function that the nature of the system imposes upon whoever undertakes to govern and it is insisted upon by the public.

If the three types of party system are analyzed in terms of the function of responsibility, it is possible to discern these differences: In Great Britain because of party discipline and of government operation by one party, the governing party must accept full responsibility for what is done. In France a governing party in the coalition can be made to accept its proportional responsibility but can reasonably argue itself out of complete responsibility, which is undertaken jointly by all of the governing parties; "there is an

---

[12] See below, Chapter 25 for a more extended discussion of party responsibility.

almost perpetual division of responsibility for what is done or not done." [13]
In the United States the situation is approximately midway between the
British and French since one party operates the government and undertakes
the responsibility but cannot implement its program as readily as a British
party because of the more lax discipline.[14] In the United States we get
imperfect realization of party responsibility when it is measured against
an absolute standard, but we get almost complete realization of party
government.

PARTIES AND NATIONAL UNIFICATION

In view of the foregoing functions of parties, it comes as no great
surprise to remark that they have generally been important nationalizing
forces. While this result has to some extent been inadvertent and unin-
tended, it has also been an inevitable consequence of an expanding power
struggle based upon the need for finding more supporters. Simultaneously,
the whole tendency of campaigns for national offices has been to emphasize
national questions at the expense of provincial questions. The greater
problems of public policy are more vividly dramatized on the higher and
wider levels of government; and as communication facilities have made
transmission of developments and ideas instantaneous, this preponderance
of national affairs has grown. In countries with constitutional federal
systems or with a strong heritage of loyalty to localisms, political parties
have helped to pull together the loose strings of decentralized practices and
thinking. Furthermore, parties tend to stress national questions because
of the constant political pressure to widen the base of parties. Eventually,
as a party becomes national, it adopts national patriotism as one of its
cardinal tenets. Thus stimulated, people are led to think of themselves
and their problems more and more in a national environment rather than
in a sectional environment.

Not only does this evolution characterize the United States, but parties
here have had another unification function which is not a contest between
nationalism and localism. The organization of American government,
both federal and state, on the plan of separation of powers created a problem in actual operations. If each of the three coordinate branches of
government remained as separated in fact as it was in Constitutional outline, there was a danger that government would break down under the
sheer strain of separatism and lost motion. The formal insurance of checks
and balances was no guarantee that the system could be saved. Into the
chasm created by a machinery operating in isolated segments, political

---

13 Ogg and Zink, *op. cit.*, p. 550.

14 See Julius Turner, "Party and Constituency: Pressures on Congress," *The Johns
Hopkins University Studies in Historical and Political Science*, Vol. 69, No. 1 (1951)
Chap. 2 for some statistical evidence of the differences in party cohesiveness in the United
States, Britain, and France.

parties poured the cement upon which working arrangements were established. By making the separation-of-powers plan work, parties vindicated the plan itself as a workable arrangement.

It can be contended that political parties do not always produce unity, but either permanently or temporarily encourage disunity and provincialism. In the first place, however, it is a mistake to conclude that party leaders are wicked ogres scheming to subvert the principles of the Republic because they get into nasty arguments with one another in the process of competing for office. Unity under free government does not mean absence of disagreements, quarrels, hot tempers, and provocative language. This kind of unity is found only when a tyrannical government can impose it artificially. At the same time, some critics of parties attack them for producing disunity during an election campaign but this criticisim is really not warranted. After the election it is obvious that the threat to national stability never was real and that a great deal of the evidence for thinking so was a misinterpretation of posturings assumed in order to get votes. In the second place, some parties never reveal a national awareness but deal always in the market of local discontents and peculiarities no matter how trivial. They cannot be described as national parties nor are they the major parties of a system. They can rarely hope to win a majority at an election. They attain their highest status in the multiparty system, and one of the clear value judgments that can be rendered in behalf of the two-party system is that the major parties are of necessity national parties and in the full sweep of their activities bind together far more people than they ever separate.

Selected Bibliography

Duverger, Maurice, *Political Parties: Their Organization and Activity in the Modern State.* New York: John Wiley & Sons, Inc., 1954.

Engelmann, Frederick C., "A Critique of Recent Writings on Political Parties," *Journal of Politics,* Vol. 19 (1957) pp. 423–440.

Herring, Pendleton, *The Politics of Democracy.* New York: Rinehart & Company, Inc., 1940, Chap. 3.

McCally, Sarah P., "Party Government in Turkey," *Journal of Politics,* Vol. 18 (1956) pp. 297–323.

McKenzie, R. T., *British Political Parties.* New York: St Martin's Press, 1956.

Neumann, Sigmund (ed.), *Modern Political Parties.* Chicago: University of Chicago Press, 1956.

Padgett, L. Vincent, "Mexico's One-Party System: A Re-evaluation," *American Political Science Review,* Vol. 51 (1957) pp. 995–1008.

Rustow, Dankwart A., *The Politics of Compromise: A Study of Politics and Cabinet Government in Sweden.* Princeton: Princeton University Press, 1955.

CHAPTER THREE

The Status of the American Two-Party System

At this point the characteristics and the functions or justifications of parties have been presented, and the context for political parties in the United States is now marked out. This particular system takes on stature as well as perspective when seen within the larger reference of parties in free governments. Now the objective is to set United States parties within their particular context by inquiring into their peculiar operations and general characteristics.

EFFICACY OF THE SYSTEM

Psychological Value. One of the advantages of a two-party system is the psychological value of an operation which produces a majority on Election Day. There is an inherent value in a system that helps to manufacture acquiescence in itself, and the ease of governing is never so great as to permit the governors to spurn any method which helps to produce consent among the governed. At some stage in the course of the power struggle a surcease of overt conflict is needed—both to relieve the tension of the struggle and to permit the advancement of constructive work.

The efficacy of this system is particularly apparent in the fact that the two parties do not engage in a life-and-death struggle with each other. In the aftermath of United States elections, there is no fear that the losers will mount the barricades or that the winners will annihilate the losers. No one is going to be shot for losing and no one is going to be made dictator for winning. This acceptance, which seems so natural and logical as hardly to need comment, gives a considerable stability to all institutions. The only time any sizable number of Americans refused to accept the outcome of an election, the result was the Civil War of 1861–1865. Neither before nor since have the losers failed to acquiesce.

EXPLANATIONS OF THE SYSTEM

Inasmuch as a unique type of two-party system dominates the American political landscape, the reasons for the system's appearance and continuation become important. In one sense it does not matter why we have the system as long as it satisfies us; knowing historical or organic causes for the system may be unimportant from the practical point of view of opera-

ting it. In another sense, however, a comprehension of how it came about
and why it was developed may be extremely important in forming judgments and evaluating the system itself. In addition, to ask the question,
Why does the United States have a two-party system? leads to further interesting questions which generally stimulate worthwhile thinking about
the whole spectrum of political parties, their functions, and the characteristics of the people who operate them.[1]

MECHANICAL-ELECTORAL EXPLANATIONS

Single Member Districts. One of the most frequent explanations of
bipartisanism is the special influence of such devices as the single-member
legislative district, the election of single executives, and the electoral-
college system. Here, the emphasis is upon certain mechanical features of
the electoral system.

One of the most ambitious attempts to explain the two-party system
as the result of the single-member district arrangement was made by Professor E. E. Schattschneider, who emphasized that the result of grouping
voters by geographical areas is to produce accidental distributions of party
support. Or, conversely, to divide voters into arbitrary districts by drawing
lines on a map is to deprive parties of a representation proportionate to
the total state vote cast for the parties. One party, theoretically, can make
a clean sweep of all the districts by polling 51% of the total vote, assuming
that in each district the party gets just a few votes more than the other
party. Actually, this kind of result is not likely to happen, but what does
happen is that a party receiving, let us say, 55% of the total vote cast in all
districts will very likely elect 60% or more of the members. There is, then,
an unearned increment in the number of seats won by the party getting
a majority of all of the votes, while the party getting less than a majority
suffers an unearned penalty by electing a smaller percentage of its members
than its percentage of the total vote. When parties have unqual distributions of strength geographically, they have strongholds to which they cling
in times of despair and weather vanes that turn to them when the wind is
in their direction. In this way the minority party can command a monopoly
in opposing the majority party in each district, for the minority (or second
party) becomes the natural rallying point for those opposed to the majority
party. Hence, no party except the two major ones has an opportunity to
develop into a genuine electoral organization.[2]

---

[1] The discussion that follows of the explanations for the two-party system assumes its
continued evolution but does not preclude the possibility of its being reconstituted by
Americans' beliefs and practices.

[2] Schattschneider, *Party Government* (New York: Farrar & Rinehart, 1942) pp. 70-84.

The single-member argument is often buttressed with the contention that it produces the two-party system when a majority is required for election. Although some states in the United States require that a candidate receive a majority in a direct-primary election in order to become his party's nominee, no state requires by law that a candidate have a majority of all the votes cast to be *elected* to an office. The fact is that with a two-party system one of the candidates nearly always gets a majority, but the majority is the result of the system, the system is not the result of having to receive a majority.

There are two basic difficulties which arise when the single-member district is associated with a two-party system and the multimember district is associated with a multiparty system. First, multiparty political systems, e.g., in France, have used single-member districts without tending to become two-party systems. Second, two-party systems employ multimember districts without encouraging additional parties. In 1954, it was found that over 12% of the members of state senates and 45% of state representatives in the United States were elected from multimember districts.[3] The most clear-cut case is the state of Illinois. The members of the lower house of the Illinois legislature are elected by cumulative voting whereby each district elects three members and each voter can concentrate his votes upon one or two candidates or distribute his votes equally among three candidates. One of the aims of this system, according to a close student of it, is to provide minority representation [4]; but the minority in each case is one of the major parties, not minor parties. Here, with multimember districts, the two-party system goes serenely on.

It is difficult to resist the conclusion that the method, instead of creating the system, is made to conform to the system.[5] This statement should not obscure the fact that the single-member district is obviously more adaptable to bipartisanism than other systems. The kind of multimember district which would be established by proportional representation would no doubt tend to weaken the major parties by encouraging splinter groups. However, the genuine weakening would arise from the existence in the first place of splinter groups demanding separate representation through multimember districts. It appears that the advocates of the two-party sys-

---

[3] Maurice Klain, "A New Look at the Constituencies: The Need for a Recount and a Reappraisal," *American Political Science Review*, Vol. 49 (1955) pp. 1107, 1108.

[4] See below, pp. 585-586.

[5] J. C. Charlesworth, "Is Our Two-Party System 'Natural'?" *The Annals*, Vol. 259 (1948) p. 6. The same conclusions have been applied to the British; see Leslie Lipson, "The Two-Party System in British Politics," *American Political Science Review*, Vol. 47 (1953) pp. 346-350.

tem and of proportional representation are not so much mortal enemies as they are principally concerned with diametrically opposite objectives in representation. Proportional representation is not advanced by those who are primarily concerned with bipartisanism, but instead, by those who are willing to have multiple parties in order to have proportional representation.

When the single-member district explanation is placed in this light, the reliance upon the mechanics of electing single executives looks less attractive, especially when the action is presented as being another selection from a single-member district, i.e., a state or the nation. However, this explanation, particularly as applied to the Presidency, does not lack worthy advocates. Professor Arthur Macmahon concludes that the influence of the presidential office "more than any other factor discouraged the development of the multiplicity of parties." [6] No one would deny that the office of President is the capstone of a system of crucial executive elections and that many politicians are preoccupied with the problems of getting and retaining these offices. However, other English-speaking nations which possess a two-party system do not have an elective office comparable to that of the President of the United States. More to the point, some countries have or have had elective presidential offices without producing a two-party system, although the requirement that the winner receive a majority of the votes cast is likely to produce two coalitions for the second or runoff election.

A similar situation occurs in city elections in the United States held under the nonpartisan system. The first city election brings out, as a rule, a long list of candidates for each office, with the result that no candidate gets a majority. It then becomes necessary to hold a runoff election between the two candidates who received the highest number of votes for each office; in this second election, with only two choices, the political forces split two ways. No one would say that the runoff election in a city gives evidence of an incipient two-party system even if the candidates were running as members of political parties. The fact that they are not frees city politics from party restrictions and makes of it something much more comparable with multiparty politics. In fact, this situation has arisen consistently in multiparty systems when a majority was required.

The single-member-district explanation has the same defects whether applied to a single-member district within a state, to a whole state, or to the entire United States.

---

[6] Macmahon in *Encyclopedia of Social Sciences*, Vol. 11 (1933) p. 598. In fact Professor Macmahon defines American parties as "loose alliances to win the stakes of power embodied in the presidency."

Electoral College System. The Presidency merits further attention because of the operations of the peculiar device for electing presidents. A majority of the electoral votes is required to elect, or if no candidate receives a majority, the House of Representatives elects. Presidential electors are chosen by the voters in each state on the at-large basis. Because a party must be organized nation-wide in order to command a majority of the electoral votes, purely sectional parties cannot hope to win the Presidency.[7] This situation is a description of what has happened in the organization of parties for the purpose of winning the nation's highest office, but the description has been accepted as proof of the cause-and-effect relation between the electoral college and the two-party system. The examination of this conclusion raises two separate questions: Is it the electoral college itself or the majority requirement that sustains the two-party system? The reasoning, in either case, rests on the belief that if victory were to depend less upon a large coalition, splinter groupings would be encouraged and smaller parties would become more numerous and more important.

No matter which of the two questions is dealt with, the insistence upon preserving bipartisanism immediately dominates the discussion. By the time the proposals have been cut to fit the cloth of the two-party system, they are little more than ravelings clinging to the fabric of the major parties. This result demonstrates that exponents of the two-party system are suspicious of experimenting with the electoral-voting arrangement, but the relationship remains obscure. There are too many loose ends, too many imponderables, too many speculative avenues of thought. However, it is possible to see some light by keeping out of the clouds of the unknown and remaining within the limited perimeter of observable phenomena.

If in the future a minor party should develop unusual strength, the assumption that one of the major parties will always get a majority of the electoral votes would have to be abandoned. Granted such a new status for one or more minor parties, the mechanics of the present electoral college could very well be a serious obstruction to their aspirations; but the new development itself would signal a breakdown of the two-party system. Would the two-party system survive if it was supported only by the electoral college system? It would be a tremendous assertion that, in the past, voters would have voted differently if there had been no electoral college, particularly in view of the unawareness of many of them that they were voting for presidential electors instead of presidential candidates.

It can even be argued that given a predisposition for the multiparty system, the electoral college could be an invitation to splinter parties to enter slates of electors, to deprive any candidate of a majority and to force

[7] *Ibid.*, p. 144. Arthur N. Holcombe, *The Political Parties of To-Day* (New York: Harper & Brothers, 1924) pp. 316-317.

every presidential election into the House of Representatives. Here, we reach bedrock. Under the two-party system, it would be useless for a minor party to carry an election to the House when it is composed only of major-party members. The present situation in presidential elections reveals various minor parties talking as if they were in the race, but if they are too weak to elect members of the House, how can they win electoral votes? Can they elect members of Congress if there are no electoral votes?

Supposing the House of Representatives to be multiparty in composition, the results of an undecided presidential election would be a fantastic confusion in which the system would completely break down or interparty negotiations would finally produce a solution—the actual procedure used by the two parties in 1877. Such goings-on would strike Americans as ludicrous. Their government and party system would be incompatible, and Americans would be incompatible with both because they habitually show the keenest resentment toward prolonged deadlock. They want the election to settle the issue and not be kept in suspended agitation while representatives continue the campaign on the floor of the House. Assessments of the results the few times the House has had to settle an election suggest that the machinations harass party leaders and antagonize the public.

A third issue is now raised, that is, the significance of the practice of electing presidential electors on the general-ticket basis. This is an all-or-none system, for in each state the slate of electors receiving more votes than any other slate is elected *in toto*. This system is not required by any federal law; and the states are quite free to elect their electors any way they choose: by districts, proportionally, or at large on a general ticket. By a natural process of political deduction, leaders in even those states that once used the district method came around to the at-large method, and the overwhelming majority of states has never used any other method. It can be said in all truthfulness that political leaders favored at-large election because it most nearly insured a majority in the electoral college and permitted one party to elect a President without dissipating itself in the House of Representatives. The constitutional provisions regarding presidential electors do not create or even presume bipartisanism, but the usages which have come to surround those provisions are clearly intended for a political system which offers just two principal alternatives.

The evidence strongly suggests a predisposition, a value judgment, on the part of both leaders and followers for the two-party system. This predisposition has led to compatible methods, to techniques which facilitate the ultimate objective. Looked at in this light, it is putting the cart before the horse to conclude that the method produced the predisposition. Rather, it is either independent of or antecedent to both the constitutional method of electing presidents and the usages associated with that method.

ECONOMIC AND SOCIAL EXPLANATION

Economic conflict as a dichotomy has been advanced as the cause of the two-party system. This interpretation springs from various sorts of evidence. It may be found in the "long standing opposition" "between independent farming and the mercantile and financial activity out of which industry grew." Given this basic struggle, American party division was "based on the reality of the conflict between wealth in the land and wealth seeking outlets in industry." [8] By extension, this division is seen in a gulf between gentlemen and commoners and in the cleavage between "liberals" and "conservatives," the classification being farmers, commoners, and liberals as one general group and merchants, gentlemen, and conservatives as the other group. Some "popular" enlargements upon this theme have added words without appreciable elucidation of the problem.

In the writing of the Constitution, generally speaking, farmers were split between those with back-country interests and those with tidewater interests; urban populations were split between artisans and the financial and mercantile interests. Tidewater agriculture and urban capital were allied in carrying through this momentous reform.[9] The Federalist Party, however, neglected the Southern planters who oriented toward the Jeffersonian Party which was coalescing around the debtor discontent of the back-country farmers. So, the first major two-party alignments were agriculture v. business, but it was also an alignment of gentlemen and commoner v. urban interests. No one has adequately explained why, if there be unity of agricultural interests, farmers joined both major parties nor, if it be argued that agriculture is not unified, how the diverse interests helped to create bipartisanism. The high tide of minor-party strength in the United States was based upon farmer discontent in the West and South in the last three decades of the nineteenth century, suggesting that diverse agriculture interests could have supported multipartisanism. It is far from clear why the diverse interests of business helped to stabilize a two-party system, or why business elements turn up in both parties. Finally, why is it that the overwhelming number of special interest groups, classifiable under as many headings as there are classifiers, have worked through two parties in the United States and through many parties in various other countries? [10]

Jeffersonianism v. Hamiltonianism. Closely related to economic determinism is the concept that everyone is born a strict or loose constructionist

---

[8] Macmahon, *op. cit.*, pp. 597, 598. In 1808 John Adams stated his belief that two parties reflect differences in wealth and are particularly found in commercial countries. ——*The Works of John Adams* (Boston: Little, Brown and Co., 1865) Vol. 6, pp. 530-531.

[9] Charles A. Beard, *An Economic Interpretation of the Constitution* (New York: The Macmillan Company, 1939) pp. 149-151, Chap. 10.

[10] Charlesworth, *op. cit.*, pp. 6-7.

of the Constitution. In this way each individual can trace his political, economic, and social lineage directly to Thomas Jefferson or Alexander Hamilton, respectively; and we have a Jeffersonian-Hamiltonian two-party system representing views toward the meaning of the Constitution based upon predestined views toward government and life generally. Perhaps this historical fountainhead doctrine can be sustained even if, in tracing the heritage of Jefferson and Hamilton, the threads of continuity get crossed as they move from one party to the other—even if the Jeffersonian Party becomes loose-constructionist and the ideological heirs of Hamilton adopt a strict-construction view. The death knell, rather, of this contention is the discovery that constitutional interpretation must not be fixed at birth because the same man from time to time can be strict and loose and can even be both simultaneously in regard to different public policies. Reactions to the powers and functions of government are not the result of temperament but of interests; and the followers of Jefferson and of Hamilton were pursuing their interests, not a constitutional doctrine. The theory was subservient to the ends.[11]

CULTURAL HOMOGENEITY AS AN EXPLANATION

Because the two-party system is looked upon as reflecting a large area of consensus in the United States, cultural homogeneity is sometimes found to be the backbone of the system itself. This homogeneity is often seen as the product of the colonizers and settlers who predominantly reflected English customs and thinking and set the mold to which subsequent migrants have conformed. The assimilation of the foreign-born into American culture, as a result, is a process of conforming. This culture, though absorbed with relative speed, is not attained instantaneously. Practices of other national cultures linger on and are sometimes insulated against the corroding process of Americanization by a voluntary segregation. Racial and nationalistic attachments to countries of origin have

---

11 See Elihu Root, *The Citizen's Part in Government* (New Haven: Yale University Press, 1920, 2d printing) pp. 46-47. Lord Bryce, *The American Commonwealth* (New York: 1908) Vol. I, pp. 16-19, concluded that two "permanent oppositions" ran through our party history: centralized v. federalized government and authority v. liberty. He was able to show some basis for putting the Federalist-Whig-Republican Parties on the sides of centralization and authority and the Democrats on the opposite sides. Yet, he carefully recorded the confusions resulting from such a classification and noted that the liberty v. order opposition "goes deeper and is more pervasive, has been less clearly marked . . . and less consciously admitted by the Americans themselves."——p. 17. If the two oppositions are related, subsequent history has only further confused the distinctions which Bryce found far from clear. It is reasonable to wonder if he would have applied the same historical opposition between the parties on centralized v. federalized government after 1933. It is no secret, surely, that both Thomas Jefferson and James Madison were at one time or another on both sides of the central v. decentral controversy. See H. J. Ford, *The Rise and Growth of American Politics* (New York: The Macmillan Company, 1898) p. 116; Beard, *The American Party Battle*, (New York: The Macmillan Company, 1928) pp. 2-5, 139.

sometimes been injected into American politics with considerable friction as a result, but through it all the two-party system has continued to develop.

If it were true, cultural homogeneity would certainly be a plausible explanation of the United States political party system. It would answer so many questions and account for so many results. Its onetime validity no longer exists. As a nation, we are a plethora of nationalities, races, and cultures which are often sources of multiparties abroad. If homogeneity be the cause of bipartisanism, we could not possibly have maintained it and would have abandoned it several generations ago.[12]

ANGLO-SAXON POLITICAL MATURITY AS AN EXPLANATION

If the cultural practices of the United States do not offer enough unity to be used as a peg on which to hang the two-party system, the search for other fundamental supports is not precluded. Presumably, the object of the search is not too far removed from the principle involved in cultural homogeneity. The problem is to find another base for the consensus, not another and unrelated kind of explanation. This other base is sometimes proclaimed as being the more advanced and sophisticated political development of English-speaking peoples.[13] Like the previous explanation, this one antedates both the Constitution and the Revolution and denies that bipartisanism relies upon post-Constitution phenomena.

The very enunciation of this thesis tends to call forth its own opposition. No doubt some people are repelled by the suggestion of racial superiority or the implication of self-satisfaction. There is one difficulty the opponents must face and that is the fact that the two-party system is characteristic of Anglo-Saxon political institutions although some Anglo-Saxon countries have more than two major parties and some other countries have, actually, a two-party system.[14] Objection can be directed to the assertion that bipartisanism is symptomatic of political *maturity*. Such a pronouncement carries a good deal of gratuitous assumption or invidious comparison. The "maturity" analysis has been used by those who are themselves conditioned by the English heritage and who strongly favor the stabilizing qualities of the two-party system as against the erraticism of the multiparty system. If this reasoning be understandable on the part of

---

[12] Charlesworth, *op. cit.*, p. 6. If cultural homogeneity were the cause of bipartisanism, it would be very disturbing to read the thesis of Samuel Lubell, *The Future of American Politics* (New York: Harper & Brothers, 1952).

[13] Charlesworth, *op. cit.*, p. 8. Root, *op. cit.*, pp. 70-77, distinguished three stages of evolution of popular government in which political division occurred on the bases, first, of what individual would have power; second, of interest and ideas; third, of fundamental differences of principles and policies. Only the last basis, according to Root, would be a two-party division.

[14] Maurice Duverger, *Political Parties: Their Organization and Activity in the Modern State* (New York: John Wiley & Sons, Inc., 1954) pp. 208-212.

those having these value judgments, objection can most legitimately be made to one of their implicit assumptions: The two-party system is the highest and most blessed level of political heaven, to which refuge all who would be saved must eventually repair. It would be a safe conclusion that the French and Italians will never reign with us in two-party glory. Bipartisanism is neither inevitable nor predestined. That English-speaking nations have it means nothing beyond the fact itself. Nations that do not have it give no promise of attaining it.[15]

At last the question of two parties is placed in its proper perspective; its principal orbit is Anglo-Saxon, not just American, practices. The late Professor Sait asserted flatly that for any explanation of the two-party system in the United States to be valid, it must also explain the system in Great Britain. Operation with only two major parties is an Anglo-Saxon characteristic, he went on, "whether it has become such through historical accident or through a racial aptitude for practical politics or through the longer experience of the English-speaking peoples with popular self-government." [16] Neither the British system nor ours grew in one piece overnight, and the characteristics associated with them in the twentieth century appeared primarily after the two countries' political separation. What we did not inherit before the Revolutionary War we developed independently thereafter. With a totally different form of government, living in a totally different environment, we also produced a two-party system; but it is a very different kind of two-party system.

If we have bipartisanism because we inherited English institutions, can we be more definite than Professor Sait as to why English institutions include bipartisanism? Suddenly the suspicion appears that to answer this question is really a function of psychology or anthropology or, maybe, biology. The best that students of politics, who are laymen in these other fields, can do is examine the political evidence and agree that "it will be conceded that, to a considerable degree, the English-speaking peoples are less doctrinaire in politics" [17] and that American voters "find pleasure in affiliation with vast if amorphous political associations." [18]

---

[15] This thesis also suffers from certain historical flaws, particularly the fact that the record of English parties is not entirely that of bipartisanism. The English tendency to waver between two or more parties led Professor Carl J. Friedrich to call it "a two-and-one-half-party system."—*Constitutional Government and Democracy* (Boston: 1950, rev. ed.) p. 414. Lipson, *op. cit.*, p. 339, takes exception to Friedrich. It is also discouraging to admit that our own American leaders of the Constitutional period, despite their Anglo-Saxon backgrounds and the cultural homogeneity of their time, were extremely dull about perceiving the usefulness of any kind of party system, to say nothing of foreseeing bipartisanism as "maturity" in the evolution of government.

[16] Howard R. Penniman, *Sait's American Parties and Elections* (New York: Appleton-Century-Crofts, 1952, 5th ed.) p. 181. Lipson contended that the causes in one country are not necessarily the only causes in other countries.—*Op. cit.*, p. 358.

[17] Penniman, *op. cit.*, p. 182.

[18] Macmahon, *op. cit.*, p. 597.

Considering the Frenchman as the apotheosis of the multiparty man, the nearly universal judgment has been that

> in his politics he tends to be theoretical; that is to say, having inherited or otherwise acquired a principle or an ideal, he holds out for it with a tenacity not so often encountered among Englishmen; and this makes it difficult for him to identify himself with a wide-sweeping political alignment which necessarily must be a product of compromise.[19]

If, as a result, it be reasonably true that politics to a Frenchman is a free-for-all fight instead of a game whereby one seeks his objectives, it is hopeless to expect him to adopt the two-party system. The French character "is traditionally one of personal individualism which tends to regard compromise as surrender of principle. Collectively Frenchmen have a highly developed sense of class interest and a marked reluctance to permit encroachments upon their class." [20]

FUNCTIONAL-PRAGMATIC EXPLANATION

The best conclusion would seem to be that the United States has the two-party system because it works according to our standards of a political system; that our "system results from an act of will, on the part of men who have sensed that it is the best way to operate a republican government." [21] Americans want one party to govern at a time; this result depends upon one party receiving a majority, and this eventuality can only be assured by limiting the number of parties to two. American government, being both federal and presidential, is more decentralized and dispersed and requires more of parties than even some other two-party systems do. As nearly as we can tell, only the specific two-party system which we have can hold together and coordinate all these loose pieces of machinery. The formally described government organization in this country would most naturally lend itself to a politics of fragmentation.

Standards for a satisfying explanation of the two-party system may vary, but to attribute the system to the accidents of mechanics or the presence of some immutable force is hardly superior to free choice and determination. If the explanation offered here is not immediately plausible, it is at least capable of further refinement and exactness. Its ultimate merit will not be its statement of the complete truth but its providing the basis for the truth.

---

[19] F. A. Ogg and Harold Zink, *Modern Foreign Governments* (New York: The Macmillan Company, 1949) pp. 547, 548.

[20] Robert C. Doty in the *New York Times,* March 1, 1953, p. 4E. For a summary of two-party evolution in England and a comparative analysis of it and the French system, see Friedrich, *op. cit.,* pp. 411-413.

[21] Charlesworth, *op. cit.,* p. 9.

DEPARTURES FROM THE SYSTEM

One-Party Systems. One of the principal features of the American two-party system is the fact that half or less than half of the states have such a system, as measured over a period of time, in either presidential or state elections.[22] The issues leading to the Civil War, the War itself and the Reconstruction following have endured for more than one hundred years as the dominant influences underlying voters' partisan inclinations. Although these influences have existed in most of the states, the strongest partisan traditions stemming from the Civil War period have persisted in the secession states of the Confederacy. The term "Solid South" is symbolical of the insistence upon voting in the twentieth century according to the issues of the mid-nineteenth century. This persistent Southern unity, equated with the one-party political system, has given an illusion of uniformity in Southern problems and conditions when the one genuine basis for the solidarity has really been the Negro.[23]

The exact nature of the Democratic Party in the South, including the degree of its factionalism, varies sharply from state to state so that the section actually presents a variety of one-party systems. In some states, e.g., North Carolina, Tennessee, and Virginia, the Democratic Party is split into two well-defined factions and normally presents a united front because, if for no other reason, the Republican Party is strong enough to win a state election if the Democrats become too disunited. In Georgia and Louisiana, since the days of Eugene Talmadge and Huey Long, respectively, the Democrats are principally divided into two factions, not because of the potential threat of the Republicans but because of basic policy differences between Democrats giving some semblance of a two-party division. In Alabama, Mississippi, and South Carolina there are neither enough Republicans nor enough well-defined issues to create unity and overcome localisms; the Democrats are divided into numerous factions based on the highly

---

22 By combining the vote for the offices of president, governor, and United States senator, 1914 through 1952, twenty-six states were classed as two-party, twelve as modified one-party and ten as one-party. See Austin Ranney and Willmoore Kendall, "The American Party Systems," *American Political Science Review*, Vol. 48 (1954) pp. 477-485. Using only the vote for governor and applying two criteria—the division in party control over a period of time and the rate of alternation between parties—nine states were classed as competitive, four as cyclically competitive, eight as one-party cyclical, sixteen as one-party predominant, and eleven as one-party. Joseph A. Schlesinger, "A Two-Dimensional Scheme for Classifying the States According to Degree of Inter-Party Competition," *ibid.*, Vol. 49 (1955) pp. 1120-1128. Partisan results in some northern states' elections are affected by various practices, such as nonconcurrent and staggered terms required in constitutions, legislative apportionments, and erratic voting behavior. V. O. Key, Jr., *American State Politics: An Introduction* (New York: Alfred A. Knopf, Inc., 1956) Chap. 3.

23 V. O. Key, Jr., *Southern Politics in State and Nation* (New York: Alfred A. Knopf, Inc., 1949) p. 315 and *passim*; O. Douglas Weeks, "Republicanism and Conservatism in the South," *Southwestern Social Science Quarterly* (Dec., 1955) pp. 253-254.

TABLE 1: NUMBER OF GENERAL ELECTIONS UNCONTESTED BY MAJOR PARTIES FOR THE OFFICES OF GOVERNOR, UNITED STATES SENATOR, AND UNITED STATES REPRESENTATIVES (1946–)

(Where party identification of D or R is not shown, unopposed candidates were Democrats. Numbers beneath states indicate gain or loss under 1950 census reapportionment)

States	1946			1948			1950			1952			1954			1956			1958		
	Gov.	Sen.	Rep.	Gov.	Sen.	Rep.	Gov.	Sen.	Rep.	Gov.	Sen.	Rep.	Gov.	Sen.	Rep.	Gov.	Sen.	Rep.	Gov.	Sen.	Rep.
1. Alabama	1		5		1	5	1	1	8			7	1		7		1	6			8
2. Arkansas (−1, 1950)			6	1		7			7			4		1	6	1		5			6
3. California (+7, 1950)	1		6D 4R			3D 9R			5D 6R			6D 7R			2			3			5
4. Florida (+2, 1950)			3			2		1	4			4			6		1	2			5
5. Georgia		1	10	1		10	1		10			10	1		9		1	9	1		10
6. Kentucky (−1, 1950)			1R		1	1D 1R			4D 1R					1	3			1			2
7. Louisiana			6	1		7			8			7 1R		1	7	1		6 1R			7
8. Massachusetts			1			2D 2R									3D 1R			6		1	3D 1R
9. Mississippi (−1, 1950)		1	7		1	6		1	5		1	4		1	6		1	4			6
10. North Carolina			1						3	1		3			2						4
11. South Carolina			6		1			1	6		1	4			1			4			6
12. Tennessee (−1, 1950)	1		6D 2R			3D 1R	1		8		1	5	1		4			4D 1R			6
13. Texas (+1, 1950)			14			12			15	1[a]	1[a]	21			17		1	17	1		19
14. Virginia			1			2			5		1	5		1	4			1		1	7
TOTALS	3	2	79	3	4	73	3	4	96[b]	2	5	88	3	5	81[c]	2	5	72[d]	2	2	96[e]
Percentage of total of House seats uncontested:			18.2			16.8			22.1			20.2			18.6			16.6			22.0

[a] Democrat endorsed by Republicans.
[b] Includes 1D in Missouri.
[c] Includes 1R in Illinois, 1D in Maryland, and 1D in Oklahoma.
[d] Includes 2D in Missouri.
[e] Includes 1D in West Virginia. One of the six seats in Arkansas was contested and won by an Independent Democrat as a write-in candidate.

SOURCES: Richard M. Scammon (ed.) America Votes. New York: The Macmillan Co, 1956 and 1958; Congressional Directory.

personalized leadership of individual men. Arkansas, too, is a case of fluid multifactionalism, but it results primarily from a consensus upon policy among the voters. Texas has moved back and forth from dual factionalism to multifactionalism, and Florida appears to be moving from the latter to the former.[24]

Irrespective of the various motivations among the Democrats in the Solid South, it is a section from which, traditionally, the Republican Party has been excluded in presidential as well as state and local elections. Although the Democrats have been consistently excluded from a few states outside the South in presidential elections, many northern and western states—led by Vermont—have long records of one-party Republican dominance or monopoly on the state and local levels.

That two-party competition is the stereotype rather than the fact in some parts of the country is suggested in the elections for the lower house of Congress. Table 1 shows the number of public offices filled without a genuine contest at the general election; either the winning candidate ran without any opposition or with only minor-party or independent opposition. Although the table includes other offices, it is in the congressional districts that the bulk of the uncontested elections occur. Of the total House membership of 435 (436 in 1958), the number of uncontested seats was never less than one-sixth and was more than one-fifth in 1950, 1952, and 1958. In over three-fourths of the congressional districts, the majority party normally receives 55% or more of the total vote. Between 1896 and 1946, one-fourth of all House members were elected with at least 75% of the total vote cast.[25] In the twenty-five elections between 1896 and 1944, the Republicans on the average failed to run a congressional candidate for 15.2% of the seats; the Democrats' average was 3.9%.[26]

Another and a different kind of trend bearing upon the two-party system has developed in New York City. The American Labor Party was formed in 1936, with the support of Franklin D. Roosevelt, to insure the Democrats' carrying the state by bringing labor directly into political organization. Within a few years the American Labor Party was so domi-

---

[24] Key, *Southern Politics*, Chaps. 2-14. Alexander Heard, *A Two-Party South?* (Chapel Hill: University of North Carolina, 1952) pp. 14-16. H. D. Price, *The Negro and Southern Politics* (New York: New York University Press, 1957) p. 95. O. Douglas Weeks, *Texas One-Party Politics in 1956* (Austin: The University of Texas, Institute of Public Affairs, 1957) p. 35.

[25] Julius Turner, "Primary Elections as the Alternative to Party Competition in 'Safe' Districts," *Journal of Politics*, Vol. 15 (1953) pp. 197-210; Malcolm Moos, *Politics, Presidents and Coattails* (Baltimore: The Johns Hopkins Press, 1952) pp. 24-29; Cortez A. M. Ewing, "Primaries as Real Elections," *Southwestern Social Science Quarterly*, Vol. 29 (1949) p. 294.

[26] *Ibid.*, p. 297; Cortez A. M. Ewing, *Congressional Elections* (Norman: University of Oklahoma Press, 1947) pp. 55-57. Out of thirteen elections in the South between 1920 and 1944 for members of the national House, an average of 43.5% of the seats was uncontested in the general election, and in a majority of those contested the opposition was negligible. *Ibid.*, p. 92.

nated by its pro-Soviet Communist faction that the Liberal Party was formed to carry on the political organization of labor.[27] Four parties operated for a time in the state of New York, but in 1954 the ALP failed to receive enough votes to remain a legal party. Few officials are elected by the Liberal Party alone, but most of the officials elected from New York City are elected either as Democratic-Liberal or Republican-Liberal coalition candidates. The affinity between the Liberal and Democratic parties is very close, and a large majority of the coalition candidates run with these two parties' endorsements against Republicans. In fact, it has become exceedingly difficult for the Democrats to win a state-wide contest (whether for President, United States senator, governor, attorney general, or comptroller) unless the Liberals endorse the Democratic candidate. The practice of coalition politics, therefore, has qualified the fact of multiparty politics, but the persistence of a separate Liberal Party supports the conclusion that the two-party system is the result of wanting the system and that highly divisive issues developed by independent leaders will produce at least a striking variant of the system.

Although it may appear paradoxical, this New York development can be seen as part of an apparently definite trend away from the heretofore one-party system in much of the United States. New York City has never really had a genuine two-party system and the Liberal Party has succeeded in presenting a challenge to the Democratic Party which the Republicans rarely have been able to do. In a real sense the shifting or weakening of traditional party allegiances is becoming characteristic of the present generation of voters. These departures are most apparent in normally Republican states where Democrats are establishing themselves in executive and legislative offices and capturing congressional seats for the first time since the Civil War. Concurrently, the Solid South looks potentially less like a Democratic bastion after being penetrated in two consecutive presidential elections and after reelecting Republicans to congressional seats which Democrats had always held following Reconstruction.[28] The prospects for the future are not all of one kind. If schisms in some places

---

[27] Hugh A. Bone, "Political Parties in New York City," *American Political Science Review*, Vol. 40 (1946) pp. 272-282.

[28] Heard, *op. cit.;* Weeks, *op. cit.*, pp. 248-256. Donald S. Strong, "The Presidential Election in the South, 1952," *Journal of Politics*, Vol. 17 (1955) pp. 343-389; William Buchanan, "Cracks in Southern Solidarity," *Antioch Review*, Vol. 16 (Fall, 1956) pp. 351-364. The following tabulation shows the Republican gains in the National House of Representatives in the South:

	1946	1948	1950	1952	1954	1956	1958
Florida					1	1	1
North Carolina				1	1	1	1
Tennessee	2	2	2	2	2	2	2
Texas					1	1	1
Virginia				3	2	2	2
Totals	2	2	2	6	7	7	7

suggest the rise of strong minor parties, schisms and weakening traditions in others places suggest that national bipartisanism may be attained.[29]

The general assumption among students of the American party system is that nationalizing the two-party system is not only desirable but also essential to the development of a more responsive and representative government. Rarely is dissent voiced to these assertions. The fact is that one of the marks of the two-party system in the United States has been the absence of a two-party system in some sections and states. To change this feature would be likely to bring other changes some of which are expected and acclaimed and some of which may be unexpected and, depending upon the standards of judgment, dubious. Because the two parties have unequal strength in different states and sections, a party is not wiped from the board when it loses a national election. It still retains its control of those governments where its strength cannot be overcome even if it suffers a national disaster; from its areas of dominance, it can recoup and prepare a springboard for the next national contest. If the two-party system in the United States extended to every hamlet and crossroads, a national landslide would conceivably wipe out a party in every state and leave it no nucleus from which to rebuild. In this situation, the minority party would indeed have to monopolize the opposition to the majority party, for the former would need all of the resources available to come back and compete on equal terms.

SOME DISTINCTIVE CHARACTERISTICS OF THE SYSTEM

EFFECT UPON THE IDEOLOGICAL FUNCTION

The kind of bipartisanism developed in the United States has ruled out the possibility of the parties providing any kind of exactness in ideological choices. Conflicts which are incompatible with the two-party system have been submerged and ignored. Potential bases of parties, those which are really bases in multiparty systems such as race and religion, are avoided or suppressed.

This de-emphasis of the ideological function is not uniformly the same either within all two-party systems or at any given time in any one system. Evidence of ideological purity can be found in the formation of United States parties: The Federalists, Jeffersonians, Jacksonians, and Republicans were deeply concerned with fundamental problems of their times and took commanding positions in regard to them. It was in the stress of developing subsequent issues that these parties became intermixed and forsook their original character. Preoccupation with winning elections triumphed over the desire to reflect crystal-clear policy positions and submerged the ideo-

---

[29] For example, see Leon D. Epstein, "A Two-Party Wisconsin?" *Journal of Politics;* Vol. 18 (1956) pp. 427-458; Earl Latham, *Massachusetts Politics* (New York: The Citizenship Clearing House) pp. 5-23; Paul T. David, "The Changing Party Pattern," *Antioch Review,* Vol. 16 (1956) pp. 333-344.

logical function.[30] There is only one difficulty with this view of American party history, and that is the troublesome matter of accounting for the Whig Party. This Party suffered from the hour of its formation from its inner ideological incompatibilities and appeared to hold itself together by its opposition to Jackson and its collective desire to get votes. The contrast of the Whigs is undoubtedly overplayed, since the other major parties were not as simon-pure in their devotion to strict policies as time and eulogies would have us think. Yet, there is some contrast, and the problem is whether to treat the Whig Party as an exception to the rule or whether to conclude that it was never a genuine major party.

What does seem to be an unbroken rule in American politics is that parties have progressively weakened their original ideological content in order to widen their appeals and attract more supporters. For over the last hundred years, since platforms have been written at national conventions, we have a record of the parties' attempts to reach out for more and more voters. In order to promote or propagate an ideology, there is need for organization, which, in time, gets in the way of the ideology; but the original ideology itself is progressively weakened and perverted by shifting political circumstances and by the appearance of new problems. Eventually the only real cement holding the original factions together is the organization and the sentiments of the glorious struggles and victories of the past. As Lord Bryce concluded from his study of American parties, "the fewer have become their principles, the more perfect has become their organization. The less of nature the more of art; the less spontaneity the more mechanism." [31]

PARTY DISTINCTIONS

Similarity. As the ideological content of the two major parties becomes more anemic and as they intrench themselves behind their organizational breastworks, another result is the tendency for the two to become more alike because they are seeking the votes of the same individuals. Two-party competition carries with it the inevitability of one party getting a majority, so politicians in the United States cannot assume that they are precluded from any significant number of voters. The party leaders seek to be all things to all men, and in this process the leaders of both parties end by being very much like each other. By having representatives of all within each party, it mirrors the clashes of interests found in the other party, while both of them mirror the clashes found generally within the body politic.

---

[30] For a general statement of this development in parties, see Robert M. MacIver, *The Modern State* (New York: Oxford University Press, 1950) pp. 401, 402.

[31] *Op. cit.,* p. 3; also pp. 22-24. It has been suggested that Sir Henry Maine's theory that party struggles are the result of a combative instinct may be a good explanation of a party's continuation if not of a party's origin.——Penniman, *op. cit.,* pp. 168-169; A. D. Morse, *Parties and Party Leaders* (Boston: Marshall Jones Company, 1923) p. 17.

Moderation. Paralleling this movement toward similarity, the parties tend to reflect moderate rather than extreme positions. The interests both parties are trying to hold together are to a greater or lesser degree incompatible as far as their extreme objectives are concerned. In order to fashion a well-rounded appeal to the maximum number of interests each party tones down its appeal to any one specific interest and attempts to convince the leaders of each such interest that they can get more from this party than from the other party. In this way each party tries to find the common denominator within the electorate, the best balance of calculated appeals and commitments which can be designed at the time to produce a majority at the polls. Furthermore the tendency to moderation is enforced by the skepticism of the general voter toward extreme positions and the resultant political disaster that is likely to result from a failure to conciliate, reconcile, and harmonize.[32]

Do the Parties Stand for Anything? Because of these characteristics of similarity and moderation, the party system is criticized and even scorned because the parties do not stand for anything. The choice between Democrats and Republicans is asserted to be the choice between tweedledum and tweedledee. There may be some choice in personalities and even some in general capabilities; otherwise, it is often contended, the voters select one candidate in preference to the other candidate for reasons probably not well known even to the voters.[33] Apparently, we cannot quite make up our minds. We want the two-party system, but we berate politicians for operating in a manner made necessary by the system. We deplore the lack of choices and the obvious posturings for votes, but we feign grave alarm when we think politicians are threatening our unity and stability by their failure to get together and agree on programs.

To leave the discussion at this point is dissatisfying and the premonition lingers that something more remains to be said. Is this concept of tweedledum-and-tweedledee parties correct or is it an overemphasis for the sake of simplicity or for lack of better thinking? The concept has been

---

[32] Penniman, *op. cit.*, pp. 161-168; Arthur N. Holcombe, *Our More Perfect Union* (Cambridge: Harvard University Press, 1950) p. 120.

[33] Arthur N. Holcombe, *The Political Parties of To-Day* (New York: Harper & Brothers, 1924) Chap. 1, surveys an arresting historical record of this disparagement of parties. In *Our More Perfect Union*, p. 401, Professor Holcombe makes a frontal assault upon this view: "If there were no differences between the parties except the personal differences between their candidates for the presidency, the system would still serve its essential purpose. Both parties would strive to find the candidates who would seem most attractive to the kinds of voters holding the balance of power in the big doubtful states. The safeguards against a perpetual monopoly of power of the 'ins' would be the disposition of those voters least dominated by habit and tradition to make a rational choice at the polls. A bipartisan system, uncomplicated by important economic and social differences between the parties, would offer these voters the kind of choice they are most competent to make intelligently." Here, at least, is a basis upon which choices can actually be made by voters despite the most perplexing issues over which even highly trained and qualified experts disagree.

rejected about as often as it has been accepted. Professor Holcombe compared parties to flowing waters which "can not greatly alter" their courses, which may slacken and dry up "leaving only a waste, a sad reminder of former greatness," and which may at flood time carry "all before it until its force is spent"—a party is channeled along a course guided by its "interests and habits and traditions." [34]

Samuel Lubell accepted as a fact the similarities of parties, but he was also convinced that there are important differences. Noting that except for the 1876-1896 period, one of the major parties has been the majority party and the other major party a minority party, he compared them to a solar system of a sun (the majority party) and a moon (the minority party). The significant struggles of each period are fought within the majority coalition, and the minority party, limited and controlled by the conflict within the majority party, revolves like the moon around the sun trying to attract enough elements to become itself the sun. Lubell conceived of the American party as a magnet drawing together conflicting elements which, by their alliance, "defy every law of logic. But, like the sun, this apparently unstable political mass has its own gravitational equilibrium." [35]

Personality Differences. The question of the differences between the two parties becomes more tantalizing the further it is pursued. Within their similarities the parties are different, but the one or the other characteristic side of their nature alternately predominates with the development of successive issues. At some times the parties seem to be, genuinely, tweedledum and tweedledee; but at other times they seem to reflect fairly sharp differences. Although their essential similarities may be seen despite the alternate choices they are presenting, there are choices even when they appear to be forced or synthetic. There are choices, at least, in the differences of the personalities of the candidates. While they may have a generally similar philosophy and may take a generally similar approach to problems, they will not react identically nor do exactly the same things in detail. Although individual differences are important, to make such differences apply to the parties, each of them would have to be linked to a given personality type.[36]

---

[34] *The Political Parties of To-Day*, pp. 348 ff.; also *The Middle Classes in American Politics* (Cambridge: Harvard University Press, 1940) pp. 117-120.

[35] Lubell, *op. cit.*, pp. 198-205.

[36] See *New York Times Magazine*, January 8, 1950; August 19, 1956, p. 10; May 5, 1957, p. 19. However, in commenting on the Washington crowds assembling for the inauguration of President Eisenhower in 1953, Arthur Krock noticed that "in their looks, their manners, their voices and their apparel the victors closely resemble the losers, and when they mix in groups the anthropologist or sociologist does not live who could tell them apart.

"This is not surprising, because they belong to the same continental breed, its members promptly recognizable as 'Americans' wherever they go. . . . It is not surprising also because, though the candidates and spokesmen of the two major parties approach

The crux of this question may actually be obscured by the conventional description of the party as simply appealing to interests in the role of a disinterested broker. This personification has some value in helping to demonstrate certain manifestations of political behavior, but its value is inherently limited because it either denies or ignores the involvement of party factions with given interests. An attempt to represent a collectivity as a unit should always be recognized frankly for what it is, a simplification for the purpose of elementary explanation. Once the point is grasped for which the simplification was employed, continuation of the figure of speech becomes oversimplification and can be misleading, if not pernicious.

Kinds of Affinities Between Parties and Interests. Major parties are not led by a single man who is a broker. They are led by a bewildering number of men and women—so many, in fact, that in the interest of the complete truth, it is impossible to say who are exclusively the leaders. These people who share the party leadership are not ideological eunuchs who have no real concern for the issues of their times. They have attachments and loyalties and vested interests of their own or they would not share in the leadership. Although the multigroup nature of American life is reflected in the parties, making them similar and moderate, affinities between parties and groups vary. Some groups have no logical antagonists or have no specifically organized opposition. These groups, particularly, give major parties an aura of tweedledum-tweedledee similarity. The special objectives of veterans organizations, for instance, are so well reflected by both parties that their differences on veterans affairs are imperceptible. Certain groups and interests have animosities for one another because of their conflicting objectives, and the predominance or submersion of such groups in a party will affect that party's ideological positions and set it off from the other party.

The two parties, like sailing ships, may list in opposite directions, but their hulls are in the same body of water and their courses are set by helmsmen with only relative differences in their sense of direction.

INERTIA OF THE VOTERS

Implicitly in the United States two-party system there has been an attitude of passivity on the part of the general public toward politics.

some problems of government from different directions, Republicans and Democrats agree more than they disagree on the nature of these problems and the objectives that must guide their solutions. The similarities in dress, in turns of language and ultimate goals make a human pattern in which—except for a few whose native latitudes are computable by their accents—only the strongest imagination could enable an onlooker to say, 'These are Capulets and those are Montagues.' . . . Even if the insides of the heads and cardiac regions of most of them could be given a doctrinal examination it is unlikely that convincing evidence would be produced of the congenital differences that are still proclaimed in the party platforms."——*New York Times*, January 20, 1953.

While the agitation and the noise at election times and even other times may be alarming or may betoken a high degree of excitement throughout the country, the actual situation is much nearer to passivity and humdrum living than the superficial evidence indicates. In part because of the areas of fundamental agreement, there is a greater necessity to manufacture enthusiasm and political spirit. The engines of partisan passions are brought to white heat for the benefit of a relative few. The peculiarly American reaction of skepticism and restraint toward things political makes its citizens appear to be blissfully unaware or callously disdainful of the hosannas and condemnations.

A form of inertia is reflected by certain kinds of voting behavior. One example is found among those citizens who habitually vote for a given party label. They usually talk like the most dogmatic partisans, as if the difference between heaven and hell were in the choice presented by the two parties. Yet when these habitual partisans lose an election (and some of them lose every election), they go on about their business in the usual way, paying off election bets and submitting to humorous remarks at their expense. Actually, they do not find life particularly different after they adjust themselves to the fact that their heroes lost and those rascals or knaves on the other side were elected. Another example is presented by those citizens who mark their ballots without any firm convictions. They vote for one candidate because a friend has urged them to do so. They vote for another candidate because he said something that pleased them or they like his appearance or his voice. A third example is the phenomenon of nonvoting.[37]

THE POSITION OF MINOR PARTIES

Variety and Impotence. Minor parties, within a two-party system, play an anomalous role. They exist, but they struggle to do even this much. They enter campaigns, but no one, practically speaking, pays any attention to them.[38] Some, like the Socialist Party, thrive on adversity; others spring up from nowhere and just as suddenly steal back into oblivion. The names of some suggest that politics is a question of what we eat and drink, e.g.,

---

[37] See below, pp. 544-553.

[38] The average percentage of the total presidential vote, 1900-1952, cast for minor parties is 6.3%. If the vote cast in 1912 and 1924 be disregarded (because of the abnormally large votes cast in those years for Theodore Roosevelt and R. M. LaFollette, Sr., respectively) the average for the other elections is 3.1%. Ewing, *op. cit.*, pp. 26-27, found a decline in the vote cast for minor parties both as a percentage of the total and in the number of seats contested. From 1896 to 1944, minor parties elected 128 members to Congress; Democrats elected 5301 and Republicans 4986. Ewing, *Presidential Elections* (Norman: University of Oklahoma Press, 1940) Chap. 3. The best any minor-party presidential candidate has done is poll 27.4% of the vote, in 1912, and then the popularity of an ex-President, supported by about half of a major party was required. "We find that the large minority votes are as a rule either Democratic or Republican, for the non-Democratic, non-Republican votes are widely scattered and few are continuous."—— E. E. Robinson, *The Presidential Vote* (Stanford: Stanford University Press, 1932) p. 34.

the Vegetarian and Prohibition Parties. The hard core of them holds stoically to the texts of their stern gospels of economic emancipation. Experimenters, proselyters and dispensers of dire doctrines of repentance, minor parties appeal to voters' political souls while major parties appeal to voters' hearts, and therefore get the votes on Election Day.

Relation with Major Parties. First among the complaints of minor-party leaders is the major-party fixation of the American people. The United States, when comprehended as a total political system, is a major-party paradise. Not only do the voters ignore the minor parties, but also the major parties can wait for the results of minor parties' experiments with issues in order to know what course to take. In this way, to borrow a theatrical term, the minor parties, by jumping into controversial issues without counting the cost in votes, "play it on the dog." When it is possible to assess the voters' reactions to these issues, the major parties are able to develop their positions with much greater safety and can, as conditions permit, adopt the proposals and arguments of the minor parties themselves without benefit of gift or question of inheritance. This type of operation requires that major-party leaders be agile, astute, and precise in their timing, for issues sometimes cannot be put aside even if they are more conveniently ignored. Major-party leaders have proved their mettle by adjusting to the facts of political life, and their flexibility in moving with the tide has helped to seal the fate of minor parties.

Minor-party leaders are consigned permanently to the dual role of being innovators and of being pressure valves for political steam when it can find no outlet in the major parties. The Socialist Party alone has taken root in some cities, e.g., in Connecticut, where Socialists dominate the municipal governments. With these few exceptions on the local level, minor parties, in the full sense, are not parties at all. They fail too many of the tests of the characteristics of a party, and definitions of parties have little application to them. They go by the name "parties," in popular vernacular, but they are variously agitational associations, educational organizations, or fiery debating societies. They are not in the same category as major parties and should not, properly speaking, be called parties at all.

From time to time, factions of a major party have broken away from their parent organizations and have attempted to become electoral organizations by themselves. Examples of such factions in the twentieth century were the Progressives of 1912, 1924, and 1948 and the State Righters also in 1948. In each case the factional leaders thought that they had some chance to win, or at least decide who would win. The outstanding characteristic of these factions is that they maintained their separate identity for one election. Thereafter, bowed in defeat, their members drifted back home to the major party from which they came, or joined the other major party, or slipped into a permanent opposition position in association with a minor party or some other group of protest. These bolting factions, while hopeless as successful parties, must be taken seriously because of the possibility that their diversion of strength will affect the outcome of the election. Their disaffection may doom the chances of the party from which they split, as was the case in 1912. In 1948, when two factions were subtracted from the same party, its defeat was confidently expected and its slim victory was all the more stunning because of these circumstances and expectations.

It is also quite conceivable that not only a faction but also a permanent minor party can affect the outcome of a close election between the major parties—especially if the faction or minor party has its following concentrated in one of the key states, as several times occurred in the two decades before the Civil War.

EFFECTS OF THE SYSTEM UPON THE POWER STRUGGLE

Inasmuch as political party leaders make the political struggle for power orderly, it is reasonable to expect that any individual party system encompasses this function in its own distinctive manner. In a two-party system, with its presentation of two choices, the dynamics of the power struggle is a contest between those who hold offices and those who do not.

Consequently, in the United States we speak very naturally of the "ins" and the "outs" and can raise little objection to Professor Holcombe's conclusion that "the perennial struggle of the 'outs' against the 'ins,' regardless of the ebb and flow of issues, seems to be the essence of the two-party system." [39] It may not be instantly apparent to a stranger just who constitute the "ins" and the "outs," but there is no doubt among those familiar with the system.[40] The "in" party is the one holding the executive positions, whether President, governor, sheriff, or mayor. The other party is "out" even if it has a majority in the legislative branch.

Object of Winning Elections. The power struggle in United States politics is distinguished not by the objective of winning elections but by the potentialities of what can be won. With only two choices, the prize is a complete victory in both the executive and legislative branch. Whichever party accomplishes this result comes into control of the government. Since one party or the other will attain this enviable position, they both

---

[39] *Our More Perfect Union*, p. 88.

[40] Rarely, perhaps, but possibly, there may be some confusion in the popular mind. In the 1948 presidential campaign, Harry S. Truman acted much more like an "out" than an "in." His savage attacks upon the Republicans who had a majority in Congress created a distinct impression that he was the challenger (the typical position of the "outs") and that the Republicans were on the defensive (the typical position of the "ins").

fight with every resource at their command to win each election. This is a constant objective nationally, and in two-party states and districts as well.

Acceptance of Loss of Elections. In one-party states and districts the minority party is perpetually consigned—and accepts the fact—to lose every contest. Sometimes in a city or a county in which one party is clearly dominant and the other party usually no more than an electoral harassment, agreements may be made between the leaders of the two parties to apportion the offices and eliminate actual electoral competition. The minority party will be permitted to elect a judge or a few councilmen or a county official or two and even be given some modicum of patronage if no candidate of the party opposes the dominant party's candidates for the other offices. This kind of arrangement is extrapolitical within the two-party system; it is not comprehended by the bipartisan philosophy, much less by democratic philosophy. It is a sign of the failure of the political system and a deficiency of some kind among the populace. Another kind of exception is that situation in which a political leader has a choice between winning an election and losing his control over the party machinery to another faction in the party; in this case, the organizational leader will almost invariably choose to lose the election and keep his position intact.

If there be exceptions to the rule of parties seeking to win elections, it can further be asked, Are there occasions when a party should not try to win? Is it conceivable that wisdom could lead responsible party officials to conclude that they should not follow the rule? Perhaps, if hindsight were foresight, the answer would be an unqualified "Yes." The winning of an election in the face of certain kinds of indications may prove to be shortsighted, but how does one read with any particular degree of accuracy what lies ahead? If political leaders were prescient, it is quite possible the Democrats in 1892 and the Republicans in 1928 would have chosen to lose the Presidency. In each case, by its victory the party inherited a depression and was deprived of office for an extended period of time. If the leaders of one party found it inadvisable to win an election, the opposing leaders would likely reach the same conclusion, so it is just as well that we do not have powers for penetrating the future. As it is, leaders want to win even when prospects are not promising because unforeseen factors may intervene. It is natural for political leaders to be optimistic by nature; their usual response is a Micawberish assumption that no matter how dreary the prospects, something may very well turn up.[41]

---

[41] Although party leaders want to win elections despite unfavorable indications for the future office holders, there are elections when leaders have no prospects of winning and go into the campaign prepared to lose. One indication of this situation is their willingness to run second-grade candidates, for, as Boies Penrose once said, "Any candidate is good enough to get licked with."——Quoted in Walter Davenport, *Power and Glory: The Life of Boies Penrose* (New York: G. P. Putnam's Sons, 1931) p. 191.

Effect upon Election Campaigns. A two-party system with its dynamics of "ins" *v.* "outs" produces distinctive features in election-campaign techniques. This fact is no doubt one reason for charging United States parties with being tweedledum and tweedledee. Each party responds one way to a set of circumstances if it is in office and another way if it is out of office. So invariable has this behavior become that from an examination of a campaign program one can determine which party—in terms of its being in or out—prepared the program.

The necessity for winning elections and especially for winning majorities creates an imperative need for orderly, regularized methods and procedures. Therefore, organization becomes inevitable as a means to the end and eventually becomes an end in itself. One of the major characteristics of the American political-party system, distinguishing it completely from other systems, is the elaborate organization constructed and the constant preoccupation of politicians with the organization.

The investigation of the American political system divides itself at this point into two major lines of development: the organizations and the bases of bipartisan support which the organizations are designed to mobilize. The first of these is considered in Section II and the second in Section III. In Section IV the synthesis of these developments will be examined as they are brought together to create the phenomena of election campaigns.

Selected Bibliography

Beard, Charles A., *The American Party Battle*. New York: The Macmillan Company, 1928.

Bryce, James, *The American Commonwealth*, 2 vols. New York: Commonwealth Publishing Co., 1908.

Duverger, Maurice, *Political Parties: Their Organization and Activity in the Modern State*. New York: John Wiley & Sons, Inc., 1954, pp. 206–280.

Ford, Henry J., *The Rise and Growth of American Politics*. New York: The Macmillan Company, 1898.

Heard, Alexander, *A Two-Party South?* Chapel Hill: University of North Carolina, 1952.

Herring, Pendleton, *The Politics of Democracy*. New York: Rinehart & Company, Inc., 1940, Chaps. 8, 14.

Hesseltine, William B., *The Rise and Fall of Third Parties*. New York: Public Affairs Press, 1948. Especially Chap. 1.

Holcombe, Arthur N., *The Political Parties of To-Day*. New York: Harper & Brothers, 1924.

——— *Our More Perfect Union*. Cambridge: Harvard University Press, 1950.

Key, V. O., Jr., *Southern Politics in State and Nation*. New York: Alfred A. Knopf, Inc., 1949.

Lubell, Samuel, *The Future of American Politics*. New York: Harper & Brothers, 1952.

Moscow, Warren, *Politics in the Empire State*. New York: Alfred A. Knopf, Inc., 1948, Chap. 7.

Root, Elihu, *The Citizen's Part in Government*, 2d printing. New Haven: Yale
    University Press, 1920.
Schattschneider, E. E., *Party Government*. New York: Farrar & Rinehart, Inc.,
    1942, pp. 70–93.
Stedman, Murray S., Jr., and Susan W. Stedman, *Discontent at the Polls*. New
    York: Columbia University Press, 1950, Chaps. 2 and 3.

SECTION
TWO

Organization

A party can not only continue to live, but
may be able to displace the other party in the
government, merely because its organization
under a powerful leader is more effective than
is that of the other party. The party lives by
the strength of its organization, and therefore
the organization is the main thing, the program a side issue.—— C. J. FRIEDRICH, *Constitutional Government and Democracy*, (1950,
rev. ed.) p. 417.

CHAPTER FOUR

The Inventions of the Machinery

The existence of party organization is dependent upon controversy, which is the occasion for parties, and the pursuing of controversy through political processes culminating in elections. These are the factors which lay behind the formation of the first political party organizations in the United States.

FORERUNNERS OF ORGANIZATION

Pre-Revolution. Controversies abounded throughout the American colonies from their founding, so parties in an incipient stage are as old as our colonization.[1] Their retardation until the last decade of the eighteenth century was caused by at least two conditions: First, the physical barriers obstructing movement and communication reinforced the political barriers which made each colonial government a self-contained unit. Second, two controversies obstructed and confused each other, not only because they created different alignments but also because only one of them was capable of becoming a tenable basis of division in American politics.

In every colony there existed a source of political controversy in the stratification of the population between the seaboard residents and the back-country settlers. Antipathies could reasonably be expected when one group could be identified by the favors it received from the royal or proprietary governors. These differences reproduced on a small scale in each colony the Tory-Whig divisions of English politics, a court and a country party.[2] The rise of the controversy between the colonies and Great Britain temporarily deferred these indigenous issues. The normally pro-British groups, the court party, had finally received whatever favors were available from the British Government and asked only to be unmolested. When they were threatened by British policies, they chose to close ranks with the country party.[3] This controversy could not be made into a durable source

[1] According to John Adams in a letter of November 25, 1812, divisions "began with human nature; they have existed in America from its first plantation."——*The Works of John Adams* (Boston: Little, Brown & Company, 1865) Vol. 10, p. 23.

[2] *Loc. cit.;* H. J. Ford, *Rise and Growth of American Politics* (New York: The Macmillan Company, 1898) pp. 3-5. This cleavage was reflected not only in antipathies but also in the trust placed in the leaders by the people.——*Ibid.,* p. 11.

[3] "Not until the irksome commercial regulations of the British ministry had harassed the merchants almost to distraction were the incompatible interest groups of the colonists combined into the improvised association that took up arms."——W. E. Binkley, *American Political Parties* (New York: Alfred A. Knopf, 1943) pp. 6-7. Carl Becker, *History of Political Parties in the Province of New York* (Madison: University of Wisconsin Bulletin, Vol. 2, 1909) pp. 7-8, 17.

of political division because any opposition would be considered pro-British and, therefore, anti-American. The attempts to organize the pro-British side were short-lived and sometimes disastrous. The contribution of this controversy to American political development was the creation of colonial and intercolonial organizations which sprang up in the Sons of Liberty, the committees of correspondence and of safety.[4]

In conformance with the original colonial concept of local self-government, the freemen or freeholders of a colony assembled in person to make their local laws. Eventually, with the growth and spread of the population, practices of representative government were adopted. Representation meant the holding of elections. This forerunner of parties was well established during the seventeenth century, although the opportunities for elections were restricted because many offices were appointive.[5] One of the major American political developments, which culminated in the period of Andrew Jackson's Presidency, was the creation of more elective positions.

Considering the many political activities preceding and during the Revolutionary War, one logically concludes that there were germs of political organization during the same period. Consultations were held prior to elections. The word was passed around and candidates previously agreed upon were elected. The prime movers in this activity were the influential men in each community and in each colony. They were what constituted the aristocracy, whether the landed gentry, merchants, or religious leaders. Whatever organization existed in New York, we are told, was "within the aristocracy as a social class."[6] John Adams in 1763 described in his diary the Boston method for choosing city officials in the Caucus Club before the election was held in the town, and this practice is assigned to Boston at least as early as 1724.[7]

These developments were impressive, but they were not *party* organizations as such. They were antecedents. They broke the ground and marked the path. They established the form and habits for organization when

---

[4] Committees of correspondence had been used previously by colonial legislatures to correspond with the agents of the colonies in London. As the name implies, they were committees created for the purpose of exchanging information through written communication. They performed an essential function during the Revolution and naturally became very powerful, not only because leading citizens were members but also because they were bottlenecks of information regarding affairs in all other colonies. The term itself was gradually dropped in favor of the single word "committee" as party organization developed during the nineteenth century.

[5] Cortlandt F. Bishop, *History of Elections in the American Colonies* (New York: Columbia University Press, 1893) pp. 1-45, 203-218. Except for Massachusetts, Rhode Island, and Connecticut, the only elected officials were members of the lower houses of the legislatures and some local officials.

[6] Becker, *op. cit.,* p. 11.

[7] *The Works of John Adams,* Vol. 2, p. 144 and Note 2, p. 144; M. Ostrogorski, *Democracy and the Organization of Political Parties* (New York: The Macmillan Company, 1902) Vol. 2, pp. 3-5.

domestic issues appeared. The genuine organization of American political parties arose from nominations and campaign machinery, both of which assume elections based upon issues which divide the electorate. These ingredients were supplied after the War for Independence was won.

Post-Revolution. The larger the electorate, the more elaborate will be the party organization. During the colonial period, suffrage was considerably restricted. Every colony had a real-estate requirement of varying amounts, although variations were introduced as early as 1750 when some colonies computed the freehold in terms of its value and others in terms of its area. By the time of the Revolution, changing conditions, particularly the increase in the number of urban dwellers, were reflected in suffrage qualifications. Five states accepted other property of forty or fifty pounds value as an alternative to the freehold, and South Carolina allowed the alternative of a ten-shilling tax payment. During the Revolutionary War New Jersey, Pennsylvania, and Georgia dropped the property requirement entirely, but the other states only reduced the amount.

The trend, once established, was continued in the direction of less stringent provisions.[8] The movement went from the land-owning requirement to personal property to taxpaying and finally to manhood suffrage. By the 1830's this process had been completed in most states, although some had skipped one or more of the steps. Of the new states admitted after 1789, only Ohio, Louisiana, and Mississippi had a taxpaying requirement. After 1817 no state came in with either a freehold or a taxation provision.[9] The overthrow of the freehold removed the major block to suffrage, for the subsequent restrictions had only slight effect. Taxpaying was almost as broad as manhood suffrage, at least in the experience of New York, where the number of eligible voters was increased only 1% when taxpaying was dropped.[10] In Virginia the religious restriction was not well enforced, for after its repeal in 1785 "the records of a considerable number of county

---

[8] Kirk Porter, *A History of Suffrage in the United States* (Chicago: University of Chicago Press, 1918) pp. 10-14 *et seq.*; Bishop, *op. cit.*, pp. 69 ff. Occasionally, provisions were less restrictive than intended: The New Jersey statute of 1776 enfranchised every one-year resident of the State who was worth fifty pounds; but in 1807 the legislature clarified what had been previously intended by specifying only free, white male citizens twenty-one years of age and over who had resided in the state for one year and were worth fifty pounds.—— George P. Luetscher, *Early Political Machinery in the United States* (Philadelphia: University of Pennsylvania Press, 1903).

[9] Porter, *op. cit.*, p. 110. The taxpaying provision may lead to some confusion in meaning, but "any kind of a tax requirement connected with suffrage since 1860 has been practically nothing but a registry fee, and several states accomplish the same by requiring that men must pay their poll taxes. . . . The old-fashioned taxpaying test as a compromise with property qualifications was gone before the Civil War."—— *Ibid.*, p. 111.

[10] Luetscher, *op. cit.*, p. 13. In 1800 and succeeding years Tammany met the New York property qualifications by having several Republicans buy property jointly; the Tammany Society probably furnished most of the money. Gustavus Myers, *The History of Tammany Hall* (New York: Boni & Liveright, 1917, 2d ed.) pp. 14, 15.

elections show that the average number of votes was not much affected, and was certainly not increased." [11]

The spirit of the Revolutionary period and the problems of the postwar period, ending with the adoption of the Constitution, began breaking down the aristocratic character of the ballot. As more and more persons were enfranchised, there was a promise that when the occasion for organization appeared, there would be sufficient numbers to justify the effort.

The multiplication of places of voting was a companion development of the suffrage and was an equally important forerunner of parties. Increasing the number of polling places not only encouraged voting but also polling places became the basic unit for organization. Except in New England, where elections were held in the towns, voting took place almost entirely at county courthouses. This practice created hardships, especially in the South,[12] mitigated only by the fact that the election was usually held on county court day when a large number of the voters would have been present anyway to transact their business affairs. The few cities then in existence made arrangements as appropriate as they saw fit; the holding of a special election in Albany in 1773 on the aldermen's front stoops may or may not have been a common occurrence, but it is certainly not a practice limited to our early history.[13]

The evidence of dissatisfaction appeared in state legislation after 1776. Colonial statutes seldom specified the polling places, either accepting the customary place or leaving the decision to the discretion of the sheriff or other election officials.[14] Among the original thirteen states—exclusive of New England—New York in 1778 prohibited further use of the county as an election unit and required that voting be conducted "by boroughs, towns, manors, districts and precincts." [15] Ten years later it established the township system, marking out 100 to begin with, but increasing the number to an average of 7 in each of the 21 counties by 1795. The township system in 7 of the 13 New Jersey counties was instituted in 1790, and the

11 C. S. Sydnor, *Gentlemen Freeholders* (Chapel Hill: University of North Carolina Press, 1952) p. 29.

12 "The voters came by horseback and wagon from all over the county, many of them having left home that morning though a few spent the night with friends or with one of the candidates who lived along the road. In the larger counties some of the voters had to ride twenty-five miles or more to an election."—*Ibid.*, p. 18.

13 Bishop, *op. cit.*, p. 233. David H. Kurtzman found, as of July 1, 1932, sixty-one Republican committeemen in Philadelphia with voting places in their own homes.—*Methods of Controlling Votes in Philadelphia* (Philadelphia: University of Pennsylvania Press, 1935) Appendix D.

14 One exception to this rule was a law of 1748 requiring two polling places for Orange County, New York, because of the difficulty of crossing the mountains. The sheriff began the election at one place and adjourned to the other.—Bishop, *op. cit.*, p. 109.

15 This state-by-state information is taken from Luetscher, *op. cit.*

county courthouse was completely abandoned there by 1797, when the legislature created 104 townships and designated them as voting units. Election of delegates to the Pennsylvania Constitutional Convention of 1776 was generally held in districts within counties, and the legislature in 1785 divided most of the counties into election districts, with the result that the number of voters increased sharply. South Carolina and several other states had from early times used the parish for certain elections; [16] the parish was also used as the regular polling place as early as 1789, but a system of 61 election districts was established by 1793. In 1799, the Maryland Legislature divided the 16 counties into 66 election districts. The remaining states did not respond so rapidly to this trend. The county courthouse remained the polling place in Delaware until 1811, when the three counties were divided into twenty "hundreds" [17] which became the election units. The following year Virginia began to designate places other than the courthouse; but this was a spasmodic, not a regular, arrangement and the district system was not adopted until 1830. North Carolina and Georgia had the district system by 1820.

There is no doubt that increased enfranchisement and greater accommodation of the voters, taken together, wrought something of a revolution in American politics, but neither would have developed if issues of an absorbing nature had not drawn more and more people into public discussions and impressed upon them the value of direct action.

The heritage of organization created during the Revolutionary period was still fresh in most adult minds when the Constitution became the law of the land, even though many of the former practices had lapsed. The so-called radicals had failed to keep up their organization after winning their objectives of independence and the adoption of the Articles of Confederation. Instead of pressing their advantage, they found themselves on the defensive in the immediate postwar period, having to meet the attacks being made upon the weak and indecisive nature of the general government. Having nothing to attain, but rather something to conserve, they had no occasion for reawakening the spirit of the masses and reactivating the committees of correspondence and the mobs of the cities. These agitational activities are typical of the strategy of the "outs," not the "ins."

The "outs" were the pre-Revolution court party—the tidewater, commercial, landed aristocracy—and they had neither the ability nor the desire to arouse the public. Their revolution, culminating in the Constitution and a new form of general government, was a more quiet and carefully

[16] Bishop, *op. cit.*, pp. 114-115, 212-215, 223-224, 229-232.

[17] This use of the word came from England, where *hundred* meant a subdivision of a county and probably referred originally to divisions of people into groups of one hundred warriors or one hundred families for military and administrative purposes. The term is still used in Delaware, but was also used in Virginia, Pennsylvania, and Maryland during the colonial period.

calculated series of negotiations. They trapped their opponents into agreeing to a convention, which disregarded its instructions and provided for a
method of ratification unconstitutional under the provisions of the Articles
of Confederation. The aristocracy had moved surely and rapidly, taking
along with them new sources of support from the urban elements that
favored a stronger government. Some of the radicals of the Revolution
tried belatedly to turn back this concerted attack. Upon the institution of
the new government with the Administration of Washington, the old
radicals had become the "outs" even though Thomas Jefferson sat in the
Cabinet. It was now their turn again to find an issue upon which they
could rouse the public and turn the aristocracy out of office. The French
Revolution presented them with the opportunity almost immediately.

There was marked interest and enthusiasm in the United States for
the struggle against tyranny in the country which had so valuably aided
the Americans in their own dark hours of revolution. In 1792 when the
French Republic was proclaimed, there began forming in the United States
sympathetic organizations called by various names but usually termed
"societies" and referred to derisively by their opponents as "Democrats." [18]
Being legally disqualified as a voter was no bar to participation in these
societies, since the base of authority as well as the personnel of organized
activity in the 1770's had been much broader than the enfranchised. If
the purpose of these societies had been limited to expressions of opinion
favorable to French democracy, they would have been of trifling importance.
But their real aim was to attack the underpinnings of American aristocracy
and orient the nation toward republican France and away from monarchical England; in some cases they also concerned themselves with
sectional, domestic issues. Obviously, their politics was Jefferson Republican,
not Federalism.

In less than two years, twenty-four such societies were formed. The
Philadelphia organization, perhaps the strongest and most active of all,
tried unsuccessfully to develop a national movement. The important
organizational feature was the degree of local control. Members met at
county courthouses at the time of the meeting of the county courts, chose
officers and a committee of correspondence, and admitted new members if
they were vouched for or were well-known Republicans. The societies
made themselves vocal by attacking Washington's Proclamation of Neutrality and the Jay Mission, and they also tried with some success to influence
the congressional elections of 1794.[19] Their political potentialities in

18 The following material on the Democratic Societies is taken from Luetscher, *op. cit.*
See also Charles A. Beard, *The Economic Origins of Jeffersonian Democracy* (New York:
The Macmillan Company, 1915) pp. 258 ff.

19 The Republican candidate was elected in the Philadelphia district by 58 votes;
two years before, the Federalists had held it almost two to one and in 1788 had had a
six-to-one margin. Even the citadel of New York City fell to the Republicans. The
Federalists held the Charleston, South Carolina, district, but by a much-reduced plurality.

getting out a vote and in maintaining a flow of propaganda were worthy of respect, but a series of developments proved their undoing.

Their excessively pro-French position boomeranged after the Reign of Terror set in, when Americans realized that what was happening across the Atlantic was not exactly the same thing that had happened here in 1776. Their radicalism and their political successes brought out a certain reaction; most men in positions of authority were threatened more or less by the societies' leveling philosophy. Correctly or not, the societies in Pennsylvania were associated with and blamed for the Whiskey Rebellion, and many members dropped out of the organization after this event. Losing prestige and suffering attacks from as high a source as the President of the United States, the societies became a handicap to the Jeffersonian Republicans. The demise of the societies also bore testimony to the importance of the physical barriers which still existed; it was a technical impossibility to succeed with such a venture without a system of national communication.

RISE OF FORMAL NOMINATING SYSTEMS

Colonial Origins. The process of making party nominations is in its history a tangled web of never-ending improvisations and experimentations whose origins are obstructed partly by insufficient records and partly by the confusion of terminology. It is impossible to say, for example, when the first nominating convention was held, although the procedures used for nominating candidates for the office of assistant [20] in the Massachusetts Bay Colony from 1644 to 1648 had some of the appearances of a state convention. Nominations during the colonial period were not party processes; instead, most of the systems amounted to a "preliminary election for the purpose of reducing the whole number of eligible candidates by a process of exclusion." In the East Jersey Colony for a time, candidates were drawn by lot.[21] In New York "candidates were . . . 'sett up' by private personal agreement among those leaders whose 'interests' were likely to carry the election." [22]

Out of these colonial practices, two methods developed. Self-announcement, whereby candidates put themselves before the electorate on their

---

In anticipation of this 1794 election the Philadelphia Society, which was vigorously agitating for repeal of the excise tax on whisky, framed an address to the citizens of the United States calling upon them to decide "how far their Representatives are entitled to public confidence by approving the good and dismissing the bad." Although this address was not issued because at the time it was written federal troops were sent into Pennsylvania to enforce the law, the appeal is interesting for its historical value and for its foreshadowing the much later technique of Samuel Gompers when he urged the AFL to reward its friends and punish its enemies.

[20] "Assistant" was the name given at this time to a member of the Governor's Council.
[21] Bishop, *op. cit.*, pp. 98, 120-127.
[22] Becker, *op. cit.*, p. 15.

own intiative, took root in the South. This was the method employed by candidates for the House of Commons in England and could have been expected to be followed in these colonies, most closely oriented toward England. For the reason that self-announcement was considered an English imitation, it was not popular in New England, where a friend of the candidate took the public initiative. The Middle States, apparently, employed both methods: self-announcement for local offices and announcement by friends for state offices.

Both methods weakened gradually under the impact of more democratic politics. First, they were instruments by which the aristocracy could pick the voters' candidates for them. Second, they were not adaptable to stormy political situations where large numbers sought to express themselves. Third, they were incompatible with party government when it finally arose. With the rise of issues and the open challenges to the aristocratic tradition, new methods were worked out, but the process did not move uniformly among all of the states.[23]

Local Nominating Methods. The connecting link between nonparty and party nominations actually had been suggested by the evolving modifications of the New England method. If a candidate could be placed in nomination by one friend, that friend could also join with another friend or with several friends in making the announcement so as to give the candidacy greater weight both actually and in appearance. This, in effect, was the caucus system, originally developed in Boston, and both there and in other colonies expanded into large public gatherings during the Revolutionary War; the objective was to broaden the base of authority and to avoid cleavages among the patriot groups. Consequently, there developed during the Revolutionary period a system of mass meetings, often dominated by the Sons of Liberty and the committees of correspondence. The term was used so flexibly, however, that any number gathered together could claim the name.[24] Mass meetings, generally adopted in the North, were retarded in the South because of the size of the counties, the smallest units from which officials were elected, and because of the greater stability of the aristocracy. One of the contributions to political processes of the Democratic Societies was the encouragement and renewed popularity they gave to this type of political action.

Certain problems of the mass meetings were never overcome. Its size could not be precisely fixed, and it was not representative in theory even though it could be in fact. No matter what its virtues, it was an assemblage of individuals each one acting for himself, and it was designed for use within a very limited geographical area. It failed to measure up to the necessities

---

[23] See F. W. Dallinger, *Nominations for Elective Office in the United States* (Cambridge: Harvard University Press, 1897) pp. 4-6.

[24] Becker, *op. cit.,* p. 18; Dallinger, *op. cit.,* Note 18, p. 9, and pp. 10-12.

of party organization, although it was in general use for years as party machinery.[25] In time the distinction was made between a mass meeting and a convention. The former was a meeting of all party members who were able to attend and take part; the latter was a meeting of those party members who had been selected previously to represent the party's rank and file. Party members indiscriminately can attend a convention, but only those individuals chosen as delegates are entitled to take part in the proceedings. On the local level of government the mass meeting served its purpose and then gave way to the instrument of the county convention, which by the twentieth century began being replaced by the direct primary.

The county convention was designed primarily by the Jeffersonian Republicans as a nominating device, but it served to a limited extent the purpose which the mass meeting served to an almost unlimited extent. The convention was a means of mass appeal, and it logically was brought to fruition by the party of the masses. Some authority was needed for Republican nominations and the only basis the party had was the people, in contra-distinction to the basis of tradition and *noblesse oblige* upon which Federalist nominations rested. Through the operation of the county convention, the efforts of smaller areas can be seen as they blended together into a synthesis for joint action.

During this formative period, the states with the earliest and most professional political backgrounds carried the county convention to its peak, particularly those states that provided for elective county officials;[26] that created township or voting precincts, which were indispensable if delegates were to be equitably elected; and that made suffrage qualifications uniform for all elective offices. Because the South lagged in enacting such legislation, the county convention was late in appearing there and self-announcement continued down to the Civil War. The convention was also retarded in New England because Rhode Island and Connecticut had no counties, and few officials were elected on a county basis in New Hampshire and Massachusetts; New England had a convenient substitute in the town meetings and an aversion for extralegal machinery.

---

25 It is still used, in fact. Compare the following: "That, for the purpose of reorganizing the County Executive Committee . . . there shall be called and held a . . . Convention [which] shall be a *Mass Convention* of the assembled Republicans of the County." "The said delegates to said [State] Convention shall be selected in county *Mass Conventions. . . ."——Call and Rules of the Republican State Executive Committee of Tennessee, 1952;* italics mine. "The Democratic Executive Committees of the various counties . . . are hereby directed to proceed with the election of delegates to the said State Convention . . . either by county Party conventions, county *Party mass meetings,* or by designation by the County . . . Committees."——*Resolution of the Democratic State Executive Committee of Tennessee, 1952;* italics mine.

26 Much of this information is taken from Luetscher, *op. cit.,* and Dallinger, *op. cit.,* pp. 21-25. Generally speaking, a convention would not be held to nominate a candidate for only one office, but the use of congressional-district conventions became an exception. As early as 1789 and 1793 such conventions were held in New York.

Irrespective of which was cause and which was effect as between bipartisan controversy and enabling state legislation, the county convention first arose and was established in all or parts of New York, Pennsylvania, New Jersey, Delaware, and Maryland between 1801 and 1822. The new era forced New Jersey, for example, to discard a most unwieldy nominating procedure which utilized two trips to the polls, sorting of ballots at the capital, and proclamations by the governor and all of the sheriffs. The most professional manifestations of all were exhibited in Pennsylvania, where in 1803 the Bucks County Republicans issued a ringing statement showing the necessity for making nominations and extolling the county convention which "may be said to hold in trust the whole elective powers of the county." Previously, the people were told, their votes "counted nothing, and you could not put into place a single officer."

> Time was in this county when a few men met at court, erected themselves into a committee, and assumed the power of forming a ticket for the county. Our tickets are formed agreeably to the representative system, by men elected and specially appointed to the service.
>
> . . . Would you merit the character of Republicans? Bow to the will of the majority, and support the ticket formed by your representatives. . . . Take the obvious means to extend your power and influence, and do not madly pull down with your own hands, the fabric you erected with so much care. . . . Make your Committees a just representation of the Republican interests—support by your votes the ticket they recommend— and take for your pole star that political maxim, United We Stand, Divided We Fall.[27]

The emergence of the county convention was spotty and erratic, but its utility was eventually recognized everywhere. There is no other tenable explanation for the surprising uniformity of its appearance. At the grass-roots level it marked the shift from aristocratic to popular politics.

State Nominating Methods. The major mechanical impediment to state organization was the lack of elective state offices. The South best reflected this condition: Governors were elected by the state legislatures; members of Congress and state legislators, within districts; and presidential electors, either within districts or by the legislatures. The only elective offices in other states were those of governor, lieutenant governor, and presidential electors. Representatives in Congress were often elected at large at the beginning, but were soon brought into the district system. The crux of competitive election activity was largely confined to the local areas: local issues involved county officials; state issues centered around the election of

---

27 The results of this kind of Republican activity are shown in the increase in the Republican vote over the two years, 1796 and 1799: Lancaster County from 619 to 2258; Chester County from 117 to 1105; York County from 139 to 2039; Bucks County from 356 to 2059.

state legislators, who by choosing United States senators were also impli-
cated in national affairs; otherwise, national issues were determined by the
election of members of the lower house of Congress.

Election of governors and lieutenant governors by the voters forced
the parties to find methods for nominating their candidates. The only
convenient and regular gathering of party leaders occurred during the
sessions of the state legislature. Politics dominated the thinking of the
legislators. Those of the same party were intent upon choosing the legislative officials, they sought to control the patronage of the legislature, and
they tried to reach agreement upon specific bills as well as upon general
policies. In order to take this joint action they would hold a *caucus,* a
word signifying a private meeting prior to the event with which it is concerned, a word that had long been in use in Boston.[28] The party leaders
in the legislature, who had already been endorsed in their localities and
considered they had won their right to take part in party management,
were in a position to seize upon the nominating function as part of the
work of the caucus. The legislative caucus was established as permanent
party organization because it found acceptance among party members, the
test of any extraconstitutional machinery.[29] It was first used in Maryland
in 1788 [30] by both parties to nominate candidates for the National House
of Representatives and appears after 1796 to have been the settled practice
in all the states outside the South, except New Jersey and Delaware.[31]

Because the caucus was limited in its personnel, its effectiveness suffered. Most counties elected only one member to the legislature and,
therefore, could be represented in only one party's caucus. It was also
possible that some influential men were not always in the legislature, and
a pure caucus would exclude them from the nominating process. It is
reasonable to suppose that ambitious political spirits who had helped to
elect the local legislative ticket were just as eager to participate as the legis-

---

[28] The origin of the word *caucus* is unknown, but various theories have been advanced;
see George Stimpson, *A Book about American Politics* (New York: Harper & Brothers,
1952) pp. 39-42; Dallinger, *op. cit.,* Note 13, pp. 7-8. The word is applied most frequently
to meetings of party members of legislatures, but some legislators use it only for those
meetings where members are committed to vote a particular way on a pending bill, not
for meetings of a general nature.

[29] *Ibid.,* pp. 25-27. Ostrogorski, *op. cit.,* p. 11; in general, pp. 10-13.

[30] This date seems well established by Luetscher; Ostrogorski's assertion that it was
first used in Rhode Island in 1790 is incorrect (*Ibid.,* p. 11). However, the Maryland
caucuses in 1788 were really mixed, not pure legislative caucuses. In this sense Ostrogorski
is correct if he is referring to the Rhode Island action as the first caucus composed only
of legislators. Furthermore, he apparently is correct in saying that Rhode Island was
the first to endorse candidates for governor and lieutenant governor through the
legislative caucus.

[31] Indicative of its inevitability where state-wide nominations were required is the
fact that Virginia Republicans held a caucus to choose presidential electors in 1800, the
one year that the state tried electing them at large during this period. North Carolina
adopted the at-large system for electors permanently in 1804, and the caucus was used
thereafter to nominate candidates until the convention superseded it.

lators. The desire for party regularity and wide appeal finally overcame
any predisposition to be exclusive, although in some states, e.g., New York,
the caucus leaders fought for their prerogatives. Almost from the beginning,
there is evidence that other party members were admitted to the caucus,
but the practice was not generally or regularly adopted until the end of
the first decade of the nineteenth century. The nonlegislators were chosen
in their own localities to go to the capital for the caucus, although it is
likely that in the first years their selection was informal, if not ethereal;
some of them may have simply managed to be in town the day the caucus
met and were invited to take part. The admission of others besides legislators was reflected in the name "mixed" or "mongrel" caucus as opposed
to the pure caucus.

The drive for representation and public support finally turned the
mixed caucus into a state convention, just as mass meetings became county
conventions, but the transition was gradual. The first conventions themselves were "mixed" by the presence of legislators who held on as long as
they could to this special function attaching to their public office. When
the pure convention was established, it was set off from its predecessors by
the formalized system of selecting its members (delegates) and the acceptance that the authority of the delegates came from the party organization
in the locality where they were selected. This is the representative system
within the party; the convention delegates are supposed to act for their
party constituency. Conventions became the end product of local organization and, in turn, were impossible without a grass-roots base. The caucus
era lasted about thirty years although it held on longer in northern New
England.[32] Otherwise, with almost precise uniformity, it was succeeded by
state conventions during the 1820's.

CREATION OF PARTY COMMITTEES

The rise of formal nominating procedures was predicated upon holding
elections for which candidates could be nominated. The official agencies
of the party, called "committees," were formed for the purpose of electing
the candidates who had previously been nominated. At both ends of the
electoral process, party organization appeared. The formation and expansion of these committees in those states for which there are records make
clear the forces dictating the organization's emergence.[33]

The Republicans in New Hampshire formed a Grand Committee
(comparable to a state committee) which in 1805 instructed the town
committees to assemble all active Republicans before the election and "cause
the town to be divided into districts, assigning each man his district, whose

---

[32] Until 1829 in Vermont, 1831 in New Hampshire, 1832 in Massachusetts and 1843
in Maine.——*Ibid.*, pp. 34-38; Dallinger, *op. cit.*, pp. 27-29.

[33] The following data are taken from Luetscher, *op. cit.*

duty it shall be that every Republican in the district be furnished with a vote and attend the town meeting." No more efficient basic plan of party warfare has ever been formulated. A point of equal historical importance is that New Hampshire had a hierarchy of party committees by 1805.

In Pennsylvania, in order to get out the vote during campaigns, township and ward committees were appointed at city and county mass meetings. Eventually, the voters in the smaller areas wanted to choose their own committees, and the party leaders were agreeable because township activities could influence more votes than the large mass meetings. The principle of homerule in party affairs was welcomed as soon as its value was perceived. The Federalists themselves held a mass meeting at Philadelphia in 1788, at which ward committees were chosen with the power to nominate delegates to a state convention.

The Republicans in Hunterdon County, New Jersey, formed an Association, with Associators in each township, where a standing committee was to be chosen twice a year. These committees met jointly to nominate county officials and could call a general meeting of the Association. The chairmen of all the committees constituted a committee of correspondence for communication with Associations and individuals in other counties, and they were to meet four times a year to carry on the work and consult with one another. This body of chairmen had some of the characteristics of an executive committee which acts on behalf of the full committee; individually, the chairmen can be compared with precinct or township committeemen. The Federalists in Gloucester County, New Jersey, finally showed some awareness by the appointment of township committees and a county committee of correspondence, but this action was taken at a county mass meeting with centralized instead of local control. The purpose of this machinery of the Federalists was to "solicit subscriptions for the purpose of raising a fund for diffusing useful political information"; to "endeavor to procure individual subscriptions for the Trenton Federalist"; and to "endeavor to obtain an accurate list of all the voters in each township, male and female, and designate them by proper marks opposite their names as Federalists or otherwise and transmit a copy of such list to the general committee as soon as possible." Any first-class political organization would be expected to collect such information.

In New Castle County, Delaware, the Republican mass meeting in 1800 appointed a committee of two from each "hundred" to superintend elections; but two years later these individuals were chosen in their own hundreds and acted as a campaign committee. In 1801 the Republicans demonstrated the most remarkable discipline when their committees of correspondence kept in such close touch with one another that the mass meeting in each county nominated the same candidate for governor—an unusual adaptation of local mechanics to state processes. Delaware is the only state in which the whole Federalist Party adapted itself to the new era of politics. For a time they retained the centralization feature in their organization, keeping the power to appoint hundreds committees in the county mass meeting; but finally even they accepted decentralization. After 1810 both parties had similar state organizations, including the state convention. This was the beginning of the period of the Federalists' demise, but the Delaware Federalists refused to die and as late as 1821 and 1822 in Kent and Sussex Counties introduced the county convention to replace the mass meeting.

ORGANIZATION: LOCAL IN ORIGIN, DECENTRALIZED IN COMPOSITION

The first fact of importance about American party organization is that it blossomed rapidly in most of the states from Maryland north during the two decades of the 1790's and the 1800's. Then, as the Federalist contestants wilted and gradually disappeared, organization was neglected, only to burst out with renewed growth in the middle of the 1820's when party warfare resumed. The so-called Era of Good Feelings was a time of disuse of political machinery, for there was no one to organize against. This was the pattern except in Maryland, where state organization fell into the discard in the 1790's because there were no at-large officials elected except presidential electors.

A second fact was the fall of the Federalist Party from the heights of 1789 to the depths of 1816, from being the only party to being nothing but a collection of unhappy and discredited politicians. The Federalists were conspicuous in their refusal to adopt an organization with appeal to the growing number of voters. They refused to recognize that new methods were the ways to power. Their policies during the second Washington and the Adams Administrations alienated numerous groups, but they failed to see the need either to win these groups back or to bring in new support. With the Jeffersonian Republicans drumming constantly upon rigorous taxes, the dangerous Sedition laws and unscrupulous financial policies, the Federalists proceeded as if they were depending upon getting their votes in heaven. They made few enough concessions to get their votes on earth. The opportunity they could have grasped was revealed in Delaware, where they accepted organization and learned how to build it by imitating their opponents. This was the only state in which they lasted long enough to be absorbed along with the Republicans in the cataclysm of the Jackson v. Adams-Clay alignments. Outside Delaware the Federalists used the legislative caucus in some states and occasionally turned to serious activities in a few counties, but organizationally they were never a political party. In the vast storehouse of political lore and party history it is always necessary to make exceptions for the Federalists. Their ailment was unadjustability to the party system, an understandable fatality among aristocrats in a free political system.[34]

The third fact is that the Republicans were a party based upon popular politics. Their strategy, their principles, their whole reason-for-being were summed up in Jefferson's cherishing of the people. Claiming to be of the people and to speak for the people, they were forced by their logic and their objectives to go to the people; and the people responded enthusiastically. The results of this grass-roots participation could not be ignored by any wise politician, and the lessons to be drawn from the techniques of mass appeal were accentuated, if accentuation were needed, by contrast with the austerity of the Federalists. Winning politics was organized politics, with identifiable leadership locally originated and controlled. The process was started at the bottom, not at the top, and the process was largely a spontaneous response from local sources. Americans revealed the same aversion for centralized authority in their extraconstitutional government that they had shown for it in their formal, constitutional government. Federalism had been adopted as a compromise between the Confederation they had tried and the unitary system Hamilton had espoused. Politics, it was demonstrated, was to be federalized both nationally and within the states themselves. Each community, each geographical unit, was an individualized unit of political power. Decentralized organization, dispersed from the capitals and county seats to the crossroads and the hamlets and the farms, is the mark of grass-roots politics; and grass-roots politics is the only kind the United States has had since the coming of the Jeffersonian Republicans.

Selected Bibliography

Becker, Carl L., *History of Political Parties in the Province of New York*. Madison: Bulletin of the University of Wisconsin, Vol. 2, 1909.

Binkley, Wilfred E., *American Political Parties*. New York: Alfred A. Knopf, Inc., 1943, Chaps. 1–4.

Bishop, Cortlandt F., *History of Elections in the American Colonies*. New York: Columbia University Studies in History, Economics, and Public Law, Vol. 3, 1893.

Dallinger, Frederick W., *Nominations for Elective Office in the United States*. Cambridge: Harvard University Press, 1897. Harvard Historical Studies, Vol. 4.

---

[34] One description of the Federalists in Connecticut points up the caliber of electioneering practiced by those privileged to govern:

"Apart in a pew sat a dozen men, the magnates of the town. In other pews near by sat still others, all staunch respectabilities. These were the leading Federalists, persons of high character, wealth, and influence. They spoke a few words to each other, and then relapsed into a sort of dignified silence. They did not mingle with the mass; they might be suspected of electioneering. Nevertheless, the Federalists had privately determined, a few days before, for whom they would cast their votes, and being a majority, they carried the day."——Quoted in Joseph B. Bishop, *Presidential Nominations and Elections* (New York: Charles Scribner's Sons, 1916) p. 4.

Luetscher, George P., *Early Political Machinery in the United States*. University of Pennsylvania, 1903. Ph.D. dissertation.

Ostrogorski, M., *Democracy and the Organization of Political Parties*, 2 vols. New York: The Macmillan Company, 1902, Vol. 2.

—— *Democracy and the Party System in the United States*. New York: The Macmillan Company, 1910.

Porter, Kirk H., *A History of Suffrage in the United States*. Chicago: University of Chicago Press, 1918.

CHAPTER FIVE

The Elaboration of Party Organization

When politicians of opposing factions of the Democratic-Republican Party (the later name of the Jeffersonian Republicans [1]) began to contend with one another for office at the end of the Monroe Administration, the fundamentals for conducting party warfare had already been established. The problem in each state was either to refurbish the machinery which had been permitted to lie unused or to develop it imitatively; by the early 1830's, these achievements were substantially realized. The character of organization during the process of revival was affected by the primary emphasis upon permanency and continuity, with the result that the committee structure took on increasing importance.

REVIVAL OF PARTY ORGANIZATION

The committees, which had been appointed at the mass meetings and conventions, became the nucleus of the party organization. In theory the committees received their authority from the rank-and-file members of the party through the duly elected conventions, but these party gatherings only met periodically. The committees in time assumed the function of leadership on a continuing basis, including the power to issue the call for conventions. There was no particular objection from the leaders to this shift in the source of power. Rather, the leaders needed organizational methods for systematizing the operation of party processes. By dominating the committees, which in effect dominated the conventions, the leaders controlled the machinery of the party.[2]

Within this general movement, practices were not entirely uniform. The influences of geography and culture created diversities, especially in the South, where the population was more spread out and the older aristocratic practices continued down to the Civil War. The political organization in new states was largely determined by the background of their settlers. Through all of these vagaries and adjustments a general uniformity

---

[1] The name "Democratic-Republican" continued into the twentieth century as the official name of the party, e.g., in 1904, Tammany Hall issued its "Rules and Regulations of the Democratic-Republican Organization of the County of New York." See Jesse Macy, *Party Organization and Machinery* (New York: The Century Company, 1905) pp. 198 and 285.

[2] Frederick W. Dallinger, *Nominations for Elective Office in the United States* (Cambridge: Harvard University Press, 1897) pp. 44-45.

emerged in the adoption of the county or district system for state legislators, the direct system for members of the National House of Representatives, and the at-large system for presidential electors. In each of these geographical electoral areas the parties' committees and conventions began to appear in the 1820's and 1830's, and this basic organizational arrangement has continued with a persistence and durability that can only be attributed to its inherent practicality.

RULES AND USAGES OF THE PARTY SYSTEM

Sources of Rules. In the years since party organization became fixed, the rules of the system have existed in three different forms: first, in the minds of political leaders who learned the procedures by observation and practice and passed them on to the next generation in the same fashion; second, in formal publication by responsible party committees; and third, in enactments by state legislatures. The first differs from the last two by being informal and even casual, if not hazy or invisible. The first two, however, proceed from the same source and mark the party, originally, as a private association completely outside official government regulation. When party rules become part of the public laws of a state, they are enforceable by public officials; yet the three forms of the rules have shown a surprising ability to exist simultaneously so that the most elaborate statutory regulations have not precluded rules from party sources.

Parties Legally Defined. One result of legislation has been to produce legal definitions of parties in terms of their strength at the polls, but the provisions vary from state to state. In some a party is required to cast a certain percentage of the vote, e.g., ten per cent of the vote cast for at least one nominee in Washington, five per cent of the vote cast either for governor or presidential electors in Louisiana. In other states the strength is fixed in terms of the number of votes, e.g., 50,000 in gubernatorial elections in New York.

Under these laws, major parties have no difficulty qualifying as parties, and if a minor party can cast the minimum vote required, it is legally a party. Problems arise when a group wants to start a new party. People have an inherent right to organize a political party, but legislatures unquestionably have the power to regulate parties. The power of regulation would, or could, be nullified unless legislatures can define what a party is. Therefore, statutory law limits the right to create a party by requiring a minimum number of members and specifying the procedures for proving their existence before candidates of the party can appear upon the ballot. Laws of most states require the organizers of a party to circulate petitions and secure a given number of signatures in order for the party to attain legal recognition. Requirements vary, e.g., in Nebraska a new party must have 750 members in a state convention, 150 in a congressional district or county convention, 250 in a city or county with 50,000 or more population, and 35 in a precinct, village, or ward.[3] Where the petition method is not used, alternative means are prescribed. It is obvious that nearly all states' regulations are designed for a two-party system, and the formation of minor parties is discouraged because of the legal difficulties involved. Minor parties are not, in reality, the equal of major parties, and the tendency of legislation is to insure that the ballot will not be cluttered with a large number of party names. The obstacles to minor parties are not insurmountable if the parties have any widespread support, but the obstacles are very real.[4]

Uniformity in Organization. A great deal of statutory law attests to the importance of party organization in both its electoral functions and its committee structure. For purposes of description it makes little difference whether the organization is governed by unofficial party rules or official government rules. The forms and functions are substantially the same in either case, since legislators are also party members and seldom have concepts of party organization beyond their own experience. No alternatives have appeared to the traditional units of organization attached to geographical and electoral divisions of a state. The substantive basis of the organizations, for which the forms are mere convenience, is determined by people and situations, not by book rules.

STRUCTURE AND FUNCTION OF THE ORGANIZATION

The lowest and smallest political unit is that area in which all of the voters go to the same *polling place* to vote. Most state laws provide that the populations of such areas be approximately equal and based on the number of voters who can conveniently use the facilities of one polling place. Legislatures usually have the power to make this determination or may be authorized to delegate the power to the county or city legislative bodies. The names given to such areas vary from one part of the country to another and between urban and rural communities. Cities throughout the United States are normally divided into wards; a ward may be a polling place by itself, but is usually large enough to be subdivided into two or more polling places called precincts or divisions. In rural areas in the North, except for New England, the township is the major subdivision of a county and either constitutes a polling place or is subdivided into pre-

---

[3] *Revised Statutes of Nebraska*, 1943, III, Ch. 32. On the general subject of public regulation, see J. R. Starr, "The Legal Status of American Political Parties," *American Political Science Review*, Vol. 34 (1940) pp. 439-455, 685-699.

[4] William B. Hesseltine, *The Rise and Fall of Third Parties* (New York: Public Affairs Press, 1948) Chap. 13; Murray S. Stedman, Jr., and Susan W. Stedman, *Discontent at the Polls* (New York: Columbia University Press, 1950) Chap. 7, especially pp. 125-129.

cincts. In the South the system is the same except that the county subdivisions are called districts, not townships. In New England the basic unit
is the town.

The conventional references to grass-roots politics usually mean the
ward or precinct, township, town, or district level. The organization at
these points consists of the legendary precinct captain or leader for each
party. In some cases there are, officially, two leaders, a man and a woman,
who may be selected directly by the voters or by a committee of which they
are chairman and vice-chairman, respectively. This leader "is the only
connecting link—the only man in the machine who has any point of direct
contact with the voters, who knows anything about them, who has any real
influence with them. . . . Without him there is no machine. He is the
indispensable cog in the wheel." [5] Not all precincts are so well staffed. In
a good many, the position is left vacant and much local leadership is
amateurish.[6]

In cities there is a *city committee* composed of the committees of the
polling-place units or, in the largest cities, of representatives from each
ward. Because of the power that has gravitated to county committees,
cities have not been nourished as separate organizations. Leaders in even
large cities dominating a county usually exercise their power through the
county organization.

The *county committee* in personnel is representative of each of the
polling-place units in the county except for those in large cities which are
represented by city wards. Outside New England the county is the key
unit of party organization, and all of the well-known past political organizations of the twentieth century—Pendergast, Kelly-Nash, Crump, Vare,
Hague, Tammany—have been based upon the control of a populous county.
Geographically the county is small enough to organize efficiently, and ad-
ministratively it is the major subdivision of the state. It is usually the
battleground in elections, which are computed in terms of the swing of
this or that pivotal county.[7] Its officials exercise significant political power.

---

[5] Frank R. Kent, *The Great Game of Politics* (New York: Doubleday, Page & Company,
1924) pp. 1-2. Kent concluded that this leader is so important that to discuss Presidential
politics without understanding precinct politics "is like trying to solve a problem in trigo-
nometry without having studied arithmetic." See Sonya Forthal, *Cogwheels of Democracy:
A Study of the Precinct Captain* (New York: Pamphlet Distributing Co., 1946).

[6] Hugh A. Bone, *Grass Roots Party Leadership,* Bureau of Governmental Research and
Services, University of Washington, October, 1952, Report No. 123. Robert L. Morlan,
"City Politics: Free Style," *National Municipal Review,* Vol. 38 (1949) pp. 485-490.

[7] "A party victory . . . is an important factor in most of the counties . . . important
most of all to party managers; . . . certain county organizations are in a position to win
or lose presidential elections." "Indeed, the distribution of the vote in 1916 is the clearest
indication . . . of the possibility of carrying elections by concentrating effort in counties

The county committee is a party agency of importance wherever the organization has power at all. Its leaders speak for the party in the county and may clear state and even federal patronage. Their decisions regarding nominations are frequently a decisive factor in their counties, and they are in most cases the main cogs in the election machinery and campaigns. Much of the power of the county committee is exercised by the county chairman. His power is rarely as autocratic as the popular accounts have suggested, for his position rests upon election by his colleagues, who demand recognition of their own interests in the decisions that are made. The county chairman is seldom so secure that he is free to antagonize them. His job is to harmonize the factions and consolidate both his personal and the party's position within the county. The more completely he accomplishes these objectives the stronger and surer voice he is likely to have in party councils above the county level.

In some states, committees are created for *districts* which may be smaller than a county or multicounty. From these districts members of Congress, judges, and state legislators are elected. Such committees have long since ceased to serve much purpose because of the use of the direct primary for making nominations. When nominations for these offices were made in district conventions, the district committees issued the call for the conventions and usually managed their proceedings. The only remaining use for congressional district committees is to call congressional district conventions to select delegates to national conventions in those states where this method is used. Sometimes what is called a congressional district committee is formed *ad hoc* as a campaign committee in behalf of a candidate for Congress but this is usually a personal organization of the candidate, not part of the regular party machinery.

At the top is the *state committee*. In most states this body is comparable to a union of the party organization in the counties, congressional district, or other geographical unit from which the committee is elected. The usual procedure is to reorganize the state committee each gubernatorial-election year. The state chairman, although chosen nominally by the state committee, is generally acceptable to, if not the personal choice of, the party's candidate for governor. In most states the selection of the state chairman is important because if the party captures the governorship, he will normally direct the distribution of patronage. For this reason, primarily, the powerful county leaders want to be consulted regarding the selection of the chairman. After all, he will come from one of the counties and may himself be a present or past county chairman or a one-time polling-place leader. The rules governing his selection, aside from his acceptability

where the margin of victory is slight."——E. E. Robinson, *The Presidential Vote 1896–1932* (Stanford: Stanford University Press, 1934) pp. 4, 19.

to the gubernatorial candidate, are his familiarity with the party leaders and the party's problems, his managerial ability, and his command of sources of political power within or without the organizational structure. Sometimes he is chosen because he has a large personal fortune and/or is able to solicit money successfully from men of wealth.

The state committee is the over-all campaign committee, and the state chairman is the campaign manager for the state ticket; this assignment usually includes coordination both of the individual candidates' campaigns and of the activities of the party committees on each geographical level. Variations of these practices are frequent. To take one illustration, candidates for governor may prefer to rely mainly on their own personal organization through which they were nominated and to relegate the state committee to the periphery of their campaign. This practice may or may not work well in winning an election, but it almost invariably causes tensions and disharmony between the personal and the party organizations. If the candidate is elected, these problems are likely to increase in the pullings and haulings over patronage and policy.

VARIETY IN METHODS AND ARRANGEMENTS

Party committees correspond with geographical boundaries or with electoral units such as legislative and congressional districts. Variations within these uniformities are numerous, and certain extraneous developments of a national and sectional character have affected organizational practices.

Arrangements for Women. The introduction of women into politics was the culmination of many years of bitter controversy over their right to vote, but as soon as the right was assured, party leaders began jockeying for their support. One manner of handling the problem was to create a women's auxiliary group during election campaigns so that women could proselyte women in behalf of the ticket. This arrangement was all right as far as it went, but it failed to integrate the sexes in the organization itself where the decisions were made. One solution was the admission of women into the various committees, either by mandatory requirement or by permissive authorization, on an equal numerical basis with men or equally represented in the hierarchy of committees through creation of the office of vice-chairman.[8]

Differences in Extent and Significance. Party organization is confused by the degree or intensity of it within states and from state to state. By and large, the stereotype of highly organized party politics is deficient as

[8] The first woman county chairman in New York was elected in 1953. See the *New York Times*, May 16, 1953.

applied to the entire country and has been primarily a phenomenon of the Eastern United States and of some large cities elsewhere. The West has been most consistently a section of loose organization and fluid operations, emphasizing leading personalities. The sharpest contrasts within states are found among those in the South where there is only a semblance of Republican organization. In Texas, for example, the laws specify the procedure for organizing parties (i.e., the Democrats) that cast 200,000 or more votes in a gubernatorial election, but the procedure is optional for parties (i.e., the Republicans) that cast between 10,000 and 200,000 votes. With the exception of the South, the diversities in organization are found in contrasting one state with another rather than in contrasting the organizations within one state.[9]

Examples of States' Organizations. The methods of constituting the various committees are too diverse to permit much generalization. Only a state-by-state description would be wholly accurate, but examples of states in various parts of the country are sufficiently suggestive.

In the state of *Washington* the party voters in each precinct elect their respective party's committeeman, and all of the party's committeemen in a county constitute the county central committee which, at its organizational meeting, elects the county's members to the State Central Committee.[10]

In *Louisiana* each parish, except for New Orleans, is divided into police jury wards which become polling places. To constitute the parish executive committee, the party voters in each ward elect as many members as the ward is entitled to on the police jury; in addition, five members of this committee are elected at large in the parish. City committees are made up of one member elected in each ward unless there are less than three wards in which case a three-member committee is elected at large. The city government in New Orleans divides the city into wards and precincts and the parish committee is composed of two members from each ward. The State Central Committee is composed of one hundred members apportioned among each parish and each New Orleans ward on the same basis as the lower house of the legislature. The Democratic state committeemen are elected on the same day the regular state-wide primary is held, but the Republicans use mass meetings and rarely elect the full number. The state

---

[9] "The two political parties in a given State are likely to have practically the same sort of organization. . . . [They] learn much more from each other respecting the outlines of effective organization than they learn from their party associates in other States."—— Macy, *op. cit.*, p. 108.

[10] *Revised Code of Washington*, Book 3, 1951, Chap. 29.42.

central committee may create any inferior committees on the district level composed of the state committeemen from parishes or wards within that district.[11]

Moving north into the Great Lakes states, where parties have traditionally been highly organized, the county committee in *Indiana* is made up of a committeeman and vice-committeeman elected in each precinct; those elected in city precincts also form the city committee. The congressional district committees are composed of the chairman and vice-chairman of each county committee within the district; and the chairman and vice-chairman of each congressional district committee jointly form the state central committee. Chairmen and vice-chairmen of all committees must be of different sexes.[12]

Massachusetts is an example of the town system of New England as opposed to the county system in other states. Each town elects a committee of at least three members, and city committees are made up of not less than three members from each ward. Both town and city committees determine the size of their committees in excess of these minimums. The state central committee consists of one member elected from each senatorial district plus as many members at large as the committee determines. The most difficult aspect of this organization for a non-New-Englander to grasp is that the populace does not conceive of the county or of any government level or district between the town and the state in the political organization.[13]

NATURE OF PARTY ORGANIZATION

INSTITUTIONALISM AND FACTIONALISM

Except for those who are directly connected with politics or specifically involved in the operations of parties, there is little appreciation and less knowledge of the actual structure and function of the organization. To the public at large, this array of committees is an invisible world existing under their noses, a remarkable example of Edgar Allan Poe's thesis in *The Pur-*

---

[11] *Louisiana Revised Statutes of 1950*, 2, Title 18, Ch. II, Sec. 285-303; A. L. Powell and Emmett Asseff, *Party Organization and Nominations in Louisiana* (Baton Rouge: Louisiana State University, Bureau of Government Research, 1952) pp. 7-10. See William Goodman, *Inherited Domain: Political Parties in Tennessee* (Knoxville: University of Tennessee, Bureau of Public Administration, 1954) Chap. 2, for a Southern state with a stronger Republican organization and with little statutory provision for any of the parties' organization.

[12] *Annotated Indiana Statutes*, 1949, 7, Part 1, Ch. 29. This arrangement is analogous to that in Texas where all county chairmen, elected at large by the party voters, form the state executive committee. An atypical provision is Nebraska's system of election of county committees by the state central committee without regard to equal precinct representation.

[13] *General Laws of Massachusetts*, 1932, I, Ch. 52, Secs. 1-4; Earl Latham, *Massachusetts Politics* (New York: The Citizenship Clearing House) pp. 25-29; Macy, *op. cit.*, Chaps. 9-14, remains one of the best available discussions of structure and function in selected states, despite the book's being out of date in many details.

loined Letter that human beings fail to perceive the most casually obvious things. Because the public is so unaware of the party organization, a great deal that happens in party politics is not at all comprehended and attempts at explanation produce very little additional awareness. What is even more difficult for the layman to grasp is that the committee structure has produced the concept of the Organization with a capital "O", an impersonal force seemingly generating a perpetual momentum. Yet the forces are those of human beings, and the Organization, like all institutions, is a composite of personal forces.

Party politics in the United States is essentially the result of individual aspirations and motivations of incalculable variety. People who are active in party organizations are seldom moved strictly by charitable or humanitarian impulses. Generally they go into politics for something specific—a job, prestige and power, money, professional advancement, and so on. It is upon the competitive personality, seeking definite ends, that political organizations depend. Jealousy is either clearly evident or just below the surface among most practitioners, although they have various ways of showing it and varying skill in concealing it. If one individual in the organization appears to be forging his way to the top, there is often a reaction against him by those who feel they are being left behind. Human acquisitiveness and combativeness are constantly displayed.

Inevitably, politics breeds cliques of likeminded individuals, factions of leaders and their followers aspiring to exercise power and to receive acclaim. Factional lines are often fluid because the individuals are trying to protect themselves either by defensive shifts of allegiance or by offensive maneuvers against those who seem to threaten them. Not only do factions change their positions under the impact of events, but also there are factions within factions; bitterness and friendliness are exhibited within and across supposedly rigid groupings. This fluidity is normally made possible by the fact that factionalism is rarely based on ideology or on any other substantive differences capable of being evaluated objectively. Quite often these struggles pit one crowd against another crowd, two or more groups seeking mutually exclusive objectives which often involve economic interests. The occasion for factionalism may be professional competition between two lawyers or two businessmen. Factions may stem from different church affiliations or different fraternal or social organizations. Factions may have no apparent basis but sheer pugnacity or stubborness. While some causes of factionalism, though seemingly irrational, may permanently bar one group from ever acting in harmony with another, in many cases individuals can conveniently find their way back and forth as the tide of political fortunes shifts in the endless motions of intraparty warfare.

Many professionals in politics complain of the desire of everyone to be leaders and never to be followers. Criticism is rife, and the followers are positive they can do better than the leaders are doing. Anyone contemplating the hazards that emerge from these clashes of ambitions, where lines of relationships are constantly changing, will find it difficult to comprehend how order and stability can exist and how constructive accomplishments can emerge.[14] The fact is that leadership does operate and that chaos never quite triumphs.

Supremacy of the Organization. It is easy to overlook the adherence of people to habitual patterns of thought and action and to forget their tendency, when checked by competition, to be reasonable. In addition, political organizations are actually held together to some extent by these very difficulties which seem to obstruct their operations. Because people want something, they accept the necessity of joint endeavor; they are forced to be practical both in their ambitions and in their methods if they are to achieve anything at all. The prima donna, the sorehead, and the bolter normally have no future in politics even if they are tolerated. Success of the organization is further insured because not all of its members want the same kind of thing or exactly the same rewards.

Finally, stability is achieved by the institutional nature, the separate existence of the organization and its traditions. Its members make it supreme and then stand in awe of its supremacy. They know that if put to the test, the united organization can discipline the unruly and impress the irreverent because, politically, individuals are impotent by themselves. The members soon learn that they need the organization far more than the organization needs them. They also learn that whatever they wish to accomplish must be done through the organization and that to oppose it is suicidal unless they have the capacity and the time to build their own organization.[15]

INTERNAL RELATIONS

Because the organization in each state consists of a collection of committees on the various government levels, reaching from polling-place areas to the state, they are habitually referred to as a hierarchy. The usual method of visualization is a pyramid drawing—a figure useful in suggesting the narrowing of the gap, the progressive reduction of the number of committees until there is only one. Such suggestions are not helpful if they convey the idea that each committee necessarily has some kind of legal or coercive jurisdiction over the committees of smaller geographical levels listed below it in the pyramid. The relationships are considerably more subtle and involved.

---

14 See Kent, *op. cit.*, Chap. 5, "The Looseness of Machine Ties."

15 Frank R. Kent, *Political Behavior* (New York: William Morrow & Company, Inc., 1928) Chaps. 3 and 4.

The selection of polling-place leaders by the party voters may have created a false impression of the status of these people. Actually they are chosen, rated, promoted, retained, or fired by their superiors solely on their ability to deliver the vote expected of them. In Philadelphia, for instance, there are two leaders elected in each division (i.e., the polling-place area) by the voters of each party; but the ward leader can substantially affect this selection by refusing to do favors for a leader. The party voters not only will be lined up for the division leader favored by the ward leader but also will want the candidate who is able to get things for them.[16] There is endless testimony to the existence of the same relationship in other cities [17] as well as in such urban counties as the Bronx.[18] The necessity for having an able producer of votes at the grass roots is just as applicable to rural counties.[19] The polling-place leader requires the con-

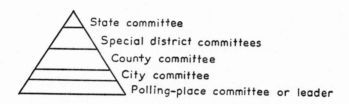

State committee
Special district committees
County committee
City committee
Polling-place committee or leader

fidence of the voters if he is to be elected by them. If the leader is successful, he is unlikely to be challenged by outsiders, whose chances of unseating him would be nil both because the force of the organization would be behind the leader and because the voters approve of him. The voters generally react the same way toward the polling-place leader as the ward leader does. In "professionally" organized cities, the same relationship applies to the ward leader and the city leader, since the former is dependent upon the latter for the favors he distributes in his ward.

The relations among the committees from the city upward to the state are marked by a certain amount of autonomy on the part of each.

[16] David H. Kurtzman, *Methods of Controlling Votes in Philadelphia* (Philadelphia: University of Pennsylvania, 1935) pp. 20 and 115.

[17] In general, see Kent, *The Great Game of Politics*, p. 14. For specific cities, see Maurice M. Milligan, *Missouri Waltz* (New York: Charles Scribner and Sons, 1948) p. 135; George M. Reynolds, *Machine Politics in New Orleans* (New York: Columbia University Press, 1936) p. 112.

[18] "Discipline in the Bronx organization is most assuredly maintained. The District Captain is held accountable for his district by the Assembly Leader. If the Captain does not produce results, if he does not run his district efficiently, invariably, he or she is replaced."——Edward J. Flynn, *You're the Boss* (New York: The Viking Press, 1948) p. 16.

[19] Kent, *The Great Game of Politics*, p. 66.

The main power of coercion lies in the use of patronage. Formal sanctions are seldom either possible or desirable. It is true that in some states the law gives impressive powers to the state committee over party policy and personnel, e.g., in Indiana the state committee has power to enforce its rules by applying for a writ of mandamus.[20] In actuality, no political party can operate long by coercion of committee by committee. Even statutory powers of supervision and regulation are often exercised with a leniency to the point of nullification. Cases of orders being issued and enforced are almost invariably the result of a fierce factional fight for power. People do many things they do not want to do, but they do them voluntarily more often than not.

In the ordinary course of operations, the relations among party committees can be shown more accurately if they are projected on a surface capable of revealing height and depth. Visualized in this way, hills and valleys represent the varying degrees of prestige resulting from the actual powers of a committee or group of committees or of persons outside the formal organization. The surface is capable of rearrangements and adjustments to show, for any given state, the evolving spheres of a group's influence. At one time a specific county committee that dominates its party's affairs may be placed so as to dominate the whole surface; within a few years its leaders may have died or have been undermined or have lost their sources of authority. Then the new pattern will show where power has gravitated—perhaps to a group of county leaders or to a clique that controls the state committee. To understand the internal relations is to understand that power moves toward power, that power begets power.

The predominant pattern of operations among the committees is consultation, exchange of information, and requests for help of one kind or another. Each leader in his own environment is important, whether he can affect seventy thousand votes or seventy. Questions are discussed with those who can supply the answers. The state chairman does not issue directives to county chairmen for transmittal through channels to townships and districts and wards. A state chairman may travel about and discuss the situation in each county with its leaders. They may have a problem he can help them with or vice versa. Each unit fits into the mosaic. Alone, any one unit and its committee would be as anomalous as a disengaged piece of anatomy in a show window. In conjunction with all of the other units' committees it has a purpose and a meaning. A party committee does not exist by issuing or obeying orders, but by fulfilling the requirements expected of it and exercising the influence its powers permit.

---

20 The powers granted in New York come closest to the hierarchical concept: Each committee may prepare rules for the government of the party within its own political subdivision and is required to file a certified copy of them with the Secretary of State, and in the case of a county committee, with the county election board.

THE IMPACT OF LEADERSHIP UPON THE PARTY

The most constant phenomenon in human behavior is the existence of leader-follower relationships, and leadership has become the most absorbing aspect of political party organization in the United States.

Autocratic Operation. Irrespective of the system for electing men and women to people the committees—whether by mass meetings, conventions, direct primaries, or other party committees—the theory is that the rank and file determine the selection, and ostensibly they do; but the actual situation is something quite different. Each committee is run by a leader or small group of leaders who determine the composition of the committees because they are seldom challenged. Recognizing that it is not the democratic theory, but the fact of autocratic operation which controls the organization, there has grown up the honorable tradition—a pastime in some cases—of condemning the leaders with the term "bosses" and the organizations with the term "machines." "Bosses" become closely associated with "politicians," those office-seekers we profess to dislike. The word "statesman" is normally used to describe an office-seeker we profess to like. The only noncommittal term for "boss" is "leader." [21] It would appear that something inherently evil attaches to organizational manipulation.

Characteristics of Leaders. The concept of a typical boss seems to be indigenous to United States politics, but such creatures have not been turned up with the regularity one would expect. Frank Hague and T. J. Pendergast fit the pattern to a considerable extent in their personal appearance and conduct,[22] but they can hardly be considered sufficient evidence to establish the pattern. Backgrounds range from those reared in the slums to those sired in families of wealth and culture.[23] The antecedents of

[21] D. D. McKean, *The Boss* (New York: Houghton, Mifflin Company, 1940) pp. 10-11. However, T. J. Pendergast called himself a boss.——Milligan, *op. cit.*, p. 79. Theodore Roosevelt preferred the moralistic differentiation: "A leader leads the people; a boss drives the people. The leader gets his hold by open appeal to the reason and conscience of his followers; the boss keeps his hold by manipulation, by intrigue, by secret and furtive appeals to many phases of self-interest, and sometimes to every base phase of self-interest." ——Quoted in Charles E. Merriam, *American Political Ideas* (New York: The Macmillan Company, 1920) p. 293. For further invidious comparisons, see M. Ostrogorski, *Democracy and the Organization of Political Parties* (New York: The Macmillan Company, 1902) pp. 190-192.

[22] McKean, *op. cit.*, Chap. 1; Milligan, *op. cit.*, p. 79.

[23] See Harold Zink, *City Bosses in the United States* (Durham: Duke University Press, 1930) *passim;* Kent, *The Great Game of Politics,* pp. 76-77; Flynn, *op. cit.*, pp. 3-6; James A. Farley, *Behind the Ballots* (New York: Harcourt, Brace and Company, 1938) pp. 6-17; Croswell Bowen, *The Elegant Oakey* (New York: Oxford University Press, 1956); James Michael Curley, *I'd Do It Again* (New York: Prentice-Hall, 1957); William T. Hutchinson, *Lowden of Illinois: The Life of Frank O. Lowden* (Chicago: University of Chicago, 1957).

Henry Cabot Lodge were certainly impeccable. When Boies Penrose "entered politics, there was quite a little rejoicing among the better element. Here, at last, was one of their own come to lead them against the plundering rabble. Here, thank God, was a young man with the will, the education, the ideals, the traditions that they could vote for." [24]

The motivations for entering politics have varied widely. Robert M. La Follette was, like many other bosses, personally honest; his objectives were those of the reformer, and he evidenced little interest in personally amassing a fortune. Some spend money for the zest of the game or for the power they win or for the positions they hold. Professor Harold Zink concluded from his study of twenty city bosses that even a fascination for politics was not entirely applicable to all of them and that they "are not a distinct species of human beings but possess the physical, mental, and moral variations of men in general." [25] Professor J. T. Salter, speaking of politicians, used the term to include both office-seekers and strictly organization men and women; he believed politicans "are likely to have political 'it'—a pungent personality that captures attention amid the rush and tumult of daily living" although he immediately admitted that some politicians did not have "it" and that they "are men and women of infinite variety and no two are the same." [26] Characteristics may vary depending upon the level on which the leader operates.[27]

A most enlightening discovery is that the leaders are not always publicly known as the leaders. Some may seek public office and others may not or may put such pretensions aside after a short career of officeholding, in order to concentrate upon the control of the organization.[28] They may be chairmen of the committees or they may be entirely outside the formal organization. Perhaps the stereotype of the boss is the leader working in his own interest behind the scenes, selecting the officials, and giving them orders. This emphasis upon avarice and peculation seems to stem from thinking only about urban bosses, although the actual examinations of them do not fully bear out the popular conclusion.[29]

It is unfortunate that the limited information available is drawn

---

[24] Walter Davenport, *Power and Glory* (New York: G. P. Putnam's Sons, 1931) p. 98.

[25] Zink, *op. cit.*, p. 65.

[26] J. T. Salter, *Boss Rule* (New York: McGraw-Hill Book Company, 1935) pp. 8-9.

[27] H. F. Gosnell, *Machine Politics: Chicago Model* (Chicago: University of Chicago, 1937) emphasizes the enduring loyalty to a party of a ward boss, but the opportunistic and turncoat behavior of precinct captains: Chap. 2 and p. 53; Salter, *op. cit.*, pp. 36-40.

[28] See Milligan, *op. cit.*, pp. 68-9; Zink, *op. cit.*, *passim*.

[29] Revelations of the suspected financial profits leaders derive from politics can be found in Davenport, *op. cit.*, *passim*; Milligan, *op. cit.*, *passim*; McKean, *op. cit.*, Chap. 7. "The individuals who devote their lives to politics are motivated differently, but an unusual number of them have an extraordinary socio-political awareness."—Salter, *op. cit.*, p. 25. Milligan, in rebuttal of any such contention, denies that bosses are humanitarian; their services to the people are expedient and "coldly calculated."——*Op. cit.*, p. 279. However, Salter finds a wide range of contributing factors that vary with the individual, as does Zink, *op. cit.*, pp. 53-54.

primarily from city rather than from rural politics where leaders get less publicity and are not so conveniently situated for the collecting of data. Perhaps the facts, if we had them, would show as much similarity as difference between the two locales. One study of ten southern Illinois counties suggested that turnover among rural precinct committeemen was "considerable," dovetailing with a study of Chicago precinct captains.[30] However, two consecutive articles in the same issue of the *American Political Science Review,* one based on city and the other on rural precinct leaders, drew mutually exclusive conclusions regarding their attitudes toward the merit system and the value of money in winning elections.[31]

A concluding feature of general differentiation is sufficiently obvious to require only a reminder. Political leaders vary considerably both in capacities and ambition. In given cases it would be quite possible to diagnose the reason why a man goes just so far and no further. In the main, it can be said that one or the other quality determines the degree of success and the range of authority a man will achieve. While capacity is a hard-and-fast limitation, ambition is self-imposed or the result of satisfaction with the degree of success achieved. Some men enter politics indirectly or use its processes for oblique rather than straight-ahead objectives. If the leader has realized those objectives which he entered politics to attain, he has no motivation to push himself further.

Insufficient Information About Leaders. The most difficult feature in studying organization leaders is the lack of pertinent and accurate information. Political leaders themselves have not been cooperative. To accompany a presentation like Edward J. Flynn's in *You're the Boss,* we have from countless thousands of other leaders either silence or explanations on a defensive note. We learn indirectly or by inference from such books as James A. Farley's *Behind the Ballots* and *Jim Farley's Story.* Occasionally, as in William F. McCombs' *Making Woodrow Wilson President,* we perceive some of the hazards of political writings from which others have spared us by their silence. The student of politics is almost entirely dependent upon descriptions and analyses of observers rather than of the participants. Such writing can be of the very highest caliber, as Frank R. Kent's two books, *The Great Game of Politics* and *Political Behavior.* Other

---

[30] Leon Weaver, "Some Soundings in the Party System: Rural Precinct Committeemen," *American Political Science Review* Vol. 34 (1940) p. 81; Gosnell, *op. cit.,* p. 51.

[31] Sonya Forthal, "The Small Fry and the Party Purse," *American Political Science Review,* Vol. 34 (1940) pp. 74-6; Weaver, *op. cit.,* pp. 81-3. The Weaver article has the advantage of tabulating committeemen's answers to a questionaire according to which 65% of the Republicans and 32% of the Democrats favored the merit system—this partisan disproportion can be accounted for in part by the fact the Democrats at the time were "ins." The questionaire also brought out that 56 Democrats and 66 Republicans believed volunteer workers were as effective, hour for hour, as paid workers or political job holders but that only 38 Democrats and 49 Republicans thought the reverse.

journalists have done quality work in more limited areas, like Warren Moscow in *Politics in the Empire State,* or have given valuable insights into specific situations and personalities through biographies like the works of David Lawrence and James Kerney on Woodrow Wilson or autobiographies like William Allen White's. From university sources, we have the highly enlightening accounts of New Orleans Democrats and Philadelphia Republicans by George M. Reynolds and David H. Kurtzman, respectively. These are not all of the works worth mentioning, but all of them are few enough. The analyses of high merit are the result of long and concentrated experience plus an ability to segregate preconceived notions or wishful thinking from the actual data discovered.[32] The work of the serious researcher is inherently handicapped by the general code which leaders have followed of putting as little as possible on paper and relying upon word-of-mouth communication, a practice which was tremendously aided by the invention of the telephone.[33]

TECHNIQUES FOR CONTROLLING THE PARTY ORGANIZATION

Dedication of Leaders. The impossibility of finding definitive classifications of political leaders' motives, personalities, and backgrounds is no denial of common characteristics of political leadership. In the first place, people enter politics because they have objectives; they want to gain or accomplish something; this fact is so generally taken for granted that it is often overlooked, but it is a fact of first importance. The objectives themselves are not subject to precise classification. They are of infinite variety and combinations and are not always so simple as to be instantly apparent. In the second place, sustained leadership cannot exist apart from organization, and the leaders have climbed the rungs of the organization to reach whatever eminence they have attained. It is the rare case for a successful and genuine leader to buy his way in at the top or capture the party organization from the outside with a competing organization, although in small communities where politics is neither a full-time job nor the direct source of his income, he may attain his political leadership by virtue of his leadership in other activities.[34] In the third place, to become one of the directors of organized politics, a person gives his time and energies to the

---

32 See W. F. Whyte, "A Challenge to Political Scientists," *American Political Science Review,* Vol. 37 (1943) pp. 692-7.

33 McKean, *op. cit.,* p. 5, testifies to this fact for a major Democratic leader, Frank Hague. Davenport, *op. cit.,* p. 200, gives us the same testimony for an equally important Republican leader, Boies Penrose.

34 For the general rule and some of the distinctions, see Frank Kent, *The Great Game of Politics,* p. 65 and Chap. 15. Among other discussions, see Zink, *op. cit.,* pp. 23-4, 52 and Chap. 5; Salter *op. cit.,* pp. 26-29; McKean, *op. cit.,* Chap. 3; Flynn, *op. cit.,* pp. 11-33 *passim*; Milligan, *op. cit.,* pp. 56 ff.; Farley, *op. cit.,* pp. 17-23. For the relationship of leaders and organization on a wider scale than just political parties, see Charles Hickman Titus, *The Processes of Leadership* (Dubuque: William C. Brown, 1950) Chap. 2.

task and does not permit himself to be diverted. Success in this pursuit does not demand genius or even superior intelligence, but it does require a desire to attain success and to apply one's talents without limit. It follows, in the fourth place, that leaders are fighters, or they would neither reach nor hold their positions, and with their pugnacity goes a shrewdness both in sense of timing and in managing others.[35] It is not a gentle game they play. They are constantly alive to opportunities and to dangers.

Integrity of Leaders. Another observation about political leadership is equally important. Leaders require integrity in their dealings with their own organization. This characteristic is not in conflict with any of the others already suggested, but instead is part of the full stock in trade of those who manage people. The precise nature of this integrity is easily misunderstood. The leader may deceive the public, and he often tries to deceive his opposition. If he wants to build confidence and support, he does not deceive his own intimates. Leaders are frequently criticised for failure to make promises, for being noncommital when requests are made for jobs or other favors. The only way one can avoid breaking his word sometimes is to refuse to give it. Political leaders are notorious for being difficult to pin down by their associates, but when leaders make a definite statement, their associates must be able to depend upon it.

Courtesy of Leaders. In addition to this practice of integrity, which has both practical and moral sanctions, leaders follow the rule of showing their appreciation for the accomplishments of subordinates. The main opportunity for this kind of expression follows election campaigns when a party has won, and the county leaders, for example, want to acclaim the captains in particular precincts where hard work brought out the full party majority. Commendation for tasks well done, through dinners or other gatherings, is a useful supplement to the more mercenary rewards with which politics abounds. The more professional the organization, the more likely rewards of this nature will be bestowed, just as appropriate punishments will be meted out for failures or slovenly work.[36]

Personal Relations of Leaders. These techniques of leadership tell us

---

[35] Kent, *The Great Game of Politics*, p. 81; Kurtzman, *op. cit.*, pp. 18-19, 23.

[36] See Titus, *op. cit.*, pp. 78-81, 266-267. An eloquent example of a leader's tribute to a lieutenant is the following statement regarding George Washington Plunkitt made by Charles F. Murphy during his tenure as head of Tammany Hall: "Senator Plunkitt is a straight organization man. He believes in party government; he does not indulge in cant and hypocrisy and he is never afraid to do exactly what he thinks. He is a believer in thorough policital organization and all-the-year-around work and he holds to the doctrine that, in making appointments to office, party workers should be preferred if they are fitted to perform the duties of the office. Plunkitt is one of the veteran leaders of the organization, he has always been faithful and reliable and he has performed valuable services." Quoted in William L. Riordan, *Plunkitt of Tammany Hall* (New York: Alfred A. Knopf, Inc., 1948) p. lvi.

something about the sources of a leader's power and influence. How can a man or woman accomplish the many tasks which arise in party management? At least one basis is a very wide circle of friends and associates to whom the leader can turn for information and for the various kinds of help he needs in dealing with his problems. He, in turn, helps others so that the political relationship is a continuous series of interdependent actions. By having a maximum number of influential people with whom he exchanges favors and by keeping in regular communication with them, the leader is able to establish and maintain his position. Other sources of power exist, but the equation of personal relations is inevitably involved in the phenomenon of exercising political leadership.

Controlling Votes. People attempt to master the techniques of whatever activity they enter. One of the basic techniques of an elective system is the manipulation of numbers in voting, and in the case of organization politics this manipulation is performed as much as possible away from the public's attention. Since the real preparations occur in private conferences and the newspapers usually print only the end result, there is a popular and understandable conviction that political leaders possess powers of an occult or superhuman quality. What we fail to see is that the leader has turned out a finished product of his craft in the same way as a mason builds or an engineer draws and designs. It is the function of the leader to produce enough votes at crucial moments. In some instances if he fails, he may cease to be the leader. It is application and specialization that triumph, and

> it is a fundamental mistake to assume that a successful politician is necessarily a fellow of great shrewdness, subtlety and resource. The fact is the amazingly adroit political mind exists only in fiction. Except in the imagination of hard-pressed political writers and credulous side-line observers there are no deep plots in politics, no dark and diabolically ingenious schemes. The clever explanations of political tactics are almost always completely false.[37]

The particular method employed for choosing members of party committees determines the particular kind of vote manipulation required in capturing the committees. The older method, which is still in use in some states, is to announce the date and time for meetings in the polling places or whatever area is used to elect local committees, such as city wards, townships, districts. This announcement is usually routine news and probably comes to the attention of a very small minority of the public. The preparations for these meetings have been going forward for some time prior to the announcement and those who want to control the outcome make every effort to line up the vote beforehand. While any bona fide

---

[37] Kent, *Political Behavior*, p. 11.

party member, resident of the area, is eligible to attend and take part, those leaders who organize the meeting in advance depend upon few if any disinterested citizens turning out. Most of those who do appear are involved in some way in the outcome. They may seek to be elected to the committee or help a friend be elected or intend to run for a public office and wish to select committeemen favorable to their candidacy. They may have a political appointment either to a party or a government office and vote to continue their benefactors in control of the party.[38]

The meeting may involve a factional fight within the party, in which case the opposing leaders will compete in rounding up adherents for the meeting. In some states or counties, strong-arm methods are in vogue, e.g., one county faction will hire a group of people and transport them from one to another of these local meetings, having them vote at each place for the committeemen the faction is supporting. Sometimes the defeated faction will bolt the meeting and elect its own committee. In this case it is up to the county committee to decide which committee to recognize in that area.

The newer method for choosing the polling-place party leader is election by the members of the party at the time of the state-wide direct primary. Each voter, in receiving his party's ballot at the polls, will find on it the name or names of candidates for this party office. Some of the aspects of this selection have already been noted. In addition to the likelihood of a disciplined and grateful vote being cast for the organization choices, one may surmise that many voters ignore this particular race altogether and that these party contests are settled by a minuscule part of the rank-and-file party members. Attempts to determine the extent of voting have generally been confined to elections for public, not party, office. The few studies of the latter type are neither conclusive nor in mutual agreement in their findings. An analysis of the voting record for Chicago ward committeemen was pronounced poor when compared with the registered vote, but this method of computation invariably produces a low voting percentage for most offices. When the more realistic figure of the number actually voting is taken as the basis for comparison, the percentage voting for ward committeemen was considered high between 1928 and 1936. The presence or absence of contests for ward committeemen is not given, but

---

[38] At a West Philadelphia ward meeting to elect a city committeeman, the leader of the city organization, Vare, stated: "Mr. D. is the candidate for the office and I want to assure the committeemen who are office holders that they are in no danger of dismissal should they cast their votes for him."——*Philadelphia Record,* June 2, 1933, quoted in Kurtzman, *op. cit.,* p. 12. A former Magistrate and candidate for the office of city committeeman made the following campaign speech: " 'I never wanted anyone to lose their bread and butter through me. If anybody who holds a public office has been threatened with dismissal, or fears he will lose his job, I release him from his pledge and he can vote either as he chooses or as he's been ordered.' There was a burst of applause at this, and a few sighs of relief."——*Ibid.,* p. 14.

lack of contests was acknowledged as a reason for nonvoting.[39] In ten
downstate Illinois counties a high incidence of voting for precinct committeemen was found, especially when there were contests; in some cases a
higher percentage of the vote was cast for this party office than for
nominees for United States senator.[40]

With the direct election of polling-place leaders, a disciplined electorate
may be more likely to follow the county or city leadership. An independent
electorate may be more unpredictable in its voting behavior if it votes.
However, in any case, a contest for the office generates greater interest and
participation. A stabilized city or county organization, where most of the
members are secure in their areas and usually are re-elected without opposition, would not be likely to produce much excitement; but a highly tense
organization, surrounded with controversy and competition, would more
likely have to contend with a shifting and mercurial electorate.

Control through Committees. By general practice, the county committee is not separately elected but is composed of these local committeemen.
After the committee members are elected, a meeting is held to choose new
officers for the county committee; when there are factional fights, the test
of strength is this organizational meeting. The existing leaders who are
completing their term of office have a decided advantage, for the outgoing
committee or its chairman almost invariably has the authority to set the
date for the meeting. The factional leaders then in control of the organization have time to work out their strategy in the light of the election of
committeemen. The most important initial advantage is controlling the
chair, since one of the outgoing officers will call the meeting to order and
preside until a temporary chairman is elected. The presiding officer knows
whom to recognize for the purpose of making the first nomination—the
person nominated will be the man previously selected by the leaders to be
temporary chairman.[41] With one name placed in nomination, the next cue
may be to recognize a member who will move that nominations be closed.
This is an open show of strength and may prove unwise if the opposing

---

39 Gosnell, *op. cit.*, pp. 34-36. Computed on the basis of those actually voting, not
the registered vote, the respective percentage of the vote cast for ward committeemen
in each of the five elections covered was: 91.1%, 90.7%, 88.9%, 89.7%, 87.7%.

40 Weaver, *op. cit.*, pp. 77-78.

41 Kurtzman, *op. cit.* p. 15, describes a particularly good example of the cut-and-dried
nature of these proceedings. In one West Philadelphia ward the "ward leader appointed
his lieutenant as temporary chairman and another worker as temporary secretary. The
temporary chairman then recognized Mr. P., who had not even asked for the floor.
Mr. P. then read from a piece of paper his speech nominating Mr. W. as chairman
of the ward executive committee, and he was unanimously elected. These nominating
speeches were prepared by someone and handed to the various people who were to
make the nominating addresses. As a further instance . . . the temporary chairman
of the meetings, when calling for the nomination of the secretary, said excitedly: 'We
will now ask F. H. to nominate Mr. C. for secretary.' "

faction or factions are strong enough to override the motion. If the dominant faction has the votes, it may prefer to prove its strength on this motion to close nominations. The desire is to complete the work of the meeting as quickly as possible to avoid unforeseen developments and to prevent the opposition's having a breathing spell.

If there is a question about the numerical strength of the faction, its leaders may give the opposition an opportunity to present a candidate for temporary chairman in order to appear fair. This maneuver gives the leaders time to line up more votes and avoids antagonizing any uncommitted members who may object to obviously strong-arm methods. In any event, the proceedings continue through the election of the county committee's officers. When the various tests come, the side with the largest vote wins, necessitating a careful calculation long before the meeting of how the members will vote. Skillful operators will know almost exactly how many votes each side will get before the votes are cast.[42] When elections at organizational meetings are not contested, the atmosphere is quite congenial and the members are relaxed. Where other methods are used for choosing the committee's officers (e.g., in Texas the county chairman is elected at large by the party's voters in the county), the techniques of the leaders will be correspondingly affected.

The importance of the selection of officers is the likelihood that they will actually run the party affairs in the county. However, the county committee may refuse to abdicate completely to its officers, so the leaders may be forced to find other means for control. One such technique is to have so large a committee that it is powerless to act and is compelled to select a comparatively small group of leaders as an executive committee.[43] The executive committee in fact takes over the operation of the organization, and its officers become the real leaders of the party in the county unless the men with the authority choose to remain in the background and have trusted subordinates elected to the positions.

County organization in New York, especially in New York City, illustrates this general type of organization. Before 1953 the statutes provided that there be at least two members from each election district, but did not specify the maximum number of members of a county committee. Any such committee, at its own discretion, could provide for additional members. The tremendous size of some county committees with as many as twenty members per election district made an executive committee necessary, and

---

[42] See E. E. Schattschneider, *Party Government* (New York: Farrar & Rinehart, 1948) pp. 38-47, for a description of these techniques of computation.

[43] Terminology is one of the most confusing aspects of party organization. An "executive committee" most frequently is used in the sense described here, a small committee chosen by the large, plenary committee and empowered to act for it. In some states the full committee itself has the word "executive" as part of its official title. The only way to learn the actual function and status of any given executive committee is to inquire among those who are acquainted with the organization's practices.

the chairmen of the executive committees exercise the power supposedly wielded by the whole committee.[44] Edward J. Flynn frankly explained these arrangements:

> Today, actual power in the Democratic party in the Bronx resides with the Executive Committee. The Chairman is, however, the real power within that committee, and for an obvious reason. There are nineteen votes: twenty-eight Executive Members with a half-vote each; the County Committee Chairman, First Vice-Chairman, Secretary, and Treasurer with a full vote each; and the Chairman of the Executive Committee (myself) with one vote. Since I choose the people who are elected officers of the general County Committee, I can always count on four full votes besides my own, which leaves me only five of the remaining fourteen to garner to assure myself of control.[45]

The New York Legislature in 1953 finally set a limit of four committeemen from any election district. The reduction will not alleviate the necessity for an executive committee and in some cases will probably have no noticeable effect at all, for the law reduces the total number of committee members in New York City only from 35,861 to 16,164.[46]

Some Factors Influencing Techniques. So far, techniques that can be considered internal to the organization have been suggested, but there are other influences which condition the kinds of techniques as well as the more general characteristics of the organization. The best that can be done is to suggest the potential range of such influences.

(1) The *size of the population* of the area within which the organization operates is highly determinative. Generally speaking, the larger and more concentrated the population, the more "professional" and more highly organized the parties. The smaller and more dispersed the population, the less need for intricacies, the less herding and shuffling of the voters, the less excitement and frenzied activities, and the more attention to individuals. There are exceptions, but people who are in a more independent position economically and socially are more likely to resent the techniques of coercive politics associated with urban organizations. For this reason rural populations are less "boss-ridden" in most cases than urban populations. However, rural organizations, within these limits,

---

44 *New York Consolidated Laws,* 1949 Legislative Issue, Article II, secs 11, 12. Warren Moscow, *Politics in the Empire State* (New York: Alfred A. Knopf, Inc., 1948) p. 56; Flynn, *op. cit.,* pp. 9-10.

45 *Ibid.,* p. 10.

46 *New York Times,* April 5, 1953. Before the law was changed, the committee in Manhattan alone had approximately 11,995 members. Most urban county committees had 200 to 400 members. The state committees in New York are required to have two members from each assembly district but may add more at their discretion. Each state committee has 300 members. The larger the size of a committee, the easier it is for the organization to elect its members because an insurgent group is at a disadvantage in finding enough candidates to run.

can be as efficient as urban organizations and the response of urban voters to machine politics will vary with the section of the city.

One significant difference between rural and urban politics has been the use of ward or city political clubs, which have been skillfully utilized in the largest cities. The clubhouses, maintained in those wards where the organizations are strong, are the home of the ward organization and the headquarters of the ward leader who controls the club just as he controls his ward.[47] The clubs are run on a neighborhood basis, offering athletic, social, and even educational opportunities for all members of the party who wish to join. Nominal dues are supposed to be paid, but many do not pay them and no one is dropped from membership for failure to pay. In some cases a club was formed to promote the interests of a party faction, as the Choctaw Club in New Orleans was used by the Behrman organization and the Jackson County Democratic Club was used by the Pendergast organization.[48] The National Democratic Club of New Jersey was formed by a group of county leaders to control the party after the overthrow of Frank Hague.[49] The most familiar club of all is the Tammany Hall Society of Manhattan. The major well-known Republican Club was the Union League in Philadelphia.[50]

(2) The *make-up of the population* may be important. Many of these distinctions are, again, urban *v*. rural, for it is natural to think of the former populations as being more cross-sectional and the latter as being more homogeneous. Granted that rural people are more similar in race, religion, economic interests, and social status, there is considerable variation in kinds among rural populations from one section of the country to another, just as there are differences within a given rural area between farmers and nonfarmers. Rural politics in a Minnesota county where the racial background is Scandanavian may well differ from politics in rural Vermont. Likewise, special problems arise in cities where minority groups are set off—in one way or another—from the population as a whole. Here political organization is likely to become involved with racial or religious representation upon committees as well as special consideration for identifiable sections of the city.[51]

---

[47] Of course, practices vary with the men. Charles F. Murphy while he was a Tammany district leader did not use the club as his headquarters, but conducted his interviews at the northwest corner of Twentieth Street and Second Aveune between the hours of 7:30 and 10:00 P.M. each night.——Gustavus Myers, *The Hisory of Tammany Hall* (New York: Boni & Liveright, 1917) p. 303.

[48] Reynolds, *op. cit.* pp. 32-34, 122; Milligan, *op. cit.* p. 58.

[49] *New York Times*, February 1, 1953.

[50] See Myers, *op. cit.*, Chaps. 1-3; Roy V. Peel, *The Political Clubs of New York City* (New York: G. P. Putnam's Sons, 1935) *passim*. On the general subject of clubs, see Kent, *The Great Game of Politics*, Ch. 9.

[51] Kent, *The Great Game of Politics*, Chap. 12. Macy, *op. cit.*, p. 110, was of the opinion that "in every State in which a considerable proportion of the population resides in one city, the politics of that city has a decided modifying effect upon the politics of the State."

(3) The limit of an organization's influence may be set by geographic, economic or psychological *barriers*. Tammany Hall has been resisted outside Manhattan Borough from time to time for one reason or another. With the genius for vivid language characteristic of politics, the attempt to keep Tammany in Manhattan was dramatized in the statement: "The Tiger shall not cross the river." Even a person who did not understand what was meant would be likely to agree. The dividing lines of the boroughs have certainly not been a barrier for Tammany, but the geographic lines have often been a convenient reason for resistance.[52] In another kind of situation, cities may have a right and wrong side of the railroad tracks—more likely in a figurative than in a literal sense. This basis of separation is often economic, as reflected in residential areas or groupings of related economic activities. In some cities and counties there is a natural rivalry of neighborhoods or sections, with or without economic motivations. In any of these circumstances the barriers place limits upon an organization's expansion and usually cause it to intensify its hold upon the area for which it speaks.

(4) Organizations are particularly influenced by the general *standards of the population*. These standards may be lax, permitting both excessive manipulation of the machinery and flagrant methods for asserting leadership. In some places a committee meeting may develop into a gang fight, and the faction that can put its leader in the chair and keep him there by brute force carries the day. In other places this kind of conduct is not tolerated, and force has to be channeled into other forms. Moral precepts have as little influence in one case as the other, but the outward conduct conforms to the prevailing modes of acceptability. Closely related is the degree to which the population insists upon consideration in the organization's operations. Does some concession have to be made to democratic procedures, or can the leaders proceed at their own pleasure? Is the leadership challenged, or is everyone, apparently, either satisfied or unaware of the possibilities for bringing the leaders under some control? [53]

Out of these and an *x* number of other factors the organizational techniques are developed, but the differences can easily be overemphasized. Basic operations, while varying in form and appearance, follow standardized patterns. A combination of complexity in the organizational structure, of general indifference and lack of knowledge about the details of politics, of proven techniques for manufacturing consent, and of the habit of

---

[52] When Edward J. Flynn entered politics, Tammany was still at its height. Because Manhattan was the largest borough and Tammany the oldest and most aggressive of the Democratic organizations in the City, its leaders "treated the other [borough] leaders less like allies than like hand-picked viceroys—which was precisely what they were."——*Op. cit.*, p. 7. Flynn's own rise to leadership in the Bronx was brought about by Charles Murphy.——*Ibid.*, Chap. 4.

[53] See E. Pendleton Herring, *The Politics of Democracy* (New York: Rinehart & Company, 1940) pp. 144-5.

acceptance of authority make it possible for leaders to operate. It is this combination of party and government which forms the complete phenomena of political operations—the end result of all the machinery and of all the human drives in American politics.

Selected Bibliography

See the Selected Bibliography for Chapter 6, pp. 119–120 below.

CHAPTER SIX

Operations Through the Organization

The public is most generally aware of that point in political operations involving public struggles for power. The furtive regions of organization management are obscured by their complexity and apparent remoteness from the immediate business of government, but the appearance of the organization in the public realms gives rise to much easily understood publicity. Nevertheless the public phases of these operations are but the projection of the operations of the organization. The party phase of the process is carried out with relatively little interference, and if the proper prior arrangements are made, even the public phases of the process can be conducted without great risk or difficulty.

Perhaps it is a normal reaction for an artist to wonder occasionally at his own success and to find himself somewhat at a loss to account for the effects he is able to achieve within his audience. It was much the same kind of reaction when a political leader once asked, "When they can't help seeing what it costs them, why in the world do you suppose they let us run it?" [1] One perfectly tenable answer is that "they" have little alternative, since some group of leaders will be required in any case. Another answer is that a large part of "they" are not aware of what the system costs them. Still a third answer, less fatalistic than the first and more utilitarian than the second, is that a good proportion who are aware of the cost think they are getting something out of the operations. A man is unlikely to condemn the *status quo* as either wasteful or immoral as long as he is prospering. This system is commonly given the name "spoils."

It is from the relationship between the organization and the government that the patterns of the spoils system are created. Spoils are more than simple patronage, i.e., appointing political supporters and their supporters to public offices. There is a network of interrelations between political leaders and the public as well as the relations within the organization. These relations are the result of government activity itself; and as the activity increases, so do the opportunities for spoils politics.[2] It is the

---

[1] Quoted in Frank R. Kent, *Political Behavior* (New York: William Morrow & Company, Inc., 1928) p. 5.

[2] L. G. Tyler, *Parties and Patronage in the United States* (New York: G. P. Putnam's Sons, 1891) pp. 2-3.

patronage system that is the most familiar application of the spoils system, for it is the most obvious connection between party and government.

PATRONAGE

There is nothing mysterious in the feature of human behavior of wanting to associate with congenial and helpful companions. When a man has a difficult assignment to perform, he wants people he can trust working with him. This understandable premise is of very limited application in understanding the sophisticated refinements of patronage, but as an impulse it is a basic explanation of the widespread process of honoring those who are politically congenial.

Background. The origin of patronage is buried deep in our history in the doctrine that rotation in office is desirable as an educational process for the citizens and as protection for the citizens against usurpers.[3] The rotation doctrine was first applied only to elective offices, but as it became an end in itself, it was applied to all offices and was reinforced by the introduction of fixed terms, whether reappointment was permitted or not.[4]

One of the most famous canards of American political history is the statement that patronage began with the Administration of Andrew Jackson. It is true that patronage was another product of the democratization of politics and the overthrow of the aristocracy, and like the other systems of this revolution, came to full flower with the rise of Jackson.[5] The significant change from the colonial concept of rotation to the spoils concept was the change from appointing personal followers who were men of presumed ability to appointing on a purely partisan basis. The stronger the concept of party became, the stronger became the patronage motive without reference to the older notions of rotation.

In State Politics. The progress of patronage can be followed in New York, where George Clinton, governor from 1777 to 1795, made skillful but not large-scale use of patronage. The John Jay governorship continued the same general procedures, but the real spoils system was established in the early 1800's.[6] The full development comprehended both appointment

---

3 See C. R. Fish, *The Civil Service and the Patronage* (Cambridge: Harvard University Press, 1920, 2d impression) pp. 80-81.

4 *Ibid.*, pp. 83-84.

5 By 1828, the year of Jackson's election to his first term, "in every state throughout the North and West the spoils system either was established or there existed an element eager to introduce it"; the frontier states were especially addicted to equalitarian ideas that everyone was capable of government service—*Ibid.*, pp. 103-104; E. M. Eriksson, "The Federal Civil Service under President Jackson," *Mississippi Valley Historical Review,* Vol. 13 (1927) pp. 518-519.

6 Fish, *op. cit.*, pp. 86-91. It is said that the idea of rotation was first introduced into New York by the Dutch——*Ibid.*, p. 80.

of partisans and removal of incumbents to make way for more appointments. In both senses of the word, the system was retarded in Massachusetts, where public opinion refused to countenance it;[7] but in Pennsylvania the full doctrine was candidly expressed by the Republican
governor in a letter to Jefferson in 1801:

> It appears that the anti-Republicans, even those in office, are as
> hostile as ever, though not so insolent. To overcome them they must be
> shaven, for in their offices (like Samson's hair-locks) their great strength
> lieth; their disposition for mischief may remain, but their power of doing
> it will be gone. It is out of the common order of nature, to prefer enemies
> to friends; the despisers of the people should not be their rulers.[8]

In National Politics. With the inauguration of the general government under the Constitution in 1789, President Washington set the standards for appointment on a high level in that he required ability; but he
also insisted upon men who were loyal to the new government. There is
no doubt about his views on this subject, for he is clearly on record: "I
shall not, whilst I have the honor to administer the government, bring any
man into any office of consequence knowingly whose political tenets are
adverse to the measures which the general government are pursuing; for
this, in my opinion, would be a sort of political suicide." [9] In the strict
sense, there were no removals to be made; but where functions were transferred from the states or from the Confederation government, the question
arose of what to do with the incumbents of those offices in the transfers.
In the case of the state officials, Washington gave them first consideration
if they had given satisfactory service; actually, many of them were not
appointed. In the case of officials of the defunct Confederation, Washington
normally continued them in office.[10]

This state of affairs gradually changed as party spirit developed, so
that Postmaster General Timothy Pickering was able to write to an applicant for office in 1792: "As vested with a *public trust,* I think myself bound
to discharge it . . . by introducing to public beneficial situations honest
men *who have claims on the public* for their services in effecting the establishment of a government of which I am an executive officer,—or against
whom, in this respect, no exception can be taken." Noah Webster wrote
three years later: "If men, who are loading the government with curses &
denouncing our Chief Magistrate, as a tyrant . . . are to be raised to
opulence and nabobship, . . . who are the friends that will maintain that

---

7 *Ibid.,* pp. 95-98; for the early beginnings in New Hampshire and Rhode Island, p. 95.
8 Quoted *ibid.,* p. 93; also pp. 92-95.
9 Letter of September 25, 1795, to Timothy Pickering, quoted in Charles A. Beard,
Economic Origins of Jeffersonian Democracy (New York: The Macmillan Company, 1915)
p. 66; see also pp. 102-107.
10 Leonard D. White, *The Federalists* (New York: The Macmillan Company, 1948)
pp. 257 ff., 271, 400-401.

govt?"[11] The federalists' use of partisan appointments was that Washington applied them to high offices and Adams to lesser offices,[12] but the use of removal for partisan purposes was unknown under Washington and extremely limited under Adams.[13]

At the beginning of the Jefferson Administration, patronage was primarily a matter of making removals, since the offices were already filled. In fact Adams had filled every office available with fellow partisans before he left office, setting a pattern for subsequent Presidents.[14] This precedent-setting action was flagrant because of the bold-faced effort to create new positions and of the rapidity with which Adams and the Federalist Congress carried out the maneuver. The "midnight appointments," so-called because Adams was busy signing commissions during most of his last night in office, were bitterly attacked by the Republicans. While the election of 1800 was being decided in the House of Representatives, some Federalists tried to get a commitment from Jefferson not to make removals "except in the great departments."[15]

Upon assuming office Jefferson blocked the delivery of those commissions, which because of the confusion during the final days of the Adams Administration had not been given to the appointees. Seeking to win over those who had not supported him, Jefferson tried to get his opponents out of office without having to make a removal; his objective was made clear in one of his letters: "I have given, and will give only to Republicans, under existing circumstances." The number of removals from 1801 to 1803 was above the normal up to that time—the total for his eight years was 109.[16]

In the remainder of the period of Republican supremacy, there was

[11] Quoted *ibid.*, pp. 272-273. When John Adams read a manuscript which contained the statement that "our administrations, with the exception of Washington's have been party administrations," he inquired of the author, "On what ground do you except Washington's?"——*The Works of John Adams* (Boston: Little, Brown & Company, 1865) Vol. 10, p. 23.

[12] A congressional spokesman for President Adams put the matter bluntly: "The politics of the office-seeker would be the great object of the President's attention, and an invincible objection if different from his own."——Quoted in Tyler, *op. cit.*, p. 20. Partisan appointments were carried into the military in 1798 during the struggle with France.

[13] White, *op. cit.*, pp. 271-278, 285-290. The actual number of removals was seventeen for Washington and twenty-one for Adams——C. R. Fish, "Removals of Officials by the Presidents of the United States," *American Historical Association Annual Report*, 1899, Vol. 1, pp. 69-70, 84-86.

[14] The counterpractice of the Senate refusing to confirm the nominees of an outgoing President in anticipation of an incoming President of a different party was established in 1829, when thirty-eight of J. Q. Adams' seventy-eight nominees were rejected. The memory of the practices of the father was certainly a cause for the action taken against the son. C. R. Fish, *The Civil Service and the Patronage*, p. 108; Eriksson, *op. cit.*, p. 527, note 25.

[15] Beard, *op. cit.*, p. 407; also p. 408, note.

[16] Fish, *The Civil Service and the Patronage*, p. 20; in general pp. 29-44. Fish, "Removals of Officials . . .," p. 70.

less opportunity to raise the question of patronage. Removals and appointments were based upon personal loyalty rather than partisanship as such,
but the struggle for office proceeded with growing frenzy. The major
development during this period was the Tenure of Office Act, which prescribed fixed terms for appointees and departed from the practice since
Washington's time of making appointments at the pleasure of the
President.[17]

Perhaps the reason for attributing the origin of these practices to
Andrew Jackson is the much greater publicity he and his advisers gave to
the spoils system, announcing a conscious and purposeful doctrine that as
in war so in politics, the spoils belong to the victor. Jackson himself did
not speak in these terms, but his message to the first regular session of
Congress in December 1829 developed the philosophy of short terms,
rotation, and no right to office.[18] The outcries by anti-Jackson men that
1981 had been removed and that many families were left without financial
support, formed the basis for the subsequent historical judgment that the
spoils system began in 1829. In the period 1829-1837, less than one fifth
of all federal officeholders were removed, or about the same proportion
chargeable to Jefferson.[19]

It was the crowds swarming the streets of Washington in the same
rowdy manner that they had been howling and hooting at political meetings all over the country which gave the Jackson Administration the
character of a completely new regime. To the simplicity of Jeffersonian
Democracy the Jackson Democrats added party management and raucous-
ness; their greater facility with familiar speech gave their party a stamp
of more genuine democracy— with a small *d*.[20] What had now been established as an overt policy could not be reversed, and the Whigs, after their
violent condemnation of the spoils system, adopted and further applied it
when they came into office in 1841. "Thus, it is seen that Jackson's administration, instead of witnessing a complete introduction of the spoils system

---

17 Leonard D. White, *The Jeffersonians* (New York: The Macmillan Company, 1951)
pp. 387-390.

18 Eriksson, *op. cit.*, p. 523. The special significance of no right to an office was the
legal doctrine, continued from colonial times, that an office was a vested right.

19 *Ibid.*, pp. 520-522, 526-530. The number no doubt would have been larger if many
Jackson men had not already been in office, although some anti-Jackson men were retained.
James A. Farley, *Behind the Ballots* (New York: Harcourt, Brace & Co., 1938) p. 223,
tells us "the whole business of patronage was pumped up into such a major campaign
issue in the 1936 election that the word came to have a sinister meaning in the public
mind." Andrew Jackson could have straightened Mr. Farley out on his historical perspective of the "sinister meaning" of patronage, but the two would have felt a kinship as a
result of their experiences.

20 Symptomatic of the times to many contemporaries would have been the remark
of a friend of Amos Kendall's: " 'I am ashamed of myself, for I feel as if every man I
meet knew what I came for.' 'Don't distress yourself,' replied Kendall, 'for every man
you meet is on the same business.' "—Quoted in Fish, *The Civil Service and the Patronage*,
p. 110.

into national politics, as has been popularly believed, merely marked another step towards the consummation of that end." [21]

Functions of Patronage. The victory of the people which was claimed for the patronage system was in reality a victory of and for the party organization. In this sense the Jacksonian practices marked a new era, for the realization of the potential services of government to party was complete at last, and all shame and restraint were unblushingly discarded. The true awakening of party spirit meant the development of organization, and the rise of both meant the utilization of government. The theory of patronage encompassed much more than the simple placing of party sup- porters in public office. The appointment, initially, was a reward for past services; but it was a continuing means of discipline since the appointees' livelihood was involved. Considered *in toto,* patronage was an ingenious invention whereby party members were paid for government work which they did not do or did in their spare time while they were doing party work for which they could not be paid directly.[22] The problem of organiza- tion for popular politics appeared to be solved.

Federal Patronage and State Organizations. The duties of many federal offices are discharged within states; so the county and state leaders of the party holding the White House parcel out these jobs as well as the state and local jobs. The federal patronage is a supplement for state patronage, helping to relieve the provincial pressures for placement, but federal patronage is much more than a supplement. It is the ultimate to be attained, and its appearance helped to foster the concept of the party as a national network. Men with national ambitions took care of their own states, but once in high federal office they were often concerned with the pressures from other states. Patronage was a mechanism for nationalizing the party by tying together the particular interests common to all states and making them dependent upon the same conditions and the same decisions in Washington, D.C.

Presidents and sometimes their close advisers were often displeased

---

21 Eriksson, *op. cit.* p. 540.
22 For an excellent account of these interrelated purposes, see D. H. Kurtzman, *Methods of Controlling Votes in Philadelphia* (Philadelphia: University of Pennsylvania Press, 1935) Chap. 2 and Appendix A. For discussions of occupations, including govern- ment positions of organization leaders, see Frank R. Kent, *The Great Game of Politics* (New York: Doubleday, Page & Company, 1924) pp. 28-29, 41; H. F. Gosnell, *Machine Politics: Chicago Model* (Chicago: University of Chicago Press, 1937) pp. 47, 54; Leon Weaver, "Some Soundings in the Party System: Rural Precinct Committeemen," *American Political Science Review,* Vol. 34 (1940) pp. 76-84; Harold Zink, *City Bosses in the United States* (Durham: Duke University Press, 1930) pp. 49-51; D. D. McKean, *The Boss* (Boston: Houghton Mifflin Company, 1940) pp. 122 ff. According to Edward J. Flynn, at the time he wrote *You're the Boss* (New York: The Viking Press, 1947), only 142 out of 1700 dis- trict captains in the Bronx had positions based on political preferment (p. 22).

and repelled by the patronage system, which harassed them throughout their administrations and diverted them from the duties of their offices; but the party organization in the states was not to be denied. It fell to the members of Congress both to protect themselves personally and to promote the interests of the organizations behind them. The constitutional provision for "advice and consent" of the Senate in the process of appointments was the recognition of the antecedent powers of Congress to create the positions to which appointments were made, as well as of the omnipresent concern over appointments among legislators. In fact this inherent advantage of the legislative branch had been apparent during the years of the Confederation Government when the practice of consulting with members of Congress regarding the appointment of postmasters in their respective states was begun. Even though the Senate did not confirm postmasters under the new Government until the Administration of Van Buren, members of Congress were regularly consulted in these appointments from the time of Washington's Administration. They also submitted lists for auditors and the revenue offices, and by the end of the Adams Administration the custom of securing congressional approval prior to nomination by the President was well established.[23]

From time to time there were flashes of opposition. After retiring from office, Jefferson insisted in his correspondence with Madison that postmasters should be appointed by the President "but without the intervention of the Senate."[24] When President Monroe was being urged to divide the appointments to the land offices in Illinois between the state's two senators, he was reported as feeling that he should not "permit himself to be influenced by considerations of local parties in a state" nor "nominate with reference to the local effect on the respective senators in their states." The effect of this position was largely destroyed when the same spokesman for Monroe suggested that the President "nominate no person whom either senator declares unworthy of an office, if he can find a deserving man in the state free from this objection." The senatorial objection should not be honored, however, if it resulted from personal feeling or factional animosity.[25] This concession opened Pandora's box, since the qualifications attached to it were meaningless and the acceptance of the procedure of consulting with a senator means very often that the senator makes the selection. This practice, first asserted under Washington and in general use by the 1870's, has become known as the custom of "senatorial courtesy."

Senatorial courtesy is the enforcement power behind the practice of

23 L. D. White, *The Federalists*, pp. 82-7. In *The Jeffersonians*, pp. 323-325, Professor White describes a major squabble that occurred in 1822 over a postmaster appointment in Albany, New York.

24 *The Jeffersonians*, p. 322.

25 Quoted in Fish, *The Civil Service and the Patronage*, pp. 100-101.

consultation. To make the executive-legislative relation effective and mutually protective for members of Congress, a senator of the same party as the President can object to a nomination for an office in his (the senator's) state on the grounds the nominee is personally offensive to him, whereupon a majority of his Senate colleagues grant him the courtesy of voting against confirmation. It is often possible that the senator involved can prevent a vote on the floor by having the committee members who are considering the nomination fail to report it to the Senate. In this kind of fight between a President and a senator, the latter can nearly always win a negative victory by defeating the nominee even if he cannot win a positive victory by having his own selection nominated by the President. The Senate occasionally disregards the custom, but it also has applied the custom in behalf of a senator of the opposite party from the President.[26]

The politically important result of senatorial courtesy is the infrequent necessity for invoking it. The general practice in making appointments is either to ask the senator for a list of possible candidates or to show the senator a prepared list from which he can indicate those acceptable or unacceptable. Even postmaster appointments, traditionally the prerogative of representatives, are protected on their behalf by the senators. When both of the senators from the same state are of the President's party, they generally try to reach an agreement for dividing the state between themselves—a decision sometimes facilitated by the tendency for senators to reside in different parts of the state. When they disagree, it is the senior senator who is more likely to be supported by the Administration or the Senate although the particular political circumstances of the moment would determine the outcome. When there is no senator of the President's party elected in a state, a frequent practice is to substitute the national committeeman and committeewoman as the patronage dispensers. The fact that a senator is the instrument through which patronage is funneled into his state, plus his six-year term of office, goes far to explain the potentialities for leadership he can exploit.

Problems of Patronage. The development of patronage on each government level created tremendous advantages for the party organization, but it also raised new and unforeseen problems for leadership. If rotation was intrinsically good, it should be constantly applied. In some national administrations, e.g., Buchanan's, and in many state administrations, removals and reappointments followed from changes in the chief

---

26 White, *The Jeffersonians*, pp. 390-393; Eriksson, *op. cit.*, pp. 534-535. For the post-Civil War struggle over senatorial courtesy, see Fish, *op. cit.*, pp. 202-208. Also George Stimpson, *A Book about American Politics* (New York: Harper & Brothers, 1952) pp. 508-511. For an account of the attempts of Senators Roscoe Conkling and Thomas C. Platt to apply the custom against Hayes and Garfield, see *The Autobiography of Thomas Collier Platt* (New York: B. W. Dodge Co., 1910) pp. 84-89, 145-159.

executive even when the party did not change. A seemingly uncontrollable force had been released. The dam had been blown up, and the dynamiters were powerless to hold back the tide that swirled about them. Confusion followed every election as the claimants were fitted into the available openings and relative claims for recognition were urged. Some succeeded, some partially succeeded, and some failed in the drive of democratic man to serve his fellow citizens. Since executives, whether Presidents, governors, or mayors, could not possibly make all of these decisions on the basis of their own information, they relied upon the advice of their political associates and upon the recommendations of party leaders.[27] From the point of view of the patronage dispenser, there are never enough jobs to go around, and political appointments themselves involve risks because those refused are disappointed and the one appointed may likely feel he deserves something better. An ancient lament of American politics, echoing a complaint of Louis XIV of France, is that an appointment creates one ingrate and nine enemies.[28] Pressures for office are considered the major cause of the death of President William Henry Harrison after one month in office.

Not only were there pressures to hold existing offices but also pressures to create offices in order to satisfy more claimants.[29] As governmental policies brought more money into public treasuries and involved more functional responsibilities, the opportunities for creating more offices were never overlooked. Sometimes desirous officeholders promoted new activities in order to fill the new positions. Inescapably, men were appointed or elected to offices who were looking out for themselves to the exclusion of any other consideration, and they rapidly developed the arts of graft, concealed by the laborious mysteries of bookkeeping, subtle nuances of the fee system, and bold demands for money and favors upon the clientele their agencies served.[30]

---

27 See Frank R. Kent, *Political Behavior,* Chap. 5. How the Democrats' clamor for office was satisfied in 1933 is described by Farley, *op. cit.,* pp. 226-227, 234-235. The results of a party change at Washington, D. C., have always created the same general situation, but Mr. Farley's contribution was the systematizing of the process. Despite the extent of federal patronage, C. R. Fish concluded from his detailed examinations that "rotation was never complete . . . there was in the service a constant residuum of trained men."—— *The Civil Service and the Patronage,* p. 248.

28 Frank R. Kent, *The Great Game of Politics,* pp. 98-99, 177-178; Stimpson, *op cit.,* pp. 483-484.

29 R. Carlyle Buley, *The Old Northwest* (Bloomington: Indiana University Press, 1951) p. 1, points out the relation of this pressure in the multiplication of counties. George M. Reynolds, *Machine Politics in New Orleans* (New York: Columbia University Press, 1936) p. 170.

30 The public perhaps was surprised to discover that the politicians' creed became more refined through the years, and in the words of George Washington Plunkitt, drew a line between dishonest graft (outright stealing or operating outside the law) and honest graft (the advantages of having advance information and thereby being able to enrich oneself legally) .——William L. Riordan, *Plunkitt of Tammany Hall* (New York: Alfred A. Knopf, Inc., 1948) pp. 3-8.

Reactions Against Patronage. Generally speaking, the attacks upon patronage came from those who were aware of it but either were not benefited by it or were not converted to it. Daniel Webster, an heir of the Federalist tradition, voiced the sentiment of the opposition by asserting that "the patronage of office, the power of bestowing place and emoluments, create parties not upon any principle or upon any measure, but upon the single ground of personal interest." [31] Of course, this was exactly the meaning of the patronage system, but its waste was not popularly condemned until the public had occasion to be unfavorably aware of it. The system, therefore, contained the seeds of its own opposition. First, its premise that public offices required only average intelligence and unspecialized backgrounds became less and less true as governments began dealing with more and more technical and scientific matters. Second, the expansion of government functions, upon which patronage thrived, brought wisdom to citizens to the degree that they realized they were paying for the extravagance. Tentative attempts were made before the Civil War to limit rotation in the federal government, but the first piece of major legislation—the Pendleton Act of 1883—was the product of years of agitation, and more immediately, of the assassination of President James A. Garfield by a disconsolate office seeker.

Establishment of the Merit System. The success of the merit system has been most widespread within the federal government. The growth has been slow but steady, both by blanketing existing patronage appointees into the system and by requiring an examination for appointments to newly created positions. The victory of civil service reform can be gauged in the shift of emphasis among reformers from merit appointments per se to building the professional character of the service by developing policies of recruitment, pay scales, promotion, retirement, protection from political intimidation—in short, in placing the government in the role of employer and applying to it the same standards as apply to private employers. In a large sense, the battle for the adoption of the merit system within the federal government has been won.

The other side of this coin is the infinitesimal percentage of outright patronage positions still remaining within the power of the President or of his subordinates to fill. Most of these positions are of such responsibility and magnitude that just any party member cannot be trusted with them. When patronage appointments require an evaluation of applicants' abilities as well as their partisanship, the selection process is based to some extent

---

[31] Quoted in Charles E. Merriam, *American Political Ideas* (New York: The Macmillan Company, 1920) p. 272. Webster's fellow-citizen from Massachusetts, Edward Everett, did not share this view; see White, *The Jeffersonians*, p. 317.

upon a merit standard. Even the appointment of federal judges—appointees who have normally been more carefully considered than other patronage officials—raises periodic storms on the ground that the judges are not properly qualified. Postmasterships have come to occupy a status between merit and patronage. Incumbent postmasters have a fixed term and can be removed only for cause; applicants, while requiring political clearance and senatorial confirmation, must place among the three highest in the examination to be eligible for nomination by the President.

It was not until a change of party administrations took place in Washington, D. C., in 1953 that the nature of the new civil service was fully brought home. Victorious Republicans anticipated a harvest of appointments but reaped frustration primarily. The Eisenhower Administration, through a White House patronage office, searched for appointees whose experience measured up to the job analyses prepared by a firm of management consultants. One major difficulty encountered at the outset was the unwillingness of many people who were considered qualified to accept the offices offered to them. Politically, the greater difficulty was the friction between the White House patronage office and the patronage division of the National Committee. Deep-seated dissatisfactions arose, first, from the unawareness or refusal to accept the fact that the number of patronage positions amounted to only a few thousand out of the approximately two million positions in the federal service and, second, from the conviction that the Administration was not interested in taking care of the party faithful. Instances of appointments being made without consulting the National Committee, members of Congress, or state political leaders merely confirmed what was already suspected.[32] It appears that the Eisenhower Administration fell between two stools. Initially, it made motions to cut down the personnel within the merit service in order to increase patronage openings; but the efforts were abandoned, with the result that civil service reformers felt threatened and the party did not benefit.

The states have adopted civil service reform to sharply varying extents. Some have adopted the merit system only insofar as it is required by federal law in state agencies which administer federally supported programs. The National Civil Service League rates only twenty-four of the fifty states as "civil service" states.[33] City governments, under the impact of local reform movements, have followed the merit system further than some states. Counties remain, on the whole, the strongest bastions of political prefer-

---

[32] In his paper, "The National Committee of the Party in Power, 1953–1958," delivered at a panel session during the 1958 meetings of the American Political Science Association, Dr. Philip Wilder, Jr., pointed out these and other problems arising from patronage aspirations in a situation devoid of patronage opportunities. Hugh A. Bone, *Party Committees and National Politics* (Seattle: University of Washington Press, 1958) pp. 103-107.

[33] Good Government *Newsletter,* March-April, 1959.

ment in appointments, having most successfully resisted or escaped the reform movements. Yet some county patronage appointees have unexpectedly low records of political activity and partisan responses.[34]

Omissions in the Merit System. Patronage still thrives in the United States, both in the absence of civil service legislation and in the skillful interweaving of the two systems so that political leaders can operate quite handily with both of them. Patronage can be practiced by ruse or by virtue of public unawareness and continue under the guise of the merit system. It is often overlooked that reform in methods of selecting government employees has generally been applied only to the executive branch of government. The other two branches are rarely included in civil service regulations. Appointments within a legislative body during a legislative session are, compared with the executive branch, minor in number, and when the legislative body is bipartisan, both parties share in the patronage. In the case of the judiciary, the appointments made by judges may be comparatively few, but some of them are extremely lucrative and politically sensitive.

Bulwarks of the Merit System. The public has generally adopted the philosophy of the merit system—at least in theory. Within this favorable climate of openly expressed opinions, the merit system has tended to be solidified. Some positions, obviously requiring particular skills or specialized training, are unquestionably left within the merit system. The head of an agency wants competent workers and will often resist making appointments on a purely political basis. There is no question that public employees themselves, because of their number and influence and union organizations, are a political factor of great weight in favor of merit hiring. Vested interests surrounding employment and its security can be aroused by threats of politically inspired personnel policies. The entry of professional men and women into government office brings to bear the prestige and political influence of national professional organizations. There is, furthermore, the growth of actual competition between government and private employment for able and intelligent presonnel. Removals under the merit system are infrequent because of the difficulty of substantiating charges against a subordinate in an administrative hearing, which is usually provided for the protection of the employees.

Need for Patronage. The statement of the undiluted orthodoxy of patronage sounds unfamiliar and unbelievable, but the basic statement of its philosophy has not changed. Edward J. Flynn reformulated the

---

[34] Frank J. Sorauf, "State Patronage in a Rural County," *American Political Science Review*, Vol. 50 (1956) pp. 1046-1056.

political view that organization is inevitable and the necessity for continuity demands a permanent organization; patronage or spoils, in the larger sense, are the only means of keeping the organization running, because they satisfy people's interests and needs.[35] James A. Farley concluded that "patronage is the test by which a party shows its fitness to govern," but he raised doubts about its being essential by asserting that patronage is not the only incentive holding a party together and that he could build a major party without any jobs at all.[36] Frank Kent looked upon patronage as the chief source of nourishment for the organization and a valuable source of campaign funds; but the absence of patronage, he felt, would restrict, not eliminate, the organization.[37]

Part of the controversy hinges on the claims that patronage appointees are necessarily inferior, if not incompetent, and the counter claim that they can be and have been extremely able government officials.[38] Political organizations in other countries operate without the extent or even the concept of patronage that exists in the United States. The system is in many respects distinctly American and it is likely to continue in one form or another as long as Americans insist upon using political parties as employment bureaus for the government. As the opportunities for patronage decline, there will be a corresponding decline in political participation where the incentive is material rewards. Increasingly, the organization depends upon other motives such as civic or "good government" interests in public affairs, the desire for some activity as an outlet for energies released by increased leisure time. This is one of the many adjustments of the organization as a politics of policy replaces a politics of patronage.[39]

If the claims of civil-service reformers were taken completely at face value, there would be no justification for hiring anyone except on the basis of strict merit, objectively determined. The most sensitive and confidential

---

[35] Flynn, *op. cit.*, pp. 20-21, 25, 26; Farley, *op. cit.*, p. 236; Reynolds, *op. cit.*, pp. 163-166.

[36] Farley, *op. cit.*, pp. 230, 237-238. In a later book, he summed up the argument in classic simplicity: "While many criticize the spoils system, I have always felt that it is just as easy to find a good Democrat as a good Republican or vice versa and that the party in power should reward its own."——*Jim Farley's Story* (New York: McGraw-Hill Book Company, Inc., 1948) p. 35. See David Riesman, "Government Service and the American Constitution," *University of Chicago Law Review*, Vol. 7 (1940) pp. 673-675; Henry A. Turner, *Politics in the United States: Readings in Political Parties and Pressure Groups* (New York: McGraw-Hill Book Company, Inc., 1955) pp. 415-420.

[37] *The Great Game of Politics*, p. 177.

[38] Farley claimed that people with political endorsement performed better than those without.——*Behind the Ballots*, pp. 235-236, also pp. 230-231.

[39] Stephen B. and Vera H. Sarasohn, *Political Party Patterns in Michigan* (Detroit: Wayne State University Press, 1957) pp. 33 ff.

positions would be given to total strangers. Such an extension, even if intended, would be out of the question. The argument on behalf of the superiority of competitive examinations can cast into doubt the wisdom of any elections. If requirements for all offices can be reduced to a systematized classification of job descriptions and if all human abilities can be accurately measured, even the White House should be occupied by the person getting the highest score on the examination for President of the United States.[40] At this point the extension of the case for the merit system breaks down. The absurdity of such a suggestion must mean the reform has limitations, since value judgments exist which are immune from the tabulating propensities of mechanical scoring devices.

Even in the midst of attacking patronage, students of government have laid considerable emphasis upon the necessity for executives to have people of their own choice working under them, helping to carry out the policies the voters endorsed at the polls. In line with this trend of thinking, distinctions can and should be made between policy-making and general administrative operations on the one hand, and technical, specialized operations on the other. This is a concept easy to apply in some cases—e.g., a member of an executive's cabinet is a patronage appointee, while officials of a health department are merit appointees—but difficult in others. The challenge of making differentiations of a delicate nature has never discouraged the human race, and the politicians, if no one else, can be depended upon to accept the task of making those nice distinctions which will preserve the system of patronage.

THE ADVANTAGES OF OFFICE

Once the party organization has won an election and exercised its patronage prerogatives, the question logically arises: Now, what happens? It is obvious that there are still operations to be carried out and that the process is not always completed by the attainment of office itself. The whole panorama of subsequent developments is too complicated and extensive for any one presentation to be complete, but suggestions of some of the possibilities can help to clarify the general circumstances.

---

[40] In a figurative sense it can be said that elections are analogous to unassembled civil-service examinations. The applicants are interviewed by their employer, the public, through speeches and interviews, and their qualifications and background are recorded in public media which constitute the personnel files. Like all employers, the voters give different weights to the various factors: some examine the personnel file closely; others depend upon the interview; and quite a number make up their minds on the basis of preconceived notions or inveterate loyalties before any data are presented.

Inspection and Regulation. One of the most routine, but one of the most effective, means for wreaking vengeance upon individuals and businesses is the inspection functions of government. They range from the provisions of a city building code to state inspection of machinery in billion-dollar corporations, but it is in the smaller-scale operations that political harassment is most frequently effective. A merchant who has failed to contribute to a campaign fund may discover someone from the city hall measuring the width of the sidewalk in front of his establishment and may be informed that his store front is two inches too close to the curb; he generally is given a "reasonable" length of time to conform with the law. All of the infinitesimal regulations for building and wiring can be loosely or strictly applied by enforcement officials. Organizations, such as lodges which maintain clubrooms, may have gambling devices for the use of members; these practices are, of course, generally known but seldom protested. Yet police may suddenly raid the clubrooms, confiscate the gaming equipment, and arrest those in charge. The reasons for the action can often be traced back to political ruptures or grudges.

Taxation. The heart of government functions is finances, and the taxing of citizens can be a major political weapon. Favoritism in taxation arises most easily in the levies upon personal property and real estate. The assessors are often close to the political organizations rather than experts in appraising the value of property,[41] and efforts to equalize taxation or to provide a review of assessments are not always satisfactory methods of eliminating abuses—particularly if the organization is able to choose the men who make the reviews. Through the organization workers at the polling-place level, efficient political leaders can keep a current check on the political attitudes of every individual or family. Friendly and cooperative citizens may never have to pay taxes high enough to complain about. On the other hand, those antagonistic to the organization are fair game for any possible kind of punishment, which may take the form of higher taxes. Occasionally, the public has an opportunity to look into these human bookkeeping operations as it had in the contents of a three-volume record of Jersey City taxpayers which had been assiduously compiled by the Hague organization and gratuitously publicized by the organization which defeated Hague.[42]

---

41 See Kurtzman, *op. cit.*, Appendix C, for a "List of Real Estate Assessors and Their Political Affiliations" as of August 1, 1934, in Philadelphia.

42 *New York Times*, January 18, 1950. Some of the comments written next to the names tell volumes by themselves: "friendly to the administration," "Republican, absolutely no good," "Republican, but friendly to us," "Republican . . . Received favors but proved ingrate," "In 1928, had Hoover in window, but I think they are okay now," "Twenty-five Democratic votes in family, but now active Republican due to fact member of family could not secure work shaving patients in jail. All votes no good." See also McKean, *op. cit.*, pp. 229, 243; Kurtzman, *op. cit.*, pp. 108-114.

Exploiting Public Offices. Basically, the wording of statutes determines what adjustments in political activities will be made and what kinds of techniques employed. Legislation confers or withholds benefits for businesses and individuals. When organization leaders are able to suggest the bills they want, to kill the bills they do not want, and to be consulted on the effect of bills under consideration, statutory law can be expected to be compatible with party objectives and favorable to the friends of the organization. In addition, the leaders themselves, from their own business connections, have direct objectives involved in proposed legislation.[43]

The whole range of political operations is made possible, directly or indirectly, by the written law. The regulations, the inspections, the crimes, the contracts, the franchises, come under the purview of men who see with political eyes and evaluate in terms of political advantages, whether they are the legislators or the men behind the legislators. After the bills are passed, there is the check of executive approval or disapproval, but more important, even, are the powers exercised by executives in conformance with constitutions and statutes. In the executive office is vested all or part of the pardoning power, with its many ramifications for the organization. In most states the governor can determine how and when to spend part of the money appropriated by the legislature. He and his subordinates are involved in much of the process of moving money from public to private hands in the payment of contracts and salaries. It is an unmistakable sign of political potency when any executive department is hovered over and coveted as highway departments invariably are because of the sums of money they spend and the sources for patronage they supply.

Services for the Masses. From these few examples of the advantages of office, it is possible to construct the synthesis which is produced by the organization's ability to provide services for the masses and favors for the influential. While each of these components can be separately analyzed, they form a totality in operation which cannot be isolated or fragmented without destroying their functional intermixture.

The organization leaders are constantly besieged by private citizens who need help which varies from fixing a traffic ticket to finding a job or getting out of serious legal difficulties. The leaders expect voting support from those who ask for and receive favors. The leaders proceed on the basis that "If I serve a man, his vote is morally mine." [44] The creation of

---

[43] Kent, *The Great Game of Politics*, pp. 135 ff. "The legislative session is the harvest season with all the bosses, big and little. They all meet there—the big city boss with his big block of voters and the individual county bosses, with their little blocks of hand-picked delegates. They trade, and deal, and dicker, join forces and get on opposite sides over the multitudinous measures that touch some financial nerves somewhere. It is a great game—bosses and lobbyists, and lawyers, and hangers-on—they all flock to the state capitol."——*Ibid*, pp. 140-141.

[44] J. T. Salter, *Boss Rule* (New York: McGraw-Hill Book Company, 1935) p. 52.

highly efficient political organizations depends upon a favorable public attitude; this attitude is created by giving people something and making them dependent upon or indebted to the organization. Dispensing these services makes it possible to mobilize the voters on a basis of reciprocity. There is give and there is take and the organizations continue to win elections. This is the process for humanizing schoolbook ideals and making principles concrete; by performing this service function, the party becomes the intermediary between the individual and the impersonal institution of government. The larger the electorate, the more requests for favors, and the larger the electorate, the greater the need to mobilize it.

Relations with the Influential. The organization's associations with the upper levels of a community differ only in the kinds of favors sought, the amounts of money involved, and the means of negotiation. Businessmen by their very nature cannot be impervious to government. Business is regulated and licensed by government officials, and business leaders seek objectives that only government can make possible. They find their way to the party leaders in pursuit of either their negative or their positive objectives, and pressures from business interests account for much the greater part of governmental policies. City ordinances to require or to prohibit various practices of retail stores are instigated by the merchants, usually working through the local chambers of commerce. Franchises and rates are matters of life and death to private bus and traction companies. Bankers seek opportunities to lend money profitably. Contractors want to build public buildings. Dispensers of goods or services used by government want government to be their customer, and one of the favorite means of punishment visited upon businessmen is to cancel their government contracts or to refuse to accept their bids. The unlimited opportunities to help business and to play favorites among business competitors exist at every government level. The return to the party organization for these considerations is, universally, campaign contributions. Election campaigns are expensive for many reasons. The masses do not have the money to give, so the politicians go to the comparatively few who do have the money.

Politicians have also made use of private businessmen as a supplemental source of patronage. When government jobs run out, it is sometimes possible to find private employment for followers, who then become indebted to political leaders as much as those in public or party employment are indebted. Finally, individual leaders personally profit from these connections with business by accepting imaginary positions at huge salaries or by accepting money for nothing in particular except the influence they exert on behalf of business. In addition, many leaders are themselves in businesses in which they profit directly from political decisions which they make or help to make. They have a unique kind of marketable commodity. They are in the position of being able to sell out without surrendering their control; they "can sell their influence and still keep it—even increase it. Actually, they do not sell it—they rent it."[45]

Unity of the Spoils System. The combination of these components, relations with the masses and with influential interests, puts the party in an admirable position. A man loses his job and despondently goes to his polling-place leader, who speaks to the ward leader. A job is found for the unfortunate in the county surveyor's office or on the janitorial staff of the city hall or in the shipping department of a manufacturing establishment. Another man is ill and cannot work. Upon representations being made through party channels, he receives medical attention, his children are clothed, food is provided, coal is delivered during the winter, the gas and electric companies do not turn off his utilities. The party is able to request these favors from business, for the party is also taking care of the businessmen through the letting of contracts, the fixing of rates, the convenient enforcement of inspection laws. A boy gets into trouble with the law, and his parents are forever grateful when arrangements are made to extricate him without disgrace and even without publicity. This is a cohesive and impenetrable process in which everyone does that which is required of him and all live together in reasonable good fortune.[46]

Bipartisan Cooperation. The advantages of spoils, if not the necessities, are far stronger than a party label. Republicans and Democrats are concerned with their respective well-being, and to be excluded entirely from the perquisites of office is too much to ask in the name of partisan purity. In some cases, one party is a permanent minority and is pensioned off, so to speak, by the majority party with a few appointments and other miscellaneous favors as long as it is congenial and does not create problems. In other cases the parties are more evenly matched and give each other some consideration so that neither will be annihilated by a defeat.[47] Some

[45] Kent, *The Great Game of Politics,* pp. 71-72; Reynolds, *op. cit.,* Chap. 6.

[46] There is an endless series of documentations of this process as it has been practiced in various cities. On the Philadelphia Republican organization, see Salter, *op cit.,* pp. 17-71 *passim* and Kurtzman, *op. cit.,* pp. 29-36, 102-108. For the Hague organization in Jersey City, McKean, *op. cit.,* pp. 132-133; for the Pendergast organization, Milligan, *op. cit.,* pp. 22-23, 47-48, 135-137; for the New Orleans Behrman organization, Reynolds, *op. cit.,* pp. 112-114; for the Bronx, Flynn, *op. cit.,* pp. 21-22.

[47] A most enlightening illustration of the absence of partisan prejudice between Republican and Democrat leaders occurred in New Jersey in 1949, although it did not come to light until four years later. John J. Dickerson, Republican state chairman, according to his own testimony, helped John V. Kenny, a Democrat, be elected mayor of Jersey City in May, defeating the Hague organization. In return Mr. Kenny held down the Democratic vote in the gubernatorial election in November to the lowest it had been since World War I and insured the re-election of Alfred E. Driscoll, a Republican, as governor.——*New York Times,* April 30, 1952. For similar arrangements in New Jersey in previous years, see McKean, *op. cit.,* Chap. 5.

leaders prefer a limited amount of opposition from the other party as a means for keeping their own party under better control; a group is more likely to hold together with less squabbling when there is a threat from the outside.

THE CHANGING ORGANIZATION

Political operations are, at one and the same time, unchanging in their basic nature and evolutionary in their forms and outward appearances. Consequently, some features of party organization which predominate in one generation are not the predominating ones in prior generations.

Functions of the Organization. What political leaders are called upon to do at any one time is determined in great part by the people to whom they appeal. The classic functions of the organization—controlling people's votes by making them dependent and grateful because of services received—presumed the existence of a group of people able and willing to establish relations with the organization and have their problems solved by party leaders. Such a population was largely made up of the economically insecure, particularly immigrants who needed financial help and sympathetic reassurance in a new land. Once people moved out of this status and no longer required such basic sustenance, the intimate relation with the organization ceased. The middle class with its more pronounced intellectual independence, greater social and economic stability, and overt interest in issues as matters of public policy have little regard or need for precinct captains and ward leaders. Because of these changes in the character of the population, the party organization is no longer able to fill some of the functions traditionally associated with it.

The depression of the 1930's brought to an end the large-scale charity services of the organization because the demand for financial assistance was so great that only an institution of the magnitude of the government could provide the stop-gap remedies. The passing of this feature of spoils politics to be replaced by the service state has been, perhaps, the greatest single occasion for the centralization of power in the federal government and for the change in our thinking about the proper role of government in the economy in general and in our individual lives in particular. The transition from private charity through the organization to public welfare through government makes it difficult to accept now the once reasonable conclusion of Lord Bryce that "in America the great moving forces are the parties. The government counts for less than in Europe, the parties count for more." [48]

The Antiorganization Heritage. An integral part of the history of party organization has been the opposition to it. This opposition has paralleled

[48] *The American Commonwealth* (New York: Commonwealth Publishing Co., 1908) Vol. 2, p. 3.

its development, and the politics of most states is a record of recurrent rebellions against dominant or ambitious party organizations. The antiorganization, even antiparty, tradition took roots in the secondary schools and carried over to the universities: students were educated to be independents and, in the process, may have formed invidious opinions toward organized politics in general. The heritage of opposition to party organization has had strong supporters among the intellectuals and reformers and they have at least perfunctory allies in the broadening ranks of the middle class. Even professional politicians themselves from time to time denounce "bosses" and "political machines." [49]

A direct outgrowth of the resistance to organized partisan politics is the nonpartisan election system used in a majority of cities and school-board districts and in Nebraska and Minnesota to elect state legislators. The official doctrine supporting the nonpartisan system is that national or state parties get in the way of intelligent solutions of local problems; that there is no meaningful Republican or Democratic method for operating a school system or repairing city streets or laying out parks and playgrounds; and that a partisan voting behavior of a community in state and national elections should not be followed in local elections.

The New Leaders. Out of the combination of forces exerting change upon the organization, new kinds of leaders have made their appearance. The new leader is not the plug-hat, thumb-in-vest, cigar-in-mouth, self-made creature who came up from "the old Fourth Ward" or from "the old North Side Gang." The new leaders are more nearly the "cart-tail orators and college graduates," to use George Washington Plunkitt's unflattering terms.[50] They are much better prepared to administer or legislate broad programs of government welfare (if necessary, to provide "bread and circuses" for relief of hardships) than to distribute a basket of food at Christmas time or outfit a destitute family with clothing, in the manner of the old leaders.

The new leaders are more inclined to think, or at least to talk, in broad terms of national and international problems and to reveal to their constituents a more pervasive and less partisan mentality. Oratory tends to become less sonorous and more carefully timed for radio and television presentation. There may be less flag waving and fewer "Fourth-of-July speeches," which seem to embarrass rather than thrill many people, some of whom may be adverse to such sentiments for fear they smack of racial superiority and of economic nationalism or of imperialism. It seems that

---

[49] James A. Farley deplored machines which put politics above morality and grew arrogant and contemptuous of outsiders. Stephen A. Mitchell, one-time chairman of the Democratic National Committee, urged Illinois Democrats to form their own clubs because "the old-time boss system" failed to give them a voice in party affairs. *New York Times,* October 4, 1955, and September 23, 1957.

[50] William L. Riordan, *Plunkitt of Tammany Hall* (New York: Alfred A. Knopf, Inc., 1948) p. 109.

the greater popularity is shown for the light and elusive touch, for sentiments couched in the kinds of generalities that are reminiscent of the prop-
ositions for social action in college textbooks and lectures.

The new leaders reflect increasingly the public's preference for independence in politics. Some candidates during an election campaign find
it advantageous to make as few references as possible to the name of their
own political party, while more and more officials conduct their offices on
at least a quasi-nonpartisan basis. These tendencies appear in both major
parties. An analysis of the political operations of the new leaders could
quite conceivably turn up much in common between Republican Earl
Warren's governorship in California (1943–1953) and Democrat Frank
Lausche's governorship in Ohio (1945–1957).[51] Among other possible examples, the contrasts between old- and new-style leaders in New York
stand out prominently. Carmine De Sapio, as head of Tammany Hall, is
a different breed from his more illustrious Democratic predecessors, e.g.,
Charles F. Murphy; the difference in national extraction is superficial compared with the substantive differences in background and in urbanity.
Among New York Republicans, there are even more startling differences
between two leaders—separated by approximately forty years—Thomas C.
Platt of the nineteenth century and Thomas E. Dewey of the twentieth century. The contrast is even sharper in the case of Nelson Rockefeller, who
is more nearly a model of the new leader than Dewey.

Trends in Organization. The failure to maintain a permanently functioning party organization can be attributed to some extent to the apathy
of leaders, the deadwood in the committees, and the refusal of leaders to
cooperate and compromise. Another aspect of the problem is excessive
statutory regulation in some states which imposes a deadly rigidity upon
the organization and which can be evaded only by a parallel informal party
organization free to operate outside the law.[52] Because of the atrophy of
the organization, other groups, e.g., labor unions, have moved into the void
and carried on the grass-roots operations. When a party has become too
weak to fight the opposition, candidates within the party can more successfully challenge the entrenched leadership. An insurgent movement may be
successful to the point that it can displace or capture the organization, at
which point the insurgents become the leaders who will be attacked by the
next wave of insurgency.

---

[51] The independent attitude among public officials is not a unique phenomenon of the
1940's and 1950's. See Harry Barnard, *Independent Man: The Life of Senator James
Couzins* (New York: Charles Scribner's Sons, 1958).

[52] Frank J. Sorauf, "Extra-Legal Political Parties in Wisconsin," *American Political
Science Review,* Vol. 48 (1954) pp. 692-704. Murray S. Stedman, Jr., "American Political
Parties as a Conservative Force," *Western Political Quarterly,* Vol. 10 (1957) p. 396.

Candidates who are not party insurgents have, over the years, established their own personal organizations during election campaigns. This method is now more frequently the rule because a candidate has no choice but to strike out on his own responsibility when the party organization is leaderless and inactive.

Other kinds of situations should be clearly distinguished. Supplemental independent committees are created purposefully in campaigns to appeal to voters who have an aversion to the regular organization but will respond favorably to an *ad hoc* group using the name of a candidate but not the name of a party. This technique reflects the importance of appealing to all kinds of people; it does not mean that the organization is weak and ineffective in its own orbit just because the area of its effectiveness is limited. Party professionals have long realized the value of volunteer workers such as housewives, who can spread the party gospel in their immediate neighborhoods. This kind of party worker is doubly valuable: he is sincere in his work, or he would not undertake it; and among those he proselytes, he is accepted on an equal footing, not as an intruder or a suspected political manipulator.

Despite the reduced status of the party organization through both internal and external changes, politics remains essentially an organized activity and the greatest successes in nearly all cases still are based on the most effective arrangement and utilization of the human resources available.

Selected Bibliography

Bone, Hugh A., *Grass Roots Party Leadership.* Bureau of Governmental Research and Services, University of Washington, October, 1952, Report No. 123.

Buley, R. Carlyle, *The Old Northwest,* 2d printing. Bloomington: Indiana University Press, 1951, Vol. 2, Chap. 9.

Carney, Francis, *The Rise of the Democratic Clubs in California.* Case Studies in Practical Politics. New York: Henry Holt & Company, 1958.

Davenport, Walter, *Power and Glory.* New York: G. P. Putnam's Sons, 1931.

Eriksson, Eric M., "The Federal Civil Service under President Jackson," *The Mississippi Valley Historical Review,* Vol. 13 (1927) pp. 517–540.

Farley, James A., *Behind the Ballots.* New York: Harcourt, Brace and Company, Inc., 1938.

——, *Jim Farley's Story.* New York: McGraw-Hill Book Company, Inc., 1948.

Fish, C. R., *The Civil Service and the Patronage.* Cambridge: Harvard University Press, 1904. 2d impression, 1920.

Flynn, Edward J., *You're the Boss.* New York: The Viking Press, Inc., 1947.

Forthal, Sonya, *Cogwheels of Democracy: A Study of the Precinct Captain.* New York: Pamphlet Distributing Co., 1946.

Gosnell, Harold F., *Machine Politics: Chicago Model.* Chicago: University of Chicago Press, 1937.

Hollander, Herbert S., *Crisis in the Civil Service.* Washington, D. C.: Current Issues Publishers, Inc., 1955.

Kent, Frank R., *The Great Game of Politics*. New York: Doubleday, Page & Company, 1924.
———, *Political Behavior*. New York: William Morrow & Company, Inc., 1928.
Kurtzman, David H., *Methods of Controlling Votes in Philadelphia*. Philadelphia: University of Pennsylvania Press, 1935. Ph.D. dissertation.
Latham, Earl, *Massachusetts Politics*. New York: The Citizenship Clearing House, undated.
McKean, Dayton David, *The Boss*. Boston: Houghton Mifflin Company, 1940.
Macy, Jesse, *Party Organization and Machinery*. London: T. Fisher Unwin, 1905.
Merriam, Charles E. and Harold F. Gosnell, *The American Party System*, 4th ed. New York: The Macmillan Company, 1949, Chap. 11.
Milligan, Maurice M., *Missouri Waltz*. New York: Charles Scribner's Sons, 1948.
Moscow, Warren, *Politics in the Empire State*. New York: Alfred A. Knopf, Inc., 1948.
Myers, Gustavus, *The History of Tammany Hall*, 2d ed. New York: Boni & Liveright, 1916.
Reynolds, George M., *Machine Politics in New Orleans, 1897–1926*. New York: Columbia University Press, 1936.
Riordan, William L., *Plunkitt of Tammany Hall*. New York: Alfred A. Knopf, Inc., 1948.
Salter, J. T., *Boss Rule*. New York: McGraw-Hill Book Company, Inc., 1935.
———, *The Pattern of Politics*. New York: The Macmillan Company, 1940.
Sindler, Allan P., *Huey Long's Louisiana; State Politics, 1920–1952*. Baltimore: The Johns Hopkins University Press, 1956.
Stimpson, George, *A Book about American Politics*. New York: Harper & Brothers, 1952.
Titus, Charles Hickman, *The Processes of Leadership*. Dubuque: William C. Brown Company, 1950.
Van Riper, Paul P., *Handbook of Practical Politics*. New York: Henry Holt and Company, Inc., 1952.
White, Leonard D., *The Federalists*. New York: The Macmillan Company, 1948.
———, *The Jeffersonians*. New York: The Macmillan Company, 1951.
———, *The Republican Era: 1869–1901*. New York: The Macmillan Company, 1958.
Zink, Harold, *City Bosses in the United States*. Durham: Duke University Press, 1930.

CHAPTER SEVEN

Nominating Systems

The complexities of republican government shift the sequence of political functions in such a way that those unfamiliar with its inherent logic look upon it as irrational. In the United States, furthermore, the all-pervading nature of the organization obscures the fact it is the creature of the electoral function of parties. Originally organization sprang from the concerted effort to elect the party's ticket, and in the form of campaign committees, the creation of organization was the next step after the naming of the ticket. Evolution of the American party system has reversed this sequence, for the organization is now antecedent to nominations and intricately entwined in nomination procedures.

Significance of Nominations. The informed and the discerning know when the crucial points of a process occur. Among those who make politics a business, more or less, there is the constant recognition of the importance of nominations in an election system. The general public may not be diverted by the political battle until the general election is upon them; but those who have the greatest immediate stake in the outcome know that the selections at the general election are made from those candidates who were previously chosen as the nominees of the various parties. The point at which candidates are nominated is one of the most important steps in the entire sequence.

Leaders, the Organization, and Nominations. The party organization stands in a peculiar relation to nominations. Its function is to control public offices through which spoils can be administered for the prestige and advantage of the leaders and for the enhancement of the organization. The leaders naturally see this relationship in personal terms, thinking of their share of organization control as a vested interest and of their hold upon public offices as a prize to win and to keep. Proceeding from this realization, we comprehend the dual nature of the problem of leadership. First, leaders seek to nominate candidates who, if elected, will cooperate with the leaders in building the regular party organization. Second, the leaders, after nominating such candidates, work day and night to elect them. It is the first problem that is of concern here, and its magnitude is clarified by the rule that leaders much prefer to lose an election than to lose their power and control within the organization. This rule can be quickly demonstrated.

If the Democrats win a gubernatorial election, the Republican organization leaders are not expected by their followers to deliver jobs and favors. The members of the losing party understand that by their loss they are to be deprived of the advantages of public office; this is the rule of the game, so they do not criticize or complain. By the same rule of the game the Democrats are to receive the rewards and advantages of office. If a county Democratic committee is ignored on patronage, on state contracts, on legislative requests, or any of the other things it asks for, the reactions of the members will range from despondency to rage. They will denounce the governor and his spoilsmen, but more to the point, they will realize that their county leaders are the source of their troubles. In the factional struggle in their county the leaders of the organization are *personae non gratae* with the state organization; it is another faction's leadership within the county that is recognized at the state capitol. The governor, by throwing the favors of his office to the opposing faction, can undermine and sometimes destroy the power of the faction controlling the county organization. A leader faced with the challenge of a rival's receiving the spoils must summon all his powers and resources to stay alive politically, for even his friends may desert him in order to survive. Those party members who want something are much less concerned with who gives it to them than they are with the fact that they get it. When they discover who is able to give it to them, they gravitate to those leaders, who become the center of strength.

When this problem of leadership is understood—and it exists on every level—the rule that leaders hold on to the machinery even at the risk of losing an election is completely understandable and simple. It becomes one of the great paradoxes of American politics that the organization, which exists to win elections, becomes more important than the object for which it was created. In American politics the necessity of organization is an even greater necessity than the party's electoral function.[1] Successful leaders are under compulsion to win elections some of the time in order to hold on to the organization, so the two necessities are usually compatible. Occasionally, local leaders can depend upon favors from the state government and are not compelled to win local elections; some county chairmen privately admit they do not dare nominate a winning county ticket for fear the resultant uproar over the spoils will unseat them. These situations are exceptional. Most leaders not only are expected to produce majorities but also need the protection of a local bulwark of spoils to permit them to weather any storm that appears. The most usual kind of refuge is control

---

[1] Boies Penrose was quoted as saying, "Governor Ben Odell . . . told me something a few years ago. He told me that when it came to deciding between losing an election and losing control of the party, lose the election. And . . . he was right by God."—— Walter Davenport, *Power and Glory* (New York: G. P. Putnam's Sons, 1931) p. 191.

of a city or county government, the so-called courthouse ring. If the leaders can hold some of these offices, they always have leverage to exert in party councils and they also have a springboard for the next state election.[2] If a leader has a domain that his party enemies cannot capture, they very likely will be forced to come to him and make peace. Succinctly, this is the situation a leader always contends with, and this is the reason he must be skilled in the techniques of committee operations and of nominating procedures. His first enemy is not the opposite party, but opposing factions in his own party.

THE CONVENTION SYSTEM

Theory of the Convention. The evolution of early nominating methods finally arrived at the delegate convention, which was universally accepted because it was universally adaptable to party government. Consequently, it developed deep roots both in its philosophical justification and in its acceptance by the professional politicians as a practical system. Its theory appeared to be impregnable. It was the epitome of democratic procedures for accomplishing representative party actions. The rank-and-file party members by their expression of opinions controlled the basic policies through colleagues whom they chose. What was done on each level of party organization was manifestly the expression of the people, and any time they did not like the course of events, they had the power to set a new course by choosing a different set of leaders. Attacks upon this system were doomed at the beginning because the defense was based upon the American ideology of grass-roots action by free, God-fearing men. Attacks were also doomed for many years because the conventions were the only means for doing what the parties were bent upon doing in any event.

Mechanics of Delegate Selection. The use of a uniform nominating system naturally produced a high degree of uniformity in the other mechanics. The first step is the "primary."[3] To make nominations for local office, each party's voters would gather on the announced date in their own separate mass meetings and select their respective candidates: e.g., members of city councils were nominated at ward meetings; justices of the peace and constables, at township meetings. At these lowest-level meetings delegates were also chosen to represent the area in the county convention. The delegate convention, strictly speaking, began at the county level,

---

[2] When the reformers finally defeated the Pendergast organization in the Kansas City elections of 1940 and 1942, it was able to survive because it still held the Jackson County offices.——Maurice M. Milligan, *Missouri Waltz* (New York: Charles Scribner's Sons, 1948) pp. 245-246. E. H. Crump was defeated in the Tennessee state election in 1948, but his operating base, Shelby County, was still firmly held for his comeback attempt in 1952.

[3] The term "caucus" was sometimes used for local nominations instead of "primary." F. W. Dallinger, *Nominations for Elective Office in the United States* (Cambridge: Harvard University Press, 1897) p. 53, note 2.

although for many years delegate conventions were used by the parties to nominate candidates for city offices, for state legislator, or for other office elected from a district within a county. The county convention both nominated candidates for county offices and chose delegates to represent the county in the party's state convention, where candidates were nominated for state-wide office.[4] An offshoot was the selection of delegates to the conventions for districts comprising more than one county, such as the congressional district; these delegates were usually chosen at the county convention. The capstone of the system was the state convention, representing the entire party in the state and generally recognized in law as the supreme authority of the party.[5]

Statutes often determine the basis of apportionment of delegates to conventions. In Texas each precinct is entitled to one delegate in a county convention for each twenty-five votes cast for the party's gubernatorial candidate at the last general election, although each precinct is guaranteed one delegate; and each county is entitled to one delegate in the state convention for each three hundred votes cast for the party candidate for governor with the proviso that every county is entitled to at least one delegate.[6] The state convention in Indiana is composed of one delegate elected from each county "for each four hundred voters" or "for each fraction of two hundred voters or more . . . to be apportioned among the precincts, wards and townships of such county by the county election board of such county as equitably as possible, and so as to give the voters of each precinct . . . representation."[7] In Wyoming, where the county central committee is composed of one man and one woman from each precinct or city ward and the state committee is composed of one man and one woman elected by each county central committee, the apportionment of delegates to the state convention is left to the state committee. The delegates assigned to each county are chosen at a meeting of the county central committee, at which time it is known as the county convention.[8]

As it is seen in this organizational chart, the convention system appears above reproach. Perhaps it is laborious, but certainly it seems to vest control at the bottom in the rank and file. Control, however, lies with those who grasp it, and the control of the convention system was from the beginning in the party's committee structure. Even when the authority for operating the system was taken from the parties and embodied in statutes,

---

[4] *Ibid.*, Chap. 2 and pp. 71-72, 88-89.

[5] See J. R. Starr, "The Legal Status of American Political Parties," *American Political Science Review*, Vol. 34 (1940) p. 450, note 67.

[6] *Texas Statutes*, 1949, Article 1334.

[7] *Annotated Indiana Statutes*, Vol. 7, Part 1, 1949 Replacement volume, Chap. 37, Sec. 29-3702.

[8] *Wyoming Compiled Statutes*, 1945, Vol. 2, Chap. 31, Secs. 31-932, 31-935, 31-936, 31-937.

the organization was designated as the motivating force to set the procedure in motion. Local committees determined the day and hour for local primaries; county committees for county conventions; state committees for state conventions; and all of the assorted district committees for their respective conventions. These announcements are officially designated the "call." Many statutes have prescribed the requirements of the call, usually making provisions either for mandamus action to force a committee to issue it or permitting other party members to issue it if a committee fails to act. The problems arise, not from failure of committees to act, but from their manner of action.

Confusion in the Process. Organization control has been facilitated by the very confusions inherent in the delegate-selection process. On the one hand, certain party members insist upon their right to be delegates. On the other hand, many of those chosen never attend the conventions. To provide for absentees among the delegates, one alternate is chosen for each delegate, the alternate having the full power to act as the delegate whenever his principal is absent from the convention proceedings. Logically, if there are no alternates, either the county would lose the votes represented by absentee delegates or those delegates present would be empowered to cast the complete vote of the delegation. The latter practice is generally followed, because alternates are as likely to be absent as delegates. All of the detail involved in these many selections for each convention was too time-consuming and tedious for a public meeting. The practice was to have the slates of delegates and alternates prepared ahead of time and ask the meetings or conventions to ratify them. Even then, the confusion was so great that the participants themselves were not always sure of what was happening.

Lack of Public Interest. The first point at which the convention philosophy broke down was the assumption that the rank and file of the party would actually take a meaningful part in the grass-roots procedures and really exercise control over the system. The primaries were ignored by the bulk of the population. Those who considered themselves independents were not eligible to participate, and those who adhered to a party allegiance very often were uninterested or even unaware of the meetings. Organization leaders were constantly aware and were working throughout the year. They were only too glad to be able to grasp the control unchallenged, and once they had things their own way, they were eager to proclaim the virtues of the system, insisting that these processes were democratically operated by the people.

Manipulations by Leaders. Many leaders had no intention of seeing their justifications become realities even if there had been any real danger of the public showing up at the primaries. The struggle was among the leaders themselves, as faction opposed faction. Through the years there emerged a series of techniques perfected by those who were contending for control. The techniques were designed to resist capture either by amateurs or by other factions within the organization. If there was any real fear of defeat, the leaders would issue the call for the primaries so surreptitiously that only their own faction would know about it; or they would have the call printed in an afternoon or evening edition of a newspaper that would go on the streets at or even after the time specified in the call. Sometimes the hour or day would be purposely misprinted. Again, a hoary device was to designate a small room for the meeting and then be sure the members of the ruling faction arrived early and got all of the seats, so that opponents or strangers could not get in. Once in control of the meeting, the leader could easily have the previously agreed-upon candidates nominated while observing all of the usual parliamentary amenities. When two rival factions were well represented, the result would likely be complete turmoil, the upshot being a gang fight which would serve as a *de facto* adjournment and/or the nomination of rival slates of candidates.[9]

Conventions offered a somewhat safer situation for the leaders if they had been successful in electing a majority of their supporters as delegates at the primaries. Quite often there were rival delegations from the same ward or township (or county, in the case of a state convention) and the contests were settled by the full convention. Before a state convention met, the state committee would hear the contests and make a decision, for the committee prepared the temporary convention roll. (The county committee performed the same functions for county conventions.) Then those disputants who had been denied a place on the temporary roll could appeal to the credentials committee of the convention. This committee was usually picked by the state committee, directly or indirectly, and would decide the contests in the same way, moving that the temporary roll become the permanent roll. In a perfunctory manner the convention usually approved this motion of the credentials committee. Once the leaders had a majority of the delegates firmly seated on the permanent roll, the big battle was over.

Next, the leaders came to a final agreement on the slate of candidates

---

9 These experiences have a long tradition behind them. The report of a Democratic-Republican caucus in a New York City ward in 1823 noted that "the meeting was held on Monday evening last. We know not how to gather the truth from the various and conflicting accounts before us, nor shall we attempt to blame any party; but it certainly appears that the meeting was exceedingly numerous and very turbulent; and there were two presidents and secretaries put up and sustained by the opposing parties, and each set did business for itself,—one ratifying the nomination [of the executive committee of Tammany Hall], and the other forming a new ticket."——Quoted in Dallinger, *op. cit.*, p. 97; see also pp. 63-71.

to be nominated. This act of negotiation, known as "making up the ticket," varied with the political situation. In those cases where a group of leaders came together as equals, the ticket was put together in conformance with their joint wishes. This procedure became known as the "smoke-filled room" technique, for the final compromises generally occurred in a private room in the convention hall or in a hotel. If the discussions were unduly prolonged, the convention might have to be adjourned for a few hours, or time-killing procedures were employed in the form of speeches and floor demonstrations. Then the "word" was passed out to the delegates from their respective leaders, and the formality of making nominations was rapidly accomplished.[10] In less frequent cases, one leader dominated the party and its convention, but he was tested by his ability to make decisions in which others would acquiesce; his knowledge, his sense of power and of forces needed to be unerring.[11] Some leaders operated so subtly and quietly that it was sometimes difficult to realize the extent to which they directed the entire process. Other leaders acted the part of the impresario, giving orders, dictating nominations and programs.

Objectives of Victory and Harmony. Whatever the relation among the leaders, whether the conventions be contemporary or historical, one objective is to put together a "balanced ticket." Balance has always meant geographical representation. If the candidate for governor is a resident of the southern part of the state, the candidate for lieutenant governor is demanded by the leaders from the northern part of the state. When the electorate is class, race, or religion conscious, each of these factors will be reflected on the ticket.[12]

---

[10] Charles E. Merriam and Louise Overacker, *Primary Elections* (Chicago: University of Chicago Press, 1928) p. 259; George M. Reynolds, *Machine Politics in New Orleans* (New York: Columbia University Press, 1936) pp. 123-124. See James A. Farley, *Behind the Ballots* (New York: McGraw-Hill Book Company, 1938) pp. 79-80 and Edward J. Flynn, *You're the Boss* (New York: The Viking Press, 1947) pp. 67-69 for reconstructions of the famous negotiations leading to Franklin D. Roosevelt's nomination for governor of New York in 1928.

[11] *Ibid.*, pp. 36-37, and Farley, *op. cit.*, pp. 32-37 describe Charles F. Murphy's making up the 1922 New York state ticket. David H. Kurtzman, *Methods of Controlling Votes in Philadelphia* (Philadelphia: University of Pennsylvania, 1935) p. 16, gives this illustration: "The former chairman of the Republican City Committee, in trying to impress upon the committeemen, at a ward rally, the importance of their ward leader, said: 'Your leader will be one of the ward leaders to sit in on the making up of the city slate, which has already been approved by the "Senator" [Vare]. This is a distinct honor'."

[12] Excellent examples of religious and racial balance are found in state tickets in New York. Both Republicans and Democrats are careful to name at least one Catholic and one Jew and usually someone of Irish and of Italian extraction. For a number of years both parties have nominated a Jew for attorney general. See Flynn, *op. cit.*, p. 223; Pendleton Herring, *The Politics of Democracy* (New York: Rinehart & Company, Inc., 1940) pp. 136-138; V. O. Key, Jr., *American State Politics: An Introduction* (New York: Alfred A. Knopf, Inc., 1956) p. 161.

Considering all the computations entering into the naming of a party's slate of candidates under the exigencies of the moment, the leaders themselves often are disappointed and dissatisfied, but they are realistic and experienced enough to know that politics is the art of the possible, not of the ideal. Although they rarely bolt, the question of acceptability is always pertinent. If they are too discouraged or dismayed, they may lack genuine enthusiasm during the campaign or may even fail to do any work at all. In the closed-door, smoke-filled-room conferences, arguments are made and issues resolved so that everyone is supposed to be reasonably satisfied. Further, it is not always as simple as it sounds to pass the word down to the delegates and expect them to stand up and vote as they are told.

Degeneration of Conventions. The theory of the democratic purity of the convention system was badly hurt by the organization's control over the results, but the degenerations of the system in many counties and states left it bereft of any justification. It was not the organization's control as such, but the means to which leaders resorted, that made conventions notorious. The association of politicians and criminals brought conventions under the physical domination of plug-uglies who were beholden to the organization for their way of life. The lowest elements of society took part in the "snap" primaries held in the back rooms of saloons to pick a local ticket and the delegates to conventions. It was no mystery why the communities' leading citizens did not take part in these grass-roots political activities. When they did take a part, it was quietly in private conferences with the leaders of the organization. The roughhouse characteristic of primaries and conventions was sometimes emphasized by gang fights and brawls in which ex-pugilists had an opportunity to prove their political usefulness. The object of the leaders was solely to nominate candidates to whom they could dictate, and any method was accepted as fair if it succeeded. Those delegates who were not quiescent lumps of clay to be voted and ordered about were approached through threats and bribes, the latter often made possible on a large scale by the close connection between the organization and large business interests.[13]

These practices both hardened that public opinion which was anti-organization and even antipolitics, and persuaded those with no firm opinions. Statutory prohibition of fraudulent practices and the specifying of voting methods at primaries did not overcome the discontent. The process of electing delegates and endowing them with the party's constituent power was, after all, an indirect primary method. The growing mood for reform was intimately connected with an increasing desire for more con-

---

13 For examples, see Robert M. La Follette, *Autobiography* (Madison: Robert M. La Follette Company, 1913) pp. 193-200; Davenport, *op. cit.*, p. 122; Dallinger, *op. cit.*, Chap. 5 and pp. 127-133.

crete public participation in political processes. Not only was this desire caused by a greater recognition of the cost of political practices but also it was encouraged by those who were ambitious to enter politics but found themselves barred or handicapped by the convention system. For a variety of reasons, the crescendo of public protest against bossism and corruption grew, and the obvious reform of the nominating convention was its abolition. Since indirect public participation ranged from being a farce to being ineffective, the solution was direct participation—i.e., the use of the direct primary wherein the voters could express their choices for party candidates for office just as they did in general elections for public officials. The eventual realization of this change created, in effect, two elections instead of one in the electoral process.

Rise of the Direct Primary. Methods of nominating candidates have always been a problem in representative government. During colonial times in the United States the diversity in practices indicated the possible kinds of solutions of which the human imagination is capable. It is probably impossible to devise a completely new method, an absolute departure from all previous experience, and the direct primary had antecedents even older than those of the conventions. A form of direct primary was adopted in the Hartford Constitution of 1638 and was introduced in Connecticut in 1689. It continued in use in that State down to 1819. By its provisions the voters went to the polls twice a year, in May and October, to elect the lower house of the legislature; in the October election they nominated candidates for the state senate to be elected the following May; during the even-numbered years, in the May election, they also nominatd candidates for Congress to be elected the following October.[14]

The first use, apparently, of the direct primary in preference to the party-convention system was by the Democrats in Crawford County, Pennsylvania, on September 9, 1842, as a means of restoring party harmony, and they continued to use it until 1850. In 1860 the Republicans in Crawford County began using it, giving rise to the expression "Crawford County system."

The direct primary system was accepted slowly but gradually. It is not surprising that it was first adopted voluntarily, without statutory requirement, in some Southern states where one-party competition for the nomination substituted for two-party competition at the general election. In 1886, voters in local primaries in Georgia determined the gubernatorial nomination in advance of the convention by their choice of the delegates. The primary was used in some Mississippi counties in the 1870's and the Mis-

---

[14] Cortlandt, F. Bishop, *History of Elections in the American Colonies* (New York: Columbia University Press, 1893) pp. 121-122. George P. Luetscher, *Early Political Machinery in the United States* (Philadelphia: University of Pennsylvania, 1903).

sissippi legislature passed a primary law in 1902. South Carolina had a law in 1896. From the South, the movement spread to the West, where it was also used voluntarily at first, reflecting the Western dissatisfaction with formal political organization. In these early stages, legislatures provided for the direct primary on an optional basis or required it in designated cities and counties where convention abuses were prevalent. The first comprehensive law was adopted in Wisconsin in 1903. Oregon followed in 1904. Fifteen other states, stretching from California to New Hampshire, had primary laws by 1910.[15]

THE DIRECT-PRIMARY SYSTEM

The history of the direct primary in the twentieth century has been a series of attempts to solve the problems it has raised. These problems can be generally divided into two groups: first, those raised by the system itself or made more acute by it, such as tests of voters' partisan affiliations, and second, those raised by the activities of the party organization.

Voters' Qualifications. If the nomination process is to be turned into an election and if political parties are to nominate their own candidates for office, a certain amount of accommodation must take place. Under the indirect primary, those who showed up at a party's local meeting or caucus were supposed to be members of the party, but the states left the determination of this fact to the parties themselves. It was presumed that those in attendance at a meeting would know if one another were of the same partisan persuasion. Where there was any doubt, it could be resolved by questions and declarations resulting in the suspected individual being accepted or asked to leave. Again, this was the theory, and it was based upon practices in agricultural communities or at least in places of stable population. Increased human mobility and the rise of large cities meant that more strangers would be showing up at the meetings, or more likely, that they would not show up at all because of unfamiliarity and disinterest. The extent to which the meetings degenerated under the control of some city organizations made the question of qualification of the participants academic inasmuch as the leaders tried to keep out opponents and admitted supporters without reference to their qualifications.

Tests of Party Membership. The question of voters' qualifications to vote in direct primaries was not so perplexing when the determination was left to the parties, for in this case the election officials appointed by the leaders exercised the discretion.[16] Part of the increasing pressure for mandatory, regulated direct primaries was to decrease this area of possible abuse. Public regulation of the nominating process threw upon the state legisla-

---

[15] Key, *op. cit.*, pp. 90-91; Merriam and Overacker, *op. cit.*, Chaps. 2-5.
[16] *Ibid.*, pp. 19-20, 30-32.

tures the necessity to prescribe what test should be required of voters to determine their party membership. Legislatures may delegate this power to party officials, if they are made directly responsible for conducting their own direct primaries, but this handling of the matter is still decided in the legislatures.

Because there is no clear distinction, legally, between party membership and a mere voting affiliation, the latter has been universally adopted in the statutes and party rules as the equivalent of party membership and as the basis for qualifying to vote in a party's direct primary. In different states this voting affiliation is determined, whenever a question arises, by requiring the voter to swear to one or more of the following party tests: *past allegiance,* i.e., that at the last general election or for a specific number of general elections in the past the voter has voted for all or most of the party's candidates; *present affiliation,* i.e., the voter considers himself at the time of the direct primary to be a member of the party; *future intention,* i.e., the voter intends to support the candidates of the party at the coming general election. One or more of these declarations, upon either oath or affirmation by the voter, is the only legal test of party membership.[17]

Closed Primary. The direct primary in those states requiring evidence of party membership to vote in direct primaries is called the "closed primary." Anyone or more of the above three types of declarations is made by the voter in the closed-primary states in either one of two ways: by enrollment before the direct primary or by declaration at the polls (the challenge system) when the voter asks for a ballot of a given party.

Enrollment is usually made at the time of registration by public officials or, separately, by party officials. When the voter appears at the polls on the day of the primary and identifies himself, he receives the ballot of the party he gave as his affiliation when he enrolled. The general practice is that a qualified voter who refused to declare an affiliation at the time of enrollment is ineligible to vote in the direct primary and is classed as an independent. However, some state laws permit an independent to vote in the primary of the party of his choice, whereupon he automatically becomes enrolled as a member of that party.

Declaration at the polls is used in a majority of the closed-primary states. With this method the voter appears at the polls and asks for the ballot of one of the parties. In some states there is a different set of election officials for each party placed in separate rooms of the building in which the election is held; in this case the voter goes to the room in which his party's primary is being held. Whether there is a room for each party or whether the ballots of all parties are given out in the same room, the voter declares his affiliation by asking for one of the party's ballots. At this point

---

[17] See Clarence A. Berdahl, "Party Membership in the United States," *American Political Science Review,* Vol. 36 (1942) pp. 16-50 *passim.*

Official Primary Election Ticket

FIRST DIVISION

DEMOCRATIC PARTY

To vote for a person whose name is printed on ticket, mark a cross X in the square to the right of the name of the person for whom you desire to vote. To vote for a person whose name is not printed on the ticket, write his name in the blank space provided for the purpose and mark a cross X in the square to the right.

NATIONAL AND STATE TICKET

For Member of Congress
1st Congressional District   (Vote for One)

ROBERT W. DOMME, Topeka   ☐

For State Auditor   (Vote for One)

LOREN BREEDING, Marysville   ☐

For Justice of the Supreme Court,
Position No. 1 Regular Term (Vote for One)

SCHUYLER W. JACKSON, Topeka   ☐

For Justice of the Supreme Court,
Position No. 1 Unexpired Term (Vote for One)

SCHUYLER W. JACKSON, Topeka   ☐

For Justice of the Supreme Court,
Position No. 2   (Vote for One)

EMMET A. BLAES, Wichita   ☐

For Governor   (Vote for One)

GEORGE DOCKING, Lawrence   ☐

For Lieutenant Governor   (Vote for One)

JOSEPH W. HENKLE, SR., Great Bend   ☐

For Secretary of State   (Vote for One)

FRANK A. MANNING, Kansas City   ☐

WILLIAM A. BELL, Franklin

For State Treasurer   (Vote for One)

JOHN H. RUPP, Ellis   ☐

GEORGE HART, Wichita

For Attorney General   (Vote for One)

JOHN STICE, Wichita   ☐

DALE A. SPIEGEL, Emporia

For State Superintendent of
Public Instruction   (Vote for One)

WILMA CHARLESWORTH, Coffeyville   ☐

For Commissioner of Insurance (Vote for One)

VIRGIL L. SMITH, Ottawa   ☐

For State Printer   (Vote for One)

LILLIE M. WASHABAUGH, Natoma   ☐

Official Primary Election Ticket

FIRST DIVISION

REPUBLICAN PARTY

To vote for a person whose name is printed on the ticket, mark a cross X in the square to the right of the name of the person for whom you desire to vote. To vote for a person whose name is not printed on the ticket, write his name in the blank space provide for the purpose and mark a cross X in the square to the right.

NATIONAL AND STATE TICKET

For Member of Congress
1st Congressional District   (Vote for One)

WM. H. AVERY, Wakefield   ☐

For Justice of the Supreme Court
Position No. 1, Regular Term (Vote for One)

CLIFFORD H. PUGH, Wichita   ☐

JOHN C. McCALL, Chanute

For Justice of the Supreme Court Position
No. 1, Unexpired Term   (Vote for One)

JOHN C. McCALL, Chanute   ☐

For Justice of the Supreme Court
Position No. 2   (Vote for One)

HAROLD R. FATZER, Kinsley   ☐

For Governor   (Vote for One)

JOHN S. STEVENS, Wichita   ☐

WALTER L. CHERRY, Galena

HARVEY F. CROUCH, Minneola

FRED HALL, Dodge City

CLYDE M. REED, Parsons

For Lieutenant Governor   (Vote for One)

J. ASHFORD MANKA, Wichita   ☐

KIMBALL L. BACKUS, Bethel

GLENN D. COGSWELL, Topeka

ROBERT H. JENNISON, Healy

For Secretary of State   (Vote for One)

PAUL R. SHANAHAN, Salina   ☐

STEPHEN N. LAWRENCE, Hillsboro

For State Auditor   (Vote for One)

GEORGE ROBB, Salina   ☐

For State Treasurer   (Vote for One)

RICHARD T. FADELY, Topeka   ☐

For Attorney General   (Vote for One).

JOHN ANDERSON, JR., Olathe   ☐

For State Superintendent of
Public Instruction   (Vote for One)

A. F. THROCKMORTON, Wichita   ☐

For Commissioner of Insurance (Vote for One)

FRANK SULLIVAN, Lawrence   ☐

ROBERT M. CAMERON, Kansas City

For State Printer   (Vote for One)

ROBERT H. STRATTON, Kansas City   ☐

ROSS E. BUSENBARK, Manhattan

JOHN DARR, Topeka

ARTHUR DAWSON, Russell·

EXAMPLE OF CLOSED-PRIMARY BALLOTS: KANSAS, 1958

he is subject to challenge by a watcher for that party, who questions the voter's affiliation. Upon being challenged the voter is required to swear or affirm any one or more of the three tests of membership. Generally, such action by the voter satisfies the requirements of the law and he is then entitled to the party's ballot he requested.

The closed primary is distinguished by tests of party membership and the voter's affiliation is a matter of public record. In six states (Illinois, Indiana, Missouri, Ohio, Tennessee, and Wyoming) the voter—subject to challenge—may change his party affiliation on the day of the primary election. Otherwise, with or without the challenge system, a change must be made at some time prior to the primary election. The closed primary is based on the theory that voters are members of parties and are willing to identify themselves as such. Although the system can be so rigid that a voter is in practice prevented from changing even if he intends to vote for the other party's candidates in the general election, the more usual operation of the closed primary does not prevent changing. When the enrollment method is used in connection with registration, voters can usually change their affiliation on their registration record upon request. Challenges are most likely to be used in closely contested nomination races when one candidate fears that voters of the other party are supporting his opponent or where a stronger sense of party loyalty and stronger organizations exist. Some voters resent having their affiliations a matter of public record or being prohibited from voting if they refuse to make a party declaration. Not only is their right to vote restricted but also their right to a secret ballot is qualified by open acknowledgment of their affiliation. Some voters contend that they fear losing their jobs or risking other penalties if their partisanship becomes known. To a considerable extent this attitude is individualistic, if not selfish, showing only a concern for personal convenience or a total disregard for orderly party government.

Open Primary. Some of these objections are overcome in eight states (Idaho, Michigan, Minnesota, Montana, North Dakota, Utah, Vermont, and Wisconsin) where the laws prescribe no party-membership tests for voting in direct primaries. The only legal requirements are that citizens be properly qualified as voters. This system of abolishing party tests is called the "open primary." When the voter appears at the polls, he selects his party in various ways, but under no circumstances is a record made of his selection and no challenge of his partisanship is permitted. He may receive all of the parties' ballots clipped together, enters the voting booth, and marks whichever ballot he wishes, puts it in the ballot box to be counted and drops the other ballots into a box for discards. He may find that all the ballots are printed on one large piece of paper, marks the candidates listed in any one of the party columns, drops the whole paper in the ballot box, or tears off the party column he marked and deposits it sepa-

SAMPLE PRIMARY ELECTION BALLOT

Yakima County

TUESDAY, SEPTEMBER 11, 1956

To Vote for a Person Mark a CROSS (X) in the Square at the Right of the Name of the Person for Whom You Desire to Vote

United States Senator	Vote for One
WARREN G. MAGNUSON	Democrat ☐
ARTHUR B. LANGLIE	Republican ☐
	☐

Congressman-at-Large	Vote for One
DON MAGNUSON	Democrat ☐
PATRICK M. "Pat" STEELE	Republican ☐
PHILIP EVANS	Republican ☐
	☐

Representative in Congress

Fourth Congressional District	Vote for One
FRANK LeROUX	Democrat ☐
LLOYD R. BOHLKE	Democrat ☐
HAL HOLMES	Republican ☐
	☐

Governor	Vote for One
EARL COE	Democrat ☐
DON EASTVOLD	Republican ☐
EMMETT T. ANDERSON	Republican ☐
ALBERT D. ROSELLINI	Democrat ☐
JOHN E. LYDON	Republican ☐
ROY DeGRIEF	Republican ☐
RALPH E. BOHNKE	Republican ☐
RODERICK A. LINDSAY	Democrat ☐
JOHN C. EDWARDS	Democrat ☐
THOMAS C. HALL	Republican ☐
	☐

Lieutenant Governor	Vote for One
JOHN A. CHERBERG	Democrat ☐
HOWARD T. BALL	Republican ☐
HOWARD S. BARGREEN	Democrat ☐
NEIL HOFF	Republican ☐
DON McDERMOTT	Republican ☐
ED ROMAN	Democrat ☐
	☐

Secretary of State	Vote for One
RAY J. YEOMAN	Democrat ☐
R. E. "Ray" MORRIS	Democrat ☐
VICTOR A. MEYERS	Democrat ☐
RODERIC OLZENDAM	Republican ☐
B. J. DAHL	Republican ☐
CARL VIKING HOLMAN	Democrat ☐
	☐

State Treasurer	Vote for One
HOMER R. JONES	Republican ☐
TOM MARTIN	Democrat ☐
	☐

State Auditor	Vote for One
THOR A. ROMSTAD	Republican ☐
CLIFF YELLE	Democrat ☐
	☐

Attorney General	Vote for One
PATRICK D. SUTHERLAND	Democrat ☐
MITCHELL DOUMIT	Republican ☐
JOHN J. O'CONNELL	Democrat ☐
HENRY HECKENDORN	Republican ☐
JAMES A. ANDERSEN	Republican ☐
JOHN P. ROWE	Democrat ☐
	☐

Superintendent of Public Instruction

Non-Partisan	Vote for One
LLOYD J. ANDREWS	Non-Partisan ☐
PEARL A. WANAMAKER	Non-Partisan ☐
HENRY W. TURNER	Non-Partisan ☐
	☐

Commissioner of Public Lands

	Vote for One
FRANK O. SETHER	Democrat ☐
CHARLES R. MAYBURY	Republican ☐
BERT COLE	Democrat ☐
WESLEY "Wes" WENDT	Democrat ☐
PAUL LEWIS	Republican ☐
O. M. CASE (Realtor)	Democrat ☐
ERMA E. CASE (Accountant)	Republican ☐

State Insurance Commissioner

	Vote for One
WILLIAM A. SULLIVAN	Democrat ☐
GARLAND D. "Tad" CONNOR, Jr.	Republican ☐
FRED C. BECKER	Republican ☐
	☐

Judges of the Supreme Court

Non-Partisan	Vote for One

Position No. 3—(6 Year Term)

JOHN F. DORE	☐
HARRY ELLSWORTH FOSTER	☐
PAUL COUGHLIN	☐
CADWELL F. CORRIGAN	☐
GEORGE ELDON SMITH	☐
WM. J. MILLARD, Jr.	☐
	☐

Position No. 3—(Short Term)

Non-Partisan	Vote for One
WILLIAM J. MILLARD	☐
H. DOANE BRODIE	☐
HERBERT H. "Herb" SIELER	☐
	☐

State Senator (14th District)	Vote for One
EUGENE D. IVY	Republican ☐
J. P. TONKOFF	Democrat ☐
	☐

State Representative (14th District)

	Vote for Three
LINCOLN E. SHROPSHIRE	Republican ☐
HAROLD J. PETRIE	Republican ☐
CATHERINE D. MAY	Republican ☐
WANETA J. STEELMAN	Democrat ☐
FRANK "Mac" McINTOSH	Democrat ☐
GEORGE M. VanAKEN	Democrat ☐
	☐
	☐
	☐

State Representative (15th District)

	Vote for Two
JIM H. NICHOLS	Democrat ☐
DAMON R. CANFIELD	Republican ☐
CECIL C. CLARK	Republican ☐
MARY C. WALLACE	Republican ☐
DORIS J. KENNEDY	Democrat ☐
	☐
	☐

County Commissioner (1st District)

	Vote for One
LEE CROSSEN	Republican ☐
	☐

County Commissioner (2nd District)

	Vote for One
ANGUS McDONALD	Republican ☐
M. J. "Mose" DESMARAIS	Republican ☐
J. P. "Pete" PAVLICK	Democrat ☐
	☐

EXAMPLE OF WIDE–OPEN PRIMARY BALLOT: WASHINGTON, 1956

rately in the ballot box. He may be required to request the ballot of one of the parties. The open and closed primaries are alike in this one respect. The voter can vote in the primary of only one party, that is, he can vote to nominate the candidates of only one party. Nebraska cannot be clearly classified, for its laws require the closed primary both in Douglas and Lancaster counties and in communities of more than 7,000 population, but require the open primary elsewhere in the state.

Blanket or "Wide-Open" Primary. The only state in which the voter can vote in more than one party's primary is Washington. By definition Washington has the open primary, but its law is so different that it qualifies as a third system of direct primary. A consolidated ballot is prepared, listing the candidates' names, not according to party, but according to the office sought. All candidates of all parties seeking the nomination for governor are listed, together with party affiliations shown for each candidate and so on for all of the other offices for which nominations are to be made. Each voter can vote to nominate one candidate for each office. He can vote to nominate candidates of only one party for each of the offices, or he can mix up his selections among the parties any way he wishes as he goes down the ballot, e.g., voting for one of the Democratic candidates for governor and one of the Republican candidates for United States senator. This form certainly gives the voter a maximum flexibility in expressing his choices. It is a blanket primary, but it has been nicknamed most appropriately, the "wide-open primary."

"Raiding." A voter may have a keen interest in the outcome of the Democratic gubernatorial nomination because the Democratic candidates have put on a stimulating campaign and the outcome appears to be close. Except in Washington, this voter cannot vote in this desirable contest unless he takes the whole Democratic ballot and votes to nominate only that Party's candidates. If there are equally interesting races in the Republican Party, the voter will have to make up his mind which party's races mean more to him. This human reaction of wanting to be a participant in all of the dramatic contests is thoroughly understandable, and the voter's intentions may be honorable and straightforward. When a party's leaders fear that its candidate for governor, let us say, will be defeated if a certain candidate is nominated by the other party, they may instruct their voters to vote in the other party's primary and vote for the weakest candidate for governor in that party. Voting under these conditions is called "raiding," and the voters' intentions are not honorable.

When raiding suceeds and a party has weak candidates nominated for it by the other party's voters, it is a helpless victim. Raiding also hurts the general public by excluding the strongest candidates from the general election. It also is disastrous for a candidate who has spent his time and efforts and his own and his friends' money to win a nomination and then is defeated by voters who are acting in the interests of the other party. It is a blow to such a candidate, and it is a blow below the belt. If the practice were carried to extremes, it could destroy parties and turn direct primaries into the sheerest chaos. The open primary permits raiding, but the wide-open primary positively encourages it. The closed primary as it actually operates in most states is no real bar to the practice. In fact the closed and open primaries sometimes are indistinguishable, not only because voters insist on switching parties from time to time but also because candidates and parties encourage raiding under certain circumstances.

The direct primary, being an election itself, employs all of the paraphernalia, techniques, and trappings of a general election campaign. The object of an election is to win enough votes to be elected, and the object of a candidate in a primary election is to receive enough votes to be nominated. The general rule in any election is that candidates are willing to accept votes from any source, and candidates in direct primary are generally willing to forego the niceties of party-membership tests in order to get votes. Candidates are too gregarious to have friends and supporters only in their own party, and they naturally want their friends in both parties to vote for them. This fact helps to explain why party lines are crossed so frequently in direct primaries.

The South's One-Party Primary. The problem of raiding disappears in the Solid South, for there is usually only one primary held; even if the Republicans hold a primary, few voters have any interest in it. On primary election day, the Southern voters are, practically speaking, all Democrats so that they may vote in the only primary that counts. The Republicans in these states vote in the Democratic primaries and are seldom obstructed by the closed-primary laws which predominate throughout the South. On the contrary, where Republicans exist in sizable numbers, Democratic candidates for nomination are particularly active in wooing them. It would be a reasonably accurate conclusion in some of these states that Democratic primaries are occasionally decided by the votes of Republicans. Rarely do any of these Democratic office seekers make any real issue of such voting practices although they may denounce them either for public effect or for fear they are not benefiting from them. There is a strong possibility that this attitude will change drastically if the Republican Parties actually begin competing with the Democratic Parties. In that case, Republicans would be voting in their own primaries and their presence, in large numbers, in the Democratic primary would raise the same kinds of questions now raised in two-party states.

Crossing Over. Voters are expected to participate in the direct primary of their own parties (according to the theory, although not always according to the practice of the closed primary) and may participate in the direct primary of the other party (according to the theory and the practice of the open and wide-open primaries). For a voter to cross over and participate in the primary of the party that he does not consider himself a member of is not necessarily raiding in the sense discussed above. His motivations in the two cases may be quite different.

Voters generally prefer to have a choice between two acceptable candidates for the same office at the general election. On occasions Democrats, for instance, are assured of a congenial candidate in their own party either because he has no opposition or because he is obviously stronger than his opponents in the primary. Let us assume, in this hypothetical case, that the Republican Party offers a sharp difference between two candidates seeking the nomination for the same office, and one of these candidates is more nearly like the Democratic candidate or, at least, more acceptable to most Democrats. Some Democrats, who have nothing to worry about in their own party, may cross over and vote in the Republican primary for the candidate they find more acceptable, not because they will support him in the general election if he is nominated, but because they do not want his opponent to be nominated and have a chance to be elected.

This practice can be better defended in the concrete than in the abstract. It undoubtedly conforms to the tradition of the parties' providing narrow choices and tending toward moderation and similarity, inasmuch as the purpose of those who cross over is to keep sharp policy issues from being presented by the candidates in the general election. The practice does not conform to the standard of party responsiveness to its own members for the simple reason a majority of those members voting in the primary are not permitted to determine their own party candidate for office. Crossing over is suggestive of raiding, not because the objective is necessarily to nominate the weakest opposing candidate, but because the selection of a party's candidate lies with members of the other party if they succeed in accomplishing what they set out to do. This practice is rare, because, as in the case of raiding, it is possible only under a very specific set of circumstances.[18]

Extent of Statutory Regulations. The use of direct primaries is now almost entirely required by states' statutes and the days of the optional use of this system or of conventions are over. In the course of this process of legislating nominating procedures through the ballot, political parties passed from the status of voluntary associations to that of legally-recognized organizations through which public officials are elected. Statutes were piled

---

[18] An example of crossing over which was strikingly successful occurred in the special United States senatorial election in Wisconsin in 1957.

upon statutes as the states successively responded to the movement and often amended their statutes every time the legislature met. Generally speaking, these laws set the date for the election, either specifically or within a certain number of days of the general election, require both parties to hold their primaries the same day or on designated separate days, make applicable (since the introduction of the Australian ballot) the laws governing the holding of general elections to the extent they are pertinent, and apply the corrupt-practices acts to direct-primary elections.

Within this general pattern of regulations there are certain deviations in the South resulting from the Democratic Party's supremacy. First, it was apparent that the same provisions could not apply equally to both parties. If the Republican Party wants to hold a primary it may do so, but it can nominate candidates some other way, by petition and/or conventions. The legislation does not distinguish between the parties by name, but classifies them according to their voting strength at the polls in such a way that the Democratic Party is required to use direct primaries and the Republicans are not. Second, a party in the South is given more direct control over the conduct of its direct primary than is generally true in other states. This result is achieved by creating an entirely separate machinery for administering the direct primary. Each party operates its own primary within the general statutory limits laid down. Third, the importance of a Democratic nomination, since it is tantamount to election, has led to the requirement that Democratic candidates for major offices receive a majority of all the votes cast. In case no candidate receives a majority, because of the large number of candidates running, a second or runoff primary is held between the two candidates receiving the largest numbers of votes.[19]

Minor Parties and Independents. The problem of minor parties intrudes again, and their situation is comparable to that of the Southern Republicans. The direct primary was not designed for a small party. The public expense of the election does not warrant the effort. Small parties seldom have candidates who can afford to conduct their primary campaigns. Most frequently, these parties are fortunate if they have one candidate to offer for each office, and holding a primary when there are no contests is pointless. The regulation of the general-election ballot necessitates a nominating method so that election officials may know whose names are entitled to be printed on the ballot. If a party meets the legal definition of a party and yet casts little more than the minimum vote required, it is permitted alternatives from the direct primary in nominating its candidates and qualifying them for the general election. The most popular alternative

---

[19] The Southern states requiring or authorizing runoffs are: Alabama, Arkansas, Florida, Georgia, Louisiana, Mississippi, North Carolina, Oklahoma, South Carolina, Tennessee (only in case of a tie vote), Texas, and Virginia.

the states provide is the use of petitions, although a number offer the additional alternative of a convention. In using petitions, the minor-party candidate is using the same method available to an independent, i.e., a nonparty candidate. Petitions must be circulated within the area of the office being sought, a specified number of signatures of qualified voters must be attained, and the signed petitions filed by a deadline. If this process is successfully completed, the name of the minor-party candidate will appear on the general election ballot designated by the party name, or the name of the independent candidate will appear without a party name.[20]

Candidate Procedures. From the point of view of major-party candidates, primaries offer peculiar kinds of challenges, although the formal procedures for getting one's name on a ballot seldom are major hurdles in themselves. In general, the states require that candidates file nominating papers by a certain date, usually fixed by statute, but in a few cases left up to the parties. Depending upon the office or upon the state, filing requirements vary. To generalize the procedures, filing entails, first, a written, formal declaration of candidacy, usually on a form legally prescribed for the purpose; this declaration merely attests to the candidate's qualifications required by law, such as age, citizenship, party affiliation, and so on. Second, the candidate is required to secure the signatures of qualified voters on petitions [21] circulated within the area of the jurisdiction of the office he is seeking. The number of signatures required on the petitions is fixed by law, being either an arbitrary number or a number equal to an arbitrary percentage of the total vote cast in the area in the last general election for governor or some other office elected at large. Third, the candidate may be required to pay a filing fee at the time of submitting his petitions and his formal declaration of candidacy. The filing fee is only a few dollars and is not refunded, unlike the British practice of charging a large fee and refunding it if the candidate receives a certain minimum number of votes. This method of weeding out frivolous candidates—those who file purely for the publicity—is foreign to American thinking and practice.

Candidates and the Organization. All of these preparations and arrangements are purely routine and mechanical. The crux of a candidacy in the direct-primary election is the support available at the polls, and normally the bulk of the support must be found within the candidate's own party. Because the direct primary is a contest *within* the party organization, entirely different forces are set in motion from those at work in the general election. The leaders do not want to disrupt the organization for fear the effects will carry over into the general election campaign, but the

---

[20] Starr, *op. cit.*, pp. 685-688.

[21] Officially these are called "designating" petitions because by filing them the candidate designates himself for a position on the ballot.

leaders want even more to protect themselves. Candidates are, as a group, optimistic about their chances to be elected once they are nominated, but to be nominated they usually need some organization support. Although they often make a virtue of appearing before the public as being untouched by the organization, their objective is to have the organization behind them. What most frequently happens in contested primaries is that the party's organization itself is divided among the candidates, with some or all having some support from it. If a candidate makes a primary race without any organization backing, running as an antiorganization candidate, the whole organization works against him.

The advantages of organization support are obvious from the nature of the structure reaching down to the polling place. The ultimate purpose of the polling-place leaders is to win elections, and a candidate who does not have their services is required to duplicate their functions in his own personal organization. The polling-place leaders hold their jobs because they can be depended upon to deliver a majority of the votes. The votes they control include their own families, the votes of the families of the election officials who get their jobs through the leaders, the votes of the families of the runners and messengers the leaders hire, and the votes of the officeholders and their families living in the area of the polling place. Frank R. Kent estimated that at rock bottom a polling-place leader could deliver sixty-five votes, and George M. Reynolds found in New Orleans that the number was nearer to a hundred.[22]

The organization leaders may take varying attitudes toward the unfolding of the candidacies. In the most highly organized states, counties, and cities, the leader may sit in his office and interview hopeful candidates as T. J. Pendergast did. After he makes a selection, he informs the other applicants, and that is all there is to it. This ability to hand-pick the candidates does not differ from the convention methods which the direct primary was designed to obliterate. When leaders are not powerful enough to hand-pick a candidate, they watch how the candidates handle themselves and what kinds of responses they get. After satisfying themselves as to which candidate is making the strongest public impression, the leaders adopt him and put their organization behind him. In some communities the leaders select several satisfactory candidates and let them fight it out among themselves at the polls, letting the voters make the final choice. The direct primary has not changed the basic fact that organization is all-important and that a slate of organization candidates prepared in advance is, for practical purposes, invincible.[23]

---

22 Kent, *The Great Game of Politics* (New York: Doubleday, Page & Company, 1924) pp. 19-21, 36-39, 219-223; Reynolds, *op. cit.*, pp. 115-116.

23 See Flynn, *op. cit.*, pp. 219-223, for a description of the Bronx Democratic Executive Committee's process of making up a slate for Borough and City offices. Also Kent, *op cit.*, Chaps. 10 and 11 and pp. 105-111.

Organization pressure can be exerted in other ways where leaders have control of the election machinery and are unsympathetic to spontaneous or rebellious candidates. In New York City, insurgents are sometimes kept off the primary ballots by the rigid enforcement of the law applying to the preparation of petitions. Somewhere in the minutiæ of legislative regulations it is nearly always possible to find some provision to use as an excuse for refusing to certify a candidate's name. In one case, when a set of designating petitions presented by an independent candidate was so perfect that nothing could be found wrong, the petitions were thrown out; they must be fraudulent, the election board asserted, because no one could do anything so well and do it legally.[24]

When the organization is especially powerful, its candidates can be aided by illegal or seemingly illegal practices. The oldest methods, like "repeating" [25] and fraudulent counts, may be used. Candidates in the primaries need watchers at the polls to protect themselves against such frauds, but a strong organization, determined to steal an election, can obstruct the appointment or the functioning of the watchers. There is no way of knowing how extensive such practices are, but they may be easier of accomplishment in primaries than in general elections because the organizations of the two parties are not watching each other and the public may be less interested. An organization practice that implicitly is fraudulent is to pile up such a huge plurality for a candidate in one county as to offset other candidates' margins in the rest of the state; this practice is especially questionable when the returns from a populous county are not reported until the leaders in that county know the vote in the other counties, and therefore know how many votes their candidates need to win. These were standard practices in the heyday of the Hague organization in New Jersey and the Crump organization in Tennessee.[26]

Competition in Direct Primaries. The influence of the organization is only one factor—obviously an important one in some states—in determining the competitive nature of the direct primary. Candidates themselves do

---

[24] Warren Moscow, *Politics in the Empire State* (New York: Alfred A. Knopf, Inc., 1948) pp. 62-66.

[25] Repeating is the act of voting more than once in an election, a practice uniformly declared illegal in the states' laws.

[26] See Dayton David McKean, *The Boss* (Boston: Houghton Mifflin Company, 1940) Chap. 4 *passim* and p. 143; *Time*, May 27, 1946, p. 21; V. O. Key, Jr., *Southern Politics* (New York: Alfred A. Knopf, Inc., 1949) pp. 60-63. In Tennessee, Crump at one time could deliver a majority between 40,000 and 60,000 votes in Shelby County, more than enough to dominate a primary in which a total of no more than 300,000 votes would be cast. William Goodman, *Inherited Domain: Political Parties in Tennessee* (Knoxville: Bureau of Public Administration, University of Tennessee, 1954) pp. 35-36.

whatever they can to discourage their own competition. Whenever a large number of candidates is contesting the nomination, they and their representatives hold frantic conferences trying to persuade some of the contenders to drop out before the deadline for withdrawing. The object of the leaders, aside from advancing their favorite candidates, is to narrow the field and eliminate a bruising intraparty battle which may weaken the party for the general election. What is good, from the point of view of the organization or of a leading candidate, is lack of competition. What, in theory, is good from the point of view of the public is a competition which will present alternative choices and clarify issues within the party. This contradiction, which often appears in an examination of the party system, is not invariably real. Both the regular party members and the general public have been made aware of public affairs by a vigorous fight for the nomination within one party and the fight itself may stimulate enough interest and support to help the whole party ticket in the general election.

To the extent investigations have been made of contested nominations, it appears that many direct primaries present little or no competition for the rank-and-file party members to resolve. The most likely situation creating a primary contest is a wide-open field for the nomination and a chance to win at the general election. The dominant party is likely to have more primary contests than the party normally in the minority.[27] Contests tend to be more frequent in urban than rural districts. Incumbents usually are difficult to defeat so are infrequently challenged within their own party.

Because so many states, in whole or in part, are one-party in partisan makeup, the direct primary becomes the only meaningful choice presented to the voters.[28] The fact they have limited opportunities even for this choice means that a large portion of American voters is consistently presented with alternatives only in presidential elections and that it is misleading to accept the direct primary as a substitute for party competition in one-party areas.[29] The South as a section, although not the only one affected by these conditions, is the one most completely involved. Of all Southern direct primaries, 40.7% were uncontested and were greater in proportion where the runoff primary system was provided for. The incidence of no contest and of close

---

[27] V. O. Key, Jr., "The Direct Primary and Party Structure: A Study of State Legislative Nominations," *American Political Science Review*, Vol. 48 (1954) pp. 3-12 and *American State Politics: An Introduction,* pp. 134 ff., also Chap. 6; William H. Standing and James A. Robinson, "Inter-Party Competition and Primary Contesting: The Case of Indiana," *American Political Science Review*, Vol. 52 (1958) pp. 1071-1074.

[28] Regarding uncontested general elections, see above, pp. 40-42.

[29] Julius Turner, "Primary Elections as the Alternative to Party Competition in 'Safe' Districts," *Journal of Politics*, Vol. 15 (1953) pp. 197-210.

races varied among offices: the higher the office, the more likely a contest, although close races were more frequently found in contests for local offices. However, of all of the contested primaries, the winner in 45% had over 60% of the vote. Almost half of the incumbents were unopposed, and only 1% of incumbents failed to finish first or second.[30]

The findings generally indicate that voters are not stimulating challengers to enter direct primaries or stimulating real contests at all in a surprising number of nominations. Although most of the studies apply only to legislative districts, the expectation is that the same general results would be obtained for other kinds of offices. People, judged by their voting rate, lack interest in direct primaries.[31] This side of the direct-primary record was not foreseen by the early sponsors of the system.

Evaluation of the Direct Primary. No nominating system can possibly satisfy everyone either within the general public or among the politicians. Conventions were denounced, but some analyses of the direct primary's operations are by no means flattering. One of the most fascinating aspects of reform is that the claims of both proponents and opponents are usually disproved by experience. Certain objections to the direct primary have not been borne out by experience. It was claimed that the urban areas would have an undue advantage; that there would be newspaper domination; that the party organization would be destroyed;[32] that so many candidates would be encouraged to enter primaries that only minority candidates would ever be nominated. Conversely, the claims that the direct primary would automatically produce "good" candidates and would destroy bosses and machines seem too ridiculous to require comment. Apparently, the pro and con arguments never took account of such actual practices as the preprimary slate and the preprimary convention.[33] The proponents could not possibly have foreseen the reaction which has developed against the direct primary.

(1) Some of the alleged weaknesses of direct primaries can be reached by legislation. One odious practice can certainly be stopped. In some states a candidate defeated in the primary can file as an independent in the general election. These "sorehead" candidates often run futile races, but they can conceivably draw enough votes away from the candidates who were

---

[30] Cortez A. M. Ewing, *Primary Elections in the South* (Norman: University of Oklahoma Press, 1953) Chaps. 3, 4, and 5.

[31] See below, pp. 574-579.

[32] This particular objection may have validity, assuming instances of the decline of party organization (e.g., in Missouri legislative elections) are attributable to the direct primary as distinct from other causes. Key, "The Direct Primary and Party Structure: A Study of State Legislative Nominations," *op. cit.,* pp. 14-15.

[33] See Merriam and Overacker, *op. cit.,* pp. 209-216.

nominated to defeat them.[34] The question of minority nominations is more complicated. The nomination of plurality candidates can be avoided by the requirement of a second primary, but this has the disadvantage of multiplying the number of elections and increasing expenses, if not confusion. Another way of insuring that candidates be nominated by a majority is the use of preferential voting, but this and other related schemes have never been popular in American politics. There is the possible use of a post-primary party convention. In Iowa, to be nominated for any office, and in South Dakota, to be nominated for the offices of governor, member of Congress, or state legislator, a candidate is required to get 35% of the total vote cast for the office in his party's primary; otherwise the candidate is nominated at a party convention.

(2) The potential chaos in which the voters can switch parties from one primary election to another, even with a closed primary law, is subject to attack. This complaint of the primaries' operations is really directed against the whole practice of independent voting and the inability to lay down objective and enforceable rules for party membership. The correction is not likely to be found in more legislation, for most closed-primary laws are sufficient if there is a will to enforce them. The problem is the result both of voters' insistence upon not being tied down to one party's primary and of the opportunistic attitude of candidates in primaries. The hopelessness of tightening up the tests for party membership is suggested by the tendency to move away, legally, from the closed primary to the open primary. The successful solution would be an operation upon our thinking, not a new operation upon the statutes.

(3) A third objection to the direct primary is the expense of holding another election. Since the total vote cast in two-party states tends to be lower at the primary than at the general election, the per capita cost of the primary can be shown to be higher than that for the general election. If there is a desire to have the direct primary, the additional expense is inevitable.

(4) A fourth indictment of the direct primary is certainly beyond legislative correction no matter what the system. It is alleged that the voters provide themselves with too many mediocrities from whom they have to choose a public official at general elections. That the direct primary should be accused of producing undesirable candidates when this was a most telling point against conventions is ironical. The difficulty with this indictment, irrespective of the nominating system, is defining terms relating to quality. What is a "good" or "bad" candidate, a "strong" or "mediocre" candidate? Views will vary. Voters themselves cannot agree in any election

---

[34] Berdahl, *op. cit.*, pp. 241-245.

upon the application of such standards. If there could be such agreement, every election would be a rout of the "bad" or "weak" candidate by the "good" or "strong" candidate. Even when elections result in landslides, the losers still think their candidate was far superior to the one elected. It can be alleged that demagogues are encouraged by the direct primary because they can utilize their spurious charms upon gullible voters whereas they would be summarily rejected by clearheaded leaders and delegates at a convention. Conventions not only turned out misfits but also demagogues, who then had a general election in which to practice their deceits upon the voters. A candidate who is a genuine fraud may expose himself more quickly if he has to go through two campaigns, whereas he may be able to get by in one campaign. The only objective evaluation of strong and weak candidates is their vote-getting ability. The relation between this ability and personal qualities is far too moot a question to detain us here. It is likely that students of politics would agree that both conventions and direct primaries have produced all kinds of candidates, some "good" and some "bad."

The remaining objections really constitute frontal assaults upon the direct primary and can be satisfied only by a return to the convention system or by a very substantial modification of the direct primary.

(5) Conducting a primary campaign, assuming there is a contest, is just as expensive as campaigning in the general election. A candidacy under these circumstances is a doubly costly undertaking, although the party is presumed to provide some of the money for the general-election campaign. Candidates who do not have the money to finance their primary are forced to depend upon contributors who are likely to expect some *quid pro quo* if the candidates are elected. Of course the direct primary did not inaugurate the practice of spending money to get a nomination. In the convention system some candidates spent large amounts of money, legally and illegally. The choice is not between an expensive system and a free system. Campaigning to win votes at the polls costs a great deal; but campaigning for convention delegates requires money too and may very well include a certain amount of public activity to convince the voters who, in turn, elect the delegates. It is true, nevertheless, that a candidate seeking nomination for a state-wide office at a direct primary is required to make a state-wide campaign, and in many states this is a tremendous financial undertaking. Unquestionably, some candidates have abandoned the race for lack of money. A few states, whether actually for this reason or not, have retained the convention system in part. New York uses the primary only for local and district offices; candidates for United States senator and state offices are nominated at state conventions. This problem will always

persist because it is part of the whole insoluble problem of campaign expenditures.

(6) It is pointed out that in the course of the nominating convention, parties also adopted their platforms, but that they experience great difficulty in carrying out this function since the rise of the direct primary. State platforms are now written in delegated state conventions or at meetings of the candidates of the party who were nominated in the direct primary. To hold an assembly of either group of party members for the sole purpose of drafting a platform is a dreary affair and likely to be sloughed off in a careless manner; or a different contention is that platform making should not be left exclusively to party candidates in those states which follow this method. It is a good question what platforms prove anyway. They are considered essential by the groups pressing for specific declarations, but as the campaigns progress, platforms fade into oblivion. The fact is that they still are being written, and one wonders if they were more satisfactorily prepared before the introduction of the direct primary. Where the conventions had developed abuses in making nominations, it was not apparent that they were any more satisfactory in drafting the statement of principles upon which the candidates were to run.

(7) The over-all objection to the direct primary is the asserted claim that it destroys party responsibility, including the opportunity for consultation which the conventions offered. There is no question that, technically speaking, the party leadership is not responsible for direct-primary nominations except in a few states and that the direct primary handicaps leaders. However, the relationship was more nearly the other way. The direct primary resulted from, rather than created, the weaknesses of the party systems.[35]

THE BLENDING PROCESS IN NOMINATING SYSTEMS

Methods for making nominations are controversial because of the crucial importance of the nomination process. Everyone who recognizes his interests are involved becomes a party to the controversy, and political leaders, whether candidates or managers, are always in the forefront in discussing the process and making proposals for its operation. Although leaders will be found on both sides of the controversy over the merits of the direct primary, organization people are likely to condemn a system which they feel challenges their prerogatives and places them at the mercy of the whims of the voters. For this reason, in part, the direct primary has not been uniformly required in every state. In some it is optional on the local level; in others either it or the convention can be used, depending upon the geographical area of the office. Rhode Island did not adopt the

---

[35] Merriam and Overacker, *op. cit.*, Chaps. 9, 10; La Follette, *op. cit.*, pp. 247-248; Key, *American State Politics: An Introduction*, Chap. 4.

direct primary until 1948 and Connecticut not until 1955. The direct primary has been held back because the same nominating method is not equally compatible with the political situation in every state; that which works well one place does not necessarily work well some other place.

Lack of Alternatives. The direct-primary controversy is to be expected and its importance can be easily overemphasized. The really significant point is the incipient evidence of real dissatisfaction with the system. However, if the direct primary is to go, what will take its place? We have exhausted our alternatives as far as distinct systems are concerned. If we do not like the direct primary as it exists, we can revert to the convention system or we can attempt to blend the two systems and effect a compromise designed to achieve the advantages of each. Whether the compromise is wanted for itself or is accepted as the best attainable, it has begun to appear in some states; and the discussions going forward in others involve the possibility of further breaks in the less-than-solid front of the direct-primary system. The compromise adopted and now in use in five states is the preprimary designation either by conventions or by party committees.

Preprimary Designations. *Colorado* has used the preprimary convention since 1910, the only state with sufficiently long experience to warrant the conclusion the blending system is a success. Any party polling 10% of the gubernatorial vote at the last preceding general election can, by party rule, provide for the election of delegates to a convention. At any convention only one vote is taken for each office for which a nomination is to be made. All candidates who receive 20% or more of the convention vote are entitled to have their names printed on the direct-primary election ballot in the order of the number of votes cast for them. In addition, other candidates can enter the primary by filing a petition with three hundred signatures for a state or district office and one hundred signatures for other offices; these candidates are listed alphabetically on the ballot following the names of the convention-endorsed candidates. Although the governor elected in 1918 was nominated by petition, this method has been infrequently used because a candidate with any substantial backing can get the support of 20% of the delegates at the convention. Actually, candidates often drop out of the race if they do not get more than the 20% minimum. In *Minnesota*, the fact that candidates are endorsed at a convention is not made known on the ballot, and such candidates are given no preference in position on the ballot over candidates who qualify by petition.

Utah adopted the preprimary convention, applicable to all offices, in 1947. A candidate files a declaration of candidacy or has filed for him a petition with twenty-five signatures, and pays a fee of one fourth of one per cent of the annual salary of the office sought. The party members at precinct mass meetings elect delegates to county primary conventions, where delegates to higher conventions, in turn, are elected. For each office to be filled each convention is required to designate two candidates, the two who receive the highest numbers of votes, with no maximum vote required. Candidates cannot get on the ballot by petition, so the voters have a choice between the two candidates for each office presented by the conventions. (See sample ballot, following page.)

Rhode Island in 1948 moved directly from the convention system to the preprimary designation system, but the party endorsement is performed by party committees, not by specially elected conventions. Only one candidate can be endorsed for each office, and the name of each such candidate is identified on the ballot by an asterisk and by being listed first. Other candidates can qualify for the ballot by petition. *Massachusetts* in 1953 readopted the preprimary convention on an optional basis, after adopting it in 1932 and repealing it in 1937. If a party chooses to use the convention, the endorsed candidates are so identified on the ballot; other candidates get their names on the ballot by petition.

Connecticut, beginning in 1956, provided for a so-called "primary by challenge." Preprimary designations are made for all elected offices by town committees, caucuses, or conventions, respectively, but no direct primary is held unless the endorsees are challenged. Challengers must file petitions signed by a designated number of party members and must deposit a sum of money equal to 15% of the annual salary of the office for which nomination is sought. If a challenger receives 15% or more of the total vote cast at the direct primary, his deposit is refunded.

The preprimary endorsement may prove valuable and useful in the states where it has been adopted, and it may eventually extend to other states. Within the Democratic Party in California an unofficial convention without statutory status made endorsements for state-wide offices beginning in 1954; this movement was prompted as a means of offsetting the effects of cross-filing.[36] The same function has been performed by the California Republican Assembly.[37] South Dakota and Nebraska [38] discarded preprimary conventions after varying length of experience; New Mexico gave it up after using it once, in 1954.

Permanence of the Direct Primary. The future of the direct primary is not as clouded as the criticisms make it appear. Even though the organization leaders are more partial to systems they can control with greater ease,

---

[36] The cross-filing system, in use for forty-six years in California, became an increasing source of contention and was finally abolished in 1959.

[37] See Hugh A. Bone, "New Party Associations in the West," *American Political Science Review*, Vol. 45 (1951) pp. 1115 ff.

[38] Adam C. Breckenridge, "Pre-Primary Trial Dropped," *National Municipal Review*, Vol. 43 (1954) pp. 186-191.

OFFICIAL PRIMARY BALLOT

DEMOCRATIC

Salt Lake County — Twenty-first Representative District

September 9, 1958

Instructions to Voters

To vote for a candidate place a cross (X) in the square at the right of the name of the person for whom you desire to vote and in no other place. Do not vote for any candidate listed under more than one party or group designation.

United States Senator	Vote For One
MOSS, FRANK E.	☐
ROBERTS, BRIGHAM E.	☐
County Commissioner (Four Year Term)	Vote For One
LARSON, W. G. (Bill)	☐
LEAVITT, RAY H.	☐
County Commissioner (Two Year Term)	Vote For One
CARLSON, WAYNE L.	☐
GUSS, MAX	☐
County Attorney	Vote For One
GILES, GROVER A.	☐
THURMAN, WILLIAM T.	☐
County Auditor	Vote For One
JONES, DAVID P.	☐
NILSSON, SVEN O.	☐
State Representative (Twenty-first District)	Vote For One
BRUSATTO, JAMES	☐
McCARTY, DARYL J.	☐

OFFICIAL PRIMARY BALLOT

REPUBLICAN

Salt Lake County — Twenty-first Representative District

September 9, 1958

Instructions to Voters

To vote for a candidate place a cross (X) in the square at the right of the name of the person for whom you desire to vote and in no other place. Do not vote for any candidate listed under more than one party or group designation.

United States Senator	Vote For One
MATTSSON, CARVEL	☐
WATKINS, ARTHUR V.	☐
County Commissioner (Four Year Term)	Vote For One
BARKER, ABRAM	☐
CASSITY, GEORGE W.	☐
County Attorney	Vote For One
ROMNEY, VERNON B.	☐
WARD, LYLE M.	☐
County Auditor	Vote For One
JAMES, GLEN T.	☐
PRICE, KENNETH B.	☐
State Representative (Twenty-first District)	Vote For One
CLARK, CARL D.	☐
KOHLER, CARL	☐

EXAMPLE OF DIRECT PRIMARY BALLOT: UTAH, 1958 (The law requires that two candidates be offered by each party for each office)

many of them appear to prefer the direct primary, or at least do not prefer a system of preprimary designations. The direct primary has benefited parties by stimulating greater voter interest in the election process. Finally, the direct primary has introduced an activity which has become sacrosanct. Few frontal assaults are made upon it publicly. The reintroduction of conventions makes them merely a prelude to the action of the voters in the polling booths. The voters may ignore the direct primary, but they give no appearance of wanting to abolish it; the habit of having it around has become as strong as having general elections. If all else fails as a justification of the direct primary, the basic case for it is still, as Charles Evans Hughes once pointed out, that it "places a weapon in the hands of the party which they can use with effect in case of need. They are no longer helpless. This fact puts party leaders on their best behavior. . . . It favors a disposition not to create situations which are likely to challenge and test." [39]

---

[39] Quoted in Merriam and Overacker, *op. cit.*, p. 239.

THE COUNTY-UNIT SYSTEM

In Georgia and Maryland the direct primary is operated according to a county-unit system which is vaguely analogous to the electoral-vote system in presidential elections. Each county is arbitrarily assigned a number of votes computed from its representation in one or both houses of the state legislature. In both states the maximum number of legislators is frozen by constitutional provision. The intended result was to restrict urban voting power in direct primaries.

Georgia. The counties of Georgia are assigned members in the House of Representatives of the state legislature on a "3-2-1 plan"; no county has more than three representatives and no county has less than one. The tradition was established in the conventions of the Democratic Party of assigning each county twice as many convention votes as it had representatives and requiring the delegates from the same county to vote as a unit. The same voting formula was continued, by rule of the Democratic Party, when the direct primary was adopted. In 1917, the legislature enacted the Neill Primary Law which made the Democratic rule mandatory for all parties in the nomination of all officers elected statewide.

Of the 159 counties, the eight most populous are assigned six unit votes each, the next most populous thirty counties have four unit votes each, and the remaining 121 counties have two unit votes each. A majority of all the unit votes is 206. A candidate who has a plurality of a county's popular vote receives all of the county's unit votes. If a tie should occur in any county's popular vote, the unit votes of the county are equally divided. Candidates for the nomination for governor and United States senator must receive a majority of county unit votes. A run-off primary is held between the two candidates receiving the highest number of votes, if no candidate receives a majority. Should there be a tie in unit votes in the run-off, the candidate receiving a majority of the popular votes is nominated. For all other offices, a plurality of unit votes is sufficient for nomination. Each party's congressional executive committee decides whether the county unit system is to be used in nominating candidates for Congress, the state legislature, judges of superior courts, solicitors general, and county officials within that district.[40]

The result of this system is a tremendous advantage for rural counties. The discrepancy between population and unit votes increases as the metropolitan areas grow and the rural areas decline. Fulton County (Atlanta),

---

[40] Lynwood M. Holland, *The Direct Primary in Georgia* (Urbana: University of Illinois Press, 1949). Attempts in 1946, 1950, and 1958 to have the county unit system held invalid in the federal courts as a violation of equal protection of the Fourteenth Amendment have been frustrated by the refusal of a majority of the judges to render a decision on what they consider to be a political question and on the additional point that relief should be sought in the Georgia legislature. Cullen B. Gosnell, "Sues to Discard County Unit System," *National Municipal Review*, Vol. 47 (1958) pp. 226-227 and "Small Counties Rule," *ibid.*, pp. 332-334; *New York Times*, April 21, 1958, and June 17, 1958.

for example, casts more than 100 times as many votes as some small counties, but casts only six unit votes compared with their two unit votes. Under this system, minority candidates may be nominated if a marked urban-rural cleavage exists.[41] This cleavage has tended to disappear in more recent gubernatorial primaries where the winners have received comparable votes from the three classes of counties.[42]

Maryland. The practice of both parties before the adoption of the direct primary was to assign convention delegate strength in proportion to representation in the lower house of the state legislature. For this purpose, Baltimore City was divided into districts and each district was separately represented. To enact a compulsory direct primary bill, a compromise was reached in the legislature to continue the convention system of voting because of fear of domination by the voters of Baltimore City. The unit vote for counties and Baltimore City districts became the number of members in both houses of the legislature, and this system of nomination applies to candidates for United States senator, governor, attorney general, and comptroller in all parties. A candidate who receives a plurality of the popular vote in a county or district receives the entire unit vote. Nomination is by plurality of unit votes if no candidate has a majority; and in case of a tie in unit votes, the candidate with the greater popular vote is nominated. Following the primary, a state convention is held where the delegates vote by ballot for the winners of the primary, who are then officially nominated.

[41] The 1946 Democratic gubernatorial primary was such an example:

NUMBER OF UNIT VOTES RECEIVED BY COUNTY-UNIT CLASSIFICATION

	Talmadge	Carmichael	Rivers	O'Kelly
6-Unit counties	6	42	0	0
4-Unit counties	60	56	4	0
2-Unit counties	178	46	18	0
Total unit votes	244	144	22	0
Percent of popular vote	43.0%	45.3%	10.0%	1.7%

From Alexander Heard and Donald S. Strong, *Southern Primaries and Elections 1920-1949* (University: University of Alabama Press, 1950) pp. 59-61.

[42] Compare these figures:

PERCENTAGE COUNTIES WON IN UNIT-VOTE GROUPS BY SUCCESSFUL CANDIDATES FOR GOVERNOR

	Six-Unit	*Four-Unit*	*Two-Unit*
1932	12.5%	57.0%	89.0%
1942	100.0	87.0	45.5
1946	12.0	50.0	74.0
1948	38.0	70.0	88.0
1954	88.0	73.0	72.0
1958	100.0	93.0	99.0

The writer acknowledges his indebtedness for these computations to Mr. George A. Condon.

In the convention balloting, the delegates are required to vote for the candidate who received the unit votes of their respective counties.

The rural advantage of the unit vote in Maryland is much less than it is in Georgia. Although Baltimore City was the only urban center when the system was established, there now exist the environs of the Washington metropolitan area. An exclusively rural appeal, therefore, is not politically feasible in Maryland as it has been in Georgia. Another factor distinguishing between the two states is the two-party system in Maryland and the one-party system in Georgia. In Georgia there is no doubt of the outcome of a general election. In Maryland, if the urban voters should be antagonized in the primary of one party, they can swing to the other party in the general election.[43] Inherently, the Maryland system does favor the primary voters in rural counties and the system is compounded (as in Georgia also) by the inability to adjust the unit vote to conform with the population except by constitutional amendment.

Selected Bibliography

A Model Direct Primary Election System. Prepared by Joseph P. Harris and a committee of the National Municipal League, 1951.

Dallinger, Frederick W., *Nominations for Elective Office in the United States.* Cambridge: Harvard University Press, 1897. Harvard Historical Studies, Vol. 4.

Ewing, Cortez A. M., *Primary Elections in the South.* Norman: University of Oklahoma Press, 1953.

Farley, James A., *Behind the Ballots.* New York: Harcourt, Brace and Company, Inc., 1938.

Flynn, Edward J., *You're the Boss.* New York: The Viking Press, Inc., 1947.

Kent, Frank R., *The Great Game of Politics.* New York: Doubleday, Page & Company, 1924.

———, *Political Behavior.* New York: William Morrow & Company, Inc., 1928.

Key, V. O., Jr., *American State Politics: An Introduction.* New York: Alfred A. Knopf, Inc., 1956. Chapters 4–6.

Kurtzman, David H., *Methods of Controlling Votes in Philadelphia.* Philadelphia: University of Pennsylvania, 1935. Ph.D. dissertation.

Latham, Earl, *Massachusetts Politics.* New York: The Citizenship Clearing House, undated.

Merriam, Charles E., and Louise Overacker, *Primary Elections.* Chicago: University of Chicago Press, 1928.

Pollock, James K., *The Direct Primary in Michigan, 1909–1935.* Ann Arbor: University of Michigan Press, 1943. Michigan Governmental Studies, No. 14.

EAGLETON FOUNDATION CASE STUDIES IN PRACTICAL POLITICS, Henry Holt and Company, publisher:

Harder, Marvin A., *Nonpartisan Election: A Political Illusion?* (1958)

Lockard, Duane, *Connecticut's Challenge Primary: A Study in Legislative Politics.* (1959)

Lyford, Joseph P., *Candidate.* (1959)

Smith, Rhoten A., and Clarence J. Hein, *Republican Primary Fight: A Study in Factionalism.* (1958)

---

[43] Robert S. Friedman, *The Maryland County Unit System and Urban-Rural Politics* (College Park: Bureau of Governmental Research, University of Maryland, 1958) pp. 10-28.

CHAPTER EIGHT

The Evolution of National Organization

It is already evident that before the Revolutionary War there was no political party organization and that the form of the first organization was set during that struggle in the committees of correspondence and in the mass meetings. More important than the form of organization, the war created for the first time among the colonists an intense feeling, skillfully stimulated by propaganda, centering around a common focus. This response was a nation awakening. Once the nation was established in fact and in law, the succeeding problem was to find a permanent form of government. From this achievement the form of national politics followed.

THE PRESIDENCY AND THE ELECTORAL-COLLEGE SYSTEM

The first opportunity for creating the politics of the nation arose under the Constitution of the United States. During the Confederation period the separateness of the prewar colonies was modified only by a voluntary arrangement among the states which permitted their representatives to consult jointly in the meetings of a central congress. Purely national functions were few under the Confederation government. The postal system was continued from the Colonial period, and foreign affairs and finance were continued from the Revolutionary period. It was far more domestic, collective government than had ever existed before, but it was not enough to stimulate significant political activity; political organization and competition revolved about state governments, where the real power still resided.

Creation of the Presidency. When the deliberations of the Constitutional Convention turned to the executive power of the new government, national politics in its true sense began to unfold. The delegates in the Convention had already decided that the members of the legislative branch would be chosen within or by states as separate entities, but the selection of the executive officials was a different kind of problem. With no real precedent, the delegates were able to deduce quite accurately from their previous political experience what would be the probable tendencies under a central executive power. There was a remarkable consensus regarding the cause-and-effect relationship of the elements they were fashioning, and the provisions finally incorporated in the Constitution were designed as much to curb the organization of parties as they were a failure to perceive the nature of the political competition which would arise. The decision to create a single, instead of a plural, executive made the Presidency national in character beyond any doubt.

Alternatives in Election Methods. The only other consequential problem was the method of election, and the debates pointed up the dilemma which the question has always produced. There were two obvious methods available: election by Congress or by the people. Since the separation of powers had been established as a guiding principle for the organization of the new government, proposals for election of the President by Congress were voted down. Direct election was also discarded for several reasons. There was some fear and distrust of the people's ability to perform such a function, but this was not the only reason, if it was, indeed, the main reason. One objection to direct election was the advantage it would give the large states. Other objections were the belief that because of the insularity of the population the merits of many men would not be widely known and that "native sons" would receive the bulk of the votes. Implicit in this last point was the inability of the delegates to conceive of national political parties springing up as a response to the creation of national offices.

Electoral-Vote System. Various compromise proposals centering around the use of an indirect election method and utilizing a select group of presidential electors, were advanced in various forms by James Wilson, Alexander Hamilton, Hugh Williamson, and Gouverneur Morris. From these and other suggestions the Convention worked its way to the plan finally adopted. The provisions are of the greatest importance in determining the particular turns and twists of national party organization.

> Each State shall appoint, in such Manner as the Legislature thereof may direct, a Number of Electors, equal to the whole Number of Senators and Representatives to which the State may be entitled in the Congress; but no Senator or Representative, or Person holding an Office of Trust or Profit under the United States, shall be appoined an Elector.
> The Electors shall meet in their respective States, and vote by Ballot for two Persons, of whom one at least shall not be an Inhabitant of the same State with themselves. And they shall make a List of all the Persons voted for, and of the Number of Votes for each. . . . The Person having the greatest Number of Votes shall be the President, if such Number be a Majority of the whole Number of Electors appointed; and if there be more than one who have such Majority, and have an equal Number of Votes, then the House of Representatives shall immediately chuse by Ballot one of them for President; and if no Person have a Majority, then from the five highest on the List the said House shall in like Manner

chuse the President. . . . The Votes shall be taken by States, the Representation from each State having one Vote. . . . In every Case, after the Choice of the President, the Person having the greatest Number of Votes of the Electors shall be the Vice President. But if there should remain two or more who have equal Votes, the Senate shall chuse from them by Ballot the Vice President.[1]

It seems reasonable to conclude that the delegates, by this method of election, attempted to make the Presidency independent of Congress, free from control by the large states alone and elective by those able to make an uninhibited and intelligent choice, or if by the House of Representatives, by the equal votes of the states.[2] These objectives were to be quickly proved ephemeral, but the first presidential election was so uncharacteristic in its nature that the impossibility of the system was not immediately apparent.

Temporary Success of the System. There is no evidence that George Washington was in any sense formally nominated for the office of President before the presidential electors voted on the first Wednesday in February, 1789.[3] The election was distinguished by the national consensus that Washington should be the first President, thus avoiding a bitter conflict at the outset of the new government. Since many candidates both for Congress and for electors were unopposed, the election had few of the attributes of a real political contest. There was, for the moment, little fight left in the opposition which had been routed by the adoption of the Constitution, and the small number of opposition candidates put forward helps to explain the general voter apathy.[4] The friends of the Constitution, the Federalists, swept the election, but the problems inherent in the selection of a Vice-President were apparent before the presidential electors assembled in their respective states to cast their votes. The two offices, it was generally agreed, should be balanced geographically, so that the Vice-President should be a resident of the North. The candidate finally decided upon was John Adams of Massachusetts. The method of voting did not distinguish be-

[1] *Constitution of the United States*, Article II, Section 1.

[2] See Edward Stanwood, *A History of the Presidency from 1789 to 1897* (Boston: Houghton Mifflin Company, 1898) pp. 2-10.

[3] James P. Boyd, *The Political History of the United States* (Chicago: J. S. Ziegler & Co., 1889) p. 277, wrote without qualification that "Washington was nominated by a Caucus of the Continental Congress," but offered no documentary support. He meant, presumably, the Confederation, not the Continental, Congress and it would not be difficult to believe that members of that body in 1788 held numerous private discussions regarding the forthcoming elections for the new government. In view of the unanimity throughout the country for Washington, it is quite conceivable that some of these gentlemen reached similar conclusions both individually and jointly and undertook to influence the presidential electors of their respective states.

[4] Charles A. Beard, *Economic Origins of Jeffersonian Democracy* (New York: The Macmillan Company, 1915) p. 99.

tween the two offices, and the assumption that Washington was to be the President was not shared by Adams, who considered his chances equal to those of the Virginian. If the understanding that Washington and Adams were to be elected was accepted by all of the electors, the result would be a tie. Alexander Hamilton, whose motives later became a subject of controversy, asked some of the electors not to vote for Adams, but the scattering of the second votes of many of them for favorite sons made such a suggestion superfluous. Out of the total electoral college of sixty-nine members, all of whom voted for Washington, Adams received only thirty-four votes.[5]

Party Divisions. The nonpartisan, nonpolitical first Administration produced the domestic issues around which parties could be created. The fiscal measures of Hamilton reactivated the court and country party alignments which to some extent had been renewed by the fight between the Federalists and Anti-Federalists over ratification of the Constitution. The Anti-Federalists, under the leadership of Thomas Jefferson, the Secretary of State, and of various members of Congress, came to life as an opposition. Their attacks were not directed at Washington but at Hamilton on the issues and at John Adams on a personal basis. When Washington proposed retiring after only one term, not only Federalists but also Jefferson and Madison urged him to reconsider. This action itself marked a precedent in presidential politics, for the supporters of the incumbent always want him to run again. The course taken by the opposition in 1791 and 1792 was in no sense a diminution of party spirit but a recognition of the continued popularity of Washington and the extraordinary stability he lent to the government.

Party politics was turned to the second office, and a botanical expedition into New York by Jefferson and Madison in 1791 produced more than specimens of plant life. From the political discussions with Aaron Burr and George Clinton, an informal alliance was established between Virginia and New York. Although the presidential electors unanimously voted for Washington again, there was a concentration of anti-Adams, i.e., Jeffersonian Republican, electors upon George Clinton for Vice-President. Adams was re-elected, with seventy-seven votes to Clinton's fifty. The theory of the electoral college began to crumble in this second election, for the electors were not acting like free agents in casting their votes. A party discipline was being exercised by a restricted circle of politicians. In 1789 a total of eleven men had shared the second votes of the electors. In 1792 Adams and Clinton received all of the second votes except for four votes for Jefferson in Kentucky and one vote for Burr in South Carolina.

[5] Stanwood, *op. cit.*, pp. 24-28. Adams' nearest competitor, John Jay, received nine votes.

Partisan Envelopment of the Electoral College. Washington's second Administration was less nonpartisan in tone as foreign policy was added to domestic policy as a source of controversy. When the President made known his firm determination to retire in 1797, the last pretenses of conducting government above the passions of party evaporated, and the two antagonistic groupings met head-on in the first contest for the Presidency. Because the passing of Washington marked the end of unanimity among the electors as well as among the people, the previous problem concerning the Vice-President suddenly broadened to include both offices. The question, from the parties' point of view, was how to prevent the electors doing what the delegates in the Constitutional Convention had intended they would do. The formation of competing parties made it necessary for each to concentrate every vote it could get, and this compulsion was brought to bear with great forcefulness upon the electors who needed guidance to avoid a chaotic scattering of their votes. Elected by partisans, they had to vote as partisans. The entire logic of presidential politics was based upon a disregard of the spirit of the Constitution while following the letter of the Constitution.

These were the political realities behind the third presidential election. In order to meet their problems, the leaders were brought to the necessity of making nominations in order to bind the party, and through it, the electors. The innovation of nominating machinery amounted to a substitution of the party leaders' judgment for the electors' judgment. With the completion of this process the position of wishful thinking about taking party politics out of government was completely surrendered.[6]

THE CONGRESSIONAL CAUCUS

The First Party Tickets. Party members in Congress, like party members in state legislatures, had been holding caucuses. Alexander Hamilton is given credit for turning to the Federalist congressional caucus as the device for instructing presidential electors. The evidence of a Federalist nominating caucus in 1796 is not overwhelming, but it can scarcely be doubted that a meeting of some of their congressional members took place, since the identity of their candidates—Adams for President and Thomas Pinckney of South Carolina for Vice-President—was accepted without question. As the whole nation had previously looked upon Washington, the Republicans looked upon Jefferson; by common consent he was the leader

---

6 *Ibid.*, pp. 10-11. This breakdown in the theory of the electoral college was in the final analysis the result of popular insistence. When a Federalist elector in Pennsylvania voted for Jefferson in 1796, he elicited the classical retort of an angry voter: "What! Do I chuse Samuel Miles to determine for me whether John Adams or Thomas Jefferson shall be President? No! I chuse him to *act*, not to *think*."——Quoted *ibid.*, p. 51. The same year, both parties in Pennsylvania had agreed upon a slate of electors, had them ratified at meetings at county seats, and campaigned for them by name so that the voters would make no mistake when they marked their ballots.——*Ibid.*, pp. 46, 47.

of the party and his presidential candidacy was a foregone conclusion; but the agreement to support Aaron Burr for second place was the result of consultations among Republican members of Congress. The difficulty in verifying these meetings is that they were secret and their decisions were quietly conveyed to the presidential electors or to others. It was much too risky to admit openly what was going on.[7]

Hamilton, continuing to play the part of a wire-puller, deemed it wise to solicit votes for Pinckney to insure the defeat of Jefferson. He also believed that a possible result of such voting would make Pinckney president in case Adams lost a few votes here and there. The friends of Adams wanted enough votes scattered to prevent a tie and to insure Adams' election. The result was positive proof of the need for better coordination of the electors. Jefferson received nine votes more than Pinckney and three less than Adams, to become Vice-President. Adams had only one vote more than the required majority. New England electors scattered their votes to keep Pinckney's total less than Adams' and South Carolina delivered the culminating blow by voting for Jefferson instead of Adams. Politically, this outcome was ludicrous, since the opposing candidates for President were elected to the first two places in the same Administration. Hamilton's scheme almost produced the one result he most abhorred, the elevation of Jefferson to the Presidency, and did produce a permanent schism in the Federalist Party between him and Adams.[8]

The Twelfth Amendment. In the fourth presidential election, in 1800, the nomination of Adams and C. C. Pinckney of South Carolina by the secret Federalist caucus was denounced most passionately by some Republicans; but that party also held a caucus, not so much for agreeing upon Jefferson as for assuring Burr that he would get the support he should have received four years earlier when, apparently, some of the Republican electors had not been instructed to vote for him. This election, which was the first great party struggle, produced the most rigid discipline. There was a tightening up all along the line as both sides girded for the showdown; in some states, methods of electing electors were changed for party advan-

---

[7] *Ibid.*, p. 44. F. W. Dallinger, *Nominations for Elective Office in the United States* (Cambridge: Harvard University Press, 1897) pp. 13-14. There is evidence for concluding that the concept of availability first appeared in these initial caucuses. Jefferson's Cabinet record was good, and he had been out of office since 1794; his prestige was formidable, and he was looked upon as the spokesman for farmers, the greatest group of dissatisfied voters. There was a good case to be made for Hamilton's leadership of the Federalists, but he had both competitors and enemies. His policies had made him controversial, and there was also the possibility of the illegitimacy of his birth being injected into the campaign. If his candidacy was seriously considered by the Federalist caucus, the members quite naturally could have concluded that it was safer to take Adams on the basis of succession through the Vice-Presidency.

[8] Stanwood, *op. cit.*, pp. 49-51.

tage.[9] The Republican electors were so imbued with the spirit of the contest that Jefferson and Burr emerged with a tie; perhaps each elector was depending upon another to cast a vote for someone else besides Burr.

The choice of a President was for the first time put up to the House of Representatives, and thirty-six ballots were required to elect Jefferson, while extensive intrigue swirled about the Congress and the candidates. A situation permitting Federalist members of Congress to decide which Republican would fill which office was so incompatible with party government that the Constitution was amended before the election of 1804, to provide that the electors "shall name in their ballots the person voted for as President, and in distinct ballots the person voted for as Vice-President, and of the number of votes for each." [10]

Effects upon the Office of Vice-President. The quadrennial headache of how to avoid a tie without needlessly wasting votes was removed, but the price paid was the scaling down of the qualifications of the vice-presidential candidate, a result the Constitutional Convention had foreseen and had attempted to avoid by the original provision. As Gouverneur Morris argued in opposing the Twelfth Amendment, if a party's candidates ran the risk of being chosen by the other party's members in the House, there would be a greater incentive for a party to nominate two well-qualified men. This logic was wasted because it had already been vitiated. The degradation of the office of the Vice-President, in the sense that one candidate of a party was obviously intended as President and the other as Vice-President, was publicly noted and accepted in 1796.[11]

Establishment of the Caucus. The year 1800 marked a milestone in the development of the congressional caucus, which was at most four years old. The Federalists, who had pioneered it, never used it again, and the Republicans thereafter made their caucus official by removing the secrecy from it and publicly justifying its actions.[12] The caucus was strictly Republican machinery after 1800 and was used regularly every four years until

---

[9] *Ibid.*, pp. 58-63, and Dallinger, *op. cit.*, pp. 14-16.

[10] *Constitution of the United States*, Amendment XII. Other changes were that the House, in electing a President when no candidate receives a majority of the electoral votes cast for President, makes its choice from the three highest on the list instead of the five highest and that the Senate chooses the Vice-President from the two highest on the list in case no candidate has a majority of the votes cast for this office. Madison's view in the Constitutional Convention that the second person voted for would likely be the best-qualified, since the electors would probably cast their first vote as a matter of state pride for a favorite son, must have sounded quaint even to him by 1800. See Stanwood, *op. cit.*, p. 6.

[11] *Ibid.*, pp. 12-13, 45, 77-82.

[12] *Ibid.*, p. 82; Dallinger, *op. cit.*, p. 16; M. Ostrogorski, *Democracy and the Organization of Political Parties* (New York: The Macmillan Company, 1902) p. 15.

1820. That year, during the so-called Era of Good Feelings, Monroe was universally conceded a second term; the caucus met, but only to adopt a motion that it would be inexpedient to make a nomination. This was the first uncontested election for the Presidency since the time of Washington, and it was to be the last. Only one other caucus, in 1824, was ever held afterwards.

The congressional caucus had a great deal, superficially, to recommend it as a nominating device. It was obviously convenient and cost nothing, since the members of Congress were already at the national capital. It was accepted because of the political advantages and prestige of members of Congress who were at the center of national politics. Furthermore, by their agreeing upon candidates, they took the initiative; as a result, opponents of the system or of the candidates could do nothing but protest. The efficacy of the caucus was an early illustration of the political rule that you cannot beat somebody with nobody. The caucus nominated somebody; it was up to the opposition to nominate somebody else, something it could not do on an equal footing with the caucus. Because of this situation the caucus candidates were accepted and the caucus method was acquiesced in under the duress of the party system. The caucus members were usually careful to avoid being offensive and they tried to make themselves appear humble in their selection of the party's ticket. In 1808 when there was serious opposition to James Madison, the caucus issued a statement which in substance was repeated in 1812 and 1816. The statement assured the country

> that, in making the foregoing recommendation, the members of this meeting have acted only in their individual characters as citizens; that they have been induced to adopt this measure from the necessity of the case; from a deep conviction of the importance of union to the Republicans throughout all parts of the United States in the present crisis of both our external and internal affairs; and as being the most practicable mode of consulting and respecting the interests and wishes of all upon a subject so truly interesting to the whole people of the United States.[13]

Reactions Against the Caucus. The extraordinary fact about the caucus was its establishment and continuation in the midst of widespread opposition among Republicans themselves. The use of the caucus created a cleavage between those in Congress and those out of Congress. It was easy enough for men on the outside to attack the mechanism as a violation of the spirit and concept of separation of powers; for it achieved what the delegates in the Constitutional Convention most faithfully tried to avoid— the dependence of the executive upon the legislature. A more practical objection was the monopolistic and autocratic character of the caucus. In effect, its members picked the President. They usurped the intended

---

[13] Quoted in Stanwood, *op. cit.*, p. 91; Ostrogorski, *op. cit.*, pp. 17-19.

function of the presidential electors and determined for the people who their chief magistrate should be. These were telling points in the opposition's indictment. They were accurate descriptions of the process despite the soft words of the statements accompanying the caucus ticket. The criticisms were sufficiently impressive to convince members of Congress and the cleavage over the caucus was persistent and progressively wider. Some members of Congress absented themselves because they did not want to be bound by its decisions; others objected to it as such. Not only were varying numbers of members absent from all of the caucuses but also there were sharp disagreements among those attending.[14]

Because of the effectiveness of the caucus the Jeffersonian Republicans replaced the Federalists as the aristocrats in politics; revolt against the privilege and prerogative of the caucus was directed at the machinery of the asserted champions of the people. The Party that had appointed itself to keep the nation free from English monarchical notions and from the centralizing tendencies in the general government had perfected the undemocratic machinery for choosing the President. Their first great leader, Thomas Jefferson, actually or tacitly nominated by the caucus three times, obviously accepted it. There is no doubt he understood its workings, because in 1808 he used it to insure the passing on of the Presidency to his Secretary of State, James Madison, in preference to James Monroe—just as Madison used it to pass on the office to Monroe, who had become his Secretary of State. The caucus, as party organization, came to symbolize to some extent the rift in the Party after the elevation of Jefferson and the demise of the Federalists. The Jefferson faction came into power and under the stress of the times gradually adopted both the Federalist policies and the Constitutional interpretation behind them. Ambitious men learned, as Monroe did, that conformance and cooperation were essential to success. The factions that could not join in this development wholeheartedly were gradually forced out of the leadership, and they constituted a great deal of the opposition to the caucus.

Abandonment of the Caucus. It would be highly gratuitous, if not naive, to conclude that all opposition, whether in or out of Congress, was based upon principle. Human motives are seldom simple and in politics are almost always disguised to some extent. Many of the reasons for attacking the caucus were probably genuine objections to it as a system, but some of the most effective challenges came from those who had nothing to

---

[14] Dallinger, *op. cit.*, pp. 16-18. The resistance to Madison and the caucus was so great in 1808 that even George Clinton, who had been nominated for Vice-President, repudiated the caucus.—Stanwood, *op. cit.*, pp. 91-92. In 1816 Henry Clay moved that nomination by the caucus was inexpedient, but when his and other similar motions were defeated and Monroe received a majority of the votes, Clay moved to make the nomination unanimous.—*Ibid.*, p. 16.

gain with it but hopes of much to gain without it. Besides, the growing restiveness under Virginia's control of the Presidency and dissatisfaction with its monopolistic character removed the basis of consent or acquiescence upon which the caucus rested. After the second election of Monroe, the revolt burst forth in all parts of the country. Every candidate who knew he could not be nominated by the caucus denounced it.

In 1824 the machinery of the caucus was geared to nominate William C. Crawford of Georgia as Monroe's successor, the man Monroe had defeated by only eleven votes in the caucus of 1816. The ascendancy of Crawford caused alarm by itself. The justification of the caucus was that it selected men of the first rank in Jefferson, Madison, and Monroe. When the candidate was to be a man widely considered unfit to be President, the caucus system was indeed in trouble. The supporters of Crawford went through the motions of nominating him at a caucus in 1824, but three other candidates entered the race against him. The measure of his and the caucus' popularity was the election returns; he ran third, behind Andrew Jackson and John Quincy Adams and ahead of Henry Clay.[15] Once the nominee of the caucus was not accepted, once he was opposed and beaten, the caucus was dead. It was destroyed by the resurgence of the democratic insistence upon a government shared by more people and upon parties organized from the grass roots.

Evolution in the Selection of Electors. During these same years the changes taking place in the method of electing presidential electors was in keeping with the progressing revolution in national organization. From the beginning, seven states (Vermont, Connecticut, New York, New Jersey, Delaware, South Carolina, and Georgia) chose electors through their legislatures. Virginia and Maryland always permitted direct election, and the other states did the same except on one or two occasions in the early elections. Originally, in the states using direct election the electors were usually chosen by districts within the states, although there was an endless number of methods for doing it: e.g., each voter could vote for three candidates for electors, the two at large and the one from his congressional district; or the voter might elect only the elector from his district, and the legislature chose the electors at large; or the state was arbitrarily divided into as many districts as it was entitled to electoral votes simply for this purpose, and the total number of electors assigned, one to each district. Under the pressure for public participation the states electing by legislatures began adopting the direct-election system. When Vermont and New York changed over after the election of 1824, only Delaware and South Carolina continued with election by the legislature; and after 1828 only South Carolina persisted with this method. In fact South Carolina carried

---

15 *Ibid.*, pp. 126-136; Ostrogorski, *op. cit.*, pp. 25-34.

on with it through 1860, and the election of 1872 was the first in which all electors were directly elected—although Colorado in 1876 used the legislature.

Along with the trend to election of electors by the people was a corresponding compulsion to elect them all at large, the predominant method by 1828. Maryland in 1832 was the last state to use the district system, although it was used once thereafter, in Michigan in 1892. The reason for this change is apparent when the partisan nature of the elections is considered. At-large election increases the power of the large states, but also concentrates the power in every state, permitting it to act as a unit. Once the at-large system was adopted in a few states, others followed suit in self-defense.

Status and Nomination of Electors. Following the gesture of William Plumer who, as a New Hampshire presidential elector, refused to vote for Monroe in 1820 on the ground that no one after Washington should be unanimously elected, the partisan status of electors was soon established. The whole system of presidential elections now rests on the understanding the electors do not exercise individual judgments in casting their votes but, if elected, will vote perfunctorily for the presidential and vice-presidential candidates of their party. This system is the more remarkable because electors are legally free under federal law and most state laws to vote as they wish. This would be the summation of the status of electors if the struggle within the Democratic Party over civil rights issues had not encouraged deviations in the laws and practices of some Southern states.

A Virginia law of 1948 permits a party state convention to instruct its electors to vote for candidates other than those nominated at the party's national convention. Georgia, in 1958, enacted a law, limited to a period of four years, providing that each party's state executive committee shall file a list of candidates for electors at least sixty days before the presidential election. The electors will be elected at large without reference to any candidate for President or Vice-President and the electors elected by the popular vote are not required to vote for any nominee of any party but may vote for candidates of their own choice.

One Democratic elector in Tennessee in 1948 voted for the candidate of the State Rights Party instead of the Democratic candidate, and one Democratic elector in Alabama in 1956, despite having taken a party loyalty oath, voted for a fellow Alabamian instead of for the Democratic candidate. These aberrations are reversions to the original role presumably intended for electors and, if more generally practiced, would raise serious questions about the compatibility of the electoral college with a system of representative government.[16]

The methods used for nominating electors are specified by law in some

---

[16] See below, pp. 609-613.

OFFICIAL SAMPLE NATIONAL BALLOT

Republican Ticket

FOR PRESIDENTIAL ELECTORS

REP

For President
THOMAS E. DEWEY
For Vice-President
EARL WARREN

Democratic Ticket

FOR PRESIDENTIAL ELECTORS

DEM

For President
HARRY S. TRUMAN
For Vice-President
ALBEN W. BARKLEY

Prohibition Ticket

FOR PRESIDENTIAL ELECTORS

PROHI.

For President
CLAUDE A. WATSON
For Vice-President
DALE H. LEARN

Socialist Labor Ticket

FOR PRESIDENTIAL ELECTORS

SOC'L
LAB.

For President
EDWARD A. TEICHERT
For Vice-President
STEPHEN EMERY

Progressive Ticket

FOR PRESIDENTIAL ELECTORS

PROG.

For President
HENRY A. WALLACE
For Vice-President
GLEN H. TAYLOR

Socialist Ticket

FOR PRESIDENTIAL ELECTORS

SOC'L.

For President
NORMAN THOMAS
For Vice-President
TUCKER P. SMITH

Presidential Short Ballot: Indiana, 1948.

OFFICIAL BALLOT

ELECTION NOVEMBER 2, 1948

PRECINCT NO. _____   _____ COUNTY

INSTRUCTIONS:

1. Each voter is entitled to vote for eight Presidential Electors.
2. To vote for all eight electors of one man for President and one man for Vice-President make a cross "X" mark within the circle above the column which contains the candidate of your choice.
3. To vote for some, but not for all, of the electors of one group of electors, do not make a cross "X" mark in the circle, but make a cross "X" mark in the square at the left of the name of every candidate printed on the ballot for whom you desire to vote.
4. To vote for any person whose name is not printed on this Ballot, write his name in the blank space provided therefor and also make a cross "X" mark in the square at the left of the name you have written.

Each ballot shall also contain the following legend, to-wit: "Explanation of symbols: The letter (D) following the name of any candidate indicates that candidate was nominated in the Democratic Primary. The letter (R) following the name of any candidate indicates that candidate was nominated in the Republican Primary."

HARRY S. TRUMAN For President ALBEN W. BARKLEY For Vice President	J. STROM THURMOND For President FIELDING L. WRIGHT For Vice President	THOMAS E. DEWEY For President EARL WARREN For Vice President	HENRY A. WALLACE For President GLEN H. TAYLOR For Vice President
◯	◯	◯	◯
PRESIDENTIAL ELECTORS	PRESIDENTIAL ELECTORS	PRESIDENTIAL ELECTORS	PRESIDENTIAL ELECTORS
OWEN L. (BUCK) ABELL (D)	A. E. ADAMSON (D)	JOSEPH P. MOE (R)	MAXINE BELL
LOUIS M. ANDERSEN (D)	HELEN HUNT WEST (D)	ROGER V FLORY (R)	PETER CASTELLANO
CLYDE W ATKINSON (D)	JOHN O JACKSON (D)	W. B. PARKS (R)	JAMES STACHAN
FRANK W HAZELTON (D)	WILLIAM L. COATS (D)	GEORGE F GUTHRIE (R)	LAWRENCE DONOVAN
JOHN PUGH	EULA M FULLER	RANDOLPH BELL (R)	MARJORIE HAYNES
WM. V ALBURY	JOHN W. MARTIN	HELEN B. LIEB (R)	JOHN M. COE
MADGE WARD	JOHN O'BANNON	MARIE GRAMM (R)	FREDERICK O. MILLER
HOLMES ALLEN	FRANK D. UPCHURCH	LESTER DICUS (R)	WALLACE MARTIN

Combination Long and Short Presidential Ballot: Florida, 1948.

states and in others left entirely to the discretion of the parties. In each state each party selects as many electors as the state is entitled to. In some states this selection is made by party committees and in other states by party members at a direct primary, but the most frequent method for nominating candidates for electors is by party conventions. Either each congressional district convention names one for its district and the state convention names two, or all of the state's electors are chosen at the state convention. Whatever the method, the party leaders see to it that dependable individuals are chosen, and the party members can be assured that the electors will vote as they are expected to. Twenty-one states use the presidential short ballot, i.e., the names of presidential electors do not appear on the ballot; the voter at the general election in November finds only the names of the candidates for President and Vice-President, and by voting for the candidates he prefers, the voter is actually voting for the party's electors, who remain anonymous. Most of the other states print the names of both the electors and the candidates, and only six states by law print just the electors' names.[17]

In the passing of the congressional caucus and the securing of party control over the electoral college, a new era appeared in American politics in the 1820's, bringing with it the establishment of a workable national organization.

ADOPTION OF THE NATIONAL CONVENTION

Alternatives After the Congressional Caucus. The congressional caucus, as a nominating system, was a conversion of an existing mechanism within each party in Congress. It was near at hand and easily adaptable to the purpose. The difficulty in finding alternatives was shown in 1824 and 1828, when several methods were used. These were years of experimentation with forms, although there is no reason to think that the leaders were looking for a permanent and regularized system. On the contrary, the sentiments of the time emphasized the virtue of spontaneous expression and fluidity in mechanics. The convention itself was one such form of expression and was universally adopted in the Jacksonian period only because of its extraordinary adaptiveness. Five alternatives to the caucus were exploited.

(1) State legislatures passed formal resolutions urging a particular man to offer himself as a candidate. Apparently, this method was first suggested in 1807 when several legislatures urged Jefferson to seek a third term and the Kentucky legislature recommended Madison. These actions were not nominations, strictly speaking, but attempts to suggest candidates to the caucus. The first formal nomination of this kind was that of Henry Clay by the Kentucky legislature in November 1822, followed by similar

---

[17] For these developments and details, see Ruth C. Silva, "State Law on the Nomination, Election, and Instruction of Presidential Electors," *American Political Science Review*, Vol. 42 (1948) pp. 523-529; Stanwood, *op. cit.*, p. 15 and *passim* for each election.

action in New England on behalf of J. Q. Adams. Even after the coming of the national convention, the Alabama legislature nominated Hugh L. White in 1835, and in 1842 Georgia and South Carolina put forward John C. Calhoun for consideration in the convention of 1844.

(2) Nominations were made in state legislative caucuses. The first use was by the Republicans in New York in 1812, but it was often employed in the 1820's and seems to have been last used by the Democratic members of the New York legislature in 1843 to nominate Martin Van Buren.

(3) The mixed or "mongrel" state caucuses sometimes assumed this function. J. Q. Adams was nominated at a mixed caucus in Massachusetts in 1823, and twenty years later Henry Clay was recommended to the national convention at a mixed caucus of Virginia Whigs.

(4) A state convention in Harrisburg, Pennsylvania, in January 1828 nominated Jackson for President and Calhoun for Vice-President and selected a list of presidential electors who gave a pledge in writing that if elected, they would vote for the candidates of the convention. This method continued into the national-convention period, but finally was limited to the practice of instructing delegates sent to the national convention.

(5) Public gatherings were used for the 1824 election to nominate candidates. At these mass meetings, ballots were cast and formal resolutions were often adopted, e.g., Jackson was nominated at such a meeting in Blount County, Tennessee, in 1823. Generally, these gatherings were more nearly like election rallies held to stir up enthusiasm after a candidate had been nominated by some other method.[18]

None of these five methods was capable of indefinite duration. Too many people wanted to have some part in the process for any of the legislative methods to survive, and caucuses were already falling into ill repute as devices for making state nominations. The appropriateness of any kind of state machinery for national organization was very dubious even if it were feasible, and mass meetings were too informal and unreliable. The transporation system of the country was improving; for the first time, geographical barriers were being surmounted sufficiently to permit a national congregation. As early as 1824 the Democrats of Lancaster County, Pennsylvania, resolved that nomination in a "convention of delegates from all the States of the Union" would be "the best and most unexceptional method," but conceded that the time was not yet propitious because of the size of the country and the expense of traveling.[19] This desire grew, and within ten years the spirit of democracy in politics finally became compatible with the physical possibilities of the nation.

Federalists' 1812 Meeting. The forerunner of national conventions was a Federalist meeting in 1812. After the Federalists had ceased using

18 Dallinger, *op. cit.*, pp. 29-35; Stanwood, *op. cit.*, pp. 126-127.
19 *Ibid.*, p. 130.

the caucus, they relied upon understandings privately conveyed in the elections of 1804 and 1808. In fact it was not until 1812 that they had much prospect of winning and then only by joining with the dissident New York Republicans who had nominated De Witt Clinton. About seventy Federalists, as self-appointed members, convened secretly in New York City in 1812. The intention òf some of the leaders was to endorse Clinton, but active opposition prevented any official action being taken. Nevertheless the group reflected a sentiment in favor of Clinton, who received the Federalists' electoral votes that year. This meeting can hardly be called a convention, but had some of the attributes of one. It was a break with the caucus system and was suggestive of the new system which would arise in the 1830's.[20]

First National Conventions. The honor of holding the first national delegate convention goes to the Anti-Masonic Party, a rare example of a minor party pioneering in the development of organization. In September 1830 an Anti-Masonic national convention was held in Philadelphia, where the decision was made to hold another convention a year later at Baltimore. This was the first call for a national convention. To this second convention, in September 1831, each state was authorized to send as many delegates as it had electoral votes; a national ticket was nominated under a rule requiring a three-fourths majority for a choice; and a suggestion of a platform, called an "Address to the People of the United States," was issued.[21]

Once the way was shown, the major parties followed. The Adams-Clay men, the anti-Jackson faction of the Democratic-Republicans, had constituted a separate party since 1824 and took the name "National Republicans" for the campaigns of 1828 and 1832. In December 1831 they held the first major-party national convention, called by the party's legislative caucus in Maryland in February 1831. The convention, after nominating Henry Clay and John Sergeant, recommended an additional convention of young men, which met the following May, endorsed the Clay-Sergeant ticket, and adopted a platform, the first one in the familiar form of a series of resolutions.[22]

The so-called Kitchen Cabinet of Andrew Jackson (Major William B. Lewis, Amos Kendall, and Isaac Hill) engineered a Democratic convention through the Democrats in the New Hampshire legislature. These members held a caucus in June 1831 and recommended a convention for May 1832

20 See John S. Murdock, "The First National Nominating Convention," *American Historical Review,* Vol. 1 (1896) pp. 680-683.

21 Stanwood, *op. cit.,* pp. 155-157. The presidential nominee, William Wirt, was distinguished by being a Mason, but the delegates refused to name anyone else.

22 *Ibid.,* pp. 157-158.

to nominate a running mate for Jackson. Before the convention met, Jackson had been nominated at a number of public meetings and by several state legislatures. The convention merely concurred in these nominations and then chose Martin Van Buren for the second place. No platform was issued; the record of the Administration was relied upon for this purpose.[23] The events of 1831 and 1832 established the use of the national nominating convention. In 1836 it was vigorously but vainly opposed by anti-Van Buren Democrats, who recognized it as Jackson's method for dictating his successor. The Whigs ran sectional candidates in 1836, so no Whig convention was held, although General W. H. Harrison, one of the Whig candidates, was nominated at an Anti-Masonic state convention in Harrisburg, Pennsylvania. The unfailing use of conventions by the parties began in 1840.

PERMANENT SUPRASTATE COMMITTEES

NATIONAL COMMITTEES

Antecedents. Considered in the long span of development, the congressional caucuses of 1808 and 1812 set the precedents for creating national committees. In both of those years, after the nominations were made, a committee of correspondence was appointed, composed of one member from each state represented in the caucus, to see that the nominations were respected.[24] The National Republican convention in 1831 adopted a resolution "that a central State Corresponding Committee be provisionally appointed in each state where none is now appointed, and that it be recommended to the several states to organize subordinate corresponding committees in each county and town in their several respective states."[25] This was not a national organization as such but implicitly the state committees would be coordinated just as they were supposed to coordinate the local committees. In 1844 the Democratic convention appointed a "central Committee," with each state represented, to "promote the election of Polk and Dallas."

The first permanent national committee was created by the Democratic national convention of 1848, composed of one man from each state and also from each territory admitted to the convention. When the Republican Party was organized nationally at Pittsburgh in February 1856, the call for the convention was issued from Washington, D.C., in the form of a

---

[23] *Ibid.*, pp. 159-162; Dallinger, *op. cit.*, pp. 36-39. Jackson needed some "popular" method of enforcing his determination to run with Van Buren, against whom there was widespread opposition throughout the party. The Pennsylvania Democrats revolted and cast their electoral votes for another candidate for Vice-President.

[24] George Stimpson, *A Book About American Politics* (New York: Harper & Brothers, 1952) p. 44; Ostrogorski, *op. cit.*, p. 15.

[25] Quoted Dallinger, *op. cit.*, p. 37.

circular signed by five state chairmen. Originally, these chairmen most nearly approximated a national committee. The Republican Association of Washington, District of Columbia, which issued a circular the same day "to the Friends of the Republican Movement throughout the United States," urging the creation of other associations to act as a "National Committee," was a Republican club, not a body representing the party as a whole. At the Pittsburgh convention—a mass, not a delegate, convention— a Committee on National Organization was created. This unprecedented group recommended that a national convention be held in Philadelphia and that a national executive committee be created with one member from each state, from Kansas Territory and from Washington, D.C. The convention followed these recommendations, which were its main purpose and accomplishment. The National Executive Committee, the first Republican national committee in effect, issued the call and made all of the arrangements for the Party's first national nominating convention at Philadelphia, where a regular national committee was provided for. It was composed on the same basis as the original executive committee chosen at Pittsburgh, and the members elected their own chairman. The Philadelphia convention gave the national committee the power to call the next national convention.[26]

Development of Functions. Since the 1860's, the history of the national committees is a gradual increment in their functions and authority, much of the power being centered in the person of the chairmen. In 1868 the Republican chairman was chosen after consultation with the presidential nominee; but the chairman was not considered to be the campaign manager until Zachariah Chandler was chosen in 1876. Four years later Chairman J. D. Cameron first began the practice of proposing the names of all of the temporary officers of the national convention; previously, the national chairman had proposed only the temporary chairman and the other temporary offices were nominated from the floor. Senator Gorman, as Democratic national chairman in 1884, concerned himself with claims for patronage, and the same function was definitely established for Republican chairmen by Matthew Quay in 1888. The Republican National Committee first chose an executive committee, in fact, in 1860, but it was not until 1888 that an executive committee was authorized by the national convention. The Republican national convention in 1884 first adopted a detailed rule for the appointment of the national committee.

---

26 Gordon S. P. Kleeberg, *Formation of the Republican Party as a National Political Organization* (New York: The Moods Publishing Co., 1911). Jesse Macy, *Party Organization and Machinery* (New York: The Century Co., 1905) pp. 66-68. After 1848 all Democratic national conventions were called by the national committee, as the Republican conventions have been since 1856. The four Democratic conventions before 1848 were called by the New Hampshire Democratic caucus. Whig conventions from 1840 to 1852 were called by the Party's congressional caucus or by state legislative caucuses.

In 1883 a subcommittee of the Republican National Committee assumed responsibility for the preparations of the 1884 convention in Chicago. The subcommittee visited Chicago and appointed a local committee on arrangements. A separate finance committee was also appointed to raise money in Chicago for the convention. The chairman of the local committee on arrangements appointed subcommittees for each specific function. Before the convention opened, the local committee turned over the hall to the national committee. This scale of operations is suggestive of the organization in both parties in preparing for a national convention. Through the years the scale has expanded as the facilities for communication have grown and as the formality of the event has increased.

Composition. Originally, national committees were composed of one man, called the national committeeman, from each state. Gradually, representatives of the District of Columbia and the territories were admitted.[27] The adoption of the Nineteenth Amendment brought both parties under pressure to recognize women. In their 1920 national convention the Democrats doubled the size of their national committee by permitting the addition of one woman, called the national committeewoman, from each state and territory. No change has been made subsequently by the Democrats. In 1924 the Republicans added women to their national committee, but additional membership was provided for in the rules adopted at the 1952 national convention at the instigation of chairmen from some of the Midwest and Rocky Mountain states.

A state chairman becomes a member of the Republican national committee automatically under any one of the following circumstances: if his state casts its electoral votes for the Republican candidate for President; if a majority of the members of Congress (both houses) from his state are Republican; if his state has a Republican governor. After each election those state chairmen who have lost the basis of their qualification cease to be members and those who qualify become members. Territorial chairmen qualify if the delegate to Congress from their territory is a Republican. The results of this new rule, adopted by a vote of 683 to 513 in the 1952 convention, are to make the number of members of the national committee variable from time to time, to increase the representation of the normally Republican states, and to increase the number of men, because state chair-

---

[27] The dates of admission of the District and the present territories were:

	Republican	*Democratic*
Washington, D. C.	1856	1892
Puerto Rico	1904	1912
Virgin Islands	1948	1928
Canal Zone	(Not admitted)	1924

men are traditionally men. The arguments made against the rule during the convention's consideration of it were all presented by women, who contended that it destroyed equal rights for the sexes and equal representation for the states.[28]

Election. Each party in each state, territory, and the District of Columbia, selects its national committeeman and woman in the manner prescribed by law, if any, or in conformance with party rules. Republican rules vary only in detail from the Democrats': in the absence of a state or territorial law relating to the manner of selecting the one man and one woman, instructions from a state or territorial convention will be enforced by the national convention or referred for enforcement to the national committee; the state chairmen who are eligible in the Republican Party are confirmed by the convention at the same time as the other committee members. Four methods are used by the states to select their national committee members: direct primary, state convention, state committee, and the national-convention delegation. The two parties in a given state do not necessarily use the same method. Technically, these actions by the party in the state are a nomination, but it amounts to an election, for all of the names presented by the states are ratified by the national convention in a very perfunctory manner during its closing minutes.

Tenure. The term of office in both parties is four years, beginning from the time of confirmation by the national convention and running through the next convention. Vacancies in the Republican committee are filled by nomination of the state or territorial committee where the vacancy occurs and by ratification of the national committee; the state or territorial committee fills vacancies on the Democratic committee. Some members are re-elected for long periods of time. On the Republican committee in 1952 the two members from Mississippi had been serving since 1924 and the man from West Virginia since 1928; on the Democratic committee in 1952 the women from Illinois and Washington, D. C., and the man, Frank Hague, from New Jersey had served since 1928. Hague was replaced in 1952.

Organization. Both committees hold their organization meeting following the adjournment of the national convention. The Democratic rules

---

[28] *New York Times,* April 15, 1951. *Official Report of the Proceedings of the Twenty-fifth Republican National Convention,* 1952, pp. 283-287. Mrs. Beryl Meyers of Idaho, attacking the rule, summed up the feminine point of view: "Why are we depriving women of the opportunity to go on with the men? If you will permit us, please, we should like very much to be shoulder to shoulder . . . . We do not want to be in between two shoulders one man to the other. . . ." All of the Southern states and most of the small states voted against the rule. Of the large states, only Illinois and Pennsylvania voted "No" and Ohio divided evenly.

require its committee to meet "not later than March 1 of each year," but otherwise only on the call of the chairman. The Republican rules require that such meeting be held within ten days of the convention's adjournment and otherwise upon the call of the chairman or upon written petition of sixteen or more members representing at least sixteen states. Officers elected by the Republican committee are chairman, four vice-chairmen (two men, two women), secretary, treasurer, and others deemed necessary; the chairman appoints a general counsel and a woman as assistant who is in charge of the women's division. The Democratic committee elects a chairman, a woman vice-chairman who may also be the Director of the Women's Division, two men vice-chairmen, secretary, treasurer, and others deemed necessary.

Supplementary Activities. Both national committees have permanent headquarters in Washington, D.C., where numerous divisions of the committees as well as nominally independent organizations are housed to carry on various aspects of the national organization. The 1952 Republican convention approved the formation "if requested by a majority vote of the National Committee, . . . [of] an Advisory Committee composed of State Chairmen, State Vice Chairmen, Finance Chairmen and State Committee Treasurers, and Republican Governors, Senators and Congressmen, and members of the National Committee, in such numbers from the various categories as the National Chairman may deem advisable." The purpose of the advisory committee is to help develop party policies and campaign strategy, and its recommendations are to be presented to the executive committee of the national committee for determination.[29]

CONGRESSIONAL AND SENATORIAL CAMPAIGN COMMITTEES

Antecedents. The functioning of national committees had little influence upon congressional campaigns. The problem of winning seats in the House of Representatives—and, indirectly, in the Senate—was for a long time an individual matter for the candidates and for their district and state organizations; but it was reasonable that each party should have an organization concerned specifically with congressional elections. In 1842 the Democrats formed "a committee of the Democratic members of Congress" to campaign for members of their party against the Whigs. Other similar committees, representing both houses, were apparently created in subsequent years on an *ad hoc* basis. The creation of permanent national machinery, when it did appear, was not carefully planned but was a response to post-Civil War partisanship.

---

[29] See *New York Times*, July 6, 1952. The details of these organization features are taken from *Rules Adopted by the Republican National Convention, 1952*, numbers 22-33 and *Democratic Manual for 1952 Democratic National Convention*, compiled by Clarence Cannon, pp. 3-9.

Congressional Committees. After Andrew Johnson succeeded to the Presidency in 1865, the schism between him and the bulk of the Republicans in Congress seemed to widen daily. When the elections of 1866 approached, the Republican congressional leaders were dissatisfied with the national committee, under the control of the President, and wanted an organization of their own. A biographer of Zachariah Chandler claimed he founded the National Republican Congressional Committee, and there is no doubt that Chandler was a leading figure in its creation. In 1866 the Republicans' purpose was to elect anti-Johnson candidates, and despite any claims made subsequently, the committee was, as Professor Macy called it, "an emergency tool."From 1866 until the adoption of the Seventeenth Amendment, this Republican committee was constituted at a joint caucus in which one member was chosen from each state having a Republican in Congress. Following the adoption of the Seventeenth Amendment, only representatives were members. The Democratic National Congressional Committee was permanently organized in 1882 to aid in electing Democrats to the House and has been composed only of representatives since that date. Between 1866 and 1882 there was a national congressional committee composed of Democrats of both houses of Congress.

The established arrangement in the Republican Party now is for the Republican House Conference every two years to select one member from each state having Republican representation in the House to serve on the committee; the Republican delegation from each state in practice picks its own representative. Each state's Democratic delegation in the House selects one of its members to serve on the Democratic committee, without any action required by the Democratic caucus. In each party no state is represented unless it elects a member of that party to the House, although women who are not members of Congress have in the past been appointed to the Democratic committee. The chairman need not be selected as his state's representative on the committee.

Senatorial Committees. The Democratic Senatorial Campaign Committee and the National Republican Senatorial Committee were created after the direct election of senators became mandatory, and these committees perform the same function in senatorial campaigns as the congressional committees perform in campaigns for the House. The Republican Senatorial Committee is created and organized by the Republican Conference in the Senate and consists of eight directors, one for each of eight geographical areas into which they divide the states, a chairman and a finance chairman; this makes a total of ten senators, with two of the eight directors acting also as vice-chairman and secretary. The chairman of the Democratic committee is appointed by the Democratic Leader in the Senate, and in turn appoints the other committee members, numbering five or seven. The practice is that the officers of the senatorial committees are shifted from time to time so that senators who are up for re-election do not have the responsibility of serving on the committees. This practice is impossible for the congressional committees, but their officers are frequently members from relatively safe districts. All four of these committees can fill their offices with nonmembers of Congress, but usually do not, except for their executive directors and permanent staff in the headquarters in Washington, D.C.[30]

In both parties these committees have no organizational connection with the national committees. They are not answerable to the national conventions, but to their respective party colleagues in each house of Congress. The general operations of these four committees are to provide campaign literature and material for speeches, including such data as individual voting records and results of research on important issues of the day; to provide popular campaign speakers for engagements in crucial states and districts; and to provide money for general-election campaigns. During presidential campaigns these committees are subordinated. The major public interest is in the presidential candidates, and the two national committees raise funds for their national tickets and for their senatorial and congressional committees as well. In the off-year congressional elections, the senatorial and congressional committees are much more important and are responsible for raising more of their own money.

In all likelihood the greatest benefit a candidate for either house of Congress can receive from his party's committee is money to help finance his campaign. Although the committees are usually able to provide several thousand dollars for a race of particular importance, their funds are never equal to the demand; candidates find the competition keen for the money each committee has available. In some cases the permanent staff of the committee can exercise preponderant influence upon the decisions. The executive directors can wield great power in the policies regarding distribution of funds and in the decisions in individual cases. The guiding rule is not to waste money on candidates who have no reasonable chance to win; this is a practical operation, and sentiment or wishful thinking plays no part in the calculations.[31] None of these four committees is supposed to interfere in any way or give aid of any kind to candidates in the direct

---

[30] *Ibid.*, pp. 10-11; Kleeberg, *op. cit.*; Macy, *op. cit.*, Chap. 7.

[31] A story is told of a candidate for the House during the 1940's approaching the executive director of his congressional committee to explain in detail all of the work he was doing to develop support in his district and to report with great pride the wonderful chances for his success if only he had some more money. The director recalled the number of the district in the state where the candidate was running and pointed out that their party had not carried that district since 1892; that he could see no reason why the voters would behave differently that year; and that the committee could not spend money in such a district.

primaries. Their machinery is to go into action in behalf of the parties' nominees after the nomination contests are settled.

It would be inaccurate to assign to other suprastate organs of the parties the same status as the national, senatorial, and congressional committees. It would also be incomplete to include only these committees and ignore other developments. The Democrats since the 1930's and the Republicans since the 1940's have made some use of regional meetings of party leaders who are directly concerned with elections and policies within the states of a specific area. These movements have been fostered for the Western and Midwestern regions and bring together members of the national committee of the various states as well as the state chairmen and vice-chairmen. Primarily, such groups have so far held meetings to popularize certain issues and to consult, hoping their efforts will be reflected in the elections in their region.

THE PRESIDENCY AND THE EXECUTIVE BRANCH

If organized machinery is regularized procedures and relationships designed to achieve both general and specific objectives, the executive branch of the federal government, heading up in the Presidency, is itself a meaningful part of national party organization. The tremendous power of the Chief Executive within the whole executive establishment is paramount; the organization begins with him and radiates out to his subordinates in the Cabinet and other administrative agencies.

President as Popular Leader. Among even cursory students of government, there is a realization of the dominant position of the occupant of the White House. A President is always a cynosure of the nation's attention, in part because news media will not permit the nation to forget him. It is the office, not the man as such, that commands the publicity, but it is the personality of the man that bends the office to the will of a party. Presumably there is a demand for news concerning the personal characteristics of each incumbent, the so-called human-interest stories. There is unquestionably a demand for leadership, for a dramatic and forceful man upon whom the nation can lean and to whom the citizens can take their troubles. In supplying the demand, Presidents depend upon publicity which creates a picture of a man and his environment that the public accepts and that deeply affects a party's political fortunes.

President as Policy Leader. A simple public statement of a President or of one of his principal subordinates can disturb the viscera of men and women both in the United States and in Chancelleries and countinghouses throughout the globe. Irrespective of theories of government, national public policy is largely determined in the executive branch. Here is the fountainhead of those decisions having the most universal effect. When this establishment is politically coordinated, the most extraordinary opportunities for partisan operation present themselves. The President, directly or indirectly, gives or takes away, and no President can forget that he is the leader of a major party which always requires election victories. Government policy becomes identified with the party inaugurating and supporting it. The choice of policies, their presentation, and their results are subjects of earnest political consultation and assessment. A determined President, however, can set a course and drag his reluctant party along. Leadership in the two areas of party management and public management becomes unified and indistinguishable. To repudiate one is to repudiate the other, and party managers have learned through the years that the party's leader in the White House cannot be repudiated if the party is to win elections. The power of the presidential office is on the side of the party whose leader holds the office, but the party is itself captured by its leader.

Presidential Advantages. The fixing of public policy through the executive branch is the most dramatic series of events associated with the presidential party, but most policies are sufficiently controversial to call into play prestige and strategy. A President automatically has certain advantages in these controversies. He can always get a hearing for his views at whatever time he chooses, through formal speeches, news conferences, or "trial balloons" sent up by advisors or visitors. Instantly, when he speaks or others speak for him, the country will be fully informed. The power of the office can be persuasive in negotiations with members of Congress or influential private citizens. In the first place there is always the possibility of presidential retaliation or punishment. In the second place the President has access to the most recent and complete information on the subjects under discussion. It is rare that other public officials openly challenge a President's information, although privately they may reject or question either the information or the conclusions based upon it.[32]

The initiative regarding policies lies largely with the President, who can pick the time and place and manner of presentation and follow up his campaign as he sees fit. The device of appointing a special commission or committee to study a problem can be used to defer or stifle it or to give it a great impetus from a new source of opinion. Such bodies can dramatize information and increase public pressure. Their appointment may temporarily pacify groups which are pressing for a decision and reassure those in doubt that the subject matter is in competent hands. In these cases

---

[32] In 1939 Senator William E. Borah of Idaho took the position that his information was as reliable as the State Department's and that he was sure there would be no war in Europe. When war did begin a few weeks later, the position of President Roosevelt and of his advisors on foreign affairs was vindicated.

the President makes some or all of the appointments, and the kinds of conclusions desired can be forecast from the people appointed. A commission on civil rights is expected to recommend new action in behalf of civil rights, not to suggest that nothing more needs to be done. A commission on education is supposed to call for more action by government to aid education. A commission to study government organization is certain to produce a plan for reorganization.

Presidents and Patronage. The patronage powers of a President are a separate source of authority and prestige and can be used to secure acceptance of his policies or adoption of cooperative attitudes within his party. Patronage becomes a supplementary means of enforcing agreement by its association with unrelated questions. Patronage is a direct means of reinvigorating the party organization in every state. Appointment to office is a recognition of past services and an insurance of loyalty and enthusiasm in the future. The whole attitude of a party is set and maintained by the patronage operations of its national leadership in the executive branch. A person who is employed in this way has a vested interest in the continuation of the party in power. He is spurred into activity to develop support for the party, and those who depend upon him are similarly motivated. Such people are the most politically alert and active.

The presidential patronage power is a matter of direct concern to state and local organizations. The factional nature of party organization always creates a problem in the distribution of jobs. The national committee, which usually acts for the President in patronage matters, normally tries to harmonize the factions in each state in the making of appointments. Success is likely to be mediocre at best, but the attempts at amalgamation go on ceaselessly. Sometimes particularly troublesome situations are carried to the White House for final settlement. Always the contestants for office try to talk with the President or with his close patronage advisors, and a constant stream of visitors may pour through the executive offices urging the merits of one or another candidate for a given office. When a situation becomes too explosively dangerous, a President may avoid talking with any of the contestants or defer making a decision, hoping that passions will cool. Nevertheless both the appointments and the channels through which they are made affect the factional relationship in a state. If one man or one group is recognized as the patronage source, his opponents are likely to lose their positions in the party while his own faction moves into the ascendancy in his state and dominates the party. Sometimes the positions of national committeeman and committeewoman depend upon patronage distribution, and in all events these party officials are intimately concerned with federal appointments in the building of their own political positions.[33]

Power of Subordinate Executives. Members of a President's Cabinet are advisors to their chief, but they are also individual administrators of their respective departments. No President, even if he so desires, can oversee in any detail the Cabinet operations. The secretaries, therefore, have a latitude in policy-making and setting the pattern in their own area of government operations. They exercise some patronage powers, the amount depending upon the department. They have extensive opportunities to make friends or enemies for the administration, and by extension, for the party. Some of their activities are unknown to the President, either because he cannot be burdened with such minutiae or because it is better that he not know. To the maximum extent possible, the President must be protected from mistakes or embarrassments which arise. One standard method for shielding him is for a subordinate to assume the responsibility for some unpopular action. The theory of administration that authority, but not responsibility, can be delegated to subordinates does not always apply in politics. Presidents have from time to time shifted the responsibility for unpopular decisions and actions upon subordinates and sloughed off all personal responsibility.

Partisan Advantages in Governmental Activity. The radiating lines of power from executive departments can be used in endless ways, legal or illegal, ethical or unethical, to the advantage of the party. This state of affairs results from at least two causes. First, the growth of the powers of the federal government has necessitated the expansion of the jurisdiction and control of the departments over large segments of the economy. Billions of dollars and millions of lives are affected by legislation conferring powers upon administrators who are, inevitably, politically motivated. As more and more decisions of economic significance are made by government officials instead of by individuals or private groups, the dependence upon government grows and the possibility of political repercussion mounts.

Second, a consequence of the growing powers of the executive branch is the growth of what is formally called "administrative discretion." Congress is not able to administer, i.e., apply general rules to specific cases; Congress can at best fix the general rules and delegate powers to administrators so that they can apply the rules with flexibility. In the case of an activity as sensitive as collecting taxes, the Treasury Department has con-

---

[33] The downfall of Frank Hague in New Jersey became complete in 1952 when he was removed as Democratic national committeeman, but by 1951 his demise was foreshadowed when the Truman Administration refused to deal with the Hague faction, which controlled the state committee, and channeled patronage through the opposing faction headed by John V. Kenny, Mayor of Jersey City.——*New York Times,* February 8, 1951.

siderable latitude in determining the taxation status of the money a person receives. If a treasury ruling favors the "in" party, who is to say whether the ruling was a political abuse or the exercise of sound discretion. The "out" party will insist that it was abuse and the "ins" will insist it was not.[34] The "ins" have such advantages inescapably, because of the discretionary powers of executive officials.

Students of public administration have shown that as an organization, the executive branch is a sprawling, unkempt, and disjointed machine. It is too large and complex for Congress to investigate and control except piecemeal or for the President to supervise except in theory and in the most remote and indirect fashion. Just the same, the executive branch, politically, can be a unit. When the President and his party are attacked or are in danger, it is possible to pull this mechanism together for a supreme effort. Any laggards or dissenters can be weeded out by removal from office or at least can be forced into silence.

An outstanding example of this kind of operation occurred in 1951 after President Truman relieved General Douglas MacArthur of his various commands in the Far East because of insubordination. In the first flare of reaction, the country condemned the manner if not the reasons for the removal, and the General came home prepared to battle the Administration on the question of how the war in Korea should be fought. The field for this policy contest was provided by the Senate and House Committees on Armed Services, which held extended hearings into the causes of the removal and the conflicts which precipitated it. Spokesmen for the Administration appeared before the committee as the officials responsible for the Korean policy, armed with all of the pertinent data; their most important advantage was the uniformity of their testimony. All of their information was coordinated and their points of view mutually consistent. While General MacArthur's testimony had a powerful impact, there was no central authority to coordinate the presentation of the opposing case. The result was confusion when numerous anti-Administration witnesses began to differ among themselves in suggesting what should be done in the Far East. They were speaking as individuals, not as officials. There was no briefing in advance for them. The final effect was a major statement of the Administration's course of action and of its basic assumptions and evaluations as opposed to a series of views related in their dissatisfactions but fragmented in their specific recommendations. The triumph of the President was complete as far as the question of policy was concerned.

---

34 There was some question about the propriety of a drug manufacturer getting a tax ruling which saved him several hundred thousand dollars when it was also discovered that he paid $65,000 to an official of the Democratic National Committee to get the ruling and that $30,000 of the fee went into the Committee's Treasury to help re-elect President Truman in 1948.——*U.S. News and World Report,* August 14, 1953, p. 24.

President and Party Machinery. The range of presidential powers within the executive branch creates a piece of party machinery of the first importance and makes all of the state machinery subservient by its dependence. State political leaders are normally amenable to presidential requests and to the extent that these leaders influence elective officials, a President can bring pressure to bear upon the officials, especially members of Congress.[35] This situation is reinforced by the President's control of the national committee. By long usage it is established that the President in fact selects the chairman of the national committee, and then the committee goes through the motions of electing the man the President has chosen. A national committeeman or committeewoman actually offensive to the President would undoubtedly be removed from the committee in one way or another. Specifically, the President is the central source of patronage which is channeled through the national committee, and in his control of this party organ he can dominate the national convention. It can be stated as a rule that a President who wants a second nomination cannot be denied, although it may be argued with plausibility that Dwight D. Eisenhower could have defeated Harry S. Truman in the Democratic convention of 1948. An especially popular President may even have difficulty in avoiding a renomination, as was the case with Theodore Roosevelt in 1908.

The position of President is a most extraordinary development and constitutes a unique advantage for those who use it skillfully. It is an office and a power that is indivisible, and the historical decline in the office of Vice-President is both a result of being an official without real duties and another illustration of the political fact that there can only be one leader at a time.

Status of the Vice-President. In the protocol of Washington, D. C., the Vice-President as the second highest titular official of the United States ranks immediately after the President. In no other respect can the two offices be compared in their importance. The status of the Vice-President has been the occasion for complaints since the first occupant of the office, John Adams, observed: "My country has in its wisdom contrived for me the most insignificant office that ever the invention of man contrived or his imagination conceived." [36] John N. Garner, a more recent Vice-Presi-

---

[35] In the very close and bitter fight for Senate majority leader in 1937 President Roosevelt favored Senator Barkley over Senator Harrison. One more vote was needed to elect Barkley, and the strategists decided they could get Senator Dieterich of Illinois to change his vote because he was uncertain about his chances for re-election. Roosevelt spoke to Edward Kelly, Democratic leader in Cook County, who in turn persuaded Dieterich to vote for Barkley.——James A. Farley, *Jim Farley's Story* (New York: McGraw-Hill Book Company, Inc., 1948) p. 92. Barkley became majority leader, but Dieterich was not re-elected.

[36] Quoted in Stefan Lorant, *The Presidency* (New York: The Macmillan Company, 1952) p. 31.

dent, who held the office the same length of time as John Adams, was of the opinion that "the Vice-President is a figure of slight importance with a title of great impressiveness. . . . There can be great Judges, great Governors, great Senators, great Representatives and great Presidents. A Vice-President may move into the Presidency and be a great President. A great man may be Vice-President, but he can't be a great Vice-President, because the office in itself is unimportant." Yet he believed that the Vice-President should be as carefully selected as the President.[37]

The popular attitude toward the Vice-Presidency was crystallized in the classic story of two brothers starting out to seek their fortunes: one went to Alaska to prospect for gold and the other became Vice-President; neither was ever heard of again. The reform of the Vice-Presidency has produced proposals ranging from its abolition to its enhancement through statutory or substantive Constitutional duties. The political impossibility of dividing the presidential powers between two individuals is generally recognized, so proposals that the Vice-President share, independently, presidential prerogatives are no more than mental gymnastics. The Vice-Presidency is politically useful since the election of two national officials permits the balancing of the ticket and provides an office to be traded in the negotiations in presidential nominations. Furthermore, the existence of the office of Vice-President creates no danger or emergency, so any overt move to amend the Constitution loses the force that is required for so ambitious an undertaking.

Evolution of the Vice-Presidency. It was not until the Administration of Warren G. Harding that the Vice-President was invited to attend Cabinet meetings, and this practice itself lapsed when Coolidge's Vice-President, Charles G. Dawes, refused to continue it. Until the 1940's it could scarcely be said that the Vice-President was really part of the organization of the executive branch. He was technically in, but not really a part of it. His influence, if any, was the result of his previous position and popularity in Congress, and in the case of John N. Garner in 1939 and 1940 this influence was used at times in opposition to the President. Both Garner and Barkley, as Vice-Presidents, sat with the Cabinet and performed valuable assignments, but the first practical recognition of the office occurred when Congress made the Vice-President a statutory member of the National Security Council in 1947. The dangers of keeping the second official in ignorance of what was going on were thoroughly demonstrated when Harry Truman became President in 1945 and groped about for months in an effort to discover the facts and commitments involved in the nation's foreign affairs.

---

[37] Quoted in Bascom N. Timmons, *Garner of Texas* (New York: Harper & Brothers, 1948) p. 205.

The elevation of a Vice-President to the status of the second executive official occurred first during the Eisenhower Administration. Vice-President Richard M. Nixon performed many crucial political and legislative tasks, represented the President on official visits abroad and presided at Cabinet meetings by authorization of the President for the first time in history. These were startling departures from custom.[38]

The dual nature of the Vice-President's position, being in both the executive and legislative branches, has always been available for exploitation. It is quite possible that the office of Vice-President will continue to grow in which case there will be another dimension added to the national organization.

Selected Bibliography

Bone, Hugh A., *Party Committees and National Politics.* Seattle: University of Washington Press, 1958.

Dallinger, Frederick W., *Nominations for Elective Office in the United States.* Cambridge: Harvard University Press, 1897. Harvard Historical Studies, Vol. 4.

Kleeberg, Gordon S. P., *Formation of the Republican Party as a National Political Organization.* New York: Moods Publishing Company, 1911.

Macy, Jesse, *Party Organization and Machinery.* London: T. Fisher Unwin, 1905.

Ostrogorski, M., *Democracy and the Party System in the United States.* New York: The Macmillan Company, 1910.

Stanwood, Edward, *A History of the Presidency from 1788 to 1897.* Boston: Houghton Mifflin Company, 1898.

Stimpson, George, *A Book about American Politics.* New York: Harper & Brothers, 1952.

---

[38] Joseph F. Menez, "The Vice Presidency in the United States," *Queen's Quarterly,* Vol. 65 (Spring, 1958) pp. 22-34. Arthur Krock in the *New York Times,* March 16, 1958, discusses some of the historical background of the office.

CHAPTER NINE

The Formal Operations of National Conventions

A national convention is the supreme authority of a political party. The delegates, or a majority of them, can declare the party's official position on issues affecting public policy and can make rules governing all aspects of the party's national organization and operations. This power of conventions is seldom appreciated because of the far more dramatic and overpowering purpose of nominating candidates for the Presidency. Among party members, both leaders and followers, the struggle for factional supremacy through nominations is the all-compelling motive for attending and fighting for control of conventions; so it is correct to say that the plenary role of conventions is an incident to and a means to the end of making nominations.

In order to proceed toward the objective of nominating a presidential candidate, certain preliminary preparations and determinations are required. By the time the first national conventions were held in the 1830's convention procedure had become generally established in the states, and it was adopted outright in the national gatherings. Because it had already been tested, it has changed very little through the years; but to the uninformed outsider the sequence and the events themselves are a series of meaningless mumbo jumbo completely devoid of common sense. The truth is that the basic process and plan of convention operations are perfectly logical.

Prior Arrangements. Inasmuch as each convention adjourns *sine die,* because it is impossible to fix the day for the beginning of the next convention four years hence, the time and place of a convention are determined by the party's national committee. The composition of a convention is the next question; each convention can determine who shall sit in the convention and what methods are to be used in computing the representation from the states and territories in the next succeeding convention. Therefore, the national committee includes in the call for each convention the apportionment of delegates as well as the time and place of meeting. When the convention convenes, three distinct matters must be taken care of before candidates can be nominated.

Essentials of Convention Management. First, the right of each delegate and alternate to participate must be determined, so a credential committee is appointed; but the convention meets before the members of this committee are selected, so the temporary roll of the convention is previously approved by the national committee. Second, a staff of officials must be elected to operate the convention processes; this function is called *organization,* being temporarily supplied by the national committee until the committee on permanent organization can be selected by the delegates. Third, rules to govern the procedure are approved temporarily by the delegates and then permanently a day or two later on the basis of the report of the committee on rules and order of business. On each of these three committees, each state and territory has one member, and the work of these three committees completes the formal organization of the convention so that it can move on to accomplish its purposes.

Essentials of Convention Procedure. Certain practices are prescribed by the rules of a convention to make its work more orderly and uniform. Each state delegation organizes itself by electing a chairman, a vice-chairman, and a secretary and any other officers it wishes to have. All of the delegates from the same state are seated together on the rows of chairs which are placed closely together on the convention floor. Even when the delegation is too small to fill a whole row, it occupies chairs from the aisle inward. Every delegation chairman is seated on the aisle, with a microphone placed beside his chair to permit him to announce the vote of the state on each roll call. Also beside his chair is the delegation's standard, a placard with the name of the state affixed to a pole which is fitted into a groove in the floor from which it can be removed and carried about during demonstrations.

All decisions in national conventions, including the nominations, are made by a majority of the delegates voting on the question. Many decisions are made by voice vote, but more controversial issues are settled by a roll call. This method of voting is to call each state in alphabetical order with the territories and Washington, D. C., called in alphabetical order after the states; the Democrats in 1952 altered this system by calling all of the states and territories together in alphabetical order. When the name of a state is called, the chairman of its delegation arises and announces the vote in the microphone. Any delegate can challenge the accuracy of the vote of his own state as announced by his delegation chairman and request that the delegation be polled, whereupon the secretary of the convention calls the name of each delegate from that state and the delegate announces his vote. Because of the time consumed in a roll call, voice votes are taken unless a roll call is demanded. Such a demand can be made by a majority of delegates of any six states in Republican conventions and by one fifth of all the delegates present if seconded by one fifth in Democratic conventions. The voting for candidates for President and Vice-President is always by roll call unless the delegates vote to suspend the rules and nominate by acclamation.

Elaboration of the Procedure. Aside from these arrangements and procedures and from the making of nominations, everything else that is done in a convention is extraneous or designed to consume time or has a political justification. First, the work of a fourth committee, that on platform and resolutions, has a place coordinate with the other three committees because of general agreement that the party should declare its principles and its positions on the issues of the day. Second, the most obvious occurrence at conventions is the endless succession of speeches beginning with the keynote and running to the time of final adjournment. The purpose of these speeches is to impress the general public and to maintain the enthusiasm of the delegates; among professional politicians, speeches are the supreme means for a person to bring himself to the attention of the party and the public and to build himself up for whatever objectives he has in mind. Incidentally, speeches serve the purpose of stimulating party spirit and of filling in those periods of time when no other business is ready for convention consideration; the alternative would be to adjourn the convention for a day or longer, and no one involved in convention operations would be likely to favor such a procedure, for psychological reasons. Third, all of the rigid protocol of speeches, demonstrations, and noise incident to the presentation of names of nominees is partly the result of meeting competition and is designed for its effects upon delegates and as means of emotional persuasion. Finally, much of this extraneous procedure is hallowed by tradition and is carried out because it is the customary thing to do.

With this general description of the background facts, it is possible to follow more intelligently each major step from the call to the acceptance speeches and the adjournment *sine die.*

PRECONVENTION PROCEDURES

Preparations for the Call. Any official action undertaken by a national committee must be authorized by the national convention which elected it. The power of the national committee to issue the call for a convention is explicitly included in the permanent rules adopted by each party's convention every four years. The rules prescribe that the call be issued at least four months before the convening of the conventions; traditionally, it has been issued in December or January preceding the convention. In 1952 the Democratic call was dated January 5 and the Republican call, January 18. The date for the convention to begin is one of the first decisions. The practice is for the conventions to meet a week apart in the months of June or July. From 1888 to 1952 the Republicans always held their convention first. In 1956 they upset tradition by deciding to meet in August, in order to reduce the time of the postconvention campaign and for the first time in sixty-eight years to meet after the Democrats instead of before.

The main issue to be resolved before the issuance of the call is the *selection* by the national committee *of the city* in which the convention is to meet. So many factors enter into consideration and the requirements are so circumscribed that the choice is at once complicated and yet limited to a very few metropolitan areas. To sift out the applications and to consider the standard for selection, a special site committee is usually appointed by the national committee. The city must be large enough to accommodate the large crowd and the demands for special facilities. A very special facility since 1952 is television. While the city itself is not chosen on this basis, the convention hall may be. The Chicago International Amphitheater was selected in 1952 over the Stadium because of the greater adaptability of the former to the new medium.

Consideration of central location for the convenience of travel is becoming less important because of airline travel and the growing political claims of the West Coast.[1] The Democrats' innovation in going to San Francisco in 1920 was an isolated case for thirty-six years. Then, in 1956, the Republicans chose San Francisco and in 1960 the Democrats chose Los Angeles.

Financial considerations are of major importance in the selection of a city. Money used to defray convention expenses and for the campaign itself is raised among businessmen in the cities bidding for the conventions. Usually hotel and restaurant businesses provide the bulk of these offers, which amount to several hundred thousand dollars. Other things being equal, the city offering the most money and the best general arrangements gets the conventions.[2]

These three factors closely limit the number of cities that compete and that are chosen, but *political calculations* present further restrictions. There is no point in taking a convention to a state that the party nearly always carries or loses. The theory, rightly or wrongly, is that the party's chances are enhanced in the city and state where the party holds its convention. Cities in doubtful, two-party states, with twenty-five or more electoral

---

[1] The shift in the center of population across the continent can almost be followed in the selection of national-convention cities. Every Democratic convention from 1832 to 1852 was held in Baltimore, but the only ones held there afterward were in 1860, 1872, and 1912. The Republicans used Baltimore only in 1864. Chicago is by far the most popular city, having been used nine times by the Democrats and fourteen times by the Republicans through 1960.

[2] In 1952 the Chicago Convention Bureau reported that $9,418,160 was spent during the two conventions; 22,819 people went to Chicago and occupied 12,010 hotel rooms. The average spent during the Republican Convention was $218.98; the average during the longer Democratic Convention was $250.88.——*New York Times,* October 1, 1952. Both Chicago and Philadelphia offered the Republicans $250,000 for the convention in 1952.——*Ibid.,* May 12, 1951.

votes, are almost invariably chosen. Holding the Democratic convention in Houston, Texas, in 1928 would appear to contradict this rule, but in 1928 the Democrats feared the Southern reaction to the candidacy of Alfred E. Smith, who was the only serious contender; the fears were borne out when Smith lost Texas and several other Southern states. Because of these limitations, the national committees look to the principal cities in New York, Pennsylvania, Ohio, and Illinois.

Joint Arrangements. The convention undertaking has grown to such proportions that the Republican and Democratic committees and national chairmen sometimes work together. The selection of the city is a subject for joint discussion, for a city will usually want both conventions and will offer the same amount of money to each party. Money and effort in decorations and other preparations can be saved if both use the same hall, as they have, in recent years, in 1932, 1944, 1948, and 1952. Both national committees announced their selection of Chicago in May 1951, for the 1952 conventions.[3] Cooperation was not followed for the 1956 conventions, the two parties choosing different cities.

Instructions and Assignments. The national committee prepares instructions to govern certain aspects of delegates' behavior, e.g., the rostrum is to be kept as free as possible and those having business there should complete it as rapidly as possible and return to their seats. The introduction of television presented additional difficulties regarding both delegates and spectators, who were frequently reminded that they might be picked up by the camera and should conduct themselves with decorum. The minutiae of preparations after the city is selected can only be suggested. To illustrate, the committee on arrangements makes assignments of hotel space. Each state delegation is housed in one hotel, as a rule, although the rooms need not be located on the same floor. Visitors who wish to make hotel reservations are usually referred by the hotels to the arrangements committee for an assignment of a room. The committee also arranges the seating of delegates and alternates in the convention hall.

Apportionment and Accrediting of Delegates. These activities seldom make news, but they are the mountain of details behind the simple designation in a national committee's call specifying the hour, date, city, and location of the hall of the forthcoming convention. The other purpose of the call is to announce the apportionment of delegates for each state, the District of Columbia, and the territories (which were granted representation in both parties' conventions in 1896). No selection of delegates is supposed to be made before this official authorization appears.

---

3 *Ibid.,* March 18, 1951; Associated Press dispatch dated June 28, 1952.

The nature of the problem of apportionment can be appreciated by a backward glance at the former practices of national conventions. The original rule was that each state could cast as many votes in the convention as it had electoral votes, but the arrangements for accrediting delegates were strictly informal. In the 1830's and 1840's because of the distance to be traveled from the westernmost states to the convention city, some of these states were underrepresented or unrepresented entirely, but states near the city sometimes sent as many delegates as wanted to go. The outstanding illustration of this contrast is found in the Democratic convention in 1835 at Baltimore. No delegates at all were sent from Illinois, Tennessee, Alabama, or South Carolina. When a citizen from Tennessee appeared during the sessions and announced himself in favor of Van Buren, he was permitted to cast that state's fifteen votes. At the Maryland state convention that year it was decided to send all of the members as delegates, with the result that Maryland contributed 181 out of the total of 626 delegates. Maryland plus Virginia, New Jersey, and Pennsylvania sent 422, well over half of the total.[4]

These kinds of irregular procedures were within the rules of the conventions up until 1852 because the states' maximum votes were specified but not the number of delegates they could send. When there were more delegates from a state than it was entitled to in full votes, the individual delegates either cast fractions of a vote or collectively cast the full state vote. In the latter case, especially when the number of delegates was not an even multiple of the number of votes to be cast, the use of the unit rule certainly simplified matters.[5] After 1852 the Democrats corrected this situation by requiring each state to send twice as many delegates as the state had electoral votes, giving each delegate one half of a vote. Conventions of the Republican Party began using the computation of two convention votes for each electoral vote and of one vote to be cast by each delegate. In 1872 the Democrats finally adopted the rule that a state was entitled to two convention votes for each electoral vote.[6]

The Republicans have a problem because of their lack of genuine strength in the South. The original philosophy of representation in conventions was that states should have votes in relation to their population to the extent it is reflected in electoral votes. The alternative philosophy is that representation should be proportioned to party strength in each state as determined by voters' declaration of party membership or by the party's voting strength. There are many mechanical difficulties in this latter method, and it undoubtedly would not be exact under any circumstances,

---

[4] Edward Stanwood, *A History of the Presidency from 1788-1897* (New York: Houghton Mifflin Company, 1898) pp. 181-182; Frederick W. Dallinger, *Nominations for Elective Office in the United States* (Cambridge: Harvard University Press, 1897) p. 39, note 118.

[5] Stanwood, *op. cit.*, p. 173.

[6] Dallinger, *op. cit.*, p. 44.

but understandably it became popular with some Republicans. Party leaders in Republican states began objecting to the large delegations from the South. Using the population basis for representation, a state like Georgia, with only a handful of Republicans, might have more votes in a Republican convention that a state like Iowa which the Party dominated. Using party strength as the basis for representation, the Southern states would be proportionately reduced in relation to the Republican states of the North.

The greatest impetus for change was produced by the Republican Convention of 1912, when President Taft was renominated by the votes from Southern states and was opposed by many delegates from strongly Republican states.[7] The reason for this situation is the fact that Southern Republican leaders who are appointed to federal office have a vested interest in the continuation of the President who appointed them. They are the only active and influential Republicans in these states, so they in effect choose the delegates to the conventions. President Taft was merely doing in 1912 what Republican Presidents before and since have done, but the revolt leading to a split in the Party in 1912 introduced a new factor. No actual change was made until 1924, but then and subsequently the changes have more and more enforced the objective of relating convention strength of a state to its Republican strength.

Present Apportionment. The existing Republican rules provide that every state is entitled to four delegates at large, each with one full vote, for the state's two United States senators. This is the only part of Republican apportionment which ignores the factor of party strength. If a state elects a member of the House of Representatives at large, it chooses two more delegates at large who have one vote each. Then, as a bonus for each state, it is entitled to an additional six delegates at large each with a full vote, under any one of the following circumstances: first, if the Republican candidate for President received the state's electoral votes at the last presidential election; second, if the last election for either governor or United States senator resulted in the election of the Republican candidate. From the congressional districts of a state, one Republican delegate is to be elected if in the last presidential election or in the last congressional election the Republican candidates received 2,000 votes but less than 10,000; if, in either case, the Republican vote is 10,000 or more, another delegate is to be elected. All district delegates have a full vote each. This apportionment is worked out by the Republican National Committee and is included in its call, so that each state is officially informed how many delegates are assigned to it.

---

[7] The usual presentation of this 1912 struggle is one of unmitigated evil triumphing over virtue. For a different presentation, see R. M. La Follette, *Autobiography* (Madison: Robert M. La Follette Company, 1913, 5th ed.) pp. 646-652, 659 ff.

The Democrats, in their conventions from 1944 to 1956, allotted a bonus of four at-large votes to a state casting its electoral votes for the Democratic presidential candidate at the previous presidential election. In 1959, however, the Democratic National Committee scrapped this system and adopted an entirely new method of computing apportionment.

Each state has $2\frac{1}{2}$ convention votes for each member of Congress, and in case the number thus computed results in a fraction of one-half vote, the state is given an additional one-half vote to bring its total to a whole number. This additional one-half vote is classed as an at-large vote. The Democrats continue a practice begun in 1952, that no state is to have fewer votes in a convention than it had in the previous convention. Votes added to a state in order to bring it to the total it had four years before are classed as at-large votes. Each state may elect as many delegates as it has votes or may elect twice as many delegates with one-half vote each.

A special feature of the Democrats' 1960 apportionment was the designation of all members of the National Committee as delegates from their respective state or territory and from the District of Columbia, with one-half vote each. The effect is to add one full vote to each delegation over and above all of the other apportionment provisions. Furthermore, the members of the National Committee designate their own alternates to the chairman of their respective delegations, whereas all other alternates are elected on the basis of one for each full vote.

Delegates from the territories and from the District of Columbia are arbitrarily fixed in both parties' rules. The Republicans now allow six for the District of Columbia, three for Puerto Rico, and one for the Virgin Islands. For those territories electing a Republican delegate to Congress there is a bonus of four delegates. The Democrats allow eight votes for the District of Columbia, six for Puerto Rico, and three each for the Virgin Islands and the Canal Zone.

METHODS OF DELEGATE SELECTION

In addition to apportioning delegates, the parties' rules also specify three methods for electing delegates: by party committee, by party convention, by direct election by the party voters. Originally, in the 1830's, various methods were used: legislatures or legislative caucus, mass meetings, and conventions.[8] The process whereby the convention took upon itself the responsibility for designating the methods was slow and difficult because of the refusal of party members to be bound by such rules. In reality, the naming of these methods is not restrictive, because they are the only ones in use anyway and because neither the national convention nor the national committee dictates which method is to be used in any state. This deter-

---

[8] See Stanwood, *op. cit.*, pp. 172-173, and Dallinger, *op. cit.*, p. 37, note 112, and pp. 43-44.

mination in each state is made either by party rules or by the state legislature. Because the number of delegates has been related to the electoral
votes, the selection of delegates has long been considered to be a function
for both the state as a whole and for each separate congressional district.
A distinction is made in most states in selecting the two groups of delegates
in each party.

Party Committees. Some states either have no statutory requirements
or give the parties a choice of methods in selecting delegates.[9] In four
states, either by custom or by statutory provision, delegates are selected by
the parties' state committees. In *Arkansas,* the law requires this method,
although the Republicans ignore it and use conventions. In *Georgia* and
Louisiana by custom and by law, respectively, the state committee can
decide what method to use. The Democrats in Georgia use the state committee and in Louisiana alternate between the committee and conventions.
In both states the Republicans traditionally use conventions, although the
small number of Republicans would be more accurately designated
"cliques" than "conventions." In *Arizona* the state committees of both
parties choose the delegates, although the size of the committee is large
and is called a convention when meeting for this purpose.

Party Conventions. In all but fifteen of the remaining states, and in
all of the territories, delegates are chosen at conventions which are authorized either by party rule or by statutory requirement. There are three ways
of proceeding with this method. (1) All of the delegates, both at large and
from districts, are chosen at a state convention composed of county or town
delegates. The convention designates which delegates are at large and
which are district delegates, but they are all elected by the same convention representing the whole state. The district delegates will be residents
of their respective districts, and the delegates at large will be party leaders
for whom no place is found on the district slates or leaders like national
committeemen and women, United States senators, and governors, who
almost always are delegates at large. (2) Conventions are held in each congressional district, where the district delegates are chosen; then a state convention is held to choose the delegates at large. (3) A variation of the previous method is to hold a state convention to choose the delegates at large;
the delegates to the state convention, after they arrive in the capital, caucus
by congressional districts to choose their district delegates. These caucuses
are usually held the night before the state convention meets.

Direct Election. All of the delegates in eleven states are directly elected
by party voters at elections.[10] All of the district delegates are elected in Il-

---

[9] These states are Alabama, Georgia, Kentucky, Louisiana, North Carolina, Oklahoma,
Rhode Island, South Carolina, Tennessee, Virginia, and Washington.

[10] California, Florida, Massachusetts, Nebraska, New Hampshire, New Jersey, Ohio,
Oregon, South Dakota, West Virginia, and Wisconsin.

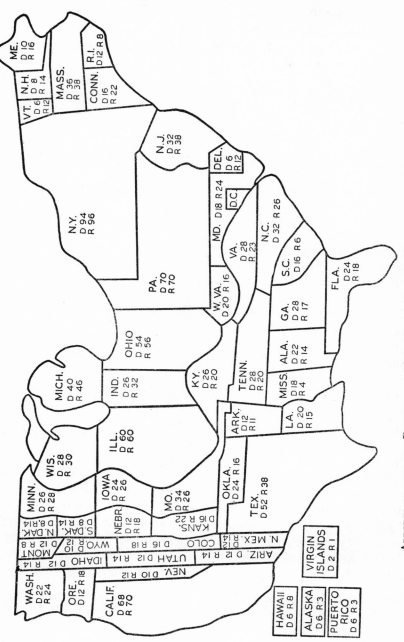

APPORTIONMENT OF DELEGATES, 1952 NATIONAL CONVENTIONS. In this distorted map the area assigned to each state is proportionate to the number of its delegates.

linois, New York, and Pennsylvania. The delegates at large are chosen at a state convention in Illinois and by state committees in New York and Pennsylvania. Under the laws of Alabama, a party casting less than 20% of the total state vote is not permitted to choose its national delegates by direct election. The Republican Party, since it seldom qualifies to use this method, uses conventions instead. A party casting 20% or more of the vote has the option (which it need not exercise) of directly electing its delegates. The Democratic Party by custom does choose its delegates this way both at large and by districts. In states electing all delegates, two general methods are used. In California, Massachusetts, Nebraska, New Hampshire, New Jersey, and South Dakota, all of the delegates are elected at large by the voters. In Alabama, Florida, Ohio, Oregon, West Virginia, and Wisconsin, the voters in each congressional district vote only for candidates for delegate from their district and for candidates for delegate at large.

PRESIDENTIAL PREFERENCE PRIMARY

It is possible in eighteen states for a voter to express to some extent his preference for his own party's candidates for the presidential nomination. This opportunity is a presidential preference primary and may be provided in either one of two forms: In some states the names of presidential candidates are listed on the ballot separately from delegate candidates; in other states the delegate candidates run pledged to a specific presidential candidate. In all of these states except Alaska, Florida, Illinois, New York, Oregon, and Pennsylvania, a candidate for the presidential nomination cannot be forced to have his name entered in a presidential preference primary against his wishes, although in New Hampshire and New Jersey, his consent may be tacit, not overt. The other ten states require a candidate for President to certify in writing his willingness to have his name presented to the voters.

Presumably, the purpose of voters' expressing a preference among their party's candidates for the presidential nomination is to bind the delegates representing these voters to vote in the national convention for the preferred candidate. Such commitment is not always required by the states' laws, and when it is required, it has only moral sanction. There is no way to enforce it legally. The best protection for a presidential candidate is to have delegates who genuinely support him and are willing to stand by him.

Without Direct Election of Delegates. Despite the selection of delegates by committees and conventions in *Arkansas,* if a state committee is petitioned by a presidential candidate of its party, the party holds a preference primary and its delegates are required to vote as a unit in the national convention for the candidate the Arkansas voters of that party prefer until the candidate withdraws or until two thirds of the delegates themselves agree to stop supporting him. No presidential primary has yet been held under this law.

Maryland delegates are elected at state conventions made up of county delegates. If a party holds no presidential preference primary, the convention can instruct the delegates whom to support or send them uninstructed. If a party holds a preference primary, the candidate preferred by the voters in each county is supported by the delegates from that county in the state convention; however, the convention must continue to vote until one candidate gets a majority, and at the national convention the Maryland delegates are bound as a unit to vote for him as long as there is any possibility of his being nominated. Actually, this instruction means the delegates are bound only on the first ballot.

In *Indiana* district delegates are chosen at district conventions and delegates at large at the state convention. However, a presidential preference primary is provided for by statute. Delegates are required to vote only on the first ballot in national conventions for the winner of their party preference primary—district delegates voting for the winner in their respective districts, and delegates at large for the state-wide winner.

In *Alaska* all delegates are chosen at state conventions, but the voters can vote for their preference for the presidential nomination in their respective parties either by writing in a name or by voting for one of the names printed on the ballot. A presidential candidate can file a declaration of candidacy and pay a filing fee, or 200 of his party supporters can file a petition in lieu of his declaration and pay the filing fee to get his name on the ballot.

With the Direct Election of Delegates. Among the states combining a preference vote with the direct election of delegates, procedures vary widely. At one extreme, in *California* all candidates for delegate must be pledged to a presidential candidate and must be grouped together accordingly, for only the names of presidential candidates appear on the ballot and a cross put by the name of a candidate constitutes a vote for all of his delegates.

The presidential candidates on the ballot in *Ohio* are those who give their written consent and authorize delegate candidates to run pledged to them. The candidates for delegate may file a pledge to support the winner of the preferential voting, but they are required to indicate their first and second choices for President on the ballot, although they do not have to run as a complete slate for a candidate. This system creates the possible situation of delegates indicating choices but not being committed to vote for them.

In *Wisconsin* the election of delegates is subordinated to the preference primary, although delegate candidates, individually or in groups, may run without a preference and may include a five-word statement on the ballot; but this statement cannot indicate a preference among the presidential candidates. The procedure of genuine consequence is taken by a presidential candidate. He can certify a list of his delegates superseding any other delegates trying to run under his name. If delegate candidates take the initiative and file papers to appear on the ballot pledged to a presidential candidate, they must obtain his consent. There can be no more delegate candidates grouped for a presidential candidate than the total number of delegates to be elected.

Election of Delegates To National Convention
REPUBLICAN PARTY

To vote for an entire slate of delegates at large and district delegates committed to the same presidential candidate, make a cross or other mark in the circle (O) at the head of the column under the name of the presidential candidate.

For Delegates At Large Republican National Convention

VOTE IN ONE COLUMN ONLY

EARL WARREN Candidate for President	GRANT A. RITTER Candidate for President	ROBERT A. TAFT Candidate for President	HAROLD E. STASSEN Candidate for President.	PERRY J. STEARNS Candidate for President
O	O	O	O	O
Delegates-at-Large	Delegates-at-Large	Delegates-at-Large	Delegates-at-Large	Delegates-at-Large
RALPH M. IMMELL	JANE GRACE BARKLEY	THOMAS E. COLEMAN	HIERON N. BIWER	WILLIAM B. BOLLES
PHILIP F. LaFOLLETTE	WILLIAM J. CAMPBELL	HARVEY V. HIGLEY	LOYAL E. EDDY	WILLIAM J. HOLICK
MARY B. LOVEJOY	ROBERT A. CHADWICK, JR.	HARLAN W. KELLEY	RAYMOND G. FREDRICKSON	GORDON E. JOHNSON
HERBERT L. MOUNT	JOHN B. CHAPPLE	DOROTHY KOHLER	LEO H. HANSEN	WILLIAM H. MacARTHUR
JOHN F. O'MELIA	JAMES A. DAUM	MELVIN B. LAIRD	ALICE JOHNSON	EVERETT M. NEWCOMB
CARL B. RIX	HERBERT A. EGGIE	ROBERT L. PIERCE	CHESTER S. McDONALD	PATRICK B. O'MALLEY
LEONARD F. SCHMITT	MADGE R. GOODLAND	CYRUS L. PHILIPP	THEODORE C. RADDE	WILLIAM C. RICHARDSON
ROY H. SENGSTOCK	MARSHALL C. GRAFF	ORA R. RICE	BETTY SHERRY	FREDERICK J. SCHWEITZER
JULIUS SPEARBRAKER	ANTHONY J. GRUSZKA	GRACE E. SYMONS	EDWARD J. SHERWOOD	CHARLES O. THIENHAUS
FRED R. ZIMMERMAN	LOUIS S. POLEWCZYNSKI	VERNON W. THOMSON	ARTHUR SORENSEN	GEORGE O. TOEPFER

Congressional District Delegates to Republican National Convention

District Delegates	District Delegates	District Delegates	District Delegates	District Delegates
AUSTIN J. BAIRD	ROY F. FARRAND	FRANK E. PANZER	HELEN EBY	ROBERT DEWA
FRED RISSER	RALPH HINCHLIFF	CARL TAYLOR	HOMER WILLIAMS	OPAL B. JUDY

The Wisconsin ballot lists delegate candidates under the names of the following candidates for the Republican Presidential nomination: Gov. Earl Warren of California; Grant A. Ritter, who is running for General of the Army Douglas MacArthur; Senator Robert A. Taft of Ohio; former Gov. Harold E. Stassen of Minnesota, and Perry J. Stearns, a perennial candidate in the state. An "X" in the circle under the candidate's name is a vote for his slate of delegates to the Republican National Convention. Because there are ten Congressional districts in the state, with two delegate candidates in each district in addition to those running at large, there are therefore ten different ballots. Unlike the system in some states, however, write-ins are not permitted on any ballots.

EXAMPLE OF PRESIDENTIAL PRIMARY BALLOT: WISCONSIN, 1952

In *Florida* any party receiving more than 10% of the total vote cast for governor at the last previous gubernatorial election or having 10% of the total registered vote must choose its delegates by direct election. Only organized slates with a chairman listed at the top of the slate can be entered in the election. While the voters elect delegates at large separately from district delegates, the slates need not be complete with candidates for delegates in every congressional district; but there must be candidates for delegates in at least half of the districts. Each slate must be evenly divided

SAMPLE BALLOT

(This number shall be torn off by
Inspector and handed to the voter)

No. 12345

MARK CROSSES (+) ON BALLOT ONLY WITH RUBBER STAMP;
NEVER WITH PEN OR PENCIL

(ABSENTEE BALLOTS MAY BE MARKED WITH PEN AND INK OR PENCIL)

(Fold ballot to this perforated line, leaving top margin exposed)

5

No. 12345   COUNTY OF SAN MATEO

TUESDAY, JUNE 5, 1956

OFFICIAL PRESIDENTIAL PRIMARY ELECTION BALLOT
DEMOCRATIC PARTY

To vote for the group of candidates preferring a person whose name appears on the ballot, stamp a cross (+) in the square in the column headed by the name of the person preferred.

For Delegates to National Convention. Vote for one group only.	
Candidates Preferring ADLAI E. STEVENSON	Candidates Preferring ESTES KEFAUVER
☐	☐
A cross (+) stamped in this square shall be counted as a vote for all candidates preferring Adlai E. Stevenson.	A cross (+) stamped in this square shall be counted as a vote for all candidates preferring Estes Kefauver.

EXAMPLE OF DEMOCRATIC PRESIDENTIAL PRIMARY BALLOT:
CALIFORNIA, 1956

SAMPLE BALLOT

(This number shall be torn off by
Inspector and handed to the voter)

No. 12345

MARK CROSSES (+) ON BALLOT ONLY WITH RUBBER STAMP;
NEVER WITH PEN OR PENCIL

(ABSENTEE BALLOTS MAY BE MARKED WITH PEN AND INK OR PENCIL)

(Fold ballot to this perforated line, leaving top margin exposed)

2

No. 12345   COUNTY OF SAN MATEO

TUESDAY, JUNE 5, 1956

OFFICIAL PRESIDENTIAL PRIMARY ELECTION BALLOT
REPUBLICAN PARTY

To vote for the group of candidates preferring a person whose name appears on the ballot, stamp a cross (+) in the square in the column headed by the name of the person preferred.

For Delegates to National Convention. Vote for one group only.
Candidates Preferring DWIGHT D. EISENHOWER
☐
A cross (+) stamped in this square shall be counted as a vote for all candidates preferring Dwight D. Eisenhower.

EXAMPLE OF REPUBLICAN PRESIDENTIAL PRIMARY BALLOT:
CALIFORNIA, 1956

between men and women. Uninstructed (no-preference) slates may be entered. If more than one slate is entered for a presidential candidate, he may select the slate he wishes; otherwise, the first slate to qualify will run under his name. The Florida law, following from specifications drawn up by academicians, is referred to as a "model." [11]

In the remaining states the presidential preference primary is an entirely separate process from the election of delegates. In *Illinois* the result of the preference voting is only advisory to the district delegates, the only ones directly elected. In *Nebraska* and *West Virginia* there are no legal instructions to the delegates to support the preference of the voters, who in Nebraska, can indicate their first and second choices for presidential candidates or may write in their choices. In *West Virginia,* presidential candidates must pay a $1000 filing fee to enter the preference primary. In both states, delegate candidates' names appear on the ballot without indication of preferences. In *Oregon* the voter may write in his preference or vote for one of the presidential candidates on the ballot, and the delegate candidates, if they file "by declaration," are bound to use their best efforts on behalf of the presidential candidate who is the preference of the voters of their party. Delegate candidates who file "by petition" can run unpledged and are not bound to the candidate who is the preference of the voters. Generally, the delegates promise to abide by the popular choice and do not state their own preferences.

In *Pennsylvania* a candidate for district delegate may, if he chooses, file a "Delegate's Statement" binding himself to support the presidential candidate who wins the preference primary. *New Hampshire,* while keeping the elections separate, permits candidates for delegate to pledge themselves to a presidential candidate and have the pledge printed on the ballot. The voter can write in the name of his preference if the name is not on the ballot. In *New Jersey* the delegate candidates may be grouped together and may have the name of the presidential candidate they favor opposite their individual names or opposite a group of names; for this purpose the presidential candidate must endorse the petitions. He need not specifically consent to have his name entered in the separate preference primary, but if his name is entered in opposition to his wishes, he may withdraw it. The candidates for delegate are obligated, if elected, to support the candidate of their own stated preference (not the preference of the voters in the separate presidential primary) until he releases them or until he gets less than 10% of the convention vote. If delegate candidates do not favor a candidate, they may have a five-word statement of principles printed beneath their names on the ballot.

---

[11] Manning J. Dauer, et al., "Toward a Model State Presidential Primary Law," *American Political Science Review,* Vol. 50 (1956) pp. 138-153. Paul T. David, *Specifications for a Model State Presidential Primary Law* (Washington, D. C.: The Brookings Institution, 1956) Reprint No. 11.

OFFICIAL PRESIDENTIAL PREFERENCE PRIMARY BALLOT	OFFICIAL PRESIDENTIAL PREFERENCE PRIMARY BALLOT
Place an (X) in the circle at the top of the column of the group of delegates for whom you wish to vote.	Place an (X) in the circle at the top of the column of the group of delegates for whom you wish to vote.

CANDIDATES PREFERRING ADLAI E. STEVENSON for President	CANDIDATES PREFERRING ESTES KEFAUVER for President

DELEGATES-AT-LARGE	DELEGATES-AT-LARGE
DOYLE E. CARLTON, Organizing Chairman	WALTER P. FULLER, Organizing Chairman
MILLARD F. CALDWELL	ED R. BENTLEY
DANTE B. FASCELL	H. C. BRAMELL
R. B. GAUTIER, JR.	WILLIAM M. BERSON
BILL LANTAFF	CECIL B. CARROLL
W. TURNER DAVIS	E. P. DANESE
ALFRED A. McKETHAN	JAMES M. GREENE
VOLIE A. WILLIAMS, JR.	JOHN F. LANAHAN
IRVING KLEPPER	G. B. (GABBY) KNOWLES, SR.
FRANCIS ANTHONY BENEDETTO	L. W. KELLOWAY
PAUL E. RAYMOND	W. RALEIGH PETTEWAY
IRVING CYPEN	ANGUS SUMNER
ROSE MARIE FLOYD	SADIE C. BETTS
MRS. J. D. ALDERMAN	DOROTHY E. CALVERT
FRANCES DAVIS GORDON	MARIE S. CHAPPELL
PHYLLIS POLLAK	ELMINA CREWS
MRS. F. ELGIN BAYLESS	FRANCES F. DALLAS
LILLIAN L. LOPEZ	NONA B. GOODE
MRS. C. J. (PAT) HARDEE, JR.	LUCILLE J. KING
MRS. JOHN M. PHILLIPS	VIRGINIA FOLEY MILLER
MRS. JOHN A. MADIGAN, JR.	ESTELLE MURER
MRS. FRANK X. CARROLL, JR.	PEGGIE GUY RODRIGUEZ
RUBY McCHESNEY	THELMA L. SHEFFIELD
MRS. MILDRED TAYLOR FELLER	MARTHA VAN PETTEN

DISTRICT DELEGATES _____Congressional District	DISTRICT DELEGATES _____Congressional District

SAMPLE PRESIDENTIAL PRIMARY BALLOT: FLORIDA 1956

In *Massachusetts* and *South Dakota* there is no separate presidential preference primary, but the delegate candidates may indicate on the ballot their preference among possible presidential candidates. In *South Dakota* the voters are required to vote for a complete slate of delegates, who collectively may favor a presidential candidate or may be uncommitted.

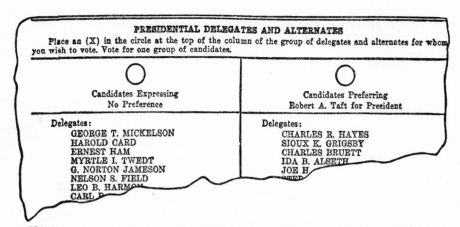

This is a cutout of part of the primary ballot to be used in the South Dakota primary election Tuesday. It shows that Taft supporters need only mark an "X" in the circle above his name, while Eisenhower voters must know beforehand that an "X" in the circle above "Candidates Expressing No Preference" is a vote for their Presidential candidate. If the voter writes in General Eisenhower's name the ballot is invalidated.

EXAMPLE OF PRESIDENTIAL PRIMARY BALLOT:
SOUTH DAKOTA, 1952

In *New York,* where the regular direct primary is held in the fall, the election of delegates takes place in the spring. The result is a smaller turnout of voters in the spring and few contests for delegate on the ballot. Candidates for delegate may state publicly which presidential candidate they favor, but they are not committed.

In each state, one alternate is chosen for each full vote, and the method of selection is the same for both delegates and alternates, except that in California, Florida, and Missouri each delegate selects his own alternate, in Wisconsin the state convention selects the alternates.

CONTESTS FOR SEATS IN NATIONAL CONVENTIONS

In those states electing delegates there is little opportunity for a contest to arise, unless losing candidates allege fraud in the voting or in the counting of the ballots. When the state convention is used to choose the delegates, contests sometimes arise from party schisms within the state. The losers may contend that the convention procedures were faulty or that there was fraud of some kind. Usually, contests are created by one faction controlling the regular convention machinery and an opposing faction holding a separate convention. In this case if all of the delegates are elected at the state convention, two complete slates of delegates may be chosen for the same party, or if the contests occur only in certain congressional districts, these will be the only ones affected. The state-committee method of selection in the South has produced the most frequent contests in Republican conventions because rival Republican factions claim to be the regular Republican organization in their state and to be entitled to recognition by the convention.

Each party's delegation from each state must be certified to the party's national committee before the meeting of the national convention—fifteen days before for the Democrats and twenty days for the Republicans. The national committee then hears whatever contests exist, decides each contest in favor of one side or the other, and makes up the temporary roll of the convention to be presented during its first session. Each side in each contest is given thirty minutes to present its arguments before the Democratic National Committee and can submit a brief either before it is heard or at the time it is heard. When the Democratic national convention meets, all of these contests are referred without discussion to the committee on credentials. The delegates who are seated on the temporary roll by decision of the national committee are entitled to take full part in the convention proceedings, serving on committees, debating, voting, and so on.[12] Until recently, the Republican procedure was the same, but a new procedure was prescribed by the 1952 convention in the hopes of ironing out some of the difficulties arising from contests, which were especially numerous and bitter in 1952.

The new Republican rule provides that the national chairman at the time he appoints the arrangements committee shall also appoint "a contest committee, consisting of seven members, the chairman of which shall be a member of the arrangements committee." The chairman, and other members if they wish, shall study all records, briefs and other documentary evidence relating to delegate contests submitted by the contestants. The chairman, assisted voluntarily by any member of the committee, shall write a report covering each contest and submit it to the full contest committee. If a majority of them approve, it "shall be filed as their report." A copy of the issue of law and fact as approved by the committee in each contest is sent to each of the contestants, who have ten days (fifteen days for contestants in the territories) to file written objections and additional statements. The contest committee then determines what it considers to be the issues in each case and submits them to the national committee, which decides each contest entirely upon these issues unless by a majority vote it decides to broaden the basis of its investigation. If the contest committee fails to state the issues, the national committee decides "upon what issues the contest shall be tried."

---

12 *Democratic Manual for the 1952 Democratic National Convention,* compiled by Clarence Cannon, pp. 29-30. Hereafter cited as *Democratic Manual.*

During these deliberations of the national committee, those members who will subsequently be on the credentials committee have a right to attend but may not vote. To make this procedure possible, each state and territorial delegation, after it is elected, is supposed to choose its member for the credentials committee. The national committee, on the basis of the issues before it, makes up the temporary roll to be presented to the first session of the convention; any contestant who is not seated by the national committee has a right of appeal to the credentials committee, but he must act within twenty-four hours after the decision of the national committee, specifying "the grounds upon which the appeal is taken, and only the grounds so specified shall be heard by the credentials committee upon such appeal; and no evidence other than that taken before the National Committee shall be taken up by the Credentials Committee unless it shall, by a majority vote of all of its members, so direct." No delegate or alternate on the temporary roll whose seat is contested may vote in the convention or in any of its committees until he has been seated on the permanent roll unless he was placed on the temporary roll by a two-thirds vote of the national committee.[13]

The objectives of these changes are, quite obviously, to clarify the issues of each contest before it is submitted to either the national or credentials committees in order that both can arrive at decisions in a reasonable length of time and speed up the work of the convention. The new rule governing the voting privileges of delegates under contest, adopted as a temporary rule in 1952 and then, with the two-thirds proviso, made into a permanent rule, reverses the standard practice of all conventions. It became the procedural bone of contention in the Roosevelt-Taft fight in the 1912 convention, and was a central feature of the Eisenhower-Taft fight in the 1952 convention.

Another change made in the Republican rules in 1952 affected the consideration of contests. The previous rule provided that contests affecting district delegates chosen at district conventions were to be settled at the state convention or by the state committee, and only contests affecting delegates at large should be presented to the national committee. Although the 1952 convention did not follow this rule and permitted the presentation of district contests previously decided in the state, it added a proviso to the rule—actually nullifying it—that thereafter contests affecting district delegates caused by "irregular or unlawful action of the State Committee or State Convention" may come within the jurisdiction of the national committee. Inasmuch as district-delegate contests are or can be related to such alleged actions, it appears that all contests from districts can be appealed to the national committee.

---

[13] *Rules Adopted by Republican National Convention,* 1952, Number 4.

The preparations and determinations, from the selection of the convention city to the make-up of the temporary roll, constitute the preconvention procedures. The remainder of the story unfolds during the sessions of the convention itself.

SESSIONS OF THE CONVENTION

Business of the First Session. Each national convention is called to order at approximately noon by the chairman of the party's national committee. After the invocation, welcoming speeches are delivered by the governor of the state in which they are meeting and by the mayor of the city. Then the national chairman makes a speech of a highly partisan nature. Next the Call of the convention is read, but to save time and avoid boredom the actual reading is dispensed with and the Call is printed in the official report. The temporary roll is then read and is referred to the credentials committee. Then the names of temporary officers of the convention, all of whom are nominated by the national committee, are read.

The proposed temporary chairman is the only officer about whose selection there is any likelihood of disagreement; but seldom is any opposing nomination made, and the names put forward by the national committee are ratified by the delegates as a matter of course. Except for their 1884 convention, Republicans have a record of always accepting the temporary chairman nominated by the national committee. The Democratic convention in 1896 refused to elect the nominee of the national committee, and the one in 1912 very nearly did the same. The significance of a struggle over this official is the jockeying for advantage by the contending candidates for the presidential nomination. If one of them feels that the national committee's candidate for temporary chairman will be unfavorable to him, he may try to elect a temporary chairman of his own choosing. A vote provides a test of strength among the candidates for the presidential nomination, and if one of the presidential candidates can successfully challenge the national committee, he achieves at least a great psychological victory.

Another technique was exhibited in 1952 when the Republican national committee picked Walter S. Hallinan as temporary chairman. He was a Taft supporter, but the Eisenhower faction, instead of opposing him with another candidate, subjected him to the most intense pressure through the press and the radio before the convention opened. Speculation ebbed and flowed regarding the degree of favoritism he would show for the Taft faction while he presided. There was no reason to think he would not be as fair as any temporary chairman, but the campaign directed against him made his every move subject to the closest scrutiny. Everyone seemed to agree afterwards that he bent over backward to be impartial. Perhaps nothing he could possibly have done to help Taft would have equaled the advantage the Eisenhower faction derived from its claims or inferences that he would be unfair.

After the temporary organization is chosen, the temporary rules are adopted. Then the membership of the four convention committees is ratified, and no convention business is in order until they report. Following the announcements of the time and place of meeting of these committees, the first session adjourns until that evening.

Keynote Speech at Second Session. The night session of the first day of the convention is devoted to the keynote address. By custom it is delivered by the temporary ·chairman, although the Republicans in 1952 made an exception when they chose as keynoter General Douglas MacArthur, who was not suited for the duties of presiding officer. The first event of importance at this evening session is the escorting of the temporary chairman to the rostrum by a committee appointed by the national chairman during the afternoon session. The temporary chairman, upon reaching the rostrum, takes over the gavel from the national chairman and becomes the presiding officer of the convention until the permanent organization is installed. At this point the temporary chairman launches into his keynote address, or if another is to give the address, the temporary chairman makes some preliminary remarks and then introduces the keynoter.

As the name suggests, this speech is supposed to set the keynote for the convention, but the keynote of every convention is substantially the same: partisan enthusiasm and the anticipation of victory in the November election. For this purpose the keynoter can be unrestrained in his oratorical passions and in presenting his views of the American political scene. He "is not expected to give quarter but hell." [14] The general idea is to claim every virtue for his party and allege every vice for the other party; to parade every past President or prominent leader of his party as a saint in spirit and a fearless warrior in action; and to denounce the contemporary leaders of the opposite party as the most incompetent, dastardly, and obnoxious individuals in the history of the human race. If there is to be a contest for the presidential nomination, the keynoter is careful to give no intimation of his personal preferences, referring to all of the candidates as an extraordinary group of upright Americans, any one of whom the party would proudly follow to inevitable victory. If it is the convention of the party which already holds the White House and the incumbent President is going to be renominated, the keynoter invariably talks a great deal about him and his many accomplishments and attributes.

The selection of the temporary chairman, assuming he will also be the keynoter, is limited by two requirements: He needs some familiarity with parliamentary procedures for his duties as presiding officer, and he should

---

14 *New York Times Magazine,* May 25, 1952, p. 38.

be an able public speaker. The latter quality is of far greater importance. His keynote is supposed to arouse the spirit of the delegates and may lead to demonstrations of several minutes duration as well as frequent interruptions by applause.

Committee Reports

Each of the four committees, after their official selection, goes into session. Because of their size, they meet in hotel ballrooms or dining rooms where facilities are provided for their proceedings, for news gatherers, and for spectators. These sessions go on more or less continuously until the committees have completed their work. Controversial issues are determined by a majority vote in each committee; if the minority wishes, it may present a minority report to the convention and attempt to carry its point with the delegates. The regular procedure is for the chairman of each committee to present his committee's report to the convention. When there is no controversy, the report is uneventful and is approved in a routine fashion by voice vote. When there is controversy and a minority report is to be presented, a prior agreement is made to divide the time for debate equally between the two sides. At the conclusion of the debate a vote is taken. In the case of each of the reports of the four committees, individual delegates have the right to propose amendments from the floor, but this action is rare. If there are any real differences involved, they will most likely be reflected on the committee itself and will be fought out in the debate between the majority and the minority of the committee.

Credentials Committee. Logically, the first committee to report is the one on credentials, and the Republican rules require that its report be disposed of before the report of the committee on resolutions is acted upon. If there are only a few, insignificant contests, the credentials committee may be able to report by the first night or during the first session on the second day. When the committee is tied up with extensive hearings on contested seats, it may not be able to report until the second night or sometime during the third day. In this case the committees on permanent organization and on rules will bring in their reports before the permanent roll is confirmed. At whatever point the credentials committee completes its hearings and makes its decision, it reports to the convention. If the credentials committee decides all of the contests the same way the national committee did, the report is to make the temporary roll the permanent roll. If the committee disagrees with the national committee on any contests, the differences are specified. In any event the entire roll of the convention is not read again. When there are differences within the credentials committee, debate is held between the majority and the minority on each separate contest concerned so that each in turn can be settled by the convention.

Committee on Permanent Organization. The committee on permanent organization makes nominations for the permanent officers of the convention. All of the temporary officers, except the temporary chairman, are nominated to hold their positions permanently, but in most conventions a new man is put forward as chairman. Because the permanent chairman presides during the most critical sessions of the convention, it is essential that he have experience with parliamentary proceedings. In exasperating and confusing situations the chairman must maintain his poise while displaying firmness and impartiality. For this reason, members of Congress are often chosen, particularly speakers of the House of Representatives. The choice of a permanent chairman may have significance for the presidential candidates, since his power to make rulings and to recognize or not to recognize delegates can be used to one or another candidate's advantage. In the 1932 Democratic convention, the Roosevelt forces opposed the nominee of the committee on permanent organization and succeeded in electing their own candidate. Normally the candidate for permanent chairman recommended by the committee is accepted by the delegates, and it is almost unheard of to oppose the candidates for the other offices such as chief sergeant-at-arms, parliamentarian, reading clerk, and so on. In the normal course of events, on the second night of the convention the permanent chairman is officially escorted to the rostrum by a committee and receives the gavel from the temporary chairman. The permanent chairman then makes a speech which is largely a repetition of the sentiments and allegations of the keynote.

Committee on Rules and Order of Business. The committee on rules and order of business reports next. If there are no rules changes of any consequence, this report is quite routine; but controversial new rules will lead to extensive debate between those speaking for the majority and for the minority reports. The order of business is standardized in conventions, but it can be rearranged by the committee as circumstances dictate and is seldom objected to on the floor of the convention.

Preparation of the Platform. The next order of business, under normal procedures, is the report of the committee on platform and resolutions. For many years the responsibility of writing the platform has required the creation of a fiction regarding the sessions of this committee. None of the four committees of the convention can undertake officially any of their duties until they have been confirmed by the convention after it convenes on the first day. The three other committees can perform their functions during the first two or three days of the convention without being unduly handicapped, but the platform committee cannot possibly complete its work in such a short period of time.

In the first place, representatives of many groups with special interests want to appear before the committee and urge that their views be incorporated in the platform. In the second place, there is nearly always considerable difference of opinion within each party over the position to be taken on the various issues of the day, and these opinions are represented by the members of the platform committee. They need time to resolve their differences and reach agreement on the several disputes among them; the product of such negotiation is, as a rule, a generally worded plank in the platform, so innocuously phrased that all shades of opinion are encompassed or mollified. After agreement is reached as to what should or should not be said about any troublesome issue, the difficult problem of writing remains. This is an occasion requiring skillful use of the English language, a delicate appreciation of the subtle nuances and connotations of words and phrases. When the purpose of a piece of writing is to be vague while giving the impression of being straightforward and specific, the choice and arrangement of words must be precise in order to avoid saying more or less than is intended.

Obviously, the work of the committee must precede the opening of the convention; so the national committee calls together some of the leaders of the party who are to be delegates to the convention and will be named to the platform committee. One of them will be chosen as chairman, and later, when the whole committee meets during the first day of the convention, the same person is usually made chairman officially. This small group begins its work several weeks before the convention meets, threshing out differences, listening to individuals who want to present their views, and drafting the preliminary form of the platform. A great deal remains to be done after the convening of the convention—at least most of the final draft is either written or approved then. The platform committee seldom reports before the third day, and its report is more likely to give rise to controversies than that of any other committee except the credentials committee. Majority and minority reports are presented on various planks, with debate time allotted between the two sides on each separate issue. Finally, the platform is adopted with or without amendments to the majority report.

At last the convention is ready to proceed to the real business at hand, the nomination of a presidential candidate, which usually begins the third night of the convention.

NOMINATING THE CANDIDATES

Procedure for Presenting Names. The procedure for putting names of candidates before a convention is now time-tested and ageless. Capable of variety in small details, its basic plan is impregnable. The assumption is that names are presented on behalf of states, so the states are called in regular alphabetical order from Alabama to Wyoming. As each state's name is called, the chairman of the delegation announces which one of four possible actions the state wishes to take:

(1) The state may wish to make a nomination.

(2) It may wish to second a nomination already made.

(3) It may wish to give its place in the roll call to another state farther down the alphabetical list to permit this state to make a nomination.

(4) It may pass, meaning it wishes to take no action for the time being and will be called again at the completion of the roll.

Traditionally, the reading clerk calls each state and it then takes the action its delegates desire, but the Republican conventions of 1948 and 1952 varied this procedure by having the states called rapidly in order, at which time each announced what action it intended to take; only those states announcing an intention to make a nomination or a second were called when the order of business of nominations was reached.

Presidential Nominating Speeches. The first state on the roll that wishes to make a nomination, or that has another state yield to it for the purpose, requests that the chairman recognize whoever has been selected to make the nominating speech. The speaker is often a delegate and almost always a resident of the state called or yielded to; he is chosen for his ability to speak and for his loyalty or friendship to the candidate he is presenting. The rules of both parties limit the time of these speeches (Republicans, fifteen minutes; Democrats, twenty minutes) but the restriction is not enforced and the time is often exceeded.

An almost ironclad ritual has enveloped nominating speeches. The general idea is to "pour it on" by detailing all of the virtues man is heir to and attributing them all to the candidate. He is fearless, strong, all-seeing and all-knowing. He is gentle, kind, and understanding. He is militantly against sin, but loves all of his fellow creatures with the compassion of a saint. As many speakers explain it, the candidate is "a man who": a man who can win the election; a man who believes in a fair return on investments and endeavors; a man who honors the working men and who believes they should be fairly paid for a fair day's work; a man who salutes the farmers and their physical labors in feeding the American public and helping them to a higher standard of living; a man who commends all enlightened employers for their efforts in the public interest to help the country progress in its material welfare. And so it goes. When there are issues of special interest, the candidate is associated with them in a favorable light. And always the delegates are assured that he is a vote-getter if he has ever run for office before.

Although everyone knows who is being placed before the convention, seldom does the speaker utter the name of the candidate until the last sentence, usually in the form: "Therefore, the State of ———— presents to this great convention the name of that indomitable patriot, that able and wise leader of men, _____ _____." By holding the name of the candidate until the very last words, the effect of the speech is heightened; it is possible to build up to a higher pitch and finish on a crescendo of emotion. Furthermore, upon the conclusion of the speech, the demonstration for the candidate begins, and his name is a good signal for its beginning. If the name is mentioned before the speech is finished, an incipient demonstration may begin, and the premature action is likely to ruin the effect both of the remainder of the speech and of the planned demonstration.

Demonstrations. The phenomenon of the demonstration consists of assorted antics such as marching about the hall waving banners and signs, shouting, whistling, using noise-making machines, dancing in the aisles if there is room. Organ music or bands are used to pep up the proceedings. Balloons are dropped from the ceiling or ascend from the floor. The whole undertaking is comparable to a college football rally, but often on a larger and more intense scale. The efforts made by the supporters of a candidate are calculated to impress the general public and the delegates. Like a football coach trying to develop a perfect play which will result in a touchdown every time, managers try to stampede a convention into nominating a candidate from the sheer weight of his support and his invincibility. The demonstration has only psychological value, and each group of supporters wants its noise to be loudest and longest. The demonstrations are carefully timed and a great fuss is made if one lasts three minutes longer than another. Both parties in recent years have tried to keep these demonstrations within a thirty-minute period; otherwise, the time consumed in presenting the candidates is so long that everyone is exhausted and the convention schedule is seriously disrupted. Some extraordinary records were set in the duration of demonstrations for Alfred E. Smith in 1924 and 1932, when his supporters maintained the hubbub for over two hours.

Seconding Speeches. After a man's name has been presented to the convention, both parties permit a maximum of four seconding speeches of five minutes each. These speeches are made on behalf of a state when it is reached on the roll call, and like the nominating speeches, are planned in advance by designated individuals, who frequently run overtime in their remarks. There is nothing new for them to say about a candidate, so they repeat what the nominating speaker said, and ovations and even short demonstrations may follow some of the seconding speeches. Toward the end of the roll call, the hour is getting late—or more exactly, early in the next morning; all of the candidates' names have been presented, and the last seconding speeches evoke less response. Generally an adjournment is taken upon the conclusion of all of the oratory, and the balloting begins at the noon session on the fourth day. The balloting goes on until one of the candidates receives a majority of all of the votes cast. On some occasions it has taken conventions an interminably long time to make a nomination. The record, which is likely to last for all time, was set by the Democrats in 1924, when it required 103 roll calls to break the deadlock between Alfred E. Smith and William G. McAdoo and produce the nomination of John W. Davis as a compromise candidate. The longest deadlock in a Republican convention occurred in 1880, when 36 ballots were required to nominate James A. Garfield. The trend since 1924 has been toward few ballots, and the prospects are that conventions will continue to complete their work within a total of six days to avoid expense and the bitterness of a prolonged balloting.[15]

Special Rules Governing Balloting. Democratic conventions have produced innovations in voting procedure, some of which remain in force. In their first national convention in 1832 they adopted a rule requiring a *two-thirds majority* to nominate a candidate for Vice-President; and this rule, applied to nominations for both offices, continued in force in all of their conventions for the next hundred years. It was finally abolished in 1936. The rule was justified as a means of showing party solidarity, and its early defenders claimed it would never be used to block the nomination of a candidate who already had received a majority of the votes. This prediction was borne out in general, and in 1856 Stephan A. Douglas withdrew from the voting after James Buchanan received over half of the vote. On two occasions, in 1844 and 1912, the prediction proved false when a candidate received a majority but failed to be nominated. In 1844 James K. Polk was nominated, but Martin Van Buren, for whose benefit the rule had been created originally, received a majority at the beginning of the balloting. In 1912 Champ Clark received a majority of the votes on the tenth through the seventeenth ballots, but Woodrow Wilson was even-

---

[15] The following list gives the years when more than one ballot was required:

DEMOCRATS		REPUBLICANS	
1924....	103	1880....	36
1860....	57	1920....	10
1852....	49	1888....	8
1912....	46	1876....	7
1920....	44	1940....	6
1868....	22	1884....	4
1856....	17	1860, 1916, 1948....	3
1844....	9	1856....	2
1896....	5		
1848, 1932....	4		
1952....	3		
1876, 1880, 1884....	2		

tually nominated. The 1860 convention in Charleston was deadlocked by the rule.[16]

A rule still in effect in Democratic conventions requires an entire state's vote to be cast on a roll call the way the majority of the state's delegates vote. This is the *unit rule* and imposes a definite restriction upon the individual freedom of the delegates. It was not formally adopted until 1860, but in 1832 there was a suggestion of it—a tendency to leave the decision up to each state or its delegation—in the rule that "the majority of the delegates from each state designate the person by whom the votes for that state shall be given."

Democratic conventions now enforce the unit rule upon a delegation whose state convention clearly instructed the delegation to use it; a "recommendation" or "request" from a state convention is interpreted as an instruction. However, the burden of proof in the form of documentary evidence is upon those who contend the rule was imposed. Wherever delegates are directly elected by Democratic voters at a primary, the delegates are considered responsible only to their constituents and are not bound by the unit rule. A majority of a state's delegates, acting under the rule, can cast the state's full vote even though some of the delegates are absent or refuse to vote. If a state convention permits its delegation to dispense with the unit rule or if the rule is self-imposed by unanimous consent of a delegation, a majority of that delegation present in the convention can abrogate the rule. The Democrats carefully distinguish between the unit rule and instructions to a delegation to vote for a particular candidate for the nomination. The action of a state convention imposing one does not imply the other; the interpretation of the latter instruction is left to the decision of a majority of a delegation. A Democratic convention may, by suspending the rules, release delegates from instructions or pledges to vote for any candidate but cannot release them from instructions to vote under the unit rule.[17]

Because of the relation between the two-thirds rule and the unit rule, the latter is less defensible since the abolition of the former. If a two-thirds majority is required to nominate, unified state voting facilitates the

---

[16] See Stanwood, *op. cit.*, p. 182; Ostrogorski, *op. cit.*, p. 271; Joseph B. Bishop, *Presidential Nominations and Elections* (New York: Charles Scribner's Sons, 1916) pp. 9-10, 52, Chap. 12. At the 1920 convention, when the rule was overlooked by the rules committee and was not included in the rules adopted, the chairman held it to be a requirement established through immemorial usage. In 1924 it was held that a motion to suspend the rules including the two-thirds rule, if agreed to, would permit nomination of a presidential candidate by a simple majority.—*Democratic Manual,* p. 42.

[17] *Ibid.*, pp. 33-36, 43-44. At the 1952 Democratic convention, seventeen states, Puerto Rico, and Washington, D.C., used the unit rule. In the 1932 Democratic convention, the chairman ruled that instructions to vote for a candidate "until released by him" included being released for the purpose of casting a complimentary vote; therefore, when Governor Murray of Oklahoma released his delegation to vote for Will Rogers on one ballot, they remained released and the instructions could not be reinvoked.

making of a choice and reduces the preponderance of the large states. If a simple majority is required to nominate, the unit rule increases the power of the large states and loses its last reason for being.

The Whigs used a very complicated application of the unit rule in their 1839 convention, with the result that Henry Clay was defeated. In 1852 for the first time the Whigs voted by a roll call of the states instead of a roll call of the delegates, the chairman ruling that each delegation could decide for itself about the use of the unit rule; an Illinois delegate, nevertheless, was permitted to cast his own vote even though the delegation had been instructed to vote as a unit. The unit rule has never been used in Republican conventions; the only strenuous effort to impose it was made in 1880 by the forces supporting U. S. Grant.

In neither Republican nor Democratic conventions does the party assume responsibility for instructions imposed upon a delegate to vote for a designated candidate. If a delegate votes in violation of any commitment, it is a matter between him and his constituents or his state party organization. Delegates themselves interpret whatever instructions are given to them. Conversely, the two parties offer a significant difference in their attitudes toward the unit rule. The use or prohibition of the rule is the result of distinctly different concepts of the powers of a national convention, i.e., the independent right of the party assembled versus the inviolability of the state party as a constituent entity. A Republican convention is considered plenary in its powers and beyond the reach of any state Republican party. A Democratic convention adheres to the Party's historical doctrine of state rights and considers itself bound by decisions at state party conventions.[18]

After each roll call the totals for each candidate are announced. If no candidate has a majority, another ballot is taken. Before the results of a ballot are announced, the states can change their votes. This is a recognized right. The chairman of the 1952 Republican convention announced before the roll call began "that he will pause for several minutes after the completion of the roll call should any State desire to change its vote" and "that after the announcement of the ballot, there will be a pause of five minutes so that the convention can make up its mind what it thinks it will do." [19] When a candidate receives a majority of the vote, the rules of both parties permit the chairman to put a motion to suspend the rules and to declare the candidate unanimously nominated. In practice, the

---

18 For the historical development, see Carl Becker, "The Unit Rule in National Nominating Conventions," *American Historical Review*, Vol. 5 (1899) pp. 64–82; Gordon S. P. Kleeberg, *Formation of the Republican Party as a National Political Organization.* (New York: Moods Publishing Co., 1911) ; Dallinger, *op. cit.*, pp. 40-43; but Dallinger was mistaken about the unit rule in Republican conventions.

19 *Official Report of the Proceedings of the Twenty-fifth Republican National Convention,* 1952, p. 388.

honor of making and seconding this motion is given to the representatives of the defeated candidates.

Vice-Presidential Nomination. Once a presidential candidate is nominated, the convention turns to the order of business of nominating a vice-presidential candidate. The procedure is identical with that for naming a presidential candidate, but there is a letdown feeling following the first nomination. The fires of enthusiasm have burned out, and demonstrations are much shorter after the presentation of the names. The psychological and political situations surrounding the second nomination are quite different from the first and discourage any extensive competitive spirit. The presidential nominee by well-established custom is considered to be entitled to a major voice in the selection of his running mate and in some cases designates him outright. Accordingly, only one candidate may be presented, or other names are presented and then withdrawn before the balloting starts. The unanimous or overwhelming selection of a vice-presidential candidate on one ballot is a usage of long standing.

The Final Actions

In the aftermath of the nominations, nothing of consequence remains to be done. The convention goes through the process of electing the new national committee from the nominations made by each state. Resolutions of thanks to everyone connected with the arrangements are adopted. The city is praised in another motion for its hospitality and courtesy.

Until 1932, upon the completion of these courtesies, personnel of a committee to notify formally the presidential candidate of his nomination and another committee to notify the vice-presidential candidate was announced by the convention chairman. Then the convention adjourned *sine die*. During the month of August, usually, on dates spaced a week or two apart these two committees made the notification at elaborate ceremonies in each candidate's home city. The chairman of the committee would make a speech informing the candidate that he was nominated by the convention. The candidate would follow with a speech accepting the nomination, covering his general views on the issues and committing himself to the platform adopted at the convention, unless he specifically wanted to ignore or repudiate some planks. The emphases in his speech would indicate the relative weight he placed upon the various issues and the ones he considered central to his campaign. This procedure for providing a forum and a platform for the candidates' first formal utterances after their nominations was abruptly changed by Franklin D. Roosevelt in 1932, when he flew to Chicago and made his acceptance speech before the delegates prior to the adjournment of the convention.

The Democrats have continued to follow this custom set by Roosevelt.

The last use of the traditional notification ceremonies was in Indiana in 1940, when Wendell Willkie was notified of his nomination. The Republicans began using the Roosevelt method in 1944. There are two ways of handling the presidential candidate's acceptance speech in conventions. In one case, the candidate appears before the convention shortly after his nomination, as Adlai Stevenson did in 1952; then the vice-presidential candidate is nominated and makes his acceptance speech, and the convention adjourns. In the other case after both nominations are made, the candidates appear together for the first time and make their addresses, as Dwight D. Eisenhower and Richard M. Nixon did in 1952; then the convention adjourns.

It makes no difference which of these or other details are carried out in the course of a convention, the experience is exhausting. Speech follows speech and words pour forth in profuse quantities.[20] Conventions are always held in summer months in cities which are both very hot and very humid, and the use of air conditioning alleviates but does not eliminate the scourge of the weather. Added to this discomfort is the physical strain of sleepless nights and constant activity, plus the emotional strain under which most participants live. It is not to be wondered that the delegates, when they leave the hall for the last time and begin checking out of their hotels, are tired and enervated; but it is all worth the effort, the expense, and the broken hearts if they can be sent home with visions of November majorities dancing in their heads.

Selected Bibliography

Bishop, Joseph B., *Presidential Nominations and Elections.* New York: Charles Scribner's Sons, 1916.

David, Paul T., Ralph M. Goldman, and Richard C. Bain, *The Politics of National Party Conventions.* Washington, D. C.: The Brookings Institution, 1960.

David, Paul T., *et al.* (eds.), *Presidential Nominating Politics in 1952,* 5 vols. Baltimore: The Johns Hopkins Press, 1954.

Farley, James A., *Behind the Ballots.* New York: Harcourt, Brace and Company, Inc., 1938.

———, *Jim Farley's Story.* New York: McGraw-Hill Book Company, Inc., 1948.

Flynn, Edward J., *You're the Boss.* New York: The Viking Press, Inc., 1947.

Manner of Selecting Delegates to National Political Conventions. Washington, D. C.: Government Printing Office. Published every fourth year.

Overacker, Louise, *The Presidential Primary.* New York: The Macmillan Company, 1926.

Stanwood, Edward, *A History of the Presidency,* 2 vols. Boston: Houghton Mifflin Company, 1898 and 1916.

Thompson, Charles A. H., *Television and Presidential Politics.* Washington, D. C.: The Brookings Institution, 1956.

The *Proceedings* of both the Democrat and Republican conventions are published by the respective national committees.

---

[20] The record for the number of words wired from a convention, including press dispatches and commentaries as well as speeches, is 9,576,000 wired from the Democratic convention in 1924. The next largest number, over 8,000,000, was wired from the Republican convention in 1952.——*New York Times,* July 13, 1952.

CHAPTER TEN

Conventions as the Operation of the Total Organization

The nature of the organization of major parties in the United States, from the precinct to the nation, is a composite of human motives and relationships. The authority dispersed within each party structure continues to be in character with its localized and decentralized origin. The examination of this organization has proceeded piecemeal unit by unit through the geographical levels. The result is an entity with a very special and peculiar kind of mechanism. Here, if nowhere else, the federal system of relationships continues. What is designated a national organization is more nearly a voluntary merger of constituent voluntary organizations with the same name, similar outlooks, and the identical objective of winning elections. This description of a party in terms of its organization is qualified by its description in terms of factional interests. These are not necessarily confined within a state's boundaries but overlap the separate state organizations and give a partially national character to a political party.

Limitations in Leadership. The phenomenon of bosses is common in precinct, county, and state politics, but no one in the history of the United States has ever qualified as a national boss. If anyone were able to, it would be the President; but Presidents with all their authority cannot boss their national parties the way that state or local parties have been bossed by such leaders as Matthew Quay, Thomas J. Pendergast, E. H. Crump, Frank Hague, Thomas E. Dewey, or Harry F. Byrd. If no President can be a national boss, it is hardly to be expected that such a leader can arise from the national organization itself. It is generally agreed that Marcus A. Hanna most nearly approached this status as Republican national chairman during the Presidency of William McKinley, but no one contends that Hanna was really a national boss. The difficulty in the case of both a President and a national chairman is the limited tenure of office as contrasted with that of local and state leaders.[1] The creation of a national boss is further obstructed by the constant preoccupation of leaders with their own localities and with the petty details of political management.

Party Operations as National Organization. There are only two occasions when the whole party throughout the country has a common

---

[1] Frank R. Kent, *The Great Game of Politics* (New York: Doubleday, Page & Co., 1924) pp. 150-152.

Roy Justus in The Minneapolis Star

DOUBLE FEATURE

focus of attention. One occasion is a presidential campaign; but even the integrative effort of electing a president is weakened by competing state and local elections. The other occasion is a national nominating convention, which is the capstone of organization and the opening of the road to the White House. Only in this event is the whole party, figuratively speaking, brought together in such a way that its total organization operates at the same time, at the same place, toward the same end. A national convention is not an occasion for making the constituent state organizations one national organization, but all of the state organizations are meshed for the same effort under uniform compulsions. Yet this one occasion for national operation accentuates or reveals the tensions of ambition and the competitiveness of faction. The most savage struggles can ensue, the most violent passions be unleashed. Nor is the unity of interest and objective complete in a national convention. Motives and specific objectives vary among the thousands of men and women who take part. Ramifications multiply as the geographical area of party operations widens. The national convention is an identifiable phenomenon and has the simplicity of concentrated action, but the magnitude of the problem of grasping its inner meaning is one of the most challenging in the scope of American political party organization.

From the political point of view the problem involved in national conventions is the control of them. This control is sought through the regular party machinery, especially in the national committee, and through the force of party and public sentiment generated by the presidential candidates. These two sources can scarcely be separated because of their interdependence, but they can be examined separately as they interact with each other. The period of time for establishing this control begins long before a convention meets and in most cases continues into the convention sessions and up to the moment the determinative decisions are made.

THE GROUNDWORK OF NATIONAL CONVENTIONS

PREPARATIONS BY PARTY ORGANIZATIONS

State and local political leaders have varying amounts of interest in national conventions. Usually, they would like to be delegates or alternates in order to be at the center of activity and to demonstrate their influence within their own state. Quite often many of these leaders go to conventions as visitors and in this status may take an active part in the affairs of the delegation. To be picked as a delegate involves some publicity, and the national convention is a place for renewing old friendships and making new ones. These are some of the motivations for participating in the quadrennial party gatherings, aside from more specific objectives which many delegates have. The leaders in the larger states, from which presidential and vice-presidential candidates are frequently nominated, may be deeply involved in these struggles, but the leaders from the smaller states are less likely to have such grandiose roles to play. The real operation of state machinery occurs at the point of delegate selection in the state, but behind this event lies a series of developments involving directly or indirectly the national committee as well as the state and county committees.

National Committee. The exact position of the national committee in the political power equation is a subject of some disagreement. From time to time its power has waxed and waned. It first achieved its height under the Republicans with the regime of Marcus A. Hanna from 1896 to 1904. A second high point in its development, this time under the Democrats, occurred during the chairmanship of James A. Farley from 1932 to 1940. In the interim between these dates, the national committee in both parties declined. It came to life and began functioning for presidential elections, following which it sank into obscurity with nothing else to do but pay off the debts incurred during the campaign. Since the 1940's both national committees have maintained headquarters in Washington, D.C., with a permanent staff. The Democrats began this system after the defeat of Alfred E. Smith in 1928, and the work of the staff in harassing the Hoover Administration is frequently assigned some of the responsibility for the Democrats' tremendous victory in 1932.

Even this amount of organization and activity fails to impress some observers. Professor E. E. Schattschneider considers the national committee to be weak for several reasons: first, its members are chosen by each state and thus are answerable to local and state bosses; second, their term of office is short; third, they receive no salary; fourth, there is frequent turn-over in personnel; and fifth, meetings are infrequent.[2] The establishment of permanent headquarters since these criticisms were voiced disposes of an additional weakness complained of. Professor J. T. Salter reached the conclusion that the national committee "is composed of the most powerful politicians in the country or their representatives. This committee is at the apex of the party structure, and is so powerful that it has been called the 'President Maker'." [3] These evaluations depend upon one's concept of what the national committee should be. Consistently with his urging a completely new kind of party organization, Professor Schattschneider is dissatisfied whenever he finds localized control of machinery. He considers four years a short tenure and disparages the changes made in the committees' membership in conformance with the shifts in factional control in the states. Others, looking at the committee in terms of what it does, agree with Professor Salter. In part, perhaps, this difference of opinion is not as great as it appears, for Professor Schattschneider agrees that individual members on the committee are powerful to the extent that they are powerful in their own states. It is his objection that the committee as an agency in its own right is not powerful. This is a general observation that can be made of all party committees, but the observation is subject to various qualifications from time to time.

---

2 E. E. Schattschneider, *Party Government* (New York: Farrar & Rinehart, Inc., 1942) pp. 158-160.

3 J. T. Salter, *Boss Rule* (New York: McGraw-Hill Book Company, 1935) p. 5.

The effectiveness of the national committee at any time is dependent upon the chairman, whose year-round functions are a combination of raising money, devising strategy and propaganda, supervising patronage (in the case of the "ins"), and traveling to keep in touch with local leaders. In presidential campaigns he has the responsibility of leading the attack to elect the party's presidential candidate. "He must have an imaginative turn of mind, and an intuitive sense of timing and of the fitness of things." [4] Nevertheless, the national committee is more than its chairman.

Dominant leaders in each state want to control the votes of their state on the national committee, and they frequently hold the office of national committeeman and dictate the selection of national committeewoman. Sometimes two party factions are represented in the two offices, but the holders of these offices are important political leaders whether in their own right or because they speak for others. In numerous cases a leader's final act in securing control of his state is to become a member of the national committee. United States senators have often held this office. Businessmen and lawyers are the most pronounced occupations found among national committeemen, and they speak for both their state organizations and the leading economic interests of their states.[5]

The operations of the national committee as such are localized in national politics, i.e., federal patronage, national conventions, and presidential elections, but the individual operations of national committee members have deep roots in their own states. It is this body of men and women, each with his individual objectives but acting in a collective endeavor, that lays out the road and marks the signs which lead to the national nominating convention. To change the figure of speech, it is the national committee that stacks the cards in the preparations for the convention. To be more exact, it is not the whole committee, for the Puerto Rican members have no influence compared with the New York members. The power of the committee is wielded through the chairman, the executive committee, and the committee on arrangements. Both of these committees are appointed by the chairman in conformance with the political power of the individuals and interests within the party. The long evolution of conventions has gradually given to the leaders of the national committee the power to control the conventions. The developments in the Republican

---

[4] *New York Times*, October 28, 1951, Section E, "Party Chairman's Job Is a Hard One to Fill."

[5] See Wallace S. Sayre, "Personnel of Republican and Democratic National Committees," *American Political Science Review* Vol. 26 (1932) pp. 360-362. In this study of 108 committeemen of both parties, substantially every major economic interest was represented in each committee, although coal and lumber companies were not found on the Democratic committee. Businessmen predominated in every section of the country except in the West Central and Lower South states, where businessmen and lawyers were about equally represented. See also P. H. Odegard and E. Allen Helms, *American Politics* (New York: Harper & Brothers, 1947, 2d ed.) pp. 287-290.

convention in 1952 contradict this rule, for the dominant faction on the national committee was overthrown in the convention.[6] The rule assumes that those who control the committee can muster a majority of votes in the convention because of their control over the machinery. The unusual developments of 1952 simply revealed the superiority of the organization of the other faction. Even the advantage of stacking the cards comes to naught if the other crowd proves to be superior in techniques of propaganda and in the strategy of getting convention votes.

Preparations by the "In" Party. To pretend that the arrangements for national conventions are made without reference to their effects upon the aspirants for the presidential nomination is misleading and unwarranted, but the analysis of these operations depends upon the party being "in" or "out." The "in" party's national committee is dominated by the President, who selects the national chairman, or at the very least approves of the man before he is elected. This relationship begins at the time a presidential candidate is nominated,[7] and if he is elected, the relationship becomes even closer. Inasmuch as a President captures his party both through its organization and through his program, he cannot be denied a renomination if he wants it. The chairman and the executive committee prepare the machinery for the convention and make their moves under the President's supervision. Only extraordinary situations produce a revolt against a President like the one that occurred in the 1948 Democratic convention against Truman, but in the end the dissidents were forced to knuckle under and nominate him.

If a President is not a candidate for renomination, it is obvious that he can direct affairs in such a way as to help or hinder those who are candidates. Usually, Presidents in this position declare that they are keeping hands off and that the convention delegates will be free to nominate whom they choose. The practice of Theodore Roosevelt who openly forced his successor upon the Republican Party in 1908 is exceptional. For a President to do nothing publicly does not mean that he does nothing quietly. His unseen moves may clearly be designed to promote a candidate, as President Truman in 1952 aided Adlai Stevenson. The moves may be so inscrutable as to create doubt of a President's genuine desire to retire. In 1920 Woodrow Wilson insisted he was having nothing to do with the preconvention campaign, but subsequent accounts of this period by some

---

6 See Jay Franklin, *Republicans on the Potomac* (New York: The McBride Company, 1953) Chap. 2.

7 Now and then, criticism arises over the practice of presidential candidates changing chairmen. At a meeting of the Republican National Committee in 1952, Clarence Budington Kelland, Arizona national committeeman, offered a resolution to prevent the practice, claiming it "has been detrimental to the last three presidential campaigns."—— United Press dispatch from San Francisco, dated January 19, 1952.

Democrats close to him make it very clear that he was deeply interested in the campaign and freely discussed the candidates. The fact that in his discussions he found something wrong with all of the candidates led some of his intimates to suspect that he wanted a third nomination.[8] The difficulty, from a President's point of view, of holding back and releasing the reins of power in the national committee is that the political forces begin to gather so much momentum that by the time the convention meets, the President may find himself unable to control the situation even if he wants to.

Preparation by the "Out" Party. The "out" party finds itself in a different position, for it has no leader comparable to the President. The organization for its last presidential campaign is somewhat discredited by the defeat of its candidate. The national chairman may continue in his post for several months or even for a year or two, but inevitably there will be attempts to remove him. The opposition to him arises from his association with the defeat and his alleged responsibility for it. Further, he is identified as the choice of the defeated presidential candidate and is assumed to be friendly to the aspirations of that candidate for another nomination. The attitude of other leaders is that this candidate had his chance and lost, and it is now someone else's turn.

Strategies and Struggles. The factional infighting, which tends to increase as time goes on, is represented on the national committee, since each of the candidates for the nomination is likely to have some supporters there. The successive decisions made in the planning for the convention precipitate conflicts and compromises. When no one candidate has enough national-committee strength to get favorable decisions, the supporters of two or more candidate may agree to work together as a coalition as far as their mutual interests coincide. If one candidate seems to be in the lead, the other candidates often combine against him. When there are two strong candidates, a basis for compromise may lie in the selection of men favorable to weaker candidates, e.g., George F. Hoar of Massachusetts was made both temporary and permanent chairman of the 1888 Republican convention because he favored neither Blaine nor Grant, the two leading contenders. When there is serious doubt as to the outcome, some leaders will be cautious and not offend any candidate; other leaders may support

---

[8] See Josephus Daniels, *The Wilson Era, Years of War and After, 1917–1923* (Chapel Hill: University of North Carolina Press, 1946) p. 553; Charles W. Stein, *The Third-Term Tradition* (New York: Columbia University Press, 1943) p. 242. Joseph P. Tumulty, *Woodrow Wilson as I Know Him* (New York: Doubleday, Page & Co., 1921) pp. 493-499. Rixey Smith and Norman Beasley, *Carter Glass* (New York: Longmans, Green & Co., Inc., 1939) pp. 205–208.

one or another candidate but refuse to take extreme actions for fear of antagonizing the faction which may eventually win.

The decisions of the national committee, whether of the "ins" or the "outs," can be read in terms of the coming fight for the presidential nomination. The selection of the convention city, the choice of chairmen, the rulings on contested delegations, the suggestions for rule changes—all of these and many other actions have significance.

The next major process in the groundwork is the selection of the delegates within the states, and the national committee may be seen in this picture in various roles. However, the impetus at this point is more directly given by the candidates and their personal organizations.

PREPARATIONS BY CANDIDATES FOR THE NOMINATION

A campaign to capture a presidential nomination may begin years before its culmination. A man who becomes President usually plans for it and works toward it as well as he can during his political career. Occasionally, party leaders feel compelled to nominate a man who has no political training and no ability to play politics because they think he can win. It may or may not be a coincidence that the men most frequently chosen under these trying circumstances have been army men, beginning with the Whig nomination of General Zachary Taylor in 1848 and continuing through the Democrats' nomination of General George B. McClellan in 1864, and the Republicans' nomination of General U. S. Grant in 1868 and of General Dwight D. Eisenhower in 1952. These examples are exceptional cases, understandable within the context of the political conditions of the time, but not characteristic of the products of national conventions.

The point at which a man begins to direct his career toward the White House is impossible, perhaps, even for him to determine. To the extent that men seek to reach the pinnacle of their professions, politicians seek to reach the Presidency. In this sense, all serious office seekers think in terms of the *one* office which is most to be desired. Party politics narrows its path the further it ascends until it abruptly culminates in one single office. The attainment of one's supreme ambition is subject to the most severe elimination process and the most rigorous test of a human being. To follow the path this far is conclusive proof of a man's deadly earnestness; he has pursued the goal so long it has become a part of him. The case of Wendell L. Willkie in 1940 is so rare as to require no comment on its outstanding exceptions to the rules.

Even though an alderman or a county clerk harbors the desire to run for President, his serious campaign for the nomination begins within a relatively few years of the date of the convention he hopes to capture. No one needs to tell him he is ready, for he has been getting ready and has finally decided the time has come. He has engineered his career to the point he has been aiming at, the point which is to be his springboard for the one great effort. Not everyone who has attained certain successes or has accomplished certain things is presidential material, however. To distinguish between the man who is and the man who is not, American politics has developed the delightful concept of "availability."

Availability. "Available," in the political sense, does not mean desirous of the office of President, for such a meaning would fail to discriminate in any way among politicians. In this loose sense of the term, everyone in politics is available. "Available" in its proper sense means capable of being elected. The concept of what constitutes availability is the concept of what is required to convince a majority of the American voters that a candidate should become their President. A whole miscellany of rules of thumb, superstitions, inferences, and hindsight thinking is packed into the word. Its outer limits have become rigid, but it is flexible and adaptable within these limits.

Explicitly in political calculations is the fixed belief that many voters act from negative, not from positive, motivations. A voter who has a dislike for a candidate is very apt to go to the polls to vote against him without too much concern as to whom he is voting for. Applying this belief in national politics produces the rule that a candidate for the Presidency should have a *minimum number of enemies* throughout the country. The fewer people and organizations that have a reason to oppose him, the better. How does a man avoid making numerous and powerful enemies? He avoids this misfortune, if in no other way, by having no record or as little record as possible on national issues of the day. He should in his immediate environment be removed from national politics.

It would be presumptuous to fix a date in history for the discovery of this rule, because it is implicit in the development of popular politics. Perhaps the outstanding early example of having too much record to run on was Henry Clay in 1844. Before the nominations were made, he opposed the annexation of Texas in order to pacify the North. When he was threatened by Southern disaffection after his nomination, he attempted to jump back and accept the annexation of Texas. The result was to alienate supporters in both sections. Politicians are highly perceptive, and this last bid of Clay's was apparently shattered by his having an irrevocable commitment on the most sensitive issue of the day.

In the light of this assumption about a record and its effects upon a candidate, the *position a man holds* at the time of his nomination has become a matter of major consequence. The desirability of holding a seat in Congress presents an intriguing question. Though congressional experience is very helpful in seeking the Presidency, yet a seat in Congress is a handicap. Only thirteen Presidents, from Washington to Eisenhower, had no service in Congress during their careers.[9] Only seven candidates were members of Congress (five senators and two representatives) at the time of their nomination; of these, one senator and one representative were elected.[10] Only one speaker of the House, James K. Polk, later became President; Henry Clay was speaker when he made his first race in 1824. It is easy to appreciate the advantages of congressional experience, for it gives a person a unique understanding of national problems and tests his competence. Congress is the great crossroads of American politics, where one can learn much from using his eyes and ears and can come to know well the outstanding political figures of the time.

As background in a politician's training, congressional service is invaluable, but it is almost always embarrassing for a man to be in Congress at the time he campaigns for a presidential nomination. On the contemporary controversies he is recorded through his speeches and votes. Irrespective of his omissions or commissions he will have made enemies in some groups, who at the outset of his campaign will oppose his nomination. If he has avoided issues by being absent when votes were taken, he is attacked for not being on the job and for not representing his constituents. Candidates whose terms in Congress have been in the past can point to their service as valuable government experience, but many of the issues on which they were previously committed are likely to be of less interest at the time of their candidacy; such candidates can more successfully tell what they wish about their records, and hair-splitting arguments by their opponents quickly become boring and can be ignored. The extraordinary fact remains that in preconvention campaigns members of Congress, especially senators, are always looked upon as formidable contenders for the nomination. When the convention is over, someone else emerges as the presidential candidate, although members of Congress frequently get the second place on the ticket. The large number of Democratic senators seeking the nomination in 1960 marks this as an unusual year and may be either a harbinger of a new trend or merely an aberration.

If congressional membership is usually a sign of unavailability, no other office except that of governor can be considered an advantage, judging from

9 The thirteen are Washington, John Adams, Jefferson, Taylor, Grant, Cleveland, Theodore Roosevelt, Taft, Wilson, Coolidge, Hoover, Franklin D. Roosevelt, Eisenhower. The early Presidents, who had no opportunity to serve in Congress, had had considerable legislative experience.

10 The victorious senator was Warren G. Harding (Republican, 1920) and the victorious representative was James A. Garfield (Republican, 1880). The four defeated senators were Rufus King (Federalist, 1816), Henry Clay (National Republican, 1832), Lewis Cass (Democrat, 1848), and Stephen A. Douglas (Democrat, 1860). The defeated representative was Henry Clay (Democratic-Republican, 1824).

"WE PROBABLY WON'T KNOW TILL THE LAST MINUTE WHO
WE'LL PUT IN ORBIT"

the evidence.[11] John Adams and Thomas Jefferson succeeded from the office of Vice-President. The only later President to do this was Martin Van Buren, and the only Vice-President even to be nominated thereafter was John C. Breckinridge, the candidate of the Southern Democrats in 1860. Six candidates were nominated while they held a Cabinet position: James Madison, James Monroe, and John Quincy Adams were each Secretary of State; William H. Crawford was Secretary of the Treasury; William H. Taft was Secretary of War; and Herbert Hoover was Secretary of Commerce. James Buchanan was minister to England. Two men were judges when they were chosen: Alton B. Parker, Chief Justice of the New York Court of Appeals, and Charles E. Hughes, Associate Justice of the United States Supreme Court. On twelve occasions since the Civil War, candidates have held the governorship of their states: one each from Kansas, Illinois, and New Jersey, and the remainder from Ohio and New York. This pattern of nominating governors is extremely significant, for it emphasizes the advantage of holding an office unconnected with national affairs. Senators may have been more prominently mentioned and were often better known, but governors were considered more available. The appearance of state executives demonstrates that the concept of availability is not static.

The requirement of being detached from the national political scene is further illustrated by the fact that twenty different candidates were nominated while holding no political position. In some of these cases they had been candidates previously, and almost all of them had had previous political experience. Eight had been in Congress; two had been in the Cabinet; two had been diplomats; two had been governors; four had been army generals. Only Wendell L. Willkie had never held any public position, civilian or military. Counting Theodore Roosevelt in 1912, one had previously been President. The over-all conclusion one can draw from these data regarding present or previous offices held is that political experience is essential, but holding office is not essential. A qualification to be added is that a man nominated and then defeated in a presidential election is usually considered unavailable thereafter. William J. Bryan, Thomas E. Dewey, and Adlai E. Stevenson are the only exceptions since the Civil War.

The evidence that a position is not essential as an immediate springboard for a presidential nomination is subject to some refinement. A candidate needs an operating base, and public office is generally the most useful for his purpose. The base should provide him with some spare time and with opportunities for traveling and consulting. The base should also make it possible for him to get publicity. A public office is important for another reason: candidates, like nearly everyone else, need to make a living. All of these advantages can be offset or duplicated by other circumstances,

---

11 See E. Allen Helms, "The President and Party Politics," *Journal of Politics*, Vol. 11 (1949) pp. 44-47.

but a man not in public office needs to have a job permitting him free time and paying him a salary or he should have sufficient money to live on without being employed. Irrespective of the candidate's current political status, he usually is considered more available if he has been elected to offices. He and his managers can claim he is capable of being elected because he has proved his vote-getting ability. Some of the most successful presidential candidates never previously ran for office, but they have always been considered exceptions to the rule.[12]

A second major factor of availability is *residence in a key state.* Presidential elections are computed in terms of electoral votes. The votes of states are added up to see which and how many each party should concentrate upon. This preoccupation of party managers naturally leads to an acute awareness of the states with large electoral votes which each party has a chance of carrying. Any state which fulfills both of these requirements is, politically, a key state and its residents are available on the basis of geography. To be large enough to be a key state, it should have more than twenty-five electoral votes and its voting behavior must stamp it as being definitely bipartisan. Pennsylvania and Texas are key states in size, but each has tended to be a one-party state in presidential elections. Washington is a close state for the major parties, but its electoral votes are too few to make its residents available. Southern states, since the Civil War, have been overlooked in picking candidates because the Democrats could always expect their votes and the Republicans could always expect to lose their votes irrespective of the candidates. Changes in voting behavior and voters' attitudes can change this situation; during the 1940's and 1950's, when the South's dependability seemed to wane, the Democrats were more inclined to consider Southern men, notably the nomination for Vice-President of Senators Truman (Missouri, 1944), Barkley (Kentucky, 1948), Sparkman (Alabama, 1952), and Kefauver (Tennessee, 1956).

The main result of this key-state strategy has been to limit presidential candidates to a very few states. New York and Ohio have traditionally been the most frequently represented on national tickets, as expressions of the sentiment of the East and the Middle West. In every presidential election since the Civil War, at least one of the candidates has been a resident of one or the other state, although John W. Davis in 1924 and Dwight D. Eisenhower in 1952 had established their New York residence late in life and in the latter case the state probably added little to Eisenhower's availability. The high tide in the dominance of the office by Ohio occurred in 1920, when both candidates came from that state.[13] Since then, no Ohioan

---

[12] E.g., famous army generals Zachary Taylor (1848), U. S. Grant (1868), and D. D. Eisenhower (1952); a famous engineer Herbert Hoover (1928), although Mr. Hoover had previously held appointive political positions.

[13] For an analysis of the Ohio tradition, see Kent, *op. cit.,* Chap. 25.

has won the nomination, although some have been active. New York continues to be a foremost key state, furnishing both candidates in 1940 and 1944. The western shift of population is bringing other states into active consideration. California, whose population began its remarkable increase after 1920, is gradually coming to rank with New York in consideration. The election of Herbert Hoover in 1928 promises to be the beginning of a line of California candidates throughout the twentieth century.

There is some reason to question the validity of the reasoning that equates availability with key states. The basic assumption is that a state is more easily carried by a resident because of personal familiarity and state pride. If a man has carried the state on a previous occasion, the argument is reinforced, and he is often accepted uncritically as being able to win the state's electoral votes. In most presidential elections the losing candidate has lost his own state, suggesting that a trend or a swing of the voters in a state is not retarded by a favorite son. Ability to campaign and to be elected are all-important factors in selecting nominees, but the assumption that a state's voters will automatically be more receptive to a fellow citizen of the state is not only subject to limitations but also needlessly eliminates other candidates who are otherwise available.

To seek a presidential nomination, a man needs a *record in some kind of affairs partaking of a public nature.* Normally, candidates have political records. Some have been military men. A few have been specialists in far-flung administration operations (e.g., Herbert Hoover during World War I) or in the exercise of judicial and administrative functions (e.g., William H. Taft and Charles E. Hughes). Wendell L. Willkie had a record in corporate finance and management. Almost more important than the field in which the record is made is the nature of the record. In the first place, it should be devoid of blemishes or major errors in judgment, tact and execution. If some act or word or failure can be turned against a man and used as a handle, so to speak, in getting hold of him for purposes of attack, he probably is not available. If he is associated with a policy which is anathema to a large group of voters, the mere reference to this fact will place him and his supporters on the defensive. In the second place, the candidate's record should contain some positive accomplishments or some facet capable of popularization to be used as a talking point; e.g., the Republicans in 1936 constantly pointed out that Governor Alfred Landon of Kansas had balanced that state's budget. A safe record devoid of mistakes is not enough if it can successfully be attacked as a do-nothing, colorless record. One incident may be enough to create the illusion of a commendable record, like Calvin Coolidge's ending the Boston police strike during his Massachusetts governorship.

Some of the requirements of availability could impress an untutored observer as being so extraneous to the requirements of the Presidency as to be frivolous and unbelievable. Nevertheless, in politics a man's *personal qualities* are always important. People are both curious and concerned about the kind of men who offer themselves for office, and particularly for the nation's highest office. A President, Americans seem to believe, should not be too different from them. He should, as we like to express it, have the common touch. While being one with his fellow citizens, he should be distinctive to the extent that the public does not resent his aspiring to the office, but is willing to look up to him. To be available, a man needs to be both like and unlike others. He should understand the practical problems encountered in daily living, but he should demonstrate an extra ability to rise above the minutiae of human experiences and achieve something the society evaluates as outstanding and constructive. His personality should be a blend of qualities: a sense of humor but not to the point of frivolity, capacity for serious contemplation and evaluation, a sense of justice and a compassion for those who excite pity. No man can satisfy the absolute requirement of poise, timing, and judgment involved in such attributes, but the candidate who can appear to approximate them most closely is at a great advantage.

Contributing characteristics are equally important. A candidate should be a *family man*. The standard newspaper picture of candidates is a group portrait of the man, his wife, and the sons and/or daughters. Implicitly and explicitly there should be a strong suggestion of a home life in the "normal" American tradition. A widower is perfectly safe, but a candidate who has been divorced still is not completely acceptable.[14] Availability requires a *religious affiliation*. An agnostic, a freethinker, an atheist would seem to be fundamentally barred. Catholic and Jewish candidates have been considered unavailable except for the nomination of Alfred E. Smith, a Catholic, in 1928. In all probability, religion was not the cause of Smith's defeat but it was a prominent issue of the campaign. By 1960, some of the reluctance to consider a Catholic candidate had apparently disappeared. *Age* is a factor of some importance in fixing availability. Roughly speaking, candidates range in age from the late forties to the early sixties. They should be old enough to be accepted as seasoned and matured. They should not be so old as to raise questions about their physical ability to discharge the duties of the office or to raise doubts about their living to the end of their term of office. This last concern was frequently voiced concerning the second-term candidacy of Eisenhower in 1956.

Finally, a man is certainly not available if there is a known *scandal* relating to his personal life that can be used against him. Whispering campaigns are fairly common in presidential elections, and there is little

---

[14] James M. Cox, Democratic candidate in 1920, had been divorced several years previously, had remarried, and was rearing another family. Adlai Stevenson, Democratic candidate in 1952 and 1956, was divorced in 1949 and had not remarried at the time of his nomination.

basis for believing that the rumors whispered, whether true or not, have ever affected the outcome. All the same, no party wants to nominate a candidate who has a reputation which must be defended. The object is to have a candidate who can be presented as a glorious example of the virtues demanded by the American society.[15]

Despite the concrete nature of the concept of availability, it contains a further elusive factor, an indefinable quality. Some candidates have it and some do not. It is an *x* quality which is recognizable but insusceptible of precise description or definition. It involves the *ability of a man to identify himself with his generation* and the spirit of his time. In some way he is able to give expression to the aspirations of large numbers of people who cannot formulate exactly what they feel but can sense in the tone of a voice or the magnetism of a face the expressions of their own muted thoughts.

Sometimes a candidate by design or by luck or by necessity becomes identified with a winning issue—identified with it both in popular understanding and in terms acceptable to powerful interests. Available candidates carefully watch public reactions to issues so as not to offend; but from time to time there appears to be a marriage of a candidate and an issue capable of sweeping all opposition aside. A case in point was William McKinley in 1896, who ran on the issue of sound money, although he had anticipated that the leading issue would be the tariff with which he had been closely identified while in Congress. The result was his identification with the "gold dollar" despite a congressional voting record that included favorable votes on silver bills. In a different category was the candidacy in 1860 of Abraham Lincoln, who could correctly anticipate and prepare for slavery as the major issue. Franklin D. Roosevelt, exhibiting a remarkable amount of the *x* factor in availability in 1932, identified himself not with any given issue so much as with a general hope and a new resolve to overcome the depression. The nearest approximation to a statement of his appeal was the famous psychological attack embodied in the words: "The only thing we have to fear is fear itself." Yet in the final analysis it was the total man, the personality, that struck the responsive chord among the voters; the quality was indefinable, but it was real. In another context, Warren G. Harding in 1920 epitomized an inarticulate longing to live a quiet, happy life; his identification was with a spirit or a theme and was most eloquently expressed in the words: "Let's get back to normalcy."

Inasmuch as all candidates actual or potential have been men, it may very well be that *sex* is the first factor in availability. Whether the sporadic comments regarding a woman candidate will in time have any real effect is beyond rational speculation. There is some likelihood that the entering

---

[15] The most famous scandals involving presidential candidates occurred in 1884. James G. Blaine was attacked for financial dealings which had been sources of contention for eight years, and Grover Cleveland was attacked for fathering an illegitimate child.

wedge, if it ever comes, will be by way of the Vice-Presidency. The day that a woman can be seriously considered as presidential timber will obviously be a day of changed thought patterns and mores of the American public.

Two concluding observations to be made about availability are, *first*, that it is an ideal and can only be approximated. No candidate fulfills these standards 100%. There is always some weakness, some deficiency in the most promising man, and all supporters of candidates have something to explain and defend as well as something to praise and glorify. To say that no one is completely available is to say that there is no perfect candidate just as there is no perfect specimen or representative of any humanly created concept.[16]

Second, availability strikes the student of American politics as being peculiarly consistent with the whole psychology of our party system. The utilitarian, sophisticated, nondoctrinaire qualities which took form under the leadership of the Jeffersonian Republicans pointed directly to such pragmatic concepts; but availability did not emerge as a fully elaborated standard until the Jacksonian period, and its high priest was Thurlow Weed, one of the outstanding Whig and Republican managers from the 1830's to the 1850's. Perhaps to him more than any other one man is due the credit for formulating the strategy of running military heroes devoid of political records. He recognized the stature of Henry Clay and of Daniel Webster as leaders of thought, but he knew they could not win the Presidency. When others were willing to follow Clay to the grave, Weed resisted because he knew there was no political future in the grave. His standard of the electability of a candidate as the primary question to be considered disgusted many of his colleagues, but it was vindicated by its inherent logic.

No Democrat of the same period is so closely associated with the development of availability, but Democratic conventions from 1844 to 1856 produced a series of candidates who were eminently available. In 1848 there began a series of three Democratic candidates conforming to the criterion of "Northern candidates with Southern principles," an open admission that the Democrats were doing their best to avoid the horns of the slavery dilemma by nominating men with a claim to the confidence of both North and South. The scientific detachment which the application of availability implies has its limits. As calculating a manager as Thurlow Weed met his nemesis in 1860, when Lincoln most nearly fitted the require-

---

[16] Public opinion polls, being used more and more as a method of measuring or testing availability, supposedly objectify the quest for determining who has the qualities to be elected. William G. Carleton, "The Revolution in the Presidential Nominating Convention," *Political Science Quarterly,* Vol. 72 (1957) pp. 224-240, develops the concept that the pressures of mass democracy require a popular candidate, if necessary a celebrity outside politics.

ments; William H. Seward, in whom Weed had centered his hopes and ambitions, was, like Clay and Webster, too much a recognized party leader to be its presidential candidate.

Challenge of a Preconvention Campaign. No matter how promising a candidate's chances are to capture a presidential nomination, the embarking upon the venture is one of the greatest gambles and herculean undertakings imaginable. James A. Farley, a master of the preconvention and convention techniques, stated the situation far more realistically than any amateur and more forcefully than most professionals do:

> The capturing of a presidential nomination is one of the most formidable enterprises the political animal can tackle. The race is not always to the swift, the wise, the able, or the prominent, or—there would be no dark horses.
>
> In politics, you can speak too often or not often enough; you can speak too loud or too soft; you can start too soon or too late; you can be too polite or not polite enough; and again you can be too friendly or not friendly enough. Any of these extremes at any given time may be fatal. Worst of all, one is frequently called upon to make split-second decisions. And, unfortunately, what may look good now may turn out disastrously six months from now. Public good will at any given moment can be as elusive as quicksilver. It is easy to offend the public by being too cocky or too upstage, or by being neither. Public good will can be as difficult to capture and hang onto as a greased pig. Many a promising political career has been blasted because an aspirant for office has, more often than not unwittingly, wounded the feelings of a party patriarch—a being who normally has a hide as impervious to criticism as that of a rhinoceros—but who displays the tender susceptibilities of a lovelorn maiden when political amenities are to be observed.[17]

These hazards are only for the courageous and ambitious and for the professionals. Some candidates have not been professionals themselves but have had the services of managers who were highly competent in using the tools of the trade. To pretend, either with wishful thinkers or with the successful candidates, that nominations are products of spontaneous developments and that the blushing nominee was drafted against his will or his better judgment is intriguing for the romantics, but is a form of delusion for serious students of politics.[18] Every move cannot be planned in advance

---

[17] *Jim Farley's Story* (New York: McGraw-Hill Book Company, Inc., 1948) p. 8.

[18] It is with considerable surprise that one discovers that even Lord Bryce could be taken in by the folklore that men who fight their way to the top are not active agents in their own behalf: "Lincoln was never a professional politician, for he continued to practice as a lawyer till he became President; but he was so useful to his party that for some years before 1860 he had been obliged to spend a great part of his time in political work, and probably some would have called him a professional."—*American Commonwealth* (New York: Commonwealth Publishing Company, 1908) Vol. 2, p. 68, note 14. See Joseph B. Bishop, *Presidential Nominations and Elections* (New York: Charles Scribner's Sons, 1916) pp. 37-39, for a sketch of Lincoln's highly professional efforts in pursuit of the nomination in 1860.

and many fortuitous events intervene, but getting nominated is the result of wanting and working for the nomination. Candidates rarely accept a nomination with reluctance. Any man who genuinely does not want to run can remove himself from consideration by the simple expedient employed by General William T. Sherman, who announced: "I will not accept if nominated, and will not serve if elected." There never was any doubt of Sherman's real meaning, but so-called reluctant candidates never speak so directly.

Although candidates are not reluctant, it is unwise for them to appear too eager. A very unfavorable public reaction is likely to be created by tactics that are openly avid and grasping. The standard pattern is to assume a certain degree of aloofness while working diligently to win. The results of asserted disinterest are incalculable upon a candidate's followers and upon the general public. In 1920 William G. McAdoo really stimulated his followers to greater efforts when he issued a statement that he did not consider himself a candidate and asked that no further efforts be used in his behalf; the politically astute observers noted that the statement failed to include an assertion that McAdoo would not accept a nomination. Calvin Coolidge's celebrated statement, "I do not choose to run for President in 1928," led to one of the interesting puzzles of American politics. Some of his supporters remained unconvinced until Herbert Hoover was nominated. There is some evidence that Coolidge really wanted another term but wanted to be nominated without any action on his part.[19] If so, he was a victim of the popular fallacy. Whatever his intentions, he proved that even a President cannot be renominated if he keeps himself shut off from his friends and refuses even to discuss the political situation.[20]

Types of Candidates. The generalizations of preconvention presidential campaigns are affected by the categories of the various aspirants. There are, in the vernacular expression, candidates and candidates. One type is not serious, but enters the campaign mostly in name for some extraneous reason, such as publicity to help him hold or win other offices, or power

---

[19] I. H. Hoover, *Forty-two Years in the White House* (Boston: Houghton Mifflin Company, 1934).

[20] The validity of this rule is subject to question in the case of Franklin D. Roosevelt's third nomination in 1940. However, the differences in procedures between Coolidge and Roosevelt are worth noting. Hoover was the almost unquestioned successor to Coolidge who not only did nothing to embarrass Hoover's campaign but even kept him in the Cabinet where his campaign was facilitated. It is now well known that Roosevelt was constantly discussing the nomination with his friends as early as 1939. While he publicly disparaged no competitor, he maneuvered them, through appointments or otherwise, into difficulties of one kind or another. In 1928 Hoover was the only candidate with a chance to be nominated, granted Coolidge's withdrawal. In 1940 Roosevelt was the only serious candidate despite competitors. The two cases are also different in that there was a well-defined feeling that without Roosevelt his party would lose in 1940, but no such feeling existed in 1928 regarding Coolidge.

to control a block of delegates for trading purposes. He may enter as a stalking-horse for another candidate, i.e., hold as many votes as possible until a psychological moment in the convention when he can release them to the candidate he is supporting. A man may have his name mentioned in connection with the Presidency as a means of associating himself with the office in the public mind so that a future campaign can be undertaken seriously. A man may enter simply to demonstrate that he can control his party in his state; he may be forced to take such action to forestall a rival faction's attempt to dislodge him and his followers from control of the state machinery. In states where the national-convention delegation chooses the national committeeman and committeewoman, control of the delegation carries the power to select these offices. One of the standard methods of controlling a state's delegation is for one of the state leaders to become a nominal presidential candidate: his opponents in his party fear to oppose him openly, so the delegation is pledged to him and follows his wishes in matters affecting organization.

There is a second type of candidate differentiated from the previous type largely on the basis of intention. It is impossible to read a man's mind and know exactly why he enters a preconvention campaign. In one sense, everyone who permits his name to be used probably harbors secret hopes that the lightning will strike him. The distinction between these two types is further confused by their generally being favorite sons and having either no support or very limited support outside their own states. This second type is motivated by the desire to win the nomination rather than by extraneous objectives and is usually designated a "dark horse." At least candidates of the second type are always possible nominees in terms of their availability. Some presidents of the first type are strictly unavailable and cannot even be flattered with the term "dark horse."

Revealing the Candidacy. In addition to these more localized and remote candidates are the men who from the outset appear to be strong contenders with support more widely distributed over the country. Most of the classic problems of candidacies apply to this third type. These candidates begin early to formulate their strategy but keep their plans of attack flexible as they carefully watch the unfolding political forces. Beginning shortly after the congressional elections immediately preceding the presidential year, the organization for capturing the convention is gradually put together. Time is of the essence, because the convention is only eighteen months away, but at this stage the candidate usually is careful not to reveal himself openly. For a number of months he will either refuse to comment on his plans or will deny he is a candidate, e.g., Thomas E. Dewey in January 1947 denied he had presidential ambitions for 1948, and early in 1951 a political manager of Senator Robert A. Taft said he would not seek the nomination in 1952.[21] The opposite method of proceeding was adopted by the Roosevelt organization for 1932. In his campaign for re-election as governor of New York in 1930 every effort was made, according to James A. Farley, "to pile up a record-breaking majority in order to impress his vote-getting ability upon the country generally." The day following Roosevelt's victory by a 725,000 majority, Farley and Louis M. Howe issued a statement, one paragraph reading as follows:

> I fully expect that the call will come to Governor Roosevelt when the first presidential primary is held, which will be late next year. The Democrats in the Nation naturally want as their candidate for President the man who has shown himself capable of carrying the most important state in the country by a record-breaking majority.[22]

The advantage of this method is that one gets a head start on competitors by grasping the initiative. The risk is that competitors will be frightened into a coalition against the candidate.

Winning Support of Leaders. When a man is expected to be a candidate, his exact method of procedure may be further complicated as was the case of Alfred E. Smith after his defeat in the election of 1928. His popularity was so great that it was impossible to dismiss him as a candidate in 1932. As the years passed, a competitor began appearing in Franklin D. Roosevelt, his successor in the governor's office in New York. Since the two men were residents of the same state, New York Democratic leaders were in a difficult situation. This dilemma was apparently dispelled when Smith announced that he was not a candidate and actually told his friends late in 1931 that he meant what he had said. Consequently, some of them, like Edward J. Flynn and Herbert H. Lehman, felt reassured and joined in the Roosevelt campaign. In the spring of 1932 Smith became a candidate for the nomination and called upon his friends to support him, but some of them were too deeply involved in the Roosevelt organization to extricate themselves, even assuming that they would have preferred to support Smith.[23] To have the support of outstanding leaders in one's own as well as in other states constitutes having support in the national committee and the committee on arrangements.

Need for Money and Publicity. After the basic strategy is selected by the candidate and his managers, the two principal problems remaining are money and publicity; they are separate but related, since success with

[21] United Press dispatch dated January 29, 1947; Associated Press dispatch dated February 6, 1951.

[22] Farley, *Behind the Ballots* (New York: Harcourt, Brace and Company, 1938) pp. 62-63.

[23] *Ibid.*, pp. 59-60, 78; Edward J. Flynn, *You're the Boss* (New York: The Viking Press, 1947) pp. 85-87.

one tends to produce success with the other. "It is the combination that is truly effective and really essential."[24] Money must be found among contributors unless the candidate himself can finance his own campaign. Both the raising and spending of money require careful handling and deft management to avoid ostentatious show or the illusion of opulence. One of the standard sources of attack upon a candidate is the amount of money he is spending and the nature of his contributors. An error in these operations can prove to be fatal if cleverly exploited by the opposition.

If money and its ramifications are secret operations, no secret is made of the man himself. No opportunity is lost to get his name before the public and keep it there. At this stage, public officeholders, notably federal officials and governors, have an advantage because they are better able to get themselves publicized. A governor can get a hearing within his own state for his views, and if they are novel enough or pushed with persistence, he will be heard of in other states. The annual governor's conference is a primary political meeting ground where the state executives sound one another out and size one another up; those who have presidential ambitions may advance themselves at these meetings, as Franklin D. Roosevelt did in 1931. Governors, members of Congress, and federal administrative officers have opportunities to accept speaking engagements throughout the country—in some cases arranging to have themselves invited to speak—and aid the nation's citizens in getting to know them. The main danger of intensive speaking tours is that frequent absence from his office may subject an official to criticism that he is neglecting his duties. The candidate without political office has a more challenging task, and different men will choose different techniques in the face of different situations. One solution was the grueling speaking tour entered into by Harold Stassen beginning months before the Republican convention of 1948.

Winning Delegates. Simultaneously with the raising of money and developing of publicity, a candidate's managers begin traveling to sound out local leaders and determine the prospects for delegates in each state. In this work it is virtually necessary for the candidate to have about him men who are well acquainted with political leaders and situations in the various states, so that there is a line of communication to state and local organizations and sufficient understanding to evaluate the information that is gathered. The candidate himself, if he is experienced, can be very effective in these negotiations, and the leaders prefer talking to him directly. However, he should avoid making too open an effort, for his movements will be well reported, especially if his campaign for getting publicity is succeeding. His managers may move freely about the country and consult without receiving undue notice.

---

24 Kent, *op. cit.,* p. 237.

The possibilities at this stage are countless. In one state the factional situation may be so intense that the safest thing to do is keep away so as not to become involved. In another state an important leader may be in need of campaign funds, and the candidate can contribute some money and win the leader's gratitude and commitments. In still another state there may be a favorite son who wants his state's delegation to vote for him at least on the first ballot, so the candidate refrains from antagonizing him but tries to become the second choice of the delegation.[25] These negotiations are almost entirely verbal and have little binding effect even when promises are made. Many local and state leaders will hedge, preferring to defer a decision until the picture becomes clearer and they have talked with other candidates. This whole process is a maze of urgings and counterurgings, reconciliation of interests and objectives at cross purposes. It is at best only partly coordinated and proceeds in a spirit of hopeful assumption and calculated bluff. Even the arrangements that are made are subject to change in the light of new circumstances.

The method of choosing delegates in a state determines the candidate's techniques. Where the convention method is used, a candidate may be well pleased if he can win some of the districts or some of the delegates at large. Among the Democrats a candidate will try to have a state convention invoke the unit rule if he has a majority of the delegates, but will fight against the delegation operating under the unit rule if he has less than a majority of the delegates. If the candidate cannot have delegates pledged to him, he will prefer uninstructed ones. Skill in convention maneuvers is brought into play. Efforts to elect friendly delegates to district and state conventions are made in order to elect friendly national delegates. Where direct election of delegates is used, quite different problems arise. If there is a favorite son, his slate of delegates will probably be elected without opposition. Otherwise, a candidate decides how good his chances are to elect his delegates and to win a presidential preference primary.

Usually, a leading candidate does not enter all primaries. To submit his name requires that he conduct a campaign among the voters in behalf of his candidacy, and the campaign costs money. It is preferable to spend money where it will do the most good. The overriding reason dictating caution is the psychological effect upon a candidate of entering a primary and being beaten. The object is to stimulate the band-wagon effect throughout the country and especially within his own party. For him to be beaten in a primary or for his delegates to be beaten suggests that the candidate is not a good vote-getter and discourages those uncommitted delegates who go to the national convention looking for a winner.

---

25 Although there have been a few cases of a candidate opposing a favorite son in his own state, they have been violations of the rule. See Clarence A. Berdahl, "Presidential Selection and Democratic Government," *Journal of Politics,* Vol. 11 (1949) pp. 37-39.

These are some of the problems of candidates for a presidential nomination as they lay the groundwork for the supreme effort of capturing a major party's national convention. The ramifications of this preliminary campaign are too large in number and too complex to permit more than the suggestion of the most standard lines of development. It is from the combined and diffused labors of candidates and leaders of party machinery meshed together in heterogeneous forms and relations that the total organization of a political party functions for a few days every four years in national conventions.

Much of the foregoing discussion and all of the following discussion in this chapter assume a convention either of the "out" party, or of the "in" party when the President is not a candidate—a convention in which there is a genuine contest for the nomination.

CONVENTION OPERATIONS

Assemblying of the Party. Amid the growing fury of political voices and the accelerated efforts of candidates and their managers, the national convention operations begin. Originally it was customary for candidates to remain at home and keep in communication with their convention headquarters instead of going to the convention themselves. There were departures from this practice, but beginning in the 1940's it was almost entirely disregarded. No longer is the candidate expected to remain at a respectful distance; he can pursue his course openly and frankly on the scene of operations, although it is not customary for leading candidates to appear in the convention hall unless they have genuine business there, as Adlai Stevenson had in 1952, when as governor of Illinois he welcomed the delegates to the state.

Days or weeks before the convention the candidates establish their hotel headquarters, and their staffs enter the final swirl of activity. Officials of the national committee move about in final preparations for the coming events, along with the members of the arrangements committee, who are plunged headlong into the maelstrom of checking everything at the last minute. The state leaders entrain for Mecca, stating banalities or making cryptic observations designed to intensify the mystery of what is going to happen. Gradually through the week preceding the opening day the delegates filter in and the movement becomes a torrent by Saturday and Sunday. The small fry of the party seldom make the headlines in the newspapers, but their physical presence increases the surface confusion.[26]

---

[26] ". . . Old political fire horses come out to rub against political hacks at conventions. Men who are big fish in their communities and states, but small fry nationally, like to look over the candidates. The high moments of bygone conventions are lived over again by the veterans. There is much dark whispering of trades and agreements. Even the least important of the party can pass judgment on the strategists. Everyone

Attitudes of Delegates. Influencing these delegates is the business of the candidates, and there are nearly as many attitudes among the delegates as there are strategies for getting their votes.[27] At one extreme are the delegates directly elected under specific pledges to support a given candidate. Such delegates have a moral obligation to perform as expected at the convention. The greatest insurance that they will so perform is their genuine belief in the candidate and their close association with his campaign in their state. From the point of view of both the candidate and the voters, the delegates are much more likely to support the candidate if he selects them and under the state's law designates them on the ballot as his official delegates. In states where delegates can "adopt" a popular candidate as their preference, they may be less loyal to him; but if they were elected with a commitment to support him, they cannot afford to give the impression of cynically disregarding their word by forsaking him too early in the fight. The sentiment of a party organization or the evidence of public opinion in some states can be equally binding upon delegates elected in conventions. If the candidate succeeds in having his real supporters chosen, irrespective of the method, he can be as sure of them as one can be sure of anything in a national convention.

The great area of doubt is represented by those delegates who are specifically uncommitted or are elected without a preference. Leaders of these delegations look about cautiously. They very likely have a personal favorite and have made this preference known, but until such leaders can see with greater clarity how the forces are developing, they cannot and will not bind themselves irrevocably to any course of action. They have their own states and localities to think of, the county courthouses and city halls and state capitols. They cannot risk making mistakes that their factional opponents can use against them, any more than they can court defeat by the opposition party. They have friends from other states with whom they would like to cooperate. They have colleagues from their own state with whom they will continue working and who cannot be alienated. Above everything else, they want a presidential candidate who can win and who will be sufficiently popular to help them carry their own tickets. Of equal importance, they want to detect who the winner will be, so that they can

---

likes to weigh charge and countercharge. Everyone enjoys assaying rumors. Many like to hold forth on what the various contenders should do and what line the party should adopt in order in win in November. Best of all, their pleasure really begins when the show is over. They begin to shine when they get home and describe convention scenes and the part they played in the nominations. They have conversational fodder for days, weeks, months, and even years. And the stories gain with each telling."—Farley, *Jim Farley's Story*, p. 260.

27 At the 1952 Democratic convention when Michael De Salle was asked if there was harmony in the Ohio delegation, he replied: "We're always in harmony. We've got sixty delegates and only fifty-four factions."—Quoted in the *New York Times*, July 22, 1952.

deal with him while the votes of their states are crucial to him.[28] This is
the point at which future arrangements are often made. Appointments to
office are promised; patronage is assured; money is delivered or pledged
for campaign and organization purposes. If a leader can come through
this ordeal with success, he has a minimum amount of explaining to do
when he goes home; the happy results are conclusive justification of his
actions.

Diagnosis and Control of Delegates. The degree of elaborateness and
professional competence of a candidate's **organization determines** the
amount and kind of preliminary analysis of delegates. In some cases card-
file indexes are made, listing each delegate and any information about him
of political usefulness. The candidates' organization can know where the
delegate is vulnerable and what his motivations are. Delegates are influenced in one way or another. Some have their convention expenses paid
for them, a relationship amounting to buying delegates. Some do not
always stay bought; if they get the money before the convention, they may
spend it and be in need of more to keep them going. For this reason the
financial arrangements are often made after they arrive at the convention
city. The delegate may have his actual room and meal expenses paid, or
if the candidate is more affluent, the delegate may be given something in
addition.[29] Delegates are invited to visit candidates' headquarters, meet
the candidates themselves, and sometimes listen to speeches. Representatives
of candidates circulate in hotels and other public places, as well as in the
convention hall, talking to delegates, striking up or renewing acquaintances,
keeping after the indecisive, and trying to shake the foundations of other
candidates while holding their own votes intact.

Political-Party Pressures. An established procedure of candidates is
to approach delegates through political leaders to whom the delegates will
listen. If one or more of the leaders of a delegation who are also, as a rule,
powerful in the party in the state can be convinced, they will attempt to
whip the delegation into line. Techniques in these cases depend upon the
leaders and the delegates. In one case, it may be tough, direct words. In
another case, more subtle or more gentle methods are preferable, and in
many delegations these are the only feasible ones. The leader may ask the

---

28 Arthur Krock once pointed out the historical success of Pennsylvania Republican
leaders in this respect by following three precepts: "1. Don't be sentimental about
Presidential candidates. It doesn't pay. 2. Reserve or scatter your support until it will
make the contribution required for somebody's nomination, or most of it. 3. Have a
good understanding with his authorized agent before you make it."——*New York Times*,
April 24, 1952. In 1940 even the Pennsylvania leaders failed to sense the drift in time
to contribute to Willkie's nomination.

29 Only North Dakota authorizes a payment of public funds for a national-convention
delegation—a maximum of $200 for each delegate.

delegates to vote for a particular candidate on the next ballot, just to see what happens. The leader may be better able to bring pressure from home upon recalcitrants. A telephone call from a county chairman or a close personal friend who is not at the convention may win over a delegate here and there.

External Group Pressures. Delegates are never free from the attempts of individuals and groups outside of the convention to influence them. Constituents back home keep up a barrage of letters, telegrams, and telephone calls. Some of these people, representing organizations with various objectives, follow their delegates to the convention city to keep them under surveillance. A candidate is always looking among the interest groups for allies who will supplement his efforts in winning delegates. Committed delegates are as likely to be besieged with communications designed to keep them steadfast and loyal to their commitments as uncommitted delegates are to be pressured to make up their minds. Delegates with varying degrees of commitments are almost constantly under fire from those who want them to break the commitments and vote for someone else. While delegates who are elected with a firm pledge to support one candidate are often conceded the right to redeem the pledge, other candidates pursue them to win their preference when and if their avowed choice weakens or drops out of the running.

One of the outstanding means of persuasion is to work through the financial and business community. A candidate favored by the Eastern money circles has at his disposal radiating lines of communication into every American city and hamlet. A very instructive case in point was the nomination of Wendell L. Willkie by the Republicans in 1940, an event often hailed in uncritical circles as a true draft, an unfettered expression of the sincere desires of the "people" brought about by amateurs. According to a woman from a Western state, "my husband and I came here [Philadelphia] as delegates for Herbert Hoover, but my husband's banker called him long-distance and told him we should switch to Willkie—and we did." [30]

Stampeding Techniques. The constant attempt in conventions to stampede the delegates, another thoroughly American touch, appears in countless forms. The Willkie nomination furnished a brilliant use of an ancient means of the stampede by filling the galleries of the convention hall with the partisans of one of the candidates. In 1940 the attempt was made to overwhelm the delegates with the constant chant of "We want

---

[30] Thomas L. Stokes, "Getting Nominated Is an Intricate Business," *New York Times Magazine*, April 20, 1952. Stokes added: "Her husband certainly knew, whether she did or not, that his own banker's call was, in turn, the result of a long-distance call to him by a representative of international finance and foreign-trade interests in New York who had an organization at work on this sort of chore."

Willkie," as though this were the fateful voice of the masses of citizens beyond the confines of the hall. One of the earlier famous uses of this technique was the attempt of the Lincoln and Seward managers to fill the galleries against each other in 1860. The Lincoln men proved far more adept, and the pandemonium of spectators yelling at the tops of their voices for the Rail Splitter was a psychological factor in his nomination.[31] Obviously, some cooperation is needed for a candidate's organization to secure enough tickets to pack the galleries. The practice of printing imitation tickets has been resorted to. More frequently, genuine tickets are received from those in charge. Large blocks of tickets are passed out to those who know what to do when they get inside.

Announcements and Endorsements. Organized gallery demonstrations unleashed upon signal illustrate the most important feature of the stampede technique: timing. The second most important consideration is to give the impression of naturalness and spontaneity. To achieve this effect, there must be careful advance planning. Unexpected announcements of support for a candidate by influential party leaders are both carefully timed and made to appear as genuine expressions of recently acquired conclusions. Thomas E. Dewey gained a great psychological advantage in 1948 when certain Pennsylvania and Indiana leaders at the beginning of the convention announced they had made up their minds to support him. Sometimes these endorsements are held back until after the balloting begins. They can be especially effective if made by one candidate withdrawing in favor of another or by someone who controls a block of votes.

Descriptive Phrases and Speeches. Slogans or descriptions to epitomize a candidate are designed to overwhelm delegates. Significant examples have been: "I like Ike," "The Happy Warrior," "The Plumed Knight." Always the candidate is associated with events or ideas designed to please the party members or stir old sentiments, as the opening words of Senator Roscoe Conkling's speech in 1880 presenting U. S. Grant:

> "When asked what State he hails from,
>   Our sole reply shall be,
>   He comes from Appomattox,
>   And its famous apple tree."

Speeches made on behalf of candidates emphasize their availability: they can carry this or that state; they command the support of these or some other groups. Rarely can sheer eloquence be depended upon to stampede a convention, and a candidate does not want too eloquent a spokesman. James A. Garfield impressed the Republican convention in 1880 so favor-

---

31 Bishop, *op. cit.*, pp. 40-43.

ably in his appearances on the rostrum in behalf of Senator John Sherman that Garfield became the dark-horse nominee. The most outstanding use of eloquence in securing a nomination was William J. Bryan's famous Cross of Gold speech in 1896, but at least Bryan was not ostensibly speaking for another candidate. Occasionally an eloquent speech can hold the attention of a whole convention, of both the friends and opponents of the candidate, but it is unlikely to win many votes for the candidate. When Senator Everett Dirksen spoke in the Republican convention of 1952 during the debate over the credentials-committee report, an attentive silence settled down upon that throng for a few minutes under the force of the senator's words and voice. The spell was shattered abruptly by the challenge he threw at the Dewey faction, a bold move that suggested the futility of winning a hopeless fight by oratory and that served only the function of catharsis in having the quiet words of a decade spoken openly and loudly.

Patterns of Voting. A stampede is produced by creating in one way or another the band-wagon psychology.[32] The insistent urgings of a candidate's managers are finally believed. One leader discovers that other leaders are falling in line. Delegates sense that something is in the wind, and they become acutely observant. The most objective and convincing evidence of a candidate's fortunes are the roll calls. Sometimes nothing definite is indicated on the early ballots taken to elect chairmen and adopt committee reports, so the proof of relative strength is deferred. If a candidate can demonstrate his strength on an early ballot involving organization or rules or credentials, he achieves a tremendous psychological advantage over his competitors; if he fears he cannot win such votes, he tries to avoid contests.

When the balloting to choose a presidential candidate begins, the leading contenders are watched closely to see if they gain or lose as each roll call is taken. There is an almost ironclad rule that the leaders must gain on each ballot. If they lose, they are considered to be doomed. If they remain stationary, they are looked upon as having reached the maximum of their strength and as being out of the running. For this reason, convention floor managers sometimes hold votes in abeyance and have them gradually added to keep up an illusion of increments of strength. This rule does not apply to favorite sons and dark horses who begin with only a modest number of votes and may lose moderately without injuring their chances. On those occasions when the balloting has gone on interminably for twenty, thirty, forty or more roll calls, the rule does not apply. In the successive votes, the uninstructed delegates may vote for different candidates,

---

[32] A band wagon has been described as something everyone climbs on as soon as they think it is going someplace.

cautiously anticipating a stampede. Under these circumstances, the totals for each candidate will vary considerably from time to time without harmful effects.[33]

At some point in the balloting occurs what is called a "break," an event that ends the deadlock. It may be the withdrawal of one of the candidates either in favor of another candidate or merely releasing his delegates. If he has a substantial following and it moves to one of the leaders in the voting, the handwriting is on the wall; this was the method by which Franklin D. Roosevelt won in 1932, following the negotiated withdrawal of John N. Garner. The break may be the shift of a large number of delegates in one state from a candidate they have been supporting to another. The break may be some extraneous event like the arrival of President Truman at the convention city in 1952 after two ballots had been taken; everyone concluded that arrangements were under way to break the stalemate on the third ballot.

The break may be that point at which a candidate is suddenly discovered to be within 20 or 30 votes of a majority after he has gradually inched forward on each ballot. In the 1920 Democratic Convention a stampede began on the forty-fourth ballot when James M. Cox was within 27 votes of a nomination. Colorado was recognized and cast all of its 12 votes for Cox. Since Colorado had previously cast 9 votes for him, this was a gain of only 3 votes, but the switch electrified the convention. As delegation chairmen all over the hall shouted above the din to be recognized, the leaders for William G. McAdoo, Cox's chief competitor, moved to make the nomination unanimous.[34] If the trend of the voting becomes unmistakably clear, the break may occur when the leading candidate is fifty to a hundred votes short; e.g., in the Republican convention of 1948, Dewey demonstrated his invincibility on two ballots and his competitors withdrew at the beginning of the third ballot.

The break may be the result of a prior agreement by the terms of which a block of votes will be switched if they are enough to make a nomination. A classic example of such an agreement occurred in the 1952 Republican convention; 604 votes constituted a majority, and those keeping a running count discovered that General Eisenhower had about 590 votes after all the states and territories had been called on the first ballot. Minnesota, which had originally cast 9 votes for Eisenhower and 19 for Stassen, was recognized for the purpose of changing its vote and cast all 28 for Eisenhower. This was enough to nominate him and immediately

---

33 Democratic conventions have been more productive of these deadlocks than Republican conventions. The two-thirds rule was frequently a cause of the Democrats' extended balloting, but the Republicans appear to be better able to reach compromises quickly and forestall a bruising fight on the floor.

34 *Official Report of the Proceedings of the Democratic National Convention*, 1920, pp. 400-450.

most of the states voting for Senator Taft created pandemonium trying to be recognized to shift their votes also.[35]

Once the break occurs, delegation chairmen, federal officials, and individual delegates begin scrambling to be the one who actually delivers the votes that make the majority. Floor managers of other candidates often fight for a microphone in order to be the first to surrender. Whether individual state delegations are asking for the floor to change the state's vote or managers are trying to get the honor of first moving that the nomination be made unanimous, the permanent chairman is able to exercise some discretion in determining who shall have the honor of being recognized.[36]

Defensive Tactics. Basically there is no defense against a stampede after the break occurs. When managers fear they are at a tactical disadvantage, they often use delaying tactics by moving an adjournment or having several individual state delegations polled.[37] The best defense is to anticipate and prevent such an occurrence. In this and in all other respects a candidate needs an efficient line of communication from his headquarters to the convention hall, so that decisions can be relayed rapidly. One of the marks distinguishing a professional from an amateurish organization is the provision for handling this elementary problem.

Strategy of Convention Managers. As distinct from the managers of candidates there are party leaders best classified as convention managers. They include the national chairman, the permanent chairman of the convention, assorted state leaders, and if the convention is that of the "in" party, members of the national administration, e.g., Harry Hopkins at the 1940 Democratic convention. These leaders need not be delegates or even publicly recognized party leaders. They can be men of wide influence in labor unions, agriculture, reform movements, business, and finance. They may or may not be openly identified with a candidate, although they invariably have favorites among the candidates. In some conventions these managers become part of one or another candidate's organization and try to guide the nomination toward him, as most of the Democratic convention

---

[35] *Official Report of the Proceedings of the Twenty-Fifth Republican National Convention,* 1952, pp. 388-406.

[36] In 1952, Sam Rayburn recognized his friend and colleague in the House of Representatives, Walter Granger of Utah, to permit him to make the change in the vote which actually gave Adlai Stevenson a majority for the nomination.

[37] These and other purposes can be served by a delegate requesting a poll of his delegation besides the ostensible purpose of determining the accuracy of the vote. The request may be intended to force one or more delegates to vote publicly so that their constituents can discover if they are abiding by their instructions. Since the introduction of radio and television, this device also gets a person's name and face before the public for a few fleeting moments.

managers in 1952 worked for Adlai Stevenson. In this kind of situation, when a candidate succeeds in getting the party and convention machinery behind him, the distinction between his managers and the convention managers is almost imperceptible. In conventions of great contention and competition, the managers may observe neutrality until they can see the forces more clearly and appreciate the full nature of the problem, as they did in the 1920 Republican convention.

The managers' supreme objective in these cases is to protect the party from self-destruction. By reaching compromises at smoke-filled-room negotiations, harmony is preserved and the best compromise candidate is nominated. Some of this work is conducted in hotel rooms, but the managers also operate out of rooms in the convention hall. Here their strategies are often devised and from here messages are sent and received. Leaders of state delegations seek access to or are called to the rooms by the managers, who also keep in communication with party and candidates' headquarters at the hotels and with leaders throughout the country. Those managers who are outside of the party organization but obtain their strength through the votes or money they control are chiefly concerned with public policies to be followed and want some kind of commitments from a candidate before they will go along.

The Dark Horse. From these maneuverings there has sometimes emerged a candidate relatively unknown to the public before the convention. This kind of candidate is called a "dark horse." The precise meaning of this term is not what is often taken for granted by the general public. A dark horse is, not someone never previously given serious consideration, but a candidate with only a slight chance to win. Nevertheless he and his managers are active in the preconvention campaign in a quiet, unassuming way, lining up supporters or presenting his strategy to leaders who will have a voice in picking the candidate. This has been the real situation behind every dark-horse nomination since the first one, James K. Polk, was chosen by the Democrats in 1844.[38]

The only opportunity for a dark horse arises from a deadlock among the leading contenders. As they progressively checkmate one another, the convention managers are forced to look elsewhere in seeking a nominee. The initiative is lost by the leading candidates and their organizations unless they can get together and pool their strength. Normally this attempt fails because each candidate wants the others to withdraw in his favor and no candidate is likely to be able to deliver all of his delegates to another candidate like a cargo of cotton. When a candidate withdraws, many of his delegates will act independently of his recommendations. While candidates

---

[38] Bishop, *op. cit.*, Chap. 3. Other noteworthy dark horses have been Garfield (1880), Bryan (1896), Harding (1920), Willkie (1940).

are helplessly casting about for a strategy to save themselves, convention managers are making their plans and calling in a succession of leaders for short, to-the-point discussions. The logic of the situation can change rapidly in a convention. The developments of a few hours can wholly transform a man's attitude toward the problem of finding a candidate. The signal that a decision is in the process of being carried out is the increased number of votes given to one of the candidates who had not been showing much promise, or votes cast for a new candidate entirely. The other candidates begin to discover desertions as their votes fall, and some of them, realizing the jig is up, throw their support to the rising star. At this point the break occurs and the nomination is made on that or the next ballot.

The Aftermath. The inherent tragedy of presidential politics and of national conventions is the bitterness that comes with defeat. Participants presumably are conditioned against disappointment, but the stakes are so high and the effort is so great that defeat cannot be sloughed off with philosophical detachment. The most highly professional men have broken under the agony and the frustrations of defeat. Every contested convention leaves some broken spirits, but the three classic figures of Henry Clay, Daniel Webster, and James G. Blaine stand out during the nineteenth century because of their successive defeats over a long period of time. The cases of Clay and Blaine became more critical after they had received nominations and then were defeated. All three evidenced bitterness at one time or another over their misfortunes.[39] The only definite example of this same kind of experience in the twentieth century was Robert A. Taft, whose three fruitless attempts in 1940, 1948, 1952 made him successively more intense. At the moment of his last, shattering loss, he was exposed to the merciless glare of television and newspaper cameras, preserving the image of a face memorable for its ill-disguised pathos.

Strategy of Presidential Nominee. Following the presidential nomination, several hours are required to decide upon the running mate. For this reason, an adjournment is taken until the next day or until that evening, as the case may be. The decision process involves the presidential candidate and his managers and the convention managers who hold conferences constantly until the decision is made. If a powerful leader has been beaten in the presidential balloting, he may be offered the second place and often refuses it, e.g., Hiram Johnson in 1920. Other defeated candidates may be considered next. The controlling factor is to balance the ticket geographically and also between contending factions. The result may be an ideological cleavage between the two candidates in order to appeal to diverse interests. Again, key states are considered as well as the

---

[39] *Ibid.,* Chaps. 4, 5, 8.

record of the men. The perfect solution is a good campaigner from a key state (geographically balanced in relation to the state of the presidential nominee) whose selection will promote party harmony and confidence. Rarely is there any evidence that the conferees think of the possibility of the vice-presidential candidate becoming President by succession.

Inasmuch as the presidential candidate is present at most of the meetings where a vice-presidential nominee is under discussion, the possibility of his death is not a delicate subject to broach; and he is perhaps less inclined to think of his mortality on this day than on any other day in his life. When Presidents have been renominated, they are consulted and kept informed of the talks but seldom are present in person. Marcus A. Hanna could raise the question of succession in casting doubt upon the wisdom of nominating Theodore Roosevelt in 1900 because President McKinley was not at the conference. In 1944 an unusual situation developed in that leaders close to President Roosevelt could anticipate that he would not live out another term. The vice-presidential nomination that year took on added interest because of these unusual aspects, and the decision not to renominate Henry A. Wallace was in its way as significant as the nomination of Harry S. Truman.

When the vice-presidential candidate has been selected by the conferees and the man has consented to run, the scene of operations moves back to the convention hall. Already the party is captured by its leader, and the delegates wait with some impatience but with docility to learn who their presidential candidate wants as a running mate. It appears that the managers' plans in the 1920 Republican convention were upset by a movement in behalf of Coolidge from the floor. Such developments are rare, and the delegates, once they are given the signal, stampede in approved fashion to do what is expected of them.

Selected Bibliography

See the Selected Bibliography for Chapter 9, p. 214 above.

Bases of Bipartisanism

As the people go, so go the politicians.

CHAPTER ELEVEN

Historical Review of the Economic Basis of Bipartisanism

The organizing of political parties is one major aspect of the total bipartisan process in the United States, but it is not the whole process. The organization is a means for administering party affairs and for mobilizing voters, but intrinsically and by its nature, it cannot win followers. Voters are motivated to support a party or one of its candidates by appeals to their interests. Organization is a mechanism through which these appeals are made and candidates are presented, but organization is not the appeal itself. The second major aspect of the party process is the analyzing of the potential voters and the gearing of appeals in conformance with the analysis. This undertaking is by no means a complete guessing game, for there appear to be certain enduring features of the bipartisan electorate in the United States.

First, each party has durable areas of support throughout the country. The hard core of professional party workers can be counted upon to support the party's ticket and work to get out the vote. Among the rank-and-file voters, each party can expect a certain number of votes from those who adhere to the party label irrespective of the candidates. Second, there are areas within the population ranging from doubtful to potential support, including at least three elements: regular voters who are not committed to either party, the occasional or irregular voters with or without a partisan tendency, and the normal supporters of a party who are temporarily disaffected. These two observable features of voting behavior have become essential ingredients of our two-party system. There may be other features, but these are unquestionable. Each party in its durable support has a base from which to operate and attempts to capture enough potential support to attain a majority. Otherwise, one party would have a permanent majority and the other a permanent minority. In making the system function, the voter with a permanent party attachment and the voter with no permanent attachment are equally necessary. They perform opposite functions, but in unison they constitute a totality.[1] This equilibrium is made possible

---

[1] It is perfectly obvious that a fundamental change from this division of the voters between the committed and the uncommitted to an amalgamation of all the voters into one or the other classification would precipitate a fundamental change in the United States two-party system. Some advocate that everyone should be a partisan, and some

by the willingness of the losers to acquiesce because they know defeat does not mean annihilation and only rarely has meant an irretrievable setback for a party.

If the population of the United States is looked at from a political point of view, certain questions can be asked: Upon what basis do the parties motivate voters? How can we classify voters in terms of the basis upon which they support one party or the other? Putting the problem another way: How do we explain the outcome of elections? i.e., Why do people vote a particular way in a given election or in a series of elections? Can we discover the difference between a Republican and a Democrat? Do they have distinguishing characteristics which are reliable? Following from questions like these, various analyses or explanations of separate elections and of party history are developed. Essentially, there are three ways in which the bases of bipartisanism can be presented. There are the analyses based upon individuals as such, upon individuals as members of distinguishable groups, and upon individuals in the mass.

It is the purpose of the present section of this book to pursue the bases of bipartisanism in successive chapters devoted to the individual basis, selected group bases, and the mass basis. Underlying many of the ramifications of these three bases is the close affinity of economic motivation and political behavior. The historical record of the parties, as seen in the perspective of an economic analysis, is taken up in the present chapter.

ECONOMICS AND POLITICS

Perhaps the analysis of United States politics most often recurring is one or another variation of an economic basis. Political explanations in terms of economic motivations are sustained by an imposing quantity of data of high quality and command widespread acceptance even when such motivations are denounced as unworthy and contemptible. Essentially, this analysis connects forms of government and political relationships with the distribution of wealth and attempts to demonstrate that political struggles, in the main, are struggles over property and economic advantages.[2]

Economic Conflict. The genius of James Madison is revealed by the tenth paper he contributed to the *Federalist,* to which students of American

advocate that everyone should be an "independent." Neither group of advocates is likely to take into account the results of his own proposals, although some appear to be unconcerned about the effects, e.g., "In order that all Americans can share equally the benefits of our nation's great wealth the voters of this country will have to realize more fully their responsibility to the nation and see to it that lifetime Democrats and lifetime Republicans no longer are a part of the American scene." See Letters to the Editor, *New York Times,* March 18, 1952.

2 For an especially clear and concise statement of this analysis, see Charles A. Beard, *The Economic Basis of Politics* (New York: Alfred A. Knopf, Inc., 1945, 3d ed.) especially pp. 7-45.

politics constantly turn. Madison in this one essay cast more light on the relation of economics and politics than any other one man has done in a comparable number of words. With the observation that people are naturally different—a generalization that has been further strengthened in the advancement of knowledge since he wrote—Madison drew the logical inference that individuals' diversities lead to conflicts.

> So strong is this propensity of mankind to fall into mutual animosities, that where no substantial occasion presents itself, the most frivolous and fanciful distinctions have been sufficient to kindle their unfriendly passions and excite their most violent conflicts. But the most common and durable source of factions has been the various and unequal distribution of property. Those who hold and those who are without property have ever formed distinct interests in society. Those who are creditors, and those who are debtors, fall under a like discrimination. A landed interest, a manufacturing interest, a mercantile interest, a moneyed interest, with many lesser interests, grow up of necessity in civilized nations, and divide them into different classes, actuated by different sentiments and views. . . .[3]

Balancing Economic Interests. Relating these endless crosscurrents of economic conflict to the problem of the general public welfare, of the nation's population taken as a whole, Madison noted that any one or more of these interests can be checked as long as it is a minority and is opposed by a majority; but a majority can sacrifice the public good and the rights of others to its own interests. A system of government by elected representatives is no conclusive guarantee of safety for the individual or for minority interests, so the check of federalism was needed, Madison argued, to disperse power through the geographical levels of government so that no one level obtained a monopoly of political power. A given interest may triumph in one state or part of a state, but it would be checked at its own territorial boundary, for it would be restricted by the limitations upon the powers of the government of the state or locality. Its dominance within its own locale may be perpetuated or may be challenged, but it would be safely sealed off from the remainder of the country; in case it attempted to extend its sway beyond its borders, it would likely be checked by other interests fearful for their safety. The machinery of government in the Constitution was, according to Madison, intended to preserve that stability of society which can only exist when property interests are safeguarded and protected. Political struggle is the clash of these conflicting interests and the objective is to insure that none will be master and none will be destroyed.

Distribution of Wealth. The obvious problem raised in this economic analysis is to find methods for simultaneously keeping the many with little

---

[3] *The Federalist* (Modern Library ed.) p. 56.

or no wealth from banding together to wipe out the wealthy minorities and keeping the few who have wealth from pauperizing and enslaving the many. The most reliable solution is the dispersal of wealth so that the majority itself has an interest in the protection of property rights. Many of the Founding Fathers hoped that under the Constitution they wrote, the checkmating of conflicting interests would proceed with sufficient success to protect the general welfare. It was for this reason that men like Madison and Jefferson looked upon agricultural pursuits by farmers working their own land as best adapted to the preservation of the dispersal of ownership of wealth, and therefore of the stability of the new Republic. This point has been made repeatedly in later years but no one has put it more clearly than Daniel Webster, who noted that conditions at the time of the colonization of the United States permitted "a great subdivision of the soil and a great equality of condition; the true basis, most certainly, of popular government." Webster was convinced that the facts of economic life, not the forms and mechanics of government, were the essential element:

> The freest government, if it could exist, would not be long acceptable, if the tendency of the laws were to create a rapid accumulation of property in few hands and to render the great mass of the population dependent and penniless. In such a case, the popular power must break in upon the rights of property, or else the influence of property must limit and control the exercise of popular power. Universal suffrage, for example, could not long exist in a community where there was great inequality of property.[4]

Durable Partisan Issues. Long before industrialization and a greater concentration of wealth in relatively fewer hands disrupted the economic society the Fathers knew, the economic basis of American politics was reflected in the political controversies arising from the powers delegated to Congress by the Constitution. Looking at the party history of the United States from the perspective of the 1920's, Professor Arthur N. Holcombe arrived at the conclusion that only a minority of the delegated powers was useful as partisan political issues. A party could ill afford to pursue voters on the basis of policies requiring a constitutional amendment because the extraordinary majorities both in Congress and among the states can be attained only by cooperation and agreement among the parties. The only exceptions were the Thirteenth, Fourteenth, and Fifteenth Amendments added to the Constitution by the Republicans but under circumstances too unusual to justify generalization. The war powers, Professor Holcombe noted, were largely unavailable for partisan use both because a treaty requires two-thirds approval in the Senate, necessitating bipartisan support, and because wars and aggressive policies have usually been unpopular or have boomeranged even when, temporarily, they were popular. The dele-

---

[4] Quoted in Beard, *op. cit.*, p. 23.

gated powers most serviceable for partisan issues are currency and financial (taxation, coining, borrowing), commerce (interstate and foreign), regulation of government territory and property, and the "necessary and proper" clause.[5]

The one issue of national consequence which has arisen since Professor Holcombe wrote, the one he did not foresee, is civil rights related to racial and religious minorities. Most of the powers he named have been expanded to include additional functions and regulations which Congress can exercise, but none of these expansions in any way invalidates his conclusions, for most of these powers had, long before the 1920's, been stretched and pulled to fit new circumstances. The unity of these powers in forming a durable source of partisan struggle is their relation to the clashing interests of creditors and debtors, merchants, manufacturers, bankers, farmers, and salaried workers. The twists and turns of political history subsequent to 1920 present more, not fewer, conflicts arising from "various and unequal distribution of property"; and the "new" issue of civil rights itself is more of an economic manifestation than a pursuit of a golden mean.

THE CONSTITUTIONAL PERIOD

Economic Sectionalism. Not only economic interests but also their sectional nature appeared with stark clarity in the Constitutional Convention of 1787. The drama and simplicity of the big-versus-little-state feud captured a disproportionate amount of attention compared with the far more basic economic conflicts involving property in slaves, shipping, tobacco, etc. During this so-called Constitutional period, the relative size of states was usually less important than the four principal sections into which they fell. The *North Atlantic Coast* was identified by its wealth derived from the commerce which passed through its seaports. Merchants and the members of professions combined to make this section a primary source of influence among the thirteen states. The *Upper South* reflected the tobacco-growing areas around Chesapeake Bay. Because of the unity of its interests and the singleness of its outlook, it exercised, perhaps, more influence than the North Atlantic Coast during this period. The *Lower South,* least influential of the three, was a region where slave interests were paramount because the nature of the crops created a greater dependence upon this type of labor. The fourth section, the *grain-growing interior,* extended from North to South, beginning in northern New England and running through the northwest frontier south to what is now eastern Tennessee. This section was the largest in area and had the largest white population, but the people were widely scattered, unorganized, and incompatible to some extent in race and religion.

---

[5] *The Political Parties of To-Day* (New York: Harper & Brothers, 1924) Chap. 2.

All four sections were either entirely or largely agricultural, but the first three differed from the fourth in their reflection of capitalistic interests.[6] They were more nearly in the creditor position to the fourth section's debtor position. The first three were represented in the Constitutional Convention, and their interests figured in the debates in that body while the back-country farmers and the mechanics in the towns were unrepresented.[7] When the people were asked to ratify the Constitution, the voting for delegates to the respective state conventions revealed an extraordinary consistency in sectional alignment.

Economics and Ratification. Just as each of the four principal sections included whole states or parts of states, sectional voting on the Constitution overlapped state lines. Its most remarkable characteristic was the contiguous pattern of the pro and anti areas. The Federalist, pro-Constitution sections began at the northeast coast line in Maine and continued unbroken, except for Rhode Island, to tidewater Virginia; southward, it included northeast North Carolina, southeast South Carolina, and Georgia. Paralleling this north-south coast-line belt were interior Federalist pockets along the arteries of water transportation and in the valleys of the highest mobility of immigrants: namely, the Connecticut Valley extending through New Hampshire, Massachusetts, and Connecticut; the valley of the Ohio River from Pittsburgh to Louisville; the Shenandoah Valley including York County, Pennsylvania and western Maryland; and the valley between the Allegheny and Blue Ridge mountains. Certain towns of Federalist sentiment were enclaves in Anti-Federalist territory: Albany and Hudson, New York; Halifax and Salisbury, North Carolina; Pittsburgh, Pennsylvania. The Anti-Federalist sections began at Lake Winnipiseogee (now Winnipesaukee) in New Hampshire and extended south, without a break of any consequence, through Rhode Island into the general northern part of Connecticut and into a group of counties in the south-central part of that state, extending northward from the coast; a second section began in upstate New York and continued through the interior highland of Pennsylvania; a third took in the interior strip running from Virginia into Kentucky, Tennessee, North Carolina, and South Carolina, including some parts of the Virginia and North Carolina coast where there were few harbors and a small population.

The characteristics of the Federalists and Anti-Federalists fall into two

---

6 *Ibid.*, pp. 44-46.

7 A. N. Holcombe, *Our More Perfect Union* (Cambridge: Harvard University Press, 1950) pp. 28-35; Charles A. Beard, *An Economic Interpretation of the Constitution of the United States* (New York: The Macmillan Company, 1935 reissue) pp. 149-151. Professor Beard denied that he considered the members of the Constitutional Convention to be working in their own individual self-interest. *Ibid.*, "Introduction to the 1935 Edition," p. xvi.

classifications. People living along highways of commerce—whether rivers, sea coast, or overland—and in cities or towns, areas dominated by professional classes and mercantile and shipping interests possessing wealth, favored the Constitution. People who were isolated from commerce and immigrations, who were primarily poor farmers of the interior—in debt, receptive to paper-money proposals, and fearful of taxes—opposed the Constitution.[8] In states like North Carolina and Rhode Island the Federalist interests were too weak to effect ratification in 1788, and in states like Connecticut, New Jersey, and Delaware there was little or no opposition from Anti-Federalists. Apparently only Georgia was united in support because of special reasons, i.e., the weakness of its long, exposed frontier could best be remedied by a stronger central government. The place of residence seemed to exert more influence than race or religion, e.g., the Germans in Pennsylvania, Maryland, and the Shenandoah Valley were mainly Federalist, but those living in interior North Carolina were Anti-Federalist.

THE FEDERALIST-REPUBLICAN PERIOD, 1789-1825

Federalist Economic Policies. The first political period in the operation of the government under the Constitution began with the unquestioned supremacy of the Federalist Party under the leadership of George Washington. For twelve years, from 1789 to 1801, the Federalists controlled the three branches of the government and set the direction of public policy with an ambitious program initiated and carried through by "the friends of the Constitution." This program was a unified and well-rounded plan designed to strengthen the government and give a central direction to the entire country. The outstanding feature of the program was the funding of the national debt at full value without making any distinctions between original holders of the securities and subsequent holders who had purchased them at varying prices below their face value. An intimate part of the funding policy was the general government's assumption of the outstanding debts of the states. Both of these policies favored speculators and holders of securities who were concentrated in the commercial section along the North Atlantic Coast and, in the South, primarily in Charleston, South Carolina. On the funding bill, eleven senators owning securities voted "Yes" and three owning securities voted "No"; the respective numbers in the House were 21 and 8. From the results of his intensive scholarly labor, Professor Beard agreed that the vote

---

[8] *Ibid.*, Chaps. 9, 10; Orin G. Libby, "The Geographical Distribution of the Vote of the Thirteen States on the Federal Constitution 1787-8," *Bulletin of the Universiy of Wisconsin*, Madison, Vol. 1 (1894) Chaps. 1-3.

certainly justifies Jefferson's assertion that had those actually interested in the outcome of the funding process withdrawn from voting on Hamilton's proposals not a single one of them would have been carried.

But it should be observed that had the security holders abstained from voting on assumption, the decision of the matter would have been left to what Jefferson called 'the agricultural representation,' speaking for the taxpayers on whom the burden of taxation for the support of public credit principally fell. The great financial centres would have been left without any representation. Whether this would have been intrusting the delicate matter of public credit to purely 'disinterested' representatives may be left to the imagination of the reader.

Finally, it should be noted that quite a number of security holders voted *against* assumption and contrary to their personal interest; and an examination of the vote with reference to the geographical distribution of the public securities would seem to show beyond question that nearly all of the members, security holders and non-security holders alike, represented the dominant economic interests of their respective constituencies rather than their personal interests. In many instances there was, it is evident, a singular coincidence between public service, as the members conceived it, and private advantage; but the charge of mere corruption must fall to the ground. It was a clear case of a collision of economic interests: fluid capital versus agrarianism.[9]

The Federalists also chartered the First Bank of the United States and enacted a mildly protective tariff measure to encourage, among others, the fledgling steel industry in Pennsylvania. The currency system was established, based on gold and silver; native shipping was encouraged by direct subsidies and by discriminatory taxation on foreign shipping; a navy was created to protect foreign commerce, and an army was encouraged for purposes both of defense and of suppressing uprisings such as the Whisky Rebellion. In foreign affairs the Federalists displayed pro-English sympathies and were unfriendly to revolutionary France. These policies, singly and collectively, benefited the North generally rather than the South, and the commercial population as a whole rather than the agrarian population. The financial implications of the strictly economic policies carried with them the need for new sources of revenue. The Federalists were wary of taxing the land, and as the only promising alternative, turned to excise taxes on distillers. Government expenditures continued to mount every year and eventually taxes were extended to land, to houses and to slaves.[10]

Development of an Opposition. Reactions to these policies were sharp, immediate, and cumulative. The center of Anti-Federalism, especially in

---

[9] Beard, *Economic Origins of Jeffersonian Democracy* (New York: The Macmillan Company, 1915) pp. 194-195; in general, Chap 5 and pp. 180 ff.

[10] Expenditures nearly doubled between 1796 and 1800. The house tax was graduated in its rates, and the slave tax was fifty cents for each slave between the ages of twelve and fifty.—*Ibid.,* p. 355.

Western Pennsylvania, was roused by the tax on whisky, which fell heaviest in terms of its burden upon the small, grain-growing farmers of the interior. The land and slave taxes naturally antagonized the Southern plantation owners. The house tax bore heavily upon the less affluent citizens of the towns. The funding, assumption, and tariff policies were particularly attacked in Congress and across the land for favoring wealthy Northern interests. The taxes, it was strenuously asserted, fell upon agriculture which was forced to pay for the benefit of the speculators, shippers, and producers. The Federalist defense that the policies created stability and solidified the position of the new government fell less and less upon receptive listeners as the taxes mounted and the term "stockjobbers" came to be more generally applied to the "in" party. The culminating blow to the prestige of the Federalist Party was the passage and enforcement of the Sedition Act, which was applied in a partisan manner to harass and punish the more irritating antagonists of the Administration of John Adams.

The accumulation of dissatisfactions was greatest among the agricultural portions of the population without regard to the economic differences within agriculture; and the party of opposition, taking the name "Republican," sprang up from the Anti-Federalist sections of 1788 and gradually drew into this orbit disaffected interests in the South that had previously been Federalist. The Republicans not only organized and led the agrarian reaction but also were themselves in large part identified with and part of agricultural interests. Thomas Jefferson, who resigned from Washington's Cabinet as an opponent of the direction of the Federalist program, set the tone of Republican strategy both by his attacks upon funding, assumption, and the Bank and by his expression of the philosophy of the inherent superiority of agriculture over commerce as a way of life. When Jefferson "cherished" the people, he was emphasizing the sufferings of the back-country farmers and the Southern planters as well as directly and indirectly castigating the "stockjobbing" Federalists for sacrificing these people to the advantage of the business and financial interests of the Northeast. Inasmuch as the Federalists based their economic program on a loose interpretation of the Constitution, the Republicans were forced to fall back upon a strict interpretation of that document, adding to their attacks upon the injustice and impropriety of public policies the additional contention that they were unconstitutional. A mobilized, discontented opposition displaced Federalists from the executive and legislative branches of the government in the election of 1800. This was the first party overturn and the end of Federalist supremacy. The remainder of this period was completely dominated by the party Jefferson led into office in 1801, the Republican, or as it later began being known, the Democratic-Republican Party.

Conflicts in Republican Policies. The policies followed by Republican administrations from 1801 to 1825 did not follow as consistently from their party philosophy developed while they were "out" as the Federalist policies had followed from their philosophy. One of the outstanding characteristics of popular opposition movements definitely showed itself after the Jeffersonian Republicans came into office, i.e., the accumulation of discontents is a highly unifying force until it moves into the positions of authority and is required to initiate policies of its own. Then the internal differences within the opposition begin to appear and disunity among former political colleagues grows. Another source of inconsistency is that problems assume a different aspect according as one views them from responsible office or from the outside where no responsibility of initiation or administration is involved; whether a man is in or out of office is extremely likely to influence his perception of the nature of problems and his conception of the role the incumbent should play. Jefferson had attacked the concentration of power in the executive, but he was a strong and forceful President himself.[11]

A third cause of inconsistency in the Republican administrations during the remainder of this period was the War of 1812, which necessitated new policies to meet conditions unforeseen when the Party's philosophy was being developed.

Republican Economic Policies. Although these observations are valid for the complete span of Republican supremacy, the first twelve years, like the twelve Federalist years, marked a discernible trend, in the main, consistent with Republican philosophy. The Sedition Law was not renewed and those imprisoned for violating it were released through executive clemency. The national debt, accumulated under the Federalists, was paid off as rapidly as possible; the excise taxes were almost entirely repealed, and to provide revenue, the tariff rates were maintained at the existing levels. Jefferson reduced the size of the navy and army, and in an effort to avoid conflicts with Britain and France was responsible for both the embargo upon American shipping and for the Non-Intercourse Act. The substance of these policies was to reverse the Federalist trend by substituting economy in government and low taxes. In his desire to remain at peace and provide an environment favorable for domestic developments, Jefferson forsook the implications of the pro-French orientation of his Party and

---

11 Hamilton wrote to James A. Bayard that "it is not true, as is alleged, that he [Jefferson] is an enemy to the power of the Executive. . . . It is a fact which I have frequently mentioned, that, while we were in the administration together, he was generally for a large construction of the Executive authority and not backward to act upon it in cases which coincided with his views. Let it be added that in his theoretic ideas he has considered as improper the participations of the Senate in the Executive authority. I have more than once made the reflection that, viewing himself as the reversioner, he was solicitous to come into the possession of a good estate."——Quoted *ibid.*, p. 406.

dealt in foreign affairs with an eye to the advancement of American interests as he construed them.

These policies likewise redounded to the benefit of agriculture, but the greatest demands of the interior farmers were for new land for expansion and for improved transportation facilities, including the opening of the bottleneck of the Mississippi River at New Orleans. The Republicans responded with internal improvements financed with money derived from the sale of public lands. Highways were built. Canals were dug. The greatest project of all in this connection was the Louisiana Purchase which added new land for settlers and once and for all opened the Mississippi River. Most of these policies involved a loose interpretation of the delegated powers of the Constitution in relation to foreign commerce (the embargo), interstate commerce (internal improvements), and government territory (Louisiana Purchase). When strict constitutional interpretation conflicted with the interest of agriculture, the latter was triumphant; but the Republicans were the essence of consistency in their loyalty to the landed interests of the country.

One of the most contentious issues between the Republicans and Federalists was the chartering of the First United States Bank, and under Madison its charter was permitted to expire in 1811. In response to the changes created by the War of 1812, excise taxes were revived and a Second Bank was chartered. The Republican Administration finally dropped the Party's constitutional and economic objections to the Federalist monetary and financial system.[12] During the war the tariff rates were raised to provide more protection for domestic production. The war spirit in 1810 and 1811 was fostered as much by expansionist interests of the agriculture frontier to seize Florida and Canada and expel Great Britain from the continent as by the impressment of American seamen. It would appear that without the latter provocation, war could have been avoided, but the land policy of the so-called "Young War-hawks" from Kentucky, Tennessee, and South Carolina in the Congress was a powerful continuation of agrarian frontier pressure in American politics.[13]

---

[12] Actually, Jefferson did not upset any of the economic policies established by his predecessors. He failed to continue some of them and ceased favoring the commercial interests, but he did not repudiate any government commitments or undermine public credit or the system of finance. In the frantic days in 1801, when the House of Representatives was balloting between Jefferson and Burr for President, the former was sounded out on his attitude and gave assurances he would preserve the Federalist fiscal system and adopt a neutral policy toward belligerent foreign powers. A third commitment the Federalists wanted, to support and increase the size of the navy, if given, was not scrupulously kept. See *ibid.*, pp. 402-414. "That Jefferson might have been elected had there been no intermediary to convey Federalist opinions to him and his views to the Federalists is entirely probable. But that his election immediately followed what the Federalists regarded as 'a proper understanding' is clearly established."—*Ibid.*, p. 414.

[13] George Dangerfield, *The Era of Good Feelings* (New York: Harcourt, Brace and Company, Inc., 1952) pp. 36-41.

Evolution of the Republican Alignment. By the 1820's the old Jeffersonian alignment was split apart even though organized opposition to it had ended with the disappearance of the Federalist Party. Political combat was conducted within the one party by factions based either upon policy questions or upon dominating personalities or, more likely, a combination of both. The election of 1824 was a battle among these factions, all claiming political kinship with the party of Jeffersonian Republicanism. The cleavages were just as deep as if different party names had been used and different political lineages had been claimed.

The Federalist-Republican conflict continued in the antagonisms between the "old Republicans" who adhered to the original strict-construction, state-rights orientation of the Party and the group of younger men who came to surround the Madison and Monroe Administrations. In a sense, the internal Republican conflict was between the "outs" and the "ins," between those who had either gravitated or been pushed away from the center of power and those who were nearest the executive vortex and were concerned with the problems of administering the government of an expanding nation. Party interrelations had been further complicated by the entrance of former Federalists or those with essentially Federalist concepts of the economic struggle. These lines of demarcation were not clearly set by the candidates in 1824, who represented similar and opposing economic interests as well as their own personal ambitions. The sign that the original party of Jefferson and Madison had traveled a long and winding road was the election to the Presidency in 1825 of John Q. Adams, the son of the last Federalist President. This Federalist-Republican period came to an end much nearer to the place it had begun than any observer of the revolution of 1800 would have dreamed, and at the termination of both the Federalist and the Republican years of supremacy an Adams of Massachusetts was, respectively, leaving the White House and entering it.

THE DEMOCRATIC-WHIG PERIOD, 1825-1852

Realignment. The confusion of multifactional politics within a one-party system was crystallized into a second period of bipartisanism by the election of 1824. To some extent, this division was a renewal of the Federalist-Republican struggle under different names. The popular designations for some time were "Adams men" and "Jackson men," to indicate the ostensible basis of separation between those who acquiesced in Adams' election and followed the leadership of his Administration and those who refused to believe that Adams' election was deserved and followed the leadership of Jackson. In 1828 the Adams men ran under the party label of "National Republicans," and the Jackson men preferred "Democrat," the first half of the compound name. In 1832 the same names were used although Henry Clay, instead of Adams, was the candidate opposing

Jackson.[14] By 1836 the National Republicans had adopted the name "Whig," and carried on with it until the party itself went out of existence. The alignment that opposed the Democrats, whether called Adams men, National Republicans, or Whigs, constituted approximately the same interests and the same grouping; so the name finally adopted is used here, for the sake of convenience, to designate the whole period.

Re-establishment of Agrarian Dominance. The Democratic appeal had the effect, at the beginning, of remobilizing the farmers of the interior, concerned with debts and hoping for easy money to pay off their creditors and to raise the price of their products; the cotton-growing interests of the lower South; and the industrial workers in the East, who by then constituted a more identifiable and formidable group than they had at the beginning of the century. The revision in policies, starting with the Jackson Administrations in 1829 and carrying through subsequent Democratic Administrations with a notable consistency, was reminiscent of the changes wrought by Jefferson in his attempt to overhaul the Federalist program. Perhaps the greatest symbol of the sectional contest and of the partisan differences was the issue of rechartering the Second United States Bank which was forced into the campaign of 1832. Jackson, like the early Republicans, refused to approve its recharter and his running fight with the interests supporting the Bank dramatized most clearly the nature of the economic cleavage represented by the two parties between the commercial, financial, industrial groups and the agricultural frontier groups. The Whigs made rechartering a cardinal tenet of their platforms, and long after the issue lost its vitality, they continued to raise it as a specter out of the past. The increased national debt was paid off by the Democrats, and like the Jeffersonians, they also lowered tariffs to make them a source of revenue so as to avoid taxing land. The steamship subsidies, which had been reintroduced, were discontinued. No interference with slavery was attempted. It is true that Jackson spoke and acted sternly for the power of the central government to enforce the law when he broke South Carolina's attempt to nullify a tariff act; nevertheless, the state-rights philosophy, stemming from one faction of the Jeffersonian Republicans, was dominant in the Democratic Party during this period.

Continuity from the so-called left wing of the Jeffersonian Republicans to the Jacksonian Democrats was most apparent in the continuation of continental expansion. Under the Democrats, Texas was annexed and the dispute with Britain over the Canadian boundary was settled, opening the

---

14 The loose use of party names during the early part of this period does not help matters any. The same candidates might run under different party labels in different states or even in different parts of a state. See F. J. Turner, *The United States 1830-1850* (New York: Henry Holt and Company, Inc., 1935) p. 409.

Pacific Northwest for stable settlement. The Lower South faction within the Party continued to agitate for annexation of Cuba and of parts of Latin America, but this policy failed to elicit Northern support and continued to be a frustrated ambition. The objective of government economy and the doctrine of states rights were merged in the Democratic attitude that the federal government's responsibility for internal improvement was limited; some projects were approved and some were not.

Characteristics of the Whig Coalition. The Whigs suffered throughout their history because of the nature of their alignment. At no time was the Party a coherent group of compatible interests. The occasion for its existence was opposition to Jackson arising specifically from the controversy over rechartering the Second Bank, and the significance of the name itself was opposition to "executive tyranny," as the English Whig Party had opposed the asserted prerogatives of the Crown. The strongest element in the anti-Jackson coalition was the industrial and financial interests of the Northeast. Other groups were the Southern nullifiers (at least during the 1830's), the large plantation interests in the South, and those Western farmers who were most concerned about internal improvement. During the few years the Whigs administered the government at Washington, D. C., their policies were reminiscent of the Federalist program in the previous century: higher tariffs, subsidies for shipping, expansion in the Pacific by establishing formal relations with China and rights in Hawaii and by opening Japan.

The Bipartisan Alignment. In this period, both parties were national in the sense that they derived support from all sections; although the Whigs were the minority party, the only states they never carried for a presidential candidate between 1828 and 1852 were Alabama, Arkansas, Illinois, Missouri, South Carolina, and Virginia. Iowa, Texas, and Wisconsin, which participated in 1848 and 1852, were carried both years by the Democrats. The Democrats held the normal majority because of their hold upon the grain growers in the West, the most numerous group in the country, and their scattered strength throughout the Northeast and their more consolidated strength in the rural parts of the cotton belt in the Lower South. An alignment of the grain growers and the cotton growers supplemented by such states as Massachusetts, New York, and Pennsylvania was a winning combination, and the party leaders fought to combine these sections in every election. The Democrats could be displaced as the dominant national party only by a division in one or more of their most durable sources of support; primarily, the greatest threat was a disruption of the unity of the grain growers, which was not accomplished until the issue of slavery brought on the Civil War.

The Whig Party was finally unable to maintain its North-South coalition, for the Southern Whigs, faced with the open political issue of slavery, eventually went over to the Democratic Party. Concurrently, the farmers and working men of the North became increasingly unfriendly to the economic implications of slavery. Not only did the South's "peculiar institution" threaten free labor but also it challenged the expansion of both workers and farmers onto free land. The extension of slavery into the territories became a divisive issue among the Western farmers, and the pressure for cheap land for homesteading created a new perspective in the United States which a new major party was able to turn to its own advantage at the outset of the third period of party evolution.

THE REPUBLICAN-DEMOCRATIC PERIOD, 1854—

Developing Nature of the Two-Party Alignment. In the sense in which we of the twentieth century think of the bipartisan system in the United States, its beginning can be traced from this period of party history. Previously, the two major parties had either been vastly unequal in their national strength or only one major party had existed. Several presidential elections between Whigs and Democrats were close, but they had to be close for the Whigs to win. From 1828 to 1852 the Democrats lost only two presidential elections. The Whig victory in 1840 was extremely short-lived, since their President, William H. Harrison, died a month after taking office and was succeeded by John Tyler, who was so much out of sympathy with the general Whig program that he is sometimes even classified as a Democrat. The most important party developments during the Democratic-Whig period were the establishment of bipartisanism in most of the states (an innovation when compared with the Federalist-Republican period) and the insistence upon an acceptance of the value of having "ins" and "outs" as permanent features of the party system.[15]

It remained for the third period, when the party struggles were carried on by Republicans and Democrats, to produce a continuing set of alignments based on durable interests. Despite this fact the period, shortly after it opened, presents an extended dominance by one party over the other

---

[15] "The great service of the Whig coalition in the development of the American political system was its contribution to the firm establishment of the two-party system. . . . the politicians who first made a virtue of opposition for opposition's sake were Clay and his companions . . . Jackson's mastery of the political scene was to be opposed regardless of the immediate prospect of turning him and his copartisans out of office and getting themselves in. Opposition not only to such a President but also to such a concept of the Presidency as Jackson's was to become a permanent rule of political action. Clay could be at times as imperious as Jackson himself, but his place in American history is due, not to his imperiousness, but to his services as the Great Compromiser. These services were a fruit of his conception of the proper function of party leadership, whether in or out of office. He made the opposition party a permanent instrument of government."——Holcombe, *Our More Perfect Union*, pp. 95-96.

because of special circumstances connected with the Civil War and Reconstruction. The justification of the view that this is the most enduring bipartisan alignment is the imperishable quality of each party, its ability to sustain overwhelming defeats and then recoup its strength. The Republicans, coming into the executive branch of the government in 1861, maintained a supremacy through the election of 1872. From 1874 to 1894, the two parties competed on even terms. In 1896, the Republicans returned to the status of supremacy which they held until 1930; in 1932 began a fourth subdivision in this period, one of unquestioned supremacy of the Democrats.

Nature of Initial Republican Alignment. The present-day Republican Party was created in the wave of reaction throughout the North in 1854 to the Kansas-Nebraska Bill. If the appearance of the Whig Party under that name can be associated with the Bank controversy during Jackson's first Administration, the Party's disappearance can be associated with reopening the question of slavery in the territories, a question presumably settled by the Compromise of 1820. In this situation, a party opposed to the extension of slavery was demanded. The name "Republican" was chosen to signify the bond with the original Jeffersonians by placing human rights above property rights and emphasizing the agrarian appeal as the predominant element in the Party's initial alignment.[16] The Party was not abolitionist but its sympathies were against slavery, so that it absorbed the minor Free Soil Party even if it did not strike a very responsive chord among the extreme abolitionists. Northern Whigs, on this presentation of the issue, went over in large numbers to the Republican Party, and northern Democrats in smaller numbers also joined. The Eastern bastions of the Whigs generally gravitated to the Republicans although the Northwest element predominated.

The Lincoln Administration was principally absorbed in the prosecution of the War, but many of the basic policies of the Party designed to appeal to Northern farmers, workers and manufacturers were begun during the War years. The tariff rates were pushed to the highest point up to that time. A central banking system was organized, and the state bank notes which the Democrats had encouraged were taxed out of existence. The railroad was extended to the Pacific Coast, and renewed interest was exhibited in trading operations in the Far East and in controlling Hawaii. One of the most significant policies and a signal departure from precedent

---

16 Consequently, the two major parties in this third and still continuing alignment are, in a sense, heirs of the one major party with the hyphenated name, Democratic-Republican. Both contemporary parties, Democrats and Republicans, were either founded upon or received an impulse from the same dynamic source—the resurgence of the human spirit in the movement which swept to political power in 1800 under the leadership of Thomas Jefferson.

was the Homestead Act offering western land to settlers at only nominal fees. The policy of expansion abroad was continued by the purchase of Alaska shortly after the War. The increase in the national debt tied the bondholders to the Republican Party as the agent committed to redemption in specie payment, not in inflated paper—a situation paralleling the relation of the Federalists to the financial community in the 1790's.

Problems of the Republican Alignment. While the Southern States were in secession or under reconstruction, the Republicans could maintain their national majority, and the political purpose of the reconstruction policies—a shift from a free soil to an abolitionist program on the part of the Party—was to ensure Republican supremacy through the Negro vote. The impossibility of this attempt to capture the South was brought home to the Republicans in the 1874 congressional defeat, and the withdrawal of the last occupation troops in 1877 marked the surrender of this project. As the native whites returned to power in the Southern States, the agrarian vote became permanently divided, North from South. The Northern grain growers could dominate the Republican Party but they needed the support of other interests to dominate the government, especially the House of Representatives. From their base in the Central States, the Republicans had the choice of moving east or west to form a coalition that would assure them of supremacy. At the same time that the Democrats came into possession of the entire South, the Party was also losing the stigma of disloyalty attached to it during the War. Its resurgency was considerably aided in the North by the excesses of the Republican Administrations. The Democrats, offering an alternative to the waste, mismanagement, and corruption of the "ins," stressed the issues of reform. The Republicans gained a respite in the Administration of Rutherford B. Hayes from the charges of malpractice, but the nomination in 1884 of James G. Blaine, who was associated with some of the practices the opposition had been berating most vigorously, proved to be too much. Grover Cleveland defeated Blaine and became the first Democratic President since the election of James Buchanan in 1856.

The first response of the Republicans to this challenge was to turn more forcefully to the Eastern industrial interests, and their victory in 1888 upon the tariff issue, which Cleveland himself had precipitated, encouraged them to look to the East. In 1889 and 1890 the Republicans enacted the McKinley Tariff Act putting rates up to a level higher than they had ever been, passed the Force Bill to recapture the South by enforcement of Negro suffrage; admitted six new Western states to the Union. The tariff legislation did not produce the desired results in the East, and the Force Bill was a fiasco. The Republicans suffered their worst defeat in the congressional election of 1890, and their bid for Western support was only partly rewarding in 1892, when Cleveland was elected to his second term.[17] Perhaps the most significant revelation of the voting in 1892 was not which candidate or party won but the widespread evidences of dissatisfaction within the electorate, notably among the Western agrarians. Over 10% of the total vote cast went to candidates of minor parties, particularly to General James B. Weaver, who received over a million votes running on the Populist Party. Harrison, as the losing candidate, received only 43% of the total vote cast, the lowest proportion for the Republicans since 1860. Cleveland, as the winning candidate, had only 46% of the total vote cast, about 3% less than he had received in his two previous races.

Political Revolt. The demands for reform were beginning to mount beyond those that even Democratic candidates had been trying to give expression to. In this climate, Cleveland himself appeared as a defender of the *status quo* hardly distinguishable from his Republican opponents. The depression which broke upon the country in 1893 both changed the course of the partisan fortunes and heightened the demand of the Western and Southern farmers for various kinds of relief. At the center of this storm was pressure for an inflated currency to relieve the sufferings of farmers in the marginal areas of the plain states. The protests were directed at the Eastern money power, the unregulated private capitalists, including the railroad companies and the storage elevators upon which farmers depended to market their crops. The urban aspect of the same unrest was the assertion of the rights of labor to protections of various kinds in their employment and to a greater share of the rewards they were helping to create for American industry. The first political harvest from this disturbed state of the voters' minds was reaped by the Republicans in the congressional elections of 1894, when the "ins" were repudiated in the midst of economic adversity in conformance with the classic rule. The turning point was 1896, the results of which were foreshadowed in 1894.

Decisiveness of 1896. With a rampaging spirit loose in the land in the name of the Populists, or People's Party, it was inevitable that it would be merged with one of the major parties and the Democrats were the obvious and logical beneficiaries of the fusion movement.[18] In order for

---

17 The six western states admitted in 1889-1890 distributed as follows in 1892: Idaho was carried by Weaver on the Populist ticket; North Dakota cast one vote each for Cleveland, Harrison, and Weaver; and Harrison carried the other four—Montana, South Dakota, Wyoming, and Washington. California, Illinois, Indiana, New York and Wisconsin were carried by Harrison in 1888 and by Cleveland in 1892. Colorado, Kansas, and Nevada were carried by Harrison in 1888 and by Weaver in 1892. In the East, Harrison lost Connecticut and New Jersey in both elections, but carried Maine, Massachusetts, New Hampshire, Rhode Island, Pennsylvania, and Vermont in both.

18 For a discussion of the Populist movement and the fusion with the Democrats in 1896, see John D. Hicks, *The Populist Revolt* (Minneapolis: University of Minnesota Press, 1931) Chaps. 9-13.

the Democrats to absorb the Populists it was necessary to adopt generous portions of their program, and not only factions of Democrats but also factions of the Populists resisted the fusing process. The issue which, above all, symbolized the discontent represented by the Populists was the proposal to coin silver in unlimited amounts of dollars in a fixed ratio to gold—the famous 16-to-1 formula. The Democratic national convention of 1896 featured a struggle between the Eastern "gold Democrats," who fought free coinage, and the Western "silver Democrats" who carried the day with the adoption of a free-coinage plank. By diverting agrarian insistence for inflation from paper-money schemes to an expanded silver coinage, the Western silver-mining interests were cleverly and effectively brought into the new alignment and gave to a labor-agriculture movement a capitalistic supporting element. The Populist program won the convention and captured the Democratic Party, whose platform carried such other basic appeals as an income tax, a tariff for revenue and an end of the labor injunction. The gold interests, routed by the Democrats' adoption of the Populists' issues, turned to the Republican Party, whose 1896 convention repudiated the Western silver wing and came out in clear opposition to the Democrats on the currency question. The victory of McKinley over Bryan re-established Republican supremacy throughout the country, with a majority alignment based upon the Eastern and the Central States.[19] The Republican Party had at last found the combination that permitted it to be the majority party without any support from the states of the Southern Confederacy.

The depression of 1893, the currency question, the Bryan campaign, had wrought a realignment and had created two fairly equal bases for the Republicans, one predominantly agricultural and one predominantly industrial. It was a commanding alignment, but in its very nature was the source of its future difficulties. For the next three presidential elections (1900-1908) the Republicans held both the executive and the legislative branches of the government, adhering to the gold standard while pursuing their historic policies of protective tariffs and foreign expansion—the latter

---

[19] McKinley carried the entire tier of states north of the Ohio River and east of the Mississippi River, plus West Virginia and twelve of thirteen votes in Kentucky. West of the Mississippi River, he carried only North Dakota, California, and Oregon. "Making a virtue of necessity, they [Republicans] accepted responsibility for the defense of the gold standard and thereby became the favorite champions of those Eastern financial and business interests which had never forgotten their distrust of, nor overcome their dislike for, the Radical Republicanism of the Party's early years. What had begun as a predominantly farmer-labor party with an incidental appeal to businessmen now developed into a farmer-labor-business party with major emphasis on the political requirements of business. The unplanned evolution of Radical Republicanism into Conservative Republicanism brought unexpected accessions of strength in the urban and industrial sections of the country."—Holcombe, *Our More Perfect Union*, p. 100; E. E. Robinson, *The Presidential Vote* (Stanford: Stanford University Press, 1934) pp. 4-7.

considerably vitalized by the Spanish-American War. The economic decline following the war sharpened the discontent of the Central States faction, and the friction between agricultural and industrial interests finally came to a head in the formation of the Progressive Party in 1912 under the leadership of Theodore Roosevelt.

Democratic Interlude. It is impossible to do more than speculate about the outcome of that election if it had been conducted between Republicans and Democrats in the usual manner. It is a fact that Woodrow Wilson was elected as a minority candidate; the combined votes of William H. Taft and Roosevelt constituted a majority of the total vote cast. If this Democratic victory was somewhat accidental and failed to shake the basic Republican alignment, the re-election of Wilson in 1916 was even more accidental, for Hughes that year carried every state north of the Ohio River and east of the Mississippi except New Hampshire and Ohio. The popular explanation of this contest emphasizes the outcome hinging upon California because that state reported its vote last and because the final result was so close. The outcome in 1916 could have been reversed by switching to the Republican column any one of a number of states Wilson carried. The victory was personal for the President, not for the Democratic Party. The war issue along with prosperity undoubtedly saved Wilson from the fate which befell the Democrats four years later when economic conditions were declining instead of advancing and the advantage in international issues was on the Republican side. Wilson's strength in 1912 was his acceptability in the East as well as the West, and his salvation in 1916 was the total mobilization of the South and the West with disaffections in each of the normally Republican areas. Domestically, Wilson followed primarily the traditional Democratic program, but succeeded in producing a far greater quantity of legislation than any predecessor in any party: lower tariffs, creation of the Federal Reserve System in preference to a centralized banking system, the income tax, the Clayton Act, the Farm Loan Act, retrenchment in the Far East but a strong Caribbean policy.

Republican Return and Eclipse. The Wilson appeal was widespread and designed to weaken the Republicans in both the Northeast and Central States, but the appeal failed. From 1920 to 1928, Republican supremacy, begun with McKinley, continued; the results of 1912 and 1916 were aberrations just as the overwhelming Republican victory in 1920 represented a wider support than that Party normally had. Republican policies of protective tariffs, foreign commerce promotion through subsidies, and a stronger Far East policy were revived. The outlook in the prosperous days of 1928 and early 1929 gave the Democrats no hope for splitting asunder the bastions of Republican strength. It was the depression, beginning in

1929, that unexpectedly changed the direction of events and brought the Democrats into control of the executive and legislative branches in 1933, but this was no temporary victory for the Party as Wilson's had been. Exploiting widespread dissatisfactions, the Democrats, under the skillful political leadership of Franklin D. Roosevelt, turned their opportunity into an extended lease of power as the Republicans had in 1896. In 1933 the Democrats reasserted their supremacy for the first time since the Civil War.

Democratic Resurgence: The New Deal. The Democratic alignment during the period of the New Deal, as has been true of all combinations of the Party since the 1860's, was based upon the dependable South even though the Roosevelt majorities in 1932 and 1936 were so huge that he would have won without the South. In the three subsequent presidential elections, the Democrats' dependence upon the South reappeared.[20] In the first four years the enthusiasm and expectations were so high, the gravity of conditions so pronounced and the wave of Democratic popularity so great there was little opportunity or incentive for internal frictions to create serious problems.

Many of the policies were dear to the hearts of farmers and seemingly threatened to alienate completely the Central States from the Republican Party. Antagonisms between the two Republican factions had grown during the Coolidge Administration and had erupted in the Hoover Administration. The depressed farm areas, resentful at what was alleged to be Republican neglect and indifference, responded so strongly in 1932 to the Democratic appeal that some prospects appeared for that Party to remobilize the grain-growing interests of South and North. Farmers were directly subsidized by the Democrats from the Treasury of the United States Government, as businessmen had been subsidized many times in one way or another. Prices for farm products were guaranteed through the legal adoption of the concept of parity. Inflation, with its historical appeal for farmers, was accomplished by depreciating the currency.

The Western silver interests were pacified by a policy of buying silver at fixed prices along with the abandonment of the gold standard and prohibiting the circulation of gold. Impetus for the economy in general as well as relief for the unemployed was undertaken in the "pump-priming"

---

[20] If the Democratic votes cast in the sixteen Southern States are subtracted from the Democrats in 1932 and 1936, they would still have had a lead over the Republicans of 2,886,731 and 6,000,298, respectively. If these Southern votes are subtracted in 1940, the Democrats would be ahead by only 689,667 votes; but in 1944 they would be 714,483 votes behind.——E. E. Robinson, *They Voted for Roosevelt* (Stanford: Stanford University Press, 1947) p. 22. The 1948 contest was suggestive of the one in 1916 in its closeness, and the doubt as to its outcome for many hours after the polls closed. In each case the winner needed just about every state he carried.

operations of the Works Progress Administration and in granting money directly to state and local governments for construction of public projects. Reciprocal trade treaties were designed to stimulate both industry and agriculture by the encouragement of foreign trade through lowered tariffs. Industry was given direct attention by continuing the lending operations of the Republican-created Reconstruction Finance Corporation and by the codes of the National Industrial Recovery Act which suspended the antitrust acts by compelling competitors to enter into formal agreements covering competitive practices. In the same legislation, labor unions were recognized through the guarantee of the right of employees to organize and bargain collectively.

Weakening Alignment. After the first shocks of this patchwork program of improvisation and planning had passed, the faint suggestions of coming troubles could have been seen in the developing duality within the party leadership and the growing antagonism between the Southern faction and the Northern, labor faction. In the Congress the established Democrats representing predominantly Southern states were in control of committees and legislative strategy. They increasingly were rebuffed and alienated by the collection of nonprofessional party leaders, the brain trust and bright young men who asserted more and more authority in the various executive departments and at the White House as well. The basic incompatibility between such men as John N. Garner and Carter Glass on one side and Harry Hopkins and Henry Wallace on the other side went deep into ideology as well as personal rivalries and clashing ambitions. Before the 1936 election the Administration's open bid for labor support was embodied in the Wagner Act, and the general climate of pro-labor-union philosophy permeated the executive branch. This bid was a logical extension of the post-Civil-War alignment of the South and the urban North. The appeal of Roosevelt and his program to urban dwellers was a plain invitation to cement once and for all this combination of sectional interests supplemented by Northern and Western farm support. These calculations assumed the continued loyalty of the South.

Open Break and Wartime Truce. The line of demarcation between private expressions of dissatisfaction and open acknowledgment of revolt was the Supreme Court Bill proposed by President Roosevelt in 1937, and the revolt against it became a continuing revolution alternately smoldering and blazing. The disruption became official when the President in 1938 embarked upon his abortive effort to defeat those Democratic members of Congress who had voted against his program. The fate of Roosevelt, if not of the Democratic Party, was saved by the outbreak of World War II in 1939 and the ability of the Party to close ranks on the issues of foreign policies. It was exactly those Southern Democrats who spearheaded the opposition to the New Deal who joined most heartily with the President in giving aid "short of war" to the Western Allies against Hitler. Still in the midst of war in 1944, there was no challenge of the Roosevelt leadership within the Party and no real chance for the Republicans to depose him in the election.

Truman and Disruption. The death of Franklin D. Roosevelt, preceding only a few months the end of hostilities, placed upon the Democratic Party the burden of postwar readjustment under a President unfamiliar with the nature of the problems and without the ability to hold a divisive coalition together. The open bolt of a faction of Texas Democrats in 1944 was followed by the bolt of four Southern states to a sectional minor party in 1948 and by the bolt of five Southern states to the Republican Party in 1952. The brightest star in the firmament for the Democrats was the absence of the normal postwar economic decline because of continued large government spending for foreign aid and rearmament.

In the main, however, the postwar issues were more favorable for an "out" than for an "in" party. One of the greatest sources of dissatisfaction was the inflated prices paid by consumers; but President Truman in 1948 succeeded in turning this liability upon the Republicans, since they had controlled the Congress in 1947 and 1948. A second source of discontent was a growing frustration over the threat to peace by the USSR and the increasing alarm over the revelations of pro-Soviet influence and espionage inside the government itself. The outstanding foreign issues involved choices among policies for checkmating the Soviet Union, the pros and cons of the foreign economic programs and the nature of treaty commitments to defend foreign countries. Domestically, standard issues were raised in struggles over the tariff rates permitted by the reciprocal trade legislation; the reaction to the pro-labor-union policies of the New Deal which culminated in the modification of the Wagner Act by the Taft-Hartley Act; and the open and specific injection into partisan politics of the status of Negroes in the successive "civil rights" proposals. The realignment of major parties envisioned in the Roosevelt New Deal program was accelerated by the post-World-War-II developments and the progressive clashes of substantial economic interests both old and new.

The Essence of the Economic Conflict. Writing immediately before the election of 1928, Professor Charles A. Beard pointed to the emergence in party history of two distinct traditions. One began with Hamilton and ran on successively through Webster, Lincoln, McKinley, and Coolidge; the tradition that first appeared in the Federalist philosophy of the native superiority of the "rich and well born" and continued to be identified with the interests of the business community, although with the Whigs it included a popular appeal and with Lincoln it took on an agricultural tinge. The second tradition began with Jefferson and was continued by Jackson and Bryan; it emphasized the agrarian interests of the frontier and the interior, but took on urban strength among workers and among capitalists who were unimpressed with Whig or Republican policies.[21] It would do no violence to this analysis to add Franklin D. Roosevelt as an exponent of the second tradition, and it probably would be reasonable to add Dwight D. Eisenhower to the first.[22] The principal alignments produced by these traditions and the economic realities behind them were, first, the Federalist combination of the Northeast and the South against the West; second, the Jefferson-Jackson combination of the West with large areas of strength in the South and some areas of strength in the Northeast; third, the Republican combination of the Northeast and West against the South; and, fourth, the New Deal combination of the South with the urban centers of the North and West.

Problems of the Republican-Democratic Alignment. At the end of the New Deal span of years, at the middle of the twentieth century, the Democratic Party sought a cogent solution to the problem of the unraveling seams in its alignment of incompatible Northern and Southern elements. If the South was too strongly appealed to, in order to reinsure its complete loyalty, there was a risk of alienating the Northern wing and losing the large electoral votes of industrial states. An alternate strategy was to attempt to produce a majority alignment without particular dependence upon the South. After the election of Truman in 1948 through the defection of a number of Central farm states from the Republicans and despite the defection of four Southern states, there was brave talk of converting the Democratic Party into a farmer-labor vehicle based on the industrial and agricultural North and West. The congressional election of 1950 and the presidential election of 1952 gave a momentary pause, at least, to such calculations.

At this same point in the development of the parties the Republican problems were even graver and the 1952 election was not a reliable indication of the degree to which the problems were being solved. From the beginning of the New Deal, the Republicans had attempted to re-establish the 1896-1928 alignment of the Northeast and the Central States. Their rock-bottom support in the electoral college was in the Northeast, but the Central States continued to elect a large proportion of Republican mem-

---

21 Beard, *The American Party Battle*, pp. 134-142.

22 Lincoln's statement that he was for both the man and the dollar but in choosing between them was for the man before the dollar could be recalled in the Eisenhower statement that he was liberal in human affairs but conservative in economic affairs.

bers to Congress, and in 1936 showed signs of reviving presidential strength. Between 1940 and 1948 the Republican difficulty was to coordinate these two sections and mobilize them to a degree sufficient to win. The debacle of 1948 convinced some Republican leaders that this strategry was doomed and that victory lay only in a successful penetration of the South. While one faction of the Democratic Party talked of abandoning the South as the foundation of their majority, some Republicans began courting the South and urging party realignment. By the middle of the twentieth century the Republicans had come full circle since 1876 in their attitude. If the 1896–1928 alignment could not be re-formed—and growing Republican defections in the Central farm states make the prospects ever more doubtful—the Republicans certainly cannot risk being entirely excluded from thirteen Southern states which, under the 1950 census, elect 120 members of the House of Representatives and cast 146 electoral votes.

THE MARGIN BETWEEN THE PARTIES

In the search for differences between the major parties, the examination most frequently turns to the area of economics. On this basis of bipartisanism, it is assumed, some contrasts in shadings and emphases between Republicans and Democrats can be found. The parties' traditions suggest economic distinctions, but something more specific should exist to justify a conclusion of economic party differences.

Differences in Labor-Management Relations. Issues raised on both state and federal levels by the problems of big labor and big business in an economy of tremendous industrial production have revealed divergent party tendencies. There is a cleavage on the basic issue of the degree of freedom or restriction to be placed on union leaders and employers in collective bargaining. The Republican Congress which pushed through the Taft-Hartley Act contended that it restored balance to labor-management relations. Union leaders and opposing Democrats contended it was a "slave labor" law. Representatives of management, especially the National Association of Manufacturers, not only supported but helped to write the bill. This issue, while showing a clear-cut party leaning, did not completely line the parties up against each other; a substantial number of Democratic votes was needed to override the Truman veto in 1947 and to save the law from repeal in 1949.

The attitude of Presidents toward strikes in major industries is a further suggestion of party differences. Under Roosevelt and Truman the White House often was the agent for final settlement on terms near to the demands of the union leaders. The leaders, knowing the likely results of executive intervention, were sometimes inclined to prolong strikes to insure such intervention. Under Eisenhower, the executive became more aloof from strikes and the federal government's role in settlements was carried out by subordinate officials.[23]

Differences in Monetary Policies. Under the Democratic Administrations and Congresses since the 1930's, the general philosophy governing taxes was "Soak the rich," with rates rising astronomically in the higher income ranges. The revision of the tax structure under the Republicans in the 1950's swung away from this policy both in rates and in the method of taxing dividends from stocks. These differences revealed a basic ideological incongruity. The Democratic-New Deal philosophy is "that industry growth can be promoted best by a system of income-leveling taxes—taxes designed to underwrite a boost in mass buying power." The Republican philosophy is "that the same purpose can be achieved most effectively by a system of profit-preserving taxes, designed to encourage investment in new plants." In the case of dividends, full income taxes were first applied to them in 1936, and subsequently rates were substantially raised. The Republicans viewed the result as giving people "little incentive to risk savings on the common stocks that industry sells for growth funds—and with too little savings to invest adequately even if incentive were there." [24]

Inflation, created as government spending shot up, has revived the traditional party disagreement about sound money. Inflation was purposely fostered to combat the depression. Later, it was accepted as the least of possible evils. The Democrats generally defend or advocate inflation. The Republicans, despite continuing a large spending program, are concerned much more about the dangers and at least pay greater lip service to deflationary policies.

Differences in Role of Government. The predominant Democratic preference is to keep the national economy going by direct and permanent government intervention in all phases of business activity, whether through regulation or supervision or through government operation and ownership. Taxation, besides raising revenue, serves the policy purposes of encouraging or discouraging various business activities and limiting profits and salaries. The predominant Republican preference has been to keep the national economy going by more direct private action, less-stringent government regulation, and less government ownership. Taxes are reduced accordingly, and the withdrawal of government is viewed as permitting people a greater measure of freedom by retaining more of their income

---

[23] Eisenhower stated his own philosophy: "It is my belief that the Federal Government, as such, the executive portion of the Federal Government, should stay out of industrial disputes as long as it is possible, and to violate that rule only when a national emergency of some kind is obviously occurring." Quoted in *U. S. News and World Report,* July 22, 1955, p. 82.

[24] *Ibid.,* February 12, 1954, pp. 96, 97.

and using their own judgment in spending it. In either case the result follows from government action as a conscious policy. Neither approach relies upon government indifference or self-abnegation. The Democrats' preference is for a relatively greater degree of socialism, the Republicans' for a relatively greater degree of private planning and initiative.

These differences appear to be very real but they may be too subtle or too obscure to be taken seriously. "Or it may be that the people do see and understand the differences but judge that they are so small that in the long run they are not very important. And also it may be that in the long run the people who make that judgment will prove to have been right." [25]

Factions and Party Differences. Upon further examination, these distinctions are valid if each party is considered as a whole. Elementary knowledge about parties makes clear that they can seldom be considered as a unit in policy matters. Parties are composed of factions which appeal to the interests upon which they depend and with which they are sympathetic. That factions switch positions changes the basic fact of factionalism not at all. The Central states Republicans and the Southern Democrats have shifted their positions regarding various policies without making their respective parties any more unified. Irrespective of the time or place of analysis, conclusions about the parties are tempered by their factional nature. Even though seemingly economic divisions are intermixed with sentiment, traditions and subjective associations, they are the divisions to be taken into account in determining the margin between the parties.

This review of the historical record is, first, frankly an economic analysis and neither refutes nor presumes that there are no other valid analyses. Second, it resolves the question of the bases of bipartisanism back to individuals, who are the component, or microscopic, entities of the whole. Within the historical context we find the possibilities for analyzing individuals whether separately, in groups, or in the mass. These three means of analysis will, in the following chapters, be taken up in order.

Selected Bibliography

Beard, Charles A., *The American Party Battle*. New York: The Macmillan Company, 1928, Chaps. 2–8.
———, *The Economic Basis of Politics*. New York: Alfred A. Knopf, Inc., 1945.
———, *An Economic Interpretation of the Constitution of the United States*. New York: The Macmillan Company, 1913. Reissued, 1935.
———, *Economic Origins of Jeffersonian Democracy*. New York: The Macmillan Company, 1915.
Binkley, Wilfred E., *American Political Parties*. New York: Alfred A. Knopf, Inc., 1943.

[25] *Wall Street Journal,* October 19, 1956.

The Federalist. New York: Modern Library, Inc. Number 10.

Hicks, John D., *The Populist Revolt*. Minneapolis: University of Minnesota Press, 1931.

Holcombe, Arthur N., *The Political Parties of To-Day*. New York: Harper & Brothers, 1924, Chaps. 5–10.

——, *Our More Perfect Union*. Cambridge: Harvard University Press, 1950.

Libby, Orin G., "The Geographical Distribution of the Vote of the 13 States on the Federal Constitution 1787–8." Madison: *Bulletin of the University of Wisconsin*, Vol. 1 (1894) pp. 1–116.

Robinson, E. E., *The Presidential Vote 1896–1932*. Stanford: Stanford University Press, 1934.

——, *They Voted for Roosevelt*. Stanford: Stanford University Press, 1947.

Roseboom, Eugene H., *A History of Presidential Elections*. New York: The Macmillan Company, 1957.

CHAPTER TWELVE

The Individual Basis of Bipartisanism

A political system is made up of the sum total of the responses of the people within the jurisdiction of the system. People are the material of politics, but the analyses of the American party system based upon individuals cannot be a study of them as separate entities, as physical and emotional hermits. In the life of an individual the many influences which condition his thinking and make him what he is are both reflections of the type of society into which he is born and indicators of the type of society he will want to perpetuate. Each society, within the confines of its inhabitants' beliefs, practices, and habits, takes on its own inimitable characteristics which become the framework of the political party system; but the diversities of individuals within the society's general structure help to determine their particular political persuasion. In this process the individual is constantly exposed to the influences of others with whom he associates in one way or another.

In the strict sense of the word, there is no such thing as an individual basis per se for the bipartisan system, but in another sense, "It is evident that the roots of partisanship extend far below the surface of political campaigns and are deeply embedded in the traditional interests and inveterate habits of the men and women throughout the land who compose the national electorate." [1] The analysis of bipartisanism in terms of individuals does not presuppose that the individuals are molded by destiny or born with political tendencies in their genes. This is an inquiry into some of the kinds of political responses that are thought of as purely individual and some of the conditioning influences which are reputed to have produced the responses. It is a consideration of the electorate as individuals solely.

INFLUENCES TENDING TO PRODUCE INDIVIDUAL SIMILARITIES

National Influences. Since the largest over-all group into which we are born and in proximity to which we are reared is the nation itself, each generation reflects to some degree a unique reaction to the unique problems of the period in which that generation lives. Uniqueness is not conformity, and the responses of individuals to the same set of circumstances

---

[1] Arthur N. Holcombe, *Our More Perfect Union* (Cambridge: Harvard University Press, 1950) p. 108.

in the same generation are infinite in number. The influences of the frontier, of the period of overseas expansion, of the development of private capitalistic enterprises, and of the doctrine of the omnipotent welfare state have variously impinged upon millions of people, causing some to achieve and others to fail, inducing some to welcome the direction of events and others to abhor it, instilling in some the highest anticipations and in others the most callous pessimism. Some generations are associated with more easily identified characteristics than others, but every generation considered as a whole has some elements peculiar to it alone.

Events of stirring and lasting importance are likely to affect deeply and permanently the political thinking of those who are at the most impressionable age. The Civil War was just such an event. Political fixations resulting from it were sharply distinguished between North and South and forceful memories have lingered well beyond the generations immediately involved. In the South the bulk of the population, irrespective of age, became Democrats and has continued in this pattern with only infrequent aberrations; at least one hundred years elapsed before any fundamental break in this continuity could be foreseen. In the North, the partisan response was much less unanimous, but the war and the issues of secession and slavery had a profound effect upon young men who were entering into political and physical maturity, as Robert M. La Follette, Sr., later testified.[2] In this Northern generation a basis for Republican voting behavior was created which continued to pay dividends to that Party well into the twentieth century. Attachments were created which could not be completely broken even by a man like La Follette who opposed much that came to be associated with the Republican Party. Conversely, the Great Depression running through the 1930's combined with the leadership of Franklin D. Roosevelt to make the Democratic Party not only a powerful attraction for young people but also the majority party. Those individuals who get their initial political motivations from such periods of time are likely to carry their initial partisanship for many years thereafter, if not for the rest of their lives.

Parental Influence. Indicative both of group influence upon individuals and of the decisiveness of early influence is the general consensus that more people get their political partisanship from their home environment than from any other one source. The general tendency toward stability in voting lends support to this explanation of parental influence in partisanship. More specific data have been collected. The survey of 9064 college graduates made by *Time* magazine in 1947 found on this point that 58% of the graduates reported they belonged to the same party as their

---

[2] La Follette, *Autobiography* (Madison: Robert M. La Follette Co., 1913, 5th ed.) pp. 15-16.

fathers; 10% said they had changed from their fathers' party. "If we disregard the Independents, and consider only the graduates who definitely consider themselves Republicans or Democrats, we find that 85% follow the politics of their fathers and that only 15% have switched!" [3] In Erie County, Ohio, 77% of those questioned said they were following the partisan traditions of their fathers and grandfathers.[4] Respondents in a 1952 survey "who remember both their parents as preferring one of the two parties tend strongly to prefer that party themselves. When parental partisanship was reported as mixed or unknown, the identification of the offspring was more evenly divided." [5] In Elmira, New York, it was discovered that families tended to vote as a unit and that a father's partisanship was followed by younger voters, especially while they lived at home, but that a person was more likely to become a Republican as his occupational status improved. Protestants were more likely to shift Republican from a Democratic father and stay Republican with a Republican father. For Catholics, the pattern was just reversed. When parents' politics was undetermined, Catholics were Democrats two to one and Protestants Republicans two to one.[6]

Traditions of Partisanship. Influences other than parents help a person to decide the party of his affiliation. A particularly good example is the one-party state or area within a state.[7] If the bulk of the voters in such localities did not continue to follow the crowd, the localities would cease to be one-party in their political complexion. Usually some kind of catastrophe is required to jar the voters out of their one-party rut, and then the movement is general rather than a rebellion of a few rugged individualists. Throughout most of the South, voters are naturally drawn to the Democratic Party because it nearly always wins elections. These peculiar circumstances have forced people of the greatest diversity and incompatibility into the same party. Some of them in presidential elections may vote Republican—the so-called "presidential Republicans"—but in all

---

[3] Ernest Havemann and Patricia Salter West, *They Went to College* (New York: Harcourt, Brace and Company, Inc., 1952) p. 117.

[4] Paul F. Lazarsfeld *et al.*, *The People's Choice* (New York: Columbia University Press, 1948) p. xx.

[5] Angus Campbell *et al.*, *The Voter Decides* (Evanston: Row, Peterson & Company, 1954) p. 98; also table, p. 99.

[6] Bernard R. Berelson *et al.*, *Voting* (Chicago: University of Chicago Press, 1954) pp. 21-25, 88-93, 133-134. Cf., however, Herbert McCloskey and Harold F. Dahlgren, "Primary Group Influence on Party Loyalty," *American Political Science Review*, Vol. 53 (1959) pp. 757-776.

[7] Warren E. Miller, "One-Party Politics and the Voter," *American Political Science Review*, Vol. 50 (1956) pp. 707-725.

other elections they vote Democratic. In Maine and Vermont the Republican predominance is so great that many "presidential Democrats" vote Republican in state and local elections. This kind of behavior reflects both a conclusion and a tradition, and the tradition, if not the conclusion, was very likely fostered in the home.

Within the similarities established by the forces of the general society, the home and the major political traditions of a community, extraordinary variety can be found. If there is substantial basis for agreeing upon the over-all likenesses among people, there is at least an equal amount of evidence that people are different. No two persons are identical, and from these individual characteristics arise further political implications. Samples of individuals, one by one, cannot be examined under a microscope, but individuals can be discussed in terms of factors and influences which divide them or which incline them in different directions.

INFLUENCES TENDING TO PRODUCE INDIVIDUAL DIFFERENCES

Sometimes in our quest for information and enlightenment we are inclined to develop rigid categories and arrangements of data permitting an orderly and simplified frame of reference. By this method we can more quickly develop answers to questions of cosmic importance. The impulse to do this kind of thing is often irresistible, but the perversity of the human mind as quickly supplies new questions or new facets of old questions; sooner or later the neatly arranged structure topples over. Inherently complex problems resist short cuts and simple answers which seem "logical." No more complex problem exists in politics than the answer to the question, Why do individuals respond the way they do? Why does this person vote this way and that person vote that way? It is only relatively less difficult to discover and agree upon the personal characteristics which exercise the determinative influences upon political conduct.

Liberal and Conservative. It has become both fashionable and scientific, or at least pseudo-scientific, to discuss voters as liberals or conservatives, and often the dimensions of radical and reactionary are added. These terms have become to a great extent symbols with highly charged emotional content. They have themselves been dragged into partisan politics as the connotation of one or the other has become pleasant or unpleasant and as politicians have fought to appropriate for themselves whichever term is popular at the moment. The contests to use these terms for partisan advantage and to give them slanted or contrived definitions have made them largely meaningless as designations of voting behavior.

According to some views, to vote for Democrats in the North stamps one as a liberal but to vote for Democrats in the South means the voter has no alternative but to vote for a conservative. Other views advance the notions that to vote for Southern Democrats is to support constructive liberalism but to vote for Northern Democrats is to encourage radicalism. In 1948 the Democrats insisted that President Truman was the liberal candidiate, but Senator Taft insisted he was a liberal in the true sense of the term, and he and Truman were at odds on most issues. In this contentious atmosphere, the only similarity in the answers was the agreement among the Truman supporters that Taft was not liberal and the agreement among the Taft supporters that Truman was not liberal. As a liberal presidential candidate, by his own definition, Truman carried Ohio in 1948, and as a liberal senatorial candidate, by his definition, Taft carried Ohio in 1950. Does one conclude that the voters of Ohio were liberal in both years because they elected self-styled liberals? How does one account for the defeated candidates in these years who also said they were liberal? Apparently, the voters were less concerned with these terms than with other things, and the responses from samplings of Ohioans' opinions suggest that they looked upon Truman and Taft as antitheses of each other.[8]

Professor Lowell's Classification and Voting Behavior. Even when we have the more exacting presentation of these standard political terms by Professor Lowell, we are not sure what has been proved. He undertook to establish two sets of opposite characteristics, permitting a four-way classification of voters. At the extremes on the vertical line are those who are contented and discontented. At the extremes on the horizontal line are those who are sanguine and not sanguine. In each right angle, Lowell saw one of the four political types, radicals, liberals, conservatives, and reactionaries.[9]

If those who are not sanguine and discontented are reactionary, we have a description of this political type, but we are not told whom he will vote for—although some may tell us he will vote States Rights Democrat in the South and Republican in the North except where "liberal" Republican candidates are running, in which case he may vote Democratic or stay home. There is the equally interesting question of permanency. Is it possible for a person to move from being not sanguine and contented to being sanguine and contented? Or from not sanguine and discontented to sanguine and contented? If people are capable of change (and we spend billions of dollars through educational institutions on the assumption that they are) do their changes involve shifts from liberal or reactionary to

---

[8] Samuel Lubell, *The Future of American Politics* (New York: Harper & Brothers, 1952) pp. 189-194. The difference in the margin with which Truman carried Ohio in 1948 (7,107 votes) and the margin with which Taft carried Ohio in 1950 (approximately 430,000 votes) further suggests that "liberalism" had nothing to do with the results.

[9] A. L. Lowell, *Public Opinion in War and Peace* (Cambridge: Harvard University Press, 1923) p. 276; see, in general, pp. 271-292.

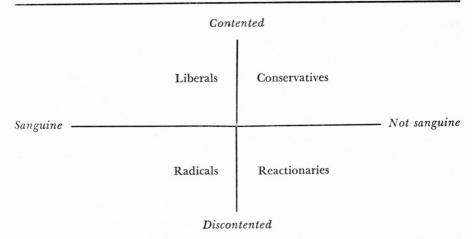

Contented

Liberals | Conservatives

Sanguine ———————————————————— *Not sanguine*

Radicals | Reactionaries

Discontented

conservative, or from conservative and radical to liberal, or from conservative and liberal to reactionary and radical? Is a person born inherently contented or discontented, sanguine or not sanguine?

Practical and Idealistic. Many people think they are familiar with certain types in those they know. Some are said to be practical in their outlook and others idealistic. The former are more inclined to think in terms of how they have known things to be or expect them to be from related experiences; the latter, to think in terms of how they would like things to be. The former in terms of what they have done or observed; the latter in terms of their own ideal mental creations. Perhaps individuals may impress us as tending in one of these directions, but few are pure examples of either extreme. It is sometimes difficult, in the case of the practical man, to separate his empirical conclusions from his hopes; and the idealistic can be extrmely practical in applying his ideals. Making this classification conform to partisan voting behavior is hopeless because both the practical and the idealistic vote for both parties for mutually exclusive reasons. For example, idealism could have led a voter to support the New Deal because of its "humanitarian" objectives or could have led a voter to vilify the New Deal because of its "cynical disregard" for people and their liberties. Practicality could have led a voter in either of these directions, depending upon his interpretation of his practical or materialistic interests.

Attitudes Toward Reforms. The analysis at this point finally comes down to a very general dichotomy. Some people can be separated at any given time on the basis of their reactions to a particular proposal for a change or changes in the *status quo*. If the vertical line in Professor Lowell's diagram be used as the dividing point, all of those to the left share to a greater or lesser degree a positive response to reforms, while those to the right of the line reflect various degrees of opposition to or suspicion of reforms. Unfortunately for the symmetry of this analysis, some people are in neither area. They either do not know about the proposed reforms or do not care how the controversy comes out. A more depressing fact from the point of view of the analyst is not only that people on both sides of the line would have to be graded in terms of the intensity of their reactions but also that a person is on one side of the line regarding one proposed change and on the other side regarding some other proposed change. An individual can simultaneously favor reform of one aspect of public policy and favor the *status quo* for another aspect. In addition, a person may move back and forth across the line as far as his general reaction to proposals for change are concerned. Attitudes toward change and toward the *status quo* are relative. A person may very well sound like a dangerous radical while he pursues an objective and then like a horrible reactionary after he achieves his objective.[10]

Other Characteristics. It is reasonable to suspect that the deep recesses of the human personality contain far more baffling possibilities than even those suggested by the potentiality of reactions to proposals for reform. There are other kinds of characteristics, whether or not closely related to attitudes toward the *status quo*. People can be adventurous or safety-seeking in different degrees, active or daring, passive or timid, young or old, rich or poor.[11] They can also be differentiated according to the amount of formal education, to religion, to race and to sex, among other possibilities. Some of these characteristics can be explored as partisan determinants in the light of the growing volume of research into the human personality.

Most people, on the basis of their own lives conclude that *age* greatly affects their points of view. In the process of growing up and growing old, we think differently about many things; we see or comprehend phenomena through "different eyes." It would be a reasonable expectation that partisan voting varies among age groups. The reservoirs of Republican strength built up in the Civil War generation in the North and of Democratic strength built up in the depression generation of the 1930's suggest that these events had a greater impact upon the young and that partisanship in

---

10 During the period of the New Deal the Democratic party became associated with reform and the Republicans with the *status quo*; but, in time, this distinction, while often asserted, became misleading. By implication at least, as more and more New Deal reforms became the *status quo*, it was the Republicans who were associated with change. Lubell, *op. cit., passim,* concluded that the fear of the changes Dewey might make helped to defeat him in 1948, and conversely, the anticipation that Truman would not make changes aided him among those who believed they had achieved something and wanted to conserve it.

11 See R. M. MacIver, *The Modern State* (New York: Oxford University Press, 1950 printing) pp. 406-416.

each period varied somewhat with age. The influence of the New Deal produced the most recently familiar pattern of age as related to partisanship. From 1932 through 1948, the generalization seemed to hold that the younger the voters, the greater the percentage of Democrats and the older the voter the less the percentage of Democrats.

The Roper polling organization found that voters of age 21 to 25 in 1952 made an initial move toward the Republicans but finally went back to the Democrats.[12] Conversely, the Survey Research Center at the University of Michigan discovered that the Republicans increased their percentage in every age group in 1952, compared with 1948, but that the most striking change occurred in the 21-to-34 group, where the Republicans approximately doubled their strength, from 19% to 37%. Since the Roper and Survey Research Center results are not for the same age groups, it is impossible to know if they are actual contradictions or not. In 1956, compared with 1952, the Republicans gained from 55% to 59% among those who were aged 21 to 34 and lost from 65% to 63% among those who were aged 55 and over.[13]

There is no clear indication of a partisanship on the basis of *sex*. According to one survey, the Republican gain in 1952 was 13% among women and 10% among men.[14] The relation of men's and women's vote in 1956 was very nearly the same as in 1952.[15] Among the surveyed university graduates, the number of Democrats was higher among women than among men, but the number of Republicans was the same among men and women because there were fewer women than men that classed themselves as independents.[16]

The *extent of formal schooling* has, like age, been associated with partisanship in that the farther one goes in school, the more likely one is to be a Republican. This relationship is a general tendency at most, not a rule. The Eisenhower victories in 1952 and 1956 were accompanied by increased Republican support among those who had not attended the university and decreases among those who had.[17]

Partisanship is related to *economic status* in terms of both occupation and income. The following table presents data bearing out this general division of the population. However, some qualifications become obvious from an examination of the figures. Groups where Republicans had been weak since the 1930's tended to give increased support to Eisenhower and some groups supposedly Republican revealed a declining Republican sup-

---

[12] Louis Harris, *Is There a Republican Majority?* (New York: Harper & Brothers, 1954) pp. 163-169.

[13] *U. S. News and World Report*, March 29, 1957, p. 62.

[14] Campbell *et al.*, *op. cit.*, p. 70; Berelson *et al.*, *op. cit.*, Appendix A.

[15] Gallup Poll, November 3, 1956.

[16] Havemann and West, *op. cit.*, pp. 109, 110.

[17] Campbell *et al.*, *op. cit.*, p. 72; *U. S. News and World Report*, March 29, 1957, p. 67.

port in 1952 and 1956.[18] Even socio-economic status has limitations as an explanation of why people vote the way they do. Yet, it is one helpful guide and explains in large measure the new Republican strength in the South.[19]

PERCENTAGE REPUBLICAN IN PRESIDENTIAL ELECTIONS BY
OCCUPATIONAL, INCOME, AND UNION–MEMBER
GROUPS, 1948–1956 [20]

	1948	1952	1956
Professional and executive	81%	70%	68%
White-collar	53	65	63
Skilled workers	27	47	56
Unskilled workers	33	33	46
Farm operators	41	64	55
Less than $2000 annual salary	39	58	60
$5000 and above annual salary	70	68	62
Union-worker families	24	44	48
Nonunion families	59	64	65

It is speculative, to some extent, to consider people as voters apart from the many influences pressing upon them from various sources. Unfortunately, not enough is known about the interrelation between group influences and individual behavior to be positive in our conclusions or even entirely clear about the process. People have many loyalties which, politically, may or may not conflict, but generalizations often assume that the individual acts the way he does because of the larger entities of which he is a part.[21] When we glibly classify people according to one association, we may fail to evaluate both the direction of the influence and the consequences of conflicting influences.[22] Individuals may take their partisanship with them into the groups they join and may become apologists for their party within their groups, as well as special pleaders for their groups within their political party. Groups which are more basic in a person's life would be

---

[18] In 1958, this trend continued as Republican losses were heaviest among groups normally Republican. Gallup Poll, January 27, 1959. Berelson *et al., op. cit.*, p. 61 note, states that women were less likely to vote according to their economic status than men.

[19] James W. Prothro *et al.*, "Two-Party Voting in the South: Class v. Party Identification," *American Political Science Review*, Vol. 52 (1958) pp. 131-139. Samuel Lubell, *The Revolt of the Moderates* (New York: Harper & Brothers, 1956) pp. 181 ff.

[20] Taken from *U. S. News and World Report*, March 29, 1957, pp. 64-67.

[21] In the case of some minorities, the interrelation between the individual and his associations may be very nearly completely compatible, helping to account for the individuals' tendency to vote the same way. It has been pointed out that minority groups are more Democratic than majority members of a community even in the South. Berelson *et al., op. cit.*, p. 62.

[22] For example, are Catholics Democrats because they are Catholics? Is a corporation executive a Republican because of his high status? What, then, should be expected of a corporation executive who is a Catholic?

expected to be more influential upon him politically. The fact that many labor unions have a clear and consistent political standard may very well account to some extent for the high degree of partisan unity among union members.[23] To become aware of demographic influences in voting poses new questions about motivations and, in turn, causes us to re-evaluate our assumptions that election victories are, per se, policy decisions.[24]

Index of Political Predisposition. Criteria were developed from a panel study of Erie County, Ohio, from which predictions of partisanship presumably could be drawn. These analyses introduced the concept of an "Index of Political Predisposition" (IPP) based upon the factors of economic status, urban or rural residence, and religion. The conclusions and predictions following from this Index are that high economic status, rural residence, and Protestantism go with Republicans, and that low economic status, urban residence, and Roman Catholicism go with Democrats. These investigators concluded that "a person thinks, politically, as he is, socially. Social characteristics determine political preference." [25] Subsequently when efforts were made to project this Index nationally, Professor Lazarsfeld

> pointed out that the IPP can be seen as an index to the political behavior of only a portion of the total population. . . . Those individuals who declare their intention to vote either Democrat or Republican are more likely to vote in line with their intentions *if* they have the appropriate Index of Political Predisposition than if their IPP fails to reinforce those intentions.

Since this qualification restricts the IPP to only those who state a voting intention,

> the IPP is not seen as an index of prediction, but . . . as a measure of reflecting the tendency in individuals who have voting intentions to follow their intentions.[26]

---

[23] This point was made in the panel paper, "Group Influence in Voting Behavior," presented by Philip E. Converse at the meeting of the American Political Science Association, New York, September 2, 1957.

[24] William Buchanan, "An Inquiry into Purposive Voting," *Journal of Politics,* Vol. 18 (1956) pp. 281-296.

[25] Lazarsfeld *et al., op. cit.,* p. 27. Social characteristics do not explain some shifts in voting, e.g., 1948 compared with 1952. Donald E. Stokes *et al.,* "Components of Electoral Decision," *American Political Science Review,* Vol. 52 (1958) pp. 368-369.

[26] Morris Janowitz and Warren E. Miller, "The Index of Political Predisposition in the 1948 Election," *Journal of Politics,* Vol. 14 (1952) p. 713. Other limitations of the Erie County study are found in the reasons for choosing this particular county in the first place. It had demonstrated political stability and had well-marked social and economic divisions. Its reported behavior was its reflection of the issues and candidates of 1940, but this same pattern was not found in 1948.—Pp. 723-724. Furthermore, rural residence may have been a sign of Republicanism in Erie County, but certaintly cannot be projected as such a sign for the whole country.

When the IPP was applied to a national sampling of voters made by the Survey Research Center in 1948, it accounted for 61% of the vote whereas 82% was accounted for by arbitrarily assigning the respondents according to their educational level.[27]

Intensity and Partisan Differences. Different people feel more or less strongly about their political commitments, and the factors which prompt them to vote one way or another can both vary from election to election as well as fail to move them to vote at all. In one presentation of a national sample of adults eligible to vote in 1948, the data were prepared to show four gradations of voting frequency (*always, usually, infrequently, never*) and five gradations of partisanship (*definite Democrats, independents tending to be Democrats, ambivalent independents, independents tending to be Republicans, definite Republicans*). While the percentage of definite Democrats who always voted was 17.5 compared with 12.8 for Republicans who always voted, the Democratic percentages were also higher in each of the other three voting categories when comparing the definite partisans: "usually"—Democrats 11.3, Republicans 3.0; "infrequently"—Democrats 3.2, Republicans 1.8; "never"—Democrats 11.6, Republicans 1.9. Out of the total sample, 28% voted infrequently or not at all, and they were subdivided into 14.8% Democrats, 3.7% Republicans, and 9.6% independents. These results indicated a preponderance of nonvoters or infrequent voters among Democrats.[28] As a cross reference to the parental influence, there is some evidence that among college graduates, children of Republican fathers are less likely to switch to the Democrats than children of Democrats are to switch to the Republicans. For the same group, the Southern Democrats who move to the North are far more likely to become Republicans than Northern Republicans who move to the South are to become Democrats.[29]

Intensity and Political Issues. In an attempt to measure the differences between Republican and Democratic voters regarding the issues of the 1952 campaign, six questions were asked which reflected partisan cleavages. The pertinent indications were that 1948 nonvoters who voted Democratic

---

[27] Janowitz and Miller, *ibid.*, pp. 717, 720. All grade-school respondents were assigned to the Democrats, all college-educated to the Republicans, and those who had not gone beyond high school were evenly divided between the parties. Only Republican voters followed their IPP scores to a degree statistically significant (pp. 717-718), and the authors concluded that the "greater power of the IPP seems to be in predicting the Republican and thereby the 'status quo' vote, rather than the protest or social change vote."——P. 723. Cf. Lubell's findings regarding *status quo v.* change in 1948, above, p. 285, note 10.

[28] Samuel J. Eldersveld, "The Independent Vote: Measurement, Characteristics and Implications for Party Strategy," *American Political Science Review*, Vol. 46 (1952) pp. 739, 740. The same general conclusions were turned up in Campbell, *op. cit.*, pp. 107-110.

[29] Havemann and West, *op. cit.*, pp. 117, 111, and 112.

in 1952 were more consistently similar to those voting Democratic both years than the 1948 nonvoters who voted Republican in 1952 were to those voting Republican both years.[30] The Republican group of 1948 nonvoters were more partisan than the Democratic group of 1948 nonvoters only on the issue of foreign involvement. There was a high degree of similarity among those voting Republican both years and among those voting Democratic both years, when the whole sample was broken down into demographic groups; but this tendency was slightly greater for Republicans than for Democrats, and the better-educated Democrats were a little more homogeneous than less-well-educated Democrats.[31]

However, marked differences appeared among Republicans when analyzed separately on social welfare activity and foreign involvements. On the former issue, Republicans of higher occupational status disagreed more sharply with the Democratic position than Republicans of lower occupational status; on the latter issue, this occupational reaction was reversed. The Democrats, considered by occupational classifications, were more homogeneous regarding these two issues than the Republicans, but the higher-occupation Democrats were stronger for Democratic positions on both issues than were the lower-occupation Democrats. In other words, so-called "blue collar" Democrats showed less support for government social-welfare activity, as well as foreign involvement, than professional and business groups who were Democrats.[32] The over-all indication that those who shifted from Democratic to Republican between 1948 and 1952 were not as partisan as the regulars in either party is consistent with the widespread observations that conditions peculiar to 1952 accounted for a sizable body of the Republican vote.

Such situations are suggestive about individual voting behavior, i.e., that it can change temporarily; but this statement tells us nothing concrete about the influences responsible for such shifts. It does introduce a new factor in the discussion of the individual basis of bipartisanism; it reminds us that the pressures and forces of the moment can only be assessed at the time they exist and cannot always be generalized for the past or always projected into the future. Finally, it should be noted that the observed relations between demographic factors and partisan preferences may suggest, in a limited way, what some of the characteristics of Republicans and

30 Angus Campbell *et al.*, "Political Issues and the Vote: November, 1952," *American Political Science Review*, Vol. 47 (1953) pp. 369, 377. The six issues were: government social welfare activity, Taft-Hartley Act, United States foreign involvement, United States China policy, United States entry in the Korean war, current United States Korean policy. These six issues clearly failed to account for all of the Republican gains among "new" voters.

31 Campbell, *ibid.*, pp. 364, 365-366, 371-372.

32 *Ibid.*, pp. 372-376. In the college-graduate survey it was discovered that 59% of the Democrats held anti-New-Deal opinions.——Havemann and West, *op. cit.*, pp. 122, 123.

Democrats are; however, to learn that a certain set of these characteristics inclines a person to one party or the other does not tell *why* these characteristics produce this result. Furthermore, correlations between partisanship and demographic factors are not sufficiently close to permit hard-and-fast identity between the two; demography may be a better indicator of the response of those who are not greatly involved either as partisans or in issues.[33]

"Independent" Voters. A final problem regarding individual voting behavior, one that is of permanent concern to party managers and that forms a part of the standard analyses of elections, is the phenomenon of independent voting. Analyses of bipartisan strength based on individuals' behavior eventually take account of those voters who presumably are committed to neither party. Discussions of the anticipated reactions of an independent voter are seldom precise or enlightening because of the confusion in the meaning of the term. The independent voter

> is a statistical rather than a mortal entity. He doesn't fit into any neat categories of wealth, social position or intellectual outlook. He's as likely to be a farmer as a small business man or a wage-earner. He has no particular habitat, has no special religious preoccupations nor any marked regional or tribal prejudices to be exploited.
>
> Nor is his independence always a matter of will and principles to be melted down by sound logic. It may be the result of simple cussedness, inner conflict or a mature judgment . . . .[34]

One of the more systematic criteria of independence that has so far been developed reveals that it can be manifested in five different ways: voting a split ticket, transferring party allegiance over a period of time, having no crystallized party predispositions, wavering in making a voting decision, and supporting minor parties. Measured on this basis of voting behavior, a 1948 sampling by the Survey Research Center classified 36.7% of the respondents as independents.[35] Other polls, relying upon voters'

---

[33] "The most interesting example of group effects to be found in our study, however, does not come from consideration of these demographic variables but from a political variable, party identification. We can make a much better prediction of how a man thinks and acts politically if we know whether he calls himself a Republican or a Democrat than if we know that he calls himself a skilled worker, a Catholic, a suburbanite, a rich man, or a pauper."——*Group Differences in Attitudes and Votes: A Study of the 1954 Congressional Election,* Preliminary Report (Ann Arbor: Survey Research Center, University of Michigan, 1955) p. 49.

[34] *New York Times Magazine,* July 13, 1952, p. 8.

[35] Eldersveld, *op. cit.,* pp. 736-738, 752-753. See also pp. 732-734 for descriptions of types of research on independent voting. Applying these five criteria, there were more independent voters, proportionally, in metropolitan cities than in other urban or in rural communities. The smallest percentage of independents and the largest percentage of nonvoters were found in rural places.——Pp. 743, 744.

Carl Rose in The New York Times Magazine, July 13, 1952

THE INDEPENDENT VOTER

self-classification, have produced a smaller percentage of independents: e.g., 20% in 1940 and 1944, and 19% in 1948, according to Gallup,[36] and 22% in 1952.[37] The identity of the independents can be inferred to some extent from existing data. Such factors as education, income, and union membership appear to have some bearing; namely, the farther one goes in school and the higher the income, the greater the proportion of independents; union members are less inclined to be independents than those workers unaffiliated with unions. It also appears that the incidence of independence among college people is highest among the most recent

[36] *Op. cit.*, p. 37. Estimates of the number of independents in 1952 ranged from 9,350,000 to 15,000,000.——*New York Times Magazine*, July 13, 1952, p. 8.

[37] Campbell, *op. cit.*, pp. 92-93.

graduates and among those getting the highest grades, declines as they get older, and is more prevalent among men than women.[38]

During the period of New Deal supremacy, estimates were made regarding the partisan division among the independents. Irrespective of the exact percentages from election to election, there was general agreement that the independent vote split in favor of the Democrats in the elections they won and in favor of the Republicans in the elections they won. From this observation, the truism has arisen that the independent voters decide elections and are the balance of power between the permanent Democrats and permanent Republicans. Certainly, if the five criteria of independency be relied upon, there is genuine validity in this balance-of-power view not only because of the numbers involved but also in their decisions to vote or not to vote. On this basis of computation, various estimates have been made of the percentage of independents each party must capture in order to win.[39] The safest conclusion is that independents, by their very nature, will be influenced by the issues of each campaign as it occurs and will be likely to move in convincing numbers one way or the other whenever there are compelling controversies which appeal to them. Personalities of people may be important in causing them to switch parties. Likewise, the application of the IPP may be of some help in anticipating the independents' behavior in the absence of unusual campaign features.[40]

It seems apparent that the reasons why some change parties between elections are different from the reasons why others do not change. Since the significance as well as the direction of this independent vote results from many crosscurrents in political life, an analysis of the individual basis of bipartisanism is, perhaps, too restrictive. For those who are more easily capable of switching their voting loyalties the following chapters are more descriptive. The independent vote lurks beneath the surface in the analyses of group and mass bases of bipartisan behavior.

Selected Bibliography

Berelson, Bernard R., et al., Voting. Chicago: University of Chicago Press, 1954.
Campbell, Angus, et al., The Voter Decides. Evanston: Row, Peterson & Company, 1954.

---

[38] Eldersveld, op. cit., p. 751; Havemann and West, op. cit., pp. 110, 120 ff.; Philip K. Hastings, "The Independent Voter in 1952: A Study of Pittsfield, Massachusetts," American Political Science Review, Vol. 47 (1953) pp. 805-810.

[39] Most such theoretical formulas have indicated that the problem of the Republicans is greater than that of the Democrats.——Eldersveld, op. cit., p. 741. Havemann and West, op. cit., p. 123, found that compared with both Democrats and Republicans, independents held views more internationalist and more tolerant regarding minorities and that they were about the same proportion anti-New Deal (58%) as Democrats (59%).

[40] "The returns [from New York City assembly districts in 1950, 1951, 1952] show that even when voters turn 'independent,' they do so within the pattern of their cultural conditioning." Lubell, The Revolt of the Moderates, p. 93.

Eldersveld, Samuel J., *Political Affiliation in Metropolitan Detroit.* Ann Arbor: University of Michigan, Michigan Governmental Studies No. 34, 1957.

Gallup, George, *The Political Almanac.* New York: B. C. Forbes & Sons, 1948 and 1952.

Havemann, Ernest, and Patricia Salter West, *They Went to College.* New York: Harcourt, Brace and Company, Inc., 1952, Chaps. 9 and 10.

Lazarsfeld, Paul F., *et al., The People's Choice.* New York: Columbia University Press, 1949.

Lubell, Samuel, *The Future of American Politics.* New York: Harper & Brothers, 1952.

———, *The Revolt of the Moderates.* New York: Harper & Brothers, 1956.

Truman, David B., *The Governmental Process.* New York: Alfred A. Knopf, Inc., 1951, Chaps. 2 and 3.

CHAPTER THIRTEEN

Sectional and Class Bases of Bipartisanism

The foregoing discussion of the individual basis carries forward the economic motivation in voting presented in Chapter 12. Out of the historical rather than the individual analysis, economic interests have been identified according to their geographical location, and sections of the country have become a familiar frame of reference for examining election statistics. By extension, the political reactions of groups of states have been developed into an explanation of a group basis of bipartisanism. Underlying this political analysis has been the presentation of American history in terms of the cultural background, psychology, and means of livelihood of the people of different geographical areas.

SECTIONS

The task of identifying a section can first be approached in general terms:

> Geographical conditions and the stocks from which the people sprang are the most fundamental factors in shaping sectionalism. Of these the geographical influence is peculiarly important in forming a society like that of the United States, for it includes in its influence those factors of economic interests, as well as environmental conditions, that affect the psychology of a people.[1]

By this test, sectionalism is a resistance to national uniformity in any of various ways and includes differences in beliefs as well as differences in economics. However much this phenomenon may suffer from the exclusion of noneconomic influences, political sectionalism becomes, sooner or later, analyses of economic interests, because economics offers the most concrete and easily managed data while other factors are more elusive and are less capable of tangible demonstration or of satisfactory formulation.[2]

[1] F. J. Turner, *The Significance of Sections in American History* (New York: Henry Holt and Company, Inc., 1932) pp. 288-289.

[2] This approach to sectionalism, by way of the main highways of economics but in view of other possible access roads seems more serviceable and certainly more understandable than to classify sectionalism as a noneconomic political influence and to present it in terms of local or sectional pride and rivalry, group sentiment, and tradition as C. E. Merriam and H. F. Gosnell did in *The American Party System* (New York: The Macmillan Company, 1949, 4th ed.) pp. 107-121. In order to account for sectional voting responses to such economic issues as the tariff, currency, and cotton growing, they admitted that "sectionalism is strongest politically when it is not merely sentimental

The South Epitomizes Sectionalism. To turn from general descriptions to specific designations of sections immediately develops a contradiction in the association of sectionalism with economics. The classic example of a political section is the South, that group of states stretching from the Atlantic seaboard to Texas and southward from the Virginia-Kentucky-Arkansas line. Historically, the South has been a foremost agricultural section, but this economic uniformity certainly does not account for its political uniformity and its sense of distinction from the remainder of the country. Some of the more intangible causes of sectionalism furnish the explanation, such as the psychological conditioning of the Civil War and Reconstruction. A related cause even more determinative of the South's sectionalism has been the intensification of the racial question and the orthodox white attitude toward the Negro. The most outstanding example of partisan sectional behavior, therefore, is based on heritage, only supplemented by economics, and has resisted bipartisanism despite a growth in the section's economic diversity and the passage of a century in time.

Three Standard Sections. The existence of a valid sectional analysis requires at least two sections. Because of the irrefutable sectionalism of the South, the remainder of the country in contradistinction is often designated the North. To lump together all of the states outside of the South as being the North may have some justification when one is thinking in a very general way and intentionally using loose terminology, but this dichotomy is useless for any practical purpose. The North cannot be expanded very well to include both New England and the states of Arizona and New Mexico. Consequently, three general sections become the basis for political differentiation: South, North, and West.

East v. West Sectionalism. These familiar classifications are a post-Civil-War arrangement. The sectionalism before that great conflict of arms was as much East *v.* West as it was North *v.* South, and the farther back in our history one goes, the greater the likelihood of emphasis being placed upon the seaboard East as opposed to the frontier West. Many states now part of the South, e.g., Kentucky, Tennessee, Arkansas, Texas, were once the "West" and reflected the agrarian and pioneer point of view of the new settlers beyond the mountains or across the rivers. To differentiate the whole South from the West was impossible before the middle of the last century, and the farthest western extensions of the South continue to reflect characteristics of the West into which they blend. Until the

but is allied with some specific issue which finds a local seat in a particular geographical location."——Pp. 108-109. This attempt to deal with economics almost incidentally, but with the admission that it is the strongest manifestation, is somewhat like arriving at an understanding of sectionalism by a switchback trail rather than by a well-traveled road.

issue of slavery became dominant, there was often more affinity of interests among groups along the Atlantic coast than among groups stretching from the Atlantic into the interior. Culture, race, religion, and psychology drew a sectional line north to south as well as east to west. As the North-South struggle took on more force, leaders on each side feared the growth of the West as a supplemental strength for the other. East-West controversies were sometimes outside the main areas of Southern interests, but most frequently the three sections interacted with one another in a series of compromises based on shifting alliances.

Part of the Western psychology has been a sectional reaction to the evidences of discriminations by the established, more highly developed East against the newer, more raucous and profane West. Legislative representation, interest rates, transportation have been constant sources of friction in East-West relations since the discontent of the back-country settlers in colonial days with the minority rule of the tidewater dwellers. As the West filled up with people and new states came into the Union on an equal footing with the older states, Eastern spokesmen in the North have returned again and again to the theme, first eloquently expressed by leaders of the Federalist Party, of representation in proportion to wealth or to numbers. The West has achieved an advantage in proportion to its population in the United States Senate and in the electoral college because of the adoption of the federal method of representation; but the basic sources of friction in unequal amounts of capital, in competition with transportation and trade outlets, in agriculture v. industry, in silver v. gold, and in debtors v. creditors have proved to be durable sectional political issues throughout our history.

A complication in the sectionalism of East and West is that the sections designated by these words have not remained static. The West, until the frontier finally disappeared with the exhaustion of the supply of virgin land, was constantly moving. Where the West once had been was a new "East" or an indeterminate or border region. The old Northwest Territory, including the present states of Ohio, Indiana, Illinois, Michigan, and Wisconsin and a small parcel of Minnesota, became a center of the nation and began being designated as the Midwest or the Central States; but these names were eventually applied also to the states running from the Dakotas to Missouri and Oklahoma; so, to differentiate, the latter group has been called the Plain States, and the states of the Old Northwest, the Lake States. More careful refinements of the Central States are found in references to East Central and West Central and sometimes North Central as well. "Midwest" is probably the most common designation for all of these Central States. The states west of the Plain States are conveniently classed as the Far West, but a basic distinction is usually recognized in the subdivision of Mountain States and Pacific Coast States. The West may include every state west of Pennsylvania, or of Illinois, or of Kansas, depending upon the meaning of the speaker.

Holcombe's Analysis. The final proof of the existence of political sections in the United States would be distinctive political behavior. The most diligent and analytical student of the manifestations of sectionalism in American political history has been Professor Arthur N. Holcombe, who first stated his case in *The Political Parties of To-Day,* published in 1924. He divided the states into twelve political sections and identified each section with a principal agricultural crop. For both presidential and congressional elections he identified the states and districts which were Republican, Democratic, and doubtful. The persistence of a partisan voting behavior was then related to the economic interests of each section, with the result that both parties were found to have urban and rural strength in approximately equal proportions. From these data, the obvious conclusion was drawn that the partisan cleavage was not urban *v.* rural, but two sets of economic interests sectionally separated. On the basis of congressional districts the Republicans were normally stronger in 161 districts located in the hay-and-pasture, rural-spring-wheat, rural-corn-belt, urban-and-metropolitan-corn-belt, and corn-and-winter-wheat regions, plus the Pacific Coast; the Democrats were normally stronger in 155 in the cotton-belt, subtropical-coast, rural-corn-and-winter-wheat, urban-and metropolitan-hay-and-pasture, and the corn-and-winter-wheat regions. Doubtful districts accounted for 117 and were found in the corn-and-winter-wheat and hay-and-pasture regions, including rural, urban, and metropolitan.[3]

With this documentation the differences between the two parties stood out, revealing good reasons why different economic interests aligned with one party or another. This is a perception of the party system which the popularizers of the tweedledum-and-tweedledee thesis apparently never discovered, although evidence of it has always been available for the researcher.[4] The moderating element in this alignment of different interests was the existence of doubtful sections which must be successfully appealed to in order to win presidential and congressional elections. In the post-1896 sectional alignment, the Democrats needed to carry the metropolitan areas in the hay-and-pasture region and the Republicans the rural areas of the corn belt and corn-and-winter-wheat regions. These problems largely explained the respective Democratic and Republican standards of availability,

---

[3] Holcombe, *The Political Parties of To-Day* (New York: Harper & Brothers, 1924) pp. 105-129. See map, p. 70, of agricultural regions.

[4] E.g., see above, Chapter 12, note 9; F. J. Turner, *The United States 1830-1850* (New York: Henry Holt and Company, Inc., 1935) for sectional analyses of voting in Congress on the tariff of 1832 (pp. 400-401), on rechartering the United States Bank in 1832 (p. 408), and on Texas annexation (p. 532); also, F. J. Turner, *The Significance of Sections in American History,* pp. 23-33 and Chap. 6.

whereby the Republicans chose presidential candidates most frequently from the Central States and vice-presidential candidates from New York, and the Democrats followed the reverse formula. As total party efforts, the Republicans had appealed with their candidates and platforms to the Northeast and West and the Democrats had generally appealed to all three major sections, with the notable exception of Bryan's attempt in 1896 to combine the West and the South.[5]

Additional Substantiation of Sections. Others have added contributions to this general subject. Professor Schattschneider saw a relative sectional stability from election to election. While party percentages varied in a state or section according to the issues and circumstances of the time, they did not appear to have much effect upon the sectional patterns, i.e., states ranked according to the degree of Republican or Democratic strength in one election tend to keep the same rank in subsequent elections regardless of the winning party; it was only in the long run that sectional transformations appeared.[6] Louis Bean found that irrespective of national issues, some states were persistently Democratic and others persistently Republican; that the pattern for the South was vastly different from that for the North or for the West; that peculiarities in patterns were usually associated with special issues as in 1896, 1928, and 1940; and that the states from Michigan northwest to the Pacific Coast were more flexible than the nation as a whole.[7]

Working in another direction, one encounters substantiation of sec-

---

[5] Holcombe, op. cit., pp. 126-127, 198 ff. As statistical support for the observation regarding Bryan, he was stronger in the following states in 1896 than in 1900 by 5% to 34%: Alabama, Arkansas, Minnesota, Kansas, North and South Dakota, Wyoming, Idaho, Montana, Washington, Oregon, Nevada, Utah, Colorado. In these states he was stronger by 5% to 12% in 1900 than in 1896: Maine, New Hampshire, Vermont, Massachusetts, Rhode Island, Connecticut, New York, New Jersey, Georgia, Florida.——Louis Bean, How to Predict Elections (New York: Alfred A. Knopf, Inc., 1948) p. 92.

[6] Schattschneider, Party Government (New York: Farrar & Rinehart, Inc., 1942) pp. 112-115. If states are ranked according to the Republican percentage of the two-party presidential vote, 1920-1952, only Vermont falls among the top twelve states for each of the nine elections; Maine for eight; Kansas and South Dakota for seven. A total of twenty-nine different states is found in the top twelve for one or more of the elections. Looking at the top fourth of the states ranked by the Democratic percentage of the two-party vote, six (Arkansas, Louisiana, Mississippi, Alabama, Georgia, and South Carolina) are found for each of the nine elections; Texas for eight; Florida for seven. A total of twenty-five different states is in the top twelve for one or more of the elections. The only two states never to appear in either the Republican or Democratic top twelve were Maryland and New Mexico. A state's rank does not necessarily determine which party carries it, e.g., Tennessee was twice carried by the Republicans when it was among the bottom fourth of the Republican states; but in four elections, when it ranked higher, it was carried by the Democrats.

[7] Bean, op. cit., pp. 80, 114-116. "Political issues that cause, say, a five-point shift in Democratic-Republican percentages in the Eastern and North Central states will cause a corresponding ten-point shift in the Northwest and Pacific states."——P. 116.

tional politics in the federal system, whose "nature . . . requires the organization of national parties upon a sectional basis." [8] Sectionalism, like the states, is older than the Constitution, or to put it another way, the conditions motivating the federal organization preceded the Constitution and created the framework within which that document was written. As the territorial limits have expanded, the nation's very size has been emphasized by the diversities from one part of the country to the other. Sectionalism is the underlying determinant of federalism, while a practice like the electoral-college system, an open and unqualified acceptance of the principle of individual state action, is a result of federalism. The manner in which presidential electors are chosen puts a premium upon carrying a state, whether by a plurality or by a majority, and concentrates attention upon carrying groups of states; but this is only one of many political arrangements reflecting the insistence upon state independence.

CLASSES

Weaknesses in Sectional Identification. The rejection of the sectional basis is something less than a rejection of the economic explanation of American politics. Sectionalism can be attacked negatively for its own inherent limitations, and positively for distorting political realities. It is not difficult to point out limitations of the sectional analysis. The accuracy of classifications is an unresolved problem which no one is any more aware of than the sectionalists themselves. The nature of this challenge is revealed in the variety of classifications which, to a greater or lesser extent, vary with each analyst. Professor E. E. Robinson in his election studies distinguishes the same nine sections used by the Bureau of the Census; Dr. George Gallup for the purposes of his national polls uses seven sections. Among popular writers all kinds of variations are found, based on the sections of East, Central, South, and West.

Professor Holcombe has made the finest and most carefully drawn distinctions, and in two of his works, *The Political Parties of To-Day* (1924) and *Our More Perfect Union* (1950), he demonstrated how sectionalism evolved in a period of approximately thirty years; he presented in his later work not only a different series of divisions but also a different scheme of classifications revealed by the accompanying chart. Elaborating upon the latter classification, he noted that the four principal sections of 1787 had been transformed into the metropolitan states of the Northeast and North Central, the corn-and-wheat-belt states of the North Central, the grazing and mining states of the West. The Border and Pacific Coast states are separately classified because they differ substantially from sections adjacent to them, not because they are internally unified; in fact, Washington and

---

8 Holcombe, *op. cit.*, p. 82; also Schattschneider, *op. cit.*, pp. 119–123.

TABLE 4: COMPARATIVE SECTIONAL CLASSIFICATIONS
OF PROFESSOR HOLCOMBE

THE POLITICAL PARTIES OF TO-DAY (p. 387)	OUR MORE PERFECT UNION (p. 115)
I. NORTHEAST (9 STATES)	**I. NORTHEAST (9 STATES)**
New England	*Predominantly Urban*

Connecticut	New Hampshire	Connecticut	New York
Maine	Rhode Island	Massachusetts	Pennsylvania
Massachusetts	Vermont	New Jersey	Rhode Island

Middle Atlantic	*Semiurban and Rural*
New Jersey, New York, Pennsylvania	Maine, New Hampshire, Vermont

II. NORTHWEST (11 STATES)	**II. NORTH CENTRAL (11 STATES)**
Central	*Predominantly Urban*
Illinois, Indiana, Ohio	Illinois, Michigan, Ohio

North Central	*Semiurban and Rural*
Iowa, Michigan, Minnesota, Wisconsin	

West Central			
		Indiana	Nebraska
		Iowa	North Dakota
Kansas	North Dakota	Kansas	South Dakota
Nebraska	South Dakota	Minnesota	Wisconsin

III. UPPER SOUTH (9 STATES)	**III. SOUTH (17 STATES)**
Upper South Atlantic	*Border*

Delaware	Virginia	Delaware	Missouri
Maryland	West Virginia	Kentucky	Oklahoma
North Carolina		Maryland	West Virginia

South Central

Kentucky, Missouri, Oklahoma, Tennessee

IV. LOWER SOUTH (8 STATES)

Lower South		*Solid South*	
Alabama	Louisiana	Alabama	North Carolina
Arkansas	Mississippi	Arkansas	South Carolina
Florida	South Carolina	Florida	Tennessee
Georgia	Texas	Georgia	Texas
		Louisiana	Virginia
		Mississippi	

V. FAR WEST (11 STATES)	**IV. WEST (11 STATES)**
Mountain	*Mountain*

Arizona	Nevada	(same states)
Colorado	New Mexico	
Idaho	Utah	
Montana	Wyoming	

Pacific	*Pacific*
California, Oregon, Washington	(same states)

Oregon can be distinguished from California as Maine, New Hampshire, and Vermont are distinguished from the remainder of New England. The perimeter of the Northern dairy interests has contracted, while the grain-growing, stock-raising, wage-earning, and capitalistic interests have expanded tremendously.[9]

To talk in terms of the political behavior of a section inevitably overlooks to some extent the sectional disunity demonstrated by large opposing votes, a disunity obscured by the electoral-college system. Except for the South, it is unusual to find a section without one or another kind of deviation in its voting, and every section, including the South, is capable of switching its partisan allegiance. To be quite exact and discriminating in isolating homogeneous states is likely to lead to the identification of many small divisions. But are they genuine sections? The other extreme is to mark off a few large regions; but in this case so many exceptions must constantly be noted that the whole value of the sectional analysis is undermined.

Sectional Inconsistency. Examinations of sectional voting behavior show that some sections vary more widely in the short run than other sections and that even relatively stable sections fluctuate very often in the same direction but not in the same proportion as the nation. These data have been interpreted in different ways. The sectionalists point out that a Democratic section in a Republican year is still more strongly Democratic than a Republcian section and vice versa. According to the opposite view, sections which swing abruptly from time to time and display a great deal of internal division cannot be considered valid sections for political purposes; and sections which reflect nation-wide influences to an extent great enough to disrupt calculations and create doubt of their political leanings are meaningless divisions of the electorate. Analyzing elections in terms of sections loses sight of the factors which are impervious to artificial boundaries shown on maps, those "waves of sentiment, resentment, conviction that transcend sectional lines." [10]

---

9 Holcombe, *Our More Perfect Union* (Cambridge: Harvard University Press, 1950) pp. 74-76, 69-70, 111. Regarding the subdividing of New England, see *New York Times,* July 23, 1950.

10 "In the face of these returns (1896-1932) it can no longer be asserted with any degree of finality that sectional interests are paramount in the minds of the voters. In 1896 and 1916 there appeared to be a sectional decision. But in New England and the Middle states there was in both elections a heavy Democratic vote; and in the West there was a Republican vote. . . . Except for approximately 800 counties, most of them in the twelve states of the South, there is as a rule a sizable minority vote in every county in every election."——E. E. Robinson, *The Presidential Vote 1896–1932* (Stanford: Stanford University Press, 1934) p. 31.

Emphasis upon Urban Voting. The results of the growth and spread of industry and the increase in size and number of cities have deeply affected political practices, and, taken in connection with the supremacy of the Democratic Party since 1932, have diverted political attention toward cities rather than to sections as such. Inasmuch as the Republican sections of East and West were never as dependable as the South was for the Democrats, the Republican sections were completely undermined when the upheaval came in the 1930's. The discontent of Western agricultural interests was a short-term development, but the progressive loss of urban strength was a long-term development. Professor Holcombe had found that while both parties tended to be strong in rural, urban, and metropolitan districts in their respective sections, there was some inconsistency in the greater Democratic strength in the metropolitan districts in Republican sections.[11]

Furthermore, an urban decline in Republican strength set in during the 1920's while the Party was still dominant, refuting to some extent the view that the urban vote went Democratic because of the depression and the personality of Franklin D. Roosevelt. The sharp break in urban voting actually appeared in 1928, when Alfred E. Smith either overcame or reduced the Republican majority in most of the larger cities.[12] The urban swing was not decisive in the 1920's because in only 6 out of 36 instances did any of the 12 largest cities cast a large enough plurality to carry its state for either party. The significant urban political development came thereafter, for in 35 out of 50 instances from 1932 to 1948 the pluralities of these 12 cities were decisive in carrying their states for the Democrats. The maximum value of this urban support occurred in 1940, when Mr. Roosevelt won 212 electoral votes in 10 states that were carried because of Democratic metropolitan pluralities. In 1932 the Republicans carried 15 cities with populations of 100,000 or larger, but they did not carry as many as 15 again until 1948.[13]

The urban vote, which never had been a Republican bulwark, became a Democratic mainstay at the very time the swelling urban populations were casting a larger proportion of the total national vote. An urban *v.*

---

[11] *The Political Parties of To-Day,* p. 120.

[12] Beard in *The American Party Battle* (New York: The Macmillan Company, 1928) p. 148, note 1, written after the major-party nominations in 1928 but before the election, pointed out the urban tendency of both parties and their relegating their rural factions to the background. The appeal of Alfred E. Smith cost the Republicans in the cities but cost the Democrats in the rural areas.

[13] George Gallup, *The Political Almanac* (New York: B. C. Forbes & Sons, 1952) pp. 29-32; Samuel J. Eldersveld, "The Influence of Metropolitan Party Pluralities in Presidential Elections since 1920: A Study of Twelve Key Cities," *American Political Science Review,* Vol. 43 (1949) pp. 1193-1196; Samuel Lubell, *The Future of American Politics* (New York: Harper & Brothers, 1952) pp. 34 ff. and 50. It was noted that both the Republicans' urban decline in the 1920's and their recovery in the late 1940's were overlooked during their process of development.——Malcolm Moos, *Politics, Presidents and Coattails* (Baltimore: The Johns Hopkins Press, 1952) pp. 30-31.

rural cleavage gave a new tone to American politics, a tone of class rather than sectional alignment.

> A new nationalizing force had clearly been injected into American politics. In the past American political realignments have always followed sectional lines. The Revolt of the City, however, had drawn the same class-conscious line of economic interest across the entire country, overriding not only regional distinctions but equally strong cultural differences.[14]

Metropolitan Sectionalism. Since 1920, when the urban population first exceeded the rural population, the growth of cities has been sharp and sudden. In 1950, 64% of the population was classified as urban.[15] The dispersal of people from large cities into the surrounding countryside—giving rise to the rapid construction of housing developments and shopping centers—has created the concept of the standard metropolitan area (SMA).[16] This pattern of movement has been so accelerated that suburban population has grown tremendously while the central-city population has declined. No longer is it possible to consider national problems only by the simple dichotomy of rural and urban, because the migration from rural to urban to suburban has expanded the geographical perimeters of human congestion and created entirely new problems of urban living.

The seemingly never-ending growth of metropolitan areas has revolutionized sectional thinking. A sectional analysis based on dominant agricultural interests is patently inadequate when over half of the population lives in standard metropolitan areas extending across the country.[17] Sectionalism, more and more, is found in the patterns of metropolitan voting. In the presidential elections of 1952 and 1956, the fourteen largest SMA cast one-third of the total national vote.[18] The improvement in the Re-

---

[14] Lubell, *op. cit.*, p. 50; see, in general, Chap. 3.

[15] The definition of urban was changed by the Census Bureau in 1950. Under the former definition, the 1950 urban population was 59%, not much more than the 56.5% in 1940. The definition adopted in 1950, although more difficult in some cases to apply, is more realistic. U. S. Bureau of the Census, *Statistical Abstract of the United States: 1952* (73d ed.) Washington, D. C., 1952, p. 2.

[16] In order for an area to qualify as a standard metropolitan area, there must be a central city with at least 50,000 population and the contiguous urban places must have a density of 150 or more per square mile.

[17] In the 1950 census, twelve states accounted for 277 electoral votes, 11 votes more than a majority:

New York	45	Michigan	20
California	32	New Jersey	16
Pennsylvania	32	Massachusetts	16
Illinois	27	North Carolina	14
Ohio	25	Missouri	13
Texas	24	Indiana	13

[18] Richard M. Scammon, "Voting for President in the Larger Metropolitan Areas, 1952-1956," *Midwest Journal of Political Science*, Vol. 1 (1957) p. 330.

publican urban vote since 1948 has been a reflection of the suburban vote, not the vote of the central city.[19] To this extent, there has emerged a potential urban sectionalism between central cities and the suburbs. This cleavage is a reflection, to some extent, of a social class difference among urban residents—suburbanites enjoying relatively higher standards of living and occupying, generally, positions of greater prestige and social acceptability. Thus, there is reinforcement for the conclusion that partisan differences among people are related to their place in the social and economic hierarchy.

Social Classes Instead of Sections. The most far-reaching conclusions have been predicated upon these political changes and trends. Stressing the effects of greater urban voting potential has simply emphasized the political appeal to groups based on their relative affluence, and the end result of some of the analyses is to substitute a class basis for a sectional basis of bipartisanism.[20] The intensified political activity of labor-union leaders, for example, has encouraged the belief that voters will progressively respond in conformance with their status in the nation's economic and social hierarchy and that this growing class division between the haves and the have-nots will form the basis of the major parties' cleavage.[21] The all-important matter becomes the ferreting out of these class alignments and identifying the class structure which supports the alignments.

Class itself, as it is thought of in this century, is a recent basis of social division; it is a product of commerce and trade and specialization of non-agricultural functions. Ancient classes were products of birth and privilege; now classes are associated with differences in income and occupation. Invariably, discussions of class take account of the Marxian stratification between the owners of the means of production and the workers, but even socialists no longer can hold to such a simple distinction.

Middle Class and the Class Concept. To apply a class analysis in the United States is to find oneself dealing, sooner or later, with the middle class, but to take cognizance of a middle class throws the whole class con-

[19] See *ibid.*, pp. 332-333 for a breakdown of the major-party vote in the fourteen areas. In 1956, Stevenson had 51.8% of the central-city vote compared with 55.1% in 1952. His percentage of the suburban vote was 37.8% in 1956 and 40.9% in 1952. *Ibid.*, Table 1, p. 331. Louis Harris, *Is There a Republican Majority?* (New York: Harper & Brothers, 1954) Chap. 8.

[20] See, e.g., Samuel P. Huntington, "A Revised Theory of American Party Politics," *American Political Science Review*, Vol. 54 (1950) pp. 676-677. Lubell, *op. cit.*

[21] This movement is epitomized in the statement of the Detroit automobile unionist in 1940, "I'll say it even though it doesn't sound nice. We've grown class-conscious."—— Quoted *ibid.*, p. 51.

cept out of focus. Does one distinguish the middle from the working class and, if so, how? [22] The middle class is found in certain occupations, such as the professions, farmers, small-scale businessmen, artisans, wives of workers, and youth, especially those in high school and universities. These categories have been augmented by managers and other salaried groups; salesmen, advertisers, credit men, and others connected with distribution; white-collar workers; other miscellaneous and expanded occupations, e.g., government employees, insurance and real-estate agents.[23] It may be equally valid to distinguish a class as

> a secondary grouping within a community, characterized by the fact that it fulfils certain functions and has a distinct place in the social hierarchy in relation to other groups. We can hardly go further than that, because the basis of differentiation varies with different societies. We might say, in a symbolic sense, that the proletarian is the slave of modern societies, but the legal status of the slave and proletarian have nothing in common. The proletarian is subject to the same law as the bourgeois, which was not true of the plebeian or slave in comparison with the patrician, or of the serf in comparison with the baron. Although men were once born nobles or burghers and generally kept that status all their life, to-day they are born the sons of bourgeois or workers but with opportunities of improving their positions which are, in law, unlimited and, in practice, limited but real.[24]

Subjective Class. The difficulty of defining a class is infinitely increased by the absence of a class consciousness upon which the definition itself depends. While Marx was profoundly mistaken in his anticipation that society would become more and more divided between proletariat and bourgeois as two coherent and all-inclusive groupings, he was eminently correct in seeing class as a consciousness of class instead of as a universally recognized set of objective characteristics. Occupations do not lend themselves easily as an objective measurement of class; different occupations can be varyingly classified according to circumstances; and some occupations defy classification. Income is a more objective measure, but severe

---

[22] Samuel Lubell, *The Revolt of the Moderates* (New York: Harper & Brothers, 1956) contended there is an economic solidarity of the middle class in the South as well as the North (pp. 184-185) and that there was a class solidarity in suburban voting in 1948 and 1952 (pp. 112-114). These conclusions were based on his definition of the middle class as "those who have climbed up out of the slums and out of the poverty of the depression to middle-income levels and who are striving to mount to the next rung of the ladder" (p. 278).

[23] Alfred M. Bingham, *Insurgent America* (New York: Harper & Brothers, 1935) pp. 49-51.

[24] Raymond Aron, "Social Structure and the Ruling Class," *British Journal of Sociology*, Vol. 1 (1950) p. 3.

problems arise again, because different types of incomes may be received by the same person or different persons may receive approximately equal incomes of different types from different sources. Private capitalism, far from developing the dichotomy of proletariat and bourgeois anticipated by Marx, has destroyed that dichotomy in the maze of cross interests produced by the dispersal of ownership through corporations and the rise of wage earners to the status of managers. If the problem of objective definition is so hopeless, subjective awareness of class is all that remains. The result is the popular and convenient division into three classes—upper, middle, and lower—but this classification is meaningless except for its political and propaganda value. Psychologically, the importance of class becomes what class people think they are in, and their self-classifications have no necessary relation to any objective class criteria or to their incomes or occupations.[25]

Self-Classifications. A sampling, just before the effects of World War II brought an end to depression conditions, permitted each respondent to specify the class he thought he belonged to. On this part of the interview, no class categories were mentioned, the respondents supplying their own descriptive words. The results showed that:

2.9% used the word "upper" or its equivalent

47.0% said "middle" or an interchangeable word

14.9% gave these words: "lower," "working," "laboring," "unemployed"

2.0% used such words as "business," "executive," "professional," "white collar"

27.5% did not know what class they were in

Less than one fourth of the factory workers and an even smaller proportion among farm and miscellaneous laborers used the words "working" or "laboring." Those respondents who did not voluntarily classify themselves as "upper," "middle," and "lower" were asked to pick one of the three as being applicable to themselves. Combining all of the respondents according to these categories, the results were: 7.6% upper; 79.2% middle; 7.9% lower; 5.3% don't know. Every group and occupation, including the unemployed and farm laborers, considered itself to be middle class.[26]

---

25 *Ibid.*, pp. 3-4, 8.

26 *Fortune*, February, 1940, pp. 14 ff. See George Gallup and Saul F. Rae, *The Pulse of Democracy* (New York: Simon and Schuster, Inc., 1940) p. 169, for similar findings. No one set of statistics nor any one series of studies can be conclusive upon a point so important or complex as class consciousness, but the findings of such surveys reinforce the almost universal observation of Americans by Americans and by foreigners as well. The drive toward middle-class status still seems to be imperishable, and even the class-consciousness that Lubell found among labor unions in 1940 appeared to be dissipated by 1948 under the impact of full employment and the attainment of gains worth conserving.——*Op. cit.*, pp. 179 ff.

This particular poll does not conform with other attempts to investigate classes. The differences in results cast a genuine doubt over the validity of the whole series of such questionnaires. The wording of questions will produce conflicting evidence, and the number of kinds of classes into which respondents are asked to fit themselves are the most important part of a survey. Other investigations reveal that large percentages of respondents will classify themselves as "working class" when the choices are: upper, middle, working, and lower. Otherwise, if there are only three choices, the bulk will fall in the "middle" category.[27] When this kind of a difference can be found depending upon the number of choices, it is only reasonable to inquire what significance, if any, such investigations have and what other means of analysis, if any, can give us an objective or meaningful classification.

Evidence of Class-Consciousness. Taking exception to the conclusions of the *Fortune* poll, one student concluded that Americans definitely are class conscious, since only an insignificant number, in his surveys, failed to place themselves in one of the four class categories, and over 90% of the respondents chose either "middle" or "working." Although a class is what people collectively think it is, in this survey the middle and working classes (as self-classified) had a separate picture of themselves in terms of the occupations they identified with their own classes. About three fourths of the business, professional, and white-collar respondents said they were middle class, and 79% of the manual workers said they were in the working or lower classes. Aside from distinguishing classes by occupation, respondents said the way a person "believes and feels about certain things" was an important difference among classes.[28]

Americans do have concepts of classes based largely on such kinds of differences as income, occupation, and education. In this sense, we are not classless, but the question is how much importance derives from these differences or our concepts of the differences. Americans tend strongly to equate class with outward symbols of what they accept as being the signs of a class. The most frequent manifestation of class has been income,

---

27 For example, the following is taken from the files of the Survey Research Center's 1952 survey:

	No.	%		No.	%
Upper class	30	2	Refused—No classes in America..	7	*
Middle class	627	35	Don't know	20	1
Working class	1039	58	Not ascertained	37	1
Lower class	39	2			

* Less than one-half of one per cent.

28 Richard Centers, *The Psychology of Social Classes* (Princeton: Princeton University Press, 1949) pp. 76 ff.

irrespective of its source. The urge of those who think they are relatively low is to rise, either personally or so as to permit their offspring to rise. Class becomes not what we are but what we think we are, and the lack of permanent insignia of class, of hard-and-fast dividing lines, becomes an outstanding characteristic of the class system. The tendency for the population to project itself into a middle ground and into the middle class as distinct from the extremes, is a denial of useful class distinctions and repudiates a proletariat psychology.

These reactions are certainly related to the nature of our national development and our nearness in spirit to the tremendous vitality of our pioneer past. The sense of equality fostered by the frontier society is still part of the national aspiration despite the passing of the frontier; and the phenomenon of mobility, both figurative and literal, continues with increased vigor. Yet the element of equality embodied in our traditions is belied by the drive for getting ahead and by the value placed upon success. The American psychology is at one and the same time neither class-conscious nor equalitarian.

For the purposes of this discussion, class is important as it is reflected politically. Whether class is objectified in income and occupation or subjectified according to people's self-classification, no class is fully mobilized politically. Whether any class is capable of being so mobilized is another and wholly speculative question. Two observations can be made. In the first place, the people as a whole have been satisfied with the established political system which is not geared to emphasize class motivations as such.[29] In the second place, political managers have demonstrated their grasp of the simple lesson that "whether a majority party be built up from the bottom or down from the top, it must be able to command the confidence of the average man, the man who is no more oppressed by his consciousness of inferiority in the social order than elated by his consciousness of superiority." [30]

---

[29] Murray S. Stedman, Jr., and Susan W. Stedman, *Discontent at the Polls* (New York: Columbia University Press, 1950) Chaps. 8, 9. The most significant evidence in 1952 of class-conscious political attitudes were statements by some workers and their families that they were Democrats because they believed that their Party did more for working people, as contrasted with statements of other workers that they were Republicans because they believed that party would do more about inflation or ending war in Korea. Angus Campbell *et al.*, *The Voter Decides* (Evanston: Row, Peterson & Company, 1954) pp. 209–210 suggests this finding, but it was more fully elaborated by Heinz Eulau, "Perceptions of Class and Party in Voting Behavior: 1952," *American Political Science Review*, Vol. 49 (1955) pp. 364–384.

[30] Holcombe, *The New Party Politics*, p. 56; also pp. 91, 102-103; Holcombe, *Our More Perfect Union*, pp. 58–70; Bingham, *op. cit.*, pp. 92–93; R. M. MacIver, *The Modern State* (London: Oxford University Press, 1950 printing) pp. 403-404; Lubell, *op. cit.*, Chap. 4.

RELATION OF SECTION AND CLASS

The relative validity of the sectional and class bases of bipartisanism presents a problem in analysis. Neither one survives examination intact, and objections offered for one can be applied equally to the other, e.g., if national influences revealed in elections override sections, they likewise transcend classes. Class and sectionalism are mutually exclusive if carried to their logical conclusions, but in fact they are not carried to such a point. Each party alignment includes both section and class bases. In one sense, the two are aspects of a single phenomenon, inasmuch as stability of voting behavior in counties, cities, and even city wards reveals a sectionalism in location. Here, "on a microscopic scale class and sectional alignments seem to be identical." [31] However, in another sense, these grass-roots voting phenomena are assumed to be a class or economic cohesion of a neighborhood, not an example of sectionalism. Both bases are not, in practice, mutually exclusive because either extreme is intolerable to practical politics. Sectional leaders need alliances because of the limits of sectional unity, and a class large enough to win an election is too large to be manageable. Class alignments create bitter, uncompromising divisions capable of creating civil strife and eventually the loss of liberty. The extremes of sectionalism magnify separatism and produce antagonisms which contributed substantially to such a tragic event as the American Civil War. Both of these tendencies are the kinds of excesses that national political parties are supposed to ameliorate.[32]

Possibilities for Durable Sections. Professor Turner, in examining the causes of sectionalism, found that some were waning—"the sectionalism due to the movement of American settlement into the wilderness is a declining sectionalism"—and he fully appreciated the nationalizing tendencies of American business activities and the growth of cities. Nevertheless, he was convinced that sectional conflicts would continue in the adoption of public policies governing national economic activities. He raised the question of the possibility of the extinction of agriculture and with it rural sectional interests, but concluded that agriculture would survive even though subordinate to industry and that the two would continue to underlie sectional differences. He contended that the growth of direct majority rule would intensify sectional resistance, and projecting sectionalism as the foundation of state sovereignty, felt it was "far from certain that it (sectionalism) would pass away though the state should be extinguished." If the nation should become more static, sectional self-consciousness would likely increase as "crystallized sections feel the full influence of their geo-

31 Schattschneider, *op. cit.*, p. 111; also pp. 116-118.
32 Turner, *Significance of Sections in American History*, pp. 45-47.

graphic peculiarities, their special interests, and their developed ideals . . . ." [33]

Persistence of Sectional Evidence. Despite the fact that sectional classifications vary, the similarity of all classifications is at least as striking as their differences. The basic divisions of South, East, Central, and West invariably appear, irrespective of other inconsistencies. Furthermore, two distinct patterns of sectional divisions outside the South have been identified in presidential elections since 1896.[34] In one group (1896, 1916, 1932, and 1948) the Democrats were relatively weak in the Northeast and relatively strong in the North Central and West. In a second group (1904, 1920, 1940) the Democrats' relative strength and weakness were just reversed.[35] These sectional swings in relative party strength are obviously related to issues of a given year. When the Democrats have gone into a campaign attacking dominant Eastern interests, the Republicans have picked up strength in the East. When the Democrats reassured dominant Eastern interests either on domestic issues (1904) or foreign issues (1940), the Republicans' strength increased relatively in the Central and Western states. This basic East-West cleavage reflected a sectionalism that transcended partisanism, and presumably class as well.

Sectionalism, 1920–1956. Additional light can be thrown upon the validity of sectionalism during the years of most intensive urbanization by studying the contrasting patterns in national and sectional voting in the accompanying graphs. The sectional classification used is that developed by Professor Holcombe at the middle of the twentieth century in *Our More Perfect Union*. Although he does not project it back to 1920, he does apply it to the Democratic New Deal period. Since the urban-rural conflict first appeared clearly in 1928, this is a reasonable classification for that year and is not entirely inapplicable to 1920 and 1924—all elections since the United States has been over 50% urban. The year 1920 is taken as the starting point in order to include years of violent swings in party dominance, the Republicans winning five elections and the Democrats five. The period is pertinent for its recency. Since percentages only are used, the results do not bear any relation to the voting turnout, and since sections, not states, are shown the result is a sectional composite. The Republican

---

[33] *Ibid.*, pp. 35-36, 287-290, 311-314.

[34] A much clearer sectionalism was usually evident during the nineteenth century, a particularly good example being 1860, when the Republicans won the Presidency because the Party dominated a section which dominated the electoral college. See Holcombe, *The Political Parties of To-Day*, p. 176.

[35] Holcombe, *Our More Perfect Union*, pp. 121, 127; Bean, *op. cit.*, pp. 93-98; Robinson, *The Preisidential Vote*, p. 24. This pattern was true in 1948 for the presidential vote, but in the congressional voting the Democrats were stronger in the industrial East and weaker in the Mountain, North Central, and West Central sections.

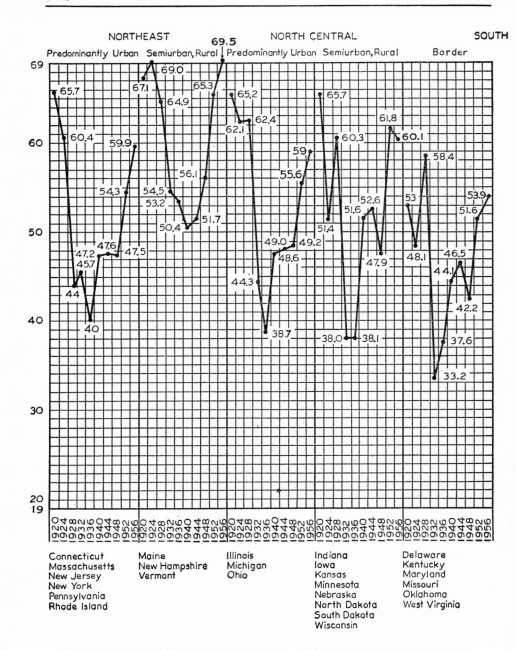

**REPUBLICAN PERCENTAGE, TOTAL VOTE CAST, PRESIDENTIAL
ELECTIONS, 1920–1956: NATIONALLY AND BY SECTIONS**

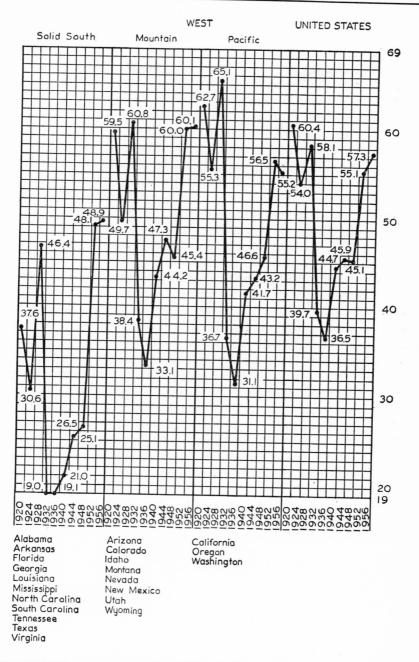

WEST

Solid South. Mountain Pacific UNITED STATES

Alabama
Arkansas
Florida
Georgia
Louisiana
Mississippi
North Carolina
South Carolina
Tennessee
Texas
Virginia

Arizona
Colorado
Idaho
Montana
Nevada
New Mexico
Utah
Wyoming

California
Oregon
Washington

REPUBLICAN PERCENTAGE, TOTAL VOTE CAST, PRESIDENTIAL
ELECTIONS, 1920–1956: NATIONALLY AND BY SECTIONS

percentage, rather than the Democratic, is used for the purpose of illuminating the position of the minority party during the greater part of the period covered and for clarifying the durability of a major party even at its lowest depths.

Nationally, the Republican high point was 60.4% in 1920 and the low point was 36.5% in 1936; the span, or difference between high and low, was 23.9 points for the whole country. The span for the seven sections, in ascending order, was 19.1 Northeast rural, 25.2 Border, 25.7 Northeast urban, 26.5 North Central urban, 27.7 North Central rural and Mountain, 29.9 Solid South and 34.0 Pacific. Only the three states of Maine, New Hampshire, and Vermont, with 18.6, had a smaller span than the nation although only the Pacific states showed a substantially larger span and were thus marked as the most mercurial. In fact the other six sections present a surprising stability, considering the political and economic strains and stresses during these thirty-two years; however, the spans should not obscure the fact that the evidences of stability are found in both bipartisan and in one-party sections. Looking at the percentages in the light of the party struggle, it appears that except for the Southern sections (and then, notably, the Solid South) well-matched parties emerge in each section. When the whole country moves up, each section is likely to move up and vice versa; inherent partisan strength in a section is revealed by the difference between the national and sectional movements up or down and by the relative differences in these movements among the sections themselves.

The deviations from the relation between the nation and section are few, but perhaps significant. Both 1924 and 1928 show up as "unusual" elections. In all sections except the urban and semiurban Northeast, Republicans were stronger in 1928 than in 1924; actually, the Republicans were weaker in the urban Northeast in 1928 than in 1932. Republicans reached their height in 1928 in three sections: Border, Mountain, and Pacific. It is obvious that something was wrong in 1928 since the general pattern was askew. The behavior of the urban Northeast, at least, can be raised as a possible example of sectionalism based on urban-class mobilization. The 1924 results found the Republicans down in the rural North Central, Mountain, and Pacific sections. Although most of the sections reflected the nation with the Republican low point in 1936, the rural Northeast was lowest in 1940 and the Border in 1932; the rural North Central and Solid South were the same in 1932 and 1936. Both the Border and Solid South show a revealing curve since 1932. The former has risen at every election except for 1948, and in 1956 exceeded its 1920 percentage; the latter has progressively increased its Republican percentage and reached its high point in 1956. The Republican failure in 1948 can be seen in its reduced percentage, compared with 1944, in the rural North Central, Border, and

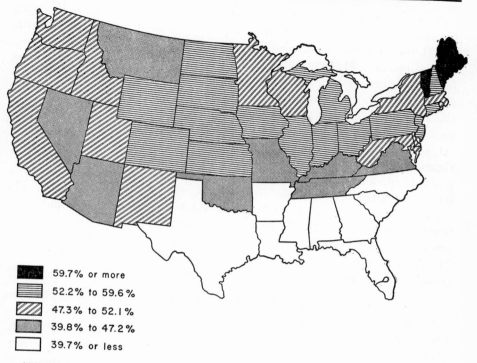

- ■ 59.7% or more
- ▤ 52.2% to 59.6%
- ▨ 47.3% to 52.1%
- ▦ 39.8% to 47.2%
- □ 39.7% or less

AVERAGE PERCENTAGE REPUBLICAN OF TOTAL VOTE CAST IN
TEN PRESIDENTIAL ELECTIONS, 1920–1956

Mountain sections while holding even in the urban Northeast and the North Central; only in the rural Northeast and Pacific was 1948 a noticeable gain over 1944.

Dealing with sectional percentages masks state diversities. The accompanying map shows state patterns for the same ten presidential elections. The average percentage of the total vote cast for Republican presidential candidates, 1920–1956, is 49.7%. Each state's percentage is averaged and classified into one of the five groups of percentages, ranging from 10% or more to 10% or less than 49.7%, and each of the five groups is indicated on the map. As was the case with the sectional composites, certain limitations should be specified. The basis of state classifications is presidential elections. No state trends can be predicted from the map, for in some cases, changing trends in states have produced the result shown here. This is a pictorial recording of the composite relation of the 48 states during the 36-year period.

Sectionalism in Congressional Voting. Presidential elections do not offer the only evidence of sectionalism in American politics. An alternative point of departure from the election-study method is the analysis of voting records in Congress. Two studies in particular were made, one covering the House of Representatives from 1870 to 1890 and the second covering the sessions of 1921, 1930–1931, 1937, and 1944.[36] The latter study did not find, as the former had, an affinity between representatives from the Democratic South and the Republican West Central states,[37] but did find a sectionalism in each party. Among Democrats, party pressures and foreign-*v*.-native-born constituencies accounted for more divisions than sectionalism; yet a North-South cleavage did appear in such issues as the Negro, state rights, executive power and administrative growth, immigration, relief, prohibition, and labor. Among Republicans, party pressures were more important than sectionalism; nevertheless, the anticipated division did show up between Republicans from the Northeast coastal region and those from the Central interior, including the Mountain section. Issues separating Republicans were foreign affairs, farm legislation, and Indian affairs; in addition, the West Central Republicans were more friendly to such groups as veterans and less friendly to government employees.

Parties and Urban-Rural Conflicts. A joint consideration of elections and party voting records was undertaken in connection with the Seventy-ninth and Eightieth Congresses and the congressional election of 1946. In rural districts, where one dominant agricultural interest existed, the parties were found to be very much the same ideologically, but very uneven in their voting strength—Republicans prevailing in the rural North and the Democrats in the rural South. In urban and suburban districts, on the contrary, there were found "two competing economic interests, one composed of middle and upper class, property-owning, capitalistic groups, the other composed of lower class, propertyless, laboring elements." While the dominant rural party is determined by tradition, urban party loyalty is determined by antagonistic interests wherein the Democrats "will not seriously attempt to win the banker and businessman vote and the Republican party will make little effort to secure the support of labor-union members and the unemployed. The parties will strive to win not by converting their opponents but by effectively mobilizing their own supporters, not by extending their appeal but by intensifying it." [38] If these conclu-

---

[36] Hannah Grace Roach, "Sectionalism in Congress (1870 to 1890)," *American Political Science Review*, Vol. 19 (1925) pp. 500-526. Julius Turner, "Party and Constituency: Pressures on Congress," *The Johns Hopkins University Studies in Historical and Political Sciences*, Vol. 69 (1951) Chaps. 6, 7.

[37] *Ibid.*, pp. 159-160. The main reason for this change is the difference in attitude among West Central Republicans who have ceased to reflect the radicalism of agrarian discontent.

[38] Samuel P. Huntington, *op. cit.*, pp. 676-677. The class stratification of one election may be tempered by shifts in percentages over a period of time or in two consecutive elections such as 1948 and 1952.

sions are valid as generalizations for urban *v.* rural partisanship as a whole, class voting is significant only in urban areas and is simplified by a clear-cut dichotomy between those who have and those who have no property. Rural sectionalism continues to thrive because of a series of dominant agricultural interests which transcend conflicting class interests.

Traditional Party Role. These conclusions are less remarkable as they touch on the urban-rural conflict. In effect, they demonstrate what has always been known. Each party is composed of conflicting interests and, as part of its function of reconciling differences, mediates between urban and rural interests as well as different rural and urban interests. Party leaders increasingly look to the urban areas for victory and here, where the clash of economic interests is most marked, we find the great battleground of American politics. It is natural that where a greater consensus exists (rural) the parties will be more alike, and where less consensus exists (urban) the parties will appeal to one or another interest. Professor Huntington's attack upon the traditional view of a national party is predicated upon a piecemeal view of the parties in congressional districts; but each party, taken as a whole, is composed of both factions, the one from the evenly and the one from the unevenly balanced districts. Reference to the above election data reveals, in the predominantly urban sections between 1932 and 1956, a variation from 40% to 59.9% in Northeast, from 38.7% to 59.0% in North Central and from 31.1% to 56.5% in the Pacific. The ability to swing this much back and forth suggests that party strength is not based entirely upon mobilization of a class.

Relative Influence of Metropolitan Voting. Despite the increased Democratic strength in cities and the growing influence within metropolitan states of the urban vote, Professor Eldersveld concluded that this situation "has not been so marked as to produce such an imbalance in the size of metropolitan electorates as to permit the use of this fact as a rationalization of big city influence in presidential elections." [39] There is no question about the importance of the large urban states' electoral votes. These have been the key states throughout the history of American presidential elections and have been a primary factor in determining availability. The unquestioned evidence of their greater importance is the more frequent appearance of New Yorkers as presidential nominees, the elevation of Californians as presidential timber, and the shift in the battleground for control of Congress to the metropolitan districts on the North Atlantic and Pacific Coasts and in the North Central States.[40]

Examination of all of the data makes it clear that there is sectional fluidity even in the Southern States, but there are distinct elements of sec-

[39] Eldersveld, *op. cit.*, p. 1192; also pp. 1199, 1202 ff.
[40] Holcombe, *Our More Perfect Union*, pp. 124-127, 129, 132.

tionalism apparent at mid-twentieth century. The changes in American life affect both the particular behavior and the relative importance of sections, but assumptions that a class-conscious industrialization has destroyed sectionalism are incorrect.

> The growth of class consciousness among the American people does not mean a radical change in the place of sectionalism in national politics. . . . The territorial basis of elections (still based on key states and districts) insures that class consciousness can do no more than infuse a new spirit into sectionalism. . . . The rise of urban industrial interests produces new cleavages but creates no better opportunities for interests incapable of carrying districts and states.[41]

Shift of Location of Middle Class. If the familiar American party system depends upon middle-class class-consciousness, the system is in evolution not revolution. The middle class has neither disappeared nor, apparently, declined in relative numbers, but it has moved in volume from a rural to an urban setting. Consequently, differences in political practices can be expected to follow from differences in points of view, habits of living, and immediate interests. The so-called Revolt of the City may simply be the latest manifestation of that well-known American drive "to keep up with the Joneses." [42] Such changes do not necessarily dictate a fundamental alteration of the party system, although parties will be more and more oriented toward the requirements of urban society. The change is not so much from sectional to class-conscious politics or from a "conservative" politics of farmers to a "radical" politics of urban masses [43] as it is from rustic to urbane politics.[44] The decisiveness of the urban middle class in expressing its political preferences is by no means inevitable. For it to act with solidarity would change both its function and the nature of the party system as well. When it divided in 1948, the balance of power lay in the grain-growing, stock-raising sections, and the rural middle class was able to play its traditional role.[45]

---

[41] *Ibid.*, p. 144.

[42] Lubell, *op. cit.*, Chap. 4.

[43] William B. Hesseltine, *The Rise and Fall of Third Parties* (Washington, D. C.: Public Affairs Press, 1948) p. 49, contended that agrarians are more radical than labor.

[44] Alfred E. Smith in 1928 "stood first and always for the urban interests of the party. But Smith did not direct his appeal to any particular class of urban society. He did not specialize in class politics, though he sponsored a brand of politics which may be properly described as urbane. . . . Urbane politics will doubtless be class politics, but it will not be based on the simple alignment of two hostile classes envisaged by the Marxists and tacitly accepted by the Fascists. Urbane politics . . . , like rustic politics, will be complex and shot through with compromise. This too will favor the hegemony of the middle class."——Holcombe, *The New Party Politics,* pp. 111-112, 115, 147.

[45] Holcombe, *Our More Perfect Union,* pp. 117-118. One feature of the 1948 election was not typical: "Always the relative positions of the factions in close states seemed to vary less than the relative positions of the factions in the strongly partisan sections outside of the South. . . . It was the factions in the close states and in the South which seemed most changeable [in 1948]."——*Ibid.*, p. 127.

Identifying Middle-Class Interests. Locating, exactly, the middle class is always challenging because of the inexactness of the term itself. In cities, one of the most convenient and reliable indicators of social status is rental area. Those who live in the most expensive neighborhoods are predominantly Republican, and those who live in the poorest neighborhoods are most consistently Democrats. These extremes were easily identified in the examination of urban congressional districts; but between these extremes, in areas of intermediate rents, populated by a diverse assortment of small business and professional men, white-collar, skilled, and semi-skilled workers, are the urban middle-class voters who can and do switch parties and candidates and force the lines of election graphs to zigzag. It is among these groups that the parties are most likely to look for the additional support which will win elections. In this at best inexact scale of measurement the approximation of the class structure is revealed in partisan voting.[46]

Moderation in Struggle. There is danger in class appeals if class is narrowly defined, for the appeal antagonizes all those who feel themselves excluded and their apprehension prompts them to combine. The tendency of middle-class Americans is to respond negatively to extreme class appeals.[47] The process of maintaining stability through a distributed ownership of wealth occurs in the competition among economic interests represented by organized groups. The business of political parties is to adjust these conflicts. The interests dominating each party tend to be extreme, and in this way each party is based on a divergent set of interests; but the party differences in practice become less perceptible than in theory because each party

[46] This pinpointing of the doubtful, balance-of-power location of the urban middle class is contributed in *ibid.*, pp. 135-136. W. F. Ogburn and L. C. Coombs, "The Economic Factors in the Roosevelt Elections," *American Political Science Review*, Vol. 34 (1940) p. 719, cited the results of an examination of the 1932 election in Chicago showing that Hoover got a majority only in areas where the rent was $80 and over. Lubell, *op. cit.*, p. 51, reports that in 1940 the Roosevelt vote in the cities he analyzed "broke at virtually the some economic level, between $45 and $60 a month rent." In *The New Party Politics*, p. 103, Holcombe concluded that the size of the middle class cannot be determined by statistical methods, but Eldersveld, *op. cit.*, p. 1206, note 40, not only assumed that the "urban middle class" thesis can be verified or refuted statistically but also suggested some factors on which statistics can be collected.

[47] "The American people are naturally a conservative people. They do not wish to touch the stable foundations of their life; they have a reverence for the rights of property and the rights of contract which is based upon a long experience in a free life . . . . No other people have ever had such freedom or property rights. They do not mean to lose this freedom or to impair any rights at all, but they do feel that a great many things in their economic life and in their political action are out of gear. . . ."——Woodrow Wilson, "Issues of Freedom" (Address delivered at banquet of the Knife and Fork Club of Kansas City, Missouri, May 5, 1911) Ray Stannard Baker (ed.), *The Public Papers of Woodrow Wilson.* (New York: Harper & Brothers, 1925) College and State, Vol. 2, pp. 283-284.

moderates its extremism to capture those interests which are needed to win elections. Most organized groups themselves, to have respectable strength, are founded on middle-class interests and try to mobilize middle-class support to achieve political objectives. In adjusting these conflicts, party leaders are appealing to the middle class, and consequently appealing virtually to everyone in one way or another. The zone of political encounter is the clash and temporary pacification of the multitude of interests which James Madison discussed, or as his thesis was restated:

> The regulation of these various and interfering interests . . . constitutes the principal task of modern statesmen and involves the spirit of party in the necessary and ordinary operations of government. In other words, there is no rest for mankind, no final solution of eternal contradictions. Such is the design of the universe. The recognition of this fact is the beginning of wisdom—and of statesmanship.[48]

Selected Bibliography

Bean, Louis H., *How to Predict Elections.* New York: Alfred A. Knopf, Inc., 1948.

Centers, Richard, *The Psychology of Social Classes.* Princeton: Princeton University Press, 1949.

Eldersveld, Samuel J., "The Influence of Metropolitan Party Pluralities in Presidential Elections Since 1920: A Study of Twelve Key Cities," *American Political Science Review,* Vol. 43 (1949) pp. 1189–1206.

Holcombe, Arthur N., *The Middle Classes in American Politics.* Cambridge: Harvard University Press, 1940.

———, *The New Party Politics.* New York: W. W. Norton & Company, Inc., 1933.

———, *Our More Perfect Union.* Cambridge: Harvard University Press, 1950.

———, *The Political Parties of To-Day.* New York: Harper & Brothers, 1924.

Lubell, Samuel, *The Future of American Politics.* New York: Harper & Brothers, 1952.

Robinson, E. E., *The Presidential Vote 1896–1932.* Stanford: Stanford University Press, 1934.

———, *They Voted for Roosevelt.* Stanford: Stanford University Press, 1947.

Schattschneider, E. E., *Party Government.* New York: Farrar & Rinehart, Inc., 1942.

Turner, Frederick Jackson, *The Significance of Sections in American History.* New York: Henry Holt and Company, Inc., 1932.

Turner, Julius, "Party and Constituency: Pressures on Congress," *The Johns Hopkins University Studies in Historical and Political Science,* Series 69, No. 1, 1951.

---

[48] Charles A. Beard, *The Economic Basis of Politics* (New York: Alfred A. Knopf, Inc., 1945) p. 99.

CHAPTER FOURTEEN

The Bipartisan Basis of Organized Interest Groups— Their Place in the Nation

Sections and classes, as concepts of group responses to partisan politics, are based on mutual interests voluntarily expressed, not on organized mobilization. Organized interest groups are, by contrast, not necessarily geographically concentrated nor limited to any one class, but are capable of more coherence in action because their organization is based on the awareness of mutual interests. The number of sections or of classes is limited, but the number of organized groups existing for the purposes of concentrating political pressure at strategic points is infinite.[1]

ORGANIZED GROUPS WITH POLITICAL SIGNIFICANCE

Organized groups can overlap endlessly in membership and they have a startling capacity for fragmentation and specialization of objectives. "In almost any field, we find not one organization but many. It often appears more accurate to say that the present era is characterized by a chaos of organizations."[2] Joining together for political advantage quickly becomes contagious. What one can do and does successfully, another can do and hopes to be equally successful. The spiral is motivated not alone by imitation but by the urge to compete with rival groups.

Americans as "Joiners." The multiplication of groups in the United States creates a presumption that we have a special genius for organization and for promotion of ideas. One stereotype of an American is the extrovert personality constantly in association with his fellow citizens on every conceivable kind of a project from a clambake to a new aqueduct. This is the picture of the so-called "joiner," and the pattern is so universal that

---

[1] Attempts have been made to compile selected lists. The Department of Commerce described 4,000 in its publication *National Associations of the United States* (Washington, D. C.: Government Printing Office, 1949). The Temporary National Economic Committee in its *Economic Power and Political Pressures* (Washington, D. C.: Government Printing Office, 1941) Monograph No. 26, listed national organizations with permanent representatives in the national capital. The list is reproduced in Frederick C. Irion, *Public Opinion and Propaganda* (New York: Thomas Y. Crowell Company, 1950) Appendix, pp. 759 ff. Particular groupings within a major classification of interests have been catalogued and discussed, e.g., Luke Eugene Ebersole, *Church Lobbying in the Nation's Capital* (New York: The Macmillan Company, 1951) Chaps. 2, 3, 4.

[2] Grant McConnell, *The Decline of Agrarian Democracy* (Berkeley: University of California Press, 1953) p. 145.

Americans have been described as a nation of "joiners." [3] The pattern itself has been called "the unique nerve of American life, which constantly stimulates and at the same time makes these people truly 'self-governed.'" The "native urge for self-government" is not satisfied by town meetings or political parties, but "spills over into all kinds of schemes for the improvement of the community, of one's self, of one's fellow man." [4] Alexis de Tocqueville concluded in the 1830's that "in the United States associations are established to promote public order, commerce, industry, morality, and religion; for there is no end which the human will, seconded by the collective exertions of individuals, despairs of attaining." [5]

Groups of Essentially Nonpolitical Character. Although the very extent of private organizations is overwhelming, not all of these groups are of equal concern in a partisan political sense. Actually a very large percentage of them are unconcerned with most of the struggles over public policy inasmuch as their purposes are in areas unrelated to government. There are people who form groups to advance their mutual interests in sports and games, in intellectual pursuits, in animals of various kinds, in endless sorts of hobbies and pastimes. Many groups exist for promotional purposes entirely. All of the contests to pick "queens" and "princesses" for carnivals, festivals, and other events of extraordinary publicity are purely attempts to exploit feminine pulchritude in behalf of lodges, businesses, and cities. Perhaps as a more democratic gesture, a large contingent of organizations bestow the designation of "Miss" instead of a royal title upon some women each year, e.g., "Miss Toadstool," "Miss Plywoodpecker," "Miss Classy Chassis" (by the UAW in the West), "Miss Melon Patch" (by the Arkansas melon interests).

In addition, there are all of the "weeks" proclaimed for promoting one thing or another. Doctors emphasize diseases during "Heart Week" and "Diabetes Week." Idealistic and humanitarian groups support such movements as "Be Kind to Animals Week," "Better Parenthood Week," "Good Will to Canada Week." The businesses involved in each of the following are self-evident: "Honey for Breakfast Week," "Pickle Week," "Cranberry Week." The American Dairy Association sponsors Cheese Festival, Ice Cream Fiesta, and Pumpkin Pie Time (the pie to be made with evaporated

---

[3] Arthur M. Schlesinger, *Paths to the Present* (New York: The Macmillan Company, 1949) Chap. 2.

[4] "The Busy, Busy Citizen," *Fortune*, February, 1951, p. 97.

[5] *Democracy in America* (New York: Colonial Press, 1900, rev. ed., Henry Reeve trans.) Vol. 1, p. 192. This urge to organize is not universally acclaimed. Orestes A. Brownson spoke for the dissenters when he complained, "Matters have come to such a pass that a peaceable man can hardly venture to eat or drink, or to go to bed or to get up, to correct his children or to kiss his wife, without obtaining the permission and direction of some . . . society."—Quoted in Schlesinger, *op. cit.*, pp. 33-34.

milk). Most of these undertakings are attempts to advertise products, localities, organizations, or drives for money; they are not, presumably, attempts to take sides between Democrats and Republicans.

Nevertheless, any organization, no matter how remote from government, can be drawn into politics if its interests are affected by government policies. A hiking club may not be aware of a presidential election if it falls on a golden autumn day when the call of the mountains is irresistible. If the club discovers that one of its favorite trails is being closed to the public for lack of money to keep it in a safe condition for walking, the club members for the first time begin inquiring where the money comes from, whom to see about it, and what all this mystery concerning appropriations and allotments is.

Dual Representation Through Groups. Politically speaking, the tendency to organize is as natural as the likelihood of humans to have wants. The organization of political parties themselves is simply a larger piece cut from the same cloth as pressure groups. An individual by himself is impotent in the face of the whole society, whether he wants to be elected to an office or to receive some special benefit or consideration from government officials. The classical theory of representative government generally assumed or postulated that men, by electing their peers to public office, were represented in a substantial sense and that the officials would take care of the interests and the needs of their constituents. The practical difficulty with this concept is not the wickedness or irresponsibility of the officials but the increasing impossibility of their playing the role assigned to them.

In agrarian communities this classical function can be approximated, but an industrial community has far more interests of a complex nature for officials to represent. A much greater effort is required to present urban problems to officials—in part because of the technicalities of the problems themselves, in part because of the maddening competition for the attention of representatives, and in part because of urban underrepresentation in legislatures. Many citizens, therefore, feel the need for a supplemental system of representation to insure they will be heard and considered by the men who enact and administer the laws. Official spokesmen of pressure groups form the cadre of this parallel representative system. They are rarely vested with public power or authority, but when they speak on behalf of their organized followers, they are both representing and competing with the constitutional representatives who are invested with the official authority.

Identification of Groups. To study groups having political significance or to study a group, e.g., union members, Catholics, farmers, Negroes, is to undertake an examination of members of specific groups to find characteristics distinguishing them from members of other groups or from the general public considered independently of group memberships. This entire discussion of organized interest groups is predicated on people's awareness of interests which can be affected one way or another by government. The actions and reactions of people are accepted as rational and logical responses to problems. A given response by an organized group of people may prove to be ill-advised or poorly executed, but for purposes of discussing groups it is accepted that the people making up and giving direction to a group are acting in accordance with their objectives and are not aimlessly moving about without knowledge or direction.

> It is because perception is so conditioned by involvement that we can dispense with a politics of disinterest as opposed to a politics of interest and can assume that every action a man takes in politics must be an interested action. All groups in which he participates are interest groups in the true sense that he is interested in them. (He may not find the interest agreeable, of course.) Some hold his interest more than others, and there must indeed be some minimum flicker of attention and reference to indicate he is a member of the group.[6]

Group classification is a different and more difficult question. Common acceptance of major economic groups may create the assumption the task of classification is easy, but difficulties soon arise. It can be said that business is an "organization of people with varied skills who use property or talents to produce something which can be sold to somebody for more than it cost. The profit . . . belongs to private individuals, who, in one way or another, have a legal claim on it."[7] This definition should distinguish businessmen, in the traditional sense, from farmers who, in another sense, are as much businessmen as retailers. The definition excludes professional men, as they are commonly thought of, that is, people with extended formal schooling, licensed by government to practice upon the passing of an examination demonstrating knowledge and skill and subject to continuing regulation for the maintenance of professional standards. Businessmen, farmers, and professional men, whatever their differences, must make a profit to survive. It would be possible to find occupations or professions which may traditionally be classified as business but which may require another definition, e.g., laundry workers, hairdressers, realtors, bankers.

Politically, buisnessmen and professional men have interests which coincide and clash, but they may coincide more with each other than with farmers. Professional men, for instance lawyers or accountants, when employed in businesses, tend to adopt the point of view of their employer. When banks or accountants provide services, such as income tax consulta-

6 Alfred De Grazia, "Nature and Prospects of Political Interest Groups," *The Annals,* Sept., 1958, p. 115.

7 Beardsley Ruml, *Tomorrow's Business* (New York: Farrar & Rinehart, 1945) p. 31.

tion, which lawyers consider to be within the scope of the legal profession, there are frictions.

No system of identification or classification can be depended upon to designate accurately the lines of alliance and opposition in group political interests.

ATTITUDES TOWARD GROUPS

The state of opinions in this country toward organized groups makes it appear that, as an abstract concept, groups do not have much prestige. Even though Americans are "joiners," they reflect in certain contexts unfavorable attitudes toward groups. Imbedded in the American concept of himself and his culture is the positive view of the whole, united in the oneness of interests and the negative view of multitudinous divisions of the whole, disunited by segmental group interests. Each person reflecting these attitudes may, if reminded of his own group affiliations, make exceptions for and defend them as not being of the type he condemns, or, less likely, he may acknowledge that his own groups are not exceptions but are to be judged by the standard he applies to all groups.

It is only fair to point out that there are groups and groups and that people draw what they consider to be meaningful distinctions among them. A man is not likely to look upon his church as the same kind of group as a labor union and he will not fail to distinguish his Saturday night poker crowd from his alumni association. Some kinds of groups are more generally disparaged in the political field than others. Occupational groups are accepted, willingly or not, as involved in partisan politics, but ethnic and religious groups still are frowned upon in this context, although people may have as justifiable objectives to attain through one kind of group as another.[8] The diversity of reactions to groups in politics is accounted for by such conditioning factors as cultural and traditional attachments, symbolisms, and personal interests.

Agriculture. In the scale of values, the farmer is perhaps the least condemned for being in politics—probably because of the prestige of farming in the abstract. One theme which has given direction to our vision and fashioned our most cherisehd beliefs is the acceptance of the rural environment and the agricultural way of life amounting at times to a semireligious and mystic attitude toward the soil.[9] The American farmer-pioneer is still

---

[8] Lawrence H. Fuchs, *The Political Behavior of American Jews* (Glencoe: The Free Press, 1956) Chap. 1. The more traditional and "respectable" attitude was expressed by President Woodrow Wilson when he told several thousand newly naturalized citizens on May 10, 1915, "You cannot become thorough Americans if you think of yourselves in groups. America does not consist of groups. A man who thinks of himself as belonging to a particular national group in America has not yet become an American." *The Messages and Papers of Woodrow Wilson* (New York: Review of Reviews, 1924) I, pp. 115-116.

[9] This theme is developed at length in Henry Nash Smith, *Virgin Land, The American West as Symbol and Myth* (Cambridge: Harvard University Press, 1950). Thomas Jef-

the institutional bedrock of a civilization which is individualistic in politics and Christian in religion. This symbolism persists in the idealistic
view of the "family farm" despite the clear realization that the farmer's
calling is less and less the idyllic life close to nature and more and more a
mechanized, scientific undertaking. Traditionally, American politics has
been rurally oriented. Farmers or spokesmen for farmers have controlled
government from Washington, D. C., to the county courthouses, and the
power of a group so basic, identifiable, and vocal has given a characteristic
tone to political campaigns. The "farm vote" is still a constant source of
concern in presidential elections, and in only the most highly urban states
can candidates for office fail to give a disproportionate share of their attention to rural areas.

Business. The prestige of agriculture has exceeded that of business,
generally speaking; but business, compared both with other American
groups and with business in other countries, has generally a high influence
and prestige. Its evaluation, as far as the stereotype of businessmen and
the operations of business, has tended to be high in times of prosperity and
low during depressions. The evaluation, as a conception or ideal of efficiency and economy, has uniformly been high. A common expression of
commendation or recommendation is to speak of doing things in a businesslike manner or of being businesslike. Politically there is often an advantage in being associated with business or in stressing the values of business. Although some businessmen have limitations as candidates for office,
they are active in public affairs. In cities they are prominent if not dominant in all civic functions, hold offices in churches and on school boards,
and organize committees for various promotional and advisory activities.
Directly and indirectly, all of the multifarious endeavors of businessmen
help to condition the public to a favorable attitude toward business for
its public-spirited and humanitarian efforts. In a more direct political way,
businessmen are active in party organizations, serving on committees on
every level. It is a commonly known fact among those with any acquaintance with party operations that the bulk of campaign contributions, at
least in state and national elections, comes from the leaders of business.

Labor. Although labor has been looked upon sympathetically, because
the great majority of people are workers, to speak of labor immediately
suggests labor unions, which have been ignored, suspected, or disliked. A

---

ferson both personalized and strongly contributed in formulating this theme. "Those who
labor in the earth are the chosen people of God if ever He had a chosen people, whose
breasts He has made His peculiar deposit for substantial and genuine virtue." Quoted in
McConnell, *op. cit.*, p. 6. In reality, John Taylor of Caroline proved to be a stronger
agrarian; Jefferson eventually qualified his views, but Taylor did not. *Ibid.*, pp. 7-9,
note 9.

distinction is frequently made between labor unions (the group, the institution) and labor (the people who work and belong to unions). The public attitude toward labor has been composed of a great accumulation of negative factors. The opposition to organizations of wage earners on the part of both employers and the general public was a distrust of labor violence and fear of the effects upon the traditional character of American individualism and liberty. The acceptance of the labor-union leader was helped considerably by Samuel Gompers who, as president of the American Federation of Labor continuously from 1895 to 1924, did much to bring labor out of the shadow of radicalism. Since the 1930's labor unions have grown tremendously in power and prestige, so that they are more completely accepted, if not wholly approved, than ever before and their strategic position promises that their status will grow as time passes. In urban and suburban areas, labor now attracts a major share of political consideration, and nationally, the "labor vote" rivals the "farm vote" as the first concern of candidates for office.

Other Groups. Public attitudes toward other groups are too diverse, even when revealed, to produce any patterns or definite tendencies. Attitudes are often the product of the moment, called into existence by a specific controversy or an association which, if deeply experienced, will be long lasting. Many groups come to public attention only occasionally and then spasmodically. During national prohibition, the Anti-Saloon League was often in the news. Since World War II, the National Association for the Advancement of Colored People has become much better known in the growing conflict to revolutionize the status of Negroes. Periodically, veterans affairs make us aware of the American Legion. Other public questions direct special attention to a church or to one or another reform movement. Any individual's knowledge of and reaction to these groups are determined by the amount and kinds of influence exerted by the group and the result upon the individual. Depending upon the person and depending upon the group, attitudes may range from friendly to antagonistic. In many cases there will be no attitude because people are unaware of the existence of the group.

MEMBERSHIP AND ORGANIZATION

The membership size and the organizational structure of groups are related to their political influence. Groups have been classed according to the number of their members, as mass-based versus selected or restricted. The pattern of organization tends to be uniform despite differences in size.

Membership. If all of the people counted as members of politically active groups were added up, the total would suggest that the whole population—men, women and children—are beneficiaries of dual representation. Any such conclusion is purely illusory because of the multiple memberships of many joiners. Instead of everyone in the United States being organized and represented, probably a majority belong to no organization of direct political or occupational significance. The general rule, especially in mass-based organizations, is that a large part of the membership is inactive. Active group membership is indicative of some kind of drive that appears to be less common among Americans than is popularly assumed. Those who affiliate are the more prosperous and/or the more active, the ones who appreciate the opportunities offered by groups and who feel they derive some benefit from membership.

Studies of agricultural groups suggest that as many as 70% of the farmers belong to no farm organization and that those who do belong are more nearly representative of higher economic status.[10] This characteristic of group membership is not confined to agriculture. Many "small" businessmen belong to no business organization or are only nominal members of trade associations and local chambers of commerce and in no case exercise influence in the policies of such groups. About one-third of all nonfarm wage earners belong to labor unions, but there is a disproportion of members from the skilled trades as opposed to the unskilled trades. It is doubtful if the members of veterans organizations exceed 4,000,000 of the more than 22,500,000 veterans in civilian life. Professional people are more likely to be members of some professional organization, but a large percentage probably is not active. If church membership is included, we have an unquestioned example of a growing membership; 62% of the total population in 1956 belonged to a religious body, compared with 57% in 1950 and 49% in 1940.[11]

---

[10] *Ibid.*, pp. 149, 215. Charles M. Hardin, *The Politics of Agriculture* (Glencoe: Free Press, 1952) p. 183, noted that "the intense activity in agricultural agencies and associations is confined to a relatively small circle of farmers."

[11]   RELIGION REPORTED FOR THE CIVILIAN POPULATION, 1957
              (THOUSANDS OF PERSONS 14 YEARS OLD AND OVER)
                   AND PERCENTAGES CHURCH MEMBERSHIP

	Protestant	Catholic	Jewish	Other	None or Not Reported	Total U. S.
Urban	44,726	24,173	3,718	1,196	2,485	76,298
Rural	34,226	6,496	150	349	1,814	43,035
Total	78,952	30,669	3,868	1,545	4,299	119,333
Percent gain, 1940-56	37.1%	38.4%	—	36.5% [a]	—	37.5% [b]

Source: U. S. Bureau of the Census, *Statistical Abstract of the United States: 1958* (79th ed.) Washington, D. C., 1958, pp. 50-52.

[a] Including Jewish.

[b] Compared with an increase in total U. S. population (1940-1956) of 21.4%.

Organization. The two basic forms of organization are unitary and federal. An example of the first is the National Association of Manufacturers, wherein the entire machinery is centralized and all of the members belong to the one organization. The American Farm Bureau Federation is an example of a federal plan based on geographical subdivisions, for local bureaus are joined together on the state level and the state bureaus are joined together on the national level. The American Federation of Labor—Congress of Industrial Organizations is an example of a federal plan based on functional subdivisions of individual unions which themselves are functionally federated in each state.

A federal plan of organization leaves a latitude of independence for the constituent member units, whereas the unitary does not. However, the central office in a unitary organization may be forced to accede to factional pressures, and various degrees of autonomy are, in practice, exercised in federations. The national leaders of either kind of organization can resist opposition from state and local chapters or from dissident individuals, although if the pressure is strong and sustained, the leaders will probably be forced to give some ground.[12] Aggressive organizations, even with a federal structure, can enforce a tremendous amount of uniformity through the pressure of the symbol of their objectives.

Internal Operations. One problem of organization is laying a basis for harmonious internal operations irrespective of the formal organization itself. Group leaders use standard techniques of persuasion for keeping members happy and satisfied, such as frequent communication, setting out the work and accomplishments of the leaders, even magnifying the importance of what has been done and the skill and patience required to do it. Members can be reprimanded by name or anonymously and can be punished in various ways ranging from wrist-slapping to expulsion. These kinds of discipline are to be avoided as much as possible in favor of positive methods for stimulating cohesion. Leaders can do favors or provide services for members, and from time to time many groups are regaled with speeches and articles pointing out the dangers posed by opponents and the need to work harder together in the common cause.[13]

Leadership is further facilitated by its exclusiveness and natural advantages in dealing with the rank and file. At each level in organizations, one officer such as a director or a secretary or a small group designated as executive council or board actually wields the power by making the day-to-day decisions. Although most groups provide in their constitutions that policies will be set at annual conventions, the leaders organize the conventions and

---

[12] David B. Truman, *The Governmental Process* (New York: Alfred A. Knopf, Inc., 1951) pp. 168-176, described such a situation in the American Medical Association.
[13] *Ibid.*, pp. 193-209.

see to it that they control the committees which make recommendations on policy. While the delegates at these conventions elect the officers, there is little choice but to re-elect incumbents or elect a slate proposed by a nominating committee. Revolt against the tailor-made committee resolutions or against the favored list of officers is likely to be abortive because the hierarchy has enough votes already committed to have its own way.

Hierarchy and the Individual. The nature of organization control becomes inevitably oligarchic. Authority, responsibility, and prestige go to those who spend their full time, almost always with a full-time salary, on the affairs of the organization. They know how it operates and how to get things done or how to prevent things being done. As the people with the aptitude and desire for leadership, they devise ways for insuring their tenure in office; they are much more compatible with one another than with the rank and file from whom they increasingly are removed and isolated.[14] One of the most important of the inherent advantages of leadership is having complete and most recent information on all matters affecting the organization. As a means of control as well as a means of group security, leaders make known only as much of their inside knowledge of affairs as they think will redound to their benefit and protect the group from attack or censure.

The anomalous situation for the individual member is that his impotence inside the organization is only relatively less than it was outside. He joins because he is powerless, but he discovers that he becomes captured by the organization. The best the individual can do is try to force his leaders to reflect his will whenever he has an opportunity to express himself. Success in insistence upon its views by the rank and file sometimes makes the leaders more intransigent in their outside dealings than they really want to be.[15] The dilemma for the individual is that his influence decreases and the organization's influence increases as the organization becomes larger.[16]

TYPES OF ORGANIZATIONS

Agriculture. Farmers have created a large number of groups reflecting both general and particular problems. There are over one hundred active or-

---

[14] *Ibid.*, Chap. 5. Charles Hickman Titus, *The Processes of Leadership* (Dubuque: William C. Brown Company, 1950) Part IV, presents a most stimulating discussion of the general problems of leaders of all kinds of groups.

[15] Edwin G. Nourse, *The 1950's Come First* (New York: Henry Holt & Company, 1951) pp. 56-57, quotes the chairman of a union committee: "I . . . would go a long way in agreeing . . . that a different course than the one we are proposing might be better for the country. But how far do you think I could carry my union with me along such a line?" Another union official: "If I even talk that way to my members, I'll be denounced as having 'sold out to the bosses.' A new man will be put in my place."

[16] The need for further examination of the relation between leaders and followers is pointed out in Samuel J. Eldersveld, "American Interest Groups: A Survey of Research and Some Implications for Theory and Method," *Interest Groups on Four Continents* (Pittsburgh: University of Pittsburgh Press, 1958) pp. 185-186.

ganizations of regional farmers or growers of a particular crop such as citrus fruits, and as many as fifty-five national farm associations [17]; but three general farm organizations stand out most prominently.

The first mass organization of farmers was made possible by the Patrons of Husbandry—now the National Grange—which was begun in 1867 by Oliver H. Kelley, a clerk in what was then the Agricultural Bureau. This undertaking was not prompted by political dissatisfaction but by a desire to give some richness to rural living through a secret, fraternal order which would draw farming families together and give them an instrument for self-improvement. The Grange grew slowly both in total membership and numbers of local orders. Its plan of organization was to form a few local granges and then establish a state grange whose master would appoint deputies to form other local granges. A ritual, with degrees modeled on the Masonic Order, was worked out for both men and women and continues to be a characteristic of the organization.[18] The rapid growth of the granges came in the 1870's under the leadership of farmers and in response to the unrest of those years. Instead of simply giving direction to farmers' social and intellectual growth, the granges very soon took up the farmers' demands for railroad regulation and precipitated what is known as the Granger Movement.[19] Since the Grange constitution forbade political discussions and the organization was intended to be kept free from partisan politics, much of the Granger political activity was done by subterfuge.

The granges' association with radical railroad legislation, failure to achieve many of their objectives, and weaknesses in organization caused the order to suffer a decline in the later 1870's.[20] Thereafter its first preoccupation was survival. Although it took positions in favor of such issues as direct election of United States senators, prohibition, highway improvements, parcel-post systems, and the Great Lakes waterway, its old spirit did not return. Its decentralized organization has given it a type of strength that has helped it to survive, in that state granges may differ widely in their positions on various policies. The collapse of the 1870's ended its stronghold in the Central states and since then its greatest strength has been in the Northeast. On many issues, whether intentionally or not, the Grange follows the lead of the American Farm Bureau Federation.[21]

Farm protest, which culminated in the Populist movement in the 1890's, continued to find an outlet in the *National Farmers Educational and Cooperative Union of America*, founded in 1902. The *National Farm-*

---

[17] McConnell, *op. cit.*, p. 214, note 1.

[18] S. J. Buck, *The Granger Movement* (Cambridge: Harvard University Press, 1913) pp. 40-52, and *The Agrarian Crusade* (New Haven: Yale University Press, 1921) Chap. 1.

[19] For the background of this conflict, see *ibid.*, pp. 23-24, and *The Granger Movement*, pp. 9-15; John D. Hicks, *The Populist Revolt* (Minneapolis: University of Minnesota Press, 1931) Chap. 1.

[20] *The Granger Movement*, pp. 52-73; *The Agrarian Crusade*, Chap. 5.

[21] McConnell, *op. cit.*, pp. 39-41, 107, 108, 143, 147.

ers' Union, as it is popularly known, is the smallest of the three major organizations and represents a class of farmers (including tenants) concentrated in the Great Plains and the South, particularly in the area between
the Mississippi River and the Rocky Mountains. These are marginal areas
where discontent is likely to be greatest because of drought, poorer land,
and fluctuating prices. The more hazardous predicament of these farmers
causes them to be suspicious of speculators in farm commodities, mortgage-
holders, and financial institutions lending money at interest. Of all farm
organizations, this one exhibits the greatest sympathy for labor unions and
its leaders give evidence of a community of interest with labor leaders.

At the beginning of the twentieth century a program was begun to
encourage diversity in farming through demonstrations upon the farmers'
land. The objective was to educate in order to raise the living standards
and the efficiency of farmers. The system of instruction, initiated in Texas,
was carried out by a county agricultural demonstration agent known popularly as the county agent. Originally, local businessmen provided funds for
the work, and in 1906 the General Education Board (endowed by the Rockefeller family) supplied the largest part of the money, which was administered
by the United States Department of Agriculture. The agriculture colleges,
challenged in the field of education, organized extension services, and in
time the county agent came into this organization with part of his salary
paid by private business sources and part paid out of public funds through
the colleges. The Department of Agriculture undertook to organize all of
the nation's farmers through the county agents, who were to establish farm
bureaus in each county. This activity gave rise to state farm bureaus and
to the formation in 1919 of the *American Farm Bureau Federation:* a private federation of farmers organized by county agents who are quasi-public
or semigovernmental officials. This relation between a private group and
government officials, including the college extension officials, is unique in
its inception and status.[22] The Farm Bureau is the largest and most politically influential of the farm organizations. It has affiliated bureaus in every
state. The heart of its strength is in the Central states although it is an alliance of interests of the Central states and the South.[23] Its leaders main-

---

[22] Hardin, *op. cit.,* Chaps. 2, 3; McConnell, *op. cit.,* pp. 23 ff. and Chap. 5; for the Bureau's organization, see pp. 151 ff. Since 1921 the relation between the Farm Bureau and
county agents has been established by agreements between the Bureau and the Department
of Agriculture incorporated in an order issued by the Secretary of Agriculture: farm bureaus participate in extension work and contribute to the salary and expenses of the
agents; the agents are not to organize farm bureaus or otherwise take part in purely organizational activities of bureaus. *Ibid.,* p. 54. County agents have continued to organize
county bureaus and in the South, especially in the poorer counties, take a major part in
conducting the bureaus' affairs. *Ibid.,* p. 153.

[23] *Ibid.,* Chap. 13, pp. 185-186. See in general O. M. Kile, *The Farm Bureau through
Three Decades* (Baltimore: Waverly Press, 1948).

tain that they speak for American farmers, a plausible contention, since many special organizations as well as the Grange are generally in agreement with Bureau policies; the Bureau tries to reconcile the differences among these organizations in order to protect its leadership prestige and to be the source of national agricultural policies.

The struggles of farmers with economic adversity led to the organization of *cooperatives* for the purposes of buying supplies and marketing commodities.[24] The general practice is that each member has one vote regardless of the amount of money he puts into the cooperative; profits are distributed to members in rebates or in other forms in proportion to their purchases or investments. Beginning with the National Grange, almost every farm movement has both advocated and organized cooperatives. The Farm Bureau early in its history devoted much attention to them and continues to be closely associated through common membership and common aims. Many cooperatives are federated in the *National Council of Farmers' Cooperative Marketing Associations.*

The cooperatives have grown in financial resources, in numbers, and in variety of functions made possible by their exemption from the antitrust laws if they meet certain conditions. They have established banks, manufacturing plants for farm machinery, grocery stores, electrical energy distribution systems, auditing and accounting services, insurance and medical care, soil conservation. One of the most remarkable examples is the *Midwest Federation of Consumers Cooperative Association,* which operates a complete petroleum industry from its own oil wells, refining plants, storage, and eventually direct sale of gasoline and tractor fuel to its members.[25] The ambitious nature of the cooperative movement suggests that in the process of protecting farmers from businessmen, it has made businessmen of farmers.

Business. The variety of American business interests exceeds that of agriculture as measured in the number of business organizations. The Department of Commerce counted 1500 national, 2000 state, and 8000 local trade associations (an organization of producers or distributors engaged in the same industry or trade) and identified an additional 300 national associations largely of businessmen.[26]

Two active and influential national organizations are the *Chamber of Commerce of the United States* and the *National Association of Manufacturers.* The former is a federation of trade associations, local chambers of commerce, corporations, and individuals. Because of the breadth of its

---

[24] See McConnell, *op. cit.,* pp. 21-22, on the organization of cooperatives.

[25] *New York Times Magazine,* January 4, 1953, p. 17.

[26] Earl Latham, *The Group Basis in Politics* (Ithaca: Cornell University Press, 1952) p. 26.

membership it is more representative of the business spectrum than any other one single organization, but the variety of interests composing it sometimes keeps its leaders from taking a position on controversial issues. The NAM, organized in 1905, is an association of several thousand corporations, for only corporations can be members. It is the older of the two and was active in the formation of the national Chamber in 1912. Members of the NAM have to a considerable extent been drawn together by their concern with employer-employee relations and, for this reason, have a greater unity in objective and operation than the members of the Chamber. A disadvantage of this common concern is a varying membership which grows when the threat of labor-union activity increases and shrinks when labor activity subsides. Like the American Farm Bureau Federation in its relation to agriculture, the NAM attempts to play the role of spokesman for American industry but with less success. In 1948, its peak year of enrollment, it had about 16,500 corporations, which constituted less than 7% of all manufacturing industries in the country.[27] Nevertheless, it represents a relatively large percentage of the productive capacity of American industry, since the bulk of the big corporations belong to it and direct its policies.

Labor. Perhaps the characteristics of overlapping jurisdictions and working against one another have been most pronounced among labor organizations. The tempo of this competition increased as unions grew in numbers of members and expanded into more industries.

The one dominating union from the time it was formed under its present name in 1886 has been the *American Federation of Labor,* which brought unions of various crafts into one central organization. Each craft has autonomous control over its own affairs, while the federation government, through its constitution, has jurisdiction over general policies and actions of mutual aid to members.[28] The AFL maintained its unchallenged position until John L. Lewis withdrew his United Mine Workers Union in 1935 and created the Committee, now *Congress of Industrial Organizations.* The basis of this split was in part the method of organization. The CIO provided for a more highly centralized form of union government and for the industrial as opposed to the craft method of organizing workers.[29]

For twenty years the AFL and the CIO were competitors for the role of labor spokesman. They fought to organize workers and raided each other's

[27] Richard W. Gable, "NAM: Influential Lobby or Kiss of Death," *Journal of Politics,* Vol. 15 (1953) p. 257.

[28] For its history and organization, see Lewis L. Lorwin, *The American Federation of Labor* (Washington, D. C.: The Brookings Institution, 1933).

[29] Actually, the AFL unions were by no means exclusively craft but they "carried over a keen sense of craft pride opposed to industrial unionism. Thus they impress upon the Federation a character of craft exclusivism, while in practice they override narrow craft lines and combine related crafts and occupations in larger units." *Ibid.,* p. 306.

members. The natural antagonism between an old established organization and a new organization trying to prove itself was intensified by personal animosities among the leaders, most of whom had a vested interest in their personal domains. The path to unification was cleared by the removal from both organizations of John L. Lewis and the rise of new men to the presidency of each in 1952. The unity which so many, including Mr. Lewis, had been calling for was finally consummated in February 1955 in the new organization, AFL–CIO. In effect, the thirty-four CIO unions entered the seventy-seven-union AFL as a special department with the understanding that the city and state central bodies of the two would gradually merge within two years. Initially, the AFL contributed $3,500,000 and the CIO about one-half of that amount to a common central treasury. The CIO maintains a separate treasury to finance its own organizing drives. The President and Secretary of the AFL retained the same positions in the merged organization and an Executive Council was created as the governing body composed of seventeen AFL and ten CIO vice-presidents. Both craft and industrial unions were recognized and raiding was to be abolished.

All unions such as the United Mine Workers, the Railroad Brotherhoods, and unions of public employees which are not affiliated with the AFL–CIO are designated "independent" or "unaffiliated." The national and international unions with headquarters in the United States in 1956 were divided into 137 for the AFL–CIO with 16,904,000 members and 52 for the independent, unaffiliated with 1,573,000 members.[30]

Veterans. Organizations of ex-servicemen who had served in the nation's armed forces go back to the post-Revolutionary War period and the formation of the Order of the Cincinnati, limited to those who had been officers in the Continental Army. The next great veteran organization was the Grand Army of the Republic, created by and for those who had fought in the Union Army during the Civil War.[31] Before the twentieth century, veteran organizations were restricted to those who fought in one specific war and none was intended to survive beyond the lifetime of the men originally eligible for membership.

Permanent organizations open continuously to veterans are now the vogue. The largest, most aggressive, most politically astute and influential one is the *American Legion,* created in 1919 by a group of army officers. It has become the foremost spokesman for veterans' affairs and enjoys the reputation it has established by its diligent and effective activity. While it long ago established a type of oligarchical control through its so-called "king-

---

[30] U. S. Bureau of the Census, *Statistical Abstract of the United States: 1958,* p. 236.
[31] Mary Dearing, *Veterans in Politics* (Baton Rouge: Louisiana State University Press, 1952).

makers" and "policy makers," its lobbying power is enhanced by the fact that the rank-and-file members largely agree with their leaders. The Legion is not only a unified but also an affluent organization, with a physical plant throughout the United States worth more than $200,000,000. Because of its prestige its leaders can use it as a springboard for a political career, and most politicians are willing to the point of eagerness to advertise their Legion affiliation. The basis of its influence, however, is not entirely its campaigns for veterans' benefits. In many communities the local Legion post is integrated into local civic affairs through work in child welfare, especially combatting juvenile delinquency. One of the most successful campaigns was the gathering of children's toys in this country following World War II and shipping them abroad to children in desolate and ravished countries under the slogan of "tide of toys." Locally, Legion posts conduct Americanization programs through school debates and ceremonies at the swearing-in of new citizens in the courts. Part of this patriotic impulse is also shown in concern for the content of public-school textbooks in the interest of fostering the Legion's concept of Americanism in the learning process.[32]

The second largest organization in membership is the *Veterans of Foreign Wars*—the name taken by three national societies when they merged in 1913. As its name implies, its members must have served abroad with one of the fighting forces. Often, in its political activities, it follows the leadership of the American Legion. The *Disabled American Veterans*, organized after World War I, has the specialized objectives of promoting the welfare of veterans with various physical handicaps and disabilities. Since a large majority of its members are also Legionnaires, it follows the Legion in most policy matters.

Two organizations combining veteran and religious interests are the *Catholic War Veterans of the United States*, founded in 1935, and the *Jewish Veterans of the U.S.A.*, founded in 1896.

In 1944, two new organizations were formed. The *American Veterans of World War II* (AMVETS) is limited exclusively to members of the Armed Forces who fought in World War II and Korea and is concerned with maintaining an identity separate from the American Legion, although it does not challenge the Legion's leadership. It has evinced much interest in international affairs and in the activities of the United Nations. The *American Veterans Committee* (AVC) has the smallest membership of any veterans organization. In a strict sense of the word, it is not a veterans organization but an organization of veterans with the motto: "Citizens first, veterans second." It has concerned itself with political and social objectives similar to

---

[32] General sources are: Marcus Duffield, *King Legion* (New York: Jonathan Cape and Harrison Smith, 1931); Richard S. Jones, *A History of the American Legion* (New York: Bobbs-Merrill, 1946); Justin Gray, *The Inside Story of the Legion* (New York: Boni & Gaer, 1948).

those of the Democratic New Deal.[33] In 1950 a *World Veterans Federation* was created with constituent veterans organizations in Western Europe and in the United States.

Religion. When people are classed according to religious beliefs, the three groups of Protestant, Catholic, and Jewish predominate. Protestants are characterized by the number and diversity of their denominational divisions, and the bewildering number of Protestant organizations concerned with decisions on public policy closely follow denominational lines.[34] Attempts to submerge doctrinal disputes in order to cooperate in fields of general agreement have succeeded in the formation of the *National Council of the Churches of Christ in the U.S.A.* (founded in 1908 as the Federal Council). This organization brings together twenty-four Protestant and three Orthodox denominations and takes positions on many political questions. It is strenuously opposed both doctrinally and politically by the *American Council of Christian Churches* which represents a group of more fundamentalist creeds. The political value of these interdenominational organizations is open to some question. Their leaders get a hearing or at least are heard, but the sounding-board function may be the greatest value.

Catholics, in contrast, have the advantage of unity, being one church. The close-knit character of the faith is reinforced by Catholic lay organizations covering many fields of social work and group interests.[35] Often there is a closer relation of an influential nature between the clergy and the laity.

Like Protestants, the Jews are divided on the basis of religion, of which there are three divisions: orthodox, conservative, and reformed. A different kind of cleavage is that between the Zionist organizations, which have worked for the creation of the state of Israel, and the American Council for Judaism, which is anti-Zionist, contending that the Zionist movement separates American Jews as an identifiable community with specialized interests.

Women. As early as the 1830's, women took part in the abolition movement and from this beginning agitated for woman's freedom along with Negro freedom.[36] The beginning of the woman suffrage movement, if a

---

[33] The American Veterans of World War II chided the American Legion in 1956 for trying to push through Congress a bill to pay all needy veterans a $105 a month pension without regard to disability and asked the Legion to shift its support to an AMVET proposal which was confined to disabled veterans. The reaction of the American Veterans Committee was to attack the Legion and the members of Congress who voted for the Legion bill under pressure and to point out that veterans were better off economically and professionally than non-veterans. *New York Times,* June 19, 1956, and letter to the Editor from Mickey Levine, National Chairman, AVC, *ibid.,* July 3, 1956.

[34] Ebersole, *op. cit.,* Chap. 2.

[35] *Ibid.,* Chap. 3 covers the activities of the National Catholic Welfare Conference and the National Conference of Catholic Charities.

[36] Women's recognition of their political and legal status antedated this period. As early as 1776 Abigail Adams urged her husband John, who was helping write the Declaration of Independence, to make some provision for woman's rights in that document. Associated Press dispatch, March 24, 1951.

particular point in time may be fixed, was the meeting at the home of Mrs. Elizabeth C. Stanton at Seneca Falls, New York, July 19 and 20, 1848. Impatient with the lack of progress in achieving suffrage, the *National American Woman Suffrage Association* was formed in 1890 by a merger of the National Woman Suffrage Association and the American Woman Suffrage Association, both of which had been founded in 1869. The new association was dedicated to securing an amendment to the United States Constitution as the only feasible solution. In 1913 a group of the more extreme militants withdrew from the Association and formed the *National Women's Party*. After the achievement of their objective in the adoption of the Nineteenth Amendment in 1920, Mrs. Carrie Chapman Catt, the President of the Association, founded the *League of Women Voters* as a nonpartisan organization to help women make use of the franchise. The Association continued in existence for thirty years, encouraging woman suffrage in other countries, and officially disbanded on January 9, 1950, the ninety-first birthday of Mrs. Catt, who had died three years before.[37]

Many women's organizations do not have feminist objectives as such, but reflect the interests of particular groups of women. The *General Federation of Women's Clubs,* which has affiliates in thirty-nine foreign countries, was founded in 1890 to encourage and promote education, philanthropy, welfare, morals, and fine arts. In its national conventions it has supported such policies as reciprocal trade, the United Nations, and military preparedness, including universal military training. It provides scholarships and sponsors fine-art festivals. Its huge size (over three-quarters of a million in the United States; over 11,000,000 world-wide) weakens its unity, sometimes causing it to avoid highly controversial issues. The *National Business and Professional Women's Clubs* is a smaller organization (less than 200,000) confined to the United States. Its greater homogeneity makes its local chapters, at least, effective because their members are active and influential in their own communities.

Other organizations to some extent can be classified by groups. The League of Women Voters is an example of a reform or "good government" organization. It organizes discussions of issues by candidates for public office and other people informed on current questions; directs and encourages analyses of specific problems; and lobbies and campaigns for changes in governmental structure and political processes. The *American Association of University Women* is more directly oriented toward education, but at times becomes concerned with reforms of a more general nature. The *Daughters of the American Revolution* and the *United Daughters of the Confederacy* are concerned with fostering patriotic and historical interests; the former has consistently opposed the United Nations and international-

---

[37] *New York Times,* January 10, 1950.

ism in its annual meetings.[38] The *Women's Christian Temperance Union,* a prohibition organization, is an example of professional reformers among women whose ardor has been directed from feminist problems to the liquor traffic.

GROUPS VERSUS PARTIES

The Business of Reform. One of the hallmarks of American society is the concern of relatively large numbers of people with reforms ranging from bus schedules to the ownership of billion-dollar industrial enterprises. Professional reformers, in the sense of people who devote their lives to uprooting some aspect of the *status quo* of their generation, are familiar figures both historically and contemporaneously; they may be professional in that they derive their living from their reformist work or they may receive no material rewards whatever for their efforts. Among those who give their time gratis, there is seldom any cause to suspect that they are not genuine in their interest; but sometimes those who earn their livelihood from the business of reform may be suspected of simulating an interest in what has become a profitable venture.

Morals and Economics. Reform is often associated with economic questions, but it would be a mistake to equate the two in all cases. Many reformers are not motivated primarily by dollars-and-cents questions, although they have related their objectives to economics in order to reach more potential supporters. The synthesis or separation of moral and economic aspects of reform is a function of human thinking, and many people themselves may not be sure of the relative weight of the two aspects in arriving at their conclusions. Both were intermingled in the free-soil agitations of the 1840's and 1850's. The issue of prohibition apparently springs from motivations of morality with economics as a subsidiary feature.[39] Slavery was either a moral or an economic question or both, depending upon individual attitudes. In the same way, problems of juvenile delinquency as well as civic and "good government" projects can be approached differently. Antivivisectionists themselves are unlikely to be economically motivated, although some of their opponents may be. Reformers, nevertheless, are most frequently concerned with problems having definite and direct economic implications.

The essence of economic reform has usually been embodied in minor parties whose leaders very often display a missionary fervor for their ob-

---

[38] Martha Strayer, *The D.A.R.: An Informal History* (Washington, D. C.: Public Affairs Press, 1958).

[39] Peter H. Odegard in his *Pressure Politics, The Story of the Anti-Saloon League* (New York: Columbia University Press, 1928) makes this point eminently clear. See Chaps. 1 and 2, especially pp. 48-56.

jectives. The impetus for additional parties, then, comes from some type of reformist motivation associated with interests capable of being organized.

Farmer-Labor Parties. Reformist movements tend to become all-embracing in their panaceas and appeals because of the interlocking nature of economic questions. Leaders who begin with agricultural reforms soon reach out to include labor questions, and those who start with labor problems soon find their way to farmers' problems. The ideal of many professional reformers has been to knit together a farmer-labor party through which they could reach positions of power and institute the basic changes they believe the nation should have. This ideal has been consistently shattered; no matter how broad the program presented by a minor party, the major parties' programs won the votes. When a minor party does approach the brink of political significance with an issue, major parties rapidly absorb and exploit it. On these occasions minor parties discover that they have been "destroyed by their own success." [40] These small parties have belied their claims to universality by their own inability to remain united upon strategy and programs—a revealing testimony to their doctrinaire, rather than political, nature.[41]

The underlying difficulty with the farmer-labor party aspiration is a basic incompatibility between the two groups, even assuming that either group can be mobilized. The post-Civil War history of minor parties, looked at from this vantage point, is a series of separate attempts to combine appeals to farmers and to workers. The Greenback and Populist parties were farmer-oriented, and the Progressive movement of La Follette in Wisconsin had a stronger agricultural than urban-industrial base of support. The efforts in 1912 and 1924 to challenge the existing bipartisan alignment were genuinely supported by both rural and urban interests, but the reappearance of a Progressive Party in 1948 revealed a strength mainly restricted to industrial centers.

Even relatively unified minor parties which develop roots are eventually absorbed into the two-party system. The Non-Partisan League, organized in 1915, first captured the Republican Party in North Dakota and then in 1956, after much partisan turmoil, left the Republicans and became affiliated with the Democrats. In Minnesota the Farmer-Labor Party, organized in 1920, was able to maintain its separate identity for approximately twenty years. In 1944 it merged with the Democratic Party and the name Democratic-Farm-Labor Party was officially adopted. In 1945 Robert M.

---

[40] A. N. Holcombe, *Our More Perfect Union* (Cambridge: Harvard University Press, 1950) p. 140; Murray S. Stedman, Jr., and Susan W. Stedman, *Discontent at the Polls, a Study of Farmer and Labor Parties, 1827-1948* (New York: Columbia University Press, 1950) pp. 112-117; William B. Hesseltine, *The Rise and Fall of Third Parties* (Washington, D. C.: Public Affairs Press, 1948) p. 33.

[41] Stedman and Stedman, *op. cit.*, pp. 104-110.

La Follette, Jr., disbanded the Progressive Party and led it back into the Republican Party.

Labor Parties. Another line of minor party development is that of labor and socialist parties. The oldest of these is the Socialist Labor Party, established in 1896, with a pure Marxist ideology, although during the 1920's it was opposed to the Stalin regime in the Soviet Union. After the break between Stalin and Trotsky, the latter was represented by a fractional party, the Socialist Workers Party, formed in 1928. While it was pro-Soviet although anti-Stalin, it suffered a division in 1940, when a group split off and took the name Independent Socialist League. A Communist Party was also on the scene following the Bolshevik revolution in Russia, but had troubles with various state laws which excluded it from the ballot; the Communists followed the policy of infiltrating and capturing existing parties, as it did successfully in the case of the American Labor Party in New York and the Progressive Party in 1948.

It is not only significant that these radical parties established no alliances with consequential labor-union leaders but also that they strenuously fight one another and vigorously oppose the Socialist Party, which attained its heights at the polls in the years before World War I under the leadership of Eugene V. Debs and again in 1928 and 1932. Initially the Socialists were strongest west of the Mississippi River, but the source of their strength shifted to the Northeast industrial centers.[42] Intense competition developed between socialists and labor-union leaders over strategy as well as leadership in the labor movement; but the Gompers type of leadership finally captured the unions and the Socialist Party was left as a fragment cut off from the body of labor political action.

The main line of union development in the United States has been incompatible with the organization of a labor party, and labor (both leaders and rank and file) have generally refused to support minor parties which make direct appeals to labor. The presidential campaign of Robert M. La Follette, Sr., in 1924 was an exception, for it developed important labor support, the American Federation of Labor officially endorsing it. When Henry Wallace accepted the Progressive Party presidential nomination in 1948, it was anticipated that much labor strength would gravitate to him. On the contrary, except for unions under the influence of the Soviet Com-

---

[42] *Ibid.*, pp. 106-108; Hesseltine, *op. cit.*, Chap. 4. Arthur N. Holcombe, *The Political Parties of To-Day* (New York: Harper & Brothers, 1924) pp. 323-342. An occasional irritant for the soul-searching, deadly serious minor-party candidates is to be outvoted by freakish candidates. In 1952, in New Jersey, both the Socialist Workers and Prohibition parties ran behind Henry Krajewski, the owner of a pig farm and beer tavern, whose candidacy was a stunt. He ran on the Poor Man's Party with a platform of "no piggy deals in Washington" and "more beer parties for the poor man."——*New York Times*, March 9, 1952, and December 13, 1952.

munist philosophy, labor leaders denounced his candidacy for splitting the labor vote and for being Communist inspired.

Groups and Parties Distinguished. The formal distinction between minor parties and organized pressure groups is that the former runs candidates for office and the latter supports Republicans and Democrats for office. The question of whether or not to run candidates in opposition to the major parties is largely a question of tactics and strategy.[43] Some movements employ both techniques: prohibition has been supported through the Prohibition Party and through various groups such as the Anti-Saloon League and the Women's Christian Temperance Union; the Townsend pension scheme of the 1930's—to pay everybody sixty years of age and over $200 per month out of the federal treasury—was frankly a pressure group organized through local Townsend Clubs, but the lack of success intermittently inspired the leaders to organize a party. Supporters of a given reform may be followers of both pressure groups and parties which are promoting the reform, so that there is some identity among the supporters of both strategies. Very likely, however, believers in a reform will support a pressure group but will not vote for the candidates of a compatible minor party, because it is more effective to vote for relatively sympathetic major-party candidates.

Movements Divided upon Strategy. The two different approaches to reform—through pressure upon major parties or by a separate political organization—often split the leaders in a movement. Generally, the group leaders and the party leaders are frankly pursuing their objective from opposite directions independently of each other rather than supplementing each other's efforts. This difference sometimes creates antagonisms, as in the case of the split between the Vegetarian Party and the American Vegetarian Union, Incorporated.[44] From time to time, after a series of defeats at the polls, the leaders of a minor party come face to face with their dilemma and begin to evidence their discouragement. Individual leaders may desert the party or the entire leadership may be split on the question of future operations. Norman Thomas, who was the Socialist Party's presidential candidate in the six elections from 1928 to 1948, concluded that the Socialist program could be better advanced by conducting educational campaigns and working in conjunction with organized labor than by running candidates for the Presidency. In the party's national convention in 1950 Thomas and his faction made a great fight on this issue of strategy but were voted down, and his era of leadership came to an end.[45]

---

[43] Minor parties "essentially are weak political interest groups that adopt this form of activity because they cannot command access to government through other means."—— Truman, *op. cit.,* p. 282.

[44] *New York Times,* April 4, 1952.

[45] *Ibid.,* June 3 to June 5, 1950; July 8 and 9, 1952; December 16, 1952; June 1, 1954.

Superiority of Groups over Parties. The record of accomplishment of reforms suggests that pressure groups have certain advantages over parties as an approach to a problem and that in many practical respects groups are vastly superior. As educational organizations, as creators of opinion, both groups and parties are and have been effective. If the objective is to create awareness and acceptance of a reform within the general public, either a group or a party can be used with some success. If the objective is to have a voice in affairs, to be consulted and to receive some of the credit for achieving a reform, the pressure group is much to be preferred. Group leaders are likely to get some part of what they want and they may well exaggerate a partial political success for the sake of their own prestige. They are not constantly frustrated, but enjoy intermittent satisfactions of various kinds. Minor-party leaders usually choose their strategy because they are too doctrinaire to be satisfied with a series of small victories; they will settle for nothing less than complete capitulation by the enemy. Since they run candidates, they antagonize major-party leaders, who will adopt a minor-party program without a kind word for the crusaders who developed that program.

Selected Bibliography

See the Selected Bibliography for Chapter 16, pp. 389–392 below.

Chapter Fifteen

Organized Interest Groups—Issues and Partisanship

ISSUES GENERATED BY GROUPS

Candidates for office and government officials deal with issues, those problems and conflicts which beset enough people to be brought to public attention. Political leaders are sensitive in searching out and recognizing issues, but the range of potential issues is too vast for anyone to give equal attention to all. Dealing with issues is selective and is dictated by the most pressing problems or by people who are able to make the most convincing noises in the competition for attention. Except on a very small geographical level, a problem must concern a considerable number of people to merit very much attention. Any time a group of people has a problem, they can be classified as a group with an interest to be mediated in the political process. The larger and more influential a group, the more likely it is to receive attention and have its problems considered. Although not all issues are generated by organized groups, a very large proportion of issues is the result of organized group conflicts or insistence, and the most stable issues over the years are those of concern to large numbers some of whom are formally organized for the purpose of insuring political consideration of their interests.

Monopoly. Particularly since the Civil War, Americans have been continually plagued with problems of monopoly in the economy. The great agrarian agitations from the 1870's onward, the emergence of labor unions, the progressive movement of the early twentieth century, the clash of contentions during and following the depression of the 1930's, have been related directly and indirectly in major and countless minor lines of cause and effect to the growth of bigness in agriculture, industry and, finally, labor. Despite the never-ending attacks upon monopoly or upon bigness susceptible of monopoly, the trend toward combinations and recombinations of power structures goes on. This monopoly trend is all-pervasive. Large organizations replace small organizations in every field, in religion as well as in business and labor.[1] Even when organizations are not merged,

---

[1] The movement to combine Protestant churches in order to eliminate competing sects is one of the characteristics of the present trend toward mergers and bigness. Methodist Bishop Gerald H. Kennedy of Los Angeles referred to this growing "lust for unity at too low a level" as a threat to religious liberty in the United States. *New York Times,* February 5, 1957.

they tend to follow the leadership of the largest and most successful among them as in the case of agricultural and veterans groups noted in the preceding chapter.

In agriculture, the number of farms is going down as the size of farms increases, because larger acreages are needed for one farmer to make a living.[2] The farm population, both owners and hired labor, has been declining slowly in absolute numbers and dramatically as a percentage of the total population (see the table below). This decline is even more dramatic when contrasted with the first census in 1790, at which time 95% of the adult male population was classified as farming. Farm labor has been drawn off by industrial employment and driven off by mechanization.[3]

FARM POPULATION, NUMBER AND SIZE OF FARMS (SINCE 1920) [4]

Year	Farm Population in Millions	Farm Population as Per Cent of Total	Number of Farms, in Millions	Average acre per Farm
1920	31,974	30.1	6,518	
1930	30,529	24.9	6,546	
1940	30,547	23.2	6,350	174.0
1950	25,058	16.6	5,648	215.3
1957	20,396	12.0	4,856	

By 1954, individual owners (the so-called family farms) accounted for 87.6% of total farm land. Corporations owned 5% and government 7.4%.[5]

Monopoly in business has attracted most of the prohibitory legislation and has been the source of most fears about the threat of bigness to the American system of liberty. Business mergers, within the limits of restric-

[2] The Census Bureau defines a farm as: 1. "All the land on which some agricultural operations are performed by a person, either by the operator or with the assistance of household or hired labor." 2. "Places of three acres or more . . . if their production is valued at a minimum of $150, exclusive of that from a home garden." 3. "Places of less than 3 acres must have sold a minimum of $150 of their production . . . ." U. S. Bureau of the Census, *Statistical Abstract of the United States: 1958* (79th ed.) Washington, D. C., 1958, p. 609.

[3] The distribution of workers between farm and nonfarm occupations over the years is clarified by the following figures:

Selected Years	Per Cent Employed (Farm)	Per Cent Employed (Nonfarm)
1820	71.8	28.2
1850	63.7	36.3
1900	37.5	62.5
1920	27.0	73.0
1950	11.6	88.4

Source: *Ibid.*, p. 202. The figures are for gainful workers 10 years old and over except those for the year 1950, which are for experienced civilian labor force 14 years old and over.

[4] *Ibid.*, pp. 611, 615.

[5] *Ibid.*, p. 612.

tive legislation, continue, and thousands of small businesses go bankrupt every year. In each industry there is a pattern of three or four large companies that dominate even though several smaller companies exist. Periodic investigations and attacks upon the size of business enterprises raises such questions as how big is big (i.e., how big is too big)? Is bigness a natural result in some industries? Are attacks upon bigness a penalty upon efficiency and a threat to consumers? What is competition?

The merger of the AFL–CIO has created a new threat of labor-union monopoly in the economy and a more powerful political force at the polls. The potentialities of this organization and the revelations of the capacities of some labor leaders to exploit their power, legally or illegally, to the point of overt abuses have stimulated arguments for further legislative restrictions upon unions, including the proposal to bring them within the terms of antitrust legislation.

AGRICULTURE

Traditional Sources of Discontent. The idealization of rural living notwithstanding, standards of living on farms have been and in some parts of the country still are below national standards. Rural areas, in comparison with urban, have suffered in sanitation, housing, medical facilities, child care, cultural advantages. Farm organizations, government agencies, extension services, and private undertakings have, over the years, succeeded in making life more pleasant and attractive. Automobiles and television have brought the rural residents to the cities and urban culture to the rural residents.

The dependence of the farmer upon transportation systems for moving his products to market and the products of distant markets to the farm was for generations one of the greatest hazards of farming. This fact explains farmers' concern with "internal improvements"—canals and turnpikes—in the early nineteenth century and subsequent battles for nondiscriminatory railroad rates, for highway systems and rural roads projects. These transportation systems have freed farmers from much of their isolation and backwoods environment, if they can afford to take advantage of the new technology.

The farmer has been sensitive to the differentials in the prices he receives and the prices consumers pay for food. Accordingly, he suspects and resents the profits of the so-called middlemen who transport, process, and distribute food. Since farmers have traditionally been debtors, they have frequently championed or supported schemes for inflating the currency, whether through the issuance of paper money or the coinage of more silver. They seek greater farm credit and an increased volume of currency, both of which go along with cheap money. Farm prices increase by restricting output and/or expanding currency faster than production. In a period of unusual prosperity, farmers are likely to prefer government economy except when expenditures are of direct benefit to agriculture, and their opposition to the real property tax leads them to favor other kinds of taxation and to urge the shifting of activities to state and federal governments whose revenues come from other sources.

Productivity and Surpluses. The basic agricultural problem, as a result of mechanization and the most advanced scientific methods, is a productive capacity far exceeding consumption.[6] Only in wartime, when great amounts of food are shipped abroad, is there a demand for all that the farmers can produce. After wrestling inconclusively with the problem of surpluses, the country embarked in the 1930's on the parity system for basic crops in order to equalize the prices farmers receive with the prices they pay.[7]

In general terms, the parity system operated by the federal government, through the Commodity Credit Corporation in the Department of Agriculture, provides for purchasing a given farm commodity at a predetermined price which in the 1930's varied from 52% to 75% of parity. The effect of government "support" of these prices was to stabilize the market at those or at higher prices so that the support price became a floor. The other side of the coin, so to speak, was governmental determination, through allotments, of the acreage to be planted in supported crops in order to reduce the supply and thereby further bolster the market price. In practice these allotments are very difficult to equalize among states and individual farmers.

To stimulate war production in 1942, Congress raised the level of support to 90% of parity for corn, cotton, wheat, tobacco, rice, and peanuts; later, this same floor for prices was extended to other commodities such as dairy products. After the war, the problem was no longer overdemand but, again, overproduction. However, there was great pressure from farmers and their organizations to continue the wartime supports indefinitely. The combination of political factors plus the partisan jockeying for farm votes resulted in the continuation of 90% supports during the immediate postwar years. The government paid billions of dollars to buy surplus commodities and other billions of dollars to rent storage space to keep the commodities after they were purchased.

The controversy grew more acrimonious over continuation of 90% parity as well as the parity system itself, an instructive example of "an eco-

[6] Grant McConnell, *The Decline of Agrarian Democracy* (Berkeley: University of California Press, 1953) p. 190.

[7] Parity is the price a farmer received for his crop during an arbitrarily selected period in the past (known as the base period), when the farmer enjoyed relatively high prosperity. The base period selected most frequently was 1909-1914, but for particular crops other periods have been selected.

nomic right turned into a political obligation upon government." [8] The leaders of the American Farm Bureau Federation were virtually the only farm spokesmen ranged against high parity, although the Federation's membership was divided on the issue. The Farmers Union was perhaps the most adamant supporter of the policy, joined by the National Grange.

The Eisenhower Administration was responsible for placing parity on a sliding scale from 90% to 75%. The philosophy of the Administration accepted price supports as disaster insurance, not as a fixed policy, and tried to encourage farmers' independence because government regulation threatens farmers' liberty. There was resort to a soil-bank program to reduce production by taking designated amounts of land out of production—a program that did not conspicuously affect the problem.

The solution for surpluses may be more instantly painful than the problem of surpluses. There are too many farmers, many of them at the subsistence level, who require support in order to produce that which is both unneeded and costly to keep off the market.[9]

Partisan Alignments. Agricultural policies have rarely been a clear-cut party issue. Farmers have generally been a major factor in sectionalism, whether they have been stable in their voting behavior (in the South and New England) or periodically unstable (in the Central and Mountain states). Representatives of farm areas, whether Democrats or Republicans, have been in basic agreement, and urban representatives have rarely identified themselves openly as opposed to the demands made on behalf of agriculture.[10] The result has been a bipartisan, almost nonpartisan, treatment of the farmer because of his power at the polls. The designation of a bipartisan group in Congress from the Central and Southern states as the "farm bloc" was a formalization of the power of agriculture whose unity transcended party lines. The farm problems of the 1950's created cleavages among farm representatives and split the farm bloc coalition as each section fought for its own crops.[11]

Between 1948 and 1954, Congress reflected a sharper partisanship in voting on price-support legislation. The Democrats in the House increasingly favored high, rigid supports, apparently in response to constituency rather than party pressure. Labor leaders, seeking agricultural alliances,

[8] Charles M. Hardin, *The Politics of Agriculture* (Glencoe: The Free Press, 1952) p. 105.

[9] Lauren Soth, *Farm Trouble* (Princeton: Princeton University Press, 1957).

[10] It was not until 1952 (*New York Times*, April 2, 1952) that a group of House members from urban districts spoke of organizing a "city bloc" and two years later that a member suggested a Department of Urbiculture in the President's Cabinet to give special attention to such problems of city dwellers as slums, juvenile delinquency, and smog. United Press dispatch, July 24, 1954.

[11] Associated Press dispatch, April 18, 1955 and *New York Times*, March 10, 1957. The Farm bloc was brought into existence in the Washington offices of the American Farm Bureau Federation in May, 1921. McConnell, *op. cit.*, p. 57.

have joined in the battle by favoring rigid supports and have brought influences to bear upon members of Congress. Republicans are more homogeneous than the Democrats and have voted overwhelmingly, especially in the House, for flexible supports.[12]

Continuing Power of Agriculture. Despite its reduced numbers and its internal differences, agriculture stands in the anomalous position of exerting an influence out of proportion to its relative strength. In addition to the districting system which gives farmers, numerically, an overrepresentation in state legislatures, the combination of strategic geographical location, basic importance to the economy, and unique national prestige makes the farmer a formidable political force. The argument that what is good for agriculture is good for America has been used to justify many policies, and the prosperity or depression of agriculture reaches out and affects business generally all over the country. The strength of agriculture will have to be much further reduced and far more thinly spread out before the peculiar problems of farmers will cease to dominate the American political scene.

BUSINESS

The issues associated with business have been as pervasive and as durable as those associated with agriculture. It would be impossible to think of American politics without these two sources of controversy. Although business issues have provided occasions for attacks from nonbusiness and antibusiness sources, nearly all of the issues have been vigorously contended within business, such are its contrasts and diversities of interests.

Business Size. One of the most important reasons for clashes among businessmen is the wide range in the size and strength of their units. Leaders of comparatively small units, fearful of being crowded out of business, adopt a defensive attitude toward big units. Some results have been the struggles over the years to limit or abolish chain stores through various taxing devices and the amalgamation of independent retailers for the purposes of pooling their own buying. Perhaps the greatest equalizer of prices among business with both large and small volume is the device of resale-price maintenance. While this practice is attacked as a means for manufacturers to keep prices high for the consumer, the practice is often stoutly supported by small retailers who look upon it as assurance that their big competitors cannot undersell them.

The Tariff. Certain traditions respecting the division produced by tariffs became truisms long ago and are now largely delusions rather than fact. Responses to the tariff depend upon the type of economic interest. Historically, manufacturers wanted high tariffs but importers of raw ma-

---

[12] J. Roland Pennock, "Party and Constituency in Postwar Agricultural Price-Support Legislation," *Journal of Politics,* Vol. 18 (1956) pp. 167-210.

terials, producers of excess commodities such as cotton, bankers handling foreign exchange, and exporters favored low tariffs. This historical division of interests has become outmoded. Many manufacturers, heretofore protectionist, are advocates of freer trade. The farthest-reaching statement from a manufacturing spokesman, perhaps, was the proposal by Henry Ford II to eliminate all tariffs as rapidly as possible.[13]

The problems raised by the tariff still exist because a substantial number of industries (e.g. mining, chemicals, glassware, hats, gloves) still insist that they need protection against foreign competitors or their business will be disrupted and their employees thrown out of work. The optical and watchmaking companies contend that peacetime protection is justified to maintain an industry whose precision skills are essential to national security in wartime. Generalization is likely to be misleading, and individual companies must be investigated separately to determine the impact of tariff rates.[14]

Since 1934, United States tariffs have come down under the impact of the reciprocal trade treaties which the President is authorized by Congress to negotiate with other countries on the basis of reducing American duties as much as 50% under the Tariff Act of 1930. Following World War II, this legislation was amended to empower the Tariff Commission to notify the President when "peril points" are reached, i.e., points at which imports will imperil domestic producers.

The tariff is one issue on which Republicans and Democrats have popularly been supposed to oppose each other. Through the years, representatives have reflected their constituents' interests with the result that exceptions to the official policy have existed in both parties. From the 1890's to the 1920's and early 1930's, the Republicans, generally speaking, favored higher rates and the Democrats lower rates. A major Republican deviation during this period was the Central farm states, where producers wanted to sell abroad and be able to buy at cheaper prices the products of foreign countries. Congressional voting in 1945, 1948, and 1949 on reciprocal trade bills followed the party pattern: 95% of the Democrats and Republicans in the House and 91% of the Democrats and Republicans in the Senate voted with their respective party. In 1951 a break occurred in the pattern: 20% of the Democrats in the House voted against their party and the Southern Democrats were the chief source of the defection. In the ten years from 1945 to 1955, the political forces finally established a new

---

13 *New York Times,* February 18, 1953. Periodically, speeches of top executives of the largest corporations are circulated and the speeches, almost without exception, contain a section advocating lower tariffs and more imports as well as exports.

14 "Tariff Cuts: Who Gets Hurt?" *Fortune,* April 1954, pp. 138 ff. Howard S. Piquet, "Would Tariff Suspension Hurt U. S. Business?" *Harvard Business Review,* Vol. 31 (1953) pp. 95-103, asserted that approximately seventy manufacturers and products are involved in maximum competition from imports but only thirty would be likely to be seriously affected by increased imports.

coalition. A majority of Republicans, the Democrats from the deep South and from West Virginia, Pennsylvania, and Massachusetts favored tariff protection for the interests they represented. Opposed to them, favoring fewer restrictions on trade, was a majority of the Democrats and Republicans from the Central states and New York. There has been a shifting in votes as a result of some business becoming free-trade advocates, the textile industry moving South, the fears arising among the coal interests in West Virginia and Pennsylvania, and the independent oil and gas operators in Texas and Oklahoma.[15] Labor interests are divided because employees follow the interests of their employers, as a general rule.

Taxes. It is not surprising that businessmen are more or less constantly on the alert to protest new or higher taxes which they will have to pay. It is true that business taxes are normally passed on to consumers in the prices charged for goods and services, but this fact does not cause businessmen to accept taxes with equanimity. Price rises may create criticism and resentment among consumers. Taxes usually complicate business operations through requirements for preparing forms, making reports, compiling and storing records, hiring corps of specialists to keep the business out of legal troubles. Businessmen usually resist a tax which they are required to collect; retailers, for instance, dislike a sales tax when it is first levied. Landlords or manufacturers would probably prefer sales taxes to property or income taxes. Any businessman is aroused if he concludes his competitors are favored by a tax system.

Government Regulations. Businessmen's attitudes toward government regulatory activities depend upon the effects of the activities, and the effects may be quite different for one business compared with another. Generally speaking, businessmen oppose government activity which involves subsidies to other groups, e.g. veterans and farmers, or which falls in the field of so-called consumer legislation (such as pure food and drug acts) because of both the restrictions themselves and the danger of creating a negative public reaction to advertising. In the long run, cooperation in the administration of regulations has benefited industries; a great deal of enforcement does not involve punitive actions.[16] A business subsidy is welcomed by the beneficiaries and opposed by their competitors or by the businessmen who find the government action competitive with their own business. A long list of enactments, beginning in 1890 with the Sherman Anti-Trust Act enforced through the Anti-Trust Division of the Department of Justice and the Federal Trade Commission, have been grounds for vigorous differences

[15] Richard A. Watson, "The Tariff Revolution: A Study of Shifting Party Attitudes," *Journal of Politics*, Vol. 18 (1956) pp. 678-701.

[16] E. Pendleton Herring, *Public Administration and the Public Interest* (New York: McGraw-Hill Book Co., 1936) pp. 232-237.

of opinion. Conversely, monopoly has been legalized through regulation of utility companies, and price competition is often abolished in effect through the decisions of the Interstate Commerce Commission and the Federal Power Commission.

Two kinds of relationships can be distinguished between government agencies and their special clientele. In one case, there exists at the outset or subsequently develops an antagonism, either because of the nature of the regulation or because of the manner in which the agency carries out its functions: e.g. the Federal Trade Commission, some utility commissions, antimonopoly agencies, tax assessment and collection agencies. In the second case, mutual interests and similar points of view eventually develop through association between the administrators and the private citizens they work with. The Interstate Commerce Commission was generally resisted and attacked by railroad companies at first, but in time most leaders came not only to accept such regulations but also to depend upon them as a means of stabilizing their business, eliminating harmful competitive practices and establishing uniformly profitable rates.[17]

Republican Partisanship. A close affinity between the Republican Party and business was established by the 1870's, born of their compatibility on such issues as tariff protection, subsidies for expansion of transportation, sound currency, and foreign expansion. Differences within business have kept its members bipartisan, but the weight of business is on the Republican side.

Despite their concern with government policies, businessmen have not engaged directly in partisan politics on a scale commensurate with their potentialities. Perhaps the clearest example of business in politics is the direct participation of Ford and General Motors' executives in the Republican Party in Michigan and the consequent orientation of the party there to the interests of the automobile industry. The more frequent pattern among executives of the larger corporations is to contribute handsomely to party treasuries and otherwise make speeches disparaging inefficiency in government and irrationality in politics.[18] As the power of union labor at the polls appears ever more threatening to business, the urging of businessmen to get into active partisan politics becomes more shrill and insist-

---

[17] *Ibid.*, pp. 115 ff., Chaps. 11, 12.

[18] In two consecutive days at the annual meeting of the American Petroleum Institute, the members were told by one speaker to stay out of politics and deplore instead of duplicating labor's political activities, and another speaker urged them to identify with either party but to "take a walk" if their ideas were disregarded or if their party thought they were "trapped with no other place to go." It is obvious the second speaker understood little of organization politics when he added that "In extreme cases of provocation the walk may have to take the individual clear over to contributing money to and voting for an even more distasteful candidate in the other party." *New York Times*, November 12, 1958.

ent.[19] The Chamber of Commerce urged its members to go "to work at the precinct and ward levels, where political decisions are made and office holders chosen.[20] If businessmen feel themselves challenged to a point of danger, they may overcome their reluctance and attempt to meet labor on common ground. Whether they can succeed as a practical matter may deter them less than the fear of alienating customers or of becoming involved in matters they cannot foresee when they embark on their political activity. For many businessmen the time involved, if not the money, may preclude their competing with labor unions.

LABOR

Differences in interests among wage earners are reflected as well as created by their responses to unions. White-collar workers have notoriously been difficult to organize compared with blue-collar workers. Differences between these groups include their own views of themselves and the consequent appropriateness of their joining a union. White-collar workers often come in closer contact day-by-day with management and are likely to reflect more nearly management's point of view. Generally speaking, the greater the sense of security, the less likely the desire to join a union; and security is largely the product of good economic conditions. All wage earners may be less receptive to union organization when they are enjoying prosperity and more receptive when in danger of losing their jobs.

Objectives of Unions. The traditional union objectives of fewer hours, higher wages, and improved working conditions have been gradually widened as the relation of living standards to government policies has become more intimate. Union leaders apply pressure in behalf of expanded social security, government housing and educational appropriations, tax advantages in the lower income brackets, and government labor departments or other agencies enforcing laws or providing services beneficial to labor. One of the most impassioned arguments in the post-World War II debates over inflation has been the relation between wage increases and price increases. Of necessity, labor leaders insist that the relation is not close and management insists it is.

Some union leadership has gone beyond the strictly bread-and-butter objectives or even the larger economic problems of wage earners. Unions have been identified with such issues as protection of small business from monopoly, women's rights, veterans' benefits, elimination of racial

[19] The tempo increased after the 1958 elections, e.g. J. J. Wuerthner, Jr., *The Businessman's Guide to Practical Politics* (Chicago: Regnery and Co., 1959); Armand G. Erpf, "Corporations Must Change Their Attitude Toward Politics," *Vital Speeches of the Day,* Vol. 25 (1959) pp. 269-272. Horace E. Sheldon, "Businessmen Must Get Into Politics," *Harvard Business Review,* Vol. 37 (1959) pp. 37-47.

[20] *New York Times,* September 20, 1958.

or religious discrimination in employment, the Zionist movement, voting qualifications, making Election Day a holiday, and foreign affairs—giving voice to the propular sentiments regarding international organization and cooperation.

Most of all, union leaders encourage organization and oppose open-shop laws or practices whereby workers do not have to join a union to be employed or to remain employed. The closed shop, requiring workers to belong to a union to be hired by an employer, is much preferred, although the leaders attain the same goal in some industries with the union shop—workers are given a certain period of time after they are hired to join the union. In extreme cases, unions have publicly declared their anathema upon those who are not organized.[21] An aid to organization is the collection of members' dues by the union, and in some companies dues are deducted from the pay checks and the money turned over to the union treasury.

Unions have fought for the rights to strike, picket, and bargain collectively with employers. They have fought the lockout, which is management's equivalent of the strike. They have opposed most strenuously the power of courts to issue injunctions against unions in labor disputes. The Norris–La Guardia Act (1932) in effect deprived employers of the injunction weapon in labor disputes in interstate commerce, although this act did not prevent the United States Government from securing an injunction when a government agency was in the employer relation to workers in private industry. The 1935 National Labor Relations Act (Wagner Act) guaranteed labor's right to bargain collectively and to negotiate the closed shop; the act also created the National Labor Relations Board to prohibit unfair labor practices by employers. The 1947 Labor-Management Relations Act (Taft-Hartley Act) greatly upset labor leaders with its authorization of injunctions by the government in certain types of strikes, its prohibition of the closed shop while permitting the union shop, and the establishment of categories in which the NLRB may find unfair labor practices by unions as well as employers.

The pros and cons of cumpulsory unionism have been presented again in the so-called "right to work" laws permitted by the Taft-Hartley Act and enacted in several states, applying wholly to intrastate commerce. The wide sweep given to the concept of interstate commerce has brought many kinds of businesses essentially local in character under the jurisdiction of the NLRB and therefore under uniform federal regulations, so that state legislation for labor as for business is restricted in its effect and scope not just to the geographical limits of the state but to the limited conceptual sphere of intrastate commerce.

---

[21] The Communication Workers of America (CIO) declared in convention that non-union workers were "untouchables," unworthy of union members' friendship and respect. *Ibid.*, February 22, 1950.

Democrats and the Unions. Labor, agriculture, business, or any large aggregate within the economy cannot afford to be unconcerned with government, because of its far-reaching regulations and of its ability to provide benefits and advantages as well as penalties and prohibitions. Farmers and businessmen work in both parties to protect themselves, except where the one-party system exists; and there they affiliate with the dominant party. Only labor-union leaders have a partisan leaning of such strength that they work for the Democrats even in predominantly Republican areas.

The national affinity of union leaders for the Democratic Party is partly a reaction to the business orientation of the Republican Party and partly the calculated courting of labor by many Democrats in the North and West and, somewhat less, in the South. Legislative roll calls, both federal and state, show that urban representatives and Democrats in large numbers support legislation pushed by labor, while rural representatives and Republicans in large numbers are found in opposition. The difference is not a one-hundred-percent party cleavage on labor issues but an uneven distribution of partisans on the two sides. The "right to work" laws have been promoted by business interests and in some cases by Republican leaders. Outside the South, Democrats seem rarely, if at all, to be among the supporters of such legislation. The list of candidates supported by labor leaders is almost exclusively composed of Democrats.

The connection between union leaders and the Democratic Party is much more than a voting support. Union leaders are in many cases active participants in the party from the grass-roots operations to the highest levels of policy councils. Democratic candidates for office are more frequently union leaders or people closely associated with them. In Michigan, following the election of G. Mennen Williams as governor in 1948, the United Automobile Workers took over in large measure the Democratic Party in the State.[22] In California, following the 1958 elections, labor's power emerged as a great part of the substance behind the Democratic Party's victory. The CIO, since its creation in 1935, has been virtually a political auxiliary of the Democratic Party. Its attitudes are epitomized in the person of Walter P. Reuther, President of the United Automobile Workers and a vice-president of the AFL–CIO. The AFL continued to adhere to the traditional Gompers policy of "reward friends and punish enemies" and avoid presidential commitments, but was gradually drawn toward the side of the Democrats. While the CIO has consistently endorsed Democratic candidates for President, the AFL did so only in 1924, when it endorsed the minor-party candidacy of Robert M. La Follette, Sr., and in 1952 when it endorsed Adlai E. Stevenson The merged AFL–CIO endorsed Stevenson in 1956.

---

22 Stephen B. and Vera H. Sarasohn, *Political Party Patterns in Michigan* (Detroit: Wayne State University Press, 1957) pp. 53-64.

At the time of their merger, the AFL and the CIO also consolidated their respective political campaign committees into one over-all unit—Committee on Political Education (COPE). Its general lines of procedure are the so-called "political education" programs regularly carried in union newspapers and other publications and in radio and television programs; the raising and spending of substantial sums of money in campaigns; the issuing of "score cards" on candidates and circularizing their voting records; the highly effective get-out-the-vote machinery which includes getting union members registered and then getting them to the polls by providing transportation and baby sitters; sending out doorbell ringers, a job the major parties often neglect.[23]

The potential for greater success in the widening area of labor-union influence brought about by the AFL–CIO merger and the high degree of labor's partisan activity have created their own reaction.[24] These developments have served as the pretext for renewing the charges that unions threaten the balance of the political system. After several years of revelations of union racketeering and underworld control in selected industries (although these abuses and illegalities in some cases were in collaboration with employers) the uneasiness about the union potential has grown and the vocal protests are louder. Labor leaders intersperse their political attacks with assurances that there is no "labor vote" or, at least, that union leaders do not control their members' votes. As George Meany, President of the AFL–CIO, expressed it, "Labor controls no votes. It wants to control none. It should control none." [25]

Unions in politics have dramatized themselves so effectively, it is easy to adopt the misconception that all labor leaders are as active partisans as the CIO and COPE. Even the AFL–CIO Council is not unanimous in its political decisions, and both state and local unions refuse to follow the lead of the parent organization on all candidates in every campaign. Outside of the AFL–CIO and the one-time activities of John L. Lewis, President of the United Mine Workers, labor leaders reflect various degrees of partisanship, including those who feel it is a mistake to identify labor so closely with one party and to expend so much energy in politics.[26]

---

[23] *U. S. News and World Report,* September 28, 1956, pp. 113 ff., and December 12, 1958, pp. 101 ff. One of the more enterprising efforts to organize members is the system of designating political shop stewards who are responsible for getting all members to register and to vote.

[24] Dick Bruner, "Labor Should Get Out of Politics," *Harpers,* Vol. 217 (1958) pp. 21-27.

[25] *New York Times,* October 17, 1958.

[26] "So long as the national community will guarantee its basic strength in the rights to colective bargaining, labor should not seek outside privileges through the ballot box. The ballot should provide equal status to labor and management, and that is all. The collective-bargaining process should take care of the rest. And I will predict that, just as in other affairs, the history of other labor groups in twenty-five years will be written very similarly to ours." Guy L. Brown, Chief, Brotherhood of Locomotive Engineers, quoted in *U.S. News and World Report,* December 11, 1953, p. 70.

VETERANS

Organizations of former members of the Armed Forces of the United States have a generally similar outlook and set of interests. While they may compete among themselves for members, they can easily collaborate in pursuing their objectives because they are not mutually exclusive. Successful achievement for one organization redounds to the benefit of all veterans, no matter which organization they belong to, if any. This unity in point of view has been extremely beneficial to veterans in a material sense. Arguments may arise regarding specific proposals and the means of implementing them, but the nation as a whole has accepted the doctrine that the ex-serviceman has valid claims for special recognition.[27]

Types of Benefits. The kinds and amounts of government assistance extended to veterans appear to be limited only by the ingenuity of the human mind and the audacity of veterans leaders. *Pensions* for veterans with service-connected disabilities or for their widows are probably the most ancient of benefits. *Land grants,* in one form or another, have often been made by state governments, but the most generous use of land for this purpose was included in the homestead policy of the federal government during and following the Civil War. Direct financial help of other kinds has been *tax exemptions* and *bonuses.* Newer forms of help, beginning with World War II veterans, were *loans* to buy farms and homes; *educational benefits* from the federal government to pay both expenses for schooling and a monthly subsistence allowance for varying lengths of time to veterans who wanted to return to school to earn a degree or to receive special vocational training; weekly *unemployment payments* during the period of adjustment after leaving service; *job reinstatement* under various circumstances for those who wished to return to the same employment after their discharge.[28]

One of the issues raised in providing benefits is the distinction to be made between veterans who were injured in service and those who were not, and that between those who did and those who did not serve overseas. Pensions, like medical services, are normally extended only to those injured in service. Bonuses have sometimes been scaled to length of service or to

---

[27] The essence of the philosophy was expressed by an official of AMVETS: since military service "by its very nature" is not universal but selective, "those who served should be treated as a select group." *New York Times,* May 11, 1956.

[28] It was estimated that veterans, who with their families accounted for nearly half of the total population, had received per capita about $3000 between 1945 and 1957—a total of $66,000,000,000 for "veterans expense." *Ibid.,* February 12, 1957. From the Revolutionary War through the 1956 fiscal year, veterans and their dependents had received more than $82,000,000,000. *Ibid.,* July 7, 1956. In 1955, total federal and state expenditures for veterans was $4,576,329,000, of which $4,457,000,000 was the federal cost, amounting to 6.9% of the entire federal budget. *Statistical Abstract of the United States: 1958,* pp. 242, 255.

overseas as opposed to continental service. Most other benefits are offered to all honorably discharged veterans without other distinction.[29]

Veteran preference in making appointments to the civil service is in force in the federal government, in all the states, and even in many local governments.[30] The preference is given in various ways: an absolute number of points is added to veterans' examination scores, or the score is increased by a given percentage, or all veterans get absolute preference, i.e., they must be hired before nonveterans. Often an injured veteran is given a greater increase on his score than an able-bodied veteran, and the preference in some cases is extended to the wife or widow of an ex-serviceman. The policy of veteran preference has become in effect a vested interest which the veteran organizations stoutly protect and which legislators are loath to tamper with. This form of favoritism really goes beyond the ordinary concept of veterans' claims for consideration and establishes the government's obligation virtually to provide employment in civil service for any veteran who can meet nominal qualifications.

Veterans in Politics. Veterans and their spokesmen have been a factor in partisan politics since the Revolutionary War. With the exception of the close connection between the Republican Party and the Grand Army of the Republic, veterans organizations have worked equally well with both political parties and can be described accurately as nonpartisan in operation and bipartisan in composition. Since the benefits are not associated with either party, veteran interests are not affected by party changes. Influential leaders in all walks of life, including politics, are veterans themselves. In the National House of Representatives, 55% of the members elected between 1950 and 1954 were veterans, although only 40% of all males 25 years of age or older were veterans. There was no consistent preference among the voters for veterans and both parties favor them. The number of veterans running as Republicans was increasing, but remained fairly constant among the Democrats. The Republican Party ran more veterans than the Democrats in marginal and urban districts.[31]

---

[29] The congressional practice of voting pensions to Civil War veterans who in many cases had no service-connected disability led to one of the great issues during the first Cleveland Administration, when the President began vetoing such legislation. The World War I bonus was paid off in 1936, after constant pressure from the early 1920's onward, intensified after the depression of the 1930's. A national bonus was much less attractive after World War II and organizations differed in their attitudes regarding it because of the total cost, the variety of other federal benefits, and a small bonus in the form of mustering-out payments. Some states have voted bonuses for state residents with a resulting strain upon taxpayers, including veterans.

[30] Veteran preference is included in all state merit laws, and in states without merit laws veteran preference is confined to appointments where merit is required under federal grants-in-aid. William E. Mosher, J. Donald Kingsley, and O. Glenn Stahl, *Public Personnel Administration* (New York: Harper & Brothers, 1950, 3d ed.) pp. 142 ff.

[31] Albert Somit and Joseph Tanenhaus, "The Veteran in the Electoral Process: The House of Representatives," *Journal of Politics*, Vol. 19 (1957) pp. 184-201.

The Appeal of Patriotism. One of the supplemental strengths of veterans organizations is the patriotic appeal which at times can rally citizens whether veterans or not. In the case of veterans, the patriotic appeal is not the principal source of strength, but in the case of some other organizations it is the only source. Patriotic societies generally have little opportunity to cause deep cleavages or create profound issues because of their sectional or local impact, although some of them take strong positions on controversial issues. Almost without exception, patriotic groups are devoted to fostering general or specific historical values in American life and to preserving and maintaining shrines, monuments, and buildings. These specialized interests are outside the stream of dynamic politics and the most frequent incursions of such groups in public affairs are to save landmarks, attain title to historic sites, and receive public support for their undertakings. Occasionally they are politically effective in alliance with other groups, but to a great extent the public is unaware of them.

GOVERNMENT BUREAUCRACY

The story of the growth of government in personnel and functions is now old and hallowed. Whether the resulting implications of the bureaucracy's political influence are equally well appreciated is doubtful, but the very massive growth of government has produced repercussions throughout the political system of the United States. The peacetime level of civilian federal employees following World War II has varied between 2,000,000 and 2,500,000; the number of state and local government employees ranges upward from 3,500,000. In 1900 one out of every twenty-four workers was employed by the United States Government, but the ratio in 1948 was one out of eight or nine.[32] The basis for this upsurge in employment has been the expansion of government services on all levels and the movement of government into new types of activities where services or regulations were demanded by one or another group of citizens.

The Issue of Bureaucracy. The amount and extent of government action is always a matter of political attention. As the bureaucracy expands in proportion to its activity, it becomes itself an issue, and candidates for office debate, sometimes heatedly, the practices, the size, and the status of the government service. The switching of terms may itself be significant. Government employees are the civil service when we speak of the technical aspects of employment policies or when we wish to reduce the controversial element of the subject. When government employees are treated as a political issue, they are a bureaucracy.

The political issues may relate to such questions as the efficient and economical use of manpower, the dangers of size in government, and the

---

[32] *New York Times,* July 10, 1949.

threats to the people of an entrenched or uncontrolled corps of public employees. The impossibility of knowing the operations of the whole bureaucracy, much more of supervising it, is a natural cause of alarm.[33] The manner of administration and the relations between government employees and private persons may be not only wasteful but also corrupt through misspending funds or highly negligent through the poor management of funds or the careless decisions regarding projects for expenditures.

Bureaucracy may be made an issue as a façade when the real issue is a controversial government activity. Those benefited by the activity defend the administration of the law and those not benefited may attack bureaucracy in general as well as the bureaucrats administering the law. In this guise the issue of bureaucracy is simply another manifestation of the pull and haul among private groups. "Governmental activity is unobjectionable to special interests when in accord with their aim, but when it is directed to other ends the cry of bureaucratic interference is raised." [34]

A Government Lobby. Although acts of Congress prohibit expenditures by federal agencies to influence congressional attitudes, many agencies have public-relations offices called by some innocuous name, distributing publicity under the label of "information" or "education." A necessary loophole in the legislation preserves the right of officers and employees to answer requests of members of Congress and to transmit, through channels, requests for legislation or appropriations deemed necessary. This communication is, generally, lobbying, and its protection by Congress recognizes the rights of bureaucrats as well as other representatives of special interests to present matters of concern to representatives of the people.[35] The lobbying activities of the bureaucracy can be divided into those relating to the internal operation of the civil service and those relating to some aspect of public policy.

There is a wide area of *internal interests* of a bureaucracy, a product of the growth in personnel and the growth in the concept of a career service on the basis of merit. The entire range of questions concerning examinations, placements, salaries, working conditions, dismissals, and retirement is of special concern to government employees. The growth of union organization within the bureaucracy attests to the feeling that unity

---

[33] Concern with one or more of these questions is reflected in studies of state and local government and a series of studies in the federal government beginning with the Taft Administration, the latest being the reports of the two Hoover Commissions. A searching examination of the many problems involved in finding the proper operational area for federal government employees is found in Charles S. Hyneman, *Bureaucarcy in a Democracy* (New York: Harper & Brothers, 1950).

[34] Herring, *op. cit.*, pp. 11 ff. An outstanding example of an agency which is supported because of valuable services it renders is the Bureau of Standards in the Department of Commerce. *Ibid.*, Chap. 19.

[35] James L. McCamy, *Government Publicity* (Chicago: University of Chicago, 1939) pp. 6-8.

is needed in order to get a hearing by government officials. Generally, public employees are not permitted to strike and union leaders cannot, in the real sense, bargain collectively with administrators or with legislators. However, the case for employees can be presented better by a unified leadership either during election campaigns or before legislative committees.

Public policy is profoundly influenced by those who administer the policy. In many cases, legislative bodies intentionally give administrators an area of discretion in order to develop standards and formulate rules. Even when the discretion is not intended, it is exercised in fact because of the inevitable effect upon a job of the person doing it.

Organized interest groups establish intimate lines of communication and interest with government officials who administer policies of concern to the group. Often, these relations are not just amicable but alliances of interests. The most effective kind of lobbying is the combination of a strong government agency and an active organization of private citizens, e.g., veterans administrations and organizations, the Department of Agriculture and farm organizations, fish and game agencies, and sportsmen's organizations. Sometimes an agency makes friends with some groups by creating enemies among other groups. The Rural Electrification Administration, attacked by private power companies, becomes more popular among those opposed to power companies.

Basically, agencies want more money to conduct more functions; appropriations are the most frequent crux of the bureaucracy's objectives both internally and policy-wise. An organized interest group allied with an agency will support its requests for funds. The collaboration can be very effective. Agencies performing direct services may threaten to curtail specific projects if funds are reduced in order to alert sections or groups adversely affected to bring pressure upon legislators.[36] Welfare agencies make sure that recipients of relief and pensions are informed about the prospects of less money for welfare; public health agencies have the support of medical groups for their programs and appropriations; the problems of state educational commissions are taken up by educational organizations which arouse parent-teacher associations in behalf of educational budgets and teacher salaries.[37]

---

[36] When the Budget Bureau cut $279,000,000 from the Veterans Administration's request for funds, that agency issued an estimate that six or seven hospitals with a total of 4809 beds, would have to be closed. *New York Times,* May 24, 1953.

[37] A different kind of pressure on the public occurred when the voters of New York and New Jersey communities defeated referendum proposals to increase salaries of city policemen. Immediately the police began writing traffic tickets. In North Bergen, parking summonses jumped from a daily average of 10 to 300. In two days, 645 traffic summonses were issued in Binghamton, more than had been issued in several years. *Ibid.,* November 11, 12, 13, 1955.

NATIONALITY AND RACE

Problems of Definition. Nationality is a fact objectively determinable under any nation's laws, since it is a legal concept capable of documentation. To consider the political significance of groups organized on the basis of similar national affinities is to toy with a sterile legalism, for the formal classification may be unrelated to the psychology of those purportedly composing the group. The concept of race presents even greater difficulties partly for the same and partly for different reasons because it is an indefinite and debatable concept. It may be a convenient means of distinguishing among the world's people and may have some practical validity, but to establish a scientific basis of race is an undertaking which many students of the subject find exceedingly perplexing.

In the first place, racial classifications vary significantly and the familiar one of white, yellow, and black has become hopelessly scrambled by intermixtures; skin color is not a reliable guide. Other characteristics such as eyes, hair, stature, shape of nose vary among members of the same race. Classification by inherited factors in the blood, which is strictly controlled by heredity, simply demonstrates anew the itinerant nature of peoples; the same blood types are found in widely separated areas among different so-called races.[38] In view of these great problems of classification and identification, this is a field for specialists. Laymen cannot be expected to grasp more than superficial or easily identifiable characteristics of race and can confuse race with nationality or religious groups. In the second place, specialists are unable to discover significant mental or biological differences among supposed races even when a pure race can be found. The types of human differences capable of sharp distinctions are not found in biologically fixed behavior but in cultural differences or learned behavior.

Political Use of Concepts. The connection among politics, race, and nationality arises from people's thinking rather than from scientific foundations. It is this psychological factor—the popular acceptance both of the importance and of the recognition—which concerns us here. If racial issues are injected into politics, the results are just as serious as if race were a scientifically pure and significant distinction. Popular concepts of nationality or race depend upon differences in speech or distinguishing physical marks or customs as in worship or in manner of dress. In the antiforeign, nativist period in American politics, foreigners were identified by their urban residence and industrial employment as well as by their language and religion.

Outward means of identity undoubtedly contribute in some cases to the coherence and unity of those who consider themselves related by nationality or race. Skin color is a badge of membership just as language or dialects.

---

[38] Ruth Benedict, *Race: Science and Politics* (Modern Age Books, 1940) pp. 11-58.

Leaders of such groups may be placed in a more enviable position because of both the groups' internal consciousness and their external recognition. In states where these groups become powerful enough to be a political factor, they have a claim to be represented on the parties' tickets, to receive a certain number of appointive positions, to be heard when they have special problems. With the upsurge of these groups in various states there sometimes occurs a genuine shift in the balance of power and new kinds of names begin to dominate the political scene.[39] To single out a race or nationality group can have multiple purposes, from expressing mawkish sentimentality to scapegoating.

Sources of Unity. Members of distinct nationalities and of accepted races may have differing motives for acting within their own groups. *Economic status* is probably the most single important reason and certainly has the greatest political impact. Immigrant generations and their offspring have in many cases been among the lower wage earners, and their unity has more often than not been the result of economic rather than racial consciousness. When race itself is the cause of the economic handicaps, as in the case of Negroes, the two factors become inseparable. By the process of evolution, racial groups develop hierarchies, so that in time economic status becomes a cause of disunity or incompatibility.

Political environment or *political issues* can fuse an ethnic group. Immigrants who took up residence in cities in the Northeast generally came under the sway of Democratic organizations and remained predominantly Democrats for generations thereafter. Immigrants who moved into the less populated Central and Western states more frequently affiliated with the Republicans, although it is noteworthy that discontent marked the activities of both groups and correspondingly influenced their respective parties in their own areas. Issues drawn from foreign affairs can divide a group into factions or may array one group against another; Italians and Yugoslavs were divided over the Trieste settlement in 1919; there were pro- and anti-Hitler Germans as well as pro- and anti-Mussolini Italians.

In some cases it appears that a basic *race consciousness* is the explanation of the group solidarity. This condition, in turn, may be involuntary through such practices as segregation or voluntary through practices of group insulation and attitudes of clannishness in order to preserve intact distinct cultural patterns.

Relations with Parties. Group unity, if the group is sufficiently large, can have political influence even when it is not highly organized. But communication is more instantaneous and effective if conveyed by way of

---

[39] Samuel Lubell, *The Future of American Politics* (New York: Harper & Brothers, 1952) pp. 48, 52, 73-75, 78-80. D. W. Brogan, *Politics in America* (New York: Harper & Brothers, 1954) pp. 105-109.

leaders of the group or through organizations which most of the group trust and respect. The general impression party leaders wish to make is that they are concerned with the welfare of the group, but quite often there are no specific group issues as such. In this situation, candidates may appeal to the group within the same context as they appeal to classes, emphasizing prosperity and employment, or to the Old World patriotism of the group, linking their heritage with that of the United States.[40] Both the Democratic and Republican National Committees appoint aides representing such groups as the Swiss, Chinese, Poles, Ukrainians, Negroes, Italians, to lead the party campaign among the respective communities. The amount of influence for any given group will vary with the relation of the group's size to the geographical level.[41]

Looking upon nationality and racial groups as a collection of minorities, the generalization can be made that, at least since World War I, the Democrats have profited much more from the votes of minorities than the Republicans have. Many minorities are urbanites and the Democratic organizations in the cities have traditionally appealed to them. The Republican Party has been based in rural rather than urban areas, has appealed more strongly to Anglo-Saxon stock and to middle- or upper-income classes. Even when opportunities have arisen for winning minorities' support, the Republican Party has either missed completely or has been less effective than Democrats. The votes of a minority group have gone in large measure to the Republicans in specific elections, e.g., the Irish in 1920 and the Germans in 1940, but the basis for this behavior was a temporary issue and was not, or could not be, permanently exploited.

THE SPECIAL CASE OF THE NEGROES

The position and influence of Negroes in the United States are worthy of more detailed examination. This group, constituting approximately 10% of the nation's total population, is unquestionably one of the most closely unified on the basis of race that can be found. Its unity can be attributed

---

[40] "My own studies of election returns since the Civil War indicate that *at all times* in our history ethnic tensions have been almost as important a voting force as sectional and economic conflicts. The successive immigrations to this country have made us a nation of divergent cultural streams, each with its own distinctive political flow, predispositions and even versions of history." Samuel Lubell, *Revolt of the Moderates* (New York: Harper & Brothers, 1956) p. 79.

[41] Clement R. Attlee, free of the inhibitions of American politics, could afford to be explicit about the situation: "In the composition of the American nation there are elements drawn from many races, but not in equal proportions. There are, for instance, more Italians than Yugoslavs, a great many Jews and practically no Arabs. It is natural that the Italians and the Jews should be more influential in America than their rivals. They are able to make their voices heard very emphatically at election time, and quite inevitably party leaders listen to them. The elections being close and the international complications being far away, home considerations may be more effective than foreign affairs." Quoted in *U.S. News and World Report,* January 15, 1954, p. 86.

to economics, since the race as a whole has been poorly educated, poorly paid, and relegated to menial occupations; but its economic position is the direct result of racial discrimination so that the basis of unity is, more properly speaking, racial. Differences in economic and social status, however, are the main sources of internal friction and division.[42]

Segregation. The issue of Negro status and position in the United States has risen and fallen. Since the Civil War and Emancipation, the fever chart of the issue shows, alternately, intense concern succeeded by a sense of futility and unconcern largely caused by intractable opinion in the South. Another upward spiral began during the 1920's and 1930's and, reinforced by World War II, desegregation burst forth upon the country as one of the major and fundamental issues of the twentieth century, shaking the unity and the power of Southern leaders.

Whereas the nineteenth century was a struggle for Negro freedom and his acceptance as a citizen in the most elemental sense, the struggle of the twentieth century is for political, economic, and legal equality. Segregation, the status imposed upon the Negro as a substitute for slavery, became the core of the issue, and the 1954 decision of the Supreme Court of the United States, holding enforced racial segregation in the public schools unconstitutional, has become the symbol for a highly emotional national issue. Actually, the school decision was one in a series of Negro victories won through federal court decisions. Others were the ending of the white primary, ending segregation on interstate carriers, holding restrictive covenants in deeds to property unenforceable in the courts. Some states and local governments prohibit racial and religious discrimination in employment and housing. Segregation, under federal jurisdiction, has been abolished in the Armed Forces and in the District of Columbia. Each new development creates its own reaction among those southerners who are adamant against racial equality in their own communities. The National Association for the Advancement of Colored People on one side and the White Citizens Council and the other Southern organizations of like persuasion on the other are implacable foes ranged against each other. There is no prospect for submerging the issue as was done in the 1870's and 1880's. It is irrepressible and party leaders must deal with it.

---

[42] "The Negro upper class is most thoroughly assimilated into the national culture, but it is also most isolated from the whites. Its members are the most race-conscious. They provide the leadership and a large part of the membership of the nationally established Negro defense organizations. . . . But they sometimes feel great difficulty in identifying themselves with the Negro masses whose spokesmen they are. . . . The Negro upper class is characterized by many of the traits that are in complete contrast to those of the masses of Negroes in the lower class. Their social ambition is to keep up this distinction. In private they are often the severest critics of the Negro masses." Arnold Rose, *The Negro in America* (New York: Harper & Brothers, 1948) p. 229.

Negroes and the South. To Negroes can be attributed the chief cause of the one-party system in the South since Reconstruction. Southern whites united in their efforts to keep the Negroes controlled economically and politically, and the most effective method was to monopolize Southern government through the Democratic Party.[43] The inclinations of pre-Civil War Whigs were not, initially, toward the Democratic Party. However, the policies of the Radical Republicans at the beginning of Reconstruction made it difficult or impossible for the Whigs to align themselves with that party, just as the policies of the Lincoln Administration in 1861 forced the Whigs into a secessionist position which many of them did not want to take.

From the end of the Civil War through Reconstruction, the Republicans in the South were allied with the Negroes who as officeholders and voters formed the backbone of the party. The first real prospect for opening the South to a two-party division based on native white Southerners appeared in the negotiations of 1876–1877 leading to the selection of Rutherford B. Hayes as President over Samuel J. Tilden. At last the Whig tradition seemed able to reassert itself within the Republican Party.[44] The actual result was that the Republican Party dwindled to a mere shell in the Lower South and to a static regional minority in North Carolina, Tennessee, and Virginia. The Party was unable either to combat white supremacy or to compete in such an environment. Even the economic appeal of Populism was finally contained in some Southern states by appeals to whites to maintain a solid front against the Negro in politics.[45]

Negroes and the Republicans. Before 1932, no group was more closely tied to a political party than the Negroes were attached to the Republicans as the party of Lincoln and Emancipation. While the bulk of the Negroes were still in the South, the primary Republican appeal to them was through federal patronage and recognition of a leadership role for them in their respective states. Finally convinced that there was no hope of Southern success in allying with the Negro, some Republican leaders began cultivating white voters and sloughing off the Negro attachment. In some Southern states the miniscule Republican parties were factionalized by dividing Negroes and whites—leading to the designations of "Black and Tan" for the

---

[43] The Democratic Party established control in all of the secessionist states within twelve years following the end of the Civil War. The dates are: 1870: Georgia, North Carolina, Tennessee, Virginia; 1873: Texas; 1874: Alabama, Arkansas; 1875: Mississippi; 1876: Florida, Louisiana, South Carolina.

[44] C. Vann Woodward, *Reunion and Reaction* (Boston: Little, Brown & Co., 1951) Chap. 2, *et seq.*

[45] John D. Hicks, *The Populist Revolt* (Minneapolis: University of Minnesota Press, 1931) Chap. 2 and *passim* for individual Southern states; Frederic D. Ogden, *The Poll Tax in the South* (University: University of Alabama Press, 1958) Chap. 1; Helen G. Edmonds, *The Negro and Fusion Politics in North Carolina 1894-1901* (Chapel Hill: University of North Carolina Press, 1951).

faction including Negroes and whites and "Lily Whites" for the all-white faction.[46] Increasingly from the 1890's on, Southern states presented the racial issue at Republican national conventions in the guise of a delegate contest; learned arguments were intoned over which group actually represented the Republican Party in its own state, but the decision depended upon political advantage, not legal hairsplitting. Lily Whites were more frequently seated in conventions and enjoyed the patronage after elections.

Negroes and the Democrats. World War I marks a high point in Negro history. In the years 1916–1919 a great migration from the South to the North was stimulated by employment opportunities in industry. The overall result, as this movement continued during the next decade, was improvement in education and economic status. Politically, the change was momentous inasmuch as Negroes in the North could qualify to vote and a potential "Negro vote" became possible.[47] Urban Democratic organizations began to give Negroes consideration, and a basis of Democratic affiliation was begun. No significant switch of party allegiance occurred during the 1920's [48] although Alfred E. Smith in 1928 did develop support in some Negro newspapers and among some urban residents. The depression of the 1930's, which broke the Republicans' hold on the nation, had a similar effect upon Negroes, who especially suffered because of their lower economic status. The resurgence of Lily Whiteism under Hoover as well as his attempt to consolidate his 1928 penetration of the South by ignoring Negroes hastened the day of realignment.[49] The real bolt did not occur in 1932 but in 1936 when Franklin D. Roosevelt finally won and thereafter held a large proportion of the Negroes. In 1948 Truman's civil rights campaign had a marked appeal, and the attraction to the Democrats continued through 1952.[50]

---

[46] According to Henry Lee Moon, *Balance of Power: The Negro Vote* (New York: Doubleday & Co., Inc., 1948) p. 79, "lily white" originated in Texas. See also V. O. Key, Jr., *Southern Politics in State and Nation* (New York: Alfred A. Knopf, 1950) pp. 286 ff.

[47] Moon, *op. cit.*, Chap. 5.

[48] The failure of the Democratic Party nationally to receive Negro support during the 1920's was the result of the party's traditional attitude. Perhaps 1920 marks the last attempt at Negro baiting on a large scale by the Democrats: an undercover campaign, bolstered by posters and "documentary evidence," was launched against Warren G. Harding, the Republican presidential candidate, alleging he had Negro blood. This campaign, which was pushed in the border states and in the southern counties of Ohio, Indiana, and Illinois, undoubtedly boomeranged. Negroes were unified in support of the Republicans but whites were not drawn to the Democrats because of the charges. The details are treated in the author's unpublished dissertation, *The Presidential Campaign of 1920* (Ohio State University, 1950) Chap. 10.

[49] In addition, Negroes were affronted by Hoover's nomination of Judge John J. Parker of North Carolina to the Supreme Court and the segregation of Gold Star Mothers during their voyage to the battlefields of France.

[50] Beginning in the 1930's Negroes' Democratic partisanship was reinforced by the policies of the CIO in admitting Negroes as members and in advocating equal rights for them. Moon, *op. cit.*, Chap. 8.

Negroes and the Balance of Power. As early as 1907 Negroes were told, "The politicians that we have known and with whom we have been in active sympathy . . . have passed out of active control of Republican politics." Consequently, Negroes should change their strategy:

> It would be futile to form a race party. It would be folly to go boldly from the Republican to the Democratic party. But if they should give support to one party or another as it shows a disposition to be genuinely democratic, regardless of race in its principles and policies, they (the Negroes) would find the support of their race largely sought for by both parties.[51]

This thesis of Negro bargaining as a means of getting what they want through government is pervasive and persuasive. Many Negro leaders have adopted it as a conscious strategy and one of them, Henry Lee Moon, expressed it in the title of a book: *Balance of Power: The Negro Vote.* The thesis gains credence by the continuing rapid migration of Negroes to the large metropolitan centers, where they become a key group in statewide voting in large, pivotal states and a dominant group in many districts. In this way, a small fraction of the total vote, by being unified, can substantially influence the outcome. The political attractiveness of Negroes is their tendency to move preponderantly in one direction even when they shift as they did following 1952. Eisenhower did better in 1956 than in 1952 among Negroes in the entire South and in many Northern metropolitan centers.[52] Even if their racial unity declines, thereby breaking their political unity, Negroes will long be in a bargaining position because both parties will continue to appeal to them as, at least, a potential balance of power.

RELIGION

Potential Danger of Issues. Despite the occurrence of great reformist and religious fervor created by political issues in our history, American politicians normally avoid religious controversy. Religious issues seldom are pleasant to deal with. The dangers are great, the benefits indefinite and unstable. The divorce of religion from politics is one of the principal differences between the political system of the United States and Europe. The aversion to group pressures in politics is often pronounced when associated with churches, and many Americans simply refuse to accept or condone partisan activity by their religious leaders. Americans, considered as church members, however, may very well demand governmental action in regard to some condition which upsets them, but such responses are not associated with religious pressure for strictly political purposes.

---

[51] Editorial in the *New York Age,* Negro weekly, quoted in Elbert Lee Tatum, *The Changed Political Thought of the Negro 1915-1940* (New York: Exposition Press, 1951) pp. 41-44.

[52] Henry Lee Moon, "The Negro Vote in the Presidential Election of 1956," *Journal of Negro Education,* Vol. 26 (Summer, 1957) pp. 219-230. See also Richard M. Scammon, "How Will Negroes Vote?" *The New Republic,* September 16, 1957, pp. 11-14.

The points of association arise over issues which people look upon as moral and expect churches to take a stand upon for moral reasons, as in the case of prohibition. Other issues touch religions differently and cause the cleavages in doctrinal beliefs to be injected into politics when there is fear of governmental favoritism, e.g., diplomatic recognition of the Vatican. Sometimes an issue alerts a religious group, but on nonreligious grounds, as the Irish opposed the Treaty of Versailles because it did not provide for Irish independence. Moral issues which may have religious significance are as likely to create divisions as to create unity. Prohibition, separation of church and state, euthanasia, and birth control divide Protestants, but generally unite Catholics. Slavery split the Northern and Southern memberships of the Methodist and Presbyterian bodies. Issues of a more directly religious nature were more prevalent in the pre-Civil War years than they have been since that time. The nativist movements were attacks upon religion, at least obliquely, in the course of opposing foreigners. Whenever a church or a religion is attacked as such, its members are most prone to be brought together and submerge their internal differences.

Partisan Alignments. If all church members could be mobilized politically, they could sweep away any opposition. If religious differences coincided with partisan differences, we would have religious parties. Since neither of these two situations exists, there is not, in this sense, a "religious vote" in the United States. However, there is evidence that members of the three major religious groups—Protestant, Roman Catholic, and Jewish—do have significantly different partisan voting records. The challenging question is the relation between the religious affiliation and the partisan vote.

Expressed popularly, Catholics tend to be Democrats and Protestants (outside the South) tend to be Republicans. Southern sectionalism again becomes a source of qualification, and the political distinction between Northern and Southern Protestants can hardly result from religion. In fact, many Protestants, North and South, have been rural residents, farmers, drys, and even opposed to high tariffs. Religion has been buttressed by many other factors which normally have some political importance. Religion apparently will not unite groups separated by economic interests.[53]

The religious unity of Catholics has been the cause for a great deal of attention given to their political unity. The question—Is there a "Catholic Vote"?—has been answered both ways. It has been labeled a "myth" and a "nonexistent commodity."[54] Even the 1948 study of Elmira, New York, which concluded "there is a strong 'religious vote' in this country," found

[53] Charles A. Beard, *The American Party Battle* (New York: The Macmillan Co., 1928) pp. 12-13.

[54] *New York Times*, July 15, 1956, reporting interview with the head of the History Department at the University of Notre Dame. Nationality differences have led Catholics to different parties. Brogan, *op. cit.*, pp. 109-111.

Catholics were Democrats because of informal social relations, not because the Church attempted to "deliver the vote." [55] Interest in the existence of a Catholic vote has revived because of the prominence of Catholics among potential candidates for President and Vice-President. Although the 1928 defeat of Alfred E. Smith is generally attributed to the Republican trend of that year and the prohibition issue, rather than his religion,[56] analyses of 1952 election statistics gave rise to diametrically opposite conclusions regarding a Catholic vote in congressional elections and a Catholic swing to Eisenhower.[57]

In the case of Jews, the evidence seems to be more clear-cut; there tends to be a "Jewish vote" whether the reason be religious, racial, cultural, or something else.[58] Only Jews were found to be an exception to the rule that voting behavior and attitudes toward issues correlate with economic status rather than with religion; irrespective of economic status, Jews reflected Democratic partisanship and receptivity to government action.[59] Historically, Jews supported Jefferson and Jackson, but in the North largely went over to the Republicans and did not begin returning to the Democratic Party until the 1920's. Their swing to the Democrats was more complete and lasted longer than in the case of any group except Negroes. However, Jews with the most associations with non-Jews are more likely to vote Republican, with the result that Jewish women are stronger Democrats than Jewish men. Jews became more independent as voters in the early twen-

[55] Bernard R. Berelson et al., Voting (Chicago: University of Chicago Press, 1954) pp. 64-71.

[56] Louis H. Bean, How to Predict Elections (New York: Alfred A. Knopf, Inc., 1948) pp. 99-102, found that in the East, Central, and South Atlantic states, 20% more Catholics resulted in about 10% more votes for Smith in 1928. Comparing the 1928 Democratic vote with that in 1924 in Oregon and Texas (which had about the same percentage of Catholics in their populations) the 1928 Democratic vote fell off 5% in the former and 33% in the latter state. This response to Smith's candidacy tells more about the Protestant vote in Texas than about the concentration of the Catholic vote.

[57] Text of an analysis of the "Catholic vote" made by backers of Senator John F. Kennedy for the Democratic vice-presidential nomination. U. S. News and World Report, August 10, 1956, pp. 41-46. "More About 'Catholic Vote' in U. S. Elections," Ibid., August 17, 1956, pp. 42 ff. While the first analysis argued there was a Catholic vote to the extent of a noticeable shift to Eisenhower in 1952, the second analysis inferentially suggested a Catholic response by pointing out that Eisenhower's 1952 vote was smaller in areas of large Catholic concentration than in areas of small Catholic concentration.

[58] The answer to the question "Is there a Jewish vote?" depends on what is meant. All Jews do not react the same way to candidates and issues. "If the query simply means, does being Jewish sometimes influence one's political attitudes and behavior, then the answer is, certainly. In this sense there is not only a Jewish vote but an Irish, Polish, Armenian, and even a Baptist and Episcopalian vote." Lawrence H. Fuchs, The Political Behavior of American Jews (Glencoe: The Free Press, 1956) pp. 13, 14.

[59] Wesley and Beverly Allinsmith, "Religious Affiliation and Politico-Economic Attitudes: A Study of Eight Major U. S. Religious Groups," reprinted in Daniel Katz et al., Public Opinion and Propaganda (New York: The Dryden Press, Inc., 1954) pp. 151-158. Maurice B. Guysenir, "Jewish Vote in Chicago," Jewish Social Studies, Vol. 20 (1958) pp. 195-214.

tieth century as a result of their interest in reform and the removal of abuses on the local level. Jewish culture, compared with Christian culture, has distinct features which help explain Jews' different political attitudes and voting.[60]

WOMEN

Organizations of women cannot be classified simply as efforts to advance the political interests of women. Neither sex is unified politically, and the range of interests and personal characteristics which divide the nation work without regard to sex. Women have developed interests peculiar to themselves because, historically, they have been placed in a special category. Militant women's groups have fostered a battle-of-the-sexes attitude, but it would seem to be axiomatic that no long-range, sustained movement of mass appeal can be geared to antipathies between men and women. The battle of the sexes may temporarily be politically feasible as a rallying cry; it can never be considered biologically sound or psychologically satisfying.

Objectives of Organizations. Women no longer confine their organizing talents to groups of women meeting as women seeking objectives of women per se. At one time this feminist type of organization predominated, and it still flourishes. The reforms associated with these organizations fall into the areas of women's legal, economic, and political status.

The *legal status* of women under English common law was markedly inferior to that of men. They could not own or manage property or enter into contracts. A married woman could not seek divorce or be given custody of the children if she was divorced. If she committed a crime in the presence of her husband, the law presumed that the husband coerced her and she was not held accountable. In a sense, her status was summed up in the marriage vow of women to "obey" husbands and one of the symbols of feminine emancipation has been the substitution of "cherish" for "obey" in the marriage ceremony. Through the years, state laws have gradually whittled away many of these legal impediments.

The *economic status* of women is intimately connected with their legal status. The reforms of the law have reflected changed attitudes toward women's place in the economy outside of the home. Except for certain traditional occupations like teaching and sewing, women had to overcome great prejudice in seeking remunerative positions in business or the professions and the resistance to coeducation was part of the obstruction to women's economic advancement. One of the basic complaints of women in business has been differential pay scales favoring men. Opportunities for

---

[60] Fuchs, *op. cit.*, Chap. 2 *et seq.*

advancement into supervisory and executive positions have been restricted. Although there is no sex discrimination in such benefits as unemployment insurance and pension or welfare payments, labor legislation contains many provisions designed to discriminate in favor of women: prohibition of night work in certain industries, minimum wages and maximum hours, maternity leaves.

In order to secure women's economic and legal status, an equal-rights amendment to the United States Constitution, providing that "Equality of rights under the law shall not be denied or abridged by the United States or by any state on account of sex," was brought forward. Inasmuch as the objective is to remove all legal distinctions between the sexes, even those designed for the protection of women, this proposal has divided women and women's organizations. Congress has periodically wrestled with the issue since 1942. Its advocates appear to have struck a position which politicians can never fully accept nor completely reject.

The *political status* of women first revolved about the issue of woman suffrage. After concluding that a state-by-state attack would not succeed, the women's organizations turned to the federal government.[61] Over seventy years of effort preceded the adoption of the Nineteenth Amendment to the Constitution on August 26, 1920.[62] Following this major victory, the principal concern for women, politically, has been voting and participation within the political parties.

Women in Politics. Political differences between the sexes is a subject of continuing discussion and disagreement. Women outnumber men in the population, but the voting rate for men is higher. The more general predisposition of the housewife is to follow the political thinking of her husband, who is more politically oriented at least to the extent that he spends more of his time in activities outside of the home. Women have, quite likely, helped to give greater impetus to welfare legislation and humanitarian policies, and political practices are undoubtedly different in many respects as a result of the presence of women. Long-overdue reforms in local and state governments have been achieved by outraged forces with women in the vanguard. Despite the most favorable view of this record, women are politically apathetic compared with men.

Among the obstacles women encounter in politics is the opposition of men who are reluctant to break with tradition and accept women as co-

---

61 Woman suffrage was first attained in Wyoming Territory. Before 1920, only seventeen states had given women the vote in some or all elections.

62 The great difficulty in ratification was the resistance of Southern states, but one of them was needed to make the necessary thirty-six. The choice fell on Tennessee where the Governor called the General Assembly into special session. Ratification was achieved after an extremely bitter fight, with charges of corruption back and forth; the Women's Party was accused of having spent $80,000 in the state. *New York Times* for the month of August, 1920, *passim*.

workers and who dislike to share the spoils of politics with women, or with any outsider, man or woman. There is a certain area of agreement that women as a whole have less political aptitude than men. Women tend to be more emotional and more subjective in their judgments. They are more likely to want to start at the top of the party and to be unwilling to go through the ranks to serve their apprenticeship. Many refuse even to join a party because of their scruples against the evils of politics, preferring to remain aloof and engage in wholesome nonpartisan activities designed to clean up government and abolish corruption. Women particularly complain that women refuse to support women candidates for office, whether from jealousy or from the same bias men have against women in politics.[63]

Whatever the evaluations of women in politics, they are now permanent participants. They are prodigious campaign workers, influencing their neighbors at a coffee hour, doing volunteer service at campaign headquarters, making chain telephone calls, delivering speeches and, from official positions, urging other women to take part in politics.

Women in Office. According to the 1950 census, women constituted 52% of the total population, but they hold no more than 1% or 2% of all public offices.[64] Women have served at the local level as mayors and members of city councils, school boards, and other special district organizations. Hundreds of women are elected to state legislatures. Two women have been governors of states: Mrs. Nellie Ross (Democrat, Wyoming) and Mrs. Miriam A. (Ma) Ferguson (Democrat, Texas). Over sixty women have been elected to the House of Representatives since the first woman, Jeannette Rankin (Republican, Montana), was elected in 1916; and a few have served enough consecutive terms to become committee chairmen.[65] Three women —Mrs. Margaret Chase Smith (Republican, Maine), Mrs. Hattie Caraway (Democrat, Arkansas) and Mrs. Hazel H. Abel (Republican, Nebraska)— have been elected to the United States Senate, although Mrs. Abel served only the unexpired two months of a term ending January 3, 1955. Four

---

[63] Some discussions of these situations are: "Key Political Force—The Ladies," *New York Times Magazine*, March 11, 1956, pp. 14 ff. "What Women Do in Politics," interviews with women representatives from both national committees, *U. S. News and World Report*, December 12, 1958, pp. 72-79. John C. O'Brien, "Women's Bid for Politics," *Sign*, Vol. 38 (January, 1959) pp. 18-20. Edward M. Bennett and Harriet M. Goodwin, "Emotional Aspects of Political Behavior; The Woman Voter," *Genetic Psychology Monographs*, Provincetown, Massachusetts, Vol. 58 (1958) pp. 3-53.

[64] Women have a better record in party conventions. They first appeared in the 1892 Republican National Convention as alternates, but there was no sizable number in either party until 1920. The trend now is upward every four years. The total number of women delegates and alternates in 1956 was: Republican 555, Democratic 650; in 1952: Republican 389, Democratic 525. See Marguerite J. Fisher and Betty Whitehead, "Women and National Party Organization," *American Political Science Review*, Vol. 38 (1944) pp. 895-903.

[65] The number of women in recent Congresses are: 83d (1953-1954) 11; 84th (1955-1956) 16; 85th (1957-1958) 15; 86th (1959-1960) 17.

women held the office temporarily through appointments. Women have held appointive federal offices as ambassadors, members of the President's Cabinet and such lesser offices as Director of the Mint and Treasurer of the United States. Each four years since 1952, there have been publicity buildups in both parties for a woman on the national ticket, but no woman apparently has been found sufficiently experienced and available.

Selected Bibliography

See the Selected Bibliography for Chapter 16, pp. 389–392 below.

CHAPTER SIXTEEN

Evaluations and Implications of Organized Interest Groups

POLITICAL TECHNIQUES

The methods employed by organized interest groups to achieve objectives can generally be classified as activities designed to influence directly government officials and activities designed to influence directly the general public. The first set of activities is lobbying and participation in election campaigns in behalf of issues, candidates, or parties. The second set involves the various techniques of public relations in order to create a climate of opinion favorable to the group and its objectives. These activities will be taken up in order.

Lobbying. Private individuals have used many means of bringing their problems to the attention of government officials. By letter, telegram, telephone, or personal contact the governed attempt to influence those who govern. All of the arts of cunning may be employed to make a favorable impression on legislators or administrators. A lobbyist may work through a friend of the official or through party leaders in order to conceal temporarily his own identity. The lobbying approach may be quite open and even blatant, e.g., a group may call in mass upon a government official to present their point of view or picket his office or, even, the capitol. Very often lobbyists are more effective in getting a hearing if they establish personal relations with officials and are able to provide services for them. In dealing with legislators, lobbyists prepare bills, provide data and advice, make requests and even threats—and always want to convince legislators that their constituents back home support the objectives of the lobbyist.

The great problems of lobbying arose when it became an organized venture, not by individuals but by many groups—whether large or small—possessing money and prestige and professional competence in plying techniques.[1] The more seriously an organization goes about influencing government policies, the more elaborate its preparations. It will employ a rep-

---

[1] In Washington, D. C., alone, 3273 different persons or organizations registered as lobbyists between 1946 and July 1956; $64,479,749 was reported as having been spent by lobbyists in the years 1947-1957. *Final Report* of the Special Committee to Investigate Political Activities, Lobbying, and Campaign Contributions, U. S. Senate, 85th Cong. 1st sess., Report No. 395, May 31, 1957, pp. 190, 193-195; Belle Zeller, "Regulation of Pressure Groups and Lobbyists," *The Annals*, September, 1958, p. 100.

resentative or, if the operation warrants, a fully staffed office at the national and state capitals in order that direct contact can be continuous and instant.[2] The knowledge of many powerful and clever groups spending huge sums working through professional lobbyists has aroused fears that American government responds to organized pressures and neglects the general public. What the actual influence of professional lobbyists is, whether they can basically change legislators' minds, has not been established by any body of substantial findings.[3] The popular fear is that the influence is real and profound.

One basis for alarm over lobbying activities is the fact that at times bribery and blackmail have been notorious, causing the prestige of legislative bodies to suffer accordingly. In all likelihood, outright illegalities are infrequent because of the needless risk and the effectiveness of legal techniques, but questionable practices are used, some of which are at least on the borderline of legality. What constitutes bribery? If those who benefit from policies do favors for a legislator who advanced the policies, is this bribery? Ostensibly, most of these situations are technically legal unless there is an understanding of a *quid pro quo*. If contributions are made to a legislator's campaign by a group with legislative interests, the circumstances determine in large part the question of legality.[4] Pressure tactics may be unethical without being illegal, for instance, sending telegrams to a legislator in someone else's name without his knowledge or permission.[5] Not every allegation of wrongdoing by a legislator is by any means proof that he did wrong.[6]

---

[2] Among many useful discussions of lobbying are the following: David B. Truman, *The Governmental Process* (New York: Alfred A. Knopf, Inc., 1951) Part III; Luke Eugene Ebersole, *Church Lobbying in the Nation's Capital* (New York: The Macmillan Co., 1951) Chaps. 5, 6; Dayton David McKean, *Pressures on the Legislature of New Jersey* (New York: Columbia University Press, 1938) Chaps. 7, 8; E. E. Schattschneider, *Politics, Pressures and the Tariff* (New York: Prentice-Hall, Inc., 1935) Chaps. 3, 4; Belle Zeller, *Pressure Politics in New York* (New York: Prentice-Hall Co., Inc., 1937) Chap. 8; David Camelon, "I Saw the GI Bill Written," reprinted in Henry A. Turner (ed.) *Politics in the United States: Readings in Political Parties and Pressure Groups* (New York: McGraw-Hill Book Co., Inc., 1955) pp. 186-194; Earl Latham, *The Group Basis of Politics: A Study in Basing-Point Legislation* (Ithaca: Cornell University Press, 1952); *Final Report, op. cit.*, pp. 9-56.

[3] See Samuel J. Eldersveld, "American Interest Groups: A Survey of Research and Some Implications for Theory and Method," *Interest Groups on Four Continents* (Pittsburgh: University of Pittsburgh Press, 1958) pp. 173-196.

[4] When an oil company offered a $2500 campaign contribution to Senator Francis Case (Republican, South Dakota) at the time the Senate was considering a bill to exempt natural gas producers from regulation by the Federal Power Commission, the Senate ordered an investigation. *Hearings* Relative to S. Res. 205, Select Committee for Contribution Investigation, U. S. Senate, 84th Cong., and S. Rept. No. 1724, 84th Cong. The company and the individual offering the contribution pleaded guilty to violation of the Federal Regulation of Lobbying Act. The Natural Gas and Oil Resources Committee raised $1,950,000 from over 1000 contributors. *Final Report*, p. 13.

[5] *Ibid.*, pp. 57-59.

[6] The contributing editor of the Bismarck (North Dakota) *Leader* admitted that he rewrote a headline referring to Senator Milton R. Young (Republican, North Dakota) voting

The basic problem in attacks upon lobbying is the fact that organized interest groups are merely exercising civil rights provided in federal and state constitutions. Political pressure tactics are a general exercise of freedom of expression by speech or by publication; specifically, they are an exercise of the right to petition the government for a redress of grievances. Even if such activity could be abolished, the result of the suppression would be the end of a system of liberty. The alarm over group activities has led to state and federal regulation designed to secure information about lobbying and campaign expenditures and to publicize these techniques. Aside from prohibiting bribery and campaign contributions from certain sources, laws usually require reports of money spent in elections and money spent for lobbying, and identification of the people carrying out these activities.[7] It is hoped that publicity will restrain the excessive tendencies toward expenditures of funds even though the amounts spent are not legally limited.

The Federal Regulation of Lobbying Act, incorporated in the Congressional Reorganization Act of 1946, requires registration with the Clerk of the House and the Secretary of the Senate and the filing of quarterly reports showing the amounts of money received and spent by any person if the money was "used principally to aid, or the principal purpose of which person is to aid" either the passage or defeat of legislation or to influence "directly or indirectly" passage or defeat of legislation. A person convicted under the act is prohibited from lobbying for three years. When the constitutionality of the Act was upheld, the majority of the Supreme Court, in effect, deleted the word "indirect," arguing that the act covered only "lobbying in its commonly accepted sense" of "direct communication with members of Congress" and that Congress must be able to protect itself by having information about the people and the money spent in bringing pressure upon Congress—"otherwise, the voice of the people may all too easily be drowned out by the voice of special interest groups seeking favored treatment while masquerading as proponents of the public weal." The civil rights issue was raised directly by the minority of the Court who, granting that Congress can regulate lobbying to some extent, considered the act unconstitutional because of vagueness and the limits placed upon freedom of speech and petition.[8]

The principal weaknesses of the act are its vagueness or confusion and its omissions. The expressions "principally to aid" and "principal purpose" do not really clarify who is required to register; some have registered al-

---

to exempt natural gas from federal regulation. "It was late afternoon. I was in a hurry, and I decided that the headline 'Young for Oil Trust' didn't have enough punch to it, and so I rewrote it in 'Young Sells Out Again.' . . . Our purpose was frankly to politically embarrass Senator Young." *Ibid.*, pp. 32-33.

[7] For information on state legislation and litigation, see *ibid.*, pp. 69-71 and insert between pp. 222-223. Zeller, "Regulation of Pressure Groups and Lobbyists," pp. 95-97.

[8] *United States* v. *Harriss* 347 U. S. 612 (1954). See Belle Zeller, "The Federal Regulation of Lobbying Act," *American Political Science Review*, Vol. 42 (1948) pp. 239-271.

though they doubted they were required to do so and others have not registered because they insisted they were not required to do so. The act covers neither lobbying with administrative officials nor public relations activities by groups. The provision of the act exempting from its requirements a person who "merely appears" before a congressional committee "in support of or opposition to legislation" has been interpreted to exempt also those who prepare statements for witnesses before committees.[9] The act was held to apply to lobbying construed only as "representations" to members of Congress as individuals or committees and not to include the power of a committee to compel the disclosure of names of people buying and distributing publications of a lobbying organization.[10]

Activities in Election Campaigns. Despite the well-publicized campaign activities of labor unions and business and agricultural organizations, most groups are much less active in election campaigns, in a partisan sense, than they are in lobbying with legislators and administrators who are already in office. No matter how strongly some group leaders feel about a particular issue, they try to follow the nonpartisan or bipartisan avenue to their objectives. To avoid antagonizing members of either party, lobbyists steer clear of partisan involvements or commitments in election contests. It has been estimated that no more than 25% of Washington lobbyists are active in politics, that over half of them have never raised money for campaign funds, and that their political activity is not related to the membership size of their respective organizations.[11] Spokesmen for groups, no matter how nonpartisan, are more than willing to appear before platform committees at national conventions to make statements regarding policies reflecting group interests and urge these positions upon the parties. Some groups, finding it difficult to strike the proper nonpartisan balance, have protected themselves through leaders closely allied with each party in order to have a foot in both camps.

Apparently, group leaders are more frequently involved in general elections than in direct primaries (except in one-party states) either because predicting the winner in a primary is more difficult or because their position is stronger if they can bargain between the two parties. Labor leaders are often an exception to this rule, for they enter primaries in order to nominate candidates they can enthusiastically support. Business leaders have been known to indicate their satisfaction with several candidates and then let the votes fall where they may.

---

9 *U. S.* v. *Slaughter* 89 F. Supp. 876 (D.C.D.C., 1950).

10 *U. S.* v. *Rumely* 345 U. S. 41 (1953). The majority of the Court was of the opinion that Congress had the constitutional authority to so extend its investigative power, but two judges considered such a power to be a violation of freedom of the press under the First Amendment.

11 Lester W. Milbrath, "The Political Party Activities of Washington Lobbyists," *Journal of Politics*, Vol. 20 (1958) p. 348. Ebersole, *op. cit.*, pp. 74-76.

Persuading the Public. One of the sharpest turnabouts in techniques of organized groups is the transition from ignoring and spurning the public to calculated efforts to make the public an ally of the group. In fact, "educating" the public may be more effective in the long run than lobbying per se.

The dispersal of voting power to the bulk of citizens twenty-one years of age and over is potentially a threat to groups because of the lack of interest and unfamiliarity with them on the part of the public at large. Group leaders feel the compulsion to make the public perceive, in a favorable light, the group's objectives. By turning to those who are uninvolved and convincing them that they are involved, these leaders can generate a political steam far out of proportion to the generating power of the size and importance of the group.[12] A parallel result of the widening of the suffrage and public concern with policies was the adoption in a large number of states of the initiative and referendum for direct legislation by the voters. Here, an entirely new field was opened to lobbyists and undoubtedly played a part in their transition to public relations techniques. By the use of the initiative and referendum, pressure groups can transcend the normal confines of the representative system by directly appealing to voters for support on an issue.

If the public becomes conditioned to and accepts the basic premises of a group, the public attitude will be communicated to government officials either in specific instances through letters and telegrams or over a period of time in general reflection of these attitudes. Government officials will be influenced, as a result, not by the group itself but by the public.[13] Even an

---

[12] "Other people in the society, who are not in the particular interest group, must exist who are predisposed in favor of the interest group's shared value.

"The interest group must then bring together for political action the largest possible number of persons who are already predisposed favorably toward the value in question. . . . the job of the interest group is to build up support for an existing value by bringing together latently disposed persons who share that value and then to channel their combined energies toward a specific goal of action.

"In general, communication between people may have a greater effect than the effect of mass media on people." Murray S. Stedman, Jr., "Pressure Groups and the American Tradition," *The Annals*, September, 1958, pp. 128-129.

[13] Labor unions have been notably successful in arguing the point publicly that higher wages benefit the whole economy and spread prosperity. Occasionally a rebuttal appears from a source other than management:

". . . whatever the element of truth or falsity in this proposition, it need only be pointed out that it is equally true (or false) for income received by any element of society, and not merely by trade unionists.

"Whoever receives a higher money income gains relative to others who do not, and there is nothing in the argument to indicate why union laborers any more than anyone else should be chosen to have the agreeable privilege of mysteriously spreading prosperity in this way.

"But since some laborers (and some other elements of society) have more power to raise their money income than others (some, such as receivers of contractual incomes, life insurance beneficiaries, pensioners, etc., have zero power), those who have more power gain at the expense of those who have less. The interest of those who gain is hardly to be identified with the whole, if the whole includes also those who lose." Professor Edward H. Chamberlin quoted in *New York Times*, January 27, 1958.

organization like the medical profession, which generally has eschewed partisan politics and is loath to bring its operations to public attention, proved
to be extremely effective in creating unfavorable attitudes toward socialized
medicine by a well-financed public relations program.[14]

With the rise of the public relations approach, experts in such matters
have been hired to direct and coordinate campaigns, and sometimes they
become the highest authority within the group in deciding what shall be
done and how it shall be presented. An overwhelming assortment of communications, from handbills to house organs, spills out of the public relations offices. Representatives of the group are constantly making speeches
which are carefully combed to delete anything offensive to the general public and to include sentiments which will identify the organization with every
conceivable human value. Speeches and other publications are released to
the press in the hopes they will be carried on the wire services and printed
widely in newspapers throughout the country. Speeches, reports, and other
information designed to have wide interest are mailed out to teachers, ministers, businessmen—to anyone who is in a position to influence others. In
addition, group leaders often are very prominent in community, state, and
national activities of a charitable or uplift character and stamp into people's
minds the association of the group, through its representative, with the public interest.

It is a job of public relations to make a group's issue the hero of the
unfolding story and to make the opposition the villain. This undertaking
is mainly a process of getting people to make associations so that the heroes
and villains they are already acquainted with in old issues can be transferred
to new issues. Each clash of group interests features a competition in the
mobilization of opinion. Being exposed to the various presentations and
forming an opinion constitute keeping up with what is going on and being
informed. People become converted on issues which sometimes they understand only in a vague and general form—issues which they can discuss only
in terms of shibboleths and stereotypes. A distinction can be made here between the actual and the apparent. The former is the province of those who
are directly and deeply affected, those who manufacture, improvise, or aug-
ment the issues. The latter is the province of those who are on the outside,
who know only what is made available for the public.

Permanence of Group Influence. The enduring qualities of political
influence vary with the type of group. Some groups seem to attain a plane
in effectiveness, or perhaps achieve an equilibrium between what they want
and do not want. Their leaders remain alert to any threat from any direction but want no particular changes in public policy; their activity is intended to maintain a *status quo*. Under different stimuli they can increase

---

[14] R. Cragin Lewis, "New Power at the Polls: The Doctors," reprinted in Turner, *op.
cit.*, pp. 180-185.

their staffs, alert their membership, and begin making the welkin ring with predictions of disaster for the Republic if some change is or is not made. The degree of aggressiveness can vary within the same organization, while other organizations are characteristically always aggressive or always relatively quiet and remote from the public.

The temper of the times or the peculiar problems of a generation may determine a group's success or failure.[15] There may be cycles of virility for some groups conforming with shifts in predominant opinion in the nation. Some movements are more prone to suffer temporary eclipse because their objectives are not as basic as those of some others. It is inconceivable that the AFL–CIO, the American Farm Bureau Federation, or the Chamber of Commerce should wither away as the once dominant and fiery Anti-Saloon League shrank in size and influence until, in 1948, its name was changed to Temperance League of America and, in 1950, it joined the National Temperance Movement of America to form the National Temperance League, Inc. Prohibition went through two extreme phases of a cycle but groups concerned with the basic economy of the country are not likely to have such a melancholy fate.

GROUPS AND THE GENERAL WELFARE

Identification of General Welfare. One question is inevitably raised whenever the totality of organized interest groups is considered: What are the effects upon the general welfare of the persistent pressures in behalf of the special welfare of multifarious groups? Implicit in the question is the assumption that a series of measures designed for segmental welfare is incompatible with the welfare of the entire nation. In order to probe this question the general welfare must be identified and delineated.[16] How does one even think about the welfare of a nation numbering its population in hundreds of millions? Illustrations of an obvious threat to the general welfare, such as a nation-wide plague, does not go to the heart of the problem because it does not pose any conflict between special and general welfare.

The only concrete way of considering general welfare is in terms of the welfare of individuals and groups. However, groups vary in size from letterhead organizations to mass-based organizations, so the interests of some groups are more general than the interests of others. Within any group classification, representation of interests cannot be complete—all American farmers do not have interests capable of being represented by one farm organization. What, then, do all Americans have in common which can be

---

15 Arthur M. Schlesinger, *Paths to the Present* (New York: The Macmillan Co., 1949) p. 85, discounted the possibility that new instruments for persuasion will permit pressure groups to change or "reverse a fundamental drift of sentiment." If group objectives coincide with the times, however, they may become more extreme.

16 See Frank J. Sorauf, "The Public Interest Reconsidered," *Journal of Politics*, Vol. 19 (1957) pp. 616-639, for a discussion of various definitions and attempts to clarify meaning.

represented collectively? Interests are many and some are conflicting and all have relevance to the individual. Who can, in reality, construct an order of welfare and fail to include himself? Who can positively believe that the general welfare is served if he is injured? General welfare is not an objective entity like a mountain or a forest. General welfare is what people think it is and they can be expected to think of it in terms of themselves.

The most significant feature of this problem is psychological—the insistence that there is an interest which everyone shares.[17] A more practical question is: How are the various special interests advanced so that everyone is served? Partisan discourse seldom comes to grips with this problem because politicians either lack the capacity or fear that too few people would give them an appreciative hearing. It is far safer to make simple appeals which overlook the complexities, like this sample from a speech of former President Harry S. Truman: "All groups in our nation depend on one another. That is what the term 'general welfare' means. The general welfare is the sum total of the welfare of all the groups in our country." [18] That this kind of expression of unsophisticated philosophy is well received suggests it is not entirely spurious even if it appears deficient by analytical standards. The happy acceptance of achieving eternal progress by the formula of one for all and all for one cannot be summarily dismissed as complete gibberish or naivete.

Results of Group Activities. The political success of group action has overcome the weakness of individual influence and the isolation of the individual in a mass society. People feel they have a place by virtue of their associations and are reassured by working with compatible associates. In combination, they are assured of being heard and being known.

The American system, made possible by a wealth of resources and the lack of restrictions upon our genius for exploiting and developing them, has created a tremendously high level of material comforts and conveniences. Production and distribution have created a need for the art of consumption. The competitive urge to mass-produce for mass tastes makes it increasingly untenable to offer an eclectic product or service for the select few. The democratization made possible by an economy of abundance and the desire to share widely the good things of life in order to increase profits and pleasures cannot be considered apart from the political efforts of individuals and organized groups which have pressed for this or that expansion until no conception—no matter how fantastic—is beyond realization. Group organization within a society in behalf of special interests and welfare has

---

[17] ". . . though no two men agree on what precisely constitutes the public interest, all agree it exists, must be respected and feel a sense of outrage when it is not." S. E. Finer, "Interest Groups and the Political Process in Great Britain," *Interest Groups on Four Continents,* p. 143.

[18] A broadcast to the women of the country, text in *New York Times,* August 28, 1949.

paid off splendidly, as almost any set of statistics gathered at random comparing the present with the past will demonstrate.

The over-all evaluation is a balance-sheet, not an exclusive phenomenon of glory and net gains. Whether material satisfactions have been accompanied by psychological satisfactions is a basic question which cannot be examined here, but the materialistic results themselves are subject to scrutiny on both sides of the ledger. The drive for special interests has increased the public debt, cheapened the currency, and raised taxes.[19] The political clash increases as some people, whether or not organized, feel the effect of the disadvantages more than the effect of the advantages.

Legislators are constantly harassed for money and spend the greatest portion of their time examining the society's practices for new sources of revenue or for existing taxes which can be increased. The "incessant pleas" for more government appropriations are periodically identified as pitting special groups against the public.[20] The hubbub over the division of the public's funds is drowned out from time to time by appeals from those who will pay the new or higher taxes, that they be spared and the blow fall upon someone else. To please those who want more money spent and those who oppose more taxes, governments borrow by issuing bonds; then when debts reach their legal limit, the limit is raised or new units of government such as special taxing districts or government corporations are created for the purpose of raising money. Judging from what people say, "Everybody wants lower taxes, more social security benefits, higher farm prices, lower living costs, better schools, better health facilities, intelligent use of natural resources, equitable labor-management laws, more and better highways, better defense for less money—all this and a balanced budget, too." [21]

The challenge to political leadership in the growing complexity of economic life seems at times to be overwhelming. In a sense, everyone needs reassurance that there is a solution which will, even temporarily, ameliorate differences and clarify standards. Political success, it has been pointed out, has often resulted from "sublimating the specific economic interests of different political factions by merging them in more general interests, which can be identified with the public interest of the whole body of people." "An excellent specimen of this technique" was Henry Clay's "American System," but "it was greatly inferior to Washington's identification of the

---

[19] According to a report of the National Industrial Conference Board, comparing purchasing power as affected by inflation and taxes, a $3000 salary in 1939 was equivalent to $6457 in 1958, $50,000 in 1939 to $159,020 in 1958. *New York Times,* April 2, 1958; "Who Gets the Big Subsidies," *U. S. News and World Report,* May 4, 1956, pp. 98 ff.

[20] Statement of Dwight D. Eisenhower in the *New York Times,* February 14, 1959. Former President Herbert Hoover estimated that 200,000 voluntary associations try to influence government and 200 of them press for expenditures; if the 200 took a two-year holiday, five to seven billion dollars a year could be saved. United Press dispatch dated March 10, 1954.

[21] Editorial "Something for Everybody," *U. S. News and World Report,* January 15, 1954, p. 104.

public interest with a more perfect Union or to Jefferson's identification of the public interest with Liberty as well as Union."

> [Stephen A. Douglas] was as ingenious a coordinator of special interests as any of the Anti-slavery Republican leaders, but he could not touch 'the mystic cords of memory,' to which Lincoln appealed in his 'First Inaugural,' in order to 'swell the chorus of the Union.' It was Lincoln who possessed the magic to call forth 'the better angels' in the nature of the American people and transmute a political campaign into a moral crusade. He gave new meaning to the vision of democracy and new purpose to Republicans of whatever extraction. The mighty force of conscience gave an impulse to the new party which swept it to heights beyond the reach of politicians who would live only by the exploitation of a leader's personality and the rationalization of their followers' interests.[22]

The confusions and the apparent intensification of problems by special interests suggest that another process of sublimation is in order. Short of this identification of a more general interest, limitations upon group conflict are a source of hope.

Checking Function in Group Conflicts. James Madison expressed the thesis that the general welfare can be safeguarded, despite the excesses of selfish groups, through the interaction or checking function of group upon group. The result could be an equilibrium—or a standoff in some cases— so that no interest gained total ascendancy and no interest was totally submerged. Some group conflicts tend to substantiate this thesis of Madison's.

Farmers and railroad companies fought over rates, services, and the results of government land grants until their feuds became legendary. The employer-employee antagonism is a feature of the economic system always present, potentially or actually. "Wets" and "drys," public power associations and private power companies, high and low tariff advocates, high and low farm parity advocates, are examples of opposing groups in operation. Temporary issues create conflicts between groups: veterans organizations and the American Medical Association have differed vigorously over policies for treating ex-servicemen in veterans hospitals at government expense. Segments of large groups oppose each other, e.g., cotton farmers in the South protest the acreage allotments of cotton farmers in California and Arizona, and each section is defended by its own representatives in Congress and within farm organizations. Differences in size and in the degree of successful operation divide businessmen and farmers.

These examples of the checking function of groups, although imperfect if judged against a theoretical model, actually provide some protection against excesses. Unfortunately, the checking function is by no means a universal phenomenon in group operations.

---

[22] Arthur N. Holcombe, *Our More Perfect Union* (Cambridge: Harvard University Press, 1950) pp. 92-93, 98.

The establishment and maintenance of an equilibrium of interests require both the opportunity for human beings to propose and oppose policies and the organizational machinery to keep excesses under control. Madison's thesis was based on the assumption that representative government by itself was not sufficient and that federalism was needed as an additional restraint. In this context the degree of concentration of power in one government becomes a factor in the success or failure of the checking function. The federal system of government is one of geographically divided powers; units of government attain certain power over a given area of land and, ideally, each unit is entrusted with the amount and extent of power required for the efficient operation of the government of that area.

Under the Constitution of the United States the government with its capital in Washington, D. C., is given powers deemed sufficient to cope with national problems, those which the states cannot deal with either efficiently or in fact. The Constitution leaves to the states all of the remaining powers which have not been either specifically denied to the states or reserved to the people directly. The result is a theoretical clarity in the lines of distinction and a practical confusion in deciding where to draw the line. It is easy to decide that the currency system should be standard throughout the United States and, accordingly, that the Congress shall exercise the exclusive power to coin money and regulate its value. It is easy to decide that the states can have their own individual systems of criminal law, each state legislature determining what will constitute a crime and the range of punishments which can be imposed upon those convicted of committing the crime. Where to draw the line between the powers of central and state governments becomes more difficult when the question is the control of large economic organizations which operate in many states. The constitutional division of powers giving jurisdiction over interstate commerce to the federal government and intrastate commerce to the states becomes a source of difficulty.

The pressure of organized groups seeking benefits and favors is constantly directed toward a government operating over a larger area, for such a government has greater financial resources, through more widely distributed taxes, and has superior powers of coercion. The push for more government spending moved to the state and then to the federal level. The concept of which activities are properly regulated on a uniform basis throughout the country has progressively widened and has resulted in a constantly increased scope of authority asserted for and by the federal government through its power to tax and to regulate foreign and interstate commerce. The delicate balance of federalism, in practice, gets out of balance quickly when people want something done and do not particularly care who does it. One of the clear and outstanding developments in American government is the decline of federalism. A major consequence of this rapidly moving trend is to centralize the bargaining of organized interest groups in the central government. The check that federalism is designed to place upon them is gradually disappearing.

Restraining excesses through the check of competition and opposition fails in the case of those groups which normally or temporarily have the field to themselves. Generally, veterans organizations are unopposed in their programs; women's groups have presented issues which men feared to resist; reformers have insisted on changes when opposition would appear to be sympathy with sin. In some cases, at least, the only check is to depend on the public's sense of outrage or on the accumulation of irritants to provide resistance. Whether or not proposals are deserving can only be determined if they are critically examined. The danger is to adopt them upon only perfunctory investigation simply because no one appears to argue on the other side. There are many kinds of situations where interests are not challenged on an equal basis by counter-interests.[23]

The checking function appears to be circumvented by the direct role of groups in government policy-making. At one level of influence, leaders of interest groups expect to select or to approve before officially appointed the administrators of governmental departments created to serve their particular interest. The heads of such departments as Agriculture, Commerce, and Labor in the President's Cabinet are almost invariably chosen in conformance with the wishes of group leaders in these respective fields. At another level, the practice of bringing representatives of groups into the government with official authority over policy is well established in both state and federal administration.[24]

Group leaders can perform useful advisory roles and can be valuable in mediating public questions in which they have special competence as well as interest. By making them directly responsible for formulating government policy they may develop new perspectives and understanding. The practice, however, may have the effect of permitting groups to fight out among themselves a policy that government officials are afraid to undertake. It is always

---

23 "Our representative system places in a more advantageous position politically these classes that can best be represented upon a geographical basis. It places in a disadvantageous position those interests which are spread so thinly over the country that they cannot control congressional districts. It militates against classes that are economically weak. It discriminates against interests that are poorly organized and that do not have an immediate and substantial pecuniary stake in governmental affairs. The working of our present democratic machinery is rigged in favor of those interests that happen to fit in with the economic system." E. Pendleton Herring, *Public Administration and the Public Interest* (New York: McGraw-Hill Book Company, 1936) p. 257.

24 Allan R. Richards, *War Labor Boards in the Field* (Chapel Hill: University of North Carolina, 1953). Avery Leiserson, *Administrative Regulation, A Study in Representation of Interests* (Chicago: University of Chicago Press, 1942). Institutional arrangements of this sort are soon created as hard and fast usages. The CIO in Connecticut was disturbed when the governor violated custom by appointing a CIO leader of his own choice as a member of the State Board of Mediation and Arbitration instead of the man the CIO leaders designated. *New York Times*, May 3, 1953.

to be hoped that the groups thus recognized are substantial enough in membership and breadth of interests to be entitled to have such a direct voice.

Resolution of the Dilemma. In the analysis and anticipations of the affairs of men, there is a margin for error because of the ability of men to work their way, logically, to the edge of the cliff and then, illogically, to refuse to take the next step and jump off into the abyss. There is a knowledge that men have about men which assures them that the worst possible will probably not happen. None of us is able to wait quite long enough to be completely sure we are correct in our happy assumptions, but we have enough historical experience of man's ability to achieve the impossible to encourage anticipations of all kinds of impossibilities again in the future.

In one sense the dilemma is resolved since no one can suggest a tenable alternative to people pursuing their interests through their own organizations. We resolve to live with a situation which appears to be inevitable and try to keep it within bounds. The recognition that something is a fact does not justify it morally, but moral strictures are meaningless if they assume a standard of group conduct unrelated to the individual conduct of the people composing the group.

In "the never-ending march and counter-march, thrust and parry, among economic groups" [25] the compromise function of parties acting through government receives its greatest test. It would be a grievous error if the discussion of the checking function of group upon group and the mediating influence of government were seen as perpetual struggles among irreconcilable interests. The reasons the limitations of the checking function have not been fatal is that the entire process does not require a formal check or an official government directive. The premonition that the worst will never happen is based on the record of accommodation and cooperation among people no matter what institutional conflicts separate them.

There is good authority in our political precedents for the conclusion that excessive selfishness creates its own reaction. All groups are checked at some point by the rule that you cannot indefinitely get more out of a system than you put into it. Interaction between the governed and the governors is not a perversion of political purity but the essence of free government. Nor are relations between government officials and representatives of private interests inherently inimical to the general welfare.

Giving expert opinions on technical questions, investigating administrative practices, recommending improvements, negotiating with officials, supplying data to their membership, and watching the execution of statutes too remote or specialized to interest the general public—in such

[25] Latham, *op. cit.*, p. 53.

matters the contact man and his Washington staff can perform work useful alike to the government and to his organization.[26]

The contrasting impressions of the effects of pressure groups sometimes suggest we are going in two directions at the same time, and we are left with the ambivalent conclusion that groups are and are not inimical to the general welfare. We recognize this dual evaluation when we refer to "good" and "bad" groups, but these vague moral judgments may be no more than distinctions between groups with which we agree or disagree. Even if there were absolutes by which to judge, they would be of little practical value. Rarely does a group fall clearly on the side of virtue or of sin.

The greatest imperative in the role of organized interest groups is that despite their power, they be amenable to public authority and answerable for their actions.

GROUPS AND OTHER CLASSIFICATIONS

The organized group basis of bipartisanism relieves to some extent the harshness of the class basis and provides a more tenable explanation than the sectional basis. The basis of bipartisanism which has the best foundation in the evidence is not necessarily the one which would be chosen as a matter of preference.[27]

Groups and the Middle Class. It is noteworthy that the bases so far considered revolve around what are considered to be middle-class interests. This theme arises from political analysis whether the point of view be the two-party system itself or one of the group bases for the system. At no place are we nearer to the essence of middle-class phenomena than in an examination of organized interest groups. To appeal politically on this basis is to distinguish, within the population, groups of interests which tend to be vertical in structure rather than horizontal.

Interest appeals are directed to all sections where a given interest exists and the growing diversity of interests in the various sections gives appeals more nearly a national quality. By combining appeals to the various interests within a section, aided by the interdependence of interests, it continues to be possible to get sectional reactions to party campaigns, just as it is possible to get all of the sections, i.e., the nation, to respond similarly to a campaign, although in different degrees. To the extent that, or in those situations where, sectionalism depends primarily upon non-economic factors, the organized-interest-group analysis will probably be less useful either to account for what happens or to guide the politicians' appeals.

---

[26] Herring, *op. cit.*, p. 36.

[27] For instance, not everyone would make the same value judgment of the conclusion of Lawrence Fuchs that ethno-religious diversity has diminished class cleavages. *The Political Behavior of American Jews* (Glencoe: The Free Press, 1956) p. 20.

Other Group Classifications. The group bases of bipartisanism—sectionalism, class, and organized interest groups—are the familiar ones usually considered in connection with the two-party system in the United States. This traditional treatment of the electorate does not preclude the possibility of other kinds of groups. As analyses of human beings push on into new concepts, other kinds of classifications are suggested. Professor Harold D. Lasswell in his *Politics: Who Gets What, When, How,* first published in 1936, noted that in addition to skill and class, leaders can be considered with reference to personality: "What is the varying fortune of the masochists, the sadists, the detached, the hysterical, the obsessive, the compulsive? . . . Special interests attaches to personality forms which are predisposed by nature and by early nurture to find satisfaction in playing particular roles on the stage of politics." [28] The same classification may be applicable to the individual voter although identifying and appealing to him as such presents an entirely new dimension in American party politics.

A more familiar kind of classification, but one which presents its own peculiar problems in practical application, is attitude groups. "The world is divided among those who are influential on the basis of shared symbols of loyalty to nation, class, occupation, person. . . . Quite different personality types may be united in loyalty to nation or class, method, policy, outlook. Thus attitude groups cut across personality classifications, even as they cut across skill or class." [29]

These other possible groups are suggestive of the penetration which potentially can be made into the still elusive realm of voting motivations. With the greater illumination of the subject it will be possible to know how valid the traditional group classifications are and the nature of their relationship to the newer classifications.

The individual remains to be examined in one more context of his political actions and reactions—the mass basis of the bipartisan conflict.

Selected Bibliography

AGRICULTURE

Buck, Solon Justus, *The Agrarian Crusade.* New Haven: Yale University Press, 1921.

—— *The Granger Movement.* Cambridge: Harvard University Press, 1913.

Hardin, Charles M., *The Politics of Agriculture.* Glencoe: Free Press, 1952.

Hicks, John D., *The Populist Revolt.* Minneapolis: University of Minnesota Press, 1931.

Kile, Orville M., *The Farm Bureau Movement.* New York: The Macmillan Company, 1921.

—— *The Farm Bureau through Three Decades.* Baltimore: The Waverly Press, 1948.

---

[28] *The Political Writings of Harold D. Lasswell* (Glencoe: Free Press, 1951) p. 303.
[29] *Ibid.,* p. 305.

McConnell, Grant, *The Decline of Agrarian Democracy.* Berkeley: University of California Press, 1953.
McCune, Wesley, *The Farm Bloc.* New York: Doubleday, Doran & Company, 1943.
Soth, Lauren K., *Farm Trouble.* Princeton: Princeton University Press, 1957.
Toward a Realistic Farm Program, Committee on Economic Development, December, 1957.

BUSINESS

Dimock, Marshall Edward, *Business and Government.* New York: Henry Holt and Company, Inc., 1949.
Lane, Robert E., *The Regulation of Businessmen, Social Conditions of Government Economic Control.* New Haven: Yale University Press, 1954.
Latham, Earl, *The Group Basis of Politics: A Study in Basing-Point Legislation.* Ithaca: Cornell University Press, 1952.
Ruml, Beardsley, *Tomorrow's Business.* New York: Farrar & Rinehart, Inc., 1945.
Schattschneider, E. E., *Politics, Pressures and the Tariff.* New York: Prentice-Hall, Inc., 1935.

LABOR

David, Henry, "One Hundred Years of Labor in Politics," J. B. S. Hardman and M. F. Neufeld, eds., *The House of Labor.* New York: Prentice-Hall, 1951, pp. 90–112.
Derber, Milton, and Edwin Young, eds., *Labor and the New Deal.* Madison: University of Wisconsin, 1958.
Fine, Nathan, *Labor and Farmer Parties in the United States, 1828–1929.* New York: Rand School of Social Science, 1928.
Goldberg, Arthur J., *AFL–CIO: Labor United.* New York: McGraw-Hill Book Company, 1956.
Harris, Herbert, *Labor's Civil War.* New York: Alfred A. Knopf, Inc., 1940.
Karson, Marc, *American Labor Unions and Politics, 1900–1918.* Carbondale: Southern Illinois University Press, 1958.
Lorwin, Lewis L., *The American Federation of Labor.* Washington, D. C.: The Brookings Institution, 1933.
Mills, C. Wright, *The New Men of Power.* New York: Harcourt, Brace and Comany, Inc., 1948.

RACE

Benedict, Ruth, *Race: Science and Politics.* New York: Modern Age, Inc., 1940.
Brogan, D. W., *Politics in America.* New York: Harper & Brothers, 1954, Chap. 3.
Edmonds, Helen G., *The Negro and Fusion Politics in North Carolina, 1894–1901.* Chapel Hill: University of North Carolina Press, 1951.
Fuchs, Lawrence H., *The Political Behavior of American Jews.* Glencoe: The Free Press, 1956.
Heard, Alexander, *A Two-Party South?* Chapel Hill: University of North Carolina Press, 1952.
Kesselman, Louis C., *The Social Politics of FEPC.* Chapel Hill: University of North Carolina Press, 1948.
Key, V. O., Jr., *Southern Politics in State and Nation.* New York: Alfred A Knopf, Inc., 1949.

Moon, Henry Lee, *Balance of Power: The Negro Vote*. New York: Doubleday & Company, 1948.

Price, H. D., *The Negro and Southern Politics*. New York: New York University Press, 1957.

Tatum, Elbert Lee, *The Changed Political Thought of the Negro, 1915–1940*. New York: Exposition Press, 1951.

VETERANS

Dearing, Mary R., *Veterans in Politics*. Baton Rouge: Louisiana State University Press, 1952.

Duffield, Marcus, *King Legion*. New York: Jonathan Cape and Harrison Smith, 1931.

Jones, Richard S., *A History of the American Legion*. New York: The Bobbs-Merrill Company, Inc., 1946.

GENERAL AND MISCELLANEOUS

Almond, Gabriel A., (Rapporteur) "A Comparative Study of Interest Groups and the Political Process," *American Political Science Review*, Vol. 52 (1958) pp. 270–282.

Bailey, Stephen K., *Congress Makes a Law*. New York: Henry Holt and Company, 1952.

Ebersole, Luke Eugene, *Church Lobbying in the Nation's Capital*. New York: The Macmillan Company, 1951.

Ehrmann, Henry W., ed., *Interest Groups on Four Continents*. Pittsburgh: University of Pittsburgh Press, 1958, International Political Science Association.

Garceau, Oliver, *The Political Life of the American Medical Association*. Cambridge: Harvard University Press, 1941.

Harris, Louis, *Is There a Republican Majority? Political Trends, 1952–1956*. New York: Harper & Brothers, 1954.

Herring, E. Pendleton, *Group Representation Before Congress*. Washington, D. C.: The Brookings Institution, 1929.

——, *Public Administration and the Public Interest*. New York: McGraw-Hill Book Company, 1936.

Higham, John, *Strangers in the Land*. New Brunswick: Rutgers University Press, 1955.

Hyneman, Charles S., *Bureaucracy in a Democracy*. New York: Harper & Brothers, 1950.

Leiserson, Avery, *Administrative Regulation: A Study in Representation of Interests*. Chicago: University of Chicago Press, 1942.

Lubell, Samuel, *Revolt of the Moderates*. New York: Harper & Brothers, 1956.

——, *The Revolution in World Trade and American Economic Policy*. New York: Harper & Brothers, 1955.

Morlan, Robert L., *Political Prairie Fire: The Nonpartisan League, 1915–1922*. Minneapolis: University of Minnesota Press, 1955.

Nash, Howard P., Jr., *Third Parties in American Politics*. Washington: Public Affairs Press, 1959.

Nourse, Edwin G., *The 1950's Come First*. New York: Henry Holt and Company, 1951.

Odegard, Peter H., *Pressure Politics: The Story of the Anti-Saloon League*. New York: Columbia University Press, 1928.

—— and E. Allen Helms, *American Politics*. New York: Harper & Brothers, 1947, Chaps. 8–11.

Shannon, David A., *The Socialist Party of America*. New York: The Macmillan Company, 1955.

Stedman, Murray S., Jr., and Susan W. Stedman, *Discontent at the Polls*. New York: Columbia University Press, 1950.

Strayer, Martha, *The D.A.R.: An Informal History*. Washington: Public Affairs Press, 1958.

Truman, David B., *The Governmental Process*. New York: Alfred A. Knopf, Inc., 1951.

"Unofficial Government: Pressure Groups and Lobbies," *The Annals*, September, 1958.

Wittke, Carl, *The Irish in America*. Baton Rouge: Louisiana State University Press, 1956.

Zeller, Belle, *Pressure Politics in New York: A Study of Group Representation Before the Legislature*. New York: Prentice-Hall, Inc., 1937.

CHAPTER SEVENTEEN

The Mass Basis of Bipartisanism

Out of the actions of human beings appear configurations, trends and rhythmic repetitions of responses to challenges. When a substantial amount of data is collected over a period of time, it is possible to detect the beginning and the end of a movement, and from such collections of materials we induce the product or end result of the mass actions of the population. Consequently, it is a natural impulse to examine the record of individuals' actions and reactions within the groupings of their society in order to discover the nature of the whole population's behavior. Applying this method of analysis to the bipartisan struggle, it becomes pertinent to speak of the mass basis underlying elections in the United States; and those who have undertaken such analyses have, assertedly, found two kinds of mass behavior: cycles and upheavals.

CYCLES IN ELECTIONS AND CANDIDATES

Extent of Cyclical Theories. It is quite possible that attempts to apply cycle theories to American politics have been inspired by, or at least are related to, general cyclical theories applied to endless phenomena in the physical world. The study of cycles has become an extensive undertaking in many fields of human activity, e.g., the rise and fall of the incidence of various crimes. Cycles are discovered in deaths from heart disease in the Northeast United States, in the abundance of salmon in New Brunswick, in real-estate and stock-market prices. Cycles are noted in the weather, in wars, and in great human disasters through the centuries. These discoveries of rhythmic recurrences in experience help to satisfy the human drive to predict the future, and in the case of short cycles, men may govern their conduct according to their anticipations of a series of repetitious events. For the purpose of this discussion it is needless to become entangled in the cosmic question of why there are cycles. Sufficient to the present point is the investigation of selected cycle theories applied to the political system of the United States.

Cycles of Elections. This system itself is based on arbitrary cycles of election dates fixed by constitutions and statutes. Every four years we have a presidential election; every two years, congressional elections. In the states two- and four-year cycles apply to practically every elective office except that of judge, where tenure is often much longer. When party leaders and candidates know exactly the date of the next election for each office, they inevitably develop a sequence of rhythmic moves and counter-moves. Immediately following an election there is a tremendous letdown in interest; for a few months thereafter the public does not wish to be disturbed with reminders of the next election, and the party leaders and hopeful candidates need a period of relative inactivity to recover their balance and re-form their lines. As the next election comes closer, more of the backstage activity breaks into the public's awareness; and when the campaign period approaches, the crescendo of activity begins to rise to the height it will finally reach on Election Day.[1]

Cycles of Weather and Politics. Because there are cycles in weather and because weather has a direct connection with elections, a relation based on weather cycles has been sought. For example, an investigation of voting behavior in Nebraska in the latter half of the nineteenth century turned up an interesting correlation between the lack of rainfall and the increased popularity of the Populist Party. In western Nebraska, where normal rainfall is required for successful farming, the lack of rain in 1890 was found to be one of the causes of the first political revolt against the Republicans after 1865.[2] Such illustrations are easily acceptable as causes for conduct which is out of pattern, but there is no cyclical theory demonstrating that drouth necessarily damages the "ins" along with the crops. When discontent exists, some evidence of protest voting is expected, but the nature of this protest is not amenable to a formulation which can become the basis for prediction. Lack of data keeps the kind of relation that was found in western Nebraska from being generalized into a statement of cyclical rule. Weather has a direct bearing upon the total vote cast at an election and therefore may directly affect the outcome, but this relation is not of permanent partisan significance since the effect may help a party at one election and hurt it at another. All of the specific factors of a given election would have to be known to be able to predict or to construct a series of positive relationships.

Cycles among Presidents. Some patterns of repetition in American politics involve, not parties themselves, but Presidents of the United States. One of these is the *cycle of zero Presidents,* from which emerges the melancholy fact that in the one hundred years from 1840 to 1940 each President elected in a year ending in a zero died in office: William Henry Harrison in

---

[1] See Jesse Macy, *Party Organization and Machinery* (London: T. Fisher Unwin, 1905) pp. 3-7.

[2] John D. Barnhart, "Rainfall and the Populist Party in Nebraska," *American Political Science Review,* Vol. 19 (1925) pp. 534–538.

1840; Abraham Lincoln in 1860; James A. Garfield in 1880; William McKinley in 1900; Warren G. Harding in 1920; and Franklin D. Roosevelt in 1940. Only one President who died in the White House, Zachary Taylor, was not elected in a zero year. Having established this rhythmic recurrence in the past, there is no immediate observation which seems appropriate. To project it into the future is hazardous from the scholarly point of view and unduly heartless toward presidential candidates of those future years. Within this cycle there are some variations apparently without any more meaning than the cycle itself. Harrison, Garfield, McKinley, and Harding died during the terms for which they were elected in the zero year (although for McKinley it was his second term). Lincoln and Roosevelt died during the subsequent term. Three were assassinated and three died of natural causes. Such unmanageable, presumably accidental events can hardly be taken into account by party managers when they lay their plans for presidential elections every twenty years.

An entirely different kind of cycle among Presidents was developed by Professor Charles H. Titus. In this case the recurrences are based upon the *backgrounds and primary political training of successful candidates.* Beginning with the election of General U. S. Grant in 1868, four types of men have sought the presidential office. (1) Reformers like William J. Bryan have never been elected. (2) Specialists who were well known for their achievements outside practical politics but who seldom had sought public offices before running for President have tended to be the least successful or least adaptive to the office, because of their general lack of political experience. (3) The Executive-Politicians have had a political background primarily in executive positions—particularly as state governors—although they may have had at some time legislative experience; in any event, their reputation as an executive or their position as an executive at the time of their nominations was a factor in their selection. (4) The Legislative-Politicians have had a political background largely in legislative bodies both state and federal. Applying the last three backgrounds, a distinct cycle applicable to candidates *elected* to the Presidency, not to accidental Presidents, appears. Three accidental Presidents, Theodore Roosevelt, Calvin Coolidge, and Harry S. Truman, were subsequently elected in their own right, and in their elections they fall into the cyclical pattern, illustrating the practice of balancing national tickets.

Table 7 reveals that from 1868 to 1948 the swing from one type of background to the next one in order followed without variation. In 1952 the cycle broke with the selection of General Eisenhower, a Specialist, when an Executive-Politician was indicated; this break is all the more noteworthy because the Democrats, in effect, depended upon the cycle by nominating a governor, Stevenson. Without knowing that the pattern would fail in 1952, Professor Titus wrote that the importance was

TABLE 7: PRESIDENTS OF THE UNITED STATES (1868-1952) CLASSIFIED
ACCORDING TO TYPE [3]

L-P Type	E-P Type	Specialist
		Grant (1868, 1872)
	Hayes (1876)	
Garfield (1880)		
	Cleveland (1884)	
		Harrison (1888)
	Cleveland (1892)	
McKinley (1896, 1900)		
	T. Roosevelt (1904)	
		Taft (1908)
	Wilson (1912, 1916)	
Harding (1920)		
	Coolidge (1924)	
		Hoover (1928)
	F. D. Roosevelt (1932–	
Truman (1948)	1944)	
	———	
		Eisenhower (1952, 1956)

not "the continuance . . . the perfection or imperfection of the pattern,
nor the universality of the behavior either in voting or nonvoting clusters.
The important aspect is that masses of people select their leaders so as to
conform, probably unconsciously, with a three-point pendulum pattern.
They either keep the incumbent in office or select one who will fit into the
next position in the pendulum swing." [4]

The cycle can have meaning for party managers when they cast about
for presidential candidates. This eighty-year swing suggests that during
those particular years the voters, when they made a change, wanted a new
type of man in background as well as personality. This suggestion, in turn,
may indicate a tiring on the part of the people of one type and a desire
for a different type. The table also tells something about the two major
parties themselves in their selection of candidates: All of the specialists
have been Republicans, and except for Truman, all of the Legislative-
Politicians have also; the Democrats as the predominant party of the "outs"
during these years have captured the Presidency with state governors. The
results in 1952 demonstrate that the clocklike regularity of the swing is not

---

[3] These data, through 1948, are reproduced from Charles Hickman Titus, *The
Processes of Leadership* (Dubuque: William C. Brown Company, 1950) p. 274; also
pp. 272-273.

[4] *Ibid.*, p. 275. That Professor Titus had neither a vested interest in nor an
emotional attachment to the unbroken continuation of the swing is revealed by his
observation in a letter to the author on February 12, 1952, months before the break
could have been known: "In terms of the 'three point pendulum swing' pattern, you
know that for some time I have been hoping that there would be a deviation—I have
never liked 100% conformity. . . ."

inevitable, but even 1952 makes clear that a change very likely will mean a swing even if one of the points is passed over entirely. It is still true that no two consecutive presidents have been of the same type. With this break in 1952, the future developments become even more intriguing. Will the next swing be to the Executive-Politician which was missed in 1952 or will this point be omitted again? [5]

Party Cycles in Congressional Voting. The foregoing material has implications for party strategy, but it tells us nothing about either of the major parties as such, since each of them can apply whatever lessons are involved. The swings in the parties' fortunes in electing members of Congress were chartered by Louis Bean for the period 1854 to 1946. He found there were three prolonged periods of Republican domination (1858-1872, 14 years; 1894-1908, 14 years; and the 12 years following World War I) and three periods of Democratic domination (1874-1892, 14 years; 1910-1918, 8 years; 1930-1946, 16 years). Computing the percentage of seats won at each biennial election for each party, he discovered that the Democratic tide in both the House and the Senate was rising, i.e., each low point in the Democratic percentage was, generally speaking, successively higher than the previous low point.[6] The elections subsequent to 1946, when the Democratic percentage was 43 in the House and 47 in the Senate, have continued to bear out this thesis; the Democrats had a majority in both houses in 1948 and 1950, but fell to 49% of the membership in 1952. In 1954 their House majority was over 53% and their Senate majority just over 50%, the margin of one seat. In 1956, the Senate division remained the same but the Democrats increased their House margin to 54%. In 1958, the swing back to large Democratic majorities occurred with over 65% of the Senate and nearly 65% in the House. This was the largest Democratic victory in both houses since the depression elections of the 1930's.

Projecting this rising tide raises interesting questions. Will the Democratic Party perpetually have a majority in Congress, since successive low points will be above 49% reached in 1952? Mr. Bean himself noted that the course of a tide is affected, in regard to both its high and low points, by economic conditions and political and social issues.[7]

Presidential and Congressional Voting. A well-known cycle in the midterm Congressional elections is that the "ins" lose seats to the "outs,"

---

[5] If anyone were inclined to rationalize the 1952 result, he can take note of the argument made in behalf of General Eisenhower's administrative and managerial ability as an offset to the alleged maladministration of Truman. Stevenson was a governor, an executive; but this fact in and of itself seemed to make little impression because the nature both of the man and his campaign did not emphasize this background.

[6] Louis Bean, *How to Predict Elections* (New York: Alfred A. Knopf, Inc., 1948) pp. 14–16, 18, 19.

[7] *Ibid.*, p. 35.

with only the year 1934 as a conspicuous exception. If the "outs" actually capture one or both houses of the Congress in the midterm election, the anticipated result is for the "outs" to win the Presidency two years later; this result has occurred twelve times in our history. On five occasions, however, the "ins" have lost one or both houses of Congress at mid-term but have held the Presidency and recaptured the Congress at the next election.[8]

That the election of a Congress and the election of a President are connected in their outcomes has long been demonstrated by the use of election statistics to show the strength or weakness of a presidential candidate as compared with the vote cast for members of Congress of the candidate's party. According to Mr. Bean whose conclusions may appear to be more precise than the actual statistics warrant, a shift of 5% in the vote for a Democratic presidential candidate resulted, on the average, in a 10% shift in the Democrats' membership in the House of Representatives.[9] Even without reliance upon such assertedly exact figures, the standard conclusion has been that a presidential candidate who runs ahead of his party's candidates for Congress has carried them into office on his coattails and vice versa. Most frequently, however, the coattail influence is seen to be the presidential candidate's, not the congressional candidates'; furthermore, the influence of the presidential candidate on the ticket is often given as the main reason why the "ins" lose seats in the mid-term elections.[10] It is a matter of record that since the last decade of the nineteenth century, the electorate has almost consistently elected a President and a majority in Congress of the same party, the outstanding exception being 1956.[11]

Difficulties with Coattail Analyses. Conclusions regarding coattail influence have not been wholly valid and have missed other factors; but they have been adopted because they seem plausible. The fact that a presidential candidate receives more votes than the congressional candidates of his party has been glibly assumed to be conclusive evidence that the former carried the latter into office with him simply because he received more votes. A successful presidential candidate runs ahead of his congressional candidates an average of 7%. If one presidential candidate leads his congressional

---

[8] The years of these five mid-term elections were 1794, 1854, 1874, 1878, 1946. See Cortez A. M. Ewing, *Congressional Elections, 1896-1944* (Norman: University of Oklahoma Press, 1947) pp. 23-26. In 1954 the Democrats captured Congress and held control in 1956 even though they could not recapture the Presidency.

[9] *Op. cit.*, p. 20. He contended the usual relation was that 69% of the Democratic candidates for Congress were elected when the Democratic presidential candidate received 59% of the popular, two-party vote. *Ibid.*, p. 68.

[10] Bean even concluded that during the Roosevelt period in the 1930's and 1940's, the Democrats' loss of seats in the mid-term election equaled the number carried into office in presidential years on the Roosevelt coattails.——*Ibid.*, pp. 32, 34, 54; Malcolm Moos, *Politics, Presidents and Coattails* (Baltimore: The Johns Hopkins Press, 1952) p. 108.

[11] "Why An Ike Win and a Democratic Congress?" C. Q. Fact Sheet, May 6, 1957.

ticket, the other candidate will trail his.[12] This situation suggests a reversed coattail influence in the two parties, a departure from the standard concept, and can only be explained in terms of the greater interest and participation generated in a presidential year.[13]

To be more strict about presidential coattail influence requires more and different kinds of information; specifically, how many voters vote for a Democrat or Republican candidate for Congress because they support the same party's candidate for President.[14] To have much confidence in any conclusions, it is necessary to know a great deal more about the voters. From an examination of election returns in New York State, it appeared that candidates for minor offices exerted the coattail influence, although they actually did not when the figures were more carefully examined.

> The independence of thought the public uses in making its choice for the top of the ticket seems to diminish progressively as its fingers move across the voting machines toward the nominees for lesser office. For example, in Democratic New York City the Democratic majorities, though not the total vote cast, increase in each assembly district the farther one gets away from the head of the ticket, so that many an anonymous assemblyman has won by a greater margin than Roosevelt. . . . And in up-state Republican territory a candidate on the GOP ticket for the same office would always win by more votes than Tom Dewey.[15]

The rule that the "ins" lose members of Congress at mid-term and gain members in the presidential-election year makes coattail influence inevitable. The measure of the influence, however, is neither the net difference between votes cast for presidential and congressional candidates nor the difference in the sheer number of members of Congress elected between mid-term and the presidential year, but the number of members carried into office by the presidential candidate.

Left-Right Cycles. Inasmuch as contrasting political developments cannot always be associated with different parties, trends and swings can be charted without particular reference to the tide of party fortunes. Professor Arthur M. Schlesinger, Sr., developed a comprehensive cyclical pattern in historical periods which were, alternately, left and right. His method of distinguishing the periods is that a leftward direction emphasizes

---

[12] Moos, op. cit., pp. 121-124; also pp. 10-13.

[13] Ibid., p. 5.

[14] Angus Campbell and Warren E. Miller, "The Motivational Basis of Straight and Split Ticket Voting," American Political Science Review, Vol. 51 (1957) pp. 293-312. Charles Press, "Voting Statistics and Presidential Coattails," ibid., Vol. 52 (1958) pp. 1041-1050.

[15] Warren Moscow, Politics in the Empire State (New York: Alfred A. Knopf, Inc., 1948) pp. 39-40. Moscow further elucidated this situation by pointing out that in a one-party unit such as a county, independent and opposition voters vote only for state offices and not for offices in the unit, while party regulars vote for all offices. Furthermore, independents are more likely not to vote for minor offices if they do not know the candidates.

human welfare through a relatively rapid movement in reform and a rightward period emphasizes the welfare of property by, relatively, slowing down reform action in order to exploit and consolidate the reforms of the preceding period. The years of these pulsating contrasts are as follows:

LEFT	RIGHT
1765-1787	
	1787-1801
1801-1816	
	1816-1829
1829-1841	
	1841-1861
1861-1869	
	1869-1901
1901-1919	
	1919-1931
1931-1947	
	(1947-1962)
(1962-1978)	
	(1978–)

The projection of these swings is made possible by Professor Schlesinger's computations of the average duration of a period. The average length of all the periods up to 1948 was 16.6 years, with the rightward periods averaging 18.2 years and the leftward periods averaging 15 years. If the two most uneven and unusual periods between 1861 and 1901 be eliminated, the average is 14.8 years and 16.2 years, respectively. It is on the basis of these figures that he predicts the approximate length of future periods.

What constitutes a left or a right position changes from time to time, and Professor Schlesinger notes that a process which is both periodic and progressive is more accurately portrayed as a spiral than as a swing of a pendulum on the same level. In any event, he concludes, the swing or spiral begins and runs its course irrespective of party changes, of foreign wars, of the size of the electorate, of the expansion of the nation across the continent, of the growth of transportation and communication systems, and of the expansion of education among the masses. There is no marked correlation between these national periods and similar periods in individual states as indicated by their rewriting and revising their constitutions. Data regarding cycles in nonpolitical phenomena, e.g., sun spots, field-mice plagues, and marriage rates, suggest that each one functions independently. In time the voters became tired or bored or disappointed with one line of development and then shift to the other line.[16]

---

[16] Arthur M. Schlesinger, *Paths to the Present* (New York: The Macmillan Company, 1949) pp. 80-92; Titus, *op. cit.*, pp. 268-271.

ELECTION UPHEAVALS

Aberrations in Voting. Human activities provide both the predictable and the unpredictable, the usual and the unusual. Habit and lethargy tie people to familiar patterns and spontaneous reactions. Occasionally some rare or unfathomable force intervenes and the normal patterns are no longer guides to the future. In politics these mass movements, under the proper stimulants, can cause an upheaval at election time and wrench the parties out of their accustomed grooves. Sometimes these upheavals are temporary and localized, aberrations in the chain of events rather than significant and fundamental breaks in the links of continuity. Candidates for office fear such developments and do not always foresee them. Now and then an incumbent is defeated for re-election and wonders plaintively what happened. There may be reasons, sufficient and substantial, for what happened, but candidates sometimes feel about the game of politics as Casey Stengel once expressed himself about the game of baseball:

> No one can explain winnin' or losin' streaks. When you're winnin', you're doin' everything right. You get every break imaginable. Even the baseball itself seems to cooperate, bouncin' away from their fielders in favor of your hitters or bouncin' into your fielders' gloves to stop their hitters. Then all of a sudden the slump comes. You seem to be doin' everything the same way, livin' right and drinkin' your orange juice. But something has happened and you can't find the handle to it.[17]

The historical, rather than the contemporary, view is often more productive for the analyst. With the advantage of perspective and a more complete record, the factors which entered into an upheaval can be better appreciated and their relative merits more accurately assessed.[18] Professor Holcombe noted the tendency of voters slavishly to follow their partisan commitments during the 1850's, and then how they broke lifetime habits in the election of 1860 by voting for Lincoln. "In all of those states . . . where the Democracy had been most firmly intrenched in power in 1852, the Republicans had become by 1860 the dominant party." Such an upheaval is important because it signifies permanent changes. "It is only great causes that can produce great effects. There must have been much thinking to have brought about this extraordinary change (in 1860) in the habits of men." [19]

---

[17] Quoted in Arthur Daley, "Philosophy of C. Stengel," *New York Times Magazine,* July 26, 1953, p. 14.

[18] A case in point was the attempt to explain the outcome of the 1952 presidential election in Michigan and Ohio metropolitan centers. Since Stevenson received more votes on the Democratic ticket than Truman had received in 1948, analysts were attempting to locate the source of the expanded Republican vote in 1952 which overwhelmed the Democrats. See *Ibid.,* November 9, 1952.

[19] Arthur N. Holcombe, *The Political Parties of To-Day* (New York: Harper & Brothers, 1924) p. 175.

These upheavals deserve respectful consideration in any discussion of bipartisanism. They are culminations of forces, the points of explosion, which commands attention for its own dramatic qualities. Upheavals are the signs that a turning point has been reached and that a new direction of events is to follow. Nevertheless, they may come stealthily or unobtrusively and those who are responsible for them may be just as surprised as anybody else. We encounter the curious situation of voters who discover after the ballots are counted that the preponderance of their fellow countrymen felt approximately the same way they did.

Business Conditions. The only political question about upheavals is what causes them. The answers are not mutually consistent, but Professor Salter expressed the view that is as near to orthodoxy as any:

> It is only depressions or catastrophes that can, as a rule, generate enough energy to arouse the people out of their lethargy, indifference, or traditional way of voting. . . . Depressions are invariably hostile to the political party in power and can effect a reform where mere revelations of corruption fail. Any economic maladjustment is sure to be a tremendously powerful agent for change, and a general house cleaning. . . . When this most sensitive pocketbook nerve is touched, . . the voter is pricked to action and he votes against the party in power. . . .[20]

From another, unrelated source, we have the unqualified observation that "prosperity absorbs all criticism" and that the "ins," if they normally have a majority, cannot be beaten unless they are unlucky or stupid.

> Proof of corruption, allegations and proof of incapacity, of waste, of false pretense and of party promises broken or unfulfilled—all fall harmlessly to the ground in times of great prosperity. The people as a whole are not interested in politics under such conditions and cannot be stirred into activity by any ordinary political issue. They lack a grievance. They have nothing to vote against . . . .
> [Conversely] to the party in power there is no greater menace than an industrial depression. When work is scarce, wages low and unemployment widely prevalent the whole temper of the American voter is changed. His interest in politics is quickened to the extent of trying to find something on which to blame his hard luck. And when he goes to the polls under such conditions he goes, as every precinct executive worth his salt well knows, 'to hit' somebody. What this means of course is to vote against the party in power. It is the natural and, in fact, the sole available target for his resentment. Just as unreasoningly as he is willing to credit the administration with good times, he cordially puts upon it full responsibility for the bad ones.[21]

Louis Bean, in applying his statistical techniques to this problem, was convinced that "our economy is in a literal sense a political economy" and

---

20 J. T. Salter, *Boss Rule* (New York: McGraw-Hill Book Company, 1935) pp. 220-221.
21 Frank R. Kent, *Political Behavior* (New York: William Morrow & Company, Inc., 1928) pp. 111-112, 117-118; see in general Chap. 11.

A depression beat Van Buren.

Hoover supporters in 1932 saw but could not lick
prosperity issue.

Gillam in Judge

William Jennings Bryan fell like Don
Quixote before McKinley's slogan and
national good times.

Poinier in The Detroit News

Democrats again bank on the historical
lift of prosperity in an election year.

THE PROSPERITY ISSUE IN PRESIDENTIAL CAMPAIGNS. Cartoons taken from
New York Times Magazine, August 24, 1952.

that "Greater economic stability in the future would mean greater political stability." In three elections since World War I every state has shifted its position—"In 1932 the Democratic vote was larger in every state than in 1928. In 1920 the Republican vote in every state was larger than in 1916." [22] In each of these years there was a depression and in each year a party over-turn occurred. In 1952, when the Republican vote was larger in every state than it had been in 1948, there was no depression. At best, one would conclude, a depression is not the only cause for such upheavals.

That people who are economically discontented engage in protest voting and that protest voting means voting against the "ins" as the most convenient symbols of responsibility is widely accepted both in major-party and in minor-party voting. Farmer and labor parties have been, universally, protest movements; their appeal has been made to farmers and workers who have been on the verge of financial collapse and of subsistence living or who have been dispossessed and unemployed. The relations between the votes for parties of protest and, respectively, wholesale prices in general, prices of farm products, business activity, and ratio of farm to nonfarm prices were chartered for a 130-year period.[23] It was found that the relation was closest when the economy was slipping in terms of both the price level and a business recession, but that before the bottom of the downward slide was reached "one or both of the major parties recognized the wide-spread character of the discontent" and then "the vote for farmer and labor parties tended to drop off sharply. Thus, the paradox that farmer and labor parties have tended to do most poorly at the very time when an economic determinist might be led to anticipate that they would do best." [24] Furthermore, according to these analyses, the relation between economic adversity and protest votes for minor parties was not so exact as Mr. Bean had claimed in major-party voting during the 1930's. "Economic man is not so carefully tuned to the times that a ten-point change in a Bureau of Labor Statistics index will result in a ten-point change in voting behavior."[25]

A further attempt to develop a formula governing the relation between economics and voting behavior was made by Professors F. A. Pearson and W. I. Myers of Cornell University. Their findings are that prosperity, for

---

22 Bean, op. cit., pp. 17-18, 57. During the depression of the 1930's Bean found that "the Democrats gained 16 per cent of the total seats in the House for every 10 per cent rise in unemployment. . . . with every increase of a million in unemployment the Republicans lost 14 seats in Congress." Admitting the presence of other factors, he was convinced that in the shift in party fortunes in congressional elections, "the business factor has been consistently dominant." Pp. 24, 55-56.

23 Murray S. Stedman, Jr., and Susan W. Stedman, Discontent at the Polls, a Study of Farmer and Labor Parties, 1827-1948 (New York: Columbia University Press, 1950) Chap. 5.

24 Ibid., p. 101.

25 Ibid., p. 100.

presidential-election purposes, is determined by high or rising commodity prices and by expanding activity in building construction; prices have been a more consistent indicator. In the thirty-two elections from 1824 to 1948, they found, the major-party battles were determined in this manner: The "ins" lost seven elections when both indicators were low or falling and won thirteen elections when both were high or rising; the "ins" lost four elections when construction was rising and commodity prices falling and won four elections when construction was falling and prices high or rising.

Four elections are left unaccounted for, those in 1824, 1852, 1876, and 1912. The Pearson-Myers formula cannot take into account other factors than the two economic indicators, and the authors freely admit that minor parties, for example, may throw off the calculations. In 1824 a price decline suggested a victory for Jackson, the bona fide candidate of the "outs." He did receive a plurality both of the popular and of the electoral votes, but not a majority, because of the division of the electoral votes among four candidates; the House of Representatives chose John Quincy Adams as President. In 1852 a price rise indicated that the Whigs, the "ins," would win, but they lost. In 1876 a decline boded ill for the Republicans who were the "ins," but in the negotiations following the famous disputed election the Republican candidate received a majority of the electoral votes; actually the Democratic candidate was conceded a majority of the popular vote, but the widespread irregularities in casting and counting ballots that year makes it impossible to know for sure which candidate should properly have been elected. Economic conditions in 1912 were favorable for the "ins," but Theodore Roosevelt's leading a minor-party movement insured the success of the Democrats, the "outs." Applying the formula to 1948, the authors saw a victory for the "ins," i.e., for Truman, but hedged in their predictions because of the potential effect of the two new minor parties of that year.[26]

Looking back upon this record, Professors Pearson and Myers found that only 1852 was a true exception because complicating factors were not present and because the price level, though low, was rising. The election exactly a hundred years later also raised a question of another genuine exception. The formula suggested that the "ins" would win, although the indicators were mixed. Prices were still high and construction falling—the situation on four previous occasions when the "ins" had won. However, prices had been declining and taxes were at an all-time peak for a peace year—an unknown factor in itself, just as were the issues of corruption and Communism against the Democrats and the personality of General Eisen-

---

[26] *New York Times*, October 31, 1948.

hower.[27] The inconclusiveness of the formula in 1952, when its authors hedged because of the other factors they could not calculate, gave rise to the rejoinder that such explanations cannot be scientifically systematized and that the formula is a "pseudo-scientific gadget," "a simple and highly obvious generalization." [28] Some of the trouble for analysts, in addition to extraneous influences which cannot be measured, is the spotty nature of prosperity or depression in some years: one industry, one crop, one section of the country may not have felt the effect of the trends by election day.

Qualification of and opposition to the "pocketbook vote" thesis have made an appearance from time to time. The fascinating feature of this disagreement is the use of statistics to support diametrically opposite cases. Using the same election-year party percentages Louis Bean had used, two writers found that the correlation of election results and business activity were either insignificant or absent.[29] Another analyst charted the turnover of the "ins" in selected congressional districts for the years 1878-1888 and 1904-1911 by a method of correlation believed to be "a rough measure of the extent to which party popularity will vary," and concluded "that party popularity does vary with fluctuations in business conditions. When elections occur during or just following periods of expansion, other things being equal, the party in power may expect a vote of confidence" and vice versa during periods of depression.[30]

The tumult and the correlations notwithstanding, there is sufficient reason for party managers of the "in" party to worry about voters who are

---

27 See news account and Arthur Krock's column in *ibid.*, October 14, 1952. The authors felt that declining taxes in 1948, increasing purchasing power, created sympathy for the "ins," but that the reverse conditions in 1952 created sympathy for the "outs." Professor Pearson noted the incompatibility of his "pocketbook vote" analysis and the emphasis upon the "independent vote," contending that the latter was "greatly overrated" and that the former, containing two to four million voters, was the deciding factor.——*Ibid.*, October 29, 1952. The confusion in interpreting the effect of economic conditions was pointed up in 1952, when average earnings of factory workers rose to an all-time high but farm prices dropped significantly after July.——*Ibid.*, October 24, 1952; October 30, 1952; January 4, 1953; Associated Press dispatch, dated September 30, 1952.

28 Edward H. Collins in the *New York Times*, October 20, 1952.

29 Thomas Wilkinson and Hornell Hart, "Prosperity and Political Victory," *Public Opinion Quarterly*, Vol. 14 (1950) pp. 331–335. Compare the figures in Bean, *op. cit.*, pp. 55–56.

30 Clark Tibbetts, "Majority Votes and the Business Cycle," *American Journal of Sociology*, Vol. 36 (1931) p. 605. An "in" was considered a representative of either party who was running for re-election, but this is a somewhat misleading view since the blame is usually party-wide for the party holding the White House. For example, applying Tibbetts' method to the congressional elections of 1930, when a depression was already in progress, either a Democrat or a Republican would be considered the "in" for a district if he was elected in 1928; however, the "ins," who bore the brunt of the blame were the Republicans, and the effect of the depression voting would be determined by computing the Republican districts captured by Democrats. Democrats running for re-election would be part of the "out" party, nationally speaking, and would benefit from the attack upon the "ins."

having financial difficulties. A vote cast at a time of economic frustration, insecurity, or poverty is likely to be against the policies and officeholders associated with the misfortune. The votes of discontented and fearful people are likely to flow in a stream to the "outs," and a large enough mass shift of voters will take place to shear the majority of the "ins" or to make them the minority. To deny the effect of the pocketbook upon voting is analogous to denying the effect of air upon the lungs. The search for patterns and precise relationships may lead us astray, but the basic importance of the voter's mental state as conditioned by his economic state cannot be ignored.

Upheavals and Dissatisfaction. Upheavals by their nature are revolts against the *status quo,* and therefore against the "ins" who are associated with and considered responsible for the *status quo.* A reaffirmation of the "ins" is normally a manifestation of satisfaction with the way things are going and in no proper sense an upheaval within the electorate. By extension, an upheaval is usually a period of political ferment—the very opposite of times of contentment when political interest and participation decline. The possibilities of stirring up enthusiasm for what already exists are decidedly limited, but in times of troubles the possibilities for arousing people to feverish activity are virtually unlimited. A sense of satisfaction does not drive a person to vote, but a sense of being mistreated or victimized certainly impels one to act to the extent of casting a ballot. Because of these distinctions in the patterns of contented and discontented voting, the election of 1936 is worth special notice because it amounted to an upheaval in favor of the "ins." Comparing 1936 with 1932, there was an increase both in the total vote cast and in the percentage cast for the Democrats; in 1932 the Republicans had been overwhelmed by the depression issue, but were even further eclipsed in 1936 when better times redounded to the advantage of the "ins." The spontaneous outpouring in 1936 was a tremendous expression by a more satisfied electorate of the benefits achieved and the promises of other benefits yet to come.

Voting Turnout. Shifts in the results of elections can in many cases be attributed to the number of voters. Lack of interest, keeping people from the polls, can result in ups and downs for the party in power as demonstrated by the tendency for the "outs" to gain in midterm elections when the total vote cast is smaller than in presidential-election years. Refusal to vote or indifference about voting affects outcomes in a negative manner, and as a phenomenon of mass inaction, it is quite as important as the opposite phenomenon of mass action. Indications of a heavy turnout often furrow the brows of party managers, particularly if the reasons for the unusual interest are obscure. An angry electorate is likely to be a voting electorate, and angry voters bode ill for some candidates or for one of the parties as a whole.

Conflicting Tensions. The complexity of mass reaction is more clearly suggested in such an election as that of 1940, when the third-term issue collided with a dangerous international situation. The first issue motivated against the "ins," while the second issue was advantageous for the "ins." Limiting the equation artificially to these two influences, the fear of the future overcame the respect for the past represented by the two-term tradition. The new high in voting participation in 1940 reflected a disturbed state of mind largely unrelated to business conditions, inasmuch as the real upturn from the depression of the 1930's was just beginning. It is remarkable that in two consecutive elections, 1936 and 1940, the Democrats, as the "in" party, were able to profit rather than suffer from the disturbed thinking of the people, although in 1940 the Democratic percentage of the vote fell sharply from that of 1936.[31]

Effect of War Issues. International issues involving the possibility of war are always sensitive questions in campaigns. While a war is going on, the "ins" have been able to hold their ground, but in the elections following the war, there is the strong prospect of at least a minor upheaval. Defeat of the "ins" associated with wars has usually occurred during the normal postwar slackening of business. When the business slump coincides with an election, the prospects of the "outs" are good, e.g., 1848 and 1920. When prosperity continues through the election, the prospects of the "ins" are good, e.g., 1900, 1948. Wars can develop a backwash of sentiment, as World War I obviously did, and the shift of sentiment from wartime idealism to postwar disillusionment was as definite a factor as the economic situation in the defeat of the "ins" in 1920.

Personalities. The personal influence and the effect of candidates' personalities are almost always a matter of importance. The personality of Franklin D. Roosevelt was so consistently referred to that an almost legendary basis was laid for the assertion that the man himself stimulated voters' support. In the same vein, the personality of Dwight D. Eisenhower was constantly advanced as an explanation for his election in 1952. Such assertions are always plausible, but are incapable of satisfactory documentation. The supporters of such a candidate emphasize the magnetism of his personality, but how many votes are won by the personality per se is really unknown. In contrast, the opponents of such a candidate may actively attack the same personality characteristics. Many great or commanding

---

[31] Bean, *op. cit.*, p. 69, estimated that the third-term issue cost the Democrats 1,000,000 to 1,500,000 votes or about 2½% of the total vote cast.

personalities who have sought the Presidency have been defeated; Henry Clay, Daniel Webster, James G. Blaine, and William Jennings Bryan lost to men who were uninspiring and stolid by comparison. A candidate is under the necessity of communicating his points of view to the electorate and will convey the main facets of his personality in the process, but the voters have accepted various kinds of men and have not insisted upon the most lucid, the most sparkling, the most charming. Personality may have a greater direct bearing in local elections, but personality alone is hardly capable of causing an upheaval at any level of government.

Disaffection and Dissatisfaction. The observation of marked trends in mass voting regularly turns up the conclusion that the causes are imbedded in discontent of one or another kind. Two discernible kinds are temporary disaffection within a party and the culmination of accumulated dissatisfactions. The first can occur within either the "ins" or the "outs," but the second naturally runs against the "ins." In 1904, the Republicans were, by any standard, likely to be kept in office by the voters. Business indicators were favorable and the Party was united under Theodore Roosevelt who had succeeded in capturing the nation's attention. The Democratic vote, however, fell off more than these factors alone warranted, and one cause can be found in the Party's internal difficulties that year. William Jennings Bryan, for the first of several times, was beaten by his opponents in the convention; the nomination went to Judge Alton B. Parker of New York, who was opposed to the Bryan wing of the Party. Because many Bryan followers either failed to vote or voted for Roosevelt in protest against Parker, their disaffection gave the election some of the characteristics of an upheaval which otherwise would have been lacking.

When general dissatisfactions finally pile up, the tide will turn against the "ins." It may be that the crowning event creating such dissatisfaction is a business depression, but not necessarily. Unquestionably, dissatisfactions existed in 1912 with the Taft Administration even though business was good. Both the Democrats and the Progressives under Theodore Roosevelt capitalized on the situation; the bolting Republicans disassociated themselves from the regular Republicans as the "in" party and ran second in the voting. In 1948 even with prosperity there were tensions capable of being developed into numerous dissatisfactions; but on this occasion President Truman succeeded in putting the Republicans in the role of the "ins" and exploited his advantage to the full—the protest voting was in many cases directed against Governor Dewey. In all previous cases where party control was divided as between the legislative and executive branches, the voters had considered the party holding the executive branch to be the "in" party; in 1948 it was the legislative branch that was held responsible.

Restlessness. Dissatisfaction may be an expression of restlessness on the part of the voters. People can grow tired of the same faces, the same names, and the same kinds of pronouncements. Boredom may produce a kind of agitation, a series of aimless movements designed to relieve the monotony. In casting about for a change, dissatisfactions are not difficult to find, and they may attach to circumstances which at other times have little influence. Charges of corruption against the Republicans in 1924 appeared to impress few voters, but the corruption issue in 1952 appeared to be a valuable issue for the "outs." In 1924 the Republicans had been in office four years; in 1952 the Democrats had been in office twenty years. The differences in the time element could have been important in the response to the corruption issue. All the evidence surrounding the 1952 election substantiates the view that an accumulation of dissatisfactions, including a type of inarticulate restlessness, can cause a party turnover. A true upheaval, in that it involved the whole population, took place in the voting booths that year, evidence of it being documented in the polls conducted by the Survey Research Center at the University of Michigan.

> The most striking impression gained from these tables is that the shift toward the Republicans in 1952 was a general one which affected many different classes of the population. Some components of the 'Democratic coalition'—skilled and semi-skilled workers, Catholics, young voters, union members—showed large scale deflections from their Democratic preference in 1948. The shift toward the Republicans was equally marked among groups which are not usually considered to be members of this 'coalition.' White collar workers, for example, went from an even vote distribution in 1948 to a ratio of almost 2 to 1 in favor of the Republicans; farmers, who had favored the Democrats in 1948, swung heavily into the Republican column in 1952. Except for the Negro group, the only groups which showed no shift in favor of the Republicans were those which already had a traditionally heavy Republican majority—the high status occupational and educational groups.[32]

LIMITATIONS OF THE MASS-BASIS ANALYSES

Insufficient Data. Whenever such assertions as some of those contained in this chapter are made, a natural response is to contest and dispute them. They are productive of dissent, first, because of the breadth of the generalities, and second, because of their challenge to those traditional values which have surrounded Americans' concept of their political system. At the outset the mass basis of bipartisanism, especially the cyclical theories, suffers from the shortness of United States history and the lack of substantive illustrations. So far there is not enough total or specific data to press

---

[32] Angus Campbell, *et al.*, "Political Issues and the Vote: November, 1952," *American Political Science Review*, Vol. 47 (1953) p. 379.

beyond certain hypotheses. In our desire to develop these analyses, we must patiently await more material evidence in the form of more swings and more causes of trends. In short, we await more history. A different kind of difficulty which more history is not likely to alleviate is the appearance of data inconsistent with main trends or cycles. At least some data cannot be accounted for by the principal generalizations. In addition, the methodology or the orientation of an analysis can turn up corroborative, puzzling, or contradictive finding regarding a political event.[33]

Separability and Interaction of Factors. Another fundamental limitation of the mass basis is the difficulty or in some cases the impossibility of segregating the causes of a result and evaluating them separately. Not only do we need to know the force of each factor affecting the outcome of elections but also the extent of their interrelatedness. Few have denied a connection between war weariness, satiation with high-flown concepts, and declining commodity prices as causes of Republican victory in 1920. In addition, normally Democratic voters, the Irish, were disaffected by the Treaty of Versailles and bolted in large numbers to the Republicans. Was this disaffection unrelated to or a tangent from the other influences? To answer a question like this, it would be necessary to hold the election over again with one of the factors eliminated. Unfortunately for the scientific impulse, the controlled experiment is impossible in such affairs; "the precise reasons why change was desired on that November day in 1920 are not recorded, not even in the memories of the individual voters." [34] No two elections are identical in their issues, their motivations, and their ideological environment. The frame of mind of the voter when he enters the polling place is still largely inscrutable to investigators and may not be entirely grasped by the voter himself. At least we cannot induce exactly the same mental condition again even if we know what it is. This struggle to separate factors, to determine their relation, and to assess their intrinsic importance will continue, but is not likely to be completely successful.

Distortions. Discussions of election trends, swings, and upheavals, whether on the national, state, or local level, are compromised by circum-

---

[33] Despite the upheavals recorded for the elections of 1932 to 1935, an analysis of the Chicago electorate in 1932 and 1934 revealed that only a relatively small part of the voters shifted parties. On relatively small differences, multiplied many times, are relatively large developments predicated.——H. F. Gosnell and N. N. Gill, "An Analysis of the 1932 Presidential Vote in Chicago," *American Political Science Review*, Vol. 29 (1935) pp. 967–984; H. F. Gosnell and M. J. Schmidt, "Factorial and Correlational Analysis of the 1934 Vote in Chicago," *Journal of the American Statistical Association*, Vol. 31 (1936) p. 518; Charles E. Merriam and Harold F. Gosnell, *The American Party System* (New York: The Macmillan Company, 1949, 4th ed.) pp. 141–145.

[34] Walter Lippmann, *Public Opinion* (New York: The Macmillan Company, 1922) p. 196.

stances which distort the total result. Every presidential and congressional election since the Civil War has to be qualified in some way by the traditional Democratic voting of the Solid South. It may be possible to measure trends in some of these Southern states by noting that the Republicans cast more or less than 15% or 20% of the votes, but these are special methods requiring special standards. The most convenient and sometimes most accurate results are obtained by eliminating the South altogether: e.g., in comparing the relative party strength in congressional voting, the Democrats always look good, even in a Republican year, if Southern votes are included, but a very different picture can be drawn by considering the votes cast in about thirty-six states outside of the South.

In analyzing party strength in legislatures, the process of districting those legislatures directly affects the data. Implicit in the act of reapportionment and redistricting is a certain amount of gerrymandering. Thus, the fact that a party captures a legislative body may prove the party's popularity or the fact may show the party's success in drawing district lines to accentuate its strength. The system of fixed terms of office obscures and distorts public political opinions. If an officeholder comes up for election at a time of discontent, he can anticipate a close race or defeat; if his term continues through the period of discontent, he may be out of danger by the time he runs. Overlapping terms in legislatures have the effect of holding back political trends. Obviously, a distortion is created when election returns are incorrectly reported, for whatever reason. Analyses simply have to be based on the assumption that the data available are accurate even though some data very likely are not.

A different class of distortions is found when state and local elections are interpreted in terms of national trends. In presidential elections, national issues are likely to permeate all parts of the Union and have some effect upon the outcome in widely separated localities. Without the unifying symbol of a presidential candidate, mid-term congressional and state elections are often decided by local and state issues. This fact explains many elections which otherwise are baffling; it also explains some cases of split-ticket voting both in presidential and nonpresidential years.

Resistance to the Implications. Finally, when all objections are pinpointed, they often lead back to one central objection. The implications of the mass basis are not nearly so flattering for man as many men would prefer. Cycle and upheaval theories, at least to some extent, carry with them the thesis that people are controlled by fate, by some kind of preordination, and that people are impotent creatures of extraneous and uncontrollable forces. The drive of the orderly mind to find and identify patterns of universal relationship is checked by the drive of the egocentric mind to assert individuality and independence. A formulation of a political system in which human beings are automatons ordered about by impersonal forces in the universe is not calculated to be received with human warmth. The attempt of a man to control or overcome the forces that beset him is always a stirring experience for both participants and observers unless they be confirmed fatalists.[35]

It can be argued that men's inability to predict what men will do should make it clear that we are not governed by impervious forces but can manage our own affairs; by rational evaluation of problems we can arrive at decisions which no one could have prophesied before the nature of the problem was known. Yet if these activities when marshaled and correlated reveal consistent patterns and demonstrate cycles, the assumed freedom of action which we think we exercise may prove to be illusory. After all, the validity of the mass basis of bipartisanism does not depend upon value judgments as to its desirability but upon the caliber of the evidence of its existence. The test is not that a particular cycle occurs *exactly* every 16.8 years or that an upheaval of a given type causes a shift in the total vote cast of *exactly* 25.2% or brings out *exactly* 20% more voters than a "normal" election. The test is whether certain relations can be perceived within the fog of multiple events; whether any kind of order can be induced from the apparent chaos of a chain of never-ending episodes. At least some leaders who seek the probable pattern of the future, so that they can anticipate eventualities in their planning, take seriously the discoveries of some of the cycles and upheavals as signs of the mass basis of bipartisanism.

Selected Bibliography

Bean, Louis H., *How to Predict Elections*. New York: Alfred A. Knopf, Inc., 1948.

Ewing, Cortez A. M., *Congressional Elections, 1896–1944*. Norman: University of Oklahoma Press, 1947.

——— *Presidential Elections*. Norman: University of Oklahoma Press, 1940.

Moos, Malcolm, *Politics, Presidents and Coattails*. Baltimore: The Johns Hopkins Press, 1952.

Robinson, E. E., *The Presidential Vote 1896–1932*. Stanford: Stanford University Press, 1934.

——— *They Voted for Roosevelt*. Stanford: Stanford University Press, 1947.

Schlesinger, Arthur M., *Paths to the Present*. New York: The Macmillan Company, 1949.

Stedman, Murray S., Jr., and Susan W. Stedman, *Discontent at the Polls*. New York: Columbia University Press, 1950.

Titus, Charles Hickman, *The Processes of Leadership*. Dubuque: William C. Brown Company, 1950.

---

[35] One of the explanations of the 1948 presidential election is that Truman by a resolute effort, overcame what was generally considered his inevitable defeat. The difficulty in passing this election off as a triumph over fate is the postelection indications that the men who measured political fate through polls and therefore helped to establish the conclusion as to what was fate, had failed somewhat in their task. According to the Pearson-Myers formula, fate was on Truman's side, not against him.

Election Campaigns

If a man solicits you earnestly for your vote, avoid him; self-interest and sordid avarice lurk under his forced smiles, hearty shakes by the hand, and deceitfully enquires after your wife and family.——ADVICE GIVEN TO FREEHOLDERS IN ACCOMAC COUNTY, VIRGINIA, 1771: quoted in Charles S. Sydnor, *Gentlemen Freeholders,* p. 46.

The influence of words over men is astounding.——NAPOLEON: quoted in Robert B. Holtman, *Napoleonic Propaganda,* p. 202.

CHAPTER EIGHTEEN

Suffrage and Voting

The two-party system in the United States operates in a framework molded by the characteristics of the people of this nation within the tradition of liberty (see Section I). The system has developed a particular set of techniques carried out through its own peculiar organizational machinery evolved out of Colonial experience with political operations (see Section II). The interaction of party and people has given rise to various methods for analyzing the political behavior of individuals and explaining the recorded results of their electoral decisions over the years (see Section III). Election campaigns are a synthesis of the parties' organizations and the bases of the bipartisan competition. It is this final area of party activity—election campaigns, including various related subjects—which is presented in the chapters of this section.

SUFFRAGE AND POLITICS

Electorate, Essential and Basic. In the philosophy of democracy which underlies representative government in the United States, there is both explicitly and implicitly a place for the individual to exercise his judgment in regard to government by exercising his voting franchise. The act of voting by the individual is intrinsically good, but as a means to an end, not as an end in itself. Voting must accomplish something, must reflect the popular will as a determinant of public policies. In order to have a party system there must be elections, and to have elections requires voters. All of these layers of functions and relations spring from and are justified as a machinery for permitting people to control their government. Voting is at the base, government at the summit. If some other form of human organization could be invented, all of this expenditure of effort and time could be dispensed with; but the only known form is the human operation controlled by the freely expressed opinions of the human being within the system. This is the relationship of the values, but practice with the mechanics often twists our perceptions and understanding. By emphasizing the party system, we see voters as cogs in the bipartisan machinery. Since the division of the electorate determines the outcome of elections, the process of influencing the electorate is the constant and the highest objective of the politician. The electorate is king, but it is made an instrument upon which its servants practice all the arts of opinion-making in an effort to lead the Ruler, in an effort to convince him which choices he should make.

Theories of Voting. Despite the emphasis in representative government upon the desirability of voting, there is an equally strong concept that eligibility should be restricted, that not everyone should be permitted to vote. This attitude toward the exercise of the suffrage clearly sets it off from the attitude toward civil rights. Generally speaking, every person, citizen or alien, irrespective of age or condition, is entitled to the protections of civil-rights provisions of the constitutions under whose jurisdiction he lives or finds himself; but specific qualifications are laid down in the same constitutions to determine which people are eligible to vote. This difference is the basis for the distinction made between civil *rights* and the *privilege* of voting, even though voting often is spoken of as a right. The legal situation is that people have no unqualified right to vote, but if a person can and does fulfill the legal requirements for voting, he then has a legal right to vote. The acceptance of this status for the act of voting, the acceptance of the doctrine of exclusion and inclusion, is found in all of the theories of voting. The earliest, that of the Greek city-states, included all citizens but excluded all those who were not citizens. Subsequent theories have distinguished not only between citizens (or subjects) and noncitizens but also among citizens. These theories have relied upon such standards as social status (e.g., ownership of land); abstract right, i.e., a person is entitled to vote as he is entitled to other rights of man; by the will of the state, whereby voting becomes a function of citizenship to be exercised for the good of the state.[1] Within the history of the United States, these last three theories have at one time or another been applied.

STANDARDS FOR VOTING REQUIREMENTS

It is the usual belief in the twentieth century that economic qualifications are indefensible because they disfranchise such a large number, and what is equally evil, disfranchise them because they have failed to acquire a sufficient amount of worldly goods. This general judgment results from the projection backward into time of current standards of values which were not the standard at the historical time being discussed. The judgment may also overlook the fact that at the time of the economic qualifications either the numbers excluded were not as great or their exclusion was not

---

[1] Charles Seymour and Donald Paige Frary, *How the World Votes* (Springfield: C. A. Nichols Company, 1918) Chap. 1. Kirk H. Porter, *A History of Suffrage in the United States* (Chicago: University of Chicago Press, 1918) pp. 5-6. As a matter of fact, some element of the Greek theory of voting was also present in the compulsory-voting laws of Colonial America. See below, Chap. 23.

as undesirable as later generations may conclude.[2] Even the theory that voting is one of the rights of men draws some lines on the basis of maturity; in addition, there is a concept that voting is an act in concert with the group or community and requires some identification of the voter with his fellow voters. Whatever the theory, the element of *acceptance* by the group is the condition required for exercising suffrage. How this identification by and acceptance of the voter is determined can vary widely. Progressively, the standard for determination has been divorced from economic qualifications. Furthermore, other kinds of standards assume more or less importance from time to time: for instance, a religious qualification was once required, but has long been disparaged and prohibited. There may also be a time lag between the existing legal requirements and those the people have come to believe are useful and worth enforcing.[3] With the passing of the freehold or other economic qualifications, voting requirements took on a new guise, for the electorate began being determined solely on the basis of individual factors and of individual equality.[4]

Federal Provisions. The first fact about suffrage in the United States is that the requirements are determined in each state by its constitution, the legislature usually being prohibited from adding to these provisions. The *United States Constitution makes no positive provisions,* but instead adopts the voting requirements in each state as the requirements for voting for federal officers, i.e., members of Congress. When the Constitution was written in 1787 the only federal officials to be elected by the voters were members of the House of Representatives, who, it was provided, should be chosen by "the electors [voters] in each State [who] shall have the qualifications requisite for electors of the most numerous branch of the State

[2] Charles S. Sydnor, *Gentlemen Freeholders* (Chapel Hill: University of North Carolina Press, 1952) pp. 29–31, 36–37, 123, concluded that in Colonial Virginia the landowning requirements were really not very restrictive because of the cheapness of land; nor did the requirements favor the rich but were intended to restrict the very rich by disfranchising their landless "tenants and retainers," who presumably would have voted as the landowners directed. "This much is plain: the political system of eighteenth-century Virginia was admirably suited to the social order which existed in eighteenth-century Virginia. And the political devices used, no matter what their theoretical value for other times and places, made this political system work."——P. 122; Dudley O. McGovney, *The American Suffrage Medley* (Chicago: University of Chicago Press, 1949) contended that "the practical effect of these restrictions . . . is that not over half of the adult white men in the United States were eligible to vote in 1787. . . . Voting was limited to the middle and upper economic levels." Slaves, Negroes, Indians, and white indentured servants were disfranchised.——Pp. 16–17. See above pp. 59–60.

[3] Sydnor, *op. cit.,* pp. 28–29, noted that the exclusion of dissenters in Virginia was not enforced, so that enfranchising them was not accompanied by a marked increase in the vote cast.

[4] Porter, *op. cit.,* pp. 20–21. Until 1851 in Virginia, a man could vote in every county in which he had enough land to qualify, if he could be present on Election Day.——Sydnor, *op. cit.,* p. 34. The rule of one person, one vote is rigidly accepted now.

legislature." [5] When the Seventeenth Amendment was added in 1913 to require direct election of senators, the identical wording was repeated regarding eligibility of voters. All other federal officials are appointed except the President, who is elected by specially chosen presidential electors.

The Constitution, however, does place *two specific limits upon the states in fixing their requirements.* The Fifteenth Amendment prohibits the exclusion of people from the franchise because of "race, color, or previous condition of servitude," and the Nineteenth Amendment contains the same provision in respect to sex. The effect of these two prohibitions upon the states is not that all races or all women must be eligible to vote, but that if they are ineligible, it must be for some other reason than their race or sex.

There are two additional limitations upon the states. First, the equal protection clause of the Fourteenth Amendment has been applied, independently of the Fifteenth, to prohibit racial discrimination in voting. Second, Article I, Section 4, of the Constitution, giving Congress the authority to determine the "times, places and manner" of choosing members of Congress has been interpreted to mean that although qualifications of individuals are governed by state law, the right to vote in a federal election is derived from the United States Constitution. Holding state and federal elections simultaneously does not limit Congress's power; rather, Congress and the states exercies concurrent authority over federal elections. The right to vote for members of Congress is protected against actions of individuals as well as actions by the states because the provision of Article I, Section 4, is stated without restriction or limitation. The Fourteenth Amendment limits only state action and the Fifteenth limits only state and federal action.[6]

State Provisions. Voting qualifications, determined separately by each state, cannot be completely uniform throughout the country, but the kinds of qualifications are generally the same. The variations are found in the detailed provisions.

---

[5] *Constitution of the United States,* Art. I, Sec. 2, par. 1. The significance of the qualification that voters were eligible to vote for candidates for the House if eligible to vote for members "of the most numerous branch of the State legislature" was the practice for a number of years in some states of having a minimum property requirement to vote for the lower or more numerous house and a larger property requirement to vote for the upper or smaller house. The provision in the Constitution, therefore, was the least restrictive of the suffrage, for it included anyone who was likely to have any voting rights. Regarding the practice of having different qualifications to vote for different offices, Porter, *op. cit.,* p. 111, noted the effort in Massachusetts in 1853 to retain taxpaying qualifications for town meeting. "They seemed not to care so much who voted for president and governor, but only the best men in the community should vote for hogreeve."

[6] *Ex parte Yarbrough,* 110 U. S. 651 (1884); *U. S. v. Classic,* 313 U. S. 299 (1941).

Voters must be *citizens of the United States* by birth, naturalization, or derivation except in West Virginia, where they are required to be state citizens. The question of the timing of admission to citizenship in relation to elections is answered by the provision of federal law that naturalization proceedings are not to take place within sixty days of a general election. A few states require that the status of citizenship be acquired from thirty to ninety days before an election.

Every state requires a *minimum period of residence* in the state and usually in the county or town and often in the election precinct. The length of time for living in the state varies from six months to two years, a one-year requirement being the most frequent; [7] county or town residence varies from twenty days to one year, the average being two or three months; election-district residence varies from requiring a person to vote in the district in which he lives, without specification of time, to as high as six months. In 1958 the voters of California amended the state constitution to authorize the legislature to permit persons to vote for President and Vice-President after living in the state only fifty-four days (the residence requirement for the election district) if they are otherwise qualified to vote under California law. Residence normally means the place of one's home or domicile, whether one is physically present at the place or not. The general rule is that residence is neither gained nor lost by presence or absence while a member of the Armed Forces or while a student at an institution of learning. Inmates of public or private institutions normally do not establish voting residence except for domiciles in soldiers' and sailors' homes and in old-age homes in some states.

The *minimum age requirement* is no longer uniform. People who otherwise qualify are eligible to vote at age twenty-one in forty-six states. The voting age is eighteen in Georgia and Kentucky, nineteen in Alaska, and twenty in Hawaii.

A *system of registration* of voters is provided in forty-eight states, and Alaska will be added when the legislature implements the provision of the state constitution authorizing registration. Arkansas and Texas do not provide for registration separately from the poll-tax system. North Dakota abolished its registration requirement in 1951.

Technically, registration itself is not a requirement for voting but is a method for determining who has met the requirements or will meet them by election day. However, a qualified voter who does not register cannot

---

[7] Three states require two years: Alabama, Mississippi, and South Carolina. Twelve states require six months: Idaho, Indiana, Iowa, Kansas, Maine, Michigan, Minnesota, Nebraska, Nevada, New Hampshire, New Jersey, and Oregon. The remaining thirty-five states have a one-year requirement.

vote; so for all practical purposes, registration amounts to a requirement. The necessity for a registration system arose with the increase in population, its density in urban places, and its mobility. In small communities where people are well acquainted, the election officials will certainly know those who appear at the polling place and will know if they are qualified under the laws to vote. Being friends and neighbors, the officials will recognize someone who comes back to repeat or to vote for someone else. In larger and certainly in the largest communities, most of the voters are strangers to the election officials, who cannot know whether the people asking for ballots are qualified or not. Registration became necessary to prevent the various election frauds which are encouraged by lack of any objective means of identification. Since this is the basic justification, registration may be mandatory throughout a state for all elections, including direct primaries and local elections; it may be mandatory only in cities or counties above a specified population and no more than optional in cities and counties under this population; it may be mandatory for general elections but not used for the direct primary.[8]

REGISTRATION PROCEDURES. A public official such as a county or city clerk or a local election commission or board is normally designated by law as responsible for registering voters and transporting the records to the voting precincts on election day. When the voter registers, he gives data to identify himself and prove his eligibility to vote; in some states he must declare a party affiliation, so that it can be noted on his record if he wishes to vote in a direct primary. He may, if there is any question, be compelled to provide legal documents or affidavits of other citizens to prove his eligibility. In any event, in the registration process the voter swears to the accuracy of the data he gives so that an ineligible person who registers commits perjury. In some states the voter is given a card to show that he registered, and he may be requested to produce it when he appears at the polls. The record of his registration is made either on a card in a card-index file or on a sheet of paper kept in a loose-leaf book. This record is taken from the central registration office to the appropriate precincts on election day so that the election-precinct officials have it before them when the voters appear. In some New England towns a list of voters is prepared and published, permitting correction before election.[9] Otherwise, a person

---

8 See Joseph P. Harris, *Registration of Voters in the United States* (Washington, D. C.: Brookings Institution, 1929) pp. 4-16; see Chap. 3 for the history of registration.

9 This method is reminiscent of the early Colonial practice in New Hampshire and Maryland of naming the persons qualified to vote in each town or district at the time of issuing writs or announcements of an election. In Colonial South Carolina all voters' names

must accomplish his own registration, although about half of the states permit him to do it by mail or through another person in the cases of members of the Armed Forces and of those who are ill or in some unusual circumstance.

Although registration usually goes on continuously, there is a cutoff date about one month before an election, after which no more registrations are taken, in order that the records may be prepared for election day. For a period of time before the cutoff date there is a publicity campaign to remind and urge eligible voters to register if they have not done so; as a part of this campaign, subsidiary registration points may be established at more convenient locations, even on street corners. In Oregon, house-to-house canvasses are used.

REGISTRATION SYSTEMS. Two general types or *systems of registration* are in operation. The more widespread type is *permanent* registration. After a voter registers once, he does not have to register again unless he moves his residence (if he moves within his precinct or county, state laws are about evenly divided on the necessity for re-registration), changes his name through marriage, divorce or legal process; fails to vote either in a given number of elections or over a given period of years. This system is less demanding upon the voter if he keeps his registration valid and is less onerous for the persons responsible for keeping the records because they need only add registrants to the rolls and delete those whose eligibility has ended. To say that the public officials in charge of registration have "only" to keep the records current is not to belittle the great amount of work this process entails. In practice the usual method of purging the rolls is to watch obituary notices and delete names of persons deceased. A more ambitious and accurate method, used in some states, is checking upon the mobility of people through the postal authorities and private transit companies; about one half of the states authorize house-to-house inquiries to determine that the registered voters are still alive and living at the same address. The implications of names of ineligible voters being left on the rolls are obvious. While the oversight may be the result of carelessness, corruption is made easier by the practices of voting the graveyard and voting in the names of those who have moved away or who habitually do not vote.

The second and less popular type of registration is *periodic*. At stated intervals all of the registration records become invalid and all voters must re-register. The valid period of time varies from annual registration in New York in towns of 5,000 and over to ten years in South Carolina. In some states, a combination of both permanent and periodic registration is used,

---

were "fairly entered in a book or roll, to prevent voting twice."——Cortlandt F. Bishop, *History of Elections in the American Colonies* (New York: Columbia University Press, 1893) pp. 107-108, 175.

(Left page)

(Right page)

Voting Registration: Precinct Roll Book, Louisiana.

depending upon the size of cities or counties.[10] Obviously, this system is likely to be very unpopular with the general public and it throws upon the registration officials a huge task for a short period of time when the bulk of the registering is done. Usually, temporary employees are used to handle the crowds, and their slowness and inexperience with the procedure often add to the general confusion and irritations. In addition, permanent registration is probably cheaper, keeps more people on the rolls and eligible to vote, and, if administered by a well-trained and competent staff, will eliminate corrupt practices resulting from fictitious or invalid names being kept on the register list.[11]

The only other feature of suffrage laws which can be considered universal among the states is the exclusion of people in certain categories. In twelve states,[12] *paupers* are excluded; but who is considered a pauper varies. Generally, inmates of public or private charitable institutions or recipients of local-government relief are ineligible except for honorably discharged veterans in a veterans home. Domicile in institutions in some states does not constitute residence and disqualifies for this reason. In forty-three states *conviction of crime* deprives a person of his suffrage; and in New York, Wisconsin, and Wyoming betting on elections even without conviction is disqualifying. In the vast majority of these states the crime is defined as any felony or as infamous—at least a crime involving imprisonment in the penitentiary. Restoration to full citizenship is attained variously by executive pardon or legislative action. In a few of these forty-three states the specified crimes are fewer in number and usually involve only violations of election laws or extreme offenses such as treason; the forfeiture of suffrage then is usually overcome within a specified time, although Utah requires a pardon and New Hampshire requires restoration by the Supreme Court. The conviction applies in some states only if it occurs in the state's own courts; others accept conviction in the courts of other states or federal courts. In the remaining seven states,[13] exclusion results, not from conviction of crime, but from *confinement in prison*, either because no provision is made for voting by prison inmates or because the law explicitly disfranchises them.

---

[10] States using periodic registration only in some areas of the state: Iowa, Louisiana, Kansas, Maryland, Missouri, Nebraska, New York. States using periodic registration state-wide: Hawaii, South Carolina, South Dakota.

[11] Harris, *op. cit.*, Chap. 4. The reverse argument, pointing out the dangers in permanent registration where powerful political organizations control the registration machinery, was voiced in a memorandum by several hundred Republicans of New York City urging retention of periodic registration. See the *New York Times*, February 21, 1952. Grand-jury investigations into registration practices in Cape May County, New Jersey, turned up some of the abuses connected with permanent registration, e.g., the number registered often exceeded the number of eligible voters.——*Ibid.*, February 26, 1955.

[12] Delaware, Louisiana, Maine, Massachusetts, Missouri, New Hampshire, Oklahoma, Rhode Island, South Carolina, Texas, Virginia, West Virginia.

[13] Colorado, Idaho, Indiana, Maine, Michigan, Oklahoma, Vermont.

At the conclusion of the prison sentence the person is eligible to vote irrespective of a pardon or other official action.[14] The states of Alabama, Connecticut, and Louisiana, besides the negative provision against prisoners, have positive provisions that voters should be of good moral character. Persons of *unsound mind* are either specifically disfranchised by law or presumably would be refused the ballot by the courts if a suit were brought. Only in Indiana does the exclusion apply only to those committed to an institution.

A *literacy* or *educational requirement* is included in the laws of twenty-one states,[15] and in Colorado the legislature is authorized, although it has not exercised the power, to prescribe educational qualifications. What is actually required by these laws varies widely from the onerous provisions in some Southern states to the practical satisfaction of the requirement if the voter can sign his name or is able to make his application in writing. In a few states the voter is required to draw a slip of paper at random from a box and read the extract of the constitution or statute he finds on the paper. The justification of a literacy requirement can be endlessly debated. One view is that taxpaying and duties of citizenship are not confined to the literate so voting should not be either. The other view stresses the necessity for possessing basic tools for acquiring both pertinent current information and general orientation in the traditional values of the nation.

Two particular applications of the literacy requirement deserve attention: those in New York and in most Southern states.

In the state of New York a standard is established either in the level of schooling completed or the ability to pass a literacy test. At the time of registration, a person either must produce proof that he has completed the eighth grade or beyond in an institution where English is the language of instruction or make an affidavit to this effect. As a substitute, he can present an honorable discharge from the Armed Forces if a New York resident at the time of entering service or make an affidavit to this effect. Inability to sign one's name, except for physical disability, is conclusive proof of illiteracy. The literacy test to qualify those who cannot prove literacy otherwise is designed by school authorities to measure fifth-grade achievement and is given, experimentally, to fifth-grade children in the schools; the median grade received by these children is the grade an adult must receive in order to pass the test and qualify to vote. The simplicity of the test is apparent from its fifth-grade level; it consists of a short paragraph followed by a series of eight questions testing comprehension of the paragraph, and the grading is based upon evidence of understanding irrespective of mis-

---

14 McGovney, *op. cit.*, pp. 54-55.

15 The states, outside the South, are Alaska (only if challenged), Arizona, California, Connecticut, Delaware, Hawaii, Maine, Massachusetts, New Hampshire, New York, Oregon, Washington, Wyoming.

spelled words or errors in grammar.[16] For those who do fail, day or night classes are offered in the public schools, where instructors can prepare the pupil to pass the test. While these standards may strike the university-educated person as ridiculously low, they at least are definite standards of attainment and give some genuine value to the literacy requirement.

The New York literacy law has become controversial because of the large number of Puerto Ricans living in New York City who are literate in Spanish but not in English. The contention is that they are citizens, not alien immigrants, and are entitled to be treated differently. Both the treaty establishing conditions for annexation of Puerto Rico and the equal protection clause are advanced as arguments that requiring literacy in English, which is not the native language of Puerto Ricans, is unconstitutional.[17] It is impossible to predict how persuasive a court would find this argument regarding Puerto Ricans, but the Supreme Court has upheld literacy laws as constitutional per se.

The literacy laws in eight Southern states can best be understood by reading a summary of the requirements:

ALABAMA	Read and write any article of the United States Constitution. Fill out in own handwriting without assistance, unless physically handicapped, a questionnaire containing twenty-one questions; they cover both personal information to establish eligibility and other information to establish good citizenship attitudes.
GEORGIA	Alternatives: 1. Persons of good character who understand duties and obligations of citizenship under a republican form of government; if this alternative is chosen, the voter must answer correctly twenty of thirty standard questions provided by law. 2. Read and write in English any section of the Georgia or United States Constitution or, if unable because of physical disability, understand and give a reasonable interpretation when the same is read to him.
LOUISIANA	Read and give a reasonable interpretation [18] of any clause in

16 *Ibid.*, pp. 65-66.

17 Dan Wakefield, "200,000 New Yorkers Can't Vote," *Nation*, February 28, 1959, pp. 183-185. This article is in error in saying that Arizona, California, Nevada, New Mexico, Texas, and Utah permit bilingual literacy. The last four have no literacy requirement and the first two require literacy in English. Louisiana and Hawaii have bilingual requirements. When a group of Finnish-speaking residents of Wyoming attempted to vote, the state supreme court held that the provision requiring a person to be able to read the Wyoming Constitution to qualify to vote meant ability to read it in English, not in translation. *Rasmussen* v. *Baker*, 50 Pac. 819 (1897).

18 A similar provision of the Alabama Constitution, requiring applicants to "understand and explain," was held unconstitutional on the grounds that it gave the registrars arbitrary power to accept or reject any applicant and therefore violated the equal protection clause of the Fourteenth Amendment; that the provision, both in objective and manner of administration, violated the Fifteenth Amendment. *Davis* v. *Schnell*, 81 F. Supp. 872 (E. D. Ala., 1949); Donald S. Strong, *Registration of Voters in Alabama* (University: University of Alabama Press, Bureau of Public Administration, 1956) pp. 21-30.

the state or United States Constitution or, if illiterate, understand and give a reasonable interpretation of any such section when read aloud and be a person of good character and reputation attached to the principles of the Constitutions of Louisiana and the United States and understand the duties and obligations of citizenship. If literate only in a language other than English, fill out the registration application from dictation by an interpreter; sign name or make mark on an affidavit, stating English illiteracy, in the presence of the registrar and two witnesses. Applicant must bring two qualified voters of his precinct to attest the truth of the facts in the application and the affidavit.

MISSISSIPPI Read and write any section of the state constitution. If unable to read, applicant must be able to understand the same when read and give a reasonable interpretation thereof.

NORTH AND SOUTH CAROLINA, OKLAHOMA Read and write any section of the state constitution. South Carolina has an alternate provision that a person who pays taxes on property valued at $300 is exempt from the literacy requirement.

VIRGINIA The registration procedure is a literacy requirement, in effect: unless physically unable, applicant must make application in his own handwriting "without aid, suggestion, or memorandum, on a sheet of paper containing no written or printed data, information, questions or words, in the presence of the registrar, stating therein his name, age, date, and place of birth, residence, and occupation at the time, and for the one year next preceding, and whether he has previously voted and if so, the State, county, and precinct in which he voted last."

Negro Voting in the South. The literacy requirements in the South suggest an effort to make laws to disqualify persons instead of qualifying them. The Southern voting problem has existed since the end of Reconstruction in the 1870's. The means of disfranchising Negroes was at first violence and fraud, but toward the end of the nineteenth century a reaction set in and the Southern states began adopting suffrage qualifications which would in fact disfranchise Negroes but which were not per se in violation of the United States Constitution. In this legalizing of evasions of the law, the South had recourse to registration of voters which was being adopted in other states to prevent corrupt practices. Registration in the South was usually connected with literacy requirements, and, taking the two of them together, the purpose was something more than corrupt practices legislation. The registration-literacy requirements permitted registrars of voters to exercise "discretion" in accepting whites and rejecting Negroes. In addition, Southern laws included poll taxes as a qualification for voting, the "grandfather clause," and the white primary. Each of these deserves separate discussion.

The *poll tax* is a hang-over from the taxpaying qualifications which, in turn, replaced property requirements of the colonial and early national period of our history. Twenty-two states levy a poll or head tax, but the revenue is a small percentage of total collections except for some local governments. The states long ago found far more productive and efficient means of raising money. The poll tax as a voting qualification in the South is not a revenue measure primarily; except in Virginia, a person is under no obligation to pay the tax unless he wants to vote. The revenue raised is relatively high in election years when people vote and relatively low in the intervening years. Nearly all of the money collected is earmarked for schools.

Only five Southern states and Vermont (for local elections only) still use the poll tax as a suffrage requirement. The Southern abandonment of the tax resulted partly because of open opposition, partly because of other methods for excluding Negroes, and partly because of changing attitudes toward the effect of the tax. The annual rate varies from $1.00 in Arkansas to $2.00 in Mississippi. Arkansas and Texas do not accumulate the tax, but Alabama and Mississippi do for two years and Virginia for three years. The maximum amount anyone would owe at one time is $4.50 in Virginia. Although local governments are authorized to levy additional taxes in Mississippi, Texas, and Virginia, none is asesssed, except in the case of some Texas cities which levy $1.00 to vote in municipal elections. All five states exempt people on various grounds such as age, physical condition, veteran status, or being members of the Armed Forces. The discriminatory operation of the poll tax against Negroes is less than it once was and it is impossible, in any event, to single out any one cause for Negro disfranchisement. The period of time that the tax must be paid before an election is perhaps most responsible for holding down the size of the vote. The periods in the five states vary from one to nine months for a general election and from three to eighteen months for a primary.[19]

In Vermont, taxpayers whose poll taxes are unpaid on January 1 each year are not legal voters in town meetings unless the individuals came of voting age after the last annual assessment or are exempt from taxation.

A much more direct slap at Negro voting in the South was the so-called "grandfather clause." Laws with this clause provided either that a voter must pass a literacy test or pay a tax or meet some other qualification unless an ancestor of his had voted in that state on or before an arbitrary date in the past. The practical effect of such a law was, positively, to enfranchise the members of ante-bellum white families who voted either before the Civil War or during a subsequent period when Negroes were excluded. Conversely, all newcomers to the state and all old families whose male members

---

[19] The most recent work on the poll tax, treating its history, present operation, and implications, is Frederic D. Ogden, *The Poll Tax in the South* (University: University of Alabama Press, 1958).

had not voted had to qualify in the alternate way the law provided. It is a good guess that if racial discrimination had not been involved in this legislation and/or if there were no Fifteenth Amendment, these laws might have stood the court tests. However, in the case testing the Oklahoma statute where the date was January 1, 1866, the Supreme Court of the United States held the effect was to circumvent the Fifteenth Amendment because the date adopted was prior to the adoption of the amendment and the surrounding circumstances created the suspicion that the intention was unconstitutional.[20]

The most effective method of keeping the Negro either from voting at all or from casting a meaningful vote has been the *white primary,* a by-product of the one-party system of the South. When bipartisanism does not exist, the electorate can only play an important part at that point of the electoral process at which the candidates of the dominant party are nominated. It is a matter of no practical concern in this situation whether the second party, which is permanently a minority, nominates candidates or not. The affinity of the racial question with the one-party system in the South was most clearly revealed by prohibiting Negroes from taking part in the nominating of Democratic candidates. Since the only significant decision for the voters was nominating Democrats for the various offices, the Democratic Party in most Southern states began relatively early permitting rank-and-file members to take a direct part in the primary, and the convention system of nomination was voluntarily put aside. In time, direct-primary laws were enacted whereby the Democratic Party leaders were given administrative control over their nomination processes, but their actions were limited and controlled by legal sanctions to prevent corrupt practices. Both before and after the formal adoption of direct-primary laws, the Democrats in charge of the nominating procedure could decide which voters were Democrats and therefore eligible to vote. It followed that Negroes could not, generally speaking, satisfy the rules governing party members. Only white people were eligible. This system was given the name "white primary."

This exclusion of Negro voting at the only point where a vote really counted was successful for many years because nobody challenged the white primary in the courts. Furthermore, the use of the word "elections" in the United States Constitution was assumed to refer only to general elections, since these were the only elections known to the Founders. By virtue of this conclusion, a direct primary might be generically an election but it was not an election in the constitutional sense, being nothing more than a new form of nominating procedure. This view of the status of nominations was given some official sanction by the Supreme Court of the United States in a decision holding that the Federal Corrupt Practices Act did

---

[20] *Guinn v. United States,* 238 U. S. 347 (1915).

not apply to a primary election involving a candidate for the United States Senate.[21] The victory for state monopoly over the nominating process was not clear-cut: four judges expressed the opinion that Congress could regulate nominations, four judges took the opposite position, and the ninth judge did not express his opinion on this issue but sided with latter four judges on the ground that when the Corrupt Practices Act was passed Congress had only general elections in mind and the act was not intended to apply to primaries. The practical result was to strengthen the presumption that the states had a free hand in the nomination process.

Accordingly, the Texas legislature passed an act of outright exclusion of Negroes from the primaries of the Democratic Party, a much further and more direct step toward official discrimination than any previous action. The Supreme Court found this legislation unconstitutional, not because of the electoral powers of Congress, but because the Negroes had been deprived of equal protection of the laws as guaranteed by the Fourteenth Amendment.[22] Undaunted, the Texas legislature gave each party's state executive committee the power to determine party membership, i.e., who could vote in the party's primary. In conformance with this statute the Democratic Executive Committee adopted a white-primary rule for the Party. The Supreme Court found these circumstances indistinguishable from the previous case and held the action unconstitutional, inasmuch as the committee was exercising state power delegated by the legislature; since it was really action by the State of Texas, it was still governed by the Fourteenth Amendment.[23] In the course of this decision, however, the Court hinted that this action would be permissible if taken by the state convention of the party instead of the state committee; therefore, in the absence of any legislation in Texas on the subject, the Democratic state convention adopted the white primary as a party rule, and the court upheld it.[24]

Texas apparently had shown the way whereby the South could exclude Negroes from the Democratic primary without infringing the federal Constitution or laws. The road leading in this direction proved to be very short. Six years after this decision, the Supreme Court held, in a case not involving discrimination against Negroes but involving fraudulent election practices in the nomination of a candidate for the House of Representatives in Louisiana, that a voter who is qualified to vote is entitled to have his vote counted and counted accurately.[25] Specifically, the Court agreed that the perpetrators of the fraudulent practices had violated the Civil Rights

---

[21] *Newberry* v. *United States*, 256 U. S. 232 (1921).
[22] *Nixon* v. *Herndon*, 273 U. S. 536 (1927).
[23] *Nixon* v. *Condon*, 286 U. S. 73 (1932).
[24] *Grovey* v. *Townsend*, 295 U. S. 45 (1935).
[25] *United States* v. *Classic*, 313 U. S. 229 (1941).

Act passed by Congress in 1886. By extension, a majority of the Court agreed, Congress (as part of its power to regulate the election process delegated by the Constitution) can regulate primaries in which federal officials are nominated if the primaries are an integral part of a state's election machinery.

With this seemingly new departure of the law relating to the status of the direct primary, another case was brought up from Texas, testing the action previously sustained. Now the Court reversed itself by holding that the action of a state party convention was state governmental action made possible by the lack of state legislation just as action by a state committee in pursuance of legislation was state governmental action. In either case the responsibility and the determination was made by the state. Furthermore, there remained some state protection and regulation in the laws relating to corrupt practices and the reporting of the vote.[26] Thus ended the legality of the white primary. The public status of the political party is now established beyond challenge, a recognition of a fact whether supported by legislation or not.

The demise of the white primary resulted in quickly increased Negro registration and voting (notably in the larger Southern cities) although not uniformly in all states and still low compared with the number of white registrants. By 1958 the estimated number of Negroes registered in the eleven Southern states was 1,266,488, virtually the same as 1956. Negro registration in Missisisppi still lags noticeably, and Alabama responded to the *Smith* v. *Allwright* decision by tightening its literacy requirement and registration procedure.[27] The growth of Negro registration in Louisiana gave rise in approximately a dozen parishes to a concerted effort to purge the rolls of Negro registrants.

---

[26] *Smith* v. *Allwright,* 321 U. S. 649 (1944). In *Terry* v. *Adams,* 345 U. S. 461 (1953) the Supreme Court went further by holding the "Jaybird primary" in Fort Bend County, Texas, unconstitutional. Jaybird was the name taken by white Democrats in the county who held a primary prior to the regular state-wide Democratic primary. Nevertheless, the Justices found that this private primary was state action and Negroes could not be excluded. Even a "Citizens Party" in Texas, operating only in local elections, which held its primary at the same time and under the same state laws as the Democratic primary, could not exclude Negroes. *Perry* v. *Cyphers,* 186 F. (2d) 608 (5th Cir., 1951). The attempt of South Carolina to maintain the white primary by making political parties "private clubs" was struck down. *Brown* v. *Baskin,* 78 F. Supp. 933 (E. D. S. C. 1948).

[27] *New York Times,* November 5, 1956, July 14, 1957, November 3, 1958. Strong, *op. cit.,* Chap. 4. H. D. Price, *The Negro and Southern Politics* (New York: New York University Press, 1957) Chap. 2; and "The Negro and Florida Politics, 1944-1954," *Journal of Politics,* Vol. 17 (1955) pp. 198-220. Donald S. Strong, "The Rise of Negro Voting in Texas," and O. Douglas Weeks, "The White Primary: 1944-1948," *American Political Science Review,* Vol. 42 (1948) pp. 500-522.

Absentee Voting. Except for Alabama, Louisiana, Mississippi, New Mexico, Pennsylvania, and South Carolina, the states make provisions, in case civilian voters are absent from their home on Election Day, to enable them to obtain a ballot, mark it in the presence of a notary public or public official competent to administer oaths, and mail it to the election board by a specified date. In most states the voter can vote absentee irrespective of the reason for his absence. The question of absentee servicemen voting has arisen whenever war and elections coincided. In fact, the first absentee-voting legislation was adopted by eleven Northern states during the Civil War. Their residents in uniform were permitted to vote in the field or by proxy; in many cases men were furloughed home in time for the election of 1864. During both the Spanish-American War and World War I, legislation was introduced in Congress to facilitate absentee voting, but no bills were passed.

Problems During World War II. By 1942 a number of states had amended their laws with the voting of servicemen in mind, and Congress also passed an act—applicable only in time of war—specifying that members of the Armed Forces should not be denied the opportunity to vote for members of Congress and presidential electors by reason of absence or failure to register or pay poll taxes. Military officials were authorized to provide postcard application blanks, and state officials were required to prepare a war ballot including federal officials, and, if state law permitted, state and local officials as well. These provisions applied only to states whose laws did not make provision for absentee voting in the Armed Forces, and the expenses involved were paid out of federal funds. The number of servicemen who voted through the normal absentee procedures cannot be determined because no separate count was made of them. However, only 137,686 applied for war ballots, and in forty states where records were made, 28,051 war ballots were counted. After a long and bitter Congressional debate a new act was passed applicable to the 1944 presidential election whereby overseas servicemen could only vote a specially prepared federal war ballot containing candidates for Congress and presidential electors, if they had applied for an absentee ballot by September 1, 1944, and had not received it by October 1, 1944, and if the governor of the state certified that the ballot would be acceptable under the laws of his state. Where a governor failed to provide this certification and the state failed to provide enough time for mailing out and returning absentee ballots, the overseas servicemen could not vote. Because all of the states provided for absentee voting for servicemen within the United States, they were ineligible to vote the federal war ballot. The two major bones of contention over this act in Congress were the fear that the federal government would usurp the power of the states over their election machinery and the fear of the Republicans that partisan favoritism in administration would work to the advantage of the Democrats.

The number of difficulties raised by servicemen voting is large. Aside from the actual residence requirements, a number of states demand registration in person, and the federal postcard, it was hoped, would be acceptable as both a registration and an application for an absentee ballot. In 1944 only South Carolina refused to accept the postcard as an application. Other requirements such as literacy could not be met by men and women thousands of miles from home. The regulations governing the date for mailing ballots and the deadline for their return made overseas voting a physical impossibility in some states. As a final difficulty, some states permit absentee voting only for general elections, not for direct primaries. The 1944 act, however, had the effect of stimulating some state legislatures to relax legal provisions on these various points and make overseas voting possible. Actual practices varied from state to state. In some, ballots were mailed at the request of relatives or friends and were even mailed without request to all servicemen whose names were on registration lists or other lists of state residents of voting age. The result was about 85,000 federal ballots cast and about 2,600,000 state ballots cast by servicemen.

Permanent Armed-Forces Voting. Since the congressional legislation as well as some state legislation applied only in time of war, and since the size of the Armed Forces remained high after 1945, a new appraisal of the situation was needed in the period after World War II to convert the numerous stopgap measures into a permanent and orderly system. A new act by Congress in 1946 left all responsibility for providing ballots with the states, continued the use of postcard applications, made provision for rapid communication between state election officials and voters in uniform, and continued the prohibitions against payment of poll taxes and personal registration for federal elections. Otherwise the act contained recommendations for state legislation. Another effort was made for federal legislation for the 1952 presidential election, but no new act was passed.[28] Responsibility for surveying and recommending appropriate action was given to the American Political Science Association, and a committee of the association submitted an extensive report covering

---

[28] See the *New York Times*, August 17, 1952, for the status of absentee-voting laws in the states for the election of that year. Only New Mexico makes no provision for absentee voting.

the recent experience with servicemen's voting and analyzing the obstacles to be overcome.[29]

Since not all of the members of the committee were in agreement on recommendations, the conclusions probably were moderated more than would have been the case with a unanimous committee. The right of the states to enforce their voting procedures was not challenged as such, and the states which had made sufficient provisions presented no problem anyway. However, the majority of the committee obviously felt that the solution was a federal write-in ballot for citizens from states without satisfactory provisions. The majority concluded that despite the difficulties in handling both the federal and the state ballots, a federal ballot was not "inevitably barred by administration considerations," which would not be as great in any case as the problems presented in 1944.

Congress relies for its power to guarantee the right to vote for federal officials upon the constitutional provision: "The times, places, and manner of holding elections for Senators and Representatives shall be prescribed in each State by the legislature thereof; but the Congress may at any time by law make or alter such regulations. . . ." [30] Proceeding from this grant of power to Congress to regulate the election of its own members, the committee majority noted the different situation regarding presidential electors, who are chosen as state legislatures determine, and hoped for an opportunity to test in the Supreme Court the power of Congress to include presidential electors on a federal ballot. While the committee agreed that "the responsibility for election administration should remain with the states," most of its members "do not agree that the Federal Government must or should stand idly by when the States fail to perform their essential functions in the administration of Federal elections." [31] The control by the states over their election procedure, including determination of their own voting requirements, may very well be at stake in the future if the demand for uniformity is not realized in individual state action.

Voting by Presidential Electors. One other occasion for casting ballots occurs every four years in presidential elections, not by individual citizens, but by victorious presidential electors in each state. When the voters cast their ballots in presidential elections, they actually are voting for the group of presidential electors of one or the other party, not directly for the party's candidates for President and Vice-President. One

---

[29] *Voting in the Armed Forces*, Message from the President of the United States transmitting the Report of the Special Committee on Service Voting (Washington, D. C.: Government Printing Offices, 1952) House Doc. No. 407, 82d Cong., 2 sess.

[30] *Constitution of the United States*, Art. I, Sec. 4, par. 1.

[31] *Voting in the Armed Forces*, pp. 49–51.

group of party electors is elected as a whole over the other group; a plurality of all of the votes cast is sufficient to elect. The successful group of presidential electors meet in their state capitol on the first Monday after the second Wednesday in December and cast ballots for the presidential and vice-presidential candidates of their party.[32] The ballots are sent, either by messenger or by registered mail, to the President of the Senate. In the following January the Congress meets in joint session and the ballots from all states are opened and counted.

SYSTEMS OF VOTING

MANNER OF CASTING VOTES

From Public to Secret Voting. The use of paper ballots or voting machines is so universal today that it is difficult to realize that elections were ever conducted otherwise. In the evolution of voting, the first stage has generally been some form of public voting, whether by show of hands, oral declaration, or dropping different-colored objects in a container in such a manner that the color can be seen and the voting known. During the Colonial period in Georgia, Maryland, New Jersey, New York, and Virginia, public voting was the general practice at one time or another, in imitation of the election of members of Parliament in England, although Massachusetts used show of hands at first, and like Connecticut and Rhode Island, permitted voting by proxy.[33] The desirability of secrecy in voting was generally appreciated as time went by. Voters could write the names of candidates and give the list to the official receiving the votes, or colored balls were used in such a manner that bystanders could not tell how anyone voted. One student of the subject concluded that the written ballot is of Roman origin and that the Puritans first introduced it, having made its acquaintance while they

---

[32] Four different meeting dates for presidential electors have been fixed by Congress over the years: the first Wednesday in December, by Act of March 1, 1792; the second Monday in January, by Act of February 3, 1887; the first Wednesday in January, by Act of May 29, 1928; and the first Monday after the second Wednesday in December, by Act of June 5, 1934.

[33] Bishop, *op. cit.*, pp. 98–99, 127 ff. *passim;* Sydnor, *op. cit.*, pp. 19–20. The fact that proxy voting was illegal at common law barred its use in those colonies most closely under royal control. Elections at county towns in New York were by show of hands, but if the count was in doubt, a poll was taken.——Carl L. Becker, *History of Political Parties in the Province of New York* (Madison: Bulletin of University of Wisconsin, Vol. 2, 1909) p. 15. The protocol public voting entailed in Virginia is described by Sydnor, *op. cit.*: "When a voter came before the table in the contest for a seat in Congress between John Marshall and John Clopton in 1799, the sheriff asked: 'Mr. Blair, who do you vote for?' 'John Marshall,' said he; and thereupon the future Chief Justice of the United States replied: 'Your vote is appreciated, Mr. Blair.' As the next voter approached, the sheriff inquired: 'Who do you vote for, Mr. Buchanan?' 'For John Clopton,' he answered; and Clopton, at the other end of the table, responded: 'Mr. Buchanan, I shall treasure that vote in my memory. It will be regarded as a feather in my cap for ever.' "——Pp. 21–22.

were at Emden, Netherlands.[34] In New England written lists were referred to as "papers," and the first use of the word "ballot" in America may have occurred in the Constitution of West New Jersey in 1677.[35] Most of the colonies upon becoming states adopted ballot-voting.[36]

Doctrine of Open Voting. Even though this theory was triumphant, some voices were raised thereafter in behalf of the practice of open voting. One of the most noted proponents of this was John Stuart Mill, the English writer and political theorist. It was his contention that secrecy was justified when voters in one way or another are slaves and a few can exercise power over the many. Such coercion declines in more advanced states, and the chief consideration in voting is that it is a public trust. The public, being entitled to have a man vote, is entitled to know how he votes. Secrecy permits a voter to vote as he feels inclined without regard for others, because they do not know for whom he voted. Mill insisted that a "voter is under an absolute moral obligation to consider the interest of the public, not his advantage, and give his vote, to the best of his judgment, exactly as he would be bound to do if he were the sole voter, and the election depended upon him alone." [37]

Secret Voting Barred by Methods. To what extent voters would vote more unselfishly if they voted publicly is a moot question. Certainly most if not all voters would contend that their secret votes are cast in behalf of "the best candidates," and therefore in the public interest. To debate this question is to beat a dead horse, because representative government today rests firmly upon the inviolate secrecy of the ballot as the first rule in voting. However, secrecy and paper ballots are not necessarily the same thing. For many years in the United States after the elective process was taken over by political parties, each party printed its own ballot containing just the names of its candidates and distributed them to voters any place they could be found. Each party would likely use different colored paper so that the vote could not be secret unless no one saw the ballot when the voter dropped it into the ballot box. Instead of privacy in casting ballots, there was usually a great hubbub of confusion about the polls. Party workers often could exhort the voter all the way up the street into the polling place and right up to the ballot box. Even legislation making the parties' ballots the same color and size corrected few

[34] Douglas Campbell, *The Puritan in Holland, England, and America* (New York: Harper & Brothers, 1892) Vol. 2, pp. 430–440.

[35] This is the conclusion of Bishop, *op. cit.*, p. 166.

[36] Campbell, *op. cit.*, Vol. 1, pp. 52–53. The last state to give up oral voting was Kentucky in 1891.

[37] *Considerations on Representative Government* (New York: Henry Holt and Company, Inc., 1882) p. 208; in general, Chap. 10. Seymour and Frary, *op. cit.*, pp. 246-252.

of the difficulties. Voters were deceived in some cases when the symbol of one party and the candidates of the other were printed on the same ballot. This experience with what amounted to open voting often disproved John Stuart Mill's theorizing, for coercion and intimidation were made much easier when the voter could be followed to the ballot box to see which ballot he dropped in and whether or not he scratched any of the names on it.

Correction in Australian Ballot. The corrective of many of these conditions was the gradual adoption of the Australian ballot,[38] beginning in both Massachusetts and Louisville, Kentucky, in 1888. The objective of this method of voting is secrecy, so certain features are rigidly prescribed: the ballot becomes an official ballot, printed at public expense, uniform in size and color, listing all of the candidates entitled to have their names printed, distributed only at polling places by designated election officials and marked in a private booth. The reception among the states has been almost universally favorable to the Australian ballot.

Corrupt Practices and Ballots. This reform was no panacea for corrupt practices. The struggle for the secrecy of the ballot revolves mainly around the practice of bribing voters and the desire to make sure they vote the way they are paid. For this type of corrupt practice to be conducted on a large scale, ballots must be identified or the marking of the ballot observed. The Australian ballot interferes with but does not prevent these illegalities. One method used to evade the intention of the Australian ballot is the "chain ballot." A person who is paying for votes obtains a supply of official ballots. When voters appear on election day to be bribed they are handed one of these ballots already marked. This ballot the voter hides in his pocket, goes to his polling place and receives the ballot he is entitled to, walks into the booth, switches the ballots, emerges from the booth and deposits in the ballot box the marked ballot he brought with him. Upon his returning to the man who is paying for votes, the voter produces a blank ballot and receives his money. In this way the voting is controlled and the buyer of votes has the same number of blank official ballots at the end of the day that he started out with. When numbers began being printed on ballots, each one could be identified individually by the election officials. Then, if the officials are not parties to the bribery, the "chain ballot" cannot be used. This is only one of many examples of attempts to nullify the secret ballot.

Voting Machines. The Australian ballot is a type of voting wherein

---

38 As the name implies, this style of ballot was first used in Victoria Province, Australia, in 1856.

secrecy and honesty are the objectives. Consequently, it need not be conducted with paper ballots. Voting machines conform with the requirements just as well. Thomas A. Edison in 1868 received the first patent for an electrical vote recorder, and the first use of a machine in an election in the United States was at Lockport, New York, in 1892. The intricacy of these mechanisms and the limited market (primarily public elections, but some use by labor unions, national conventions of groups like the Business and Professional Women and state political party conventions, e.g., Indiana) has kept the competition confined to two companies, Automatic Voting Machine Corporation (organized 1898) and Shoup Voting Machine Company (organized 1938).

Over one third of the voters in the United States now vote on machines, but they are concentrated in the larger Eastern cities. Machines are not used on a large scale in any other country. Since they are entirely mechanical, there is no paper used except for rolls attached to the machines in some places for writing in names not appearing on the machines. Each vote for each candidate is recorded progressively during operation, so that at the end of the day the totals are simply copied from the machine. A curtain encloses the front of the machine while the voter is manipulating the levers; when the voter has moved each lever by the names of the candidates he is voting for, he turns the master lever or switch, whereupon his vote is recorded and the curtain opens. When the next voter enters, he turns the master switch back and the curtain closes. There are various sizes of machines appropriate for different cities, and the machines are extremely flexible in that they can be set for almost any kind of an election involving any number or kinds of complicated choices.[39]

Paper v. Machines. Proposals for adopting voting machines have usually encountered opposition based on two arguments. (1) It is contended the machines are too difficult to operate and voters will be disfranchised by their failure to cope with the mysteries of the levers and the curtain. At first sight a voting machine is likely to be baffling, but officials can readily explain how it works. Once a person understands it, there is no further trouble and usually one complete explanation is enough. (2) Machines are resisted because of their high cost. The different sizes and models vary from approximately $1000 to well over $1400. The initial outlay by a city or county will be high because at least two machines per precinct are needed, and to provide for several hundred precincts puts the purchase price well up into six figures. The average cost of an election with machines, however, is estimated at about half the cost of using paper, although reports of savings vary from city

[39] George Stimpson, *A Book about American Politics* (New York: Harper & Brothers, 1952) pp. 413-414; *Business Week,* October 30, 1948, pp. 25-26.

to city. The saving arises from the smaller printing costs, fewer precincts (because more people can vote in a given time where machines are used) and the tremendous reductions in the cost of recounts.

Corrupt Practices with Machines. The grandiose claim has been frequently made that machines will prevent corrupt practices and that honest elections will always result. Unquestionably the illegalities connected with paper ballots will not be usable on machines, but the only sure cure for lawbreaking is people who do not want to break the law. Where there is a will there is a way. Most corrupt practices with paper ballots depend upon the participation or connivance of election officials. If they are dishonest, machine voting can be dishonest. One method is to rig the machine so it will not record votes for certain candidates. Another method is to manipulate the counters before the voting starts so that favored candidates are given a certain number of votes to begin with. In this case the totals at the end of the day may exceed the number of voters, but no correction can be made because there is nothing to recount. Should there be litigation, the entire precinct may be thrown out because of the corrupt practice.

A weakness of machines is the possibility of their breaking down during an election. The companies train local workers in the maintenance and repair of their machines, but on occasions machines have had to be abandoned and the voting continued on paper ballots. In the final analysis, machines excel for their efficiency, their accuracy in the count, and the reduced expense over a period of time. They have at last released from bondage the election officials, who often toil through the night counting the votes cast on paper ballots.

FORMS OF BALLOTS

Party Column or Office Block. The manner in which names are arranged on general-election ballots leaves the states various alternatives.[40] All the introduction of the Australian ballot accomplished in this respect was the decision to print all candidates' names on the officially prepared ballot. How they were printed was unrelated to the objective of a secret ballot. Massachusetts, the first state to adopt the new ballot, arranged the names in groups according to the office sought and printed the party affiliation of each candidate by his name: all candidates for governor were listed under that designation, candidates for United States senator

---

40 It is assumed in this discussion of ballots that the reader is aware of the differences between direct-primary and general-election ballots and will grasp the fact that ballot problems sometimes apply to both kinds of elections and sometimes only to general elections. The form of the ballot is a question primarily for general elections, since candidates in the direct primary are already separated on the basis of party and the names are arranged in the office-block form.

under that designation, and so on. Following each name is a small square in which the voter puts a mark to indicate which candidate he votes for. This manner of listing candidates is familiarly called the "Massachusetts ballot" but is descriptively designated the "office-block" or "office-group" ballot.

The year after Massachusetts, Indiana also adopted the Australian ballot, but continued to list candidates' names by party designation in the traditional manner. In this form, the ballot is divided into vertical columns, each party being given a column for its candidates. At the top of the column the name of the party is printed, and if emblems are permitted, the party emblem appears below the party name. Below the emblem is a circle or a large square; if the voter puts a mark here, he is voting for all of the candidates in that column, i.e., all of the candidates of that party. The names of candidates for each office are listed side by side across the ballot; if candidates for governor are listed first, for example, then each party's gubernatorial candidate is listed as the first name in the party column and so on for each additional office. This form of ballot is familiarly known as the "Indiana ballot," but is descriptively named the "party-column" ballot. Of the forty-seven states using the Australian ballot, eighteen have adopted the form of the office block, the other twenty-nine using the form of the party column.[41]

Long ago value judgments began to attach to one or the other form, and the debate has swirled between the advocates of party solidarity and the advocates of independent voting. The party column obviously makes it easier to vote a straight ticket because the act of voting can be completed by making one mark. The office block offers no advantage to the straight-ticket voter, for he must go through the ballot and place a mark after the name of each candidate he wants to vote for. Consequently it takes just as much time and as many marks to vote a straight ticket as a split ticket. The distinction between the two ballot forms is the relative ease of voting for all of the candidates of one party or candidates of different parties. Of course a split ticket can be voted on a party-column ballot, but the temptation to make one mark at the top of the column is presumed to be very great. To vote a split ticket on the party-column ballot the voter must either go down the list of candidates in the columns and place a mark in the square opposite each name he wishes to vote for, or in a few states he must place a mark at the top of the party

---

41 Appearances in ballots can be deceptive. Although Pennsylvania is one of the eighteen states using the office-block form, it nullifies the effect by printing separately the names of the parties with a square after each; a straight ticket can be voted by making a mark in one of the party squares. Four states—New Jersey, North Dakota, South Dakota, and Wyoming—use the party-column form, but there is no circle or square at the top of the columns; a voter has to go down the columns and vote for candidates individually whether voting a straight or a split ticket.

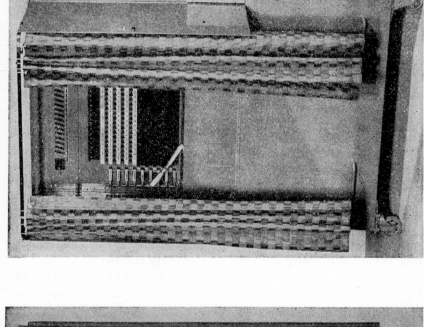

Courtesy, Automatic Voting Machine Division, Rockwell Mfg. Co.

Courtesy, Shoup Voting Machine Corp.

TYPICAL VOTING MACHINES READY FOR THE VOTER

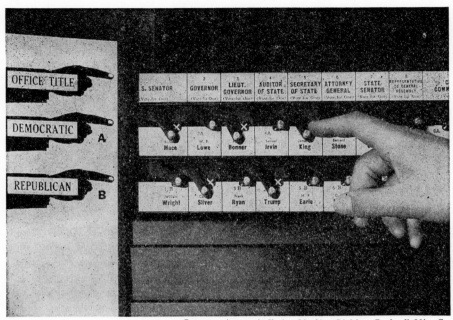

Courtesy, Automatic Voting Machine Division, Rockwell Mfg. Co.

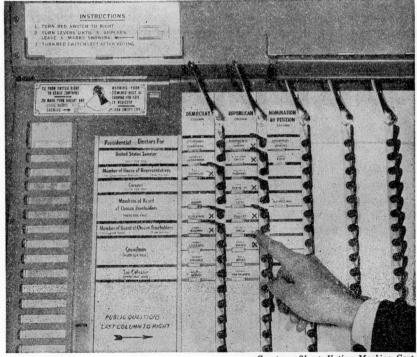

Courtesy, Shoup Voting Machine Corp.

THE VOTER INDICATES HIS CHOICE

Courtesy, Automatic Voting Machine Corp.

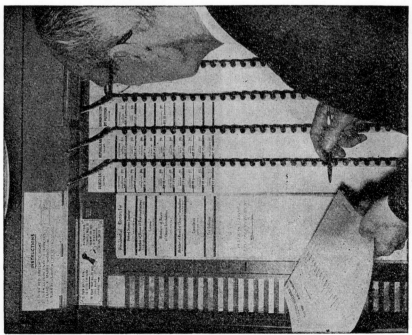

Courtesy, The Shoup Voting Machine Corp.

AT THE CLOSE OF VOTING MACHINES SHOW THE TOTALS TO OFFICIALS

column and then scratch out the names of candidates in that column for whom he does not want to vote. On a voting machine he can pull the party lever and then adjust the candidate levers as he wishes in order to split his ticket.

The issue, then, is whether voters should be encouraged to vote for all the candidates of one party, implementing a total party victory and insuring more complete party responsibility for conducting the government, or be encouraged to vote for candidates irrespective of party on "the best man for the job" philosophy. The reactions within the states have varied, although the party-column form is definitely favored. There seem to be no distinct sectional preferences either way, although a relatively higher number of Western states use the office-block form.

The order in which names are printed on ballots involves two distinct kinds of problems.

(1) The first arises in connection with general elections using the party-column form. By law in each state it is decided what the order of the offices on the ballot will be. The usual arrangement is candidates for President and Vice-President and/or presidential electors; next, candidates for United States senator and governor, or vice versa, followed by candidates for other state-wide offices, congressional district, judicial and legislative districts, and finally, county. The popularity of the names of candidates at the top of a column may cause some voters to vote a straight ticket in that column—the bandwagon effect. The consistent vote-getting power of Franklin D. Roosevelt caused Republican-controlled legislatures in some states to amend the ballot law, providing for two separate ballots. On one, only the presidential candidates and/or presidential electors are listed; on the other all the remaining candidates are listed. This system is known as the "separate presidential ballot."

(2) The second kind of problem arises in general elections using the office block, in direct primaries and in nonpartisan elections. The distinguishing feature common to all of these is that several candidates for the same office are listed consecutively. As a rule each candidate wants his name to be first on the list. Different states use different methods for listing the names, and different methods may be used in a state for different elections. One method is to print first the name of the incumbent, if he is seeking re-election, and then the other candidates in an order determined by the kind of election it is. In general elections, by this method the second name listed will be the candidate of the other major party with minor-party candidates, if any, listed thereafter. In a direct primary or nonpartisan election, other candidates may be listed in the order that they have qualified on the ballot or be listed alphabetically or by drawing lots. A second method is to list all candidates, including incumbents, alphabetically. A third method is for all candi-

dates to draw lots. A fourth method, perhaps the most justifiable, is to rotate the order of names so that on every so-many thousand paper ballots or voting machines each candidate will appear in each position in the list.[42]

Write-in Candidates. The law in most states makes provisions for the voter to write in the names of candidates if he does not wish to vote for the candidates listed on the ballot. On an office-block ballot an extra space is left under each office for writing in, and on the party-column ballot the column on the extreme right of the ballot is blank. This is one aspect of voting to which paper ballots are more adaptable than voting machines. With machines it may be possible to leave spaces where a voter can write a name and then pull the lever or a roll of paper is provided on which the names are written. In some states the name need not be written on paper ballots: the voter may paste on a label with the candidate's name. In any event a write-in campaign for a candidate is usually a hopeless endeavor. In states where a stamp is used to mark the ballot or where voting is on machines, no pencils are provided at the polling place. The write-in candidate would be a trusting soul, indeed, to depend upon the voter bringing his own pencil; so one device is to pass out a pencil to each voter as he enters the building where the voting is conducted. An even greater hazard is depending upon voters to spell the name correctly. Laws vary in their severity on the accuracy of spelling. In some states both the first and last names must be written, but in others only the last name. In the final analysis the laws leave the question of whether or not to count a write-in vote to the discretion of the election officials. If they have any feeling in the matter, they are likely to be unsympathetic to the write-in candidate. Occasionally a candidate is elected to a local or district office by a write-in vote. One of the seven wonders of American politics was the election of J. Strom Thurmond to the United States Senate from South Carolina in 1954 as a write-in candidate. Nothing of the sort had ever happened before in the history of the country.

Length of Ballots. The tendency in American government since early in the nineteenth century, and especially since the period of Andrew Jackson, has been to elect officials wherever possible rather than having them appointed to office by other officials. This practice was for many years considered an intimate part of the representative system, keeping government close to the people by making the maximum number of

---

[42] See Henry M. Bain, Jr., and Donald S. Hecock, *Ballot Position and Voter's Choice* (Detroit: Wayne State University Press, 1957).

To vote for a Person, mark a Cross X in the Square at the right of the Party Name or Political Designation. **X**

SENATOR IN CONGRESS — Vote for ONE

JOHN F. KENNEDY – of Boston — Democratic
Candidate for Re-election

VINCENT J. CELESTE – of Boston — Republican

LAWRENCE GILFEDDER – of Watertown — Socialist Labor

MARK R. SHAW – of Melrose — Prohibition

GOVERNOR — Vote for ONE

FOSTER FURCOLO – of Longmeadow — Democratic
Candidate for Re-election

CHARLES GIBBONS – of Stoneham — Republican

HENNING A. BLOMEN – of Somerville — Socialist Labor

GUY S. WILLIAMS – of Worcester — Prohibition

LIEUTENANT GOVERNOR — Vote for ONE

ROBERT F. MURPHY – of Malden — Democratic
Candidate for Re-election

ELMER C. NELSON – of Mendon — Republican

HAROLD E. BASSETT – of Clinton — Prohibition

FRANCIS A. VOTANO – of Lynn — Socialist Labor

SECRETARY — Vote for ONE

EDWARD J. CRONIN – of Peabody — Democratic
Candidate for Re-election

MARION CURRAN BOCH – of Norwood — Republican

FRED M. INGERSOLL – of Lynn — Socialist Labor

JULIA B. KOHLER – of Boston — Prohibition

TREASURER — Vote for ONE

JOHN F. KENNEDY – of Canton — Democratic
Candidate for Re-election

JOHN E. YERXA – of Dedham — Republican

WARREN C. CARBERG – of Medway — Prohibition

JOHN ERLANDSSON – of Boston — Socialist Labor

AUDITOR — Vote for ONE

THOMAS J. BUCKLEY – of Boston — Democratic
Candidate for Re-election

THOMAS H. ADAMS – of Springfield — Republican

JOHN B. LAUDER – of Revere — Prohibition

ARNE A. SORTELL – of Randolph — Socialist Labor

ATTORNEY GENERAL — Vote for ONE

CHRISTIAN A. HERTER, Jr. – of Newton — Republican

EDWARD J. McCORMACK, Jr. – of Boston — Democratic

CHARLES A. COUPER – of Attleboro — Socialist Labor

GUSTAF B. NISSEN – of Concord — Prohibition

DEMOCRATIC PARTY ◯

For United States Senator **FRANK E. (TED) MOSS**	☐
For Representative in Congress **DAVID S. KING**	☐
For State Representative **KEN W. GARDNER**	☐
For County Commissioner 4 yr term **VERN R. BURTON**	☐
For County Commissioner 2 yr term **G. EVAN TAYLOR**	☐
For County Sheriff **LELAND NALDER**	☐
For County Clerk and Auditor **HARRY L. STRONG**	☐
For County Assessor **CHARLES BLAKE**	☐
For County Recorder **EMILY T. ELDREDGE**	☐
For County Treasurer **BRIANT JACOBS**	☐
For County Attorney **MILTON J. HESS**	☐
For County Surveyor **E. W. ISHAM**	☐
For Constable	☐
For Justice of the Peace **C. KENNETH BURTON**	☐

REPUBLICAN PARTY ◯

For United States Senator **ARTHUR V. WATKINS**	☐
For Representative in Congress **WILLIAM A. DAWSON**	☐
For State Representative **JOE KNIGHT**	☐
For County Commissioner 4 yr term **EUGENE TOLMAN**	☐
For County Commissioner 2 yr term **THOMAS AMBY BRIGGS**	☐
For County Sheriff **LE ROI DAY**	☐
For County Clerk and Auditor **ROBERT TELFORD**	☐
For County Assessor **DAVID E. COOK**	☐
For County Recorder **HELEN H. BROWN**	☐
For County Treasurer **LEROY H. DUNCAN**	☐
For County Attorney **CHARLES E. BRADFORD**	☐
For County Surveyor **HAROLD J. TIPPETTS**	☐
For Constable	☐
For Justice of the Peace **B. M. ANDERSON**	☐

CITIZENS FOR LEE ◯

For United States Senator **J. BRACKEN LEE**	☐
For Representative in Congress	☐
For State Representative	☐
For County Commissioner 4 yr term	☐
For County Commissioner 2 yr term	☐
For County Sheriff	☐
For County Clerk and Auditor	☐
For County Assessor	☐
For County Recorder	☐
For County Treasurer	☐
For County Attorney	☐
For County Surveyor	☐
For Constable	☐
For Justice of the Peace	☐

◯

For United States Senator	☐
For Representative in Congress	☐
For State Representative	☐
For County Commissioner 4 yr term	☐
For County Commissioner 2 yr term	☐
For County Sheriff	☐
For County Clerk and Auditor	☐
For County Assessor	☐
For County Recorder	☐
For County Treasurer	☐
For County Attorney	☐
For County Surveyor	☐
For Constable	☐
For Justice of the Peace	☐

EXAMPLE OF OFFICE–GROUP BALLOT: PORTION OF MASSACHUSETTS BALLOT, 1958

EXAMPLE OF PARTY–COLUMN BALLOT: UTAH, 1958

officials directly accountable to the voters at election time. The result in most states and counties was to elect a long list of officials ranging from important policy offices to routine and even trivial offices. When voters were highly conscious of local government and took an active interest in local politics, they could know the candidates and the duties of the multitude of offices. In practice many voters ignore entirely the candidates for lesser offices. This situation is expressed in the statement that the vote falls off as you go down the ticket, for as you go down the ticket the offices become less important. The result is that candidates for these lesser offices receive far fewer votes than candidates for major offices and are elected with far fewer votes.

A growing dislike for these long ballots is displayed by the voters who only vote the top of the ticket and by students of government. In some elections, ballots have attained tremendous proportions—as long as six feet, and in some direct primaries containing over a thousand names. The increase in the number of measures submitted in referenda to voters merely adds to the length and to the responsibility that the voter is supposed to assume. The corrective is a shorter ballot, attained not by limiting measures to be voted on, but by making such state offices as secretary of state, treasurer, auditor, and attorney general and such county offices as coroner and tax collector appointive by executive or legislative officials. The demarcation between election and appointment, it is generally agreed, should be the difference between officials who directly determine public policies (chief executives and legislators) and officials who make little or no public policy, whose duties are defined for them and beyond their discretion. This is one of a number of reforms where little headway has been made. The difficulties in the way are vested interests in the *status quo*, the lack of dynamic motivation among the people to make the changes, and the amount of support necessary to amend state constitutions.

ELECTION ADMINISTRATION

Development of a National Election Day. Except for special elections, e.g., local elections to approve the issuing of bonds for capital improvements and elections called by the governor of a state to fill a vacancy in Congress or the state legislature, all elections in the United States today fall on designated dates fixed by constitutions or statutes. This situation is now taken for granted, although it has not always been so. In Colonial America elections in the royal colonies were held upon the issuance of writs by the royal governor. The writs specified the date of the election. The frequency of elections varied with the laws of the colonies. For instance, the legislative assembly had to be elected once in seven years in New Jersey, once in three years in Virginia and Maryland, once in two years in North Carolina, and once each year in Pennsylvania. In the Puritan colonies election days were fixed, but writs authorizing the election were issued. In colonies with counties the writs were sent to sheriffs, and in New England to the town constables. The main problem was informing or reminding the voters well in advance of the election day. The usual method was by poster notice at public places; in Virginia, Maryland, and North and South Carolina, the notice was either read at the end of church services or posted on the church. Quite often in the South the election day coincided with county court day when many people would be at the county seat to transact business anyway.[43]

It first became necessary to fix a national election day after the Constitution was adopted. Congress passed the first Presidential Succession Act in 1792, in pursuance of its power under the Constitution to determine the day when presidential electors were to cast their votes for President and Vice-President; the day Congress agreed upon was the first Wednesday in December. In order to avoid confusion, Congress also provided that the electors be chosen within thirty-four days before the first Wednesday in December. As long as a large number of states chose electors through their legislatures, it was not important what day the electors were chosen. After 1824, when all of the states except South Carolina began permitting popular election of electors, problems multiplied. The states, left free to pick the date as long as it was within thirty-four days of the first Wednesday in December, picked a variety of days in November.[44] The result of elections occurring on different days in different states was to encourage repeating, and in 1840 and 1844 both parties organized gangs of voters who were taken from state to state.

In response to pressure, Congress in 1845 set the uniform day of the first Tuesday after the first Monday in November for the election of electors.[45] The same day is also required for the election of members of

---

[43] Bishop, *op. cit.*, pp. 99–101, 110-112; Sydnor, *op. cit.*, pp. 14–15, 18. It was discovered in Virginia that going from house to house to give notice was not satisfactory.

[44] In two states, the second Monday; in fourteen, the first Monday; in two, the second Tuesday; in two, the first Tuesday; in two, the Friday nearest the first of November; in New York, Tuesday after the first Monday; in New Jersey, the first Tuesday and the day following.

[45] The reasons for adopting this day were understandable in the 1840's. The date should be as close as possible to thirty days before the first Wednesday in December. Public sentiment was opposed to voting on Sunday or to traveling on Sunday, which many would have to do if the election were held on Monday, because of the distance and the slow transportation. These considerations fixed Tuesday as the day of the week. However, if the second Tuesday of the month were picked, the election could be held as late as November 14, leaving only twenty-two days for the electors to assemble in December. The first Tuesday may fall on the first of November, an inconvenient day for businessmen. The first Tuesday after the first Monday conformed to all of the requirements and could not be later than November 8, always leaving about thirty days for the electors to meet and vote. It was further pointed out that by this time harvesting was over but roads were usually passable. Most of these reasons no longer

Congress unless a state constitution prescribes a different day. In the interest of economy and lessened confusion in holding elections, the states gradually adopted the first Tuesday after the first Monday for election of state officials and sometimes for county officials as well. Alaska holds general elections on the second Tuesday in October but must choose presidential electors on the same day as other states.

Hours of Voting. Since the voter today knows or can easily find out what day the election will be held, the only other information he needs is the time the polls will be open. Again we find that elections in our early history were not held during set hours. The polls would stay open until the officials knew that all of the voters had appeared or assumed that no more voters would appear. Then the sheriff or other official in charge would announce that the polls were closed.[46] When the states began setting hours for the polls to be open, the result was a great variety of times from state to state and even within a state, depending upon the size of the community or upon the nature of the election, whether a direct primary or general election. The earliest time for opening the polls is 6 A.M. and the latest closing hour is 9 P.M., with the earlier hours usually followed in rural areas, the later hours in the larger cities.[47]

When there is a definite legal time for closing the polls, the problem arises of how to deal with those voters who arrive before the deadline but must wait their turn and are thereby prevented from receiving their ballots before the deadline. In some states when there is a line of voters waiting at the hour to close the polls, those already in line may vote, but those arriving after the closing hour may not vote. A device sometimes used to keep out the latecomers is for a policeman to get in line at closing time; everyone ahead of him can vote, anyone behind him cannot. In other states some kind of arbitrary rule is used to determine how many waiting voters will be permitted to vote.

Twenty-eight states make some kind of provision for workers to have time off during voting hours to cast their votes. These laws lack uniformity in many respects but follow a general pattern. If an employee is qualified to vote, he "may upon prior application to the employer, absent himself from work for a specified period (usually one to four hours) without penalty, and without deduction from wages, the time of absence to be designated by

---

have any pertinence, and Congress in 1934, after the adoption of the Twentieth Amendment, set the day for the electors to vote farther into December, further nullifying the previous reasons for selecting the first Tuesday after the first Monday.——Stimpson, *op. cit.,* pp. 29-31; Edward Stanwood, *A History of the Presidency from 1788-1897* (Boston: Houghton Mifflin Company, 1898) pp. 36 ff.

[46] Sydnor, *op. cit.,* pp. 23-25; Bishop, *op. cit.,* pp. 113-114.

[47] Bertram M. Bernard, *Election Laws of the Forty-Eight States* (New York: Oceana Publications, 1950) pp. 86-87.

the employer. . . . The laws usually also provide penalties in case an employer refused an employee the privileges conferred under the laws." [48]

Distractions and obstacles are removed from voters by law. Generally, all liquor establishments must be closed during voting hours—a policy inspired by the revolt against the historical practice of mixing liquor and politics, especially when election polls were located in saloons.[49] In some states, in order to prevent intimidation, voters are exempt from arrest while going to or from the polls.[50]

Personnel for Elections. For the individual voter the challenge of an election is deciding how he will vote and getting himself to the polls, but this is infinitesimal compared with the challenge to those responsible for organizing and conducting an election. The general practice is to create a bipartisan state board or commission with various responsibility for the over-all conduct of elections. (Usually the one organization operates both direct primaries and general elections, although in Southern states the political party organization operates its own direct primary.) Party representation is not always equal, for the party holding the governorship or some other designated office may have an extra vote.[51] In one-party states the minority party may be legislated into a permanent minority status. State legislatures have universally ignored third parties and have either turned the entire administration over to the major parties or have provided for "nonpartisan" administration. The members of the state board have the power to select a bipartisan county board although the local authorities are sometimes designated by law—the county clerk or some other official. Duties of the county officials include registration, transporting ballots or voting machines and supplies to the polling places, supervision of the voting, interpretation of election laws.

The practice is to give these county authorities the power to appoint

---

[48] *Time Off for Voting*, U. S. Department of Labor, Bureau of Labor Standards, Bulletin No. 138, 1958, rev., p. 1. The constitutionality of the Missouri law which is generally typical was upheld by the Supreme Court in *Day-Brite Lighting, Inc.* v. *Missouri*, 342 U. S. 421 (1952).

[49] "In eighteenth-century Virginia elections, the plentiful supplies of liquor, occasional fights, and 'drunken loungers at and about the Courthouses' marred the assemblages of 'the good people and the industrious.' "——Sydnor, *op. cit.*, p. 18.

[50] The ruse of arresting voters on a fictitious charge or subpoenaing them as witnesses to prevent their appearance at the polls was an English practice at one time as well as American.——Seymour and Frary, *op. cit.*, p. 106.

[51] In Indiana (as an example) the state election board is composed of the governor as ex-officio chairman and one person from each of the two parties (casting the largest number of votes for secretary of state at the last preceding general election) chosen by the governor upon nomination by the chairman of each of the two parties' state central committees. The clerk of each circuit court is the secretary of the county election board and appoints two others who are nominated, respectively, by the chairman of the county central committees of the two parties casting the largest vote in the county for secretary of state at the last preceding general election.

the election officials in each voting precinct. This responsibility can be onerous because of the number of precincts and the number of officials required at each. In 1952 there was a total of 146,274 precincts or voting units in the United States. Connectitcut, because the counting is done by towns, had the smallest number, 169; California had the largest number, 20,746. The precinct officials are called by such names as judges, inspectors, commissioners, and each major party is supposed to be equally represented. They take an oath before beginning their duties for the day and are required to be qualified voters in the precinct in which they serve. In many states a person is disqualified for this post if he is in any way involved in the outcome of the election by being a candidate, being related to a candidate, or having placed a wager on the outcome. These officials are assisted by clerks and are responsible for maintaining order at the polls, if necessary calling upon the police for help.

Only in rare cases are these precinct officials required to pass a test to demonstrate their knowledge of election laws. Their chief qualification is often political, for they are frequently recommended by ward and precinct leaders. In this way the task of finding people to serve is accomplished with much less difficulty than would otherwise be the case. The tendency is to reappoint the same officials over and over so that they do develop a great deal of know-how through experience. These officials are usually paid a fixed sum for the day's work, ranging from $5 up, and are sometimes paid overtime for the number of hours worked after an arbitrarily fixed time in counting paper ballots and preparing the returns from the precinct.

Watchers. The only other people authorized by law to be in attendance at the polls to observe the day's proceedings are watchers appointed by the parties or candidates. The number of watchers permitted by state laws varies from one to five. They usually are required to have credentials to prove their right to be present. While they are forbidden to interfere with the legitimate work of the election officials, including the counting or recording of the vote, they are entitled to see what goes on and to make objection to practices or decisions that they deem inimical to the interests of the candidates or parties that they represent.

Preparing Ballots. For the general election the first preparation is ascertaining which candidates were nominated at the direct primary or at conventions or by petition, and are therefore entitled to have their names appear on the ballot. Local authorities responsible for preparing the ballots have in some cases a complicated task because of the large number of districts from which legislators and judges are elected. Many of these districts include one or more counties, while heavily populated counties contain various districts. Consequently the county election authorities must be sure that the ballots or machines sent to each precinct contain the names of candidates the voters of that precinct are entitled to vote for. When using paper ballots, the authorities must estimate the number to order from the printer, and depending upon the election, the number will vary. From experience, rules of thumb are worked out as guides in making these estimates. Normally, the number ordered will far exceed the number of voters, so that many unused ballots will be destroyed. On those rare occasions when the number of voters exceeds the supply of ballots, any kind of available paper may be pressed into use for the emergency. When machines are used, the authorities are responsible for their maintenance, for preparing the name plates of candidates and affixing the plates to the machines, and for transporting the machines to the precincts. Generally there are two machines per precinct, permitting each party's candidates to appear on a separate machine at the direct primary and both machines to be prepared identically at the general election. In case a machine fails to work during the election, crews of repairmen are supposed to be available for summons by the precinct officials.

Sample Ballots. Whether paper or machines are used, some sample ballots will be printed and distributed before election to acquaint voters with the nature of the ballot they will be voting. In a few states, e.g., California, a sample ballot is mailed to every registered voter; in other states, e.g., Ohio, to every fourth voter. In most states the voter must depend upon reproductions of ballots printed in newspapers. Finally, any additional supplies or equipment, including pencils, stamps and pads, forms to be filled out, ballot boxes, voting-machine models, sample ballots, must be delivered to each precinct by the county election authorities.

Voting Procedure. In each precinct a place is selected for the polls. Usually, public buildings—schools, fire houses, courthouses—are used although private homes are sometimes chosen. In some states a movable structure is transported to a designated spot in each precinct and parked at the curb. The voter, upon entering a polling place, identifies himself with a poll-tax receipt in poll-tax states or gives his name so it can be checked in the registration book or card index. If he is discovered to be entitled to vote, he is given a ballot or told which machine to go to. A voter is subject to challenge at a direct primary on the grounds of party membership—a challenge he can overcome usually by taking a party oath. He is also subject to challenge on the grounds that he is not qualified, and the decision then is left with the officials who determine the facts as best they can. The voter may be turned away or permitted to vote either without qualification or subject to future determination of his right to vote. Before casting his vote he has an opportunity to inspect a model of a voting machine or a sample ballot and can ask for instruction in using the machine or in marking a paper ballot. He can also ask for help in voting because of physical infirmity, illiteracy, etc.; in which case representatives of both parties are entitled to be present. In some states a friend or relative, instead of an election official, may render this help, and a voter may be entitled to it if he simply requests it irrespective of any physical inability.

Usually, a voter is permitted to take a sample ballot or piece of paper to guide him in marking the ballot. There is nearly always a time limit on the voter. Usually one to three minutes are allowed when voting machines are used, approximately five minutes for marking a paper ballot. If the voter makes a mistake in marking a ballot, he is allowed, as a general rule, as many as three paper ballots. In machine voting the process is over when the voter turns the master switch, thereby recording his vote and opening the curtains. When using paper, the voter returns the ballot to one of the officials, who checks the number on the stub of the ballot to make sure it is the same one issued to the voter. The official detaches the stub and drops the ballot in the box.

Counting Procedure. The determination of the number of votes cast for each candidate or the number of votes cast "Yes" or "No" on referenda is simple when machines are used. At the conclusion of the voting, when the polls are closed, the totals are simply copied from the machine, certified by the officials, and returned to the county election authorities. In the case of paper ballots, the procedure is much more onerous. Each ballot is unfolded by one of the officials while others, including the party watchers, observe; and the vote cast on each ballot is called out and marked on large tally sheets by clerks. Usually, as a double check, two clerks each keep a separate tally and the two tallies are compared for discrepancies. Various technical questions can arise in the reading of the votes. If a ballot has any other mark on it than the marks to indicate candidates voted for, the ballot may be thrown out and not counted. Most states require the voter to mark an X in the square after a candidate's name or in a party circle, although some states will accept a check mark or a plus sign. Whatever mark is used, it must be kept completely within the square or circle; otherwise, that one vote or even the whole ballot will be thrown out. Some laws require a voter to indicate his vote by crossing out the names of candidates he does not want to vote for, and then he may or may not be required to place a mark after the names of candidates he is voting for.

Ballots in some states do not contain squares after candidates' names, and the voter makes his mark opposite the names. The difficulty with this arrangement is that the voter may be careless and put his mark between two candidates' names. The election officials then must determine the voter's intention. Whatever the ballot arrangement, the officials from time to time exercise discretion in deciding which candidate a vote should be counted for as well as whether a ballot is acceptable in whole or in part. Appeals can be taken from these decisions to the county officials or to the courts or to both, but such protests are futile unless the election is challenged and a recount is demanded. Often, counting cannot begin until the polls are closed, and the workday is considerably extended if all the ballots have to be counted after that time. In the interest of greater efficiency—to avoid the mistakes caused by weariness—and of uniformity in exercising discretion, central counting boards are established in some cities; all ballot boxes are taken to the one place, opened, and counted there by a special group of employees.

Indictment of Election Administration. Most citizens have no contact with election administration except when they register or pay their poll tax, and when they vote. They have little if any comprehension of the machinery in operation, and they seem to be very little concerned about it. Their ire is aroused by crowded conditions at the polls, and they may carp occasionally about the officiousness in the way someone does his job. Nevertheless there appears to be considerable dissatisfaction with both the philosophy and the methods of the administration system among those who have much specialized knowledge. The main points of criticism are:

(1) The election laws are too complicated, too detailed, and too conflicting and uncertain. It is impossible for an average precinct election official to read the many pages of the applicable statutes and sufficiently understand them for his own purposes. Obscure meanings may baffle even lawyers, and it is sometimes difficult to get clear rulings from county or state attorneys.

(2) State supervision is scanty or completely lacking. The state election officials do little more than appoint county officials (assuming they have this power), publish the election laws, issue special regulations, and in some states, compile the state returns. Counties and larger cities become almost autonomous in conducting elections and sometimes proceed by disregarding provisions of the law. One very unfortunate consequence is that standards governing the whole voting process vary within the same state.

(3) The appointment of personnel all the way up and down the line according to partisan affiliations is attacked for placing emphasis upon patronage rather than competence and inviting corrupt practices by officials who are more concerned with winning an election than with an honest

election. The bipartisan system of appointment breaks down where one party is a hopeless minority and either fails to furnish its quota of officials or supinely acquiesces in the manipulations by the majority party.[52]

Corrupt practices acts intended to maintain honest elections and accurate reporting are in many respects violated, or at least nullified. Cases constantly arise revealing both loose methods and corruption, so that one often accepts election statistics with mental reservations. Errors of many kinds can be made, and it is not always possible to know if they were willful or inadvertent. The more extreme cases of fraud, however, are identifiable and can seldom be passed off as honest mistakes. Representative types of fraud and errors are: padding registration lists either by adding fictitious names or by failing to delete the name of the ineligible; the many kinds of corruption permitted in actual voting, such as repeating, impersonation, chain voting; the willful violations by precinct officials as evidenced in deluding voters when giving them assistance, stealing elections by tampering with machines and stuffing ballot boxes; errors in counting or purposely defacing ballots so as to disqualify them; "counting out"—stealing votes during the count by giving votes for one candidate to his opponent; delayed count—holding back the report of a vote until other reports are in; errors in the tally. It was the conclusion of the students of two Michigan recounts that most errors occurred in one-party and rural areas where officials were least competent, and that the number of errors was not related to the number of voters.[53]

Problems in Reform. The correction of many of these weaknesses lies in the administrative system, and increasingly the consensus favors a single state election official, independent of the legislature, governor, or other executive official, who actually has supervisory and enforcement power over a single responsible county official. These officials would have permanent tenure under a merit system, and both the state and county offices would have permanent staffs selected through examination procedure. The correction of many election errors can be realized by the use of voting machines and by improved systems of administration. However, it is at the precinct level that the frauds and errors are committed, and the chief problem is encouraging more competent people to study election laws and pass a test all for one day's employment. Just the increase in pay alone is not necessarily going to encourage people to accept all of this work or undergo the sometimes exhausting ordeal of conducting an election.

---

[52] Samuel J. Eldersveld and Albert A. Applegate, *Michigan's Recounts for Governor, 1950 and 1952: A Systematic Analysis of Election Error* (Ann Arbor: University of Michigan Press, 1954) University of Michigan Governmental Studies, No. 30, pp. 22-23. The basic work in this field remains Joseph P. Harris, *Election Administration in the United States* (Washington, D. C.: Brookings Institution, 1934).

[53] Eldersveld and Applegate, *op. cit.*, pp. 23-24, 119; Chap. 10.

The final problem is not deciding that appointments will not be made on a bipartisan basis, but successfully divorcing election administration from the parties. People who are involved in the outcome of elections are concerned with all of the preparations for voting and the procedure for counting and reporting the votes. It should be borne in mind that the frequent failure to prosecute violations of corrupt practices under the present system is attributable to the difficulty in persuading people to testify and in assembling sufficient evidence to make a case in court. These are the difficulties even when there is a will to prosecute, but prosecutors are themselves in politics and involved in the outcome of elections. They are sometimes loath to rouse the public's anger by unveiling in court what has been occurring behind the scenes. If a prosecution falls particularly upon one party, its leaders will claim—perhaps with some justification— that they are being pilloried for partisan purposes and that the guilt lies more heavily on the other side. No nerve of the political system is so sensitive as the control of elections, for upon it may hinge the future of men and parties as well as the future of the system itself.

Selected Bibliography

Bernard, Bertram M., *Election Laws of the Forty-Eight States*. New York: Oceana Publications, 1950. Legal Almanac Series, No. 24.

Bishop, Cortlandt F., *History of Elections in the American Colonies*. Columbia University Studies in History, Economics and Public Law, Vol. 3. New York: Columbia University Press, 1893.

Harris, Joseph P., *Election Administration in the United States*. Washington, D. C.: Brookings Institution, 1934.

——— *Registration of Voters in the United States*. Washington, D. C.: Brookings Institution, 1929.

McGovney, Dudley O., *The American Suffrage Medley*. Chicago: University of Chicago Press, 1949.

Ogden, Frederic D., *The Poll Tax in the South*. University: University of Alabama Press, 1958.

Porter, Kirk H., *A History of Suffrage in the United States*. Chicago: University of Chicago Press, 1918.

Price, H. D., *The Negro and Southern Politics*. New York: New York University Press, 1957.

Report of the United States Commission on Civil Rights 1959. Part II.

Seymour, Charles, and Donald Paige Frary, *How the World Votes*. Springfield: C. A. Nichols, 1918, 2 vols.

Stimpson, George, *A Book about American Politics*. New York: Harper & Brothers, 1952.

Strong, Donald S., *Registration of Voters in Alabama*. University: University of Alabama Press, Bureau of Public Administration, 1956.

Sydnor, Charles S., *Gentlemen Freeholders*. Chapel Hill: University of North Carolina Press, 1952.

Chapter Nineteen

Public Opinion, Propaganda, and Campaigns

Politics is an activity in which people compete for objectives by getting the support of other people. To speak of politics is to assume the existence of human beings and to take for granted that some of them are looking for followers among other beings. The processes of party politics are applied to one or another group of people with whom party leaders are concerned at one stage or another. In fact, partisan political competition follows the line of what leaders believe to be the interests and ideas of the public, or put another way, politicians are constantly searching for and trying to express public opinion. This assertion raises two immediate questions, which will be taken up in order: What is or should be the role of public opinion in the operation of government? What is meant by public opinion?

RAW MATERIALS—PUBLIC OPINION

Role of Public Opinion. Perhaps the most distinctive feature separating philosophies of government is the place assigned in the total scheme of things to the opinions of the ruled. Two extremes are found in the philosophy of authoritarian government, in which, theoretically, public opinion counts for nothing, and in the philosophy of democracy, in which, theoretically, public opinion one way or another counts for a very great deal. This antithesis in philosophy is ancient; it is clearly a definitive difference between the thinking of Plato and the thinking of Aristotle in the field of public organization of men. Put in its simplified garb, these two approaches are revealed in assertions that some men know what is best for all men versus assertions that all men know what is best for themselves if they have the opportunity to grasp the necessary data.[1]

---

[1] One of the most pertinent comments of this school of thought is the one attributed to the late Raymond Clapper: "Never underestimate the intelligence of the American people; and never overestimate its knowledge of the facts." Typical of endless statements distinguishing between the two types of regimes is: "It is a consoling thought that democracy is a sound device for substituting muddling for straight-line action. Experience and history have demonstrated that human beings, particularly *en masse*, are not capable of well designed straight-line action. It is more likely than not to be in the wrong direction. That's why totalitarian states, which have the powers to impose straight-line action, invariably fail. They move straight—but go the wrong way."——Dr. E. A. Goldenweiser, quoted in Edward H. Collins, *New York Times*, June 2, 1952.

In another view of the field, it becomes clear that arguments so extreme are completely unrealistic, since in practice government cannot be operated independently of public opinion. Even the violent tyrannies of an Adolph Hitler and a Josef Stalin took some notice of their publics and made concessions to opinions. The real differences in this respect between tyrannies and free governments are the differences in degrees and in methods of consulting public opinion. Napoleon concluded that "government is nothing unless supported by opinion." [2] Consent, which is a manifestation of opinion, is the proclaimed basis of representative or of free government. Yet some representatives use appeals to public opinion hypocritically as a means of ingratiation. To proclaim the sovereignty of the people may be sheer lip service. The crux of the problem, where public opinion is openly recognized and specifically sought, is to find the area of competence of public opinion. What can the people intelligently determine for themselves and what should be determined for them? [3] Answers to this question prove that there are wide differences of opinion about the extent of the competence.

Definitions. Definitions of public opinion abound. Some are similar or consistent. Some appear to be dissimilar and contradictory. Many seem to emphasize different factors, depending upon the interest and the orientation of the one making the definition.[4] One way to attack the problem is to separate the phrase into its component parts. An *opinion* is an expression by an individual on a controversial subject. The key elements are that an opinion is held by an individual, that it becomes an opinion when there is an overt manifestation by the individual through expression, and that the subject matter involved is recognized as being controversial. It can be said that before an opinion is expressed, it is an attitude; hence, an attitude upon being expressed becomes an opinion. *Public,* in the sense of public opinion, is really a misleading word, for it implies everybody, the whole population. If public opinion meant an opinion held by everyone, it would mean nothing. Really, public opinion refers to group opinion, but the fixing of the word "public" in the phrase seems to have become permanent and to talk about "group opinion" as

---

[2] Quoted in Robert B. Holtman, *Napoleonic Propaganda* (Baton Rouge: Louisiana State University Press, 1950) page v. Mao Tse-tung put the case more crudely: "We must follow wherever the masses go. In no other way can we lead them."

[3] Harwood L. Childs, *An Introduction to Public Opinion* (New York: John Wiley & Sons, 1940) pp. 26 ff.

[4] See Walter Lippmann, *Public Opinion* (New York: The Macmillan Company, 1922); Marbury B. Ogle, Jr., *Public Opinion and Political Dynamics* (Boston: Houghton Mifflin Company, 1951) Chap. 3; Daniel Katz *et al., Public Opinion and Propaganda* (New York: The Dryden Press, 1954) pp. 3 ff.; Curtis D. MacDougall, *Understanding Public Opinion* (New York: The Macmillan Company, 1952) pp. 12-32. Leonard W. Doob, *Public Opinion and Propaganda* (New York: Henry Holt and Company, Inc., 1948) Chap. 3.

a reform in semantics would likely create more confusion than it would dispel.[5] The word public, in the sense of public opinion, is collective, at least a joining together of two or more persons. They form a public because of mutual interest through a common focus of attention. In the widest sense, a public can be any two or more, but in the case of a public whose members express an opinion, those members have a common focus of attention on a subject which is controversial. *Public opinion,* then, is the expression by a group on one side of a controversy.

Further refinement and expansion of this definition is required to clarify and isolate the phenomena. (1) A public is not a concrete thing, so a public, properly speaking, cannot have an opinion. (2) A public can exist regardless of whether its members are physically together or dispersed, or whether they are all known to one another; the test is their sense of compatibility and belonging together, not their propinquity. (3) The size of publics varies widely, depending upon the kinds of interests their members express. Generally speaking, the degree of abstraction of the focus of attention is inversely related to size. The greater the abstraction, the smaller the size, and vice versa. Where controversy is not involved, this rule would apply as well—one would expect to get more members for a golf club than for a philosophy club. When controversy is involved, the general rule is that the more concrete the issue, the more and larger the publics that will be involved. The publics involved in the controversy of liking or not liking the New York Yankees are undoubtedly far larger as well as more expressive than the publics involved in the controversy over the question of Plato's authoritarianism.[6] (4) Understanding the meaning of public as a synonym for group, the number and kinds of publics seem to be infinite—even for those involved in controversy—and nearly everybody is a member of various publics, some engaged in controversy and some not. In this manner we find our way back to the phenomena of pressure groups which are involved in controversy and in a specialized type of controversy called political.

---

[5] The recognition of the distinction between "public" and "group" in public opinion, but the refusal to accept as a convention the established phrase "public opinion" led the late Professor Sait to one of the most outspoken denunciations in the literature in this field.——*American Parties and Elections* (New York: Appleton-Century-Crofts, Inc., 1952, 5th ed.) pp. 75-76.

[6] On the New York Yankee controversy and its publics the reader probably feels the need for no citations. On the antidemocratic side of the Platonic controversy, see Warner Fite, *The Platonic Legend* (New York: Charles Scribner's Sons, 1934); R. H. S. Crossman, *Plato Today* (London: G. Allen & Unwin, Ltd., 1937); A. D. Winspear, *The Genesis of Plato's Thought* (New York: The Dryden Press, Inc., 1940); K. R. Popper, *The Open Society and Its Enemies* (Princeton: Princeton University Press, 1946). On the prodemocratic side, see John Wild, *Plato's Modern Enemies and the Theory of Natural Law* (Chicago: University of Chicago Press, 1953); John H. Hallowell, *The Moral Foundations of Democracy* (Chicago: University of Chicago Press, 1954); R. B. Levinson, *In Defense of Plato* (Cambridge: Harvard University Press, 1953).

The opinion in public opinion is the opinon of the individual members of the public. It becomes a combination or average of their opinions shared jointly, but not separate or distinct from individual opinions.[7] It is very quickly discovered that the opinions of members of a public are similar rather than identical. Each person is likely to have different perceptions and different motivations and to see aspects of the controversy, if not the entire controversy, in different contexts. Since the public expresses its individuals' opinions for the purpose of effectiveness in winning the argument, the public wants to speak with unity. At this point the role of group leaders often becomes treacherous. A leader is, of course, a spokesman, and he wants to speak powerfully for his followers. They also want him to be forceful, but clashes may occur as to just what opinion he is to express. The mark of success is the ability to give voice to the cross section or average of the opinions of the public capable of being considered in the aggregate. The leader is constantly seeking common denominators to hold together the opinions of his followers. One way of holding down potential differences and creating greater unity is through the use of high-level generalizations, speaking in terms of the members' objectives in abstract terms so that all will readily agree. Differences in opinions are more likely to appear within a group or public as questions for decision become more specific.

Compulsion to Have Opinions. With the growth of human knowledge, the pyramiding of data, and the ever-growing perception of complexities, people would presumably be increasingly reticent to voice opinions in fields of learning in which they are laymen. The exact reverse seems to be true. Everyone appears to believe that the mark of a free man is the possession of a precise opinion on every conceivable subject. To admit that one does not know is to risk censure if not ostracism. There is probably more verbalizing by more people on matters they know nothing or little about than any of us would care to admit. The recognition of this social compulsion to have opinions can be grasped by leaders and turned to their advantage. For those people who feel an obligation to have an opinion, a thoroughly uncompromising and compelling leader may appear the most heroic and attractive. If such a leader can succeed in convincing others that he actually expresses the only proper or authentic opinion, they may adopt the opinion, deluded into thinking it is their own. To express doubt or to suspend judgment or freely to admit ignorance of a mass of data is even more untenable for leaders than for followers.

---

[7] "The locus of the subjective events is still individual. The Group is not a super-individual phenomenon but a many-individual phenomenon."——Harold D. Lasswell, *Psychopathology and Politics*, in *The Political Writings of Harold D. Lasswell* (Glencoe: Free Press, 1951) p. 241.

Simulated Opinions. Another observation about people together in groups is their tendency sometimes to lose their sense of individuality. As a result, they may for the moment accept identical opinions and conduct themselves in an uncharacteristic fashion. This kind of response is most typically found in those groups called "mobs," which are emotionally inflamed, but there are some such stimuli in all group associations. The very fact that a person is joining with others is likely to give him a greater sense of power and self-esteem. When an individual's action becomes anonymous because of the total action of a group, the person may feel the protection of numbers and a consequent loss of his individual sense of responsibility. He may, upon later reflection, repent in humiliation for his antics as well as for the opinions he accepted and expressed. The influence of others not only shapes our opinions but also may urge us to have opinions. In these ways, opinions may be superficial and may even be pure pretense. One of the most important considerations in gauging another's opinion is determining the intensity with which it is held and the likelihood of its being changed under stress. After all of these side issues are explored, the basic conclusion remains that public opinion depends upon individuals because individuals alone are capable of having opinions.

Observable Characteristics of Individuals. The process of managing people depends upon acting in conformance with people's opinions. Yet opinions vary from person to person, so that in operations of any magnitude leaders find that they must deal with aggregates and averages, since they cannot possibly solicit each individual's opinion and attempt to relate every one to a consistent line of action. Leaders, who must be managers of others' opinions, are reduced to the alternative of observing people in the mass and thereby concluding how best to deal with them. It is impossible to say how many observable characteristics of people can be found, but it is possible to point out some. It should also be realized that some of these characteristics probably do not occur to a leader, but may be assumed to exist because they are so basic or because the leader himself is too immersed in them to see them as a factor in human management. We can begin with some observable limitations which are common to people generally. They live within the *confines of a physical universe* which they accept so unquestioningly that it hardly seems like a limitation at all. Dissatisfaction with this situation may increase as people become more conscious of it and yearn to extend their activities into outer space or to other planets. Scientific developments begin to suggest that the perpetual exploits of some comic-book characters may eventually become reality. For the immediate future, anyway, our actions, our thinking, our anticipations are confined to the environment of the earth. Upon the earth there are additional limiting factors in such phenomena as climate, upon which we depend for food, resources, and physical and mental energies.

A different kind of limitation, one we are much more likely to be aware of, is the social-value system of the society. These standards are more flexible and evolutionary, perhaps, than the environment of our physical universe, but they do mark off for us in general ways the permissible area of personal conduct. A careful distinction should be drawn here. People often act and think outside the area of social values, but they are not supposed to, and leaders normally must treat them as though they never do. This permissible area can be described as including any person, act, or thing which inspires a positive reaction in the public. What do people apparently put value on? What do they seem to seek? At any time there will be some confusion in discovering the answers, because people often appear to be going in different directions at the same time. These inconsistences must be expected and accepted even though they cannot confidently be predicted.[8]

A nation which officially lionizes the homely virtues of simplicity and humility can be sold glamour and elegance to the point that a movie celebrity is not safe in public without a police escort. Leaders of various kinds, seeing the value placed upon such glamorized persons, seek them out to be photographed with or employ their publicity value for advancing controversial issues. It is sometimes possible to get a clue to what has social value from history books and general literature (What is featured? What is commended? What is condemned?), from stereotypes of "good" and "bad" as heroes and villains,[9] from slogans, from newspapers and periodicals (Who and what is news? How is each person or subject presented? Which news stories are obviously expected to create sympathy or animosity?). Odd and obscure facts about things unknown may be of interest to us, while we would look upon the same kind of information about ourselves as trivial.[10]

Irrespective of time, place, or circumstance, *people have certain wants for which they demand satisfaction.* All people have nutritional and sex

---

[8] One is sometimes at a loss to explain, much less predict, what people will consider appropriate; e.g., at a time when the Bikini bathing suit seemed established as fashionable beachwear, clothing-store managers were receiving protests from irate window shoppers who were scandalized at the sight of nude manikins in the display windows. This illustration may not so much reveal inconsistency as prove that the Bikini bathing suit's technical repudiation of nudism is essential in the American scheme of social values.

[9] One of these stereotypes, taken from the famous melodramas of a bygone era, was the expectation that villains would wear mustaches. Apparently, Thomas E. Dewey did not believe this stereotype either extended into the mid-twentieth century or was transferable from the stage to politics.

[10] " 'Some Mongolian tribes put salt in their tea,' says a filler item. Still, editors keep rejecting our article about a neighbor who puts sugar on his watermelon, probably because he isn't a Mongolian."—Senator Soaper, August 18, 1953.

demands which, in the most elementary sense of human management, are assumed and exploited. More subtle types of demands are capable of more sophisticated treatment. People at some point in respect to some problems demand authoritative answers because they cannot remain in permanent mental suspension. This demand includes having things explained for them, having certain immutables established for them, having reassurance that their personal worlds are in harmony and that they have definite things to look forward to. People also demand security, but not exclusively in the narrow sense of financial security. Rather, this demand too is for assurance—the assurance that tomorrow will be like today. There is also a demand for freedom, but it is often unfathomable and is counterbalanced by other demands which restrict a person's freedom of action. What is accepted as being freedom or regimentation is sometimes determined by habit. Denial or restriction of a particular freedom may create a tremendous uproar immediately, but may gradually be accepted as people get used to it. The nature and extent of the response depends upon the freedom and the restriction. Finally, people demand or insist upon making value judgments. To be human is to acquire concepts of right and wrong, good and bad. Value judgments are often affected by time, place, and circumstance, but the making of such judgments is universal. They are so strong that they dictate or at least restrict how we satisfy our other demands.

Word Symbols. The process of forming opinions is by means of communication, i.e., the use of symbols. The most commonly recognized symbols are words, whether written or spoken, but words are by no means the only or necessarily the most effective symbols. In fact, words have both tremendous advantages and limitations. Their advantages are definite and quite self-apparent: They are capable of standardization in meaning, yet of infinite flexibility in use; they are cheap and easy to use. Their limitations can be equally appreciated. While words have standardized meanings, many words have various meanings or shadings of meanings and these connotations often confuse rather than clarify when words are used carelessly. The knowledge that conflicting meanings can attach to words may be applied in two different ways: When the intention is to be clear and precise, words will be selected for their exactness and meanings will be carefully described to avoid confusion. When the intention is to confuse or to gloss over difficulties in an effort to win an argument, words may be used for their vagueness in meaning. Attempts to influence public opinion usually exhibit examples of both methods, although the second may be used unintentionally because the communicator himself is a victim of the confusion.

These limitations of words almost always are involved in controversies over public policies. The very context in which we discuss issues is either inherently in or easily adaptable to the realm of emotionalism, and even those issues capable of calm discussion are frequently given emotional motivations as part of the art of argumentation. Almost the whole lexicon of the social sciences is emotionally charged in such words as "democracy," "justice," "the people," "social welfare." Even the act of teaching is complicated by the fact that scholarly analysis runs afoul of the emotional connotations attaching to the words which are analyzed or which are incidental to the analysis. At some points the communicator is baffled in his search for words with exact meanings, words which are not so emotionally charged that people will resent their being examined objectively. Although the emotionalism attaching to words is a grave problem in many kinds of situations, the recognition of the fact can be used to advantage in other situations. The very indefiniteness of such words becomes a weapon for manipulators of public opinion, in calling forth signal responses in their audiences. It does not matter if each person receiving the communication has a different definition or idea of what "democracy" is as long as all of them have a positive reaction to the word. Then by the use of it a generally uniform signal response is achieved.

Conversely, some kinds of words have no emotional connotation and refer specifically to the phenomenon intended by the communicator.[11] The words of the physical and natural sciences fall into this category, for they represent or describe particular things or ideas with no emotion or sentiment attached.[12] It would indeed be remarkable to witness a political argument over the correct formula for water or hydrochloric acid. If these formulas are to be revised, it is the responsibility of chemists. The general public is unconcerned with the symbols and even with the properties of water and acids; most people want sufficient water for their use, and they hope that it does not have to be shot full of chemicals which make it unpalatable or hazardous to clothing in laundering. Mathematics, the symbolical language of these sciences, is nonemotional. If some one adds 2 and 2 and gets 5, his difficulty is a lack of basic learning, not an emotional conviction that 5 is the correct answer.[13] It is entirely possible that

---

[11] This distinction between words on the basis of the definiteness of their meaning or their referent and the basis of the degree of emotionalism attaching to them is comparable to the distinction between intentional words and extensional words, respectively, discussed in Ogle, op. cit., pp. 70-72.

[12] In fact, most people understand little if any of this communication, e.g., "Heavy Particle Detection Using an Electron Multiplier" or "Chromosome Breakage and Mitotic Inhibition Induced by X-Rays at Known Mitotic Stages of the Grasshopper Neuroblast" —titles of university dissertations in physics and zoology, respectively.

[13] A fascinating attempt at expressing political concepts in mathematical symbols and formulas is to be found in the two articles by Profesor Charles H. Titus, "A Nomenclature in Political Science," American Political Science Review, Vol. 25 (1931) pp. 45-60, 615-627. Aside from the remote possibility that this kind of language would be accepted, it is doubtful if the substitution of unemotional symbols for the names of emotional concepts would be rewarding. Very likely, as the association was made, people would look upon π, the symbol for politics, with the same emotional attachment they now have for the word itself.

some symbols in the arsenal of science can produce emotional responses. Certainly the words "atom bomb" and "hydrogen bomb," which are popular terms, are in this category, although the technical term, thermonuclear, is too scientific-sounding to acquire emotional attachments. All words cannot be permanently classified as emotional or nonemotional, for many can be given either connotation depending upon the context in which they are used. The word "people" can be purely a referent when speaking of population—100,000 people live in a particular city—or it can be a word of intense emotion in political language as applied to welfare or human suffering.

Other Types of Symbols. The oldest means of communication in the history of man are *pictorial* symbols, be they beacon fires, smoke signals, pictures, or reflection of the sun's rays. While the use of pictures or other visual appeals have limitations in their accessibility and the precision of their meaning, they are the most simple, and if used effectively, can be most powerful in their impact. The recognition of their value is revealed in the dependence upon visual aids in the learning process at all levels of instruction. The effects of motion pictures and television are almost incalculable in the kinds of influence they can exert upon attitudes and opinions. The use of the political cartoon, which is almost entirely visual, has become an intimate aspect of the party battle and has a recognized place in political chronology.[14] The ability to convey instantly the idea of a party by the symbol of an animal has probably had considerable effect upon people's political understanding, especially by the subtle presentation of an attitude in the way the animals are drawn and the epitomizing of an idea through this symbolism.

Other types of symbols with more limited but highly effective use are *music, color,* and *odors.* Everyone understands the association of music with events in their lives, with sentimental attachments, with stirring emotional experiences; national anthems are supposed to arouse patriotic fervor, and many pieces of music, as the *Marseillaise,* have had controversial ideological associations. The selection *Marching Through Georgia,* because of its associations, has limited appropriate uses in the United States. Colors have immemorially been associated with status or conditions: black for mourning, white for purity, red and purple for royalty. The simplicity and ease in being able to communicate a whole complex

---

14 The symbol of the Democratic donkey was first published in 1837.——Stefan Lorant, *The Presidency: A Pictorial History of Presidential Elections from Washington to Truman* (New York: The Macmillan Company, 1952) pp. 146–147. The symbol of the Republican elephant was created by Thomas Nast in 1874 in his drawings in *Harper's Weekly.* Nast also popularized the donkey beginning in 1870.——George Stimpson, *A Book about American Politics* (New York: Harper & Brothers, 1952) pp. 281–284; letters column in the *New York Times Magazine,* January 23, 1955.

series of ideas by color is too obvious to need elaboration. Odors can remind us of food, warn us of danger, gratify our esthetic urges, and (according to perfume manufacturers) arouse us to passions.

Symbols are far more complicated in meaning and more flexible in use than this short discussion suggests. A large part of our living is predicated upon the recognition of the meaning represented by symbols. There are symbols such as crosses associated with salvation, although the location of the cross or its form may variously suggest a church or a grave; white crosses are symbolical of military cemeteries. Other symbols connected with religion are: an apple for Eve's sin, a pearl for salvation, an eye in the hand for the Lord. A shock of wheat means abundance. Insignia displayed on clothing immediately convey military rank, as clothing itself is taken to represent status. Some symbols appear to be universal and standard in their meaning, while others are accepted temporarily and then their significance passes. The stars and stripes can never be mistaken in its symbolism, but the generations following the heyday of Alfred E. Smith will never appreciate the symbol of the brown derby hat which had so much real meaning to Americans in the 1920's. Symbols are not only inevitable but indispensable. Yet, one should realize that a symbol often stands for a congeries of things which become lumped together without regard to the differences among the units making up the totality. Furthermore, symbols stand for things but are not the things themselves, just as a map represents land and water but is itself merely a piece of paper.

Basis of Opinions in Beliefs. Communication is the means for both discovering and attempting to change or influence public opinion, but the likelihood of success in the second is dependent upon success in the first. To know what opinions people hold is to know where to begin in efforts to convince them. More basic is the investigation of *why* people hold particular opinions, since it is highly unlikely that they will accept just any opinion presented to them. Again, the individual nature of opinion must be remembered, as well as the fact that public opinion arises from individuals sharing common or similar opinions on a given subject. Since opinions are expressions regarding controversies, there is a problem in semantics, if not in actuality, in discussing the condition and the process of opinion formation. Many subjects are capable of being controversial, but are not so because there is a general consensus among people. It can be said that theism versus atheism is controversial, but the controversy rarely flares up because most people are theists; at the same time, there are endless religious controversies among theists. Leaders must never overlook this distinction. By adhering to one religious doctrine they do not alienate believers in opposing doctrines except where there is complete lack of religious tolerance. However, no leader could expect to accomplish much among theists if he were an atheist. He would be challenging, not opinions about religious practices, but the consensus about a Supreme Being.

When a consensus exists, we often refer to it as a belief unless it is in the realm of objective phenomena, like the existence of a mountain or the dimensions of a house. We can distinguish between what is accepted as a fact (I am sitting at a table; I am walking down the street) and what is a matter of truth (All free men are better off than slaves; representative government is the best government). A fact has practical validity because by the arbitrary standards we adopt we can "prove" or "demonstrate" it. Truth becomes such if we accept it as truth, if we believe the substance of the assertions. That which is accepted as fact is beyond controversy. That which is accepted as truth is considered beyond controversy although the most virulent controversies have been clashes of opposite beliefs. Opinions, therefore, are products of what we believe to be true.

Beliefs are distinguishable from techniques and skills employed in the physical world to harness the forces of nature, to invent laborsaving devices which increase the ease and joy of living. The beliefs by which men live give meaning as well as impetus to the development of skills and are the cement which holds a society together.[15] Our system of beliefs cannot be approached in terms of good or evil, truth or falsity, since beliefs are the energizing forces behind men in relation to which they measure the value of the objectives they strive for and accomplish. Through his beliefs, a man understands the world about him, seeing his own relation to his environment, and develops his aspirations for what he considers to be "the good life." The tremendous value of beliefs is setting up goals or ideals for which men strive even though the very sublimity of the goals precludes their being attained.

Belief in authority is a prerequisite to human organization. The demands for authority and for security are satisfied by institutions of authority and by the leaders of the institutions who symbolize the authority. Government as an institution has become the central authority since the rise of the nation-state, for its leaders exercise or authorize the supreme coercive power. Yet, the power of government ultimately relies upon acceptance, and its authority is represented and enforced by the whole arsenal of commonly identified symbols such as music, color, pictures, and words, as well as by the use of ceremony and ritual. Here is part of the secret of consent by the governed in the establishing of habitual responses and consensus toward the symbols of the authority of government. The use of legend, which itself has some basis in historical fact, is never put to more effective purpose than in bolstering belief in governmental

---

15 Robert M. MacIver, *The Web of Government* (New York: The Macmillan Company, 1947) pp. 3–12.

authority. In fact, history itself is legendized for popular consumption and gives the controversial values of the present greater authority by the simplified presentation of the past. Belief in authority is found in all highly esteemed institutions, churches, schools, clubs. The symbolical representation and reinforcement, even when depending upon different symbols, serves the same purpose in all institutions.

Evolving Beliefs. While beliefs are not static, they normally change slowly and at any given time may appear to be immutable. Since they are affected by environment, they evolve even when they are not openly challenged; but a belief is only shaken when it no longer explains phenomena, when it is no longer compatible with new experiences. People may conclude that some of their beliefs obstruct rather than facilitate the solution of problems. Even as our beliefs evolve, a great deal of the old remains with the new, so that the changes are most frequently to be compared with a slight veering in a road rather than a sharp reversal of direction. In some cases, beliefs are challenged and attacked in the hopes of speeding up the process of change. Our beliefs are not capable of being logically demonstrated like a hypothesis in geometry, and to demand this kind of "proof" would in itself be a denial of the beliefs. People will be repelled by attacks upon their beliefs unless they already are beginning to lose their validity. Beliefs are destroyed by opposing beliefs, and to overcome one system, another system must be supplied. It is in this context that the onslaught of the tyrannical system of the USSR proceeds against the system of democracy.

Measurement of Public Opinion. These analyses of people stimulate a tremendous interest in going beyond the surface of the phenomena in order to explore the unknown and to measure its characteristics. The entire structure which is now being reared in the academic world under the title of the behavioral sciences is based upon the concept that at last the final mysteries of the human personality can be dispelled and that opinions can be not only measured but also anticipated. The quantification of people was applied to the world of commerce before it was systematically applied in the political realm. Manufacturers have an understandable desire to learn what consumers think about their products and are willing to pay large sums of money to find out. There is a growing industry in the field of conducting commercial surveys and telling corporations how their goods and services should be advertised. These are investigations of specific opinions about one or another commercial product. In the wider reaches of opinion measurement, universities are increasingly active. Both party organizations and candidates are willing to spend money for pre-election surveys. The demand both in academic and commercial fields for personnel trained in the skills of statistics, survey procedures, and quantification methodology is bringing in its wake new curricula in the social sciences and the invention of a new esoteric language in which these new concepts and measurements are communicated.

Surveys are undertaken to find out what people are thinking, what their opinions are on given subjects, and why they hold those opinions. Election surveys are sometimes used as a basis for prediction, e.g., those of the Roper and Gallup organizations; but other surveys are more concerned with analysis and interpretation and with advancing the total area of dependable information about people. These measurements depend more frequently upon the use of open-ended questions, i.e., questions for which alternative answers are not provided the respondent, but he is asked to answer in his own words exactly what he thinks. This kind of question is supposedly capable of bringing out both predominant opinions and the multitude of individual reactions, motivations, beliefs. A logical extension of this technique will be more and more into psychoanalysis, impelled by the drive to probe more deeply than is possible by the customary interviewing procedure.[16]

Limitations in Measurements. This grandiose vista of the possibilities for exploring opinion, its formation, and its roots depends upon the rigorous application of procedures which themselves are subject to constant review and revision. There is lack of agreement about methods of sampling which after all are based on mathematical laws of probability and are statistical questions. Initially, however, the concept of the entire procedure relies upon the acceptance of a sample as being representative of the group or area—called the "universe"—to be investigated. Admitting that in most cases everyone in the "universe" cannot be interviewed because most "universes" are too large, it then follows that the sample must stand for the "universe." A completely random sample may be satisfactory if it will give the results the investigator wants; thus his only problem is making sure the sample is random and not inadvertently overrepresentative of one characteristic of the "universe." For many purposes a random sample is not satisfactory because it is assumed that people falling in certain categories will have significantly different opinions. These purposes lead to stratifying the population within the "universe" and sampling from each stratum on an equal basis or on a proportional basis. Gallup and Roper have used the quota wherein the United States, as the "universe," has been stratified by age, education, economic status, sex, size of community, etc., and a predetermined number of respondents is found in each category.

---

16 For example, Harold D. Lasswell, *Power and Personality* (New York: W. W. Norton & Company, Inc., 1948) ; Else Frenkel-Brunswik, "Interaction of Psychological and Sociological Factors in Political Behavior," *American Political Science Review*, Vol. 46 (1952) pp. 44–65.

Another method is to stratify by area and then select at random from each area.[17]

To frame the questions for a survey requires knowing exactly what information is sought. The more elaborate the undertaking, the more questions can be designed to extract more information. Next, the most challenging problem occurs in the framing of the questions. The objective is simple and clear words which are at the proper vocabulary level of the respondents and are unequivocal in meaning. From the previous discussion of words it is obvious that this objective is never thoroughly achieved. Experimentation with questions by pretesting and rewording them is often helpful. The choice between open-ended and closed-ended questions depends upon the ambitious nature of the survey, the skill of the staff and the amount of money available. The possibilities of the open-ended question have already been suggested, but its limitations are found in interviewing and tabulating. The interviewer must have great skill and considerable time for his work, and he should make every effort to record the response without injecting either extraneous material or his own projection of what the respondent meant. Furthermore, the tabulating and coding of the responses is a serious challenge in capturing the essence of the opinions. While the closed-ended questions lack the possibilities of depth interviewing, they are the way to measure responses to a direct question such as, "What candidate are you going to vote for?" Here the respondent has the choices of available candidates or saying he does not know or will not vote. All conceivable answers are foreseen and supplied so that either the interviewer or the respondent can check the applicable answer. The interviewing is much simpler, and the tabulating is purely routine. The two kinds of questions bear some relationship to the distinction between the words "polls" and "surveys." Polls are, properly speaking, a process of counting heads on a question. Surveys are more than a counting; they take in depth interviewing, probing for motivations and beliefs. A survey depends much more upon open-ended questions, but of course makes use of the closed-ended kind as well.

In commercial surveys, interviewing precedes or parallels the sales campaign. There is no fixed point, as there is in election surveys where everything points to the day the voters cast their ballots. In election surveys, two distinct techniques have been used. In one kind a single interview is conducted at some point before the election and the results are tabulated. In the second kind a group of respondents is selected and asked if they will agree to being reinterviewed a given number of times before the election. This is known as the panel-type interview.[18] It permits the

---

[17] See Angus Campbell *et al.*, *The Voter Decides* (Evanston: Row, Peterson & Company, 1954) pp. 227-230.

[18] The pioneer in this technique was Professor Paul Lazarsfeld, who first used it in the United States in his 1940 survey of Erie County, Ohio.

charting, so to speak, of each respondent during an election campaign, noting when he crystallized his opinions and why, when he changed his mind if he does change, what campaign events had the greatest impact, what issues predominate at one time or another or consistently throughout the whole campaign. In either kind of interview technique, much depends upon the interviewer. He should limit himself to asking just the questions provided and avoid injecting his own opinions in any way. He should be diplomatic but insistent in getting the information and should establish rapport with the respondent. The respondent must be relied upon to give truthful answers as well as genuine answers, i.e., the opinions should be actually held, not suddenly adopted for the purpose of answering a question.

A science and a scientific method are distinguished by the ability to attain the same results under the same controlled conditions. A science of human behavior encounters special difficulties. One test of success arises in the attempts to predict, and the question to be answered is whether these phenomena lend themselves to accurate predictions.[19] The trust-worthiness of respondents is the first problem. Can they be depended upon to tell the truth, to remember accurately, to reproduce the same data for different interviewers in different interviews? Contradictory findings by different survey organizations point up, among other things, this difficulty.[20] In predicting election outcomes based on polls and surveys, another trouble-some decision is accounting for the total sample, including who will not vote as well as who will vote and for whom. Since the sample represents the "universe," the entire sample must be considered. Therefore, when a respondent says he will vote for Candidate A, the investigator must decide whether the respondent will actually vote, and if he does, whether he will carry out his announced voting intention. When a respondent says he has not made up his mind, the investigator again must decide if he will vote and for whom. When a respondent says he does not intend to vote, the question is whether he will carry out this intention or will finally decide to vote, and for whom. It becomes more understandable why investigators attempt to correlate demographic factors with voting behavior and seek to find combinations of personal characteristics, such as the Index of Political Predisposition, as clues in predictions.[21] The greatest aid in forecasting

---

[19] One of the principal doubters has been Lindsay Rogers: see *The Pollsters* (New York: Alfred A. Knopf, Inc., 1949). Hadley Cantril *et al.*, *Gauging Public Opinion* (Princeton: Princeton University Press, 1944), discuss most of the problems in this field, but not as doubters.

[20] For example, in their 1952 surveys the Survey Research Center and the Roper organization arrived at different conclusions regarding the women's vote in the presidential election. For a cataloguing of consistent and inconsistent findings of various election studies, see Bernard R. Berelson *et al.*, *Voting* (Chicago: University of Chicago Press, 1954) Appendix A.

[21] See above, Chap. 12.

is the fact that people normally make up their minds how they will vote and actually vote that way.[22] As for the exact forecast of the vote, most pollsters have conceded an error of 2% to 3%.

The greatest loss of prestige for the survey techniques occurred after the 1948 presidential election when the nationally publicized polls were wrong in their predictions. Here, apparently, was an election where the voters did not behave the way they were supposed to. Not only did a substantial number of voters report that they would vote for Dewey and then change their minds and vote for Truman, but also a larger than average number kept putting off their voting decision.[23] The election also revealed the ability of the pollsters themselves to be swept along with the popular assumption which their own polls had helped to create. Having been burned so badly in 1948, the pollsters refused to accept the implications of their figures in 1952, predicting that the result would be close. In its way this prediction was even wider of the mark since the forecasting of a close election like that of 1948 is obviously more difficult. Even in 1956, memories of 1948 were still fresh enough to produce hedges and extreme caution in predictions.[24]

Objectives of Quantification Methodology. The last question to be asked about so ambitious a movement as the behavioral sciences is, Where are they moving? At the outset it should be noted that they are not the beginning of either an interest in or investigations of behavior, for the social sciences have generally been directed toward people's behavior in various kinds of situations. The departures of these sciences are into new realms of techniques. They proceed from the assurance that all human phenomena can be measured quantitatively if the proper methodology is employed. If this position is not asserted, it is certainly implicit. To what ends are these measurements directed?

Dr. George Gallup insists that polls as miniature referenda or plebiscites are supremely justified as an *aid in the operation of representative government;* that they make the town-meeting type of direct democracy applicable to the twentieth century. His conclusion is based on the discovery in his polls that the people are often ahead of their leaders regarding public policy and that leaders can and should consult the polls to discover public opinion on the issues of the day. The result will be more precise and effective representation and less guessing about what people want

---

[22] Robert Bower, "Public Opinion Polls and the Politician," *The Annals,* September 1948, pp. 104-107. The experience cited here indicated about 87% in this stable category.

[23] For an analysis of the polls, see Frederick Mosteller *et al., The Pre-Election Polls of 1948* (New York: Social Science Research Council, 1949). See also Ogle, *op. cit.,* pp. 262 ff.

[24] *New York Times,* May 27, 1956. Associated Press dispatch, November 8, 1956.

done.[25] Leaders are not likely to be surprised to find a time lag between the expression of desire for changes and the realization of the changes. Leaders like to make sure of their ground before they move, or they may cease to be leaders. Their dependence upon polls varies, although the trend toward dependence is likely to be on the increase, as we have new leaders conditioned to the acceptance of the polling techniques.

An entirely different level of conception about the new techniques takes as its point of departure their *tremendous contributions to civilization*.[26] By refinements in methodology, in testing, in examining, people can be placed in the professions to which they are best adapted and can be more socially useful. We can learn the maximum about ourselves and finally comprehend how to live in the most satisfying and productive manner. Superstitions and ignorance can be abolished. Intelligence can gradually replace muddling, and the rational can replace the irrational in human affairs.

Indictment of the Methodology. There are many questions to be asked about the future implications of these new measurement techniques, but before these questions have any pertinence, the compatibility of phenomena and the methodology must be assured. If inappropriate measurements are used or if the phenomena do not completely lend themselves to quantification, the techniques will in reality be limited in their usefulness. At the outset, one can ask, *What is being measured?* [27] The commercial pollsters, if not the university surveyors, often speak of measuring public opinion. To ask respondents closed-ended questions and count the responses for each possible answer is a measurement of those opinions elicited from respondents. These tabulations are or are not public opinion depending upon the definition of the term. If public opinion is a collection of individual opinions on a question where all possibilities are foreseen in the alternative answers, this measurement is as accurate as the distribution of respondents' answers reflects the actual distribution of answers in the "universe."

In turn, other assumptions are made; e.g., the opinions (or lack of them) expressed by respondents are their real opinions. However, not

25 See particularly, George Gallup and Saul F. Rae, *The Pulse of Democracy* (New York: Simon and Schuster, Inc., 1940) Chapter 21. Who is ahead of whom on what issues can be a matter of opinion itself and certainly is exceedingly more complex than Gallup's thesis suggests. See Doob, *Public Opinion and Propaganda*, pp. 62–63. An ambitious survey of both leaders and followers revealed that leaders would grant more freedoms to those working on behalf of the Soviet international conspiracy than the general public would.——Samuel A. Stouffer, *Communism, Conformity and Civil Liberties* (New York: Doubleday & Company, Inc., 1955).

26 For a popularly written presentation of this case, see Stuart Chase, *The Proper Study of Mankind* (New York: Harper & Brothers, 1948).

27 Rogers, *op. cit.*, Chaps. 3, 4.

everyone says openly what he thinks privately. Others have no actual opinion, but would as readily be caught without their hair combed as without an opinion. The compulsion to have an opinion may be increased by being interviewed. There is the fear the interviewer may look down upon those who do not give the "right answer." A poll or survey reveals useful information when the respondents understand and know something about the questions and give answers neither simulated nor deceptive. It is safer still if the questions have only a limited number of possible answers whether they are elicited open-ended or closed-ended. To poll regarding a contemplated action, like voting in an election, permits checking up on the polling after the action is taken.

A great deal of polling and surveying cannot be checked in this fashion. To ask an open-ended question, Why are you going to vote for candidate X? may produce a pattern in the answers showing that certain characteristics of the candidate or the campaign predominate. However, open-ended questions establish the *individuality of opinions,* and the coding process may itself beg the question of why. One answer may be classified as candidate-oriented and subdivided in the category that he is doing a good job in the office and should be retained, while another candidate-oriented answer may fall in the category of personal qualities of the candidate apart from the way he conducts his office. These are both outwardly and potentially meaningful differences in responses, but the possibility for different categories of candidate-oriented responses may result in a tabulation of almost as many categories as there are respondents in this general classification. To analyze this measure of public opinion in terms of each individual response becomes nugatory unless the objective of the survey is to demonstrate the atomization of opinions and the resulting complexity of the public reaction and evaluation. Normally, similar responses are grouped together and given an identical code number, so that a large enough number of respondents become available in each category for analysis and possible generalization.

This type of question which calls out individual responses raises more annoying problems when *applied to matters of public policy.* Should the Government of the United States take a certain kind of action regarding a particular problem? Too frequently such questions are closed-ended, forcing respondents to classify themselves Yes, No, Undecided, No Opinion, or with the added benefit of some qualifications of Yes or No. To ask the question open-ended risks bringing down a deluge of unrelated answers, as well as consistent answers based on mutually exclusive reasons. Nowhere does the problem of language appear so great as at this point, for the selection of key adjectives and nouns with favorable or unfavorable connotations can virtually predetermine the side of the majority.[28] Many such questions are analyzed without giving sufficient consideration to the number of respondents having no opinion. In some cases this classification may hold the key to the significance of the public's reaction. The most unhappy evidence of the problem of polling on issues is the contradictory answers elicited to different questions.[29] Americans generally back away from any proposal contemplating war but often strongly favor proposals which could readily lead to war, as long as the question refers to "maintaining peace" or fails to refer to the war potential of the proposal. On a series of small scales, people reaffirm their opinions on the major issue of economic policy: Many want more money spent for their interests but want financial solvency, less inflation, and a balanced budget at the same time. To make these discoveries is not particularly enlightening to government officials who are making decisions.

The town-meeting concept of policy determination by polling is qualified by the fact that majority opinion as measured by the polls can shift suddenly from No to Yes on an issue after the issue is settled by government action; i.e., *the bandwagon effect* can operate powerfully upon people who had a weak opinion either way, no opinion, or even a strong opinion on the other side.[30] This behavior is itself essential to the operation of representative government. The minority at some points must acquiesce in the majority decision, and the result, in time, may be a consensus. The function of leadership, occasionally at least, is to act contrary to the apparent opinions of the majority when the leaders have the data, the comprehension, and the perspective of a problem which the public does not and perhaps cannot have. The fact of taking action may convince some that they were wrong and cause others to suspend their judgment while they wait and see. The action may also cause a tornado of verbal attacks, and government leaders usually time such actions so that the storm of abuse will have blown over and a favorable reaction will have set in before the next election.[31]

---

28 At a referendum in South Carolina, August 27, 1940, the determination of public policy was largely settled by the wording of the question: "Are you in favor of discontinuing the legal sale of intoxicating liquors, wines, beers, or other intoxicating beverages, and the imposition of new taxes to replace lost revenues as a result of repeal of present liquor laws?"

29 See, *e.g.*, Thomas A. Bailey, *The Man in the Street* (New York: The Macmillan Company, 1948). Frederick C. Irion, "Public Opinion Research—An Opportunity for Political Parties," *American Political Science Review*, Vol. 44 (1950) p. 921.

30 Rogers, *op. cit.*, pp. 39 ff.

31 In 1832 the opposition to Jackson injected the issue of rechartering the Second Bank of the United States into the campaign four years before the charter expired. This act illustrated the reverse situation in timing, an attempt to embarrass the Jackson Administration by Jackson's veto of the rechartering bill. Jackson won the issue and the election, the two obviously being connected. The election also settled the issue once and for all. Whether the bank advocates were the majority or the minority in 1832, they eventually had to acquiesce.

This characteristic of the problem is related to another even more fundamental difference—*the intensity of opinion*. Even those who actually have opinions and are willing to state them vary in the degree of intensity with which they hold the opinion. Different levels of intensity can be described. For instance, an opinion may be casual, the person maintaining it, but without enthusiasm or even deep conviction; at this level the opinion can be modified or even dislodged by the proper amount and kind of counterpersuasion. A person may have a stronger opinion which he wishes to discuss and advance; this can be designated the exhortatory level, and the opinion can be changed only by some fundamental experience. On a third level is sacrificial opinion, the highest intensity, for which the individual would sacrifice himself; this is the position of the genuine martyr, and his opinion cannot be changed by any foreseeable circumstances or techniques. These three levels are clear in theory but cloudy in application. The sacrificial opinion may be identified only by offering to put the respondent to death and then determining if he will recant. Whatever levels or degrees of opinion exist, the knowledge that there are meaningful differences in intensity is one of the first considerations in evaluating polls on issues.

The problem of intensity is a perfect example of one of the indictments of the measurement techniques. To measure the state or condition of intangible factors must depend upon *subjective judgments* of respondents, interviewers, coders, etc. To ask two respondents to classify their political partisanship on a scale ranging from very strong Democrats to very strong Republicans is to depend upon the words having the same connotation in both cases. A person may classify himself as an independent and vote consistently for the candidates of one party, or he may classify himself as a strong partisan and be antagonistic to the party's current leaders. A man who had once split his ticket and admitted the outside possibility of doing so again may consider that he could not be a *strong* partisan, although another who splits his ticket more frequently may think of himself as a pillar of granite of his party. The larger problem is confronted in attempts to be precise about subtle nuances, to be exact about the inexact, for the undertaking of such tasks assumes what is palpably not so.

That these measurement techniques are adaptable and even essential for mastering some types of data [32] does not automatically make the techniques adaptable to all types of data. This is a problem of the horse and the cart; for "measurability is an intrinsic property of the subject matter; we can measure only that which is measurable." [33] The largest problem

---

[32] Irion, *op. cit.*, pp. 916–919, discusses practical uses and possibilities as well as conceding limitations.

[33] Quoted in Rogers, *op. cit.*, p. 54; see, in general, Chaps. 5, 6.

posed by these techniques is the attempt to arrive at insight by a process of methodology, to enthrone the way of doing above the peculiar substance of the thing done. By implication, then, there is no configuration in human affairs which cannot be broken down completely into its component parts. The parts are those for which a method of weighing and measuring can be found. There are no other parts. All of the recognized intangibles, including psychic factors, must be as amenable to the techniques as the cranial measurements of the respondents. Finally, the entire phenomena can be presented as a series of total parts and facts arranged like a periodic table of human behavior. To seek such powers through methodology is not to seek a key to unlock hidden meaning but to pounce upon it by squirming through the crevices around the door without even bothering to pick the lock. "We should then be content to think of government rather as an art than as a science. Like every art it makes use of the appropriate sciences. . . . But no science can tell men how to govern, as the science of engineering can tell men how to throw a bridge across a river." [34]

TECHNIQUES OF OPINION MANAGEMENT—PROPAGANDA

Communication. Propaganda is the name given to the techniques for forming and changing opinions. Propaganda is communication. In its widest sense, communication is the use of symbols for the exchange of ideas among humans. It is difficult if, indeed, it is possible, to conceive of humans being in proximity without communicating.

> The problem of the definition of man is an odd one. . . . It will not do to say that man is an animal with a soul. Unfortunately, the existence of the soul, whatever it may mean, is not available to the scientific methods of behaviorism; and although the Church assures us that men have souls and dogs do not, an equally authoritative institution known as Buddhism holds a different view.
>
> What does differentiate man from other animals in a way which leaves us not the slightest degree of doubt, is that he is a talking animal. The impulse to communicate with his fellow beings is so strong that not even the double deprivation of blindness and deafness can completely obliterate it. . . . There are animals besides man which are social, and live in a continuous relation to their fellow creatures, but there is none in whom this desire for communication, or rather this necessity for communication, is the guiding motive of their whole life. . . . [35]

Definition of Propaganda. This necessity to communicate is not always a necessity to engage in propaganda, for communication is the all-inclusive term. Propaganda is communication undertaken for a specific kind of purpose. It is the expression of an attitude relative to a controversial issue

---

[34] MacIver, *op. cit.*, pp. 11-12.
[35] Norbert Wiener, *The Human Use of Human Beings* (Boston: Houghton Mifflin Company, 1950) pp. 2-3.

regarding which some kind of opinion and/or action is proposed. The essentials are that the person conducting the propaganda have an opinion and attempt to persuade others to accept the opinion and act accordingly. Propaganda is really a matter of techniques as far as analysis is concerned. Although propaganda techniques are legion, they can be identified with ease if a person is alert to them. To evaluate their effectiveness is much more difficult and requires a knowledge of the objectives of the propagandist.

The word "propaganda" contains intrinsic propaganda value because it has come to have the connotation of lies, deception, and trickery. Used as an epithet directed at a competitor, it implies or alleges that he engages in deceit; as such an epithet, it is often bandied back and forth in election campaigns. Because of the widespread acceptance of the evil meaning, the word's usefulness is restricted to those who can treat it as a designation for a field of inquiry and for the application of techniques directed toward an objective. To use the word only for evil purposes in persuasion would require the choice of another word to indicate good purposes. Then disputants would have two words instead of one to argue about, and analysts would have no objective criteria to guide them in using the two words, since the moral value or purpose is often not revealed or ascertainable. Analysts would inescapably become propagandists, for they would have to rely upon their own biases in deciding which word to use. The only useful concept of propaganda is that it is a tool in the art of managing opinions and is used by leaders upon followers most consistently. As a tool it can be studied apart from good or bad purpose, since it can be used for either; but the tool itself is amoral.[36] (Note that it is the purpose at this point in this book to propagandize the reader regarding the definition of propaganda.)

Audiences. To be more specific about propaganda, it is necessary to be more specific about those being propagandized, i.e., the audience. In numbers it can range from one to an indefinite number. Professor Doob distinguishes audiences ranging from one influential person that a propa-

---

[36] "Propaganda is a method, a device for conditioning behavior. It represents nothing new in human affairs, except a refinement of techniques and the appropriation of new instruments for exerting the stimuli. Propaganda has no doubt always existed and will continue to exist so long as human beings contrive to formulate new goals and purposes.

". . . If there is a right and a wrong in propaganda, it is to be found in the relation between means and ends, methods and purposes, not in the propaganda itself. At any rate, in a relatively free society it is to be assumed that each individual or each group which has a purpose also has the right to propagate that purpose, that is, to win converts." Introduction by the Institute for Propaganda Analysis in Harold Lavine and James Wechsler, *War Propaganda and the United States* (New Haven: Yale University Press, 1940) pp. vii-viii. See also Ogle, *op. cit.*, Chap. 12. Some of the most outstanding thinking in this field has been done by Professor Leonard W. Doob. See *op. cit.*, Chaps. 11-17, and *Propaganda* (New York: Henry Holt & Company, 1935).

gandist wishes to win over, to small groups where the communication is still informal and largely man to man, and to large groups where the communication is considered public speaking.[37] The last situation Doob calls "propaganda," the first two he calls "persuasion." This distinction can be useful in denoting situations significantly different in size and caliber of audience and in particular techniques of argumentation employed. The distinction becomes one without a difference if the process and the objective are considered, for in each case it is the *same kind* of thing occurring. Nor are the techniques completely different. It is not the size of an audience per se which dictates all of the techniques to be used, but the nature of the audience which is often classified as friendly, unfriendly, or neutral.

In the majority of propaganda situations the audience is partly or largely unknown because it is unselected. To communicate through newspapers, magazines, radio, and television is to reach an indiscriminate number of unspecified kinds of people. To speak personally to a large audience is to face a similar situation with the exception that the speaker knows the audience is composed of people who are interested enough to be present. In all of these cases the element of doubt about who composes the audience affects the techniques used in propaganda and leads to the so-called buckshot method of scattering appeals on a wide front. Conversely, communicating to a known group of people permits a shotgun method of straight-line development relying upon appeals found to be effective with these people.

Propaganda Adapted to Audience. To be entirely uninformed of the kind of people in the audience is a rare situation. The propagandist can reasonably anticipate who some of them will be, and by drawing on his experience with people, can devise appeals for a wide cross section, first, to get their attention, and second, to impress them favorably. The more nearly he can pinpoint the kind of people he wants and expects to reach, the more precise he can be in the form and the type of appeals in his communication. For reaching the total public, the extreme in unselected audiences, the propagandist can assume that some will respond positively, some negatively, and some not at all.[38] However, the communication content must be simple enough for all to understand, and its vocabulary is often no higher than sixth to eighth grade reading levels. Increasingly, com-

---

37 Doob, *Public Opinion and Propaganda*, pp. 253–255.

38 When propaganda is widely distributed and comes to the attention of people for whom it is not intended, it may have a reverse effect. A great deal of commercial advertising is directed at people relatively less inclined to analyze or to question what they see and hear. For this reason, those whose education has given them more resistance to the claims of advertisers are repelled by a great deal of this hucksterism. One result is a widened gulf between business and teachers. See the exchange of articles: Bernard De Voto, "Why Professors Are Suspicious of Business," *Fortune*, April, 1951, pp. 114 ff., and "Says Business to Mr. De Voto," *ibid.*, June, 1951, pp. 99 ff.

munication is intended for specific areas of interest and varying levels of reading ability. This is one way to select a predetermined audience. According to whom the propagandist wants to reach, he will fashion both the content and the style.

If one communicates too simply to some audiences, permitting all the members to grasp the meaning too clearly, they may conclude that the communicator is stupid. Some audiences want to be flattered with preposterous words whose meanings are often obscure and indefinite. They accept technical jargon as evidence of erudition and profundity. They look upon simple language as the babbling of the multitude and therefore emitted only from fools.[39] A particularly prevalent manifestation of this kind of communication is the language of government administrators called "gobbledygook," an elaboration of simple thoughts into involved language by use of big words which cloak or soften the meaning when they do not actually obstruct it.[40] In politics the use of less precise language is often cultivated consciously in self-defense to avoid an open commitment or the blunt assertion of a fact.[41] One of the standard techniques of propaganda is to find words with noncontroversial connotations to refer to highly controversial subjects, e.g., the use of the term "parenthood restraint" instead of "birth control."

Some Basic Propaganda Techniques. The number of techniques in propaganda is limited only by the number of situations and the ingenuity

---

[39] In this connection Lindsay Rogers quoted the sociologist, Louis Wirth: "The findings of social science are sometimes regarded as elaborate statements of what everybody knows in language that nobody can understand." Professor Rogers continued, "Mr. Wirth might have added that the language is such that the reader frequently is unaware that what is being said is something that he already knows." See "Notes on the Language of Politics," *Political Science Quarterly*, Vol. 64 (1949) p. 490, note 1.

[40] For example:

"To eliminate internal or external illumination, obscuration may be obtained by blackout construction or by termination of the illumination." *Translation:* To keep light from shining through windows, cover them or turn off the lights. See Rogers, *ibid.*, p. 503, note 3.

A plumber asked the Bureau of Standards if it was all right to clean clogged drains with hydrochloric acid and was told, "The efficacy of hydrochloric acid is indisputable but the corrosive residue is incompatible with metallic permanence." *Translations* "Don't use hydrochloric acid—it will eat up the pipes."——*New York Times Magazine*, March 29, 1953.

Patrick D. McTaggart-Cowan, assistant controller of the Canadian Weather Service: "There are those in our midst who have in recent scientific utterings claimed an intransigence for the development of extratopical cyclones which would in perpetuity defy man's ability to prognosticate." *Translation:* "Some people say the weatherman will never be able to prepare accurate forecasts."——George Dixon, syndicated column, May 23, 1955.

[41] The late Senator Robert A. Taft occasioned considerable adverse comment when he suggested "Eat less" as the solution to a food shortage. Thereafter, this suggestion from an administration official sounded like a statemanlike utterance: "Economy in the use of foods through personal restraint."——Quoted in Rogers, *op. cit.*, p. 504, note 2.

of man. No cataloguing can be either orthodox or complete. Generally speaking, successful propaganda depends upon getting the attention of those to be convinced and then finding ways of reinforcing the message to convince them and keep them convinced. At the same time the kind of action desired is constantly suggested. While propaganda proceeds by repetition, there should be variation in the methods of presentation and the kinds of appeals. Repetition without variations can become monotonous, thereby lessening interest, and monotony also may hit a blind spot on some whereas a varied presentation will more likely bring home the point to more people. In addition, propaganda sometimes achieves its objective by limiting or withholding communication. The propagandist gives only his own side of the controversy. He avoids talking against himself or confusing his audience with too many things to think about.[42] He prefers the simplicity of his own argument and tries to proceed with a minimum of extraneous or diverting impressions.

In order to simplify, the propagandist may leave out data and rely on all-embracing generalizations; this treatment is often used to present a mass of complex data to a large audience, especially in spoken communication. Simplicity of presentation can create distortion, although the distortion may be consciously achieved by selection and rearrangement of data. Both of these may constitute censorship, the purposeful and direct withholding of data. Censoring may simplify and distort; it can certainly give an entirely different impression from the one that would be given if all the data were presented.[43] As the last resort the propagandist uses fabrication in his communication, i.e., he deceives by lying. This technique presumably would be avoided unless the propagandist is immoral or unmoral and also shortsighted. The amount of deception in a propaganda program would be expected to vary with both the degree of integrity of the propogandists and the long-term or short-term nature of the program. A fast promotion scheme may succeed with lies, but a long-range development can succeed only if its leaders create a foundation of confidence.[44]

---

42 An exception to this statement is the propagandist's objective of creating confusion in some cases in order to prevent any action being taken. To bombard an audience with questions bearing on the implications of a proposed change is one technique that can be used to preserve the *status quo*.

43 Censorship is popularly associated with government, especially in wartime, but censorship is a means of enforcing taboos and is constantly present in social intercourse. For a delightful description of the use of censorship in rearing children, see "Topics of the Times," *New York Times*, March 17, 1951.

44 Several techniques have become well known by their frequent use or frequent publicity. In the study of Father Coughlin's speeches in the 1930's by the Institute for Propaganda Analysis, seven techniques were identified: name-calling, glittering generality, transfer, testimonial, plain folks, card-stacking and band-wagon. See Alfred M. Lee and Elizabeth B. Lee (eds.), *The Fine Art of Propaganda* (New York: Harcourt, Brace and Company, Inc., 1939). Throughout the mammoth literature in the field, techniques with examples are plentiful.

Predictability of Propaganda. In a sense, any propagandist begins by shooting in the dark. Assuming a receptivity to his program, he may fail to touch the responsive chord or may be elbowed aside by another who got his program in operation earlier or was more effective in presenting it. By its nature a propaganda program involves a challenge to some extent of the *status quo*. There is no need to organize an ambitious program supporting what already exists except as a counterpropaganda program to repel attacks upon the *status quo*. The initiation of a program depends for its success upon the mental state of people. When they are comparatively happy and secure, they are much less inclined to react positively to propaganda. When they are tense, unhappy, insecure, the propagandist has much greater promise of receptivity. It is the problem of the propagandist to find where tensions exist and to play upon them. However, any program takes time, and the amount of time, as suggested above, is related to the amount of integrity. Further, the propagandist can neither foresee the future nor fully control the effects or the development of his program. There are limits in time, place, and circumstance which the propagandist has to take into account. People cannot be made to believe in anything or adopt any opinion. While people at one time in designated places and circumstances will respond in one way, those people differently situated may respond otherwise. The passage of time may work for or against the propagandist, just as place may affect his success. To predict the outcome of a program involves a knowledge of people, forces, and events. Rarely can a propagandist know more than a part of each of these ingredients.

Propaganda and Election Campaigns. The act of politicians campaigning for votes involves the use of propaganda techniques, since competition for public office is a constant and central source of controversy. To ask people to vote for a candidate who, if elected, will help to govern the people is one of the most sensitive processes, depending upon extensive knowledge of the particular people concerned—upon their specific sense of values, their general beliefs, and their resultant opinions. The entire process of appealing for votes is an art, and the men and women practitioners devote their lives to the pursuit and refinement of the techniques constituting the art. There are many kinds of political artists in the sense of novel adaptations of techniques to specific constituents, and the differences in kinds should not be confused with differences in ability. The techniques used by a candidate in Massachusetts may be so unlike those used in Alabama that from superficial observation the process may be considered to differ as much as the techniques. Of course the processes of politics are the same, since there is only one kind of politics; but the application of specific techniques is determined by the voters according to what kinds of conduct and presentation will dispose them to vote one way or the other.

Campaigning for office, like all propaganda, is based on the fact, perceived by Napoleon but probably known to leaders since the beginning of social organization: "The truth is not half so important as what people think to be true." [45]

Selected Bibliography

Doob, Leonard W., *Propaganda*. New York: Henry Holt and Company, Inc., 1935.
—— *Public Opinion and Propaganda*. New York: Henry Holt and Company, Inc., 1948.
Cantril, Hadley, *Gauging Public Opinion*. Princeton: Princeton University Press, 1944.
Gallup, George, *A Guide to Public Opinion Polls*. Princeton: Princeton University Press, 1944.
Gower, Sir Ernest A., *Plain Words*. London: H.M. Stationery Office, 1948.
—— *ABC of Plain Words*. London: H.M. Stationery Office, 1951.
Holtman, Robert B., *Napoleonic Propaganda*. Baton Rouge: Louisiana State University Press, 1950.
Lasswell, Harold D., *Power and Personality*. New York: W. W. Norton & Company, Inc., 1948.
Lippmann, Walter, *Public Opinion*. New York: The Macmillan Company, 1922.
Lowell, Abbott Lawrence, *Public Opinion in War and Peace*. Cambridge: Harvard University Press, 1923.
Mosteller, Frederick, *et al., The Pre-Election Polls of 1948*. New York: Social Science Research Council, 1949.
Katz, Daniel, *et al., Public Opinion and Propaganda*. New York: The Dryden Press, Inc., 1954.
Parton, Mildred, *Surveys, Polls, and Samples: Practical Procedures*. New York: Harper & Brothers, 1950.
Rogers, Lindsay, *The Pollsters*. New York: Alfred A. Knopf, Inc., 1949.
—— "Notes on the Language of Politics," *Political Science Quarterly*, Vol. 64 (1949) pp. 481–506.
Wallas, Graham, *Human Nature in Politics*, 3d ed. New York: Alfred A. Knopf, Inc., 1921.

---

[45] Quoted in Holtman, *op. cit.*, p. v.

CHAPTER TWENTY

Candidates and Managers

The word "politician" is a standard term in the vocabulary of all kinds of people. The frequency of its use actually reveals the many and often contradictory meanings attaching to it. No standardization of the word's exact connotation is possible nor is there likely to be widespread acceptance of any one frame of reference for its meaning. In the present chapter, arbitrary meanings must be assigned to the word in order to focus attention on the discussion. "Politician" will be used to designate candidates for public office and managers of candidates or of party tickets. There may be other classifications of politicians in the sense of people in public affairs and in political party operations, but their omission is unavoidable. The concept of politicians as office seekers or as managers is both sufficiently discriminative and inclusive for the immediate purpose. The differences between them are suggested by taking up each type separately.

POLITICS AS A WAY OF LIFE

At one time or another, everyone is likely to express an opinion about politicians as candidates for public office. While the word is very frequently used in an unflattering sense, citizens almost invariably make it clear that regardless of their value judgments they look upon politicians as being different from themselves. This seeing of politicians as a group set apart is both implicit and explicit in popular discussion. Office seekers, despite their unceasing efforts to identify themselves with their constituents, are equally aware of their distinctiveness because they pursue a set of highly specialized objectives. They run with and against one another for office, but they know and their constituents know that they walk by themselves. Their way of life is not the same as their constituents'. Politicians live in a world apart.

DISTINGUISHING CHARACTERISTICS AND PROBLEMS OF OFFICE SEEKERS

It is in the nature of leadership that this strange galaxy of contradictions and tacit understandings should exist. The phenomena are easily recognized when seen in totality, yet the identification of the characteristics peculiar to politicians and their world is difficult. Many plausible distinctions are not *the* distinctions. It contributes nothing to say that politicians live at a rapid pace, because almost everybody else does the same. To say that they are the holders of office is to evade the question by jumping beyond it to the result of being a politician. To say they are the seekers of office is not sufficiently discriminatory, because it includes candidates who run for nonpolitical purposes such as advertisement, stunts, and hoaxes. To say they are the ones who want to hold office is to declare that no one except actual candidates harbors dreams of office.

The Lure of Politics. The distinction is, rather, the desire for office and the compulsion to get into politics in order to win office. At some point in this process the would-be politician senses the life of the politician and accepts it joyously, wholeheartedly. He finds in this way of life "The Lure" which Frank R. Kent described.[1] If it be slightly ridiculous to contend that exceptions prove rules, it should be as readily granted that a rule is not nullified by exceptions. To discover a politician who neither has found "The Lure" nor has learned to like politics is a rare departure from the pattern. It is frustrating and enervating to live a life one does not like. Politicians have many frustrations and enervations, but they are not the result of efforts to get out of politics.

Purpose and Drive. No hard and fast line separates politicians from either the hangers-on at party headquarters or the vicarious workers in campaigns who may sense "The Lure" without sharing the life of the politician. The way of life obviously depends upon other essentials, among which are ambition, ability, opportunities. When such qualities and conditions combine with intense drive, the product is a politician, but the drive is the determining characteristic. "The Lure" becomes a kind of obsession, an affliction, or in a figurative sense, a virus infection. The control of the disease varies with politicians, but the therapy cannot be prescribed by outsiders. If there is a cure, the politician must discover it and heal himself. The virus is of such a highly specialized type that the patient rarely wants a cure, much less seeks a cure. Once exposed to and infected with this virus, neither age nor physical condition deters politicians. What an ordinary mortal would consider a handicap, they consider an impertinence. They can be youthful or aged, crippled, blind, deaf or paralyzed;[2] they can survive amputations or removal of vital organs. The

---

1 *Political Behavior* (New York: William Morrow & Company, Inc., 1928) Chap. 29.

2 In one of the poignant accounts of American politicians, James Kerney described Woodrow Wilson, still a partial invalid after his retirement from the White House, reacting to the suggestion that he run for the United States Senate from New Jersey: "I am going to try and look at myself as though I did not exist, to just consider the whole thing in an impersonal way. From the messages I get I realize that I am everywhere regarded as the foremost leader of the liberal thought of the world, and the hopes and aspirations of that liberal thought should find some better place of expression than in the Senate. There is only one place, you know, where I could be sure of effectively asserting that leadership."——Quoted in Kerney, *The Political Education of Woodrow Wilson* (New York: The Century Company, 1926) p. 469.

only obstacle apparently they cannot overcome is the loss of speech, but a weak physical constitution or chronic illnesses are a hazard to a full political career. Among men and women so completely and unquestionably dedicated, one would expect to find a distinct set of values, a particular way of thinking and of acting.

By the layman's standards, politicians pay a price over and above the heartaches and yearnings which become transitory events in their lives. They have at best a very limited private life and are deprived of many family associations which other people enjoy as a routine of living. They have tremendous demands made upon their time and their physical and financial resources. After what most people would consider a full day's work, politicians must still be alert and active, doing what is expected of them and avoiding mistakes in their talk and their acts. They travel a great deal both during and between campaigns. In this way they become acquainted with all parts of the country and with many politicians far and near, discussing their mutual problems and speculating on who will run for what office and who will be elected. It is all exhilarating but it is also exhausting.[3]

Financial Problems. In one respect politicians are like everybody else. They have to support themselves and their families, and many politicians must do so on their salaries while simultaneously saving money for their campaigns. Solicitors for all kinds of worthy projects quickly call upon politicians, and the pressure to contribute money and/or time is usually irresistible. A real crisis develops for a politician who senses the loss of his office. Aside from the compulsion to remain in politics, he has the additional necessity to earn a living. If he knows he is going out of office, he pursues all possible avenues for securing employment. This is the reason certain kinds of professions, particularly law practice, are conducive to a political career, for the politician has a job to turn to immediately when he loses office and he often has income from it even while he is in office.[4]

---

[3] "Think of the impromptu speeches on hot, steamy mornings on court-house steps . . . . Consider the evening meetings in village halls with a group of sniveling, inattentive youngsters on the front seats and a scattering of citizens . . . in the rear—with poor lighting, deplorable ventilation, and noisy echoes from the street and slamming doors. . . ."——Raymond Moley, syndicated column, November 22, 1954. At least the life of the politician is rarely as hazardous as that of an Ivory Coast member of the French Senate, whose grassroots tour of his district was abruptly halted when some of his constituents ate him.——*New York Times*, July 12, 1953.

[4] As Franklin D. Roosevelt so aptly expressed the situation: "Either the individual should have enough money of his own safely invested to take care of him when not holding office . . . or else he should have business connections, a profession or a job to which he can return from time to time."——Quoted in Raymond Moley, *27 Masters of Politics* (1949) p. 31.

Attention and Concentration. If the form and outline of political life seem unappetizing to many, their full ramifications are still unseen. The substance of the politician's work is (1) the handling of public affairs and (2) the constant attention to personal political affairs. The two are separable for the public but inseparable for the politician. Both of them, whether considered apart or together, involve the politician with never-ending minutiae as well as with broad, general decisions.

> To a philosopher, a scientist or a great lawyer, the preoccupations of a politician seem to be the interests of a person too lazy to apply himself to serious things. This is a gross underestimation of the politician's job. For beneath the surface he is applying his mental faculties to exceedingly complex subject matter, and if he is to be successful he must labor with incessant energy and meticulous care. For political genius is the capacity to give continuous, undivided and sedulous attention to matters that to most serious people seem too trivial to bother with.[5]

By doing this job well, he hopes to remain a politician. Thomas Jefferson's remark that "Few die and none resigns" was a cogent observation of politicians' living behavior, whether or not it was a correct conclusion regarding their longevity. The vast majority of politicians stay on as long as they possibly can, and when they retire, more often than not they go involuntarily. Many who are long out of office and forgotten by the public still try to make their voices heard in party councils and insist upon being consulted whenever decisions are to be made.[6]

Publicity. Finally, the life of politicians is a life of publicity and of seeking publicity. Public affairs are news, and politicians are news. They thrive on publicity professionally as they thrive on food physically. This feature of their lives has two sides. There is no future in politics for anyone who hides his light under a bushel. Instead of being retiring or reticent, the politician needs to keep pushing himself and telling what he wants people to know. He cannot justify his existence by being modest

---

[5] *Ibid.*, p. 33.

[6] "The old principle that an 'ex' in politics is truly an 'ex' is a verity. Once power has been relinquished, it is difficult either to regain it or to exercise authority through others."——Edward J. Flynn, *You're the Boss* (New York: The Viking Press, 1947) p. 226. "It is my deliberate judgment that, since Andrew Jackson returned to the Hermitage . . . no President has willingly left the White House. There is something about the office and place that intrigues the least ambitious of its incumbents, that makes all afterlife lack that something which only the White House gives."——Josephus Daniels, *The Wilson Era, Years of War and After, 1917–1923* (Chapel Hill: University of North Carolina Press, 1946) p. 557. It is doubtful if lesser officials greet retirement any differently. "Big men, of course, accept the turn of the political wheel with philosophic calm, but at heart, the President of the United States has the same feeling as the county sheriff when the time comes to relinquish his power and authority."——Kent, *The Great Game of Politics* (New York: Doubleday, Page & Company, 1924) p. 218; also Kent, *Political Behavior*, p. 341.

and letting others have the spotlight. At the same time he usually enjoys publicity. He would want it and seek it even if it were not necessary to his career. He delights in being the center of attention wherever he goes. This quality may appear early in the life of a politician or he may cultivate and develop a taste for it. In any event he is able to absorb publicity both in happy times and in unpleasant times and is able to say what he wishes, parry with reporters, and thrust back at his enemies.

Antagonisms and Accommodations. These characteristics fill out in important respects the picture of the political way of life and help to distinguish the politican from the nonpolitician. The picture in turn explains some of the antagonism between the two groups. Because of publicity the politician is always before the public. He is set apart, not precisely because he seeks or holds office, but because he has propelled himself into the political way of life. The sum total of his existence is out of the ordinary, eventful, and nerveracking, and his composure may be only a pose. Few other professions subject the sensitive personality to so much torture from envy, malice, and the inscrutable future. "Politics can lift men higher and faster than a rocket flames its way into the sky. It can also plummet them down to earth, never to rise again. Each man must learn this for himself." [7] The public senses some of these ordeals, but mainly is aware of the exciting and stimulating elements. Frank Kent was of the opinion that there is a universal desire to hold office and that the scorn expressed for politicans is actually envy.[8] One of the author's students stated this case in an examination paper: "The average person admires the person who is able to get elected, is envious of him, proud to know him, and mistrusts him deeply." If this were all there is in the relation of politicians and people, politics would be a deathly profession. Fortunately, there is an accommodation between them based on acceptance of mutual interest and a sense of identification.

> A basic fact about the politician is that he is like the people and knows what the people like. . . . Now the common man may not himself know, but he may be able to discover who he is by the politician whom he elects. The people's choice is the mirror of ourselves against our own backgrounds. A candidate may be elected because he has the same faults and weaknesses that we have. . . . The citizen in the United States votes for someone like himself, or as he imagines himself to be, or as he would like to be. I do not mean solely as the voter might outwardly profess to want to be, but as in his secret heart he unerringly wishes to be. Of course, this is not true of everyone in the electorate or of every politician, but the politician who is elected term after term is likely to

---

[7] James A. Farley, *Jim Farley's Story* (New York: McGraw-Hill Book Company, Inc., 1948) p. 305.

[8] *Political Behavior*, p. 341.

be as descriptive of his constituency as the sidewalks are of the streets. He is, however, likely to have special markings so that he may the more readily be recognized.[9]

MAKING USE OF ISSUES

Politicians are constantly communicating, and the bulk of their communication is propaganda. Even when they communicate on a subject not directly controversial, they are indirectly involved in controversy because they use such subjects to advance themselves in their fellow citizens' estimation for the purpose of winning elections. To engage in communication requires something to talk and write about, and politicians communicate in the field of issues. Their selection and treatment of issues is the hallmark of their profession, distinguishing them from laymen and determining their degree of professional competence and attainment. In the selection of issues, politicians are concerned with the timeliness or popularity of issues and with their own personal association in respect to the issues. In the treatment of issues, an endless number of problems can be isolated.

Flexibility in Selecting Issues. Hegel once observed that "political genius consists in identifying yourself with a principle." The subtle truth in these words is realized only by precise application and sensitive discrimination. The state or condition of possessing principle is the first principle to be identified. Politicians are at pains to be on the "right" side of issues, so that in a world of fleeting issues they create the lasting impression of always standing for the "right" and the "just" on every question. The epitome of success is being considered a person of principle without regard to specific issues, so that people will listen and be receptive on all occasions.

Issues change like fads, and politicians must change with them. Having a principle is not to have a fixation or dedication about any one issue. As an actual or potential representative of his constituents, the politician follows their interests in public affairs, not his own. When new interests are evidenced, the politician accepts them as the content of his communication despite his genuine concern for other issues and interests. Some people in politics who refuse to be deflected from issues in which they believe, fail to adjust to the moving tides of interest within the public. Such people are consummate politicians while their interests coincide with the popular

---

9 J. T. Salter, *The Pattern of Politics* (New York: The Macmillan Company, 1940) pp. 115–116. "The habits, manners, and attitudes of these men who came to the polls played a part in determining the nature of political leadership in eighteenth-century Virginia. The successful candidate was a man who understood the voters and who was willing and able to practice the arts by which their approval could be won. He was not necessarily like the men who elected him, but he had to possess qualities that they approved."——Charles S. Sydnor, *Gentlemen Freeholders* (Chapel Hill: University of North Carolina Press, 1952) pp. 27–28.

interest, but if the popular interest passes on, they very likely come to grief. This rule of flexibility in accepting current issues as the content of communication was pungently expressed by Frank Kent, "When the Water Reaches the Upper Decks Follow the Rats." He further quoted a politician's illuminating comparison: "Do not foolishly drown with a doomed ship. The rule of the sea, acknowledged manly and brave, requires every sailor when the water gets to the second deck to put on his life preserver and swim for the shore. A coward deserts a ship as soon as it springs a leak; the brave only when it is doomed, a fool never." [10]

Positions on Issues. In many cases, but by no means in all, politicians must decide not only what issues to discuss but also how they want to be associated with the issues. The political way of life would be considerably different and presumably far simpler if politicians could merely take a position for or against an issue. Instead, however, they often try to create supplementary perceptions, either to divert attention or to find stronger ground on which to stand. It is not enough to discuss a popular issue. Politicians must avoid being jockeyed into a disadvantageous position which would cost them support. Impressions conveyed to the public become all important. Unfavorable impressions are easily created but slowly removed, and most politicians cannot survive many of the unfavorable kind. It is a much happier and safer situation when a politician can be clear about which side he is on and can depend upon powerful allies to support him. Association with issues can be perplexing in another way. A position on an issue may at a later time become untenable. Faced with this dilemma, the politician may take any of several courses: try to obscure his previous opinions; rationalize his different opinions to prove they are not inconsistent; admit he has changed his mind and make a virtue of necessity.

Methods for Handling Issues. Finally, the politician brings to bear upon the issues the actual ideas he will communicate. While he knows what impressions he wants to create, he often does not voluntarily choose the issues; consequently, he may have little interest and less information about them. It is his business to inform himself at least superficially, and for this purpose party organizations provide research facilities. The greatest research undertaking of this nature is the Library of Congress. Some politicians can employ a staff to dig out material, prepare digests of the data, write speeches or statements, and keep their chiefs briefed on developments and implications. Rarely do politicians have the time to become authorities on the subjects they discuss. They rely on specialists in the various fields for facts and analyses and employ staff members to

---

[10] *Political Behavior*, pp. 155–156, see all of Chap. 15.

write speeches, while they contribute to the process the ability to communicate and to popularize the data and conclusions.

Not only is the problem one of what to say but also the problem of prolific communication, for politicians are constantly making speeches before various groups. A great deal of speaking is on radio and television, so the speeches have to be adjusted to fit the time limits. In order for speeches to be well covered in the press, advance copies are given to reporters. To meet all of these demands as well as to protect the speaker by having a record of exactly what he said, it is essential that the speech be written well in advance. Few politicians of wide activity and prominence can hope to do all of this work on their own speeches. They rely more or less on others and in some cases have the complete speech prepared by others. People who do this kind of work are called "ghost writers." The practice of "ghosting" speeches has grown rapidly in Washington, D. C., but is resorted to increasingly on the state and local levels. Ghost writing, as a popular expression, usually means completely writing a speech for someone else, but how much assistance has to be given for it to become ghost writing is not clear. The practice is often condemned, and most politicians are sensitive about it. Under the existing conditions it is impossible to see any diminution of the practice whether it be popular or not.[11]

Some of the variety of situations for using data can be suggested. When his constituents are generally on one side of an issue, the politician has no problem in deciding his position and merely casts about for good arguments to support what his constituents want supported. When his constituents are unconcerned and uninvolved with an issue, the politician may ignore it or take whatever position strikes him as being sound and reasonable. In a majority of cases, the politician either does not know how his constituents react to the issue or knows that they are divided. This situation increases as people's interests become more diverse and there is less unanimity of opinion within a constituency. It is this situation which has produced the classic concept of politicians' treatment of issues. In fact the problem may be further complicated now that the direct primary is used. This nominating procedure requires candidates to campaign, and they may have to campaign differently on the issues in the primary than in the general election. The difference arises when the party constituency, which votes in the direct primary, has decidedly different interests from the total constituency which votes in the general election. Candidates first

---

11 On the subject of ghost writers, see *New York Times Magazine*, March 27, 1949, and August 17, 1952. The late Supreme Court Justice, Robert H. Jackson, in the course of one of his opinions from the bench, expressed some of the popular feelings on the subject: "Ghost-writing has debased the intellectual currency in circulation here [*i.e.,* Washington, D. C.] and is a type of counterfeiting which invites no defense." He labeled "phantom authors and ghost writers" as "legal frauds" and "disguised authorship" a "deception."——*Ibid.*, November 22, 1949.

must satisfy their own party's voters in order to get the nomination, even at the risk of losing the final election. Often if a candidate wins the nomination, he can safely anticipate that his party's voters will support him in the general election, so he is free to appeal to independents and opposite party members.

Whatever else politicians do about issues, they must appear to be sincere in their utterances. To convince someone, the propagandist first creates the distinct impression he is in earnest and believes what he is arguing. By extension, sincerity is presumed to be the handmaid of seriousness; for this reason the bulk of political communication is dry and even dull. Politicians fear that humor or frequent lightness will be misinterpreted as unconcern, cynicism, or smartaleckness.[12] Because they are frequently charged with insincerity, they counteract the effects by cultivating a solemnity which in some politicians becomes pomposity. No matter what is discussed, if it is important enough to talk about, it is important enough to take seriously even if intrinsically it is so trivial as to be ludicrous. The politician wants people to believe that he is serious and not communicating purely for political purposes or expressing judgments for their calculated effect. "To eschew political motives is a first rule of politics." [13]

The politician may be forced to simulate enthusiasm and seriousness about issues which bore him. On issues which divide his constituents he has the additional challenge of developing "The Art of Seeming to Say Something Without Doing So." He develops "a facility in the use of resonant and meaningless words, the cultivation of a style impressive, seemingly profound, but actually platitudinous, evasive, vague." [14] The political way

---

[12] There is no rule prohibiting constituents from being humorous or witty about issues, as a member of Congress demonstrated in reading an epistle from back home to his colleagues: "Send our dollars to Europe, then give Asia some more; but you won't get back to Congress in 1954."——Associated Press dispatch dated July 22, 1953.

[13] Moley, *op. cit.*, p. 44.

[14] *Political Behavior*, pp. 73–74; Chap. 8. Sometimes it appears that platitudes come cheaper by the dozen. "The new law should establish beyond a doubt the basic rights of working people to organize, bargain collectively and to strike if they are dissatisfied with their wages or working conditions. I believe in those rights 100 per cent. They are part of the fundamental human freedoms in which I believe intensely and in defense of which I am waging this campaign. . . . The new law should provide for freedom of speech for labor and management alike, provided that that freedom is not used to coerce or to intimidate."——From campaign speech of John Foster Dulles, Republican candidate for the United States Senate; text in the *New York Times*, October 5, 1949.

"I am familiar with the general average of men who belong to clubs like the Exchange Club. They are part and parcel of the community. They belong to the warp and woof of our society. They are law-abiding men. They occupy a responsible position in their community, not only in business, but in church, in education and in community life. They believe in free enterprise. They believe in initiative, individual initiative."—From a speech of Alben W. Barkley, Democratic candidate for the United States Senate; text in *Exchangite Magazine*, January, 1955.

of life is one of realism and hard knocks for its participant politicians, but they themselves create illusions about themselves and their life in order to attract and hold a following. They have a constant struggle before them in appearing to take a decisive stand on the shifting, treacherous ground of issues. Sometimes the best they can do is cover their equivocation on the substance of an issue by conveying a precise attitude about its general nature. The politician selects his words

> not because they are the most forceful or descriptive in conveying exact facts and situations, but because they will produce in the minds of hearers or readers the reaction desired by the speaker or writer. . . .
>
> Ultimately, the considerations of a politician are not based upon truth or fact; they are based upon what the public will conceive to be truth or fact.
>
> This produces what is called a 'political mind.' It is an adaptation enforced by the necessities of environment and survival, just as is the fur of a polar bear or the coloration of a ground-hog. A sort of natural selection operates in the political environment which promotes the survival and success of minds capable of what some may call dissimulation and others call insincerity.[15]

This is the feature of politicians' way of life which most people dislike and some people clearly detect. It is the basis for the distrust, the scoffing, and the excoriation of politicians by the public in general. It is largely responsible for the odious connotation of the word "politician," and people who respect some particular man or woman in politics belligerently assert that this person is different, is not a politician. Here is one reason for seeking other names, like "statesman," for those politicians we want to hold in high esteem and to avoid seeing as manipulators and schemers. Yet the choice of these illusions is based on necessity, not on a free choice. Unquestionably, politicians wish they could speak frankly and give up the game of verbal fencing, but they dare not. To say directly what they think will anger or alienate some voters who may be won by the use of finesse. James A. Farley reported the universal experience of politicians when he described the wrath which descended upon him when he frankly admitted and explained how he was distributing patronage to Democrats.[16]

Politics is a keenly competitive profession, and every time a politician leaves himself open by refusing either to dodge issues or to say the ingratiating things people want him to say, his opponents magnify and exploit his words to the full. The truth may be disillusioning and discouraging, but voters want hopes and uplift. Their demands for authority, security, and freedom are more surely satisfied by the familiar political methods than by brusque honesty and unadorned frankness. Political appeals take

---

15 Moley, *op. cit.*, p. 43.

16 *Behind the Ballots* (New York: Harcourt, Brace and Company, Inc., 1938) pp. 224–225.

into account what people believe and what they want to believe. Modern civilized society produces many groups each of which has its own values and beliefs. The politician is caught in the cross fire among groups and protects himself by trying to appease all of them at once and by falling back upon the democratic doctrine which recognizes and accepts conflicting beliefs.[17] Whatever the politician can do to relieve the pressure on himself, he can be expected to do. The voters themselves thus encourage their own deception and place a premium upon humbuggery in campaigns. Some politicians maintain more and some maintain less self-respect by the amount of humbug they engage in, but "there has to be some compromise with conscience, some 'pussy-footing,' 'trimming,' and evasion." [18]

From these inductions concerning the way of life of politicians, it is possible to see politics as a highly refined art based on great skill and constant application of the techniques of opinion influencing. Yet, unlike other artists, the politicians must be content only with the acclaim they merit in the parts they play, never as the actors who create the parts. The complete illusion of politics depends upon politicians denying or disparaging their own profession. After spending a lifetime of intense concentration becoming a master in persuading people, a politician feigns outrage or amazement if anyone publicly suggests that he has succeeded.

THE MANAGEMENT FUNCTION IN POLITICS

Management Distinguished from Office Seeking. Some politicians do not make their mark by running for office. In the division of specialized labors in politics, there are many other tasks to perform. Conducting an election campaign is analogous to the production of a stage play.[19] Only the action on the stage is meant for the audience, but behind the scenery, outside the public view, are many workers doing their part to make the production a success. The sum total of the seen and unseen activities requires skill in planning and management, for one of the most highly specialized and distinct functions in politics, as in play production, is direction of the total performance.

Some candidates may be effective managers for themselves, but the functions of campaigning and managing are so separate and specialized

---

[17] Robert M. MacIver, *The Web of Government* (New York: The Macmillan Company, 1947) pp. 50–51.

[18] *The Great Game of Politics*, p. 252 and Chap. 31. Some candidates "are of real conviction and courage, but the very best of them have to go through the ballyhoo stage, playing the game of hide and seek, howling over 'outrages' in which they do not believe, appealing to prejudice, straddling issues, concealing their real feelings—to get the votes. They have to do it. There is no way out of it. It is not the candidate's fault. It is the system—the growth of many decades—the price we pay for universal suffrage, or, rather, part of the price."—*Ibid.*, pp. 232–233; *Political Behavior*, pp. 86–87.

[19] Warren Moscow, *Politics in the Empire State* (New York: Alfred A. Knopf, Inc., 1948) p. 51.

that remarkable skill in both is seldom found in one and the same person. Candidates, before they go very far in politics, are almost certain to find managers who can direct them either through a few campaigns or throughout their entire career. The sharpness in the distinction of the two functions is partially inherent in the roles themselves, a specialization resulting from differences in aptitudes and personality. A manager has the capacity for administrative work, which includes looking after details, organizing undertakings, and handling people. Management also includes planning, which involves anticipation and timing. The management function is, finally, coordination. Even though candidates have such abilities, they have not the time or opportunity to develop them and must to some extent depend upon colleagues who can give their full attention and energies to this function.

STATUS AND PROBLEMS OF MANAGERS

Isolation of Managers. The virus of politics infects managers as well as candidates, but the result of the infection is likely to be fatal for the manager who, not content with this role, yearns to move out from the shadows of the director's corner and to stand in the limelight of a candidate's publicity. The infrequency of success in changing roles is traceable, first, to the manager's developing skills which are different from those required of candidates, second, to the suspicion he arouses in other politicians, and third, to the public's attitude of distrust. The management function in politics has universally tended to isolate its practitioners. The frequent demonstration of this truth has been formalized in the maxim, "The kingmaker can never be king." [20] The greater his success in behalf of his candidate, the more his colleagues, and perhaps the candidate also, distrust him and fear him.

One of the ways most laymen reconcile their repugnance of politics with their acceptance of candidates for office is by a process of disassociation. Much of the popular concept of wickedness in politics is applied to managers or "bosses" or "backstage wirepullers" or some other unflattering name. The citizen sees or at least senses the management of political forces in conventions and campaigns, to the extent that he is aware of politics at all. He is told in his newspaper and by his news reporter or commentator about the juggling, the machinations, the scheming behind the events of the day. Even if managers try to break out of their political limitations, they bear the infirmity of their association with undercover manipulations, and the public can more easily be persuaded to repudiate them.

---

[20] Charles Hickman Titus, *The Processes of Leadership* (Dubuque: William C. Brown Company, 1950) p. 371; Machiavelli, *The Prince* (Modern Library ed.) p. 14.

Anonymity of Managers. The functions of management cannot be performed in front of the public, and the manager both keeps to the background in doing his work and is further obscured by the outward developments and successive events of campaigns. The manager may be perceived dimly and can be devastated when brought to the public's attention by his enemies because the public will quickly grasp and accept the stereotype presentations of him. Therefore the manager, in trying to become a candidate, suffers from his lack of publicity, his unfamiliarity to the voters; and the publicity he is likely to get is not the sort conducive to his being elected. "Perfect virtuosity in the political art demands that most of its processes elude the eye and ear. . . . Such artistry demands that he [the manager] know Americans. It also demands that Americans know only a part of him." To be a manager is to keep to oneself and to be relatively unknown. "Once a manager, always a manager." [21]

Preparation and Training. The preparation of a politician to become a manager follows no prescribed course. Managers possess many kinds of backgrounds and move through different channels in the organization. The common factor among them all is their experience in politics, whether it has been gained directly through the organization, in newspaper and advertising work, as secretaries to politicians, in business, or in labor unions. Some enter politics as candidates and then change roles. Some give their full time to politics, and others divide their time between politics and earning a living in some other activity. The direction and the occasion for a person's entry into politics often determines whether he becomes a manager of a candidate as such or is associated with an organization as a manager of the party's slate of candidates.

Chairmen of committees in the organization structure are managers of the whole party ticket during a campaign, or are supposed to be. The primary exception is the national chairmen who specifically manage presidential candidates. Since the establishment of the manager function of the national chairman, he has been in many cases the manager of the presidential candidate who wins the party's nomination; but not all managers of Presidents have become national chairmen. These managers have had various backgrounds. Marcus A. Hanna came from the business world to manage William McKinley in 1896, as John J. Raskob did in 1928 to manage Alfred E. Smith. Edward M. House, virtually the *alter ego* of Woodrow Wilson for much of his Presidency, but not the national chairman, came up from political management in the state of Texas. Walter Brown was never the Republican chairman, but from his long experience in Ohio politics played an important part in managing Herbert Hoover into the Presidency. Some national chairmen were largely unknown

21 Raymond Moley, *op. cit.*, pp. 97, 99.

and untried as managers, e.g., George White, who managed James M. Cox in 1920. Others, like James A. Farley, who managed Franklin D. Roosevelt in 1932 and 1936, were organization leaders with experience in running party campaigns. Managers associated with organization management usually come up through the ranks to establish themselves as leaders of the organization. These are the ones usually called "bosses." They concern themselves with the party ticket in their own domain whether county, district, or state. They may exercise the formal power by holding the office of chairman of the committee or may exercise it with greater anonymity by holding no party position.

Group or Staff Management. The entire function of management is rarely delegated to or assumed by just one individual. The function is performed by various people around the candidate or organization including the candidates themselves. Generally, one man is designated or understood to be *the* manager, but he works in constant association with the candidate's and the party's organization. The planning and execution of strategy is a group endeavor, the size of the group varying according to the magnitude of the undertaking. Everyone around a candidate or the organization, ranging from personal friends to the hangers-on, attempts to take part in management. People in politics invariably fancy that they are strategists, just as spectators at football games offer the quarterbacks free advice on each play. The chief managers and candidates are always plagued with the constant forays upon headquarters by all and sundry imparting the latest piece of advice about how to win this block of votes and how to handle that issue. This problem must be controlled either by a manager or by the candidate in order to keep down the chaos and avoid following a series of strategies which go in all directions at the same time. The problem is magnified by the personal jealousies and rivalries to be at the center of power and be associated with the candidate. Managers who are not alert to this danger and deft in handling the aggressive extroverts around them may be elbowed out of their place and the whole campaign strategy brought to grief.

Earning a Living. Candidates are financially able to remain in politics through the salaries they earn from the positions they are elected to or from the appointive positions they hold while waiting a chance to run for office. Managers are unlikely to hold elective office, at least while they are managing others, so their only source of income in politics is from appointive office. Some managers, like some candidates, have independent incomes or are well-to-do, but they are in the small minority. For the bulk of managers there is the problem of earning a living, and effective management is difficult, if possible, when this living is earned in an occupation outside of politics. The management function is performed best when complete concentration can be applied to the shifting forces in the political world. The happiest arrangement for a manager is to have an appointive political office which is largely routine, demands little of his time, and whose functions can be delegated to subordinates. In this way the manager is relieved of much of the responsibility of his office and can give most of his time and attention to the problems of winning the next election for his party or his candidate. On every level of government patronage positions are necessary so that candidates can fill them with men in the party organization or in their personal organization who devote themselves to political management.

Sometimes these positions are obscure, and the public misses the significance of the appointment. As long ago as the Administration of John Q. Adams, the President relied upon a fourth auditor of the Treasury Department "as a sort of 'handyman.' " [22] Executives can appoint managers to their secretarial staff or as subordinates in their departments. Members of Congress have an office staff of secretaries and administrative assistants where they place men and women who are concerned with the management of campaigns; increasingly, with the patronage provided by the staffs of joint congressional committees, committee chairmen can find additional places for a politician they want to keep near them. The problem of managers of presidential campaigns is solved when the manager's candidate wins the election. The practice has been followed with some regularity of appointing the national chairman of the winning presidential party to the office of Postmaster General—although in the Eisenhower Administration when Summerfield was appointed to this Cabinet post, he resigned as national chairman. The postmaster generalship is a logical repository for the President's chief manager because the office makes fewer demands than others in the Cabinet and its functions can be discharged with less time and effort and with more delegation of authority.

MANAGERS WITHIN THE PARTY SYSTEM

Organization Leaders. Not only is the management function separate and distinct in politics but also the role and attitude of managers are different in varying degrees from those of candidates. This distinction is likely to be greatest when candidates are compared with organization leaders. Men and women who become established in the organization have a continuity in their leadership and exercise influence until they die, are overthrown, or are compelled to retire. In their time they see a constant procession of hopeful office seekers; candidates come and go, rise up and

---

[22] E. M. Eriksson, "The Federal Civil Service under President Jackson," *Mississippi Valley Historical Review*, Vol. 13 (1927) p. 531.

even pass beyond into higher and higher offices. Names and faces in the news are fleeting, but the organization is eternal. The leaders of the organization, if they succeed in holding their power, often have a career overlapping two or three generations of candidates. This class of managers is not concerned solely with one candidate's fortunes but with the fortunes of the party in holding the offices on the same level of government as the organization.

As long as these leaders keep their control of the organization, they can survive the loss of an election and try to put together a winning combination at the next election. They can absorb defeats which are sometimes fatal to candidates. The leaders, discovering that certain candidates are not vote getters, can turn to or seek out more promising candidates. Therefore, organization leaders seldom evidence the same amount of disappointment or bitterness when an election is lost, for defeats are part of the game. In the face of electoral reverses, especially when they are anticipated, organization leaders can be philosophic and magnanimous as long as they retain the base of their own power. They seldom have any disposition to argue with election returns.[23]

Managers of Individual Candidates. To manage one candidate, instead of the whole party ticket, is to stand in an entirely different position in the party system. Such managers usually rise and fall with their candidates and generally see elections as their candidates do because the status and future of these managers depend upon the success of the candidates. When a manager hitches his wagon to a candidate's star, he is very unlikely to go any further than the candidate. The manager goes up and goes out with his principal.[24] Actually, he may not go all the way up with the candidate. Frictions and clashes often develop between manager and candidate, and after the latter has attained some success, he may break with his original manager and choose new ones. During the ascent other would-be managers are drawn to the candidate, for success is always a magnet in politics. The original manager has to be on his guard to prevent being undermined and frequently is jealous of others who share the confidence of the candidate.

---

23 For example, in 1920 Charles Murphy, leader of Tammany Hall, obviously expected the Democrats to lose the presidential election. After the returns had set the trend to the Republicans on election night, Murphy issued a statement: "Governor Cox has made a vigorous and dignified campaign. His defeat would be regrettable. However, the people have cast their votes . . . . The agitation of the campaign should now be forgotten . . . . We must stand behind our new President and help him to promote our country's interest and repose."——*New York Times*, November 3, 1920.

24 An exception to this general rule was Herbert Brownell, who managed Thomas E. Dewey and then moved into the circle of Eisenhower managers. This case itself was the result of the highly unusual situation of one man turning his personal organization, including his press secretary, over to another man.

There is another possible source of embarrassment and frustration for managers if their candidates reach the height of the Presidency. The unique status and requirements for fulfilling this office deprive the President's manager of full access and association with the President. Presidents themselves, with the realization of their responsibilities, are likely to separate into tighter compartments the various roles they play. They become more and more disposed to exclude their managers from all except the political-strategy phase of their lives. This was a lesson which both Marcus A. Hanna and James A. Farley learned the hard way. A final source for deteriorating relations is the tendency of managers to look upon candidates as their own creations, as a "front man" or even a "stuffed shirt." [25] That some antagonism would develop is inevitable, for the planner-director and the executor each sees himself as the more necessary partner of the team.

THE POLITICIAN AS CAMPAIGN STRATEGIST

Candidates make commitments to individuals and groups in order to secure support. Such agreements entail promises to appoint campaign contributors to offices, to support or oppose specified policies, to exercise favoritism in letting contracts, and so on. One of the functions of managers is to make these commitments either directly or indirectly. Consequently, the candidate is shielded by not being present during these negotiations. He can honestly say he has made no promises, that he is not "owned" by anybody. He may even be misled himself, for his managers may have made commitments and refrained from telling the candidate about them.[26] While the candidate is protected, the result is sometimes a great confusion about what was promised. Recriminations fly back and forth, with the candidate and his supporters claiming they are being subjected to blackmail and the individuals claiming they were double-crossed. In some cases a contributor or a representative of a large group pledging its support refuses to reach a final agreement until the candidate personally makes the commitment. In this way the candidate not only binds himself but is fully informed of the agreement.

Sources of Information. Because of the continuing nature of elections, managers make it their business the year around to sound out opinion. They rely to some extent upon reports from organization leaders regarding sentiment in their respective areas and upon reports of various kinds from politicians, newspaper reporters and group leaders and inferential evidence derived from fads and current interests and reactions. From time to time managers themselves make trips to consult the opinions of the man in the

25 Moley, *op. cit.*, p. 99.
26 Farley, *Jim Farley's Story*, p. 91. Kent, *The Great Game of Politics*, p. 232.

street and of influential figures. The more experienced the manager, the more reliable the sources of information he has and the keener his eye for straws in the wind. He develops critical faculties and a well-balanced sense of judgment of events and of the people who make reports to him. He will know if full credence should be given to the estimates of one informant or if this person tends to be too optimistic, while someone else tends to be pessimistic in analyses and may understate the situation.[27]

Managers examine and evaluate polls, both those conducted by outside agencies and those conducted through their own organization. When polls are favorable, managers and candidates give them wide publicity, hoping to stimulate a band-wagon psychology.[28] When polls are unfavorable, they ignore them publicly or explain them away. Privately, however, they may be disturbed and try to counteract the weaknesses revealed by the polls. One indication of the outcome of an election is the betting odds posted by professional gamblers. While this source of information is not infallible, it is much more frequently accurate than inaccurate unless the odds are manipulated by the losing side covering bets to bring down the odds and thus reduce the band-wagon influence.[29]

Traditional, Marginal, and Bellwether Areas. Managers' estimates and computations include the histories of voting behavior of the electorate. The traditional voting pattern of sections within a constituency can be appraised by analyzing past performances. These subdivisions, which can be roughly classified as friendly, unfriendly, and doubtful, are usually the wards of a city; the cities, towns, and unincorporated areas of a county; the counties of a state; and the states themselves. In some elections, when the party organization can be depended upon to produce a given number of votes, the objective is to get an approximately even split in the remaining vote.[30] Depending upon the election and the area, this kind of calcula-

27 One of the dramatically accurate forecasts by a manager based upon all of the available indices was James A. Farley's prediction in 1936 that the Democrats would carry every state except Maine and Vermont.

28 Creating a band-wagon psychology is as much within the function of management as it is a function of the candidate's campaign techniques, and every campaign organization tries to make use of it. While the announcement of the outcome of polls by candidate and party headquarters, by newspapers and other sources concerned only with one campaign, can be utilized to create a band wagon, the professional pollsters deny that their polls have this effect. This question is considered at length in George Gallup and Saul F. Rae, *The Pulse of Democracy* (New York: Simon and Schuster, Inc., 1940) Chap. 20, where the band-wagon thesis is refuted by the contentions that polls do not discourage voting and that the percentage of a leading candidate does not keep increasing after the results of a poll are published. The limited awareness of polls by the public is frequently given as another reason. See Moscow, *op. cit.*, pp. 226–233 for different views.

29 *Ibid.*, pp. 225–226. In presidential elections the odds were incorrect during most of the 1916 and 1948 campaigns.

30 See George M. Reynolds, *Machine Politics in New Orleans, 1897–1926* (New York: Columbia University Press, 1936) pp. 121–122.

tion may or may not be useful. Whenever the parties compete on relatively even terms, there are doubtful areas in which the pattern of voting is a close race with either party able to win by a small percentage. These areas in congressional elections are spoken of as "marginal" and in close elections for the House of Representatives the marginal districts can determine which party has a majority.[31] Doubtful or marginal areas get special attention during campaigns, for here a relatively high proportion of money is spent and the most effective campaign speakers make one or a series of speeches. Certain of these doubtful areas may get a bellwether reputation. The difficulty in putting too much faith in such areas is that from time to time some of them fail to live up to their reputations.[32]

Headquarters Organization. Managers, whether of individual candidates or of a party ticket, must have real organizing ability, or their success will always be qualified and their potentialities for advancement severely limited. In the midst of turmoil and confusion, managers take over a headquarters, divide up the work of the campaign into such divisions as speakers, publicity, finance, women, labor, business, nationality groups, and so on. The number of these divisions and the elaborateness of their separately operated subdivisions increase with the larger area of the campaign, reaching the zenith in presidential campaigns.[33] This challenge to administrative skills is first of all a problem in handling people, getting them to do what is required of them and to work cooperatively. The manager coordinates the several divisions so that they are not working at cross purposes or duplicating one another's work. Delegations of authority should be clear, and as far as possible, overlapping of authority is to be avoided. Managers must constantly be prepared to deal with attempts of subordinates to intrude upon functions outside of the sphere delegated to them and with attempts of division or subdivision heads to expand their authority and engage in empire-building. Many decisions both on organization and strategy are fluid and rapidly arrived at. The pressure of time is

---

31 Malcolm Moos, *Politics, Presidents and Coattails* (Baltimore: The Johns Hopkins Press, 1952) pp. 24 ff. and 109, classified 105 districts as marginal, the margin of victory or defeat being in the 55–45% range; 40 of these 105 he classified as critical marginal because the margin varies within the 51.5–48.5% range.

32 Only eight counties in the United States have returned a majority for the winner in every presidential election from 1896 through 1956: Crook, Oregon; Larramie and Albany, Wyoming; Jasper and Palo Alto, Iowa; Vanderburgh, Indiana; Coos and Strafford, New Hampshire. Before the 1952 election, eleven counties had this distinction, but three of them were carried by Stevenson that year. See the *New York Times,* November 11, 1952. Among bellwether states in presidential elections, Louis Bean found that "Ohio is probably the one state in which more than any other the Democratic vote has approximated the actual national percentages."——*How to Predict Elections* (New York: Alfred A. Knopf, Inc., 1948) p. 106.

33 See, e.g., Theodore Milton Black, *Democratic Party Publicity in the 1940 Campaign* (New York: Plymouth Co., 1941) pp. 29–31.

constant, and only during the months between elections can managers take the time to analyze problems carefully and devise workable solutions.

Sharp Practices. Political management often includes meeting problems with questionable practices. The compulsion to win is sharpened by the keen competition, the mounting pressure and nervous strain as Election Day approaches. In both state and federal statutes certain corrupt practices are singled out and declared to be illegal, but these proscriptions can never be exhaustively catalogued. Many standard practices can be legislated against, but the ingenuity of the mind of man, challenged and harassed, cannot be fully anticipated. In fact, some practices may be unsusceptible of legislative prohibition through difficulty of either definition or detection, and the fine line between legal and illegal is always difficult to locate precisely.[34]

Ultimately the problem of honesty in conducting campaigns includes more than following legal practices and avoiding illegal ones. Various kinds of trickery or deception, when they appear, may be capable of being prohibited in the particular case. The difficulty is foreseeing and providing for them without unduly restricting campaigns or without leaving loopholes which nullify the legislation. The objective can be partly achieved by legislating prohibitions, but in the fullest sense depends upon making candidates responsible for the conduct of their campaigns. When these sharp and deceptive but apparently legal practices occur, the opposition is the real policeman, and the punishment is bringing the situation to the attention of the voters. If the voters tacitly encourage or condone the practices by electing the offending candidate, the problem becomes something else entirely and undoubtedly cannot be reached effectively by any kind of legislation.

Corrupt-practices acts have always aimed their fire at bribery of voters,[35] and in time coercion and intimidation were included. In some cases, however, voters are deceived without being bribed or coerced. For instance, a party organization may issue sample ballots with the names of approved candidates for a coming direct-primary election as instructions

---

34 In Colonial Virginia the law prohibited giving anything, including food and drink, as inducements to voters, but actual bribery was openly carried on. If a candidate had a reputation for hospitality, he could more easily avoid the appearance of bribery, especially if he explained that refreshments were free to all men regardless of how they voted or if he had someone else provide the treats in his name. Candidates also kept open house for those citizens who had to travel a great distance to the county seat to vote."——Sydnor, *op. cit.*, pp. 51 ff.

35 During the Colonial period, only Rhode Island among New England colonies had legislation on bribery, but all of the other colonies, except New York and Maryland, had such laws. Cortlandt F. Bishop, *History of Elections in the American Colonies* (Columbia University Studies in History, Economics, and Public Law, Vol. 3, 1893) pp. 192 ff.

to party voters; there usually is no law to prevent a group supporting a candidate not on this list from putting out a sample ballot identical in every way except for the substitution of the one name. Party voters, seeing the spurious ballot, are misled and vote for the candidate, thinking that he is endorsed by the organization. There are many variations on this practice, through instruction cards and ballots; but its very nature makes it almost impossible to reach by means of legislation. Actions may technically be within the law, but be a violation of its spirit. The locating of polling places in precincts is usually governed by rules of accessibility and central location, but local officials or boards in making the decisions on locations can follow the political rule of making the polling place convenient in friendly precincts and inconvenient in unfriendly precincts.[36]

Corrupt Practices. In the realm of frauds, of corrupt practices covered by statutes, the voters themselves bear as much responsibility as politicians, if not more. In poll-tax states, the practice of paying the tax for someone else is usually illegal. Nevertheless, many voters in effect require the organization to pay their tax if the organization leaders expect them to vote. Open violations of the law are sometimes tolerated to the point that the law has no real sanction in public support.[37] The most common classes of corrupt practices occur in connection with registration, petitions, and the vote-casting processes. Forging names is used in padding registration rolls and preparing petitions. Standard practices in the casting of ballots have been repeating, voting those illegally registered, voting phantoms or ghosts (i.e., nonexistent or deceased persons),[38] and giving illegal assistance to voters or coercing them. In the counting of paper ballots, corrupt practices include miscounting so as to "count out" a candidate, altering ballots, having voters identify their ballots by special marks, and stuffing ballot boxes. Some county organizations have been strong enough to prepare prearranged totals or to wait for the returns from the rest of the state and then announce their vote, which is large enough to elect their candidates. In these cases the actual voting is carried out in an orderly and legal fashion because the ballots cast are never counted. The quintessence

---

[36] See D. H. Kurtzman, *Methods of Controlling Votes in Philadelphia* (Philadelphia: University of Pennsylvania Press, 1935) pp. 116–118.

[37] In 1771 in Lunenburg County, Virginia, forty men were allowed to vote even though they were ineligible; candidates were loath to challenge doubtful voters for fear of antagonizing the public.——Sydnor, *op. cit.*, p. 21. New Mexico law requires that voters mark their ballots with ink or indelible pencil inside a booth, but a senatorial investigation revealed that both of these requirements were widely disregarded in 1952.——*New York Times*, May 31, 1953.

[38] Voting in the name of the dead is commonly referred to as voting the tombstones and has led to the witticism that in some communities candidates would be well advised to make their campaign speeches in the cemetery, since that is where most of the voters are.

in coercive corrupt practices is the use of force and violence to frighten voters and watchers away from the polls.[39]

Bribery. One kind of corrupt practice which election officials are not necessarily aware of or responsible for is the outright purchasing of voters. Bribery can take various forms. Paying a voter's poll tax amounts to a form of bribery. Transporting voters to the polls is an ancient and honorable practice, but can be used as a substitute for outright bribing. The most familiar practice is directly paying voters to vote for a given candidate or party ticket. Money is handled in two different ways and both ways may be used simultaneously. One way is for candidates or managers to make arrangements either with a precinct leader or with a person outside of the formal party organization who can deliver a block of votes. In this case a lump sum is handed over and no questions asked, but the person receiving the money is expected to produce results by whatever means he employs. He usually parcels the money out by sharp negotiation with individual voters unless he has a very large sum, for whatever he saves he keeps for himself. Dealing with a purely venial intermediary involves the risk of his selling out to the other side for a larger amount of money. When both sides are buying, a brisk and even violent struggle may ensue in the race to carry the precinct.

The second way is to deal directly with the voters without intermediaries. Buying the votes is a testimonial to the culpability of some voters who refuse to vote unless they are paid.[40] It also involves the problem, from the point of view of the briber, of being sure he gets what he pays for and has been solved by the chain ballot and schemes for identifying ballots. Most of these practices require the cooperation and connivance of election officials.

Effectiveness of Corruption. Quite aside from the moral aspects of corrupt practices is the question of the practical effectiveness of them. In the first place, the pressure upon local organization leaders is one cause

---

[39] The following sources include general and specific descriptions of the types of corrupt practices referred to: Kurtzman, *op. cit.*, pp. 123–136 and Appendix E; Maurice M. Milligan, *Missouri Waltz* (New York: Charles Scribner's Sons, 1948) pp. 134–166; Dayton D. McKean, *The Boss* (Boston: Houghton Mifflin Company, 1940) pp. 139 ff. For illustrations of the more extreme practices in unreformed English elections, see Charles Seymour and Donald Paige Frary, *How the World Votes* (Springfield: C. A. Nichols Company, 1918) Vol. 1, Chap. 5; on nineteenth-century American practices, see pp. 256–265.

[40] A variation of this attitude was reported in Kent, *The Great Game of Politics*, p. 68: During an uneventful election, when there was no need to spend money, a local party leader encountered a voter. "Hello, Ben, have you voted yet?"

"No, Mr. Carey . . . ."

"Well, Ben, here's fifty cents. Go on and vote."

"No, Mr. Carey, if I don't get a dollar, I'll vote my principles."

for their using frauds, bribery, and coercion, a recognition of inadequacy at one or another point in the organization. As one leader described the problem, those who are dishonest

> operate upon their own initiative and at their own risk. They are either too lazy to do the practical hard work that produces the votes, and try to make up for that laziness by cheating, or they figure they can get away with crookedness and make a big showing which will bring them easily-earned recognition and power. I am dead against that kind of politics. The hard way of producing votes is the easiest in the long run.[41]

In the second place, the more extreme the practices on one side, the more extreme on the other. At some point, flagrantly corrupt practices produce their own reaction. While many forms of relatively petty violations can well be continued because of general acceptance, it is unlikely that the more vicious forms will be tolerated indefinitely. In the third place, the use of many and excessive corrupt practices may be superfluous. "Bribery, ballot-box stuffing, padded registration lists exist . . . and . . . swell the total vote that the party receives, but the organization, in times of tension, survives if it survives at all without these aids." [42]

Selected Bibliography

See the Selected Bibliography for Chapter 21, below, pp. 540–541.

[41] Quoted in Kurtzman, *op. cit.*, p. 115; see also Milligan, *op. cit.*, pp. 137-138.
[42] J. T. Salter, *Boss Rule* (New York: McGraw-Hill Book Co., 1935) pp. 50-51.

CHAPTER TWENTY-ONE

Leaders in Search of Followers

Politicians must make the decision to go into politics for themselves.[1] They can receive all kinds of help and encouragement, but finally the decision is up to them. Sometimes a candidate is launched by his friends pushing him into a race, but he must want to go on or his friends can be of no more help to him.

INITIATION AND MOTIVE POWER OF CANDIDATES

Many young men and women who go into public life start preparing themselves by the time they enter high school or the university. The politically ambitious are often aware of their bent early in life and begin doing those things which prepare them for their profession. The more people they know and understand, so much the better; the more experience they have in electioneering in school, the less they have to learn thereafter. When they finally graduate, they are simply following a continuous process but applying it on a wider stage of action. Those who do not go so far in school make the same kinds of efforts to propel themselves into the political world. Those who plunge into the party organization without much real experience receive all of their hard knocks in professional politics itself. In any case the newcomer has the problem of being noticed and then accepted by the organization leaders. A few politicians get started because they have money, but organizations also need service and loyalty, which far more people can supply. It is give and take. The politician offers the organization something to get something in return. Progress is usually slow, but there is an escalator going up if one can get on it. Most of those who want to get on will succeed.[2]

Sooner or later the neophyte sees himself in a clearer light. He sees a perspective of running for offices in a continuing series throughout his career. His view may be broad or narrow, but he should have some idea of where he would like to finish. It may be enough finally to monopolize

---

1 Again, the problem of definition arises. In this chapter "politician" is used in the sense of office seeker.

2 Frank Kent, *Political Behavior* (New York: William Morrow & Company, Inc., 1928) Chap. 6. Two outstanding examples of politicians who went all the way up the escalator from the bottom were President Calvin Coolidge and Governor Alfred E. Smith. For one description of a beginning, see Arthur W. Bromage, "Running for the City Council: A Case Study," *American Political Science Review*, Vol. 43 (1949) pp. 1235–1241.

a sinecure in the county courthouse, or it may be that nothing less than the panoramic vistas of the Presidency will satisfy him. The distance from the starting line to the finish should be gauged in rough calculations. The whole endeavor begins and continues with organization, whether that of the party or some other. The higher a politician rises, the more he tends to build a personal organization composed of the people he has drawn about him on the way up, people who are loyal and/or dependent upon him. The relation between a personal organization and the party organization can vary from being almost one and inseparable to being both separate and unfriendly. It is the mark of the greater man not to be entirely dependent upon the party. Governors often have personal organizations and United States senators almost invariably do. Candidates for local offices often receive the same help from what is called a personal following, recruited from their places of employment, their churches, their clubs, and their civic associations.

Launching a Candidacy. This development of organization support can be called, for convenience, *internal* operations by the candidate. He has decided upon the office he wants and sees it in terms of two hurdles, the nomination and the general election. He consults party leaders, personal friends, business men, leaders of organized interest groups, and perhaps other potential candidates to determine how many will be in the direct-primary race and whom he may have to beat to be nominated and elected. Judging by the amount of encouragement and the kind of advice he receives, the politician decides whether or not to run.[3] If he does decide to—usually before he has decided—he begins his *external* operations, which consist of preparing himself for public inspection. There are two general methods of approach to the voters at large: be eager or be reluctant. The latter method seems to be far more popular. It has the advantage of not fully exposing the politician until he is positive he will run, so he is saved embarrassment in case he decides not to. In addition, he keeps his opponents guessing and protects himself in the earlier stages from either sniping or outright attacks and coalitions by his opponents. Reluctance is also presumed to have more favorable effect upon the public. If a politician acts too eager, the voters may distrust him and turn against him. In either case he must have prepared some acceptable reasons why he should be a candidate. He develops them in his personal discussions, and directly or by inference, in the groups he is invited to address.

---

[3] Of course, circumstances determine the procedures. A politician may not have much competition if the office is not desirable or if his party has little chance to win the office. As James A. Farley discovered at the beginning of his political career, it is easy to get a worthless nomination.—*Jim Farley's Story* (New York: McGraw-Hill Book Company, Inc., 1948) p. 19.

Stage-managing a "Draft." All candidates like to believe they are wanted by the voters. This mark of vanity dovetails with reluctance to appear eager. Most politicians want to simulate a draft and create the illusion they are being forced against their will to offer themselves for the office. The politician sometimes succeeds so well with his illusion that he too is taken in—an expected side disorder for one infected with the political virus.

> Once let his friends or a newspaper so much as mention a man's name as 'available material' or the 'right sort of man for this job,' or speak of him as having behind him 'a considerable public sentiment,' or say that he is 'specially well qualified' to represent the city, or state, or nation— and from that time on he is running.
>
> He never stops. Perhaps no one but himself knows about it. Perhaps the people or paper that mentioned him have forgotten all about him. That makes no difference. He is in a 'receptive frame of mind' for the balance of his life.[4]

He and his friends work frantically to stimulate the draft he says he is trying to resist. He finally permits himself to be quoted for publication "that he has not made up his mind—that it is a matter requiring earnest consideration, that becoming a candidate would involve a heavy sacrifice of his time and money, that he has no desire for public office, that he hopes he will not be forced into the fight." [5] However, there is a point beyond which it is foolhardy to be reluctant; so eventually the politician becomes eager, if no sooner than the time he files his qualifying petitions for the direct primary.

The illusions in launching candidacies should not blind us to distinguishing circumstances. Incumbents of an office sometimes can be renominated without much activity on their part. The party leaders and the candidate's own personal advisers want to avoid the disruption of picking a new candidate, want to maintain the *status quo* as far as their arrangements and employment are concerned, and argue that the party will be defeated with another candidate. This situation has often arisen in regard to the Presidency, beginning with George Washington.[6] The incumbent has only to consent to run for re-election and the wheels are set

---

4 Frank R. Kent, *The Great Game of Politics* (New York: Doubleday, Page & Company, 1924) p. 218. All manner of witticisms have been directed at the faked drafts of candidates; one representative sample is: "If you listen carefully in the spring you can hear the buds pop open, and if your ears are even sharper you can hear what the politician describes as the public's irresistible clamor that he run for office."—Senator Soaper, syndicated, April 19, 1954.

5 *The Great Game of Politics*, pp. 224–225.

6 Alexander Hamilton, among others, urged George Washington to run both in 1788 and 1792 to get the government established and to secure it from its enemies.—Charles A. Beard, *Economic Origins of Jeffersonian Democracy* (New York: The Macmillan Company, 1915) pp. 89–91.

in motion for him.[7] If he is challenged for the nomination, he must take an active part in his own fight and cannot rely entirely upon the efforts of his friends.

Continuity of Campaigning. Once a candidate is in the open avowedly seeking an office, analysis is applied to the techniques he employs in winning the office. The period of time these techniques are applied is called the campaign, but, in the proper sense of the word, campaigning never ends once a politician begins it—"Once a Candidate Always a Candidate."[8] Upon entering the profession of seeking public office, campaigning for office goes on continuously. In the nature of things the situation cannot be different, because the politician naturally does those things which are part of campaigning and he no sooner wins or loses one election than he begins preparing for the next. Nor would representatives of pressure groups permit him to rest if he wanted to.[9] No matter by what name the activity is called, generically it is the same: an activity designed to win votes from the citizens.

The designation of a special campaign period is really the recognition of the intensification of campaigning immediately prior to the judgment day at the polls. It is the climax of the electoral process, the culmination of all the preceding efforts and calculations. It is the time when candidates drop all extraneous activities of the public's affairs to concentrate on the public's state of mind. Neither the public nor the candidates could endure the intensity of a formal campaign for very long. Everyone welcomes the relief from the grueling routine. In between elections candidates can campaign with greater relaxation and ease and the citizens are less aware of the electioneering.

Acceptance of Campaigning. The acceptance of an intense campaigning period when the candidates frankly do little else but solicit votes is now so firmly established that it is difficult to comprehend how at one time in our history it was considered undignified for a candidate to appeal directly for votes. This inhibition was part of the aristocratic tradition in

---

[7] Referring to Calvin Coolidge's refusal to indicate receptivity to another nomination in 1928, Kent, *Political Behavior*, p. 13, observed that "one of the simplest rules in politics is that when a thing you want is yours for the asking you do not risk it by appearing to back away from it." Whether Coolidge wanted the nomination is a moot question if one confines himself to circumstantial evidence, but in the political world it would be assumed that had the convention offered the nomination, Coolidge would have accepted it. Possibly, a politician may be nominated for an office he would prefer not to have: a conceivable example was Theodore Roosevelt's nomination for vice-president in 1900. However, such cases are too rare to merit more than passing attention.

[8] *The Great Game of Politics*, Chap. 34.

[9] *Ibid., pp.* 253-254, 263; George M. Reynolds, *Machine Politics in New Orleans, 1897–1926* (New York: Columbia University Press, 1936) p. 127.

politics, summed up by John Q. Adams: "I never had asked, and never should ask, the vote of any person for any office." [10] On the local level there was more open campaigning, but in seeking higher offices the taboos against vulgar appeals held on until the popularization of politics made campaigning essential.

The Presidency was the last office to come under the sway of the obviously eager candidate. The theme that "The Presidency is not an office to be either solicited or declined" was honored in the sense that candidates made no campaign speeches, ostensibly, but operated entirely in the background. Charles C. Pinckney of South Carolina toured New England in 1803 in behalf of his candidacy in 1804, but this departure failed to set an immediate precedent. Candidates reached the public through personal letters, which were widely circulated and quoted. The ice was finally broken by Whig candidates William Henry Harrison and Henry Clay in 1836, 1840, and 1844. The Whig candidate in 1852, General Winfield Scott, made a "nonpolitical tour" to select a site for a soldiers' asylum. The first Democrat to campaign actively was Stephen A. Douglas in 1860. The first "swing around the circle," i.e., a carefully planned campaign trip throughout the country, was made by Andrew Johnson in 1868 to rally his faction of the Republican Party. Garfield in 1880 stumped the country in the most active personal campaign up to that time, but Bryan's campaigns, beginning in 1896, eclipsed anything that had been done before in both intensive and extensive appeals to the voters. The most ambitious speaking tour by a President was conducted by Truman in 1948.[11]

The remainder of the discussion about politicians' problems in being elected to office can be confined to the area of general practices used by candidates to win votes—the techniques employed in campaigns to attract and hold the voters.

CAMPAIGN TECHNIQUES

Elections as Instruments for the "Outs." Elections are occasions peculiarly advantageous for the "outs." The "ins," meaning the incumbents, have nothing new to gain by an election campaign; at the maximum they do no more than hold their own by keeping the office they already have.

---

10 Quoted in George Stimpson, *A Book about American Politics* (New York: Harper & Brothers, 1952) p. 398. Charles Sydnor, *Gentleman Freeholders* (Chapel Hill: University of North Carolina Press, 1952) pp. 42, 44, 49, noted the problem this inhibition created for candidates in Colonial Virginia and the many violations of the code of never soliciting votes.

11 *Ibid.*, pp. 394–405. Theodore Roosevelt holds the record for the number of speeches in a single campaign—673 in 1900; but Bryan holds the record for the most speeches in several campaigns—1500—and for the most speeches in one day—36.——*New York Times Magazine*, September 7, 1952.

It is the challenger of an incumbent (or both candidates when the incumbent is not running) that has something to gain, and only the holding of an election permits him to gain it. When the skill of an incumbent and a challenger are approximately equal, the latter has an advantage in being able to criticize, to appeal to dissatisfactions and to make unrealistic promises. The incumbent, in these circumstances of equality in skill, needs to have large numbers loyal to him and support his record, and the best ally he can have is a general atmosphere of satisfaction. It is difficult for an incumbent to profit from tensions and discontent unless they run against the party represented by the challenger. A man or woman with several terms in an office depends upon his constituents' habits, their traditional voting; and he hopes they are contented with the existing relations of organized interests. A challenger depends upon offering something new in personality and/or relations of organized interests and upon sentiments for a change.

PRELIMINARY AND PREPARATORY CONSIDERATIONS

Analyses of Constituency. An over-all problem for a candidate in devising the strategy of his campaign is the analysis of his constituency as a whole. What kind or kinds of people are they? What kinds of interests do they have? How can their interests be related to the candidate's campaign? This problem of analysis is somewhat simplified by the rules, either statutory or customary, requiring local residence. Before a candidate is ready to run, he often knows much about his constituents because he lives among them. His political qualifications making him available follow from his legal qualifications making him eligible. The size of the constituency affects directly the ease or difficulty of the analysis. The larger it is, the more heterogeneous and the more difficult to analyze, although there are complications and conflicting interests even in a constituency as small as a city ward or precinct. The candidate concludes, on the basis of his own knowledge and of any additional information he can get, what the predominating characteristics and interests of the constituency are. Most frequently he will find them diverse and will realize that his campaign communication goes to an unselected audience, reaching beyond the confines of his constituency.[12] The result in most campaigns is for candidates to make multiple appeals to this audience. Sometimes they can pinpoint a segment of citizens and use the shotgun technique of driving home exactly the points these people are concerned with. Generally, candidates have to use the buckshot technique and hope the scattered shot will hit

---

[12] Because of absentee voting, a constituency is not entirely confined to one geographical area; *e.g.*, in 1952 Republican campaign material was directed at Americans in Italy through advertisement in an English-language newspaper in Rome.——*New York Times*, October 20, 1952.

home in many directions. Issuing statements and making well-publicized speeches, the candidate must calculate the effects of his words upon all of the constituents.

Conflicting and Embarrassing Promises. The time is long past when a candidate could make conflicting or contrary promises to different groups of constituents without fear of being called to account. The invention of the telegraph first put a damper on such conduct, and the subsequent developments in communication systems make a speech delivered in Seattle, Washington, instantly available for citizens' inspection in Miama, Florida. Some of the contradictions in a campaign are kept out of print because candidates make secret commitments to organized groups, but the human tongue is always busy, and the deepest secrets soon begin to come to the public's attention.

The ability to straddle issues is only one feature of dealing with issues. A candidate who refused to make any commitments to constituents would likely do badly. Issues have ramifications which complicate and also ease the candidate's job. By the use of promises to different interests the candidate may gain multiple support and yet avoid outright contradictions. His promises may be more or less definite. He may eventually have to admit that he cannot deliver everything he promised or that his constituents misunderstood the promise.[13] These efforts in about-facing seldom increase the politician's popularity, so rationalization or diversion is usually resorted to when such embarrassments arise. In spite of all the ifs in issues, people want to hear something which sounds definite, so the candidate probes to find out what will motivate each person or each group and then appeals to them in terms of these interests and motivations.[14] As a rule the candidate is in no doubt about the wishes of groups, for their leaders seek him out to get a commitment, not waiting for him to come to them.

Individual v. Group Appeals. The analyses of a constituency are almost always in terms of identifiable groups of voters. It is simply impossible in most cases for a candidate to compute his strategy in terms of each individual voter. True, if the constituency is quite small, a campaign may consist wholly of personal contacts and appeals, but even here the candidate depends more upon influential individuals and also depends upon

---

13 During his Administration, President William Howard Taft explained to some audiences that when he promised tariff revision during the 1908 campaign, he did not necessarily mean *downward* revision as most people assumed.

14 As the late United States Senator, Henry F. Ashurst (Democrat, Arizona) stated the case, "Above all things, he [the politician] should not forget that voters never grow weary of illusory promises."——From "The Care and Feeding of Politicians," delivered in the Senate.

the groups to which he belongs. Appeals in a campaign, in the full sense of the word, are to groups. In fashioning or calculating appeals, candidates think in terms of the receptivity of particular kinds of groups of people. Some of this thinking may unavoidably be stereotyped. A frequent use of stereotypes is revealed in efforts to foresee what a whole class of people thinks and how they will react. Candidates envision how factory workers or farmers or housewives or white-collar workers or retailers will respond to an appeal. These visions may be pipe dreams, but the more improvising the candidate must do, the more of these calculations he may be forced to make.

Strategy Adapted to the Office. The kinds of campaign techniques a candidate uses depend upon the general strategy he adopts for getting himself elected. The strategy adopted is largely determined by the importance of the office he seeks. The voters want to hear from candidates for President, for Congress, for governor; to a lesser extent, from candidates for the state legislature, sheriff, attorney general; and almost to no extent at all from candidates for secretary of state, county recorder, or justice of the peace. In most states, candidates for all of these offices are elected the same day, and the voters simply have limits upon the number of candidates they can listen to during the same period of time. Candidates running for offices at the top of the ticket merit most of the general attention, so they are the ones who make the speeches, issue the statements and travel extensively about the constituency. The candidates running at the bottom of the ticket appear at rallies and are introduced to the crowds but usually make few speeches. Their general strategy is to follow the head of the ticket and depend upon organization. Again, it becomes clear why good vote getters are needed at the head of the ticket to help carry it.

A candidate for a lesser office can be independent of the top of the ticket only if he has his own following or a constituency that usually elects candidates of his party. The distinction is not that candidates for lesser offices utilize no campaign techniques, but that their techniques are more unobtrusive. They engage in more personal-contact campaigning and make fewer public speeches of a formal nature. They usually have less popular issues to discuss so have little to talk about except themselves or their records in office. Organization plus the standpat party voters are of cardinal importance.

GENERAL PRACTICES

Techniques Infinite, but Standardized. Getting to the specific question of the techniques themselves, two observations should be made at once. First, to enter a caveat, techniques can never be fully catalogued and exhaustively described. Differences in particular campaign problems and in particular candidates preclude any final or all-inclusive treatment. The really remarkable fact about campaign techniques is that definite patterns of general practices emerge from the confusion. The discovery of these patterns attests to the basically similar character of all campaigns over time and to the possibilities for orderly approaches to the problems by politicians despite the outward appearance of haphazard and petulant responses. Only when there is a basic order in operations can there be a systematic description and analysis of what goes on.

Individual Differences in Candidates. The second observation comes directly from the first. The differences in techniques and the skill in their application reflect personal differences among the candidates. No two politicians are exactly alike any more than any two individuals are. Some politicians are better adapted to the work of campaigning, finding it less of a chore and having fewer rules to learn consciously. All fish may swim with the same ease and natural aptitude, but not all politicians campaign with the same grace and aplomb. Some of these personal qualities necessary in campaigning can be learned or assimilated; others are functions of the personality and can never be mastered by certain campaigners. Inasmuch as campaigning involves so much communication, and a great deal of that oral, personal characteristics like voice and general appearance are always important. The use of radio, motion-picture, and television media has progressively placed a premium upon these qualities. Anyone can improve his speech (including pronunciation, enunciation, voice pitch, and resonance) and his appearance (including stance, posture, gestures, and facial expressions).

The capacity for improvement is itself dependent upon the individual, his native abilities and intelligence, and the intensity with which he applies himself. No standard of excellence in these matters of voice, body, and total expressiveness can be set definitely. For each man and woman there are the peculiar nuances of personality to be developed and transmitted through the learned skills. Everyone should be himself with modifications. He should appear, *in toto,* appropriate for the occasion, which includes the place, the purpose, and the audience. People can quickly sense artificiality and pretense, and to convey such impressions in campaigns is almost always fatal for candidates. People appreciate diversions and welcome individuality in politics as much as they do in other kinds of performance. No politician would be likely to succeed if he were a carbon copy of another. Relief from monotony is provided as much by stimulating personalities of different sorts as by variation in techniques.

Showmanship. Cultivating mannerisms or employing unusual tricks can distinguish an individual candidate and at the same time make him personable and his appeal unforgettable. In the middle of a speech, a candidate may remove his coat and drop it on the platform or remove his shoes or snap his suspenders or display a patch on his trousers. These gestures are not the kind taught by elocution teachers, but can be appropriate none the less. A candidate may use objects like a water pitcher, or the Bible or the flag as a stage prop for more dramatically presenting his appeal. These features are bits of hokum, but they help a candidate to "give a good show." [15] Humor itself is effective in its place for putting an audience at ease and for variety. Humor must be directed only at persons or things properly to be laughed at or about. The treatment of issues should be serious, and poking fun at an opponent can easily be overdone and actually create sympathy for him. The candidate avoids at all costs being a wisecracker or appearing smartalecky.[16] Once he creates the picture of himself he wants his constituents to see, the politician should neither overplay nor underplay his part.

Getting Attention

The first great problem to which techniques are applied is securing the attention of the voters. This is more troublesome for new and strange candidates than for older and familiar ones, but the problem always exists for every politician. How does a man make himself stand out so that the voters become aware of him? What does he say or do to impress them that he is worthy of their support? Most frequently, candidates try to solve this problem by finding something to say about issues, something which will sound different but sensible, something which will be associated with the candidate and no one else. Stunts of various kinds are used to get publicity and cause the voters to single out, in a favorable context, this one candidate.[17] Unusual campaign techniques can be very helpful, e.g., candidates make a personal tour of their constituency to meet voters, shake their hands, talk with them, and ask for their votes. Constituents

---

[15] Kent, *Political Behavior*, Chaps. 10, 14.

[16] A great deal of discussion in the 1952 presidential campaign revolved about Adlai Stevenson's use of humor. Some of it may have been lost on his audiences, and he tended to tone it down as the campaign advanced. The only time he skirted around dangerous territory was during a visit to Washington, D. C., following his nomination. When photographers asked him to make a gesture, he replied, "If I gave the gesture that comes to mind, it would not be reproduced." When photographers insisted that a group of four, including Stevenson, get closer together, he said, "That's close enough. If we got any closer people would think we were going to start shooting craps."——*New York Times*, August 13, 1952, and Ruth Montgomery, syndicated column, August 17, 1952.

[17] As an ingenious device to get voters to read his campaign pamphlet, a candidate running in a field of twenty-two for the common council of Everett, Massachusetts, put a photograph of the voter's house on the pamphlet. The candidate finished first in the race.——United Press dispatch dated October 10, 1953. Peculiarity in names can bring attention, as the case of John S. Angel filing for the Democratic nomination for treasurer of Paradise township in Arkansas. Associated Press dispatch dated June 18, 1954.

are sometimes impressed by the candidate's interest, noting that no other candidate has actually come to them as individuals.

One device formerly used far more than now is the debate between candidates, and some used it to excellent advantage not only to get their appeals over to the voters but also to bring themselves to the voters' attention. The classic example of this device was Abraham Lincoln's challenging Stephen A. Douglas to a debate for the United States senatorship from Illinois in 1858. Douglas was the incumbent, a popular and powerful national politician. Lincoln was a local and state politician, a prosperous attorney and a former member of Congress, who was watching his chance to get into office again. Lincoln had everything to gain by the debates, for they would bring him to the attention of the voters, unmistakably. Douglas had nothing to gain by accepting the challenge. He needed no device to get attention and realized the benefits Lincoln might derive. To use your opponent to your own advantage is a mark of skill because the opponent will understand the maneuver and will try to counteract it. The skill is the creation of a situation the opponent cannot escape. Douglas may have felt trapped by Lincoln's challenge. If by refusing he had given the impression of fearing or insulting Lincoln, the result could have been more disastrous than any occurrence in the debates. Candidates try to play the martyr, and should they convince the public, they may need no other issue to run on. This kind of technique, making use of your opponent, is limited because it is difficult to jockey a candidate into such a position. A prerequisite for success, even when the opponent is trapped, is knowing what to do next and doing it well.

Publicity

Means of Identification. Getting attention and holding it is merely an aspect of the greatest weapon in the armory of campaign techniques, getting publicity. While a candidate concentrates upon getting specific information about his constituents, they gather vicarious impressions about him from newspapers, newsreels, and news telecasts or broadcasts. Stray bits of descriptions and fleeting glimpses of a face or body constitute much of the public's knowledge of their candidates. The more frequently they are shown or mentioned, the more they become familiar. It is highly desirable that the publicity be favorable, but even if it is unfavorable, it is better than none. "It is an old but a true saying in politics that 'it is better to be roasted than ignored.' " [18] Candidates are aware of the problem of making their names and faces known. A name already well publicized is referred to as a good vote-getting name, either among the

---

18 Kent, *Political Behavior*, p. 252.

public at large or within one party or the other.[19] Names then become important, and candidates show care in which given names and initials they use.[20] Nicknames can be endearing identifications as "Andy" for Andrew Jackson, "Old Rough and Ready" for Zachary Taylor, "Abe" for Abraham Lincoln, "Teddy" for Theodore Roosevelt, "Al" for Alfred E. Smith, "FDR" for Franklin D. Roosevelt, "Ike" for Dwight D. Eisenhower. Descriptive terms may be associated in a flattering sense as "The Plumed Knight" for James G. Blaine and "The Great Commoner" for William Jennings Bryan. In these ways, candidates become known and hope voters will recognize their names on ballots, since people generally prefer to vote for familiar names and some haphazard voters make up their minds how to vote in some races after they get to the polls.

Presidential Publicity. Some rules and conclusions in politics are either restricted or expanded when applied to the Presidency. The campaign technique of publicity requires some special attention in connection with that office. First, the President need not worry about getting publicity, for he is always a source of news. On the contrary, some Presidents and their staffs try to avoid publicity which they think will create unfavorable impressions. Sometimes a President says or writes things that are embarrassing, and efforts are made to cover up. The subject of Presidents' physical exercise is news but not always welcome news at the White House. As a case in point, President Eisenhower became associated with golf, and his avidness for the game was made so plain that his press secretary put a damper on this publicity. Second, the President's news value is an asset to his political party. He can get a message to the public more easily, as a rule, than anybody else. Third, the status of the presidential office is a partisan advantage. Presidents receive free radio and television time to address the nation in their capacity as Chief Executive. When does the President speak as President and when as a politician? The distinction is meaningless, for the President plays both roles all the time, whether he wants to or not. The combination of publicity and status makes it difficult, if possible, for any opposition leader completely to counter the President as a political publicity force.

Candidates and the Press. Because of their dependence upon publicity, candidates cultivate newspaper reporters, editors, and publishers.

---

[19] Theodore Roosevelt first popularized that family name, and this fact was taken into account when Franklin D. Roosevelt was nominated for Vice-President in 1920. After Franklin became President, however, the partisan association shifted quickly from Republican to Democrat. A particular name can be so popular within a party that anyone with that name will run well in the party's direct primary.

[20] Woodrow Wilson dropped his first given name "Thomas" and Herbert Hoover allowed his middle name "Clark" to fall into disuse. For a semiserious discussion of names in this connection, see George Dixon, syndicated column, April 18, 1953.

This is one reason for buying advertising space in newspapers, a practice generally agreed to be ineffective in winning votes. The best publicity is human-interest, personal-information stories. Those members of the news-gathering profession who interview politicians and who find out what is happening behind the scenes have a tremendous amount of information and know the candidates very well personally. There is an interdependence, in fact. Politicians confide in reporters and give them background material for stories. Otherwise the reporters would get no news. Politicians want to establish friendly relations with reporters in order to get publicity. Even more, by these associations politicians can keep their names before the public in a favorable light and can keep unpleasant references to them-selves out of the papers. The reporters often have more information than they can print; either they cannot violate confidences, or the stories may make the papers liable for suit. When a paper favors a candidate, he can be helped immensely by constant publicity of a favorable nature, having his picture printed, getting his name into the headlines, being written up on the front page. When a paper opposes a candidate, he may be ignored or relegated to the back pages as well as presented in an unfavorable light.

The concentration of newspaper ownership has affected directly all news presentations. The number of independent newspapers has been de-clining steadily, so that many cities have access only to different editions of the same paper even though the papers may be separately operated under different names. The growth of newspaper chains and the dependence of most papers upon the wire services, except for local and regional news, in-crease the standardization of stories and the angles from which they are written. The selection of what to print, even without the intention of cen-sorship, is inevitable because no paper is large enough to print all the news received from the wire services. In the first place, the news services on the national and state levels decide what is sufficiently newsworthy to put on the wires to their newspaper customers. In the second place, each editor decides which stories and how much of a story from the tremendous mass received will be printed. In the third place, the members of chains receive certain features syndicated through the chain and editorials to be run in all of the chain's outlets. In the fourth place, the widespread use of syndi-cated features by both chain and independent newspapers gives them all a similarity in content.

Decisions about inclusion and exclusion are related to demands of sub-scribers and to building circulation, to fear of a law suit and to a sense of good taste. By these means, selection is not uniform, e.g., a story about a United States senator may be featured in most papers in his own state and largely ignored in other states. Yet, with the growth in ownership concen-tration, selection tends to be more uniform in a city or an area served by one paper. Politicians want very much to be mentioned or discussed on press-wire stories with the hope of wider publicity, and they like the support of chains or of newspaper monopolies. They often make news timed correctly for particular editions of newspapers which receive the story by wire.

Pressure from Reporters. On the highest government levels, reporters are under pressure to get news, and the pressure is applied in turn upon politicians and their staffs. As a result, skill in handling reporters and getting the candidate's story across to the public varies with politicians.[21] At the presidential level, relations with reporters is one of the chief problems of the office, and press relations have varied sharply with different Presidents.[22] The pressure for news in Washington, D. C., is so intense and so much material is demanded by columnists and reporters that they must produce whether there is any real news or not. Officials often find it the lesser of evils to give out news anonymously or give what is called "background," for fear that writers will otherwise turn out stories based on hunches or scraps of information. In this case, misinformation gains currency, officials get into hot water, and a general furor ensues.[23] This side of press relations in the federal government can be called "government by news-gathering agencies." [24]

Newspapers and Partisanship. During campaigns, if not the year around, most newspapers support candidates or parties more or less heatedly. The practice of the nineteenth century of parties directly owning or subsidizing newspapers as official organs has passed. Newspaper publishers, editors, and reporters are often active in politics at the local, state, and national levels, and many are associated with one of the parties; nevertheless, the support is based upon similar interests, upon local situations, or upon factors directly related to the newspaper such as circulation and advertising. The predominant partisan predilection of the press is Republican. This predominance has been turned to account by the Democrats with the

---

[21] Warren Moscow, *Politics in the Empire State* (New York: Alfred A. Knopf, Inc., 1948) pp. 32-35, noted that the New Yorkers' concept of Governor Dewey's record in office was partly a product of pro-Dewey publicity and lack of counterpublicity by the Democrats. Members of Congress have found that to call for an investigation is almost a sure-fire way to get publicity for themselves. See Arthur Krock, *New York Times*, December 28, 1954.

[22] See James E. Pollard, *The Presidents and the Press* (New York: The Macmillan Company, 1947).

[23] The following explanation by a London newsman becomes more understandable: Confidential "information is shared [by the British Foreign Office] with the [London] *Times* not for direct use but to inform its editors and leader writers, and to keep it from saying things that might embarrass the government. In short, the *Times* is not official, but is treated as though it were, in order to prevent misunderstandings based on the erroneous assumption that it is."——Quoted in *Time*, February 23, 1948, p. 61, note.

[24] Douglass Cater, "Government by Publicity," *Reporter*, March 19, 1959, pp. 14-23.

slogan "the one-party press." [25] This contention is based in many cases upon the editorial policy of newspapers, but the implication is that the bulk of newspapers support Republicans in their news columns either by featuring them and ignoring Democrats or by injecting pro-Republican propaganda into straight news reporting. The actual situation is by no means so simple. If the injecting of partisanship into news reporting is wrong in principle, a violation is as serious among the minority of papers that support Democrats as it is among the majority that support Republicans.[26]

Value of Newspaper Support. An equally important but different kind of question is the effect of newspapers in election outcomes. Despite newspaper opposition to Franklin D. Roosevelt from 1932 to 1944, he was elected four times, indicating what had been known long before the 1930's, that predominant newspaper support is not necessary for a candidate to be elected. The rule on publicity, to repeat, is to get it, and Roosevelt always was well publicized even in papers which opposed him. The Republicans inadvertently helped Roosevelt during his campaigns by emphasizing their opposition to him rather than their support of their own candidates; since the Democrats also emphasized him with their constant praise, he was the featured attraction, the center of the campaign. This same situation worked to the advantage of Eisenhower in 1952, when the Democrats by attacking him publicized him, and the Republicans ignored Stevenson as Roosevelt's opponents had been ignored.[27]

The manner or the degree of support of candidates by a paper becomes more important than the counting of papers on each side in a campaign. Support may mean only editorial support, and comparatively few people read editorials. Featured or syndicated writers in a paper may differ from

---

[25] In August, 1953 the Democratic National Committee began publishing through a separate corporation a monthly publication, *Democratic Digest,* as a "magazine that would be the answer to the One-Party Press." Of 1773 daily newspapers in 1952, 67.34% supported Eisenhower according to a poll by *Editor and Publisher. New York Times,* October 31, 1952. However, Stevenson conceded he had generally received impartial treatment in the news columns. *Ibid.,* April 8, 1953. In the 1956 campaign, between September 11 and November 1, the percentage distribution of 38,000 front-page headlines for the presidential and vice-presidential candidates showed: Eisenhower 50%, Nixon 9%, Stevenson 36%, Kefauver 5%. *Ibid.,* November 4, 1956.

[26] See Nathan B. Blumberg, *One-Party Press? Coverage of the 1952 Presidential Campaign in 35 Daily Newspapers* (Lincoln: University of Nebraska Press, 1954). In this analysis, 18 papers evidenced no partiality in their news columns (15 supported Eisenhower, 2 Stevenson and one was independent); in the case of 11 papers, there was no conclusive evidence of partiality (7 supported Eisenhower, 3 Stevenson and 1 independent); there was evidence of partiality in 6 papers (4 supported Eisenhower and 2 Stevenson). Blumberg also discussed the difficulties in establishing criteria for determining partiality.

[27] The fact that Eisenhower was already familiar to the general public and Stevenson was not could have been more important than the campaign publicity itself.

its editorial policy and are likely to have far more readers. The presentation of the news on the front page is perhaps the most crucial factor. While the policy of papers is set by publishers and editors, reporters have some influence upon what is printed even though they angle their stories to please their employers.[28]

Kinds and Extent of Influence. The general reactions of people toward what they read in newspapers are by no means uniform. One long-time newspaperman was of the opinion that

> it often arouses sympathy to be opposed by the newspapers. Many a man has found the opposition of the press an asset instead of a liability— particularly if their criticism is of a violent nature, and if they make a practice of denouncing him as dumb. Large, powerful and rich newspapers are always unpopular in their communities. People read them but hate them. When you consider that there is not a day in which the most decent and conservative newspaper does not have to print news personally offensive to many of its readers and which futile efforts are made to suppress, this is not surprising. And it is also easy to understand why an attack on the press by a politician, a claim that he is being persecuted and abused, an allegation of unfairness, invariably strikes a popular and responsive chord, no matter how silly his allegations may be.[29]

This view, too, is probably overstated. There is not enough information available about newspaper political influence upon readers to be adamant about any conclusion.

Basically, the complaint about press support is a matter of ideology more than partisanship as such. Because newspapers are capitalistic enterprises run for profit, their owners support policies in their and the system's interest. They tend to favor the *status quo* and to resist reforms costly to them or their associates. The dangers from newspaper excesses lie more in this direction, for the news presentation over a period of time can affect

---

[28] An example, perhaps rare, of reporters and writers clearly being at odds with editorial policy was found in the *New York Times* during the 1952 presidential campaign. From the news columns an uninformed reader could have guessed that the paper was neutral or supporting Stevenson, for most of the *Times'* writers were pro-Stevenson. In order to quiet rumors the publisher finally had to announce that his paper was not going to change its editorial policy but would continue to support Eisenhower.——*Ibid.,* October 31, 1952. Of thirty-one reporters on the Eisenhower 1952 campaign train, twenty-four favored Stevenson.——*Ibid.,* September 11, 1952. The late Senator Robert A. Taft once asserted that most news writers and columnists in Washington, D.C. "tend to be anti-Republican."——*Ibid.,* April 7, 8, 1953. James Reston, Chief of the *New York Times* Washington Bureau, who had frequently been anti-Republican himself, gave some point to the Taft assertion by attacking the Democrats' one-party press concept with the claim that Washington newsmen had been ahead of Democrats in criticizing the Eisenhower Administration. See his column, *ibid.,* April 17, 1955.

[29] Frank R. Kent, *Political Behavior*, p. 270.

readers' opinions even without their knowing it.[30] In an election campaign, the activities of candidates are news and will generally be reported irrespective of the newspaper's editorial policy. People who have no definite opinions may be influenced by their newspapers, but people who have already made up their minds probably cannot be changed so easily.

Other Media. The correction of the ills of one medium lies largely in access to other media. The powerful influence of Franklin D. Roosevelt on the radio led to a conclusion that this medium was more advantageous for the Democrats, as newspapers were for the Republicans. In part this judgment was based upon the facts of partisan strength and weakness during the 1930's, for Mr. Roosevelt was a far superior communicator.[31] To the extent that the candidates of one party speak more effectively in presenting their side of a case and in capturing people's interest, those candidates will be able to exploit the radio and television media. Comparatively, the newspaper is impersonal, and radio and television are personal in their impact. This difference itself is variously helpful or hurtful to different candidates, depending upon their forte in communicating; the difference is also important as an influencing factor upon individuals, singly or in groups. "What is one man's meat is another man's poison" applies both to the candidate as communicator and to the citizens as recipients of communication.

The growing reliance upon television and its expanding opportunities for publicity changes some of the established campaign techniques. Governors and members of Congress use both live and filmed presentations on television networks. The intensity and frequency of their reminders of themselves to the voters are substantially increased, and for members of Congress in particular this medium is heaven-sent as a substitute for returning to their states while Congress is in session. The potential in television was further advanced by the telecasting of presidential news conferences. The use of a "telethon" (the candidate stays before the camera for several consecutive hours answering questions, interspersing comments) has been accounted the difference between victory and defeat for some candidates. The conclusions about the value of a technique are often unbalanced because they are based on one or two dramatic examples. If a candidate is personable and makes a good impression, if he is experienced in handling himself under critical inspection, if he can think fast and talk extemporaneously with feeling and knowledge—then such devices as the "telethon" are likely to help him. From the point of view of a candidate or of a board of

---

[30] "Many of our private thoughts and personal opinions, many of our secret hopes and intimate fears can be traced back to the publishers of newspapers and to the people who write for them. In consequence, we are more influenced by the way some event is interpreted than we are by the event itself."——Quincy Howe, *The News and How to Understand It* (New York: Simon and Schuster, Inc., 1940) p. 3.

[31] Arthur Krock characterized this period as reflecting "The Superior Articulation of the Left."——*New York Times,* July 13 and 14, 1949.

strategy, the objective is to exploit every medium of communication, to be both in the headlines and on the air waves. Success in this objective is referred to as "saturation." [32]

Turning to the media of commercial advertising causes politicians to rely more upon public relations experts, leading to the charge that Madison Avenue runs campaigns. There are substantial fears that getting a candidate elected will become analogous to selling a breakfast food; that campaign techniques will take on the qualities of advertising jingles, spot announcements, and the vibrancy of a commercial in the discussion of public problems; that the most available candidates will be those who televise to advantage and create the best image of what the voters want or think they want. [33] The ad men dispute these conclusions, contending they do not make campaign policy and cannot sell people simply by use of advertising techniques.

> Very simply, you can't sell a politician like a bar of soap. People won't elect a detergent to public office. . . .
> . . . People vote less for an issue than an image. TV is the greatest image purveyor of all time. But let's be clear what we mean by image. We mean a total impression. That total impression is the result of many random, casual and not so casual impressions.
> What TV can do is strengthen the impression. Clarify it if it is blurred. TV can concentrate, focus, emphasize, but it cannot create an image that is not at least embryonic already. It cannot make a fat man appear thin, it cannot make an inarticulate man silver-tongued, it cannot create sincerity where sincerity does not exist. . . . What a man is, how he really feels, come through on the 21-inch screen. The image you see may not be one you admire. But if the voters accept it you can feel pretty certain they are getting what they want, they aren't being fooled by what they see. They may be wrong but they are not misled. [34]

Irrespective of who plans the campaign strategy, the objectives are the same and the most modern techniques merely permit strategists to do the same old things in new ways before audiences of millions instead of scores or hundreds.

Sense of Timing

Few activities requiring finesse, judgment, and artistry can be carried out fully without an awareness of when an action should or should not be

---

[32] For examples of saturation, see Theodore Milton Black, *Democratic Party Publicity in the 1940 Campaign* (New York: Plymouth Publishing Company, 1941) Chap. 3. The same type of technique was used as early as 1748 in New York when letters and broadsides were employed to define the issues.——Carl L. Becker, *History of Political Parties in the Province of New York* (University of Wisconsin Bulletin, Vol. 2, 1909) pp. 19-20.

[33] Vance Packard, *The Hidden Persuaders* (New York: Pocket Books, Inc., 1958) Chap. 17; Stanley Kelley, Jr., *Professional Public Relations and Political Power* (Baltimore: The Johns Hopkins Press, 1956); *New York Times Magazine*, September 2, 1956, p. 10.

[34] "Madison Avenue Techniques in Political Campaigns." Paper presented at a panel of the American Political Science Association, St. Louis, September 6, 1958, by Lloyd G. Whitebrook, Executive Vice President, Kastor, Hilton, Chesley & Clifford. See also *New York Times*, October 27, 1958.

taken as well as what kind of action it should be. Success in making this type of decision is often referred to as "having a sense of timing." The objection to this description is the implication that the skill is a mysterious quality impossible of explanation, much less of being taught and passed on. The most remarkable fact about timing is its unfailing relation to experience and knowledge. Some well-known entertainers have mastered the art of timing, but no one assumes that they were born with this ability as an innate characteristic of their personalities. A sense of timing in one kind of activity is not necessarily transferable to other activities inasmuch as it is a product of concentration, application, and insight. Whatever element of seemingly intuitive judgment is involved can likely be traced to a mastery of the subject and its processes even though the practitioner himself may be unable to explain how he knew what to do at the correct moment.

In politics, timing has many applications. It involves, to begin with, an awareness of the audience, literally and figuratively. Candidates need to know what their constituents want to hear and how much they want to hear. Candidates also want to determine when to raise an issue and when to leave it alone. They develop abilities to decide when to accept a challenge or answer a charge. The sense of timing depends as much upon inaction at the right time and place as upon action. What is sometimes condemned as indecisiveness, drifting, or lack of vigor in public officials may be a marking of time until the judicious moment for action arrives. Candidates have a sense of the public in not wanting to satiate people or wear them out. This application of technique applies both to the things a candidate discusses and to the candidate himself.

Here is to be found a qualification of the rule of publicity. It is possible to be so constantly publicized that people grow bored with the same person and begin ignoring his publicity. In cases of candidates (the President, for instance) who always are news, it is wise from time to time to give the public a rest. After a lapse of time with little publicity, the re-emergence of the candidate in the news is a fresh note and people will perceive him and be glad to hear of him again. Obviously in this kind of timing the periods of withdrawal will be well in between elections so that the return of the candidate to the headlines will coincide with the official start of a new campaign period. Candidates work out a timing operation for their formal campaigns. Most nominations are made in the spring or early summer, a period of strenuous campaigning except when nominations go by default through lack of opposition. Then, the nominees spend a few weeks preparing for the general-election campaign. The last big effort begins about a month to six weeks before election day. As this final campaign proceeds, there is an increase in tempo, in concentration, in excitement culminating on the day of election. The climax is reached at the end through a careful building process.[35]

The nature of a sense of timing precludes its being a separate technique by itself. Instead, it is an ability which permeates the entire campaign and becomes a property of many techniques. It is applied to the formal campaign and to the entire existence of the politician.

The Strategy of Attack

Holding the Initiative. Although few unqualified statements are justified about campaigning, a rule of extremely high validity is that the candidate should attack rather than defend. To take the offensive is usually helpful in getting publicity, and the impression made by this publicity is more likely to be favorable than unfavorable. To be on the defensive is to be in the position of having to explain, and most citizens are impatient with explanations in politics. They also are likely to become suspicious of the explainer since his defense will reach some who did not hear of the charge he is answering, and they may very well wonder what it is all about. To begin explaining is likely never to end, because the opposition will keep fueling the fire by demanding ever more explanations. The voters will lose interest and the defensive candidate will appear as a man without any strategy of his own, without any line of attack, and without any record or positive arguments.[36] He is controlled or victimized by events managed by his opponents and presumably would conduct public affairs in the same manner if elected. This is not a picture that people want to have of the candidates they elect. Even unaggressive people are not likely to be enamored of unaggressive candidates.

The use of the attack can become monotonous, so candidates will vary their approach and presentation. They will as much as possible choose the issues on which to attack both to create the impression of being fighters and to slide over questions they prefer not to discuss. It is also in this way that candidates try to create illusions of victory, the band-wagon technique, by making themselves appear as the inevitable winners. When one competitor seems to be on the run, his opponent tries to convince the public that they can sense his victory "in the air."

---

[35] A classic example of a failure in this kind of timing was the campaign of Wendell Willkie for the Presidency in 1940. He brought his campaign to its high point about two weeks before the election and thereafter had no place to go but down. The fact that Willkie was a novice in politics largely explains his incapacity to appreciate this factor.

[36] Boies Penrose stated this rule of attack in another way: "In politics it's a fine thing to apologize to an individual. But never apologize to a mob. The first is gracious; the second is cowardly."—Quoted in Walter Davenport, *Power and Glory* (New York: G. P. Putnam's Sons, 1931) p. 105. As the Governor of Alabama reportedly told the Governor of Tennessee, who inquired what kind of a speech to make before a particular audience: "Rough, governor. Rough as a cob. Go out here guttin', cuttin', and struttin'."——Quoted in the *Saturday Evening Post*, January 29, 1955, p. 22.

Ignoring the Opponent. The advice Abraham Lincoln is reputed to have given a young man (that to be elected you have to ask people to vote for you) amounts to taking the offensive. Using direct methods, speaking directly of a candidacy and a desire to serve are elements of the attack. As an additional part of this strategy a candidate tries to advance his own campaign along the lines he chooses and counteract the campaign of his opponent without giving him any aid. This technique is largely a throwback to the discussion on publicity. The object is to avoid giving an opponent any personal publicity or helping him communicate his campaign appeals. The most elementary rule is never mention the opponent's name in a speech or other campaign material. If an opponent must be referred to, the word "opponent" is used or some other term which will suggest that there is another candidate for the office. Candidates carefully select these terms and occasionally can develop a descriptive reference which creates an unpleasant association with the opponent, as Wendell Willkie referred to Franklin D. Roosevelt in 1940 as "the third-term candidate." This practice in American politics is one of the products of individuals campaigning by themselves or only in company with party colleagues; it could not have been followed in the days when opposing candidates traveled together, talked from the same platforms, and slept in the same hotel rooms each night. The modern practice of ignoring the opposing candidate personally is paralleled by the practice of ignoring his campaign; but in fact his campaign can and cannot be ignored. Circumstances alter cases and dictate the kinds of countermeasures to be taken. No one can compile a complete list of such circumstances. Only examples can be given.[37]

Counteracting Opponents' Appeals. Incumbents, in particular, have to keep a sharp watch on the charges made against them by challengers. When a charge is made the first time, it may be ignored or the incumbent may save up his answers for a major speech. In one great effort he will answer both directly and obliquely by asserting his accomplishments and "setting the record straight" about what has and has not been done. No candidate wants to help spread his opponent's charges, and if a charge creates no response the side instigating it will drop it, and the other side proved itself wise by having ignored the charge. To deny or counter a charge helps to give it life and keep it circulating. When a charge gets a public response and the candidate knows he cannot ignore it, the best technique is to counter it forcefully through the illusion of attacking, not defending, and if possible, to couple the answer with a charge which the other side must answer. The case arises with some frequency when one candidate takes at least a semblance of a stand on an issue and challenges

---

[37] Examples from one campaign are discussed in Black, *op. cit.*, Chap. 4.

his opponent to announce where he stands. The illusion created is that the issue embarrasses the opponent, and sometimes it does. The opponent may answer by stating a position and accusing his opponent of talking weasel words. One of the oldest charges in election campaigns is for each candidate to accuse the other of evading issues.

Attacks are often called "smears" by the recipients of the attacks, and attacks or charges should be associated with persons, things, or events usually considered unpopular. A candidate often attacks his opponent for being dependent upon the "bosses," for owing his nomination to them, for having agreed to let them have their way if he is elected. The attack may be launched in terms of issues, so that clichés and stereotypes can be dragged endlessly back and forth for the edification of the voters. A candidate can be excoriated for being a party to "the squeeze on the farmer"; for being an advocate of "excess profits" in business; for aiding and abetting the "demands of labor." Opposing candidates, figuratively speaking, spar with each other, looking for openings and trying to find weak points to attack. Sometimes the only talking point is the other fellow's inexperience or his failure to demonstrate any abilities required in the office. In case a candidate is known to be popular, the opposition avoids direct attacks upon him personally and may even try to benefit from his popularity by associating themselves with him, as many Democrats treated President Eisenhower and as some Republicans previously treated President Roosevelt. When it is dangerous to make charges against a candidate, the strategy is to attack beyond him so as to isolate him: attack his party, his associates; shame him for being in such unsavory company; shame them for being unworthy of the candidate. Another unique form of attack is through the political cartoon. This method of campaigning has reached a highly developed stage in the United States. It is used to belittle candidates, to accuse them of scandal and wrongdoing, and to caricature them.[38]

Avoiding Embarrassments. Because the history of campaigns is attack and defense, charge and countercharge, candidates are constantly embarrassed by their opponents. The golden rule for a candidate under these conditions is to preserve his composure and display no annoyance or fear. Frank Kent graphically stated this rule as "Never Handle a Hot Poker on the Front Porch."[39] The candidate tries to ignore the charge, or if it is deadly and true, he may answer it by playing the martyr, by accusing the other side of "slinging mud," by firing countercharges and generally con-

---

[38] Joseph B. Bishop, *Presidential Nominations and Elections* (New York: Charles Scribner's Sons, 1916) Chaps. 19 and 17, discusses the development of both cartoons and caricatures.

[39] *Political Behavior*, Chap. 16.

fusing the issue so that the public is not quite sure what to think.[40] At the other extreme, candidates have been responsible for having a charge made against them so that they might answer it with a forceful and smashing attack and by implication dispose of all the genuine charges as well. On the federal level a frequent charge against the "ins," since Thomas Jefferson organized the first "out" party, is that a policy or proposed policy is unconstitutional. How influential upon the voters such arguments are is very problematical, but such a charge sometimes puts the "ins" to the inconvenience of having to reply at length.

Campaign Strategy in Presidential Campaigns. Since presidential candidates have begun openly campaigning, two types of techniques have been discerned in the strategy. One is the so-called "front porch" campaign associated with William McKinley in 1896.[41] In this type the candidate stays at or near his home (whether "home" is the White House or his own personal residence) throughout the campaign, making speeches from time to time. The second type is a personal tour on a private train over much of the country, the "swing around the circle," making several short speeches each day in the communities through which the train passes and making major addresses every two or three days in larger cities or at major points on the itinerary. The swing has been most frequently used during the twentieth century because of the fear of candidates that they hurt their chances by failing to get out and let people see them. Essentially, it is this fear combined with the natural disposition to attack that impels candidates to carry their appeal in person. Also there is the contention by those candidates who do make tours that in a representative form of government the peope are entitled to see their candidates and hear from them directly.

The actual preference of most candidates, in all probability, is to avoid making long tours because of the grueling physical strain and because to stay at home is asserted to be more dignified. Since McKinley's time no candidate has completely avoided some traveling, although Harding in 1920 conducted basically a front-porch campaign at Marion, Ohio, with short trips into nearby states during late September and October, and Coolidge in 1924 stayed close to the White House. In 1940 and 1944 Roosevelt, late in the campaign, made major speeches in larger Eastern cities and also campaigned in 1944 by his "nonpolitical" trips to inspect

---

[40] One man in this predicament complained, "I don't mind his charging me with doing all these things. What I object to is the damned fellow proving them on me."—— Quoted *ibid.*, p. 172.

[41] When candidates did not campaign openly, they could have been said to use this strategy, e.g., Buchanan in 1856 and Lincoln in 1860. The similarity in appearance is largely superficial, for the tradition of remaining aloof also forbade the appearance of campaigning except writing letters and receiving visits from party and personal advisers. The front-porch technique, properly speaking, is overt campaigning and is not distinguishable from traveling except as a difference in technique.

war plants and military installations. The practice in 1896 of having Republican delegations travel to Canton, Ohio, as the occasion for McKinley to make a speech, had to be curtailed even in 1920 because of the higher traveling expenses and the discomfort and difficulty in assembling and transporting a large group. In short, it is cheaper and far less troublesome for the candidate to go to the people than to bring the people to the candidate. The introduction of radio seemed to have little influence on the decisions to make a tour, but television creates the opportunity for a candidate to be seen as well as heard nation-wide. Differences of opinion have developed over the relative values of television campaigning and of personal contact with the voters. Although the former has become a standard method of seeking votes, its effectiveness can easily be overestimated.[42] The use of air instead of rail travel now makes it possible for candidates to take a series of shorter trips, pinpointing the localities they want to visit.

Campaigning for Colleagues. The strategy of attack can be considered apart from the candidate himself when it is used by one politician in behalf of another who is a candidate. In every campaign, candidates within the same party are constantly urging the election of one another: Candidates for governor and United States senator speak on behalf of candidates for the national House, for the state legislature, for county offices, and for each other; candidates for the lesser offices urge the election of those at the top of the ticket. Presidential candidates campaign for the party ticket in each state they travel in. Certain advantages attach to this campaigning for a colleague. Some things a candidate would like to have the voters told would not be appropriate for him to tell. He would be embarrassed saying it, and the voters would probably resent it coming from him. A man cannot eulogize himself, but his running mates can eulogize him. This speaking for one another is a mutual back-patting operation, permitting a more aggressive attack than if each candidate were speaking for himself.

Presidents Campaigning for a "Friendly" Congress. The consummate use of this technique is for a candidate to have the President speak on his behalf. The distinction between a presidential candidate and a President who is campaigning is substantial. The latter has the prestige of the office with its symbolism of secret-service men, of a special musical selection, *Hail to the Chief!*, of limousines and chauffeurs and a bevy of photographers and reporters. The only question that has been seriously raised about the wisdom of Presidents campaigning for party colleagues is whether or to what extent a President should campaign for his party's candidates for Congress during the mid-term elections when the President himself is not a candidate.

---

[42] See, e.g., *New York Times Magazine*, April 29, 1956, p. 13 and Section E, October 21, 1956.

A President is always presumed to want his party to keep control of Congress, but the practice has been for Presidents to say little specifically or publicly of a direct partisan nature during the campaign period in the middle of the presidential term.

The leading case bearing on this question goes back to 1918, but a peculiar element involved in that election was its occurrence while the United States was at war. President Wilson was finally prevailed upon to issue an appeal to the country on behalf of a Democratic Congress, asking for continuance of unified counsel and leadership in civil action as well as on the battlefield. He accused the Republicans, not of being unpatriotic or anti-war, but of being anti-Administration. This injection of the President was seized upon by the Republicans, and they won a majority in both houses of Congress about two weeks after the statement was issued. The universal judgment in both parties, even among some Democrats who had originally argued for the appeal, was that it proved to be a blunder.[43] Wartime, it was concluded, was no time for the strategy of attack by the President.

The next mid-term election held during war was in 1942, when President Roosevelt, who was always mindful of the experiences of the Wilson Administration, refused to take a partisan stand and even keyed his own campaigns of 1940 and 1944 to defense and prosecution of the war, rather than to the kind of partisan issues he became famous for in 1932 and 1936. In 1950 if it had not been for the war in Korea, President Truman probably would have toured the country on behalf of a Democratic Congress as he had done in the spring of 1950. The international situation in October and November 1950 was not conducive to a vigorous presidential campaign on partisan issues. In 1954, a peacetime year, President Eisenhower went into a number of states to speak for Republican congressional candidates. The universal judgment this time was that his campaign helped the Republicans to hold down their losses.[44]

The success one politician has in campaigning for another is always difficult to assess. It is hoped that a popular official will help his party colleagues, but one person's popularity will not necessarily rub off on someone else. Too many other factors are involved in campaigns to place exclusive credence in this one.

---

[43] Arthur Krock, *New York Times,* February 17, 1950, and James P. Tumulty, *Woodrow Wilson as I Know Him* (New York: Doubleday, Page & Company, 1921) Chap. 35. Some of the precedents Tumulty cited to justify Wilson's action were not apt, applying to private statements of Presidents or to appeals made by men who were not President at the time. The only parallel was a speech made by McKinley in Iowa in 1898, after the armistice with Spain, asking for a Republican Congress to insure unity.

[44] This discussion does not take into account the results of a President openly taking sides in the nomination of candidates in his own party. Since the disastrous experience of Franklin D. Roosevelt in 1938, when he set out to "purge" certain Democratic members of Congress in the primaries, this technique is considered taboo.

Limits to Partisan Attacks. All campaigning, whether by the candidate or by others on his behalf, lapses into extreme partisanship at times. While excess is understandable under the pressure of a campaign, its degree of usefulness should not be overestimated. Candidates would do well to remember that honey is a more agreeable inducement than vinegar. Voters who consider themselves independent are either unimpressed or repelled by excessively partisan appeals, and the opposition is indignant or outraged. These appeals can please only intense partisans. The result is not likely to win the candidate new or different supporters, and such appeals may help the opposite candidate by making him a martyr.[45] The strategy of attack can be used quite apart from intense partisanship, and candidates, usually aware of the difference, use both kinds of attack. The public likes a fighter as long as they can become interested in the fight. Candidates can appear as fighters without always emphasizing partisanship, which much of the public considers petty or immoral. The best theme for the strategy of attack was expressed by Franklin D. Roosevelt when he formally entered the fray in 1940, "I am an old campaigner and I love a good fight."

Maximum Support

The object of a candidate is to receive as much support as he can, both among rank-and-file voters and among leaders who can be expected to influence voters. Probably no candidate who finds himself in a genuine contest ever feels he has sufficient support. Candidates almost always "run scared" whether they show it or not, and the perpetual dread and fear they have of making a blunder stays with them throughout their careers, in between as well as during campaign periods.[46] The pressure to attain and hold more supporters leads candidates into various acts of desperation, some ill-advised. As the day of election approaches, the emotional mercury measuring degrees of nervousness keeps moving up and the pace is quickened accordingly. There is the fear of making a mistake and the fear that the opposition will make a last-minute charge which cannot be answered adequately before election day. Any weaknesses in his armor begin looking bigger to the candidate. Sometimes in these frantic days a candidate begins to worry about the groups he was previously assured of and may make new appeals and concessions to them, doubly to insure their support. The use of buttons, stickers, and streamers identifies supporters and publicly commits them to the candidate, in addition to giving him publicity and helping him get attention. The sense of com-

---

[45] The excesses of the attacks upon General Harrison in 1840, accusing him of living in a log cabin and drinking hard cider, inspired the Whigs to adopt these symbols for their campaign.

[46] Kent, *The Great Game of Politics*, p. 257.

petition also causes candidates to spend money on personal cards, campaign literature, handbills, and paid advertisements in newspapers, because these things have been done traditionally and the opponent is doing them. No device dare be overlooked if it can conceivably reach voters and keep the candidate on a par with his rival.

The winning over of leaders associated with the opposition is always considered a net gain for a candidate, no matter at what point in the campaign it occurs. The fluidity of loyalties as they follow personal ambitions in politics is reflected in the adage, "Politics make strange bedfellows" and in the supplemental observation that politics "is no game for grudges." [47] Men who one day are pouring the most virulent scorn and vituperation on each other may shortly thereafter be allied by their interests. Usually when such reversal of form is noted, the principals explain that their previous antipathies were not personal but were based entirely upon the issues of the past, which are over and forgotten about; now, they point out, they always had the highest regard for each other individually, so their present association is perfectly natural. A dilemma for a candidate is to have, or be able to get, the support of individuals or groups who are unpopular and would cost him support elsewhere. If he cannot keep this support secret and the knowledge of it would damage his chances, he must denounce it. Just because a candidate speaks out against a group does not mean he had a chance for its support, although in either case he is trying to prove his innocence or virtue by his opposition. Candidates in or out of office are always shoring up their support, so that they are engaged in the two-way operation of holding their ground and moving on, all at the same time. "When he isn't mending fences, the average politician is putting up lightning rods.[48]

Another product of the fear of defeat and the embittered relations between contesting candidates is the spreading of rumors. The remarkable character of rumors is how they can be started and how their content is drastically changed as they spread.[49] When used in politics, the rumor is often purposely started and leaves little to be enlarged upon. Rumors are difficult or impossible to answer. They cannot be nailed down, and to try to counter them is to give them currency and even some plausibility. Rumors are not always false, and even the vicious ones may be based on truth. Those which are not vicious may strike the candidate on a highly

---

47 *Political Behavior*, p. 298; in general, Chap. 26. One of the most remarkable examples of strange bedfellows was the alliance of some of the leaders of the Anti-Masonic movement with leading masons like Henry Clay. See G. G. Van Deusen, *Thurlow Weed* (Boston: Little, Brown & Company, 1947) pp. 44-45.

48 Farley, *op. cit.*, p. 166. Mending fences is a peculiarly American term—see Stimpson, *op. cit.*, pp. 257-258—and corresponds to the term "nursing a constituency" which is used in England.

49 See, e.g., Gordon W. Allport and Leo Postman, *The Psychology of Rumor* (New York: Henry Holt and Company, Inc., 1947).

sensitive nerve, e.g., "born with a silver spoon in his mouth," "he is a Catholic," "he lived abroad most of his life." [50] Rumors in one and the same campaign can work both ways. In 1796 rumors were instigated by newspaper articles that Washington was supporting Jefferson and other rumors were set off by anti-Jefferson appeals for a *"Christian* President." [51] The rumor that an opponent is going to withdraw from the race is easily disproved, but can create the impression he has not enough support to justify his running.[52] The end result of rumors is to give undertones of whispers to every campaign and to make some campaigns on every level of government notable for the amount of malicious scandal. The value of rumors is speculative. No one can point to a campaign, unless it involved a small constituency, won by the use of rumors. The net effect of them may be a boomerang or entirely nil.

Slogans

As a means of getting attention, publicizing the candidate and his appeal, and putting the opposition at a disadvantage, slogans have constantly been coined either accidentally or by those with a facility with words. Slogans are of course completely different from rumors or scandals. Slogans are adopted with the intention of featuring them in the campaign. Candidates are glad to have slogans to use, but must publicly repudiate any resort to rumor or other surreptitious tactic. The purpose of a slogan is to provide a catchy series of words, easily understood and easily repeated. The words should epitomize the campaign theme of the candidate or party, and preferably embarrass the opposition at the same time. If a slogan conveys a popularly accepted idea, the opposition is hard pressed to counter it. The essence of a slogan should be an unanswerable, unassailable assertion or implication. The more unrelated to campaign issues and the more related to personalities slogans are, the more difficult to cope with them.[53]

The presidential campaign of 1840 produced two excellent examples, both favorable to the Whigs. General Harrison, the Whig candidate, was famous for his victory over the Indians in the battle at Tippecanoe. Ap-

---

[50] *Political Behavior,* Chap. 24. J. T. Adams, "Our Whispering Campaigns," *Harper's,* September, 1932, p. 447.

[51] Edward Stanwood, *A History of the Presidency from 1788–1897* (Boston: Houghton Mifflin Company, 1898) p. 46.

[52] This and other standard rumors were used in Colonial Virginia.—Sydnor, *op. cit.,* p. 46.

[53] During the intra-Republican fight over the presidential nomination of 1952, some pro-Taft Republicans poked at General Eisenhower and his managers with this doggerel:
Here's to the me-too Party
The home of the phony and bluff
Where the Lodges can't speak to the General
And the General won't speak to Red Duff.

pending this nickname to him was inevitable, and to account for John Tyler on the ticket, a man who was really not a Whig, the slogan frankly exploited the obvious and let it go at that: "Tippecanoe and Tyler too." To sum up Martin van Buren's difficulties in running for re-election with a depression on his hands, the Whigs disposed of him with "Van, Van is a used-up man." Of a similar nature because it was entirely personal was the 1924 Republican slogan, "Keep cool with Coolidge." Some slogans have been useful for dramatizing issues: "Fifty-four forty or fight" used by the Democrats in 1844; "the full dinner pail" in 1896, and "a chicken in every pot" in 1928, both used by the Republicans. The last one is a good example of a slogan that can boomerang when the expected conditions do not materialize: during the depression of the 1930's, the witticisms and sarcasm poured upon the "chicken in the pot" cooked it beyond edibility.[54] A similar fate awaited the 1916 Democrat slogan emphasizing the pacifistic nature of the Wilson Administration: "He kept us out of war." Republicans in 1920 hammered at the deception of this slogan, although its deception could have been dispelled and the slogan recognized as a statement of fact if the 1916 voters had remembered their English grammar and noticed that the verb was in the past, not the future, tense.

A type of rumor which finally broke through the veil of anonymity to become a slogan was "Rum, Romanism and Rebellion," a reference to the Democratic Party made by a minister in the course of introducing James G. Blaine, the Republican presidential candidate of 1884, to a New York City audience. This indictment of a whole party is popularly credited with losing the election for Blaine. Intangible issues or deeply stirring sentiments were touched by such slogans as "Back to normalcy" used by the Republicans in 1920; "Martin, Barton and Fish" used by Democrats in 1940 to symbolize and discredit the opposition; "Had enough? Vote Republican" used in the congressional elections of 1946. The slogan "Time for a change" is recurring as a theme of the "outs," and in 1952 the Democrats, wanting to emphasize their long record as being responsible for the nation's material progress and prosperity, countered the slogan with "You never had it so good" and a song entitled *Don't Let Them Take It Away*. Following the 1952 election the battle of slogans continued with such examples from the Democrats as, "Don't blame me, I voted Democratic," and from the Republicans, "Keep the change."

---

[54] Occasionally, a slogan can be countered immediately by an effective counterslogan. In the 1952 Democratic primary contest in Tennessee between McKellar and Gore, the former's supporters exhibited posters bearing the observation: "Thinking feller vote McKeller." The Gore forces quickly tacked their own posters alongside: "Think some more and vote for Gore."

EVALUATION OF TECHNIQUES

The most impressive discovery about campaign techniques is their standardization. They are perpetuated generation after generation with only the adaptation that new inventions in communication media and transportation systems make necessary. To slice into the party contest for office at any point in time illustrates "the great and abiding truth" that "professional politics is the most conservative of all trades. The same words continue to be used as the same weapons, and the tactics remain basically the same." [55] We have inventions which make the handle on the pump obsolete; but in the activity of managing people the same fundamental techniques constantly reappear throughout the centuries. In politics a complete distinction is made between the old and the antiquated.[56] Two different kinds of questions can be raised about campaign techniques—their effectiveness and their inevitability.

Effectiveness of Formal Campaigns. After just a partial cataloguing of campaign techniques, a person may well ask what they prove, how effective they are, whether they win and lose elections. Considering the formal campaign period after the nominations are made, there is evidence to indicate that the whole show is put on for the benefit of a small minority of voters in so far as the campaign changes or crystallizes voting intentions. Of those who vote, only a minuscule number make up their minds during the last two weeks before election day.[57] It also appears that voters with maximum interest in the election and with fewer conflicts in their approach to it make up their minds sooner than voters with relatively little interest or involvement or with conflicting pressures to resolve.[58] These findings simply make more concrete and reliable what had generally been assumed to be the state of the electorate during a formal campaign. If, in fact, it is conducted for those least interested, the techniques are justified

---

[55] Arthur Krock in the *New York Times*, June 21, 1949.

[56] The perceptions of purposeful methods in the handling of followers by leaders illustrate the universality of the methods as a reading, e.g., of Machiavelli's *The Prince* demonstrates.

[57] Louis Bean, *How to Predict Elections* (New York: Alfred A. Knopf, Inc., 1948) pp. 138-139. "Most of the independents who always vote apparently decided early."—— Samuel J. Eldersveld, "The Independent Vote," *American Political Science Review*, Vol. 46 (1952) p. 738; also pp. 740–742.

[58] Paul F. Lazarsfeld *et al.*, *The People's Choice* (New York: Columbia University Press, 1948) pp. 52-64; Warren E. Miller, "Party Preferences and Attitudes on Political Issues: 1948-1951, " *American Political Science Review*, Vol. 47 (1953) p. 59. Morris Janowitz and Warren E. Miller, "The Index of Political Predisposition in the 1948 Election," *Journal of Politics*, Vol. 14 (1952) pp. 721-722; Angus Campbell *et al.*, *The Voter Decides* (Evanston: Row, Peterson & Company, 1954) p. 20. Actually, these and other studies do not come up with consistent findings. See Bernard R. Berelson *et al.*, *Voting* (Chicago: University of Chicago Press, 1954) p. 336, for comparison of findings on voters who change their intentions during the campaign.

in a practical sense because they bring the contest to the attention of those most unaware of politics, those who see the least direct connection between their interests and the outcome of the election. Those voters who are interested but are in a quandary should find the campaign helpful to some extent in finally making up their minds.

Effectiveness of Continuous Campaigning. For those who have already decided before the formal campaign begins, the question remains: When did they decide? Leaving out the hard-core partisans, the point of decision can fall anywhere between elections, and most of the election surveys do not tap the respondents until the election year is well begun. Because of the continuing nature of the voters' decision process, politicians have always campaigned continuously but with varied intensity. They have realized the great difficulty of starting from scratch and winning an election in two or three months. During the in-between years is the time to become known through publicity and to develop issues in public speeches, interviews, and articles. Officeholders, in addition, are making a record and keeping their activities before the public. The result is a continuity from nonelection year to election year. In all of this time span, voters are forming impressions of candidates, reacting to issues and beginning to be conditioned for their next voting decision. The growing reminders of the coming campaign begin to attract attention by late winter and early spring, when those with firmer attachments and loyalties will assert their intention. The continued saturation of the news with politics brings more and more people to a realization and to a decision.

Reassuring Supporters. Through all of the stages in the election year, candidates ply techniques assiduously. It is not enough to depend upon their supporters' remaining firm. Candidates want to keep reinforcing the decision of their supporters. If one candidate campaigned up to election day and his opponent stopped campaigning after his nomination, there is no question but that the latter would be seriously handicapped, if indeed he could be elected at all. Supporters of a party or candidate have different degrees of loyalty and steadfastness. If they were exposed only to the propaganda of the other side, the least loyal among them would begin weakening and eventually only the die-hards may be left. Partisans need the encouragement of their side's arguments, slogans, and attacks.

Effectiveness Related to Individual Elections. The findings of pollsters have contributed greatly to the discovery and demonstration that normally many voters apparently decide early in the election year and hold to the decision. When these decisions fall approximately evenly between the two parties, the problem of predicting is analogous to the candidates' problem of winning. How will the undecided swing and what will cause them to swing? In close elections the late deciders may hold the key to the outcome, and their decisions are directly or indirectly caused by the campaign and its techniques. Not all elections follow the same pattern, for those undecided in September may be larger one year than another. These variations are themselves products of the circumstances surrounding elections, the issues presented in the campaigns, and the effectiveness of the campaigns themselves. No one can very well believe that election patterns do not vary, and some who did so believe were left speechless after the votes were counted in the 1948 presidential election. That year the campaign itself appeared to be the determinative factor, but 1948 was not unique in this respect. The managers of the Whig campaigns between 1840 and 1852 were masters of techniques, but the Whig Party was so deeply rent by conflicting interests that none of the leaders associated with any of these interests could be elected President. However, when the Whig managers could work with a military man as the candidate, a man representing no identifiable faction, their astuteness in campaign operations twice were rewarded with victory. In these cases, campaign techniques even triumphed over the organized-interest-group basis of the bipartisan struggle.[59]

Alternatives to Campaign Techniques. The party system depends upon the existence of a free government operated through the representative system. The assumption that these pre-existing circumstances are necessary for a party system as we think of it underlies this entire book.[60] In order for this system to function, a method must be found for presenting issues and channeling discussion of the problems with which the public is concerned. Election campaigns rely on the assumption that techniques of presentation are just as important as the substance of the presentation; that the problem of organizing and managing people precedes or parallels all other problems in human affairs. Campaign techniques even create interest in as well as awareness of public problems and in this way make an independent contribution. Techniques, nevertheless, appear to be irrational appeals and, by extension, seem to be based on an assumption of irrationality in people. The difficulty with a "rational" approach to these problems is, first, finding what is universally accepted as rational, since diversities in people produce diversities in their concepts and many elections are fought on mutually exclusive positions, each side insisting it alone is right, reasonable, and rational. The second difficulty is finding time and creating the desire to study and analyze the complex data involved in public problems, inasmuch as relatively few people have much

---

[59] Arthur N. Holcombe, *Our More Perfect Union* (Cambridge: Harvard University Press, 1950) p. 92.

[60] See above, pp. 1-2.

specific or general information on questions outside their daily experience.

"Rationality" in Propaganda. To compel people through violence is diametrically opposite to the methods of free government. People either must determine what they want to do or be persuaded that such and such should be done. But the line between the rationally induced conclusion and the propaganda-induced conclusion is very tenuous. The difference between the two is largely dependent upon the definition of the terms. It is irrational to be tricked, let us say, but is it irrational to become aware of a problem through an attention-getting device or trick which permits us to perceive the problem out of the whole mass of phenomena competing for our attention? Even granting our awareness of the problem, to proceed by individual analysis and inquiry takes much time. Many solutions will not wait for this kind of a reasoning process, and there are at any one time too many problems requiring solutions to dispose of them all at one time. The most discouraging observation is that some problems are immutable and have challenged the best minds in the history of the human race. The seemingly illogical method of propaganda and the logical hodge-podge we often find in the solutions attributable to propaganda are sometimes refreshingly surprising. People often accomplish more than they realize. The fault, if there be one, in the reliance upon emotion, sentiment, and prejudice instead of upon reason, logic, and knowledge is in ourselves, not in the methods people have used to manage people. If another method is preferable, no leaders using that method are likely to arise until they have some prospects of finding followers.

Selected Bibliography

Bishop, Joseph B., *Presidential Nominations and Elections.* New York: Charles Scribner's Sons, 1916.

Black, Theodore M., *Democratic Party Publicity in the 1940 Campaign.* New York: Plymouth Publishing Company, 1941.

Bullitt, Stimson, *To Be a Politician.* New York: Doubleday & Co., Inc., 1959.

Bush, Chilton, *Newspaper Reporting of Public Affairs.* New York: D. Appleton-Century, 1940.

Farley, James A., *Behind the Ballots.* New York: Harcourt, Brace and Company, Inc., 1938.

—— *Jim Farley's Story.* New York: McGraw-Hill Book Company, Inc., 1948.

Flynn, Edward J., *You're the Boss.* New York: The Viking Press, Inc., 1947.

Howe, Quincy, *The News and How to Understand It.* New York: Simon and Schuster, Inc., 1940.

Kent, Frank R., *The Great Game of Politics.* New York: Doubleday, Page & Company, 1924.

—— *Political Behavior.* New York: William Morrow & Company, Inc., 1928.

Kelley, Stanley, Jr., *Professional Public Relations and Political Power.* Baltimore: The Johns Hopkins Press, 1956.

Kurtzman, David H., *Methods of Controlling Votes in Philadelphia*. Philadelphia: University of Pennsylvania, 1935.

Lorant, Stefan, *The Presidency: A Pictorial History of Presidential Elections from Washington to Truman*. New York: The Macmillan Company, 1952.

McCamy, James L., *Government Publicity*. Chicago: University of Chicago Press, 1939.

—— *Government Publications for the Citizen*. New York: Columbia University Press, 1949.

Machiavelli, Niccolo, *The Prince and the Discourses*. New York: Modern Library, Inc., 1940.

McKean, Dayton D., *The Boss*. Boston: Houghton Mifflin Company, 1940.

Merriam, Robert E., and Rachel M. Goetz, *Going Into Politics*. New York: Harper & Brothers, 1957.

Merritt, Le Roy C., *The United States Government as Publisher*. Chicago: University of Chicago Press, 1943.

Michelson, Charles, *The Ghost Talks*. New York: G. P. Putnam's Sons, 1944.

Milligan, Maurice M., *Missouri Waltz*. New York: Charles Scribner's Sons, 1948.

Moley, Raymond, *27 Masters of Politics*. New York: Funk & Wagnalls Company, 1949.

Moscow, Warren, *Politics in the Empire State*. New York: Alfred A. Knopf, Inc., 1948.

Packard, Vance, *The Hidden Persuaders*. New York: Pocket Books, Inc., 1958.

Pollard, James E., *The Presidents and the Press*. New York: The Macmillan Company, 1947.

Rosten, Leo C., *The Washington Correspondents*. New York: Harcourt, Brace and Company, Inc., 1937.

Salter, J. T., *Boss Rule*. New York: McGraw-Hill Book Company, 1935.

Stimpson, George, *A Book about American Politics*. New York: Harper & Brothers, 1952.

Sydnor, Charles S., *Gentlemen Freeholders*. Chapel Hill: University of North Carolina Press, 1952.

Thomson, Charles A. H., *Television, Politics and Public Policy*. Washington, D. C.: The Brookings Institution, 1958. Reprint No. 25.

Titus, Charles Hickman, *The Processes of Leadership*. Dubuque: William C. Brown Company, 1950.

CHAPTER TWENTY-TWO

Financing and Regulating Campaigns

The crux of the problem of regulating elections and prohibiting corrupt practices very frequently is found in the various uses of money in politics. The financial side of politics is subdivided into the sources of money, the sources and extent of expenditures, and the results of the receiving and spending of money.

MONEY IN POLITICS

Sources of Campaign Funds. Two principal sources of contributions are *assessments* on candidates and officeholders and *contributions* from friends and supporters. The reliance upon one or the other depends upon the geographical level of an election campaign. In state and local elections the candidates themselves are often assessed on the basis of a certain percentage of the salary of the office they seek or their ability to pay. Officeholders are assessed either every year or during the campaign year, often on a sliding scale, the percentage varying with the size of their salary. In some states this practice is regulated by law with the percentage of assessment fixed. The 1883 Civil Service Reform Act prohibited a United States official or employee from soliciting or receiving from another official or employee any "assessment, subscription, or contribution, for any political purpose whatever." Although this law does not apply to members of Congress, it has otherwise largely eliminated assessment in the federal government.[1]

In campaigns for at-large offices within a state, assessments on those holding patronage positions is an important source of funds, but contributions from individuals and organizations are more heavily relied upon than in local contests. In presidential elections, both individuals and organizations contribute directly to the national committees and to other committees. From time to time efforts have been made to broaden the base of contributors and raise enough money even for a presidential campaign from a large number of small donations. The Democrats between 1916 and 1920 and the Republicans in 1920 tried such a system, but wound

[1] See Dayton D. McKean, *The Boss* (Boston: Houghton Mifflin Company, 1940) pp. 145–147; Kent, *The Great Game of Politics* (New York: Doubleday, Page & Company, 1924) Chap. 20; James K. Pollock, Jr., *Party Campaign Funds* (New York: Alfred A. Knopf, Inc., 1926) pp. 113–125; Louise Overacker, *Money in Elections* (New York: The Macmillan Company, 1932) pp. 100–105, 233. As far back as the Lincoln Administration, Gideon Welles, Secretary of the Navy, complained about the assessment of officeholders.

up their campaigns with large deficits. The average citizen is not disposed to give much of anything,[2] and the cost of reaching many thousands of reliable party members is prohibitive. The quickest and easiest method for getting large sums in an economical manner is through contributions by a few individuals capable of spending several thousand dollars.[3] Managers and candidates have enough difficulties without soliciting the public at large.

Other sources are of varying importance at different levels of government. National, state, and sometimes local committees raise money with party *banquets,* such as the Jefferson-Jackson Day fetes for Democrats and the Lincoln Day festivities for Republicans. Tickets are sold for as much as contributors will pay, ranging from $10 per person at local and $25 per person at state banquets, to $100 and up per person at banquets sponsored by national committees.[4] National committees *distribute money* to state, congressional, and senatorial campaign committees just as state committees may pass money down to county committees. However, the process may work in reverse whereby lower committees raise money and divide it with higher committees for distribution elsewhere. Both candidates and managers, at all levels of government frequently have to *borrow money* either from individuals or from banks to get through a campaign. After most campaigns there is indebtedness either from direct loans or from bills for goods and services.[5] Among minor parties, money is raised by *selling literature* or passing the hat at rallies, and in the case of the Socialist Party, collecting *dues* from members each month.[6]

---

[2] In a nation-wide survey, only 7% of the 8,000 respondents said they had given money to a party or candidate in the previous four years. This figure is probably high.——Julian L. Woodward and Elmo Roper, "Political Activity of American Citizens," *American Political Science Review*, Vol. 44 (1950) p. 874.

[3] See Pollock, *op. cit.,* pp. 68–82 and 125 ff., and Overacker, *op. cit.,* Chap. 6. In 1916–1920 the Democrats' national chairman wrote as many as three letters to each of thousands of Democrats, soliciting money.——*Ibid.,* pp. 113–115. The Republicans' 1920 plan, while not so costly, emphasized maximum contributions of $1000 for the year or before and after the national convention. Men experienced in money-raising drives were hired at large salaries. They raised a great deal of money, but their expenses were also great. Suggestions have been made for bipartisan fund raising through a committee headed by a Democrat and a Republican. Citizens could send money designated for one party or the other to the committee which would turn the money over to the appropriate party's national committee.

[4] Interesting questions of tax liabilities arise for the group sponsoring the banquets. Apparently, if nothing is sold, in the strict sense of the word, admission and sales taxes do not apply; the interpretation in this case is that the diners do not buy tickets but merely make contributions. See the *New York Times*, February 17, 1950, for the application of the distinction between the Democrats' banquet and the Republicans' box supper, where admission was by ticket.

[5] Pollock, *op. cit.,* pp. 80, 139–140. A rare exception to the tradition of postcampaign deficits was the Republicans' surplus after the 1924 presidential campaign.

[6] *Ibid.,* pp. 84–89; Overacker, *op. cit.,* pp. 109–110. Charging dues is a regular minor-party practice. See Clarence A. Berdahl, "Party Membership in the United States," *American Political Science Review*, Vol. 36 (1942) pp. 259–261.

Special Aspects of Contributions. As government becomes more active in the ordering of the economic life of the nation, more organized groups and influential individuals are willing to spend money to select legislators, executives, and judges who will control governmental policies. Since the 1930's, expenditures by or on behalf of labor organizations have gone up sharply in order to influence the voting of union members and of other people allied or sympathetic with labor. Businessmen have traditionally contributed money to campaign organizations to defray general costs or to special organizations of their own to proselyte among those favorably disposed to business interests. Some individual contributors specify the candidates or the campaign for which their money is to be spent. This practice has been followed for years in the South, where money is given to Republican committees with the stipulation that it be spent only in presidential elections or in congressional elections in states outside the South. Contributions from wealthy individuals and organizations, many of them in the area of New York City, are made for congressional campaigns in various states where a particular senator or representative is either strongly supported or opposed by the donors.

Continuing Funds. Variations of the practice of contributions, indicating the artificial designation of a few months before an election as "the campaign," made dramatic headline news in the revelations of the Nixon and Stevenson funds in 1952: Richard M. Nixon, the Republican vice-presidential candidate and Adlai Stevenson, the Democrat presidential candidate. In each case, over $18,000 had been expended from funds made possible by private donations. The Nixon fund defrayed the costs of his between-election campaigning as a United States senator and differed only in size from other funds for members of Congress raised by solicitation or by outside activities such as writing articles for magazines. The Stevenson fund was paid by him to supplement the salaries of eight officials serving in his administration in Illinois.[7]

The specific attitude of givers to an election campaign determines the extent of their generosity. They must see their interests involved in the outcome to pay extensive amounts. Some individuals or groups may contribute small sums in unimportant elections just as a matter of practice or as a gesture. The motivation to give is not only the affinity between the interests and the candidates but also the likelihood of the candidates' success. If a candidacy appears to be hopeless or if it appears to be a sure

---

[7] For these stories, see the *New York Times,* September 19, 1952, *et seq.* Contributions to the Nixon fund ranged from $10 to $1000; to the Stevenson fund, from $1 to $7100. Nixon spent some of the money in sending out 41,500 Christmas cards in 1950 and 1951, a venerable practice among American politicians. For a discussion of precedents for such funds in the case of Daniel Webster and Walter Hines Page, see Arthur Krock, *ibid.,* October 17, 1952.

winner, the general disposition to give will probably be decreased. When interests are intimately involved and the election appears to be close, the motivation to give is undoubtedly at its height. There is, of course, the reverse situation of those who are more inclined to contribute to a prospectively successful campaign in order to be associated with the winners, just as some give in desperation to help save what looks like a lost cause. The interaction of cause and effect between prospects for winning and the disposition to contribute is by no means clear.

Sources of Expenditures. The amounts of money spent in campaigns have probably always appeared excessive. From generation to generation and even election to election, the sums seem to increase. The compulsion to win elections is demonstrated in the pressure to raise money and more money for fear of losing because of the opposition's greater affluence. In addition, the necessity for expenditures keeps increasing because of more occasions for spending and the higher costs of services and communication media. The use of radio and television alone has caused campaign expenses to increase enormously. For example, if open time is taken on a national television hookup, the cost approximates $1,000 a minute for thirty minutes, but rises higher if a commercial program is displaced, depending upon the viewer rating of the program. The total for presidential candidates' national broadcasts in 1956 was reported at $9,501,000.[8] With a mass, nation-wide electorate, people must be reached with mass media. Half or more of campaign budgets are devoted to the mass media, radio and television; about one fourth to printing, mailing, newspaper, and billboards; and the remainder to the incidentals of rent, telephone, telegraph, stationery, professional workers' salaries, hiring of halls. The principal drain on campaign treasuries can be attributed to activities of a publicity and direct-communication nature.[9]

Whatever the campaign demands, something must be saved for Election Day expenses. This money is distributed at the precinct level on or

---

[8] *Ibid.,* February 3, 1957. During the 1952 campaign an odd rate schedule was discovered in the state of Washington: a 25-second spot announcement cost $135, a 1-minute spot announcement cost $170, but a 5-minute show cost $160.—*Ibid.,* December 1, 1952.

[9] Pollock, *op. cit.,* Chap. 6, writing at the beginning of the radio era and well before the advent of television, assigned the following percentage distribution to a campaign budget:

Publicity	25-40
Headquarters	15-25
Grants to committees (for Republicans)	20
Speakers, radio	10-15
Field workers	5
Election Day .... up to 50% in some cities	
Miscellaneous .... 15 (national) .... 5 (local)	

The 1916 campaign resulted in the greatest use of advertising up to that time.

shortly before Election Day to pay for transporting voters, employing help-
ers who will round up votes on their own, paying special workers, and, where
it occurs, bribing voters.[10] The avarice of people in the organization must
also be taken into account, for some of the money is not passed along as intended but is kept by the individuals up and down the line. For anyone to
refund any excess money is a rarity. Special expenses may become necessary
in case a candidate wants a recount of the vote, for the expense is usually
borne in part or in whole by the side demanding the recount. Inevitably,
in any operation accompanied by the haste, confusion, and harassments of
a formal campaign, money will be wasted. The circumstances do not permit careful decisions making for economy, but put a premium upon haste
and snap judgments.[11]

Extent of Expenditures. Table 8 contains some of the evidence of
campaign spending over a period of 40 years in national elections although
the data are admittedly incomplete. Compared with any of the entries in
the "Total Expended" column, the $100,000 spent to elect Lincoln in 1860
seems so modest as to be insignificant; yet in terms of purchasing power,
$100,000 in 1860 would a hundred years later be worth many times more.
The end result of investigations in expenditures is that no one knows how
much is spent in campaigns. Published figures do not include in most cases
what was spent in local areas in state and national elections, much less what
was spent in local elections. Estimates of presidential-election expenditures
at $50,000,000 in 1952 were suspected of being too low. The total expendi-
tures in both the presidential and congressional campaigns of that year and
1956 have been estimated in excess of $100,000,000 each.[12]

Although the national and state party organizations have elaborate
financial arrangements, the official treasurers handle only the money to be
reported under the laws. Treasurers, chairmen, and candidates scrupulously
keep themselves or are kept from knowing about any other money. Committees often have unofficial treasurers who handle additional sums for
which no accounting is made. Consequently, most politicians themselves
do not actually know the full extent of expenditures. Everyone knows

---

[10] *Ibid.*, pp. 160-162; George M. Reynolds, *Machine Politics in New Orleans, 1897-1926*
(New York: Columbia University Press, 1936) pp. 117-121; Kent, *The Great Game of Politics,* pp. 66-68 and Chaps. 19, 21; and *Political Behavior* (New York: William Morrow &
Company, 1928) pp. 207-216; Flynn, *op. cit.,* p. 22, noted that district captains got from $20
to $50 for the day's expenses.

[11] Pollock, *op. cit.,* pp. 163-168.

[12] See the *New York Times,* June 29, 1952, October 12, 1952, December 1, 1952, and
November 6, 1956. Expenditures in 1952 reached or exceeded the $1,000,000 mark in Cali-
fornia, Connecticut, Illinois, Indiana, Massachusetts, Michigan, New Jersey, New York,
Ohio, Oregon, Pennsylvania, Texas, Washington, Wisconsin. Nationally, expenditures
equalled at least 54c per vote; in Connecticut it was $1.19 per vote.

that the published figures are incomplete, but no one knows exactly how incomplete.[13]

TABLE 8: NATIONAL CAMPAIGN EXPENDITURES, 1912–1956 *

Year	Parties	Total Expended	Number of Contributors	Percentage of Total in Gifts of $5000 and Up
1912	R	$ 1,076,548	2,600	44.8
	D	1,134,848	89,815	33.3
	P	665,420	—	—
1916	R	2,441,565	34,205	41.4
	D	2,284,590	170,000	34.4
1920	R	5,417,501	50,777	0.1
	D	1,470,371	†	26.2
1924	R	4,020,478	90,227	26.2
	D	1,108,836	†	45.2
	P	236,963	—	—
1928	R	6,256,111	143,749	45.8
	D	5,342,350	90,456	52.7
1932	R	2,900,052	39,950	40.0
	D	2,245,975	26,581	43.7
1936	R	8,951,602	85,000	24.2
	D	5,164,741	54,818	26.0
1940	R	18,864,177	39,169	3.8
	D	8,052,898	37,998	13.1
1944	R	16,195,376	12,500	†
	D	9,997,935	54,739	†
1948	R	2,127,296	†	†
	D	2,736,334	†	†
1952 ‡	R	18,769,848	17,900	†
	D	6,847,725	22,500	†
1956 ‡	R	20,685,387	21,150	†
	D	10,977,790	70,000	†

* The total expenditures include in most cases money spent in congressional and senatorial campaigns as well as in presidential campaigns. The figures for 1948 include only expenditures of the national committees in the presidential campaign, where the limit was $3,000,000. Sources: Pollock, *op. cit.*, p. 27; Overacker, *op. cit.*, pp. 73, 132-133; Overacker, four articles in the *American Political Science Review:* "Campaign Funds in a Depression Year," Vol. 27 (1933) pp. 770, 772-773; "Campaign Funds in the Presidential Election of 1936," Vol. 31 (1937) pp. 476, 481-482, 484; "Campaign Finance in the Presidential Election of 1940," Vol. 35 (1941) pp. 706, 713, 716; "Presidential Campaign Funds, 1944," Vol. 39 (1945) pp. 900, 906, 907.
† Figures not available.
‡ Estimates in 1952 were put at no less than $32,155,251 (*New York Times,* December 1, 1952) and in 1956, $33,185,725, according to Senate Subcommittee on Privileges and Elections. The Republican member of the Subcommittee disputed this party disparity in spending, contending that if all spending were known, the amounts for each party would be substantially the same. *Ibid.*, February 3, 1957.

13 Kent, *Political Behavior*, Chap. 20.

Concern about Expenditures. The sensitivity to money in politics can be traced to at least two fears. One is a deep-seated conviction that the raising of large sums of money is evidence of corruption through the favoritism granted by government officials to those who are wealthy enough to contribute. Those who give have access to the candidates and are consulted and specially considered in operating government. When a party is left with a large deficit after a campaign, one or a few benefactors have often come to the rescue, giving themselves a special status by their largesse. By extension, the possibilities for corruption in government to repay campaign contributors are increased.[14] The greatest danger in this respect has become the tie-up between politics and the underworld, where the objective is *ipso facto* corrupt in one way or another.[15] It should not be assumed that all large contributors expect something in return. Some give without any expectation of receiving favors. Parties occasionally have wealthy supporters, called "fat cats," who have no further need for making money but want prestige and honor through appointment to positions of distinction. The problem of probing motives here is as great as it is elsewhere in politics.[16]

The second fear is that poor candidates are excluded from office, or an extension of the first fear, that most candidates must make improper commitments in order to raise the money they need.[17]

These two implications of the use of money are disturbing, and the huge sums being spent simply intensify the fears, despite the legitimate nature of most of the expenditures. In consequence of the antagonism to large expenditures, candidates and their managers usually stress their limited budgets and charge the opposition with corruption or at least with big "slush funds" in attempts to "buy" the election. Generally it is poor campaign strategy to engage in ostentatious expenditures which come to public attention. Especially, the appearance of spending with a free hand is a handicap in justifying official reports of small expenditures.

Effectiveness of Money. Finally, these fears, implicitly or explicitly, rest on the assumption that money itself wins elections. Some qualifications

---

[14] A classic example of this sort of corruption was involved in the infamous Teapot Dome oil scandal in the 1920's, but frauds and mismanagement of various sorts have made their appearance over the years at all government levels. Another aspect of the same problem is political leaders selling jobs, whether for personal profit or to replenish the party treasury; *e.g.,* Guy B. Hathorn, "C. Bascom Slemp—Virginia Republican Boss," *Journal of Politics,* Vol. 17 (1955) pp. 248 ff.

[15] Overacker, *Money in Elections,* pp. 105–107.

[16] Louise Overacker, *Money in Elections,* p. 109 and Chap. 70.

[17] Henry V. Poor, "What It Costs to Run for Office," *Harper's Magazine,* Vol. 208, No. 1248 (May, 1954) pp. 46 ff.; Sonya Forthal, "The Small Fry and the Party Purse," *American Political Science Review,* Vol. 34 (1940) pp. 70–71. An independent candidate for mayor of New York City withdrew because he estimated he needed $1,000,000 for a winning campaign.——*New York Times,* August 2 and 9, 1953.

are in order. In the first place, money per se is not the sole standard for determining relative advantages. The "ins" may have perfectly adequate substitutes for direct campaign spending through the organization they create by use of patronage and the dispensing of government favors. Political activity by government officials and employees whose jobs depend upon winning an election is directly translated into votes from their families and friends. The growth of government welfare spending, replacing relief spending during the depression of the 1930's, creates attachments and loyalties on the part of voters.[18] There has also been a remarkable increase in government communication, some of which is strictly of a factual nature and some of a propaganda nature favorable to the "ins."[19] To the extent that such communication is politically helpful, it supplements campaign publicity without expense to the party.

Another sort of qualification is the record throughout the 1930's and 1940's of Republican expenditures exceeding Democrats' expenditures in presidential elections by various margins, but the failure of Republicans to capture the Presidency. Even granting the offsetting advantage to the Democrats of being the "in" party during this period, few would be likely to believe that Roosevelt could have been defeated if the difference in expenditures had been even greater. There are factors of skill in management and strategy, of enthusiasm and psychological approach by the organization workers, of effectiveness in campaign techniques, of advantages in campaign appeals. The one substitute for money is familiarity with the voters, for the more a candidate is a stranger, the more he needs to spend to bring himself to people's attention. The exact balance in this relation is elusive, but the relation clearly exists.

> Probably there is a point in politics beyond which money is not effective—though exactly where that point is remains yet to be definitely determined—and if one side has enough for reasonable 'current expenses' it is possible successfully to compete with an opposition better equipped with funds sufficient to meet every contingency and supply every demand.
> But when the money is overwhelmingly on one side, then successful competition on a large scale is out of the question. In a single ward, in one county, even in a congressional or legislative district, there have been occasional instances of candidates without money defeating candidates with money . . . .[20]

---

[18] One of the areas of charges and denials surrounding the New Deal was the political effects of the expenditures for relief and recovery. For an analysis, see *Life*, May 23, 1938, pp. 22–23.

[19] For work on United States government communication, see James L. McCamy, *Government Publicity* (Chicago: University of Chicago Press, 1939) and *Government Publications for the Citizen* (New York: Columbia University Press, 1949); L. C. Merritt, *The United States Government as Publisher* (Chicago: University of Chicago Press, 1943).

[20] Frank R. Kent, *Political Behavior*, p. 197.

THE CONTROL OF MONEY

State Legislation. The march of protest against the evils of money has resulted in regulatory legislation of some kind in every state in the Union except Rhode Island. These laws establish a definite pattern. (1) Statements of money handled must be filed with the secretary of state or other designated state official. Most states require declarations of receipts and disbursements from both the party organization and the candidates for both direct primaries and general elections, although there are some variations—Mississippi, e.g., requires filings only for the direct primary. Reports are to be made during a campaign and then a complete accounting after the election is over. The time of these reports varies generally from within thirty days before an election up to thirty days after an election, with parties sometimes given more days for the final accounting than candidates are given. (2) Most states restrict the character of expenditures so as to prohibit bribery. (3) Most states prohibit contributions by corporations and other selected groups or associations, although only Indiana, Pennsylvania, and Texas prohibit contributions by labor unions. (4) Most states restrict the total expenditures a candidate for a given office can make, but few states restrict the total expenditures in behalf of a candidate.[21]

A departure in this pattern of legislation is the "Who Gave It—Who Got It" law in Florida. Whether it will set new precedents cannot be determined, but it points in a new direction long advocated by many politicians and students of the problem. The first outstanding feature is that the law places no limits on the amount spent by candidates, except those for municipal office. Contributions from various sources are prohibited, e.g., liquor sellers, horse and dog race owners, public utilities. An individual can contribute a maximum of $1,000 to a candidate but is forbidden to spend any money on his own responsibility. His contribution must be made to a treasurer of a political organization. All money received by a treasurer must be deposited and accounted for within twenty-four hours of its receipt. In this way the distinction between money spent by a candidate or on his behalf is wiped out, for he is forced to spend all of the money on his own behalf or violate the law. It was concluded after an experience with the law in one gubernatorial direct primary that the opposing candidates effectively enforced the law by their strict scrutiny of one another's activities.[22]

---

21 The current provisions are summarized in *The Book of the States* published annually by the Council of State Governments, Chicago. Older but more detailed collections are available, e.g., Pollock, *op. cit.*, Chaps. 2, 8; *Corrupt Practices at Elections, a Compilation of the Laws Relating to Corrupt Practices at Elections in the United States*, Sen. Doc. No. 11, 75th Cong., 1st Sess., 1937.

22 See Elston E. Roady, "Florida's New Campaign Expense Law and the 1952 Democratic Gubernatorial Primaries," *American Political Science Review*, Vol. 48 (1954) pp. 465–476.

ELECTION FINANCIAL STATEMENT

Name of Candidate, Personal Campaign or Party-Committee, or Club; ----------------------------------

----

Name of Secretary of Candidate, Committee or Club; --

STATEMENT of amounts received, disbursed, etc., in the interests of ----------------------------

candidate for { nomination / election } to the office of ------------------------------------ on the --------------

ticket at the { primary / election } to be held on the ---------------- day of -------------------- A. D. 19------

made pursuant to Section 12.09 of the Wisconsin Statutes.

DATE	FROM WHOM RECEIVED	FOR WHAT PURPOSE	AMOUNT
-------------	Amount previously reported ---------		$------------
		Total received -----------	

DATE	TO WHOM PAID	FOR WHAT PURPOSE	AMOUNT
-------------	Amount previously reported ---------		$------------

DATE	TO WHOM OWING	FOR WHAT PURPOSE	AMOUNT
			$------------

STATE OF WISCONSIN
County of ------------------------- } ss.

-------------------------------- and ---------------------------- being duly sworn, on oath says that he is

{ a candidate / a chairman / a secretary } for the { nomination / election } of ---------------------------- for ----------------------------

voted for at the { primary / election } held on the ----------- day of ----------------------, A. D. 19-----, and

that the foregoing is a true and complete financial statement of every { receipt / disbursement / obligation } by ----------------------------

-- for political purposes for the period ending on the------------

day of ----------------------------, 19----, together with the name of every person to or from whom such
{ amount was received / disbursement was made / obligation was incurred }, the specific purpose for which and the date on which each was made or received, to-

gether with the total amount of such { receipts / disbursements / obligations } in any amount or manner whatsoever.

Subscribed and sworn to before me this----------day   --
                                                        (Candidate or Chairman of Club)

of ----------------------------A. D. 19-----   --
                                                        (Secretary of Candidate, Committee or Club)†
--   P. O. Address ----------------------------

Notary Public ---------------------------- County   Village / City } of ----------------------------

Note.—In the event there are no receipts, disbursements or obligations this fact should be stated across the face of
the blank and affidavit executed in the usual manner. 12.09 (3) (e).
† The secretary of a personal campaign committee should not execute affidavit of his candidate's personal statement.

Financial Statement by Candidate for Office, Wisconsin.

Federal Legislation. Congress passed its first corrupt-practices act in 1907, prohibiting contributions in federal elections by any corporation or in any federal or state election by a national bank or a corporation organized under federal law. Another act in 1910, amended in 1911, required political committees and candidates for Congress to file with the Clerk of the House and the Secretary of the Senate, as the case may be, statements on receipt, disbursement, and contributors of campaign funds for direct primaries, nominating conventions, and general elections. The candidates were further limited to maximum expenditures of $5,000 for a campaign for the House and $10,000 for a senatorial campaign unless a state law fixed a lower amount, which would then apply. Although the Supreme Court in *Newberry v. United States* in 1921 cast serious doubt on the validity of limitations applied to primaries, each house in Congress could enforce such a rule by refusing to seat a member for whom an excessive sum was spent in the nominating process; in two cases, Frank L. Smith (Republican, Illinois) and William S. Vare (Republican, Pennsylvania), the Senate did refuse to seat members for this reason. After the decision of the Court in *United States* v. *Classic* in 1941, Congress clearly had the power to apply its regulations to direct primaries, but has not done so, except for placing a ban on corporation and labor-union contributions and expenditures.

While the limitation on direct primaries was still applicable and in order to insure the laws' application to candidates for the Senate (after their direct election was required by the Seventeenth Amendment), Congress passed the Federal Corrupt Practices Act of 1925, applicable only to general elections. The act broadened very markedly the category of persons required to make statements. Any treasurer of any political committee influencing the election of members of Congress or of presidential electors in more than one state must file, at specified times before and after elections,[23] with the Clerk of the House detailed information of all contributions over $100 and of all disbursements over $10. Every candidate for Congress must file with the Secretary of the Senate or Clerk of the House, between ten and fifteen days before an election and within thirty days after an election, itemized accounts of all contributions to and disbursements by him or anyone else with his knowledge and consent. Limitations on expenditures are set at $10,000 for a senatorial candidate and $2500 for a House candidate. These amounts can be increased through an alternate provision permitting 3c per vote for each vote cast at the last general election for the office, but the most that can be spent under this system is $25,000 for a senatorial and $5,000 for a House candidate. If a state has a maximum lower than these figures, candidates must abide by the state law. However, these limitations do not include filing fees, personal or traveling

[23] The times are March, June, September, then twice before a general election, and on the first of each year, covering the entire previous year.

expenses, stationery, postage, writing or printing for distributing letters, circulars, or posters (except billboards and newspapers), telephone and telegraph. A 1944 statute prohibits circulation of any campaign literature or advertising through the mails or in interstate commerce unless the material contains the names of those distributing it.

These provisions are still in effect but have been supplemented by additional restrictions legislated in 1939 and 1940, popularly known as the *Hatch Acts,* intended to prevent "Pernicious Political Activities." No political committee operating in more than one state is permitted either to receive or to spend, with the knowledge and consent of its chairman or treasurer, more than $3,000,000 in any calendar year. No individual is permitted to contribute more than $5,000 in any calendar year to any such committee or to any candidate for Congress or for President. The major objective of the legislation, originally, was to obstruct the political activity of people employed on the Works Progress Administration, who, it was widely alleged, were being exploited for the benefit of the Roosevelt Administration. Most of the provisions, therefore, cover limitations of the political activities of federal employees and of state government employees any part of whose salary is paid from federal funds through the innumerable grants in aid to the states.

Because of the breadth of coverage of the Hatch Acts, it is simpler to point out those government officials within the executive branch not covered by the prohibitions on political activities: the President, the Vice-President, anyone paid from appropriations for the office of the President, heads and assistant heads of Cabinet departments, executives appointed by the President and confirmed by the Senate who hold policy-determining positions in the United States government, ambassadors and ministers of the United States. The acts do not apply to the legislative and judicial branches. Detailed regulations of the Civil Service Commission distinguish some classes of temporary or irregular federal officials who are not covered. Violations of the statues by federal employees are punishable by the Civil Service Commission, penalties ranging from ninety days' suspension to outright dismissal. In the case of state employees the punishment is suspension for eighteen months. In case an offending state employee is not discharged or is employed in another position within eighteen months, the state loses federal funds equal to two years' salary of the employee.

Ambitious attempts have been made to specify what *political activities* are *permitted or denied employees* under the acts. Generally the only clear rights they have are to vote and to express personal political opinions. If state laws permit, they may serve as election officials, conducting themselves in an impartial manner. While they may wear a campaign button or display a sticker or political picture, they are not to make a partisan display while conducting the public business. Voluntary contributions continue to be legal as long as the money is not given in a federal building or to some federal official or employee. Employees covered by the acts are not permitted to be politically active by serving as party workers at the polls, holding party office, or actively campaigning.[24]

The implications for government workers are that their freedom of activity can be restricted at the same time that they are ostensibly protected from coercion or loss of employment by refusing to contribute to campaigns. Greater difficulty has arisen in enforcing the Hatch Acts' standards of clean politics in cases of state employees. Detecting violations is sometimes more difficult. The disposition of state officials to comply is noticeably weak in some cases, and the jurisdictional question itself is not always clear. Furthermore, subterfuges are fairly easy, for an official can resign his government position and then, unencumbered by the law, can engage in a political campaign and later be appointed to the same or another position.[25] Although the legislation prohibits such maneuvers, each specific case has to be shown to be an actual violation of the terms of the law.

Limits on Business. In addition to these special legislative prohibitions upon government employees, private groups have been singled out by Congress for special restrictions. Contributions to federal elections by corporations were prohibited by the first regulatory act on the subject in 1907. Before that time corporations had given large sums to both parties but particularly to the Republicans. The high point in the use of this source of money was 1896, when Marcus A. Hanna raised a fund variously estimated from $10,000,000 to $16,500,000 to elect William McKinley President. This campaign has become a landmark in large-scale collections

---

24 These rules are taken from Statement by Civil Service Commission with Concurrence of Department of Justice, October 17, 1940, and *New York Times,* October 21, 1952. The Civil Service Commission is authorized to permit political activity in municipalities or other political subdivisions in Maryland and Virginia, within the vicinity of Washington, D. C., or wherever federal employees constitute a majority of the voters. The constitutionality of the Hatch Acts was upheld as they applied to both federal and state employees. See Ferrel Heady, "The Hatch Act Decisions," *American Political Science Review,* Vol. 41 (1947) pp. 687–699.

25 See Moscow, *Politics in the Empire State* (New York: Alfred A. Knopf, Inc., 1948) pp. 68–69, and Milligan, *Missouri Waltz* (New York: Charles Scribner's Sons, 1948) p. 233. Some sample cases of attempted enforcement of the Hatch Acts among state employees: Despite a Civil Service Commission finding that a state forester in Tennessee solicited funds during a primary campaign three years previously, the Governor refused to discharge him and the penalty to the state for 2 years' salary was $9,000; five subordinate employees were also involved, but the Commission considered their violations "less aggravated" because of influence exerted on them and did not require their removal.—— Associated Press dispatches, dated March 21 and April 7, 1951. A charge against a Mississippi official appeared academic, since he no longer held the state position in which he was barred from political activity.——*New York Times,* November 21, 1952. A candidate for Congress in New Jersey presented a clearly academic question, since he was a nonsalaried member of a housing authority at the time he ran, and neither he nor the state was subject to any penalty.——*Ibid.,* December 31, 1952.

and expenditures and has been popularized as the stereotype of wealth given in behalf of vested interests. Some campaigns subsequently have equalled or exceeded the 1896 scale of finances, but it was the largest up to that time and represents relatively a larger expenditure because of the greater value of money in the 1890's than in subsequent years. The fact that corporations almost universally opposed William J. Bryan and contributed to the Republicans created a partisan aspect which had not previously existed. Wealthy contributors had given to the campaigns of such Democratic presidential candidates as Samuel J. Tilden and Grover Cleveland on a scale equal to their gifts to the Republicans of those years.[26] When corporations moved in force to the Republicans, the insistence upon regulation grew stronger because of the tremendous advantage derived from their support.

The formal result of both federal and state laws outlawing corporation money in elections has been a technical compliance in that contributions are not made from corporation treasuries; but individual businessmen contribute. The line between personal money and corporate money is not always clear. Reduction in total amounts from business sources has not been a result. Furthermore, when businessmen generally favor one party, their contributions will go to it, just as corporation contributions did before the prohibitive legislation. There is no way to regulate in advance what the relative partisan advantage of business money will be, although the weight of it is toward the Republicans.[27] The $5,000-per-year individual limitation imposed by the Hatch Acts appears to prevent huge gifts from the wealthy, but in actuality it does not. A person can give $5,000 each year to each committee which is organized to influence a federal election. He can give to state committees without limit, unless a state has set a maximum that its committees can receive from one person. He can give in the names of members of his family $5,000 for each member to each committee. An employer can give the maximum on behalf of employees to a committee. There remains the possibility of illegal amounts being given without any record of the transaction so that the money cannot be traced either from the giver or to the receiver.

---

[26] Pollock, *op. cit.*, pp. 62–65.

[27] For example, in 1928 many men of wealth supported the Democratic presidential candidate, Alfred E. Smith; four of these men together gave over $1,000,000. In 1936 the favoritism was more one-sided, with the DuPont and Pew families giving jointly over $1,000,000 to the Republicans. There are some interesting partisan divisions within business. Computed as a percentage of the total campaign fund for the presidential elections 1932 through 1944, contributions from manufacturers and bankers amounted to two or four times the percentage of the Republican budget as of the Democrat budget. Conversely, brewers' and distillers' contributions constituted as much as four times the percentage of Democrat budgets as Republican. See Louise Overacker's four articles in the *American Political Science Review*, Vol. 27 (1933) p. 776; Vol. 31 (1937) p. 485; Vol. 35 (1941) p. 723; Vol. 39 (1945) p. 916.

Limits on Labor Unions. With whatever success has been achieved, the issue of contributions directly from or in the name of corporations has been settled. The ascending curve of labor-union political influence in the 1930's and 1940's created a degree of concern with the financial power of these organizations reminiscent of the alarm over corporations' political power at the turn of the century. The partisan connections of labor have been almost entirely with the Democratic Party, at least as far as large-scale giving of money is involved, so that restrictions upon labor have more partisan implications than those upon corporations, except in the Bryan campaigns. The arguments in behalf of restrictions or prohibitions upon labor unions giving money are in part similar to those previously advanced against corporations—following from the fear that large organizations with financial resources will dominate government by their contributions to candidates' campaigns. The source of the fear in the case of labor unions is their large membership, which, like stockholders of corporations, will be involuntary givers to campaigns if money is allotted to parties directly from union treasuries. The position taken on these arguments depends upon one's concept of what constitutes improper influence and of the relative rights of majorities and minorities as applied to labor membership.[28]

The size of union contributions brought the matter to a head—about $750,000 was given to the Roosevelt presidential campaign in 1936.[29] The effect of the second Hatch Act's limitations on spending affected labor unions in several ways: A union was limited to the $5000 rule in contributing to a candidate or committee operating in more than one state, but was not limited in its contributions to state and local committees; however, if a union established a political committee, it could spend up to the maximum of $3,000,000 a year in behalf of one candidate or party. These were hardly to be considered restrictions of any consequence.[30] The War Labor Disputes Act eventually passed with a section prohibiting labor organizations from contributing in connection with any election in which candidates for presidential elector or for Congress were being voted for. This act did not apply to direct primaries, so a union could contribute $5000 toward a candidate's nomination and unlimited amounts for use in purely state and local elections if state laws permitted. Otherwise, political committees could still spend $3,000,000 a year. The response of the Congress of Industrial Organizations was to set up its Political Action Com-

---

28 See Joseph Tanenhaus, "Organized Labor's Political Spending: The Law and Its Consequences," *Journal of Politics*, Vol. 16 (1954) pp. 467–470.

29 *Ibid.*, p. 441; Overacker, "Campaign Funds in the Presidential Election of 1936," *op. cit.*, Vol. 31 (1937) p. 489. The United Mine Workers alone contributed or lent $469,000.

30 Tanenhaus, *op. cit.*, pp. 442–443.

mittee, and approximately $650,000 was transferred to the PAC from union treasuries. After both national conventions were concluded in 1944, the $170,000 remaining in the fund was frozen in technical compliance with the law and as a gesture to public sentiment. During the general-election campaigns of 1944 and 1946, the CIO activities were financed by voluntary individual contributions, but after Election Day union money was again directly expended.[31]

The Labor Management Relations Act (Taft-Hartley Act) expanded the restrictions on union political spending contained in the War Labor Disputes Act, which expired six months after the end of World War II. The new restrictions covered both labor unions and corporations, forbidding direct contributions from either to affect the outcome of direct primaries as well as general elections, and applying the prohibition to expenditures as well as to contributions. The crux of this law was the breadth of definition of "expenditure," for presumably it included the use of labor-union newspapers in affecting federal elections, although the distinction between political (illegal) and educational (legal) publications cannot be made objectively. In a test case of the right of union newspaper publishers to editorialize in support of a congressional candidate, the Supreme Court held that the act should not be construed as limiting freedom of expression and found that such use of newspapers was permissible within the act if they were issued regularly, distributed to union members, and aroused no opposition among members by the political editorials.[32] In two subsequent cases, one involving union political advertisements in a commercial newspaper and the other, union expenditures to aid its president's election to Congress, lower federal courts dismissed the actions, in effect, on the ground that minor violations of the law would be ignored.[33]

Despite unions being prohibited from spending money directly to affect a federal election (either during the primary or the general election) and the consequent necessity to raise all money voluntarily through contributions of members or sympathetic outsiders, the amount of union spending has remained large. In addition, political publicity can be conducted without limit through regular union publications, and union money can be used for campaigns to get union members registered and to urge

---

[31] *Ibid.*, pp. 443–450. In 1946 in the absence of national nominating conventions the PAC set an arbitrary date as the beginning of the general-election campaign. In addition to the CIO-PAC, there was also created the National Citizens' PAC to raise money outside the CIO. Sidney Hillman, President of the Amalgamated Clothing Workers, was chairman of both Political Action Committees at their inception.

[32] *United States* v. *Congress of Industrial Organizations*, 335 U. S. 106 (1949).

[33] Tanenhaus, *op. cit.*, pp. 450–461.

them to vote. Finally, in the absence of state legislation, unions can spend directly to affect state and local elections.[34]

Deceptions of Financial Regulations. To survey state and federal legislation bearing upon money in elections is to find an almost endless number of loopholes permitting unlimited amounts of money to be raised and spent. Many provisions seem to be unblushing attempts to give the outward appearance of regulation without any actual limitation or hindrance. Individual contributions are only limited, at most, to giving to one candidate or to his committee, and they can be made virtually without limit to various candidates or to various committees supporting the same candidate. Candidates and committees are responsible, when they file financial statements, only for money to them, i.e., money received and expended with their knowledge and consent. The national committees were limited by the Hatch Acts to the receipt and disbursement of $3,000,000 per year, but state committees are used for financing parts of a presidential campaign. The possibilities for juggling accounts between national and state committees are boundless.

Finally, the $3,000,00 limit can be reached by as many supplementary committees as supporters of a party want to create, and the practice of both parties since 1940 has been to organize or have organized other groups which can raise and spend to this legal maximum. One result, especially in the case of labor and business, has been to compartmentalize presidential campaigns by interest groups forming their own committees and handling their own money separately from the party organization. In this way the interest-group basis of politics is encouraged and accentuated and complete information is more elusive than if spending were centralized within the party.[35] A development paralleling this $3,000,000 maximum has been increased costs of campaigns, so that expenditures have mounted under legislation superficially directed toward decreasing the amounts being spent.

Political Sensitivity about Campaign Funds. Infractions of the laws are ignored or condoned. While the leaders of the two parties constantly berate each other for their financial practices, a great deal of the expostulation is sound and fury signifying nothing.[36] Charges of excessive sums or

---

[34] *Ibid.*, pp. 462-463. It was estimated that total labor expenditures in the 1958 election were about $3,500,000. *New York Times*, November 17, 1958. There is constant disagreement regarding the total amount of expenditures on behalf of candidates by labor unions and what kinds of activities should be included in computing the expenditures and reported as such. See *Final Report* of the Special Committee to Investigate Political Activities, Lobbying, and Campaign Contributions, U. S. Senate, 85th Cong. 1st Sess., Report No. 395, May 31, 1957, pp. 159-162.

[35] Moscow, *op. cit.*, pp. 66-67.

[36] Pollock, *op. cit.*, pp. 130-132.

irregular practices are often fishing expeditions where the attacker has no real information. Sometimes the charges imply what the attacker knows to be false. The pressure for the constant drumming on the subject is the sensitivity of politicians, the possibilities for gaining an advantage by making charges against opponents, and the likelihood of capturing attention because of the publicity value of campaign finances. Despite the political uses of these charges, politicians have a reluctance to enforce the laws against themselves, and the laws often proceed from the insistence upon some kind of long-overdue reform or from the hopes of gaining partisan advantage by the restrictions or the publicity.

Alternatives in Regulations. The problem of regulating money in elections is partly caused by these pious avowals of personal restraint as a means of currying public favor. Most citizens do not understand the need for large amounts of money and are unsympathetic with serious and realistic analyses of the problems involved in bringing to them the discussions of the issues of the day. Because this use of money is peculiar to the political way of life, citizens are unfamiliar with it and politicians are wary in their public discussions of it. Quite regularly, before, after, and even during campaigns, congressional committees launch investigations of what is spent or is being spent and elicit testimony from managers and candidates on the subject of wise legislation for curbing the money demon. Aside from partisan sniping back and forth, the proposals come down to "full publicity and reporting" of funds and to one of two attitudes toward the amount of money. Both of these attitudes follow from dissatisfaction with existing limits on spending, but there they split. One attitude is that ceilings should be raised so as to be "realistic"; the other, that there should be no legal ceilings and complete reliance should be placed upon reporting. All manner of incidental and supplemental regulations are suggested from time to time; e.g., a proposal to restrict the amount of editorial space devoted to a party or candidate in newspapers and other publications and a proposal to require a committee to register if it spends more than a certain amount in behalf of a party or a candidate. All seem to agree, in the words of Arthur Krock, that " 'There Ought to Be a Law,' but Saying What?" [37]

Basically, the choice is between a continuation of the present practice of setting limits and then exceeding them or recognizing that the only "realistic ceiling" is the amount that can be raised and repealing the laws which unrealistically set ceilings. Every scrap of evidence points in the

---

[37] Column in the *New York Times*, December 2, 1952. See, in addition, the issues of December 3, 4, 5, 1952, and January 25, 1953, for some of the testimony and the committee report following the 1952 presidential election. The proposal to restrict editorial space undoubtedly would conflict with the First Amendment and the reaction of newspaper spokesmen was immediate and sharply critical.

direction of continued high and progressively higher expenditures in all campaigns. To set ceilings which are realistic for one year is to predetermine the future. The only way to keep them realistic is to revise the law constantly to keep pace with practice. The result would be an onerous task for legislators, possible confusion much of the time, and a tacit recognition that ceilings really cannot be set after all or that they are set so high as to fail to be limiting.

Government Aids in Campaigns. A different type of proposal, going back to Theodore Roosevelt and William J. Bryan, is for campaigns to be financed partly or wholly out of the public treasury. Either way, the problem is to decide how much to give a party or candidate. Proposals to supply the full amount of campaign funds would set ceilings automatically in the sums appropriated, but proposals for government to supply only a minimum amount for a party may or may not limit the contributions from other sources. Although the adoption of such a plan would be a radical departure, official government contributions to campaigns do exist. Issuance of pamphlets, reports, press releases, and so on may be and frequently is exploited by the "ins" to their advantage the year around. More specifically, the franking privilege in the federal government is often used indirectly for electioneering purposes. This privilege, most widely known in its use by members of Congress but used throughout the executive branch as well, is frequently a source of controversy because of the uses officeholders can make of it. A member of Congress is forbidden to employ it directly in his formal campaigns, but he can use it constantly for mailing personal letters as well as copies of speeches, articles, and miscellaneous material capable of influencing voters. Of a different nature is the law in the state of Oregon whereby publicity pamphlets containing pictures of candidates and campaign arguments are distributed free to the voters at least ten days before election. Space is sold at the rate of $50 a page. Independent candidates are allowed to buy two pages each and a political party twenty-four pages. In addition, both Oregon and New Jersey permit candidates to have slogans printed on the ballots.

Beyond these existing practices, proposals have been made for government to *provide a limited amount of free campaign help* to all candidates on an equal basis. Besides these aids the candidates could raise money from private contributions for their campaigns if they chose. Suggestions have included extensions of the franking privilege; free use of public buildings for campaign rallies; publicity pamphlets so that a candidate can present "the fundamentals of his program without placing himself under any obligation . . . to any private contributor"; and free radio and television time, necessitating the government buying the time or operating its own stations.[38]

Entirely different questions are raised by proposals for government to *provide all of the money to be spent in campaigns.*[39]

(1) The treatment of minor parties is a dilemma. On the one hand, they should not be entitled to the same amount of money as a major party, but on the other hand, to devise a formula to pay them proportionate amounts would be unlikely to please anyone. To simply appropriate money only to major parties would be a serious discrimination even if it were sustained in the courts. In particular elections such discrimination would be ludicrous, e.g., had such a system been in effect in 1912, the Republicans and Democrats would have received the money, but the Progressive Party, which ran second in the presidential balloting, would have received nothing. If minor parties were included and given a generous amount for a campaign, splinter groups and malcontents would be inspired to form a party and run candidates simply to be eligible for money with which to air their grievances. Incidentally, legislation providing for appropriations would have to deal with the vexing question of defining a political party and establishing the procedures for organizing new parties in order to qualify for the money.

(2) By spending public money, all voters would be contributing involuntarily to campaigns. If Republicans and Democrats would have no legitimate complaint about financing the opposition as long as their own party received the same treatment, independents quite conceivably could protest that they were contributing financially to parties neither of which they supported.

(3) The question of the appropriation for the major parties would be, Should they be given exactly equal amounts, or as in the case of the short-lived Colorado law of 1909, should each party be paid so much for each vote it received at the last election for the offices to be filled.[40] Equal amounts could be justified for essentially two-party elections, but so much per vote could well be insisted upon by one party or the other. If the amount was subject to computation, long and loud arguments may develop

---

[38] Overacker, *Money in Elections*, pp. 382, 389-390. Professor Overacker appeared to place much reliance on the usefulness to candidates of publicity pamphlets. In Oregon all of the available pamphlet space has not always been purchased by the parties. Furthermore, even where parties pay some of the expense, the costs have been high. It was for this reason that a similar law in Montana was repealed.——Pollock, *op. cit.*, pp. 104-105, 107.

[39] See in general *ibid.*, pp. 93-110.

[40] *Ibid.*, pp. 89-93. This Colorado law was held unconstitutional before it was enforced. Each party was permitted a sum equal to 25c per vote cast for the party two years previously. The effect of this method of computing would have based the amount of money for a presidential election year upon the voting turnout in a nonpresidential year and vice versa. In any event, the per-vote computation would place a severe ceiling on spending.

over how much each party was entitled to, and the suspicion arises that the "ins," by their control of the treasury and the public disbursements, may find ways to favor themselves, just as favoritism could arise in the legislature which would be required to appropriate the money.

(4) Some question can be raised as to the possibility of actually preventing private individuals and groups from contributing to campaigns. If the prohibition were too strictly enforced, the courts might invalidate the legislation. If the prohibition were loosely enforced, or if "minor" violations were overlooked, the scheme for making government the exclusive contributor would fail. The perpetual question would arise: What is a campaign contribution and what is a contribution for an educational or informative program? The distinction would have to be made to avoid violation of civil rights, but it would be a distinction without a difference. The record of judicial treatment of labor contributions and the practices of business, agriculture, veterans, and other organizations as well make plain that private efforts to influence the outcome of elections cannot be suppressed, and as a matter of value judgment, should not be suppressed.

(5) To deal exclusively in terms of money would leave some campaign practices and abuses untouched. At all levels of government, candidates exchange commitments with individuals and group leaders where no money at all is involved. Promises of support are given for promises to pursue certain policies if elected. To put the relationship crudely, the payoff to some groups and individuals is to reward them with legislation or lack of legislation if they contribute money and/or voting support. To prohibit the giving of money does not really strike at this practice but just removes one of two sources of aid that can be given candidates. In fact, the result may be to increase the political leverage of mass organizations which can make a show of directing their members' votes one way or the other.

(6) To provide a complete system for government support, the campaigns of candidates in the primaries would have to be underwritten. A complicated question arises here analogous to the one involving minor parties. Should every candidate seeking a nomination be paid the same amount as his competitors for the same office? To answer "Yes" would encourage many candidates who were not even serious contenders but were seeking publicity for themselves or their business or some other activity. To answer "No" raises the specter of allotting money on some sliding scale.

(7) To provide money for the formal campaign is to overlook the need for expenditures, and therefore contributions, between elections. To underwrite year-round electioneering expenses would create a real burden on public treasuries, and apparently could only be done for incumbents, giving them another advantage over challengers, who would have to wait

for their nomination or declaration of candidacy to receive any money. To turn candidates loose on their own financial initiative after an election would create an artificial distinction between the formal campaign period and the rest of the year and in-between years.

(8) The problem of the federal system arises again. Assuming that one state could enforce such a law, it is doubtful if federal legislation would be very effective unless all of the states had compatible statutes so that the regulations would dovetail and not conflict.

Selected Bibliography

Hayes, Isabella Mallory, *Financing Presidential Campaigns*. College Park: University of Maryland, 1953. Mimeographed.

Heard, Alexander, *The Costs of Democracy*. Chapel Hill: University of North Carolina Press, 1960.

Overacker, Louise, *Money in Elections*. New York: The Macmillan Company, 1932.
—— *Presidential Campaign Funds*. Boston: Boston University Press, 1946.

Pollock, James K., Jr., *Party Campaign Funds*. New York: Alfred A. Knopf, Inc., 1926.

Van Doren, John, *Big Money in Little Sums*. Chapel Hill: Institute for Research in Social Science, University of North Carolina, 1956.

A great deal of primary data on campaign practices, especially financing, are available in the many congressional hearings which are frequently held during or after election campaigns.

Reforms

Ah, Love! could thou and I with Fate
  conspire
To grasp this sorry Scheme of Things entire,
Would not we shatter it to bits—and then
Re-mould it nearer to the Heart's Desire!

RUBAIYAT OF OMAR KHAYYAM, *Quatrain
LXXIII*, first edition of the Edward Fitz-
gerald translation.

CHAPTER TWENTY-THREE

Can We Redirect the Dynamics?

The preceding section concluded the discussion of the two party system in the United States considered in terms of the operation of a political system. At various points throughout the foregoing chapters disadvantages and disparagements of the existing operations were considered when they arose in the course of the discussion. The specific consideration of reforms is reserved purposely for this final section in order to set them against the background of the whole system. The reforms included in this and the following two chapters are not all-inclusive but take in questions of fundamental importance. These reforms fall into two main categories—attacks upon the dynamics of the two-party system and attacks upon various organizational features of the system.

To speak of dynamics is to risk the unhappy fate of transferring a term from one discipline to another with loss of any useful meaning or with misapplication of the concept in its new surroundings. Dynamics as used here means the forces within the American society producing or governing the partisan-political activity of the society. Dynamics comprehends a multitude of influencing forces or factors contributing to the creation of the two-party system in the United States. The relation between the reason-for-being of a system and how it mechanically operates is too close to be separated except artificially for the purposes of examination. The considerations of dynamics invariably burst forth in designs upon the machinery, and the considerations of machinery inevitably touch at some points the dynamics. One set of proposals for reform, however, can be distinguished by being directed primarily at one or more of these forces, with organization relegated to a subservient status; just as another set of proposals reverses this emphasis. Reform of dynamics is grounded in the belief that the forces which produce our peculiar political system can be changed or redirected.

Hovering over or underlying this discussion of reforms, both of dynamics and of organization, is the assumption of evolution which brings changes inevitably. Evolutionary changes may or may not be reforms in the sense of improvements, and such changes may occur as a result of minute deviations which combine to produce a new situation no one really foresaw, planned, or willed. Consequently, some of the reforms may be riding with or against the evolutionary stream of changes. Reforms of the dynamics present special questions of the possibility of making such changes at a given time and of the likely results if the changes are really accomplished.

POLITICS AS SIN

Moral Evaluation of Politics. One of the observations throughout this book has been a tradition of opposition and antagonism to politics as such. The manifestations of this reaction are many and varied, but they often coalesce into a pattern of thought which can best be epitomized as a judgment that politics is sinful. This judgment may be related to or spring from theological evaluations, but it may be quite unrelated to the spiritual life and simply emerge as a layman's identification of an activity as secular sin. This welling up of protest and even antipathy toward the whole subject of partisan politics springs from a refusal to admit or to recognize the adaptability of practical methods to practical situations. To hold that politics is sinful is to deny not only any element of inevitability in the chain of political events but also to believe that either political objectives are unworthy or that they can be pursued by "virtuous" means. The person who judges politics to be sin projects his own preconceived standards of ethical conduct as a criterion for those who operate in a field with which he is either unfamiliar or incompatible. Such a person may or may not try to apply his own standards to himself in his own fields of activity, but he believes that his standards are practical in the business of seeking public office and operating government.

Condemnation of Organization. The tradition of opposition to politics goes back into the Colonial period of the United States, and in its earliest manifestations was an opposition to political organization as such. Perhaps the best-publicized spokesman of this school of thought was George Washington, whose *Farewell Address* contained the most sweeping condemnation of parties and, by extension, their organizations.[1] In 1835, thirty-six years after Washington's warning, objection to the popular election of governor was expressed in the constitutional convention of North Carolina:

> When large bodies of men are drawn out to act for some common purpose, their action cannot be effectual without organization and discipline. Establish the scheme of an election of Governor by general ticket, and we shall soon have our Grand Central Committees, District Committees, County Committees, and Captain's Company Committees, and all that vile machinery by which the freemen of the State are drilled into the slaves of factious Chieftains—by which they are deluded into the belief that they are fighting for themselves, when, in truth, they are only quarreling for the selfish interest of designing and unprincipled men. . . .[2]

---

[1] See above, pp. 11–12.

[2] Quoted in George P. Luetscher, *Early Political Machinery in the United States* (Philadelphia: University of Pennsylvania, 1903).

Condemnation of Permanent Organization. The acceptance of organization could hardly be questioned when political parties were finally established as instruments for operating government and when organization itself was understood to be a response to the popular impulse in governmental affairs. Subsequent attacks were forced to move into new channels. Gradually the theme of sin was heralded in the discoveries of the iniquities of a permanent party organization.[3] Marching under this banner, various reformers have sought alternatives. Although Ostrogorski admitted the necessity of parties, he was constantly aware of the deceitful manipulations of party "bosses" made possible by the oligarchical nature of permanent organization. In this cross fire of a practical conclusion and a moral judgment, he propounded a system of multiple parties, each organized around a single issue. In this way he provided organization for achieving objectives but avoided traditional party organizations which exist for their own sake irrespective of what they stand for.[4]

Herbert Croly attacked the party system because traditional partisanship creates "artificial" majorities and minorities at the sacrifice of citizens' convictions. Like Ostrogorski, he believed the nature of the decisions made was more important than the manner of making them, i.e., majority rule was not enough by itself.[5] Frank Crane, who held up the intentions of the Founders as a renewed warning against the parties (which result, he contended, from lack of civic conscience and organization) expressed his ideal of a federated "organized Democracy." [6] Continuing the thesis of multiple local organizations, M. P. Follett was sure that "an effective neighborhood organization" would deal "the death blow to party" through a real unity, genuine leaders, and responsible government. The neighborhood groups would culminate in individuals creating their own state in a some-

---

[3] James Bryce, *Modern Democracies* (New York: The Macmillan Company, 1921) Vol. 1, pp. 116–118, sums up the case against permanent party organization.

[4] *Democracy and the Organization of Political Parties* (New York: The Macmillan Company, 1902) Vol. 2, p. 650 ff. In effect Ostrogorski undermined his own system by permitting candidates for office to belong to more than one party. The result, it would seem, would be to transfer the present ambivalence of tweedledum-tweedledee qualities from parties to candidates who could be associated, for purposes of getting support, with organizations whose positions on separate issues would clash or be basically incompatible. Even if such organizations were temporary, the result would be a continuation of much that Ostrogorski found objectionable. For one of the few analyses of Ostrogorski's work, see Austin Ranney, *The Doctrine of Responsible Party Government* (Illinois Studies in the Social Sciences, Vol. 34, No. 3, 1954) Chap. 7.

[5] Herbert Croly, *Progressive Democracy* (1914) p. 311. Ranney, *op. cit.*, Chap. 8 and pp. 154–158.

[6] Frank Crane, "Party Government a Failure," *Forum*, Vol. 49 (1913) pp. 698–702. His own form of organization was to be "the entire body of citizens in any community, without respect to varying opinions, in order to get those public goods which the majority want." The chain would continue with "the federation of these districts into larger groups and into a nation, for the same purpose." Either he did not reread what he had written or he was thoroughly confused. A system whereby a majority organizes to get what it wants "without respect to varying opinions" is either a fantasy or a tyranny.

what mysterious kind of organization wherein the state would be "built up through the intimate intertwining of all." [7]

These reformers would agree that "as long as we have a two-party system of government, we will have machines." [8] Their point of departure is insisting that machines can only be bad, never good. The general acceptance of the parties' permanent organizations, however, precludes anything but a detached interest or curiosity in these plural-grouping political organization schemes. Whether or not the majority of citizens can fully state the premises for their acceptance, some who are more articulate can isolate and spotlight the kind of a stone wall these reformers are encountering. The corrections must be vast and profound, we are told, so that the whole system can be renovated, but "every substantial evil that has been experienced under the electoral clauses of the Constitution was introduced by politicians for party purposes, and might be cured—granting the desire to cure it—without altering these clauses. If any scheme can be presented which politicians might not pervert, it may be well to consider it." [9]

It is encumbent upon those who attack permanent organization to show how *ad hoc* organizations will generate the public interest and activity which the party system with all of its emotional and dramatic sound and fury does not arouse. To prove what is already known, that organization tends to become oligarchic with the result that the rank and file are unable to exert any real influence and are often excluded even from consideration, does not tell us how new organizations will avoid the same process or how an organization intended to be temporary can be prevented from becoming permanent. Some opponents of permanent political organization give voice to a yearning for emancipation from institutional authority which besets most of us at one time or another, but people usually throw off this mood and accept the confines of society as essential to the existence of society. "Human society is organized society, and without organization there can be no advancement. . . . Political organization is as inherently sound and essential as any other form of organization. Only its excesses and abuses are bad, not the thing itself." [10]

To suppose that civilization can function in its "political" activities by temporary organizations or without a genuine hierarchy is in fact to invite chaos. Permanent organization alone provides the continuity we require for living, and the situation could not be different if we tore down

7 M. P. Follett, *The New State* (New York: Longmans, Green & Company, Inc., 1918) pp. 217, 255; in general, pp. 216–257.

8 Edward J. Flynn, *You're the Boss* (New York: The Viking Press, Inc., 1947) p. 231.

9 Edward Stanwood, *A History of the Presidency from 1788 to 1897* (Boston: Houghton Mifflin Company, 1898) p. 19.

10 Frank R. Kent, *The Great Game of Politics* (New York: Doubleday, Page & Company, 1924) p. 322; also pp. 320–321.

the existing structures and began to build anew from the community or the neighborhood or from current public issues or from individual convictions. There is no reason to assume that the dynamics behind the operation of the new edifice would be substantially different no matter how its outside appearance may be changed.

Acceptance of Permanent Organization. The nature of the problem of reform of our system is just as clearly revealed by those who would keep its basic structure but improve or purify its operations. Most politicians do not question the need for permanent party organization, but some of them do believe it can be changed in variously desirable ways. Aware of graft and corruption in politics, these participants have no time for complex or sophisticated commentaries but deal in plain words about justice and honesty. "Clean government is so simple most people miss it. All we need, to have it in any community, is honestly elected officials who have the moral courage to abide by their oaths of office when tempted to violate them. When that happens bossism comes to an end." [11] Others take a different tack and seek to shield the public from the rigors of uninhibited political competition, condemning the excesses of campaigns and the degrading effect of "mud-slinging" and demagoguery. A more extreme form of this point of view is the appeal to unity as a repudiation of political combativeness and the proposal now and then that no contest should be made for the Presidency because of the temper of the times.[12] It is rare, indeed, for anyone, much less a politician, to speak as Senator John J. Ingalls (1833–1900, Republican, Kansas) once did:

> The purification of politics is an iridescent dream. Government is force. Politics is a battle for supremacy. Parties are the armies. The decalogue and the golden rule have no place in a political campaign. . . . The commander who lost a battle through the activity of his moral nature would be the derision and jest of history. This modern cant about the corruption of politics is fatiguing in the extreme.[13]

Wider Activity Within Permanent Organization. Perhaps the most persistent appeal for reform within the tradition of the two-party system is the urging that all cititzens, in effect, be in politics. These proposals, in various forms and in differing degrees of intensity, try to make a representative form of government more nearly a democratic form of government

---

[11] Maurice Milligan, *Missouri Waltz* (New York: Charles Scribner's Sons, 1948) p. 279.

[12] Senator Paul Douglas (Democrat, Illinois) suggested that Dwight D. Eisenhower be nominated for President in 1952 by both the Democrats and the Republicans with a different running mate in each party. "You still would have separate tickets. We are in a great struggle. We need national unity. Why, this would merely mean a common candidate at the top."——Quoted in the *New York Times*, April 24, 1951. The same proposal on behalf of Eisenhower was made by David Lawrence for the 1956 presidential election.——Syndicated column, November 17, 1955.

[13] Quoted in Charles E. Merriam, *American Political Ideas* (New York: The Macmillan Company, 1920) p. 304.

in that mass participation would transcend the mere casting of a ballot. The pathetic aspect of these aspirations is the failure of the public to respond. Probably no more than 6% of the population is found among the active party workers.[14] One of the "bosses" himself noted, "It would be a fine thing if all officeholders felt under obligation to all types of citizens and hence based their judgments on the rule of the greatest long-term good for the greatest number. But we will never reach that Utopia unless or until all the citizens resolve to work three hundred and sixty-five days a year at being citizens." [15]

The facts about lack of participation and activity are not accompanied by acceptance of the implications of the public's neglect. It is difficult, in view of our beliefs about government fostered from the cradle to the grave, to accept the proposition that politics is a profession in the sense that it requires specialization and aptitude. Every profession, for its practitioners, is a full-time job. Laymen enter only on a part-time basis, if at all. Every citizen is supposed to enter into government processes, but inherently he cannot enter on a full-time basis because of the limits to his interest and abilities and because politics is only one function to be performed. In the division of labor, everyone cannot do the same thing. Some run for the offices as their specialization, but many others can do no more than vote and discuss.

> But it does not follow, from the fact that people can, that they *should* deploy in politics the abilities they can muster in other spheres of culture. There are many people who, choosing among their various needs and potentialities on the basis of their temperament, their situation, and their gifts, can build a very satisfying life without the slightest attention to politics. Their gardens are enough, and their osmotic pressure against the news of the day, coupled with their intense activity in other fields saves them from anxiety. Until conditions become far more desperate, and in some circumstances even if they do, it would seem ascetic, a kind of secularized Puritanism, to suggest to such people that they concern themselves with politics when it is evident that their lives are full and rich and adequately oriented without it. Since we do not live forever, no one can satisfy all his human needs on all levels of living, all the more so as these needs develop with the growth of civilization and the greater ease and length of the average life. And in these people there is choice to avoid politics, not flight from it.[16]

---

[14] Frank R. Kent, *Political Behavior* (New York: William Morrow & Company, Inc., 1928) pp. 6–7. Clarence Berdahl, "Party Membership in the United States," *American Political Science Review*, Vol. 36 (1942) pp. 245–248.

[15] Flynn, *op. cit.*, p. 235. Far from working all year around, most citizens do well to vote and discuss public affairs with one another. Using a scale for measuring political activity for 8000 respondents throughout the country, 10.3% were classed as very active, 16.8% as active, 34.6% as inactive, and 38.3% as very inactive.——Julian L. Woodward and Elmo Roper, "Political Activity of American Citizens," *American Political Science Review*, Vol. 44 (1950) p. 876.

[16] David Riesman, *Faces in the Crowd* (New Haven: Yale University Press, 1952) p. 48. Italics in the original.

Lower Voting Age. As a tangent from some of this thinking about improving citizens' political activity, we find various kinds of evidence of dissatisfaction with existing voting requirements. Proposals vary from standardizing the requirements through an amendment to the United States Constitution to eliminating specific requirements such as the poll tax. One proposal, frequently discussed following World War II, is the lowering of the voting age from twenty-one to eighteen. Georgia first took this step in 1943, and Kentucky followed in 1955.[17] Alaska came into the Union in 1958 with a 19-year voting age and Hawaii, in 1959, with a 20-year minimum voting age.

The pro-and-con arguments are well defined if not fully standardized. The leading contention in behalf of a lower age limit is that men of eighteen are taken into the military forces and that to be old enough to fight is to be old enough to vote. In rebuttal, the element of maturity in voting is stressed and the analogy between qualities of good fighters and qualities of good voters is claimed to be false. Numerous other reasons were found by both sides in Georgia [18] and will continue to be found wherever the issue is debated.[19] Regarding the contentions on both sides of the probable influence of teen-age voters upon elections, two general characteristics of voting behavior are pertinent. First, sons and daughters tend to acquire their partisanship from their parents, and families tend to vote as a unit. Second, the incidence of nonvoting is generally greatest, considered by age groups, among those under thirty. There is no reason to assume that these characteristics will be noticeably different at age eighteen than at age twenty-one.

---

[17] Franklin L. Burdette, "Lowering the Voting Age in Georgia," *South Atlantic Quarterly,* Vol. 44 (1945) pp. 300-307; *U. S. News and World Report,* January 22, 1954, pp. 26 ff. An interesting sidelight on the vote in the Georgia house was that the youngest legislator voted against the amendment and the oldest voted for it.

[18] Burdette, *op. cit.,* p. 305. The supporters insisted: Youth at eighteen is now better educated and informed, has idealism and demands higher ethical standards, would counteract the vote of the special interests of the aged, and would give a new incentive for citizen education. The opponents insisted: If fighting qualities be the test, those too old to fight should be disfranchised; peacetime policies should not be adopted for reasons agitated in wartime; eighteen-year-olds lack practical experience, are more easily deceived, and have only vague political interests; the question of the status of minors at law would be clouded. For further supporting arguments, see Hearing of Subcommittee of Senate Judiciary Committee, 82nd Cong., 2d sess., June 27, 1952, pp. 59-68.

[19] The reason age is used to determine maturity is that some kind of definite and arbitrary standard is needed, even though age is not always a reliable guide to maturity. Since it is maturity, not any given age as such, which is the objective, a desirable procedure would be to find a measurement for maturity. To do so would require some agreement about the properties of maturity and about the methods of measurement. In view of these difficulties, substantial support for a universal minimum age requirement is likely to continue.

NONVOTING

Extent. In the background of proposed reforms based on assumptions of more extensive and enlightened citizen participation in government stands the stark fact that the United States has one of the highest rates of nonvoting among countries having free elections.[20] The difficulty in making comparisons is that other countries report voting turnout as a percentage of the total number of people eligible to vote. It is not possible to make a similar computation in the United States because not every state reports the total number registered or eligible to vote. The best we can do is use the concept of the potential vote, i.e., the number of citizens of voting age.

The accompanying graph of voting turnout in presidential elections reveals several facets. Although the total number voting has increased because of the growing population, the percentage of the potential vote being cast has tended downward except for spurts of voter interest in individual years. Woman suffrage contributed to the increased nonvoting percentages because it approximately doubled the potential vote without doubling the number of voters. Since 1920, the largest proportion of voters casting ballots has been 62.7% in the presidential election of 1952.[21]

Nation-wide figures for voting are composite and mask wide state diversities. In 1956, the voting rate ranged from the high of 77.3% in Idaho to 22.1% in Mississippi. Five states cast over 75% of their potential vote and five, less than 35%. Three-fourths of the states cast over 50% and forty states, over 45%. Comparing the states for the two presidential elections,

---

[20] The writer is indebted to Richard M. Scammon, Director of Elections Research, Governmental Affairs Institute, for the figures of voting turnout in selected foreign countries.

Country	Percent	Total Electorate	Total Vote Cast (Excludes Blank, Invalid Ballots)
United Kingdom (1959)	78.7	35,080,000	27,608,000
Metropolitan France (1956)	80.3	26,772,000	21,491,000
Germany (1957)	87.8	35,403,000	31,073,000
Canada (1957)	74.2	8,902,000	6,606,000
Iceland (1956)	92.1	92,000	83,000
Sweden (1956)	79.8	4,887,000	3,902,000
United States (1956)	60.4	?	62,025,000

[21] A further complication in measuring nonvoting, if one is attempting to be precise, is determining the actual turnout at any given election. Usually, the highest vote cast for an office is taken as the total turnout, but not every voter who goes to the polls is given credit in official reports of election statistics. Unfortunately, some voters do not have their votes counted because of errors they make in marking paper ballots or because they do not vote for the office receiving the highest vote.

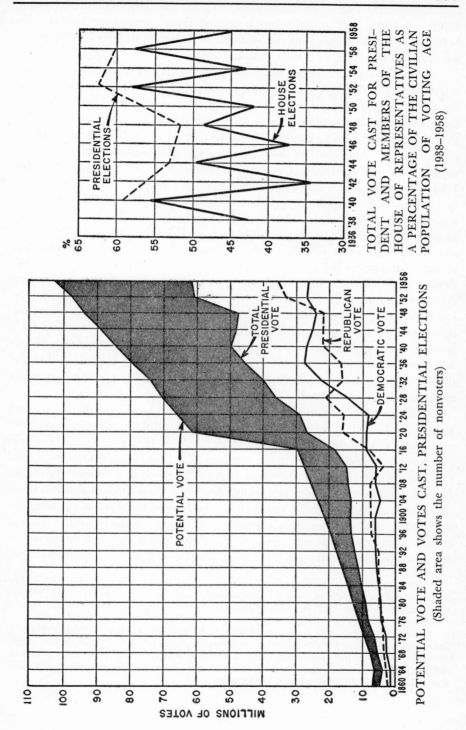

TOTAL VOTE CAST FOR PRESI-
DENT AND MEMBERS OF THE
HOUSE OF REPRESENTATIVES AS
A PERCENTAGE OF THE CIVILIAN
POPULATION OF VOTING AGE
(1938–1958)

POTENTIAL VOTE AND VOTES CAST, PRESIDENTIAL ELECTIONS
(Shaded area shows the number of nonvoters)

1952 and 1956, only seven states increased their percentage, the greatest being 3.6% in Alabama and the smallest 0.5% in New Jersey. The greatest decrease was 9.7% in North Dakota.

Not only do voters stay away from the polls but they are also often selective when they go. If we take presidential and congressional voting for the House of Representatives for comparative purposes, we begin with the assumption that millions more will turn out in a presidential election than in the intervening congressional election. In addition, a marked discrepancy exists between the total vote cast for presidential electors and for members of the National House of Representatives in the same election. Both this discrepancy and the lower turnout in non-presidential years can be seen in the accompanying graph, which, it should be noted, is a measurement of the civilian population and so includes aliens who are not eligible to vote. Voters brought to the polls by a presidential election will, at the same time, cast votes in other races which by themselves do not stimulate enough interest to bring out these voters. The high point in both presidential and congressional voting occurred in 1952 when the respective percentages were 62.7% and 58.7%.[22]

General elections, almost without exception, bring out more voters than direct primaries.[23] At general elections themselves, voters do not express a judgment in all races for office and, typically, are more interested in voting for candidates than voting on questions submitted to the electorate for decision. Occasionally a question on the ballot may attract a degree of voter attention comparable to that for candidates.

Within states there is a general pattern of larger turnouts to elect state officials and lower turnouts to elect local officials. One investigation of turnout in city elections in Kansas from 1920 to 1951 revealed an extreme range for the cities selected: from 1.1% to 92.1% of the potential vote, and a range for one city from 15.8% to 74.8%. The voting rate was highest in commission-governed cities, especially those that were cities of the first class. Turnout was higher when a number of members of the governing body was elected biennially rather than annually, and when a majority of the governing body was elected at one time. It was possible, for three of the cities, to compare turnout in city elections with that in national and state elections

---

[22] Between 1896 and 1916, 95 or 96 out of each 100 voters who voted for presidential electors voted for candidates for the House of Representatives; between 1918 and 1948, the ratio was 89 or 90 to 100. Malcolm Moos, *Politics, Presidents and Coattails* (Baltimore: The Johns Hopkins Press, 1952) pp. 16-18.

[23] V. O. Key, Jr., *American State Politics: An Introduction* (New York: Alfred A. Knopf, Inc., 1956) pp. 134-140. Between 1928 and 1948, this rule held even in the South: the voting rate per 1000 inhabitants for all Southern states was 144.3 in direct primaries and 158.4 in general elections. Cortez A. M. Ewing, *Primary Elections in the South* (Norman: University of Oklahoma Press, 1953) p. 104.

between 1932 and 1950. The median percentage in the former was 27.3 and in the latter, 65. The median percentage in city elections for the three cities, over all, was 42% of that in national and state elections; but again extremes were found for individual years where the percentage varied from 80% to 13%.[24]

As a generalization regarding the American voters, it appears that they will turn out for elections to fill offices in governments farthest away, elections featuring issues accepted as most dramatic and engrossing, although the voters may actually have less ability and opportunity to understand the issues. Voters most frequently neglect elections for offices closest to them, the elections in which they can actually be most fully informed about the issues.

Causes. Obviously, there must be reasons which account for the extent of nonvoting in the United States. These can be classified as conditions which disqualify people from exercising the franchise and as attitudes of indifference in specific elections or apathy regarding government in general.

Disqualifying conditions are usually temporary: illness, change of residence,[25] ineligibility to vote absentee, failure to pay poll taxes, previous felony convictions, inclement weather. A few may in fact be permanent: illiteracy and residence in Washington, D. C.[26] Disqualification may result from neglect or inconvenience: neglect to arrange for an absentee ballot, failure to register, dislike of crowded conditions at polling places or the difficulty of reaching them. Fears or social pressure may keep some citizens from voting. In one category is the Negro in some parts of the South who is afraid to register or vote. Other kinds of fears are that the ballot is really not secret and that the disclosure of one's vote will cause loss of business,

---

[24] Clarence J. Hein, *Voter Participation in City Elections of Cities with Populations between 5,000 and 50,000 in Kansas* (Lawrence: University of Kansas Publications, Governmental Research Series No. 18) Chapter III and pp. 59-61.

[25] In addition to California, *supra*, p. 421, four other states have relaxed the residence requirement for voting for presidential electors. Connecticut and Vermont permit absentee voting for a fifteen-month period following a move from the state; Wisconsin and Ohio permit residents of less than one year to vote, if otherwise qualified, if they were either qualified or would have been eligible to vote in the state from which they moved. See Morris S. Ogul, "Residence Requirements as Barriers to Voting in Presidential Elections," *Midwest Journal of Political Science*, Vol. 3 (1959) pp. 254-262.

[26] Since the nation's capital city is not a state, it elects no presidential electors or members of Congress. It is governed by Congress through an appointed commission, so there are no city elections. Until 1874 there was an elected city government, but Congress then provided for the present appointive one. Many employees of the federal government live in Maryland or Virginia and can vote, but no one whose residence is in the District can, with the possible exception of the informal party elections every four years to choose delegates to the national conventions.

limit job opportunities or retard professional advancement. Finally, some people report they do not vote because of disgust with political corruption or of opposition to political action per se.[27]

These causes account for some but only a minority of the nonvoters. The most important single reason can be labeled indifference or apathy. People do not often admit this reason, but it can be inferred from the excuses they give. Some of the above reasons may be only alibis or rationalizations. Some people give the naive answer that one vote out of thousands or millions is impotent, so why bother to cast it? If everyone took this view, there would be no elections. It may be genuine, but it is highly unprofessional, for no one connected with politics in any capacity is likely to agree. Every candidate is glad to get every vote he can. Pleas are often made to precinct workers, pointing out how easily past defeats could have been turned into victories by just one more vote in each precinct. There is no such thing as an impotent vote if it is counted. The search for reasons brings us to the question of interest or involvement in elections as the major determinant of voting turnout. The degree of interest affects the varying number of votes cast from year to year at different government levels, depending upon the issues involved and the sense of being directly affected by the outcome.

The evidence of differences among people which give rise to differences in frequency of voting is some measure of who is and who is not, relatively, interested and involved. These differences are not the reasons for voting or not voting, but they reveal the groups who are more likely to have or make up reasons for ignoring elections.

People who are most likely to be interested and therefore to vote are men with university education, in the upper economic levels, in their middle thirties and above, living in urban areas. Factors motivating those with less interest to vote are memberships in organizations and contacts with party workers during a campaign. People who spend comparatively more time reading about the campaign and listening to speeches and discussions are more likely to vote. The voting rate is significantly higher among those

---

27 It was estimated by the American Heritage Foundation that 17,000,000 persons were either ineligible to register or discouraged from voting in 1956 for one or another cause. *New York Times,* November 28, 1956. One of the growing problems is how an increasingly mobile population can meet residence requirements. Ralph M. Goldman, "Move—Lose Your Vote," *National Municipal Review,* Vol. 45 (1956) p. 6. In a nation-wide sampling in 1952, the ratio of those who said they failed to meet voting requirements equaled about 3 in every 100 adults but 26 in every 100 in the sample did not vote. Angus Campbell et al., *The Voter Decides* (Evanston: Row, Peterson and Co., 1954) p. 37. In Elmira, New York, in 1948, as the campaign progressed, fewer respondents said they would vote and fewer finally voted than had declared an intention to vote in October. Bernard R. Berelson et al., *Voting* (Chicago: University of Chicago Press, 1954) p. 31.

who feel strongly about the issues of a campaign; who are better integrated in their communities through such ties as home-owning and the belief that they have an obligation as a citizen to vote; and who feel that voting is worthwhile as a means of giving direction to public policy and choosing the better qualified candidates.[28] A qualification should be added that under some circumstances interest in an election may lead to nonvoting if the interest reaches a state of conflict between opposing sets of motivations. An interested person, thus torn between loyalties or desires, may resolve his dilemma by staying home from the polls.

The South as a section is consistently low in voting turnout compared with the remainder of the country. Even the low rate of Negro voting does not account for the whole phenomenon of Southern nonvoting. Southern whites vote in smaller proportions than Northern whites because the distinctive political system of the South is less conductive to stimulating interest in elections. Although restrictive suffrage provisions eliminate white as well as Negro citizens, low turnout in the South is probably more directly caused by the one-party system which by itself engenders apathy. The lack of contests both between parties in general elections and in the Democratic primary discourages voters, especially those who do not identify themselves with the dominant political party. The one-party system and the repression of contests which run the risk of whites appealing to Negro voters (as was the case during the Populist period) isolates the South from organization and campaign activities of the two major parties. The result is that Southern voter interest is reduced even in presidential elections.[29]

What to Do about Nonvoting? The implications of nonvoting are disturbing from the point of view of those who philosophically place value on the majority-vote processes of government and see minority rule in the widespread refusal of citizens to vote, a minority rule which is essentially evil. If the percentage of participation were to decline steadily, the majority of the small fraction which voted would indeed control public policies. As long as the actual electorate is large in absolute numbers and does not show a precipitous percentage drop over a period of time, these theoretical

---

[28] These findings are reported and discussed in *ibid.*—see especially pp. 336-337 for a compilation of findings in additional studies; Campbell, *op. cit.*, pp. 187-206; Paul F. Lazarsfeld et al., *The People's Choice* (New York: Columbia University Press, 1948) pp. 40-41; William A. Glaser, "Intention and Voting Turnout," *American Political Science Review*, Vol. 52 (1958) pp. 1030-1040. Charles E. Merriam and Harold F. Gosnell, *Non-Voting* (Chicago: University of Chicago Press, 1924), confined to the City of Chicago, was one of the earliest studies and helped to pioneer the field.

[29] V. O. Key, Jr., *Southern Politics in State and Nation* (New York: Alfred A. Knopf, 1950) pp. 505-508, 533-535. Warren E. Miller, "One-Party Politics and the Voter," *American Political Science Review*, Vol. 50 (1956) pp. 707-725. Ranking the states according to the percentage of their potential vote cast in the 1956 presidential election, the Southern states are the eleven lowest in rank.

dangers are more remote. The dissatisfaction with nonvoting has other over-
tones. There are predictions of doom for the American people if they do
not arouse themselves and evidence a keener appreciation of their birthright.

As a result, during election campaigns there is often a parallel campaign by various nonpartisan organizations to get citizens to vote. These
promotional activities are most marked during presidential elections when
people have the message drummed into them that their duty as citizens
demands that they vote. Casting a ballot becomes a badge of social re-
spectability. With all of the urgings from every source imaginable, it is
difficult to understand how anyone could fail to vote because he forgot
it was Election Day. Sometimes these campaigns give the unfortunate impression that knowledge or understanding is unimportant as long as the
voting totals are increased. This emphasis can give to voting the quality
of a mechanical process where the value lies just in going through the
motions.[30]

From time to time the alarms of reformers have given rise to proposals
for more vigorous measures to get people to the polls. One type of proposal
is to *offer an incentive,* usually through the application of tax laws either
by granting an additional deduction for voters or depriving nonvoters of
some part of their deductions or exemptions.

> Would it not be simple to arrange to deduct, say, only one half of
> this exemption (on income taxes), or three fifths, from the income of the
> taxpayer who does not vote at all elections simply because he is slothful
> or forgetful? The difficulties involved of checking up would not be great,
> because the tax collector could take the voting list, and in the absence
> of adequate explanation from those who do not vote, simply increase
> the tax bill.[31]

Actually, incentives are of two distinct types. In one type, the voter may
receive something he is not otherwise entitled to if he votes. In the other,
he is penalized in some way if he does not vote, i.e., he is *deprived* of something he is otherwise entitled to.

This second possibility is more than a simple incentive system, for the
law would require the overt action of voting. At this point, voting becomes
compulsory. The only feasible penalty for enforcing voting is a special

---

[30] By extension, duties of citizenship become equated with incidental benefits such as
muscle coordination (in marking a ballot or handling a voting machine) and testing one's
vision (in finding the levers on the voting machines or the squares on the paper ballots).
In another sense there is a hucksterism in these campaigns: "Go, now, before you forget,
to your friendly neighborhood election booth . . ."——Eric Larrabee, "Not the Number,
But the Quality of Voters," *New York Times Magazine,* September 28, 1952, p. 48.

[31] Samuel Spring in the *Atlantic Monthly,* quoted in Kent, *The Great Game of
Politics,* p. 190.

EXAMPLES OF ADVERTISEMENTS URGING CITIZENS TO VOTE.

Courtesy The Advertising Council, Inc.

New York Times Magazine, Sept. 28, 1952

tax or an increase in existing tax liability. This method is the reverse of the poll tax which one pays in order to qualify. Systems of compulsory voting first appeared in the American colonies in Plymouth in 1636. Virginia adopted it in 1646. Maryland had it from the beginning of its colonial history, and Delaware later adopted it. In Virginia and Maryland the punishment upon conviction was 200 pounds and 100 pounds of tobacco, respectively; in Plymouth and Delaware, a fine in money. The record of enforcement was very poor because of the excuses of having to do farm work and of having to travel great distances. Juries often failed to convict when an arrest was made, and in Virginia, at least, the law was steadily ignored with impunity.[32]

The case for compulsory voting is strengthened among those who want to swell the actual electorate as a positive and inherent good by drawing conclusions from foreign experience. In Australia after compulsory voting was adopted in 1925, the electorate swelled from less than 50% to 95% or more; in Belgium after compulsory voting was incorporated in the constitution in 1893, voting rose from 10% to 92% and over.[33] Furthermore, it is contended that to tax nonvoters will not necessarily bring to the polls a larger number of indifferent, uninformed, and thoughtless voters, because with the compulsion will go an incentive to be interested and informed. The forcing of a voter to the polls is made analogous to forcing children to go to school—compulsory voting and compulsory public education are alike since "the main idea is to get the schoolboy to the school, and the voter to the polls."[34] It is this attitude which distinguishes the advocates of compulsory voting. It is a personal right, true. But it is also a duty and can be enforced by the government because it is beneficial to society as a whole. Since eligibility to vote is determined by the sovereign power, it can also decide positively who is to vote and see that the voting is done.[35]

[32] Cortlandt F. Bishop, *History of Elections in the American Colonies* (Columbia University Studies in History, Economics and Public Law, Vol. 3, 1893) pp. 190-192; Charles S. Sydnor, *Gentlemen Freeholders* (Chapel Hill: University of North Carolina Press, 1952) pp. 32-33. North Carolina used compulsory voting in parish elections. In Providence, Portsmouth, and New Haven, those arriving late for town meetings could be fined.

[33] Robert Cobb Myers, "A Proposal to Tax Those Who Don't Vote," *New York Times Magazine*, November 6, 1949. In Australia the penalty for each violation is a set fine. In Belgium a series of graduated fines is provided through the first four convictions; the penalty thereafter is disfranchisement.

[34] *Ibid.* It is generally conceded that compulsory voting should apply only to general elections. To make it applicable to direct primaries would force voters to declare a party affiliation in most states.

[35] Although the contention (*ibid.*) that the essential ingredient between free societies and tyrannies is the method of arriving at decisions and that a coercion-free society

Objectives in Voting. By the same token, without the emphasis upon "duty" and the public right to compel individual conformance in this area of conduct, it can be equally contended that "the right to vote subsumes the right not to vote. . . . Under our system, in any case, the universal suffrage has not been universal, and was not meant to be. We exclude the immature and the unfit; why not also the indifferent?" [36] The difference is really one of objectives. Why is it desirable that people vote? Do we want a larger number of voters on the assumption that the bigger the better? Is this a further revelation of the American value judgment that improvement can be measured by the number of percentage points a line ascends on a graph? Is there an intrinsic value in the size of the vote itself? Do we actually want people to vote if they do not want to vote? The answer is that we want people to want to vote. This brings us full circle to interest and involvement as motivating voting. So, how do we get people interested and involved?

First, is there real doubt about the outcome of an election? Is it a genuine contest? There is little need to vote when one's ballot will not affect the outcome. Inevitably there is a sporting element involved in elections. If it is a race, with the factor of doubt present, the interest is likely to increase. Supplemental stimuli are the personalities of candidates for whom voters have strong likes and dislikes. To mobilize one's followers may also mobilize one's opponents. Interest in candidates and issues, even when the choices are not great, can stir citizens to action. Sometimes the choices are overdrawn, for one function of the candidate's campaign is to give good reasons for voting for him instead of his opponent. Second, does the outcome of an election matter? It it does not, then the incentive to vote is low. If it does, if one sees his interests involved some way, the incentive to vote is high. The two-party system, by its very nature of agreeing upon most fundamentals and arguing mostly about incidentals, often diminishes the incentive to vote because many citizens see no connection between their interests and the outcome. They know they will go on much as before and life will be neither intolerable nor a bed of roses despite the warnings of campaign speakers. The moderation and similarity of the two-party system are a depressant upon tense excitement or nervous disturbance about the outcome.

The question goes to the core of the dynamics of bipartisanism. If the objective is more voters, the parties should offer sharper choices. What

---

would be anarchic, not democratic, the fact remains that coercion is coercion whatever the form of government. The issue of compulsory voting properly involves the question of whether or not this kind of additional coercion is desirable.

[36] Larrabee, *op. cit.*

kinds of choices do we want and how extreme do we want them? Obviously, the presentation of more mutually incompatible choices by parties will be a sign of greater discord within the public, and the pursuit of those choices will not decrease the discord but will contribute to further disunity. It is not surprising that very high percentages of the electorate in other countries come out to support a variety of extreme and moderate programs involving issues of religion, the form of government, and ownership of property. It is instructive that the results produced by these high-percentage turnouts is quite similar to the results of smaller-percentage turnouts in the United States. The extreme forces contending for power are checked by their own and one another's limited support, and the government is taken over by a coalition which picks its precarious way through the gun emplacements of the cannonading warriors on both sides. Heretofore the unity of the United States has been more basic and compromise has flourished. If the objective of more voters overrides all others, it can be considerably achieved by the intensified opposition of segmental interests.

Significance of Nonvoting. To label nonvoters "apathetic," "indifferent," or something worse is an oversimplification of people and a misinterpretation of American society and its party system. The exhortatory personality is always likely to see lack of comprehension and dangerous passivity among those who do not respond positively to his appeals. The act of nonvoting is subject to generalities which fit only some of the nonvoters.

> Where is the line to be drawn? Is it apathetic not to vote when you literally dislike all the candidates? Is it apathetic not to vote in an area so heavily overbalanced by one party that you know it makes no difference? Is it less apathetic to vote for a hopelessly outnumbered party than not to vote at all? Does apathy necessarily imply a lack of passion or conviction? When the fanatical devotees of a man who has failed of nomination at a party convention say they will sit on their hands they, too, may abstain from voting, but they are not apathetic.[37]

Voluntary nonvoting can tell us a great deal about a nation, and its message is not necessarily unpleasant.

> In an age of well-organized constitutionalism there is reason for political abstention, since the values which motivate political conduct are secured under the organization of the limited, liberal state. The ballot is a form of protest which may be used as occasion demands in order to enforce a somewhat negative yet effective responsibility upon those who are the elected representatives of the people. A realistic view of the be-

---

[37] *Ibid.* See the discussion in Riesman, *op. cit.*, pp. 55-69.

havior of democracies leads one toward the belief that there is no danger in the continued absence of a large number of the legally established electorate from the voting booth. When men have what they want from the political order, there is insufficient excitement in campaigns to draw all of them to the ballot box on election day.

. . . Government by the few voters who make an appearance on election day may be corrupt, it may be the very foundation of the continuance of the old party oligarchy, but at least it is certain that the political waste is less than the mass of the people will stand.[38]

REFORMED REPRESENTATION

Proposals for getting more votes, if necessary by compulsion, find some parallel in proposals to reform the election system by making it possible for minority groups or parties to be more securely represented in legislative bodies. The theme behind these proposals is that votes cast for losing candidates or excess votes cast for winning candidates are "wasted" votes as opposed to "effective" votes cast for winners who need the votes in order to win. The objective is to reduce to an absolute minimum the number of "wasted" votes. When applied to the election of legislative bodies, these systems require the abandonment of the single-member district system because it results in a large percentage of "wasted" votes even when a majority of all the votes cast is required for election.[39] When a plurality alone is sufficient to elect, a clear majority of the total vote may be cast for losers and be "wasted." "Effective" votes are increased when a voter has an opportunity to concentrate his voting power (as in cumulative voting) or to express choices among the candidates (as in preferential voting and proportional representation). The assumption unifying the arguments behind the proposed systems is that a voter wants his vote to count for a winner and that a scheme which increases this likelihood will result in a fairer system of representation.

Cumulative voting as used to elect the lower house of the Illinois legislature is the oldest existing system in the United States based on these reform proposals. It was adopted in Illinois in 1870 in order to break up the pattern of the Republicans sweeping the northern half and the Democrats the southern half of the State in every legislative contest. Under this system the single-member district was replaced with three-member districts on the assumption that the majority party in each district

---

[38] Francis G. Wilson, "The Inactive Electorate and Social Revolution," *Southwestern Social Science Quarterly*, Vol. 16, No. 4 (1936) pp. 75, 76; Francis G. Wilson, "The Pragmatic Electorate," *American Political Science Review*, Vol. 24 (1930) pp. 16-17; Moos, *op. cit.*, p. 156.

[39] See Ewing, *Presidential Elections*, pp. 174-188, for illustrations of wasted popular and electoral votes in presidential elections where a majority is required.

would elect two members and the minority party, one member. Each voter can cast a total of three votes—the number of candidates to be elected in each district—in any one of four ways: three votes for one candidate, one vote for each of three candidates, two votes for one candidate and one vote for another, or one and one-half votes for each of two candidates.[40] Illinois law gives political party committees in each district the power to determine how many candidates of its own party are to be nominated. In 52% of the district elections between 1920 and 1952, there was actually no contest in the general election because the Republicans and Democrats nominated between them only three candidates.[41] In proportion to the number of votes cast for the two parties state-wide in all districts, each party elected approximately its proportionate number in each election from 1940 to 1952.[42]

A second system, *preferential voting,* can be used in either single-member or multimember ditsricts. The voter can indicate his choices among candidates, usually without limit, by placing a mark in the columns after each candidate's name. A mark in the first column is a first choice, in the second column a escond choice and in the third column a third choice (which can be indicated for any of the remaining candidates). In fact, it is usually first or second choices which elect. If a candidate has a clear majority of first choices, he is elected. In case no candidate has this many first choices, either of two plans can be followed. By the *Bucklin plan* (long used in and associated with Grand Junction, Colorado) all second choices are added; then if a candidate has a majority of the combined number of first and second choices, he is elected. Each voter in this plan is counted twice. If necessary, the winner is determined on the basis of the number of all choices. By the *Ware plan,* the candidate with the least number of first choices is eleminated, and the ballots on which he was first choice are counted for the candidate marked as second choice; this procedure, known as the single transferable vote, is continued until a winner is produced on the basis of combined first, second, or sub-

---

[40] George S. Blair, "Cumulative Voting: An Effective Electoral Device in Illinois Politics," *Southwestern Social Science Quarterly,* Vol. 34, No. 1 (March, 1954) pp. 3-4.

[41] *Ibid.,* pp. 15-17. In 13 district elections, 1920 to 1950, voters had a choice of three out of five candidates; in 410, a choice of three out of four candidates; and in 453, no choice. A party committee would be loath to nominate so many candidates that the scattering of votes would defeat them. The practice is to nominate the number of candidates the party voters can elect by cumulating their votes, and by tacit agreement at least, the minority party in most districts elects one member. "Since the election of 1872, one party has succeeding in electing all three representatives in only thirty-two districts or in only 1.5 per cent of the district elections."——*Ibid.,* p. 11.

[42] *Ibid.,* p. 13. Consequently, the minority party is always well represented, and only in the sessions of 1875 and 1913 did neither major party have a majority of all seats. For additional comment on these features, see George S. Blair, "The Case for Cumulative Voting in Illinois," *Northwestern University Law Review,* Vol. 47 (1952) pp. 344-357.

sequent choices. Preferential voting is now at a low ebb of popularity after a period of extensive use early in this century.[43] The success of the system depends upon voters making more than one choice, and their failure to do so helped to bring about abandonment of the system. It is also subject to manipulation and then becomes self-defeating.

Proportional Representation (PR). While preferential voting eliminated the need for a direct primary and reduced the number of "wasted" votes by requiring majorities, it failed to attain the highest standard of mathematical exactness. Proportional representation (or PR, as it is familiarly known) with the single transferable vote, is frequently referred to as the "Hare system," after the Englishman Thomas Hare whose book— *The Election of Representatives, Parliamentary and Municipal,* London, 1859—first popularized the subject.

To begin with, a formula is worked out for application to a multimember district to determine the electoral quota. The *electoral quota* is the minimum number of votes a candidate needs to be elected. By comparison, in a single-member district the electoral quota is a plurality of the vote if that is sufficient to elect, or a majority of the vote if that is required. In the case of PR, the electoral quota is arrived at by dividing the total vote cast by the number of candidates to be elected plus one, and adding one to the answer: Thus, in a hypothetical case, if three positions are to be filled and 120,000 people cast ballots, the computations are:

Number of candidates plus one: $3 + 1 = 4$
$120,000 \div 4 = 30,000$
$30,000 + 1 = 30,001$, the electoral quota

The electoral quota is 30,001, since no more than three candidates can receive this number of votes and the "wasted" votes are held to the irreducible minimum. The voters express choices for as many candidates as they wish by writing numbers 1, 2, 3, etc. by separate candidates' names. Only one choice can be expressed for one candidate, as in the case of preferential voting, but the use of numbers instead of marks makes the procedure more exact, and ultimately no more than one vote is counted for each voter.

At the conclusion of the election, after the electoral quota is computed, *the ballots are separated into piles according to the first choices and a count of each pile is made.* If any candidate has the quota on the basis of first choices, he is elected. In case this unlikely event should hap-

---

[43] At one time or another, ten states used it in direct primaries but gradually gave it up: Alabama, Florida, Idaho, Indiana, Louisiana, Minnesota, North Dakota, Oklahoma, Washington, Wisconsin. It was also used for varying periods in as many as seventy cities, among them Cleveland and Toledo, Ohio; San Francisco, California; Newark, New Jersey; and Denver, Colorado.

pen, he would undoubtedly have not exactly the quota, but more than the quota; and the problem would be to take away from him the excess ballots, because they are not needed and are "wasted" on him. One method is to select at random the number of ballots in excess of the quota and distribute them to the candidates marked as the second choice. A more exact method of distribution is by proportion. Take the hypothetical case used above, where the quota is 30,001. Assume that candidate A receives 40,000 first choices. His surplus is 9,999 ballots. All of the 40,000 ballots are examined to discover which candidates received the second choices on them. Assume that candidate B is the second choice on 20,000 of the ballots, or on 50%; that candidate C is the second choice on 12,000 of the ballots, or on 30%; and that candidate D is the second choice on the remaining 8,000 ballots, or on 20%. Then candidate B receives 50% of the 9,999 excess ballots, candidate C, 30%, and candidate D, 20%.

A much more likely discovery after the ballots are initially arranged according to first choices for candidates is that no candidate has attained the quota. The procedure then is to eliminate the candidate with the least number of first choices and distribute his ballots to the candidates marked as second choice on each of them. This process goes on until the number of candidates to be elected receive the quota, and by the redistribution of ballots as candidates are successively eliminated, choices as high as tenth or more may eventually be counted for a winner and become "effective." [44]

PR apparently has passed its peak of popularity and has been on the decline for several years. Whether it will ascend to another peak is, of course, a matter of prophecy. Its greatest long-time victory was in Cincinnati, Ohio, where it was adopted in 1926 and abolished in 1957. Its greatest short-term victory was in New York City from 1937 to 1947.[45] This bruising defeat seemed to signal a temporary eclipse, at least for the movement. At no time has PR been a sweeping success in the United States. Its

---

[44] In order to simplify the explanation of PR, its advocates have adopted the analogy of an election held without ballots where the voters sit in chairs, each under the banner of his first choice candidate. The same number of chairs, equal to the electoral quota, is placed under each banner. If all the chairs under a banner are taken by voters, that candidate is elected and any additional supporters he has go to the banner of their second-choice candidate and sit down, if chairs are still empty. When voters under one banner recognize from the number of empty chairs that their candidate cannot win, they disperse to their respective second choices and so on. See George H. Hallett, Jr., and Clarence Gilbert Hoag, *Proportional Representation—The Key to Democracy* (New York: National Municipal League, 1940, 2nd ed.) pp. 38-42.

[45] See Belle Zeller and Hugh Bone, "The Repeal of PR in New York City—Ten Years in Retrospect," *American Political Science Review*, Vol. 42 (1948) pp. 1127-1148. A variation in New York was a fixed electoral quota of 75,000 for each Borough.

complexity has not endeared it to the general public. Even when people have understood the explanations of the system's mechanical operation, they have sensed their own inability to appreciate or anticipate the implications. By and large the problem of "wasted" votes and the lack of minority representation have not greatly impressed large numbers of citizens. The two-party orientation and lack of speculative thinking have been further bars to more widespread consideration. Leaders of the two major parties have almost without exception opposed PR with fierce tenacity, and its reception is usually clouded from the moment the subject is introduced.[46]

In the Western European multiparty systems, PR is very popular, since it permits representation in accordance with splinter party strength more nearly than single-member districts would. Many variations of it are in vogue in Europe, including the List System previously used exclusively and now used partially in Germany.[47] The list is the names of the parties without names of candidates on the ballot. Voters mark the ballots for a party, and for every so many votes it receives, the party is entitled to a member in the legislative body. Party leaders designate which members are elected, and the voters have no control over this selection. This system dehumanizes and deglamorizes elections about as fully as possible.

PR has been especially heralded in the United States as a cure for corruption and bossism in city governments, the outstanding example being Cincinnati. While it has not been based on the doctrine of the right of the state to order that groups of a given size be permitted to elect a representative, the possibilities for minority representation have been constantly claimed as one of its virtues. PR proponents accept and believe in organization by and for candidates, but the values of minority representation and the elimination of "wasted" votes are considerations which override any value in the two-party system. While this reform has been urged at the municipal level, its advocates make it plain that their system applies equally well to all elections and they constantly draw examples from statewide and district elections to illustrate the unfairness of the single-member-district system.[48]

---

[46] It is clear that the constant enmity of Democrat and Republican leaders in New York City contributed substantially to the repeal of PR, since PR deprived them of their control over nominations. The immediate entering wedge in helping to achieve repeal was the election of two members of the Communist Party to the New York City Council during the period when awareness of and opposition to the Soviet International Conspiracy was on the increase in the United States.—*Ibid.*, p. 1137.

[47] James K. Pollock, "The West German Electoral Law of 1953," *American Political Science Review*, Vol. 49 (1955) pp. 107-130.

[48] Cortez A. M. Ewing, *Congressional Elections, 1896-1944* (Norman: University of Oklahoma Press, 1947) Chap. 6, found that the size of the United States tends to nullify the inequities of the single-member district as between Republicans and Democrats be-

Additional merits allegedly are the representation of compatible constituents who can be served by one person instead of a heterogeneous geographical area composed of conflicting interests which one person cannot serve simultaneously; the freedom of voters to have a wider selection of candidates instead of the ones provided by the party organization; the ending of problems of reapportionment and of the abuse of gerrymandering (i.e., arranging districts for the benefit of one political party); [49] the opportunity for able people to be elected and exercise leadership, particularly in view of the tendency toward longer tenure under PR; the increase in voter interest both before and after the election.[50]

PR is a change in the electoral system of great moment. However, if it is only the application of a system to a condition already in existence, it is the change in the dynamics of society that is most noteworthy. Some of the acrimony stirred up by PR is really reflective of a difference over fundamentals lying back of election systems. Yet, the machinery is not entirely a thing apart from the underlying conditions, and the controversy over PR is directed toward its effects rather than its causes.[51]

The main objection to PR is that it magnifies differences within the population and puts a premium upon intransigence. Representatives have a vested interest in constantly dramatizing their solidarity with their ideological constituents and their opposition to other groups. The success of the representative, it is alleged, depends upon his constantly fostering and appealing to the real or manufactured interests of those he depends upon for votes. Looked at in reverse, "a despotic constituency" [52] is adamant in wanting its interests advanced, and excesses are fostered by permitting groupings of extremists wherever they live.

---

cause of the unequal distribution of party strength in one-party states and one-party sections. Republicans won more seats than they earned in the East, Middle West, and West; the Democrats in the Border and the South. Minor parties, taken as a whole, suffered most, but the inequality was not so striking when they are considered individually as splinter votes.

49 On this problem, see "Symposium on Legislative Reapportionment," *Law and Contemporary Problems,* Vol. 17 (1952). Charles W. Shull, "Revitalizing Representation," *Social Science,* Vol. 25 (1950) pp. 234–238, suggested that apportionment of state legislatures be based upon the voting turnout rather than population.

50 Hallett and Hoag, *op. cit.,* Chap. 4. Zeller and Bone, *op. cit.,* give considerable attention to the pro-and-con arguments in New York City, but they make clear their own preference for PR, so they tend to appreciate the sympathetic arguments.

51 Walter Bagehot, *The English Constitution* (1892, rev. ed.) pp. 216–226, made an effective attack upon PR. The outstanding contemporary opponent of it in the United States is Ferdinand A. Hermens, who has spoken and written against it in both books and articles. See *Democracy or Anarchy: A Study of Proportional Representation* (Notre Dame: University of Notre Dame, 1941) and *Europe Between Democracy and Anarchy* (Notre Dame: University of Notre Dame, 1951).

52 Bagehot, *op. cit.,* p. 224.

The effect of proportional representation is to fill the legislature with men who are immoderate and uncompromising. For under proportional representation the constituents of a Representative are not the people living in a geographical area but an abstract group of voters who all think alike. A Representative does not have to consider those who may differ with him. He is merely the delegate of those who think alike. Therefore, he is not predisposed to moderate views and to compromises but to irreconcilability and extremism.[53]

A PR constituency is a like-minded group which makes internally consistent demands, so is less inclined toward external compromise. A geographical constituency is a multiminded group which compromises internally and is thereby prepared to compromise externally. A PR constituency can be formed on any kind of mutually compatible basis—race, nationality, religion, or class.[54]

The second objection, which follows from the first, is that to encourage people to fragment themselves for the sake of an isolated representative or two is to destroy the two-party system and with it responsible government. In the babbling of minority voices in legislative bodies no coherent program can be carried through, because there is no effective majority or leadership. The result is the same confusion and chaos that is found in European multiparty systems. Although the answer is usually given that the multiparty conditions preceded PR and that the system is not revolutionary but simply an adaptation to the conditions,[55] it is difficult to see how PR would contribute to strengthening the two-party system—"it is certain that proportional representation always coincides with a multiparty system: in no country in the world has proportional representation given rise to a two-party system or kept one in existence." [56]

PR is not always a confusion of minorities, for—as in Cincinnati—it was

---

[53] Walter Lippman, syndicated column, reprinted in Hearings before a Subcommittee of the Senate Judiciary Committee, 83d Cong., 1st sess., August 1, 1953, p. 192.

[54] The argument over PR's encouragement of ethnic voting goes on unceasingly. Warren Moscow, *Politics in the Empire State* (New York: Alfred A. Knopf, Inc., 1948) pp. 48-49, pointed out evidence of ethnic voting in New York City. Zeller and Bone, *op. cit.*, pp. 1140-1141, found the picture was mixed. On religious voting they found that Catholics constituted 22% of the population but had 53% of the representation on the council; Protestants, 46% of the population but only 21% of the representation on the council; Jews' representation was about equal to their proportion of the population.

[55] Hallett and Hoag, *op. cit.*, pp. 97-98.

[56] Maurice Duverger, *Political Parties: Their Organization and Activity in the Modern State* (New York: John Wiley & Sons, Inc., 1954) p. 245, see also pp. 242-255, 304-317, 328-330, 358 ff., 383 ff. Ewing, *Congressional Elections, 1896-1944*, p. 99, showed statistically how the two-party system has made for a safe party majority in the House of Representatives. For every 1% of the popular vote polled by a major party, it won 1.33% of representation. That is, the "majority-party vote percentage took its proportional share and one-third of another seat, which by the proportional standard belonged to minor parties."

used where minority representation was not the predominating problem. If a unity already exists, PR would not neecssarily destroy it; but PR is a handy tool for disrupting unity. The least that can be said is that a concern for the preservation of the two-party system will not be demonstrated by the encouragement of PR. Where the necessary conditions for a two-party system do not exist, as in New York City, support for PR is not as such inimical to the two-party system. Just the same, even in this case the support is an acceptance of the formalizing and compartmentalizing of disunity which is less subect to restraint with PR.

Caution should surround the use of the word "wasted" when referring to votes. It should be used only in the very limited meaning of votes cast for candidates who are defeated. There is an easily understandable tendency to impart additional meanings, so that "wasted" becomes a synonym for "useless," or "ineffectve." If thought of in this sense, the concept of "wasted" would lead to the docrine that only votes cast for winning candidates are of importance and—by extension—that everyone should be able to vote for a winner in order not to waste his vote. To permit everyone to vote for winners would give elections the appearance of unanimity or acclamation, everybody wins and nobody loses. There is a salutary psychological effect upon a winner of knowing that many of his constituents preferred the losing candidate.

Voters should be presumed to have integrity, to support their candidates and party even if they do lose. Second or subsequent choices may be only desperation, blind or unthinking choices, marked on the ballot because the rules allow the voter this leeway. Voters who are steadfast supporters of a candidate really have no second choice. If they are confused and uninformed about the candidates, no choice, whether one or up to infinity, can be described as anything other than a guessing game. PR is helpful, first, to voters who actually have alternative choices because they have no overwhelming choice; and, second, in situations where the candidates are not sufficiently different or divided as to intensify political controversy. At best it is limited in the kinds of political situations in which it promotes intelligent voting and in which it does not tear down more than it builds up.

PR is something more than a simple election reform to rid the citizens of evil politics. It raises basic questions and it involves, both as a cause and an effect, the whole dynamics of the political system and the society.

Selected Bibliography

Abraham, Henry J., *Compulsory Voting*. Washington, D. C.: Public Affairs Press, 1955.
Bagehot, Walter, *The English Constitution*, rev. ed. New York: D. Appleton & Company, 1892.

Follett, M. P., *The New State.* New York: Longmans, Green & Company, Inc., 1923.

Hallett, George H., and Clarence G. Hoag, *Proportional Representation—The Key to Democracy.* 2d ed. New York: National Municipal League, 1940.

Hermens, Ferdinand A., *Democracy or Anarchy? A Study of Proportional Representation.* Notre Dame: University of Notre Dame, 1941.

—— *The Representative Republic.* Notre Dame: University of Notre Dame, 1958.

McGovney, Dudley O., *The American Suffrage Medley.* Chicago: University of Chicago Press, 1949.

Merriam, Charles E., and Harold F. Gosnell, *Non-Voting.* Chicago: University of Chicago Press, 1924.

Ostrogorski, M., *Democracy and the Organization of Political Parties.* 2 vols. New York: The Macmillan Company, 1902.

—— *Democracy and the Party System in the United States.* New York: The Macmillan Company, 1910.

CHAPTER TWENTY-FOUR

Should We Overhaul the Machinery?

The constant attempts to improve the caliber of government in the United States in terms of the value judgments of the various reformers are evidence of ferment in thinking. Despite differences in motives, varying from highly idealistic to calculated schemes for self-advantage, the ferment is a vocal testimony to dissatisfaction with the *status quo* and to the belief that human institutions can be improved in their manner of operation. Even among those reformers who accept permanent political organization and traditional political processes, there is the pale cast of the politics-is-sin doctrine in the open suspicion of political leaders and the objective of promoting greater participation by and representation of individual citizens. Instead of setting out to abolish politics, these reformers would cleanse politics by reorganizing its procedures. In this chapter these reforms will be considered as they apply to the machinery of presidential nominations and elections.

PRESIDENTIAL NOMINATIONS

Value of National Convention. The outstanding fact about the national nominating convention is its extralegal character. It is purely an evolution of political-party usage, neither required nor described in any federal legislation. The congressional caucus appeared briefly and then succumbed to the widespread opposition and dissatisfaction it created among politicians and the citizenry. The national convention was created as a more workable system than any other alternative to the caucus.[1] On its comparative record, the national convention has done well. Its unbroken use since 1840 has established it by the pragmatic test of time. It has worked without statutory regulation or violence beyond epithets and occasional fisticuffs. As an invention it has filled the void created by necessity.

Dissatisfaction with National Convention. If this much can be said positively, a great deal more can be said negatively. Its long history has been paralleled by frequent castigations from both professional and lay sources. The life of the convention has been one of frequent change in its procedures and composition, but these reforms, far from quieting the reformers, have tantalized or goaded them on to make new demands for

---

[1] For the rise of the caucus and the transition to the convention, see above, pp. 157-170.

procedural improvements. In some respects these thrusts against the national convention are reminiscent of those against the congressional caucus; but in the meantime the popular impulse has grown stronger, the effects of political power more far-reaching and deep-seated, and the stakes in the contest much higher. As more general attention has been given to the machinery, the attacks have grown; when few knew or cared how it worked, dissatisfactions were few. The nation-wide televising of both conventions in 1952 made a greater public impact than any other one development. Many people, little impressed with verbal descriptions, opened their eyes both literally and figuratively. "So," the general response seemed to be, "this is what has been going on all of these years!"

When the indictments of the national convention are surveyed, they suggest unhappiness both with the convention machinery and with the convention itself. It is not surprising that politicians should be leaders in a reform movement affecting methods of nominating candidates for office. Their motives may result from personal convictions, from following a popular ground swell, from the desire to have machinery they can more likely operate. Politicians attack the national convention as a device of other politicians to exclude the people from participation, and urge that the citizens be permitted to nominate their own presidential candidates. They, like many others, denounce the machinery of the smoke-filled room as unresponsive and cumbersome. These sentiments are echoed in letters-to-the-editor columns of newspapers, in editorials, in the writing and speaking of columnists and commentators.

The specific suggestions are as varied as the people who make them. The voter is far removed from the nominating process; the existing "primaries are only partly democratic and bosses control conventions." [2] There should be "some uniformity in the primaries," but at least the delegates should be protected from both the bosses and the public gallery at conventions by being permitted to vote secretly on the roll calls.[3] Not all presidential candidates are entered in any state's primary, so the voters are limited in their choice; the independent voter is excluded from primaries; delegates should be bound by the state-wide preference vote.[4]

---

[2] Clayton Knowles writing in the *New York Times*, February 24, 1952.

[3] George Sokolsky, syndicated column, July 17, 1952.

[4] Thomas L. Stokes, syndicated column, March 6, 1952. For a wide variety of expressions by politicians and journalists, see *Preference Primaries for Nomination of Candidates for President and Vice President,* Hearing before the Subcommittee on Rules of the Senate Rules Committee, on S. 2570, 82d Cong., 2d sess., March 28, 1952 (hereafter cited as Hearing on Preference Primaries). When President Harry Truman referred to presidential primaries as "eyewash," the reaction was wholly adverse or bitter, and he reversed himself soon thereafter. See *New York Times*, March 2, 1952. Fifty-three Democratic members of Congress petitioned their party's platform committee to include a plank favoring a nation-wide presidential primary law.——*Ibid.,* July 15, 1952.

Alternatives. The objections, in following one of two directions, can be satisfied by either one of two corrections. Mere opposition to "bosses," to their selfish political motives, and to control of the machinery by professional politicians can conceivably be removed in large part by reforming methods of selecting delegates, controlling the delegations, and operating the conventions. In the second direction, this opposition is so strong and the insistence upon maximum voter participation is so intense that no alternative but a nation-wide direct primary for presidential candidates is acceptable. The objections and proposals do leave a choice between reforming the convention and abolishing the convention or curtailing its role. Each of these in turn will be taken up.

CONVENTION REFORM

Original State Legislation. The most outstanding change in the national convention system would be the election of the delegates by the party voters in each state. The initiative in this movement was taken in Wisconsin in 1905 under the regime of Senator Robert M. La Follette, Sr., with a law requiring the direct election of delegates. Pennsylvania provided for electing district delegates in 1906. The first law providing for a preference vote on presidential candidates was adopted in Oregon in 1910, although the practice was first suggested in Alabama in 1908. Both election of delegates and the presidential preference primary spread until by 1916 they seemed on their way to becoming nation-wide. A reaction set in, and the movement not only stopped but also receded when the legislation in several states was repealed or invalidated.[5] During the 1940's and 1950's the movement came to life again, but this time it was not developed piecemeal in the states only. A uniform national system was the major center of interest.

Attempts at Federal Legislation. In 1951 and 1952 Congress seemed to bustle with the activity of proposing constitutional amendments relating to presidential nominations. Because of the lateness of the interest, an improvised bill was introduced in the Senate authorizing the Attorney General to conduct primaries for presidential and vice-presidential candidates of parties polling more than 10,000,000 votes in 1948. Each state would have been able to take part through a voluntary agreement and would have been paid 20¢ for each vote cast in its primary.[6] Neither this stopgap measure nor any of the proposed constitutional amendments came to a vote in either house, and a bill providing for a more permanent system

---

[5] See Louise Overacker, *The Presidential Primary* (New York: The Macmillan Company, 1926) Chap. 2, for the history up to the time of her book.
[6] See Hearing on Preference Primaries, pp. 1–2, for text of this bill.

of voluntary agreements died in committee in the next Congress.[7] If to do were as easy as to wish, the selection of delegates by popular vote could be accomplished and bring an end to the troublesome subject.

To decide that delegates should be elected is merely to begin a chain of questions.

(1) Should all delegates be elected at large, or should those delegates to which a state is entitled by virtue of its House members be elected within districts? [8] This choice poses the traditional value judgments of preference between the all-or-none system or permitting definable areas within a state to select delegates separately. The at-large system strengthens the party organization, assuming it can win a state-wide primary election, by permitting the state to operate and negotiate as a unit at a convention. It does mask any minority views, and when election is by a plurality, may give representation to only a minority. The combination of at-large and district election more accurately mirrors factional and sectional sentiments, but as a consequence may encourage and magnify them by giving them expression at a convention. No solution to this problem can be considered either orthodox or ideal. Results produced by either system will vary from state to state and from time to time. Political evaluations are very likely to be made on the basis of the circumstances of the moment.

(2) Can or should the party organization be prevented from controlling the election of delegates? A body of "popular" opinion strongly maintains that the organization *should* be prevented, and since it should, it can be. The way to do it is for the voters to elect the delegates directly. This line of reasoning proceeds on the assumption that the motives of organization leaders are unworthy and at odds with the general welfare; that, properly speaking, the organization should be frozen out of the process as far as possible; and that the selection of delegates is the people's business anyway, not the "bosses'." These premises have great popular persuasive force, but the assertion that party processes should be divorced from party organizations is both fanciful and self-defeating. Election of delegates requires organization. If the party organization is neutralized, the void will be filled by presidential candidates' organization within a state. The organizations of these candidates are aligned with and dependent upon existing organizations of the party and of permanent or temporary private groups. Often the party organization is itself split, with factions supporting different candidates and forming part of those candidates' organizations. Where a party organization exists, it cannot be suspended by fiat of the advocates of unhampered "popular choice." The desirability of the competing presidential candidates fighting for support in a state without any

---

[7] See Paul T. David *et al.*, *Presidential Nominating Politics in 1952: The National Story* (Baltimore: Johns Hopkins Press, 1954) Vol. 1, pp. 217–218.

[8] For a pro-and-con discussion of this question, see Overacker, *op. cit.*, Chap. 5.

use being made of the state's party organization can be debated endlessly. The possibility is not open to question, for no such possibility exists.

(3) What should be the position of delegates when the balloting begins at a national convention?[9] It is highly desirable that voters, when they have a choice of candidates for delegate, know which are pledged to which presidential candidates and which are unpledged. It is essential that the delegates, when giving a pledge, have the integrity to carry it out by voting for the presidential candidate at the convention. These objectives are balanced by the possibility that between the time the delegates are elected and the time for voting in the convention various events may completely change the picture. If they had known the new situation, the people might have voted differently. Even when the time between election of delegates and convening the convention is short, convention developments themselves may require a complete reorientation of attitudes. A great deal of invective is expended upon the candidacy of uninstructed delegates and upon pledged delegates switching their allegiance during the convention balloting. The uninstructed delegation is rarely encouraged and little more than provided for as a means of last resort in most proposals for electing delegates. After all, it is argued, the objective is to give voters a choice among presidential candidates of their party. The candidate for delegate running unpledged or unbound by a preference vote offers no alternative to the voter except a void, an invitation to elect political schemers to bargain away the people's interests for selfish political interests.

What if all of the elected delegates are pledged, but no presidential candidate has a majority of the delegates? For the convention to make a nomination, some delegates will have to switch candidates. Are the delegates to be prohibited from switching without the consent of the candidate they are pledged to? If the candidates refuse to release their delegates, the convention would be permanently deadlocked, and the bitterness of the fight would threaten the party's chances to win the election. If delegates, either on their own initiative or under the leadership of their respective state party organizations, cannot maneuver, all vitality in the convention machinery is destroyed. Supplemental practices also intended to permit flexibility would for better or for worse become difficult or impossible. Reformists' opinions are generally unfriendly to "favorite son" candidacies as encouraging "deals" and contributing to delegate manipulation for personal gains.[10] A favorite son may at times be the best answer to the problems of the party leadership, and the rank and file may be willing to support him in preference to any other candidate on the horizon. In fact, the handicap of a favorite son may be his unfamiliarity in other

---

[9] David, *op. cit.*, pp. 213–224.
[10] See Clarence A. Berdahl, "Presidential Selection and Democratic Government," *Journal of Politics*, Vol. 11 (1949) pp. 35–40.

states, and his candidacy is a means of overcoming the handicap. This may be the only way for an aspirant from a relatively small state to get a start. Not only favorite sons but also any candidate without immediate vote appeal in a large number of states would be eliminated if delegates were all directly elected and unreservedly bound by commitments.

The process of negotiating and reconsidering is often damned as "selling out" and "making deals." The virility of words should not blind us to realities. Of course, delegates make "deals" or "agreements." What do we expect them to do? Complicated situations, which arise because so many factions must be placated, cannot be brushed off as exhibits of immorality or meaningless confusion. This machinery for accommodation, for harmonizing disputes and conflicts, is one of the chief functions of parties because it is a prime function of government. It will be performed at some point under compromise conditions despite denunciations. Human beings cannot remain suspended indefinitely in an idealistic atmosphere which creates a vacuum in the practical affairs at hand. Whether intended or not, delegates cannot avoid exercising independence as the necessity arises.

(4) What will be the effect of not permitting candidates to select the states in which they enter their names? Under current practices, presidential candidates determine which states' presidential primaries to run in, according to their prospects for winning. Unless a preference vote is mandatory in all states for all candidates, they can continue to pick and choose their battlegrounds. If all states elected delegates at the polls and if these delegates were usually committed at the time of their election, a presidential candidate would have to enter a large number of states in order to win enough delegates to have a real chance of being nominated. Nevertheless, he would not have to enter all states. If the election for delegates should be held on the same day in every state, presidential candidates would not have to worry about a poor showing in one state hurting them in another, as they do with the present system.

A further question (assuming that candidates, as either a legal or a practical matter, do not have to be entered in every state) is the policy regarding "popularity contests." A few states have provided that candidates can be entered in a preference primary without their consent and even in opposition to their wishes. The result can be a large number of candidates, each one testing his popularity against the whole field. Wherever this practice has been permitted, it has been a continual source of contention and generally has been repealed after some experience. While it is argued that the voters of a state should be able to express themselves on all of the presidential candidates of their respective parties, some candidates may be damaged seriously by being compelled to submit themselves to voters where no groundwork in publicity has been laid.

(5) A fifth question can be asked, looking to the underlying assump-

tion of primaries: Should all delegates be selected in the same way? Specifically, should they be elected in every state? Frequent affirmative assertions appear. It was contended that preference primaries as guides to delegates would produce "better Presidents. . . . They will not be obligated in the way they are now, to small groups; but they will know when they speak to foreign countries and at home, for that matter, that they have back of them the guys in the drug stores as well as the people in Wall Street offices. . . . When a candidate goes before the people to ask their endorsement, there is more chance that he will be selected on his merits than where he must run the gamut of deals, tricks, and convention ballyhoo." [11] This point of view assumes that no other machinery except direct election of delegates will achieve these high purposes and that all states must fall into step. The passion for conformity vies with the passion for a particular method. This insistence presumes that all citizens want to have primaries, and no account is taken of differences in people or the effectiveness of dissimilar processes from state to state. On the other side, machinery which works satisfactorily for those directly involved should be respected on the basis that when it is unsatisfactory, it will be changed. These two views are and always will be strangers to each other.

In the congressional hearings on the preference primary bills, only the question about uniformity was answered. Aside from agreeing on the superiority of primaries, the members of Congress preferred to pass the responsibility for dealing with the details to others. As Senator Paul H. Douglas (Democrat, Illinois) frankly admitted regarding his bill, "there are a lot of these difficulties which we shunt aside, so to speak, and put them on the shoulder of the Attorney General." [12] Discretion properly is left to administrative officials, and statutes should not fix details or make government too rigid. In the case of the various questions about operations

---

11 Statements of Representative Charles E. Bennett (Democrat, Florida) in Hearing on Preference Primaries, pp. 22, 23.

12 *Ibid.*, p. 6. A Model State Presidential Primary Law drafted by Richard S. Childs, chairman of the executive committee of the National Municipal League, and distributed by the League in mimeograph form, contained features pertinent to some of these questions. Voters would register their party affiliation by November of the year preceding the election year, and the primary would be held in June of election year to allow maximum time for voters to inform themselves. The state committee of either party, by majority vote, may certify a slate of uninstructed delegates. If this slate is uncontested, no election is held. A presidential candidate may file a slate of personal delegates without petition, but must deposit $1,000, to be returned if he receives 10% or more of the vote cast in his party's primary. Voters must vote for a single slate, and a number of delegates are elected from each, in proportion to the vote the whole slate receives. The delegates on each slate are numbered consecutively to establish the order in which they will be elected. A delegate can run on both the uninstructed and a presidential slate. If elected on both, he would have two votes in the national convention. Childs testified regarding his plan in *Nomination and Election of President and Vice President*, Hearings before a Subcommittee of the Senate Judiciary Committee, 83d Cong., 1st sess., June 11, 1953, pp. 38–45 (hereafter cited Hearings on Nomination and Election).

of preference primaries there are no answers forthcoming, and many of the questions deal with something more than details, e.g., Should runoff primaries be provided, or should nominations be made by plurality? The solution of passing the questions on to someone else in no way contributes to clarification but attests to the complications. To undertake this system will mean that at some point these questions will be answered one way or another. The continuing discussion may well be a further testing ground for developing answers and new evaluations.

MANDATORY NATIONAL DIRECT PRIMARY

Variety of Provisions. Various proposals in the form of constitutional amendments were presented in the early 1950's to substitute a national direct primary for national nominating conventions. This reform is really the logical end of the anticonvention tradition. Even popular election of delegates voting on presidential candidates cannot overcome the allegedly undesirable characteristics of conventions, which have been indicted simultaneously for being meaningless, immoral, and a threat to democracy.[13] The zeal to achieve this reform has been tempered by practical considerations for attaining the two-thirds congressional majority and the three-fourths majority required. Outlines of the prospective procedure include presidential candidates' filing, with some federal official, petitions bearing signatures equalling approximately 1% of the total vote cast in the previous presidential election. Whether nomination should be made on a plurality or on a majority basis is openly at issue. Sometimes provision is made for independent candidates to get on the general-election ballot by filing a petition with a federal official; sometimes such candidates are ignored. There is no question of setting a uniform primary date for all states, and the proposals usually fix a date no later than July 1, but would give Congress power to fix a different day.

A variation, designed to appeal to some states, was the proposal that the electoral votes be used instead of popular votes in making nominations. The presidential candidates in each party would receive the proportion of the electoral vote which their popular votes entitled them to in each state, and the nominee in each party must receive a majority of all of the electoral votes, if necessary through a runoff primary.[14] One proposed amendment simply would give to Congress the power to provide for nomination of

---

13 See Herbert Agar, *Pursuit of Happiness* (Boston: Houghton Mifflin Company, 1938) pp. 128–136.

14 This system would produce a new sort of inequity. For example, Republicans running in Alabama would be at an advantage because they would divide the entire Alabama electoral vote among them on the basis of the very small popular vote cast by the Republican voters in the State.

President and Vice-President by primary elections in the states, territories, and Washington, D. C.[15]

Some of the questions already raised in considering the direct election of delegates and preference primaries for presidential candidates are pertinent again, but some different questions also come to mind.

(1) A question that applies with or without conventions, but more acutely without, is: What will be the results upon campaign costs and public costs? Here are two separate questions. Candidates would have to finance their own campaigns in every state in the Union, just as each political party does for its ticket in the general election. If party organizations in the states helped out particular candidates, other candidates would be at an even greater disadvantage without a large amount of money. There would likely be spirited competition for contributions from those people with money to give. The undertaking would be stupendous for a candidate and his own organization unless he had access to such sources. All of the perennial problems of limiting expenditures and contributions would reappear in a more accentuated form. Each candidate who won the nomination may still be compelled to put up money for the general election and still be in debt from the primary. Comments on this point either evade the issue or amount to saying it is a tremendous problem which should be re-examined.[16]

The costs to the public of holding nation-wide direct primaries would be substantial, but not prohibitive nor objectionable, if people wanted to use the method. No doubt, the federal government would bear some of the expense, relieving the states of some of the burden, and incidentally making state officials more receptive to the idea. By combining this direct primary with the regular one held in the states, costs could be reduced. This practice, in turn, could create new problems. Assuming that a national direct primary is held on a specified date, the states would have to coordinate their own direct-primary dates to make the two coincide. In one fell swoop, voters would have the responsibility of choosing all nominees for all offices on the same day, an extension of the long ballot.[17] Finally, the result would be a direct infusion of national and state issues into the state and presidential races, whereas one of the objectives sought by some

15 For texts and testimony on these several resolutions, see *Constitutional Amendments*, Hearings before a Subcommittee of the Senate Judiciary Committee, 82d Cong., 2d sess., March 26 and June 27, 1952, pp. 23–46; Hearings on Nomination and Election, pp. 1 ff.

16 Senator Estes Kefauver (Democrat, Tennessee) argued that direct primaries would give a poor man a better opportunity than conventions because he could find enough money to travel and news media would cooperate by giving him free time.——*Ibid.*, p. 34. See also Hearing on Preference Primaries, p. 10.

17 While this situation may be undesirable in many ways, Overacker, *op cit.*, pp. 30–31, showed that more votes were cast in presidential primaries when held in conjunction with state direct primaries.

of the advocates of a presidential direct primary is to free presidential politics from the influence of state politics now found in the national convention. The scale of relative values would obviously have to be agreed upon in working out these features of a national direct primary.

(2) The question of how to avoid "raiding" is the most difficult to answer. The various proposals are consistent in specifying that voters be limited to their own political party, but the determination both of partisan affiliation and of eligibility to be a voter is left to the states. The qualifying provisions merely state that voters be members of their parties or of the party of their "registered affiliation." The implication is that states not already registering affiliations will be forced to adopt such a system.

Unless the entire voting machinery of the United States were nationalized, each state would continue to determine party affiliation for all direct-primary elections held under its jurisdiction. There is no reason to assume that the existing practices regarding switching affiliations would or could be changed substantially. In fact it is doubtful if the practice would be materially affected if Congress enacted the statutes, except that the open primary would be officially abolished. The results of raiding in a presidential direct primary could be extraordinary, and the occasion for switching affiliations would be presented every time an incumbent President was a candidate for a second term and was too strong for anyone else in his party to challenge him in the primaries. There being no contest in the "in" party, some of its voters would be wanting to vote in the "out" party's primary. The general effect may be a periodic advantage for the "in" party. If those switching their allegiance voted in the best interests of the other party and did not raid, the results would not necessarily be so unhappy. If a successful raid were conducted, the results may well be momentous to the victimized party. What constitutes a permissible occasion for switching is sometimes a matter of opinion, as the Republicans demonstrated in Texas in 1952 when Democrats were encouraged to attend Republican conventions to elect Eisenhower delegates.

In any event, confirmed party members should not be voting in the other party's primaries, and a national direct primary would be likely to lead to a campaign to enforce a system of closed primaries, while the open-primary supporters would probably remain adamant in opposition. The plight of the independent voter would be different, but not necessarily any happier. He would still be excluded from the nominating process unless he chose to become affiliated, and by this act would cease to be an independent. Perhaps it would be the independently inclined voter who would be most likely to switch his affiliation from time to time, and, it would be hoped, would enter a primary as a qualified convert not as a raider.

(3) If a national direct primary were adopted, what would happen

to the national convention? It could be abolished for the reason that its real purpose had ended. In this case the process of preparing a party platform would be undertaken either by the victorious nominee and his advisors or by some type of party gathering other than a convention, e.g., the party's members of Congress. The national convention may be continued as a platform-writing conclave, but as such it would be a tame affair if convened after the nomination was made. It would of necessity be dominated by its candidate, and the platform would be the one on which he wanted to run. A convention to write the platform could be held before the direct primary. The competing candidates could appear before it and make suggestions for planks and pledge themselves to run on the platform as it would be adopted. Some assessing of the nomination situation could be made, and the candidates would have this opportunity to make an impression on party colleagues and to use the convention as a sounding board in speaking to the nation. A final possibility is the adoption of a preprimary convention to pick one presidential candidate to go on the ballot in all states, other candidates to be qualified by petitions. Conversely, a postprimary convention could be utilized to select the nominee if no one received a majority of the votes in the direct primary.

Whether the convention met before or after the nomination, its composition would presumably command less popular attention and controversy if the delegates had no control over the nomination. Perhaps the delegates would be chosen by party process rather than election. If the convention met before the candidate was chosen and the delegates were directly elected, the competition undoubtdely would center around the competing presidential candidates. Then if delegates ran formally or informally pledged to specific candidates, the election would provide some forecast of the impending national direct primary. If the delegates had the power to make a preprimary designation or a postprimary selection, the choice of delegates would be crucial enough for a contest at the polls. The piling up of elections in presidental years—for delegates, for presidential candidates, for a runoff (if required) for state direct primaries, for Southern runoffs in the Democratic Party, and for the general election in November—would indeed make it an election year in the fullest sense of the word.

(4) The method of nominating vice-presidential candidates is a consideration. Some of the proposals for nomination by direct primary include both offices and presume that candidates for Vice-President would come forward just as presidential candidates and that a dual contest may be waged in each party. The practice of the past is not especially reassuring on this point. Few politicians announce for the second place on the ticket, even

if that is their ultimate hope, but make nominal bids for the presidential nomination. They are found in the ranks of the favorite sons, as delegates, or as bystanders who have made no public announcement. Sometimes they are important contenders in the presidential balloting. To expect politicians openly to court the second spot on the ticket is to revolutionize politics and raises the question of what caliber of Vice-Presidents we would have.

An alternative method is to nominate only presidential candidates at the national direct primary. Either the candidate could select his running mate or suggest him to a postprimary convention which would ratify the choice. Whatever else is done, it is highly probable that the presidential nominee will continue to have a part in the selection of the second person. The potential importance of the Vice-President would justify separate selection at a primary, but the usage of over a century stands in the way. To make the candidate running second in the presidential direct primary the candidate for Vice-President would most likely insure a more desirable person, but would risk incompatibility between the two candidates of a party. In addition, the possibility of extraordinary results, embarrassing to the party but impossible to change, is enough to preclude this method.[18]

THE CASE FOR THE CONVENTION

Intensity of Opposition. It would be possible to conclude from the survey of literature uttering deprecations upon the national convention that it has nothing to recommend it. Few pieces of political machinery have been subjected to such unending criticism. Some opponents, like Ostrogorski, have observed and revolted. Others have seen the byplay, the holiday spirit, the "immorality," and have been aghast.[19] Constantly there are variations on the theme that the convention is not representative, that it ignores the public, that its selections are made in a vacuum and on the basis of finding amenable candidates.[20] If the people are insistent upon changes, they will come, irrespective of the many harassing questions to be decided in setting up the new machinery or even the entire accuracy

---

[18] For example, in a national direct primary in 1948 the Democrats of the nation may have preferred some other candidate to President Truman, and it is conceivable that he would have come in second. Thus the incumbent President would have become a candidate for Vice–President.

[19] Agar, *op. cit.*, p. 130, wrote that the delegates to the Democratic convention in 1936 "wondered whether the way to run a great political party is to get drunk and ride donkeys into hotel lobbies, or to scream hideously for half an hour because the chairman has just announced" something everybody has known for months. The point overlooked here is that no "great political party" has been run this way. This kind of conduct is likely to accompany conventions, but it does not determine their outcome.

[20] Hearings on Preference Primaries, pp. 8, 84, 87, where Senator Paul H. Douglas indicted the Democratic conventions of 1904 and 1924 on these grounds.

of the charges.[21] To read tributes to or praises of conventions is a breath out of the past no matter when the words were written.

> To me a convention has all the drama inside and outside of a spectacle in sports, like the world's series, a championship fight or an Army-Notre Dame game. I love the holiday mood of the crowd. I love the restless surging of the delegates, part actors and part spectators. I thrill to the marches and songs. I am fascinated by the activity in the press sections. I delight in the oratorical cadences. I love the bustle of the platform, heavy with political notables. I am enthralled by the drama of a roll call. I am carried away by the color and frenzy of a demonstration. To me the waving state standards are more beautiful than a field of tossing grain. I love the popping of flashbulbs, the endless surge of noises, and the thick and often simmering atmosphere. To me it's *the* great American show. There's not a dull moment in it.[22]

Competition and Struggle. The final question to be raised is the standard for determining what is efficacious in presidential nomination machinery. Since struggle and controversy are parts of representative government, it is not in the realm of the possible that nominations can be made by a process of sweetness and light. On this point an instructive contradiction is often revealed by Americans. Although they are repelled by political competition, considering it dirty or degrading, they seem to respond to suggestions that issues and candidacies should be brought into the open for discussion and decision. The latter process cannot be accomplished without conflict and even bitterness. The fights which we all at one time or another disparage are inherent in our kind of government. Sometimes we may be inclined to overlook this inevitability. The refinement of our civilization tends to obscure and submerge competition, making it more difficult to detect and more indefensible to assert. Competition goes underground when objectives can be better attained by denying that there are any objectives which only competition can achieve.

The challenge in finding nominating methods is to balance popular control of the government and of parties with the opportunity for integrity

---

21 "The Presidential Primary," editorial in *New York Times*, July 15, 1952. The editors of the encyclopedic survey of nominating processes in 1952 concluded that the evidence of bossism in the two conventions that year was mostly among some Southern Republicans and in delegations under the control of governors who depended upon their public offices for their authority and who were not likely to continue to have that authority when they left office. An observation unconnected with "bossism" was that participation in delegate-selection processes was not widespread largely because citizens would not take part.—— David, *op. cit.*, pp. 170 ff.

22 James A. Farley, *Jim Farley's Story* (New York: McGraw-Hill Book Company, Inc., 1948) pp. 273-274. Sidney Hyman, "Where the 'Man Who' Will Come From," *New York Times Magazine*, March 1, 1959, pp. 60-62. Two Democratic leaders, Adlai E. Stevenson and Robert B. Meyner, put themselves on record against the presidential preference primary as it now exists. *Ibid.*, April 4, 1956 and June 2, 1958.

and responsibility within the parties, not to repress struggle. Achieving this end is neither easy nor capable of being systematically blueprinted. The higher degrees of success are the result of the spirit operating the machinery, and the spirit is often far more important than the machinery itself.

"The main argument for the convention," in the words of Professor James MacGregor Burns, "is simple. It works." [23] It works by providing the arena for adjustment in the task of nominating candidates for President of a continental world power. The stirring up of emotions, the appeals to party tradition and to meaningless symbols of party doxology, repel some observers as failing to reflect the bookish maxims of the rationality of men. These emotional techniques are proven and effective means for arousing people and getting them to act. Not only is the national convention useful as an emotional purgation, but also in the process it creates the enthusiasm among the party workers necessary for winning an election. These features are in the nature of human beings and are not to be attributed to the machinery of national conventions, which have merely exploited and harnessed these human characteristics.

Evaluation of Candidates. Many people see presidential candidates in terms of the stereotypes created by news media, of their own preconceived notions of what kind of person a statesman is, of their partisan biases. Speeches, press hand outs, and carefully timed letters or articles do not permit people to know candidates, but only to know what is told or shown about candidates. Impressions can be formed by the new techniques of persuasion.[24] This problem is frequently enough raised in choosing candidates on a state-wide basis, where information can filter down more readily because it has less distance to go. On the national level who knows the candidates? Most citizens in the country do not, but the men and women who have worked with the candidates in politics do. The party leaders, the "bosses," know them and can evaluate them as no mere voter in the primaries can.

When the leaders make a nomination, they are testifying to their acceptance of the candidate, and the voters in the general election have some recommendation to go on in making their final selection. It is not correct as a generalization that the practice of party leaders is to nominate candidates for their amenability even at the risk of losing the election. When an election appears hopeless, leaders may make a different selection than if they were confident of victory, but the fates are too undependable to

---

[23] "The Case for the Smoke-Filled Room," *New York Times Magazine*, June 15, 1952.
[24] Malcolm Moos, "New Light on the Nominating Process," *Research Frontiers in Politics and Government* (Washington, D. C.: The Brookings Institution, 1955) pp. 156-159.

be toyed with, and a stand-in candidate may be elected. Leaders do not, as a rule, care to risk an undesirable candidate on the assumption that he will lose. The examples of 1904 and 1924 in the Democratic Conventions are not especially convincing. What alternatives did the Democrats have in 1904? Only Mr. Bryan, who was then a two-time loser. The nomination of Alton B. Parker can hardly be classed as presenting a mediocre man or a wheel horse of the organization. What were the Democrats to do in 1924? The convention was deadlocked between Alfred E. Smith and William G. McAdoo, neither of whom could win. A compromise choice was the only solution; and John W. Davis was not a vacuum candidate who could be manipulated at will by the "bosses," nor was he a second-grade man by any standards.

Challenge of Understanding the Machinery. Sometimes the discontent with political processes is an expression of citizens' frustration because they do not understand what is happening or how it happens. The view amounts to saying, "Politics must be made simple enough for me, or I won't play." [25] The reason they do not understand the machinery may be inability to understand or disinterest or literal lack of time and opportunity for understanding. Intelligent participation by citizens is obviously based on a comprehension of what is being done and what their part in the process is; but complicated political machinery is a by-product of large-scale representative government. It is part of the price to be paid. If simplicity is the over-all objective, some other form of government will have to be adopted. To sweep away caucuses and conventions in order to get a simple system that everybody can understand without effort will lead to disillusionment.

Modifications of Conventions. If the national convention is to survive, the reform of its procedures must continue to conform with contemporary opinion. Although the basic form and procedure of conventions cannot be changed, they can be reformed in many respects, e.g., the elimination of prolonged delegate disputes. One of the great advantages of direct election of delegates is settling once and for all who is properly elected and entitled to a seat in the convention. There is no reason why certificates of election cannot be issued by a state government official to delegates selected in conventions. Disputes could then be aired and settled in the first instance in the state courts or by administration action instead of being left to factional infighting. These decisions even by state officials would not be binding on a national convention, but may discourage the losing side from appealing to the national convention, since its case would be embarrassed from the start. The real correction lies, not in the con-

---

[25] Eric Larrabee, "Not the Number, But the Quality of Voters," *Ibid.*, September 28, 1952.

vention nor its procedures, but in party organization in the states. When there is no longer any question as to what body constitutes the Republican hierarchy in such states as Georgia and Mississippi, most of the delegate disputes will come to an end.

Much of convention procedure is slow and can be speeded up. When marking time for a committee to complete its work, an afternoon or evening session can be omitted or kept off the air so as not to exasperate the public with long-winded speeches instead of the regular commercial programs. Too many and repetitious speeches are delivered with no one paying any attention anyway. Now that the convention can be brought into any home, the monotonous interludes must be reduced wherever possible or the national convention will be overthrown by the demand of a bored and irate television public.

PRESIDENTIAL ELECTIONS

Status of Presidential Electors. The electoral-college system has been vastly changed by usage since the adoption of the Constitution. Originally, presidential electors were considered a constitutional branch of the federal government and as representatives of the people in choosing the President— a responsibility given to them instead of to the Congress.[26] This machinery, while retaining its function superficially, has been thoroughly overhauled in the course of the development of the political system. Members of legislatures are conceded a representative status. On some occasions they are expected to exercise their own judgment and not always act entirely as agents of their constituents. Convention delegates actually play the representative's role from time to time despite a body of opinion that they should only act in conformance with the wishes of the party voters electing them. Long ago presidential electors were, in effect, deprived of any independence of action and were made agents of the voters pure and simple. The function of representation is accepted in legislative bodies, grudgingly admitted in conventions, but completely outlawed in the electoral college. The three gradations of voting—on measures involving general public policy, on nominations, and on general elections—are not considered comparable for the use of representative institutions.

The official seal of approval has been placed upon the agent status of electors, both in state and federal courts. In 1944 threats of rebellion by electors of the Democratic Party were quelled: in Texas by the state supreme court's holding that electors must vote for the party candidates, and in South Carolina, by direction of the state committee. In 1952 the Alabama

---

[26] Lucius Wilmerding, Jr., "Reform of the Electoral System," *Political Science Quarterly*, Vol. 64 (1949) pp. 15-16.

Democratic Executive Committee exercised the power delegated by act of the Alabama legislature and required electors to pledge themselves in advance to the nominees of the party. When one of the electors specifically refused to be bound, an unsuccessful effort was made in the Alabama courts to remove him from the ballot. The Supreme Court of the United States reversed the decision on the ground that the Constitution does not prohibit such action nor does it require a state party to accept as an elector a member who refuses to be bound by the official nomination. Even the Alabama court threw out the contention that the legislature lacked the power to make such a delegation of power to a state committee.[27] Where the state legislature has neither directly nor by delegation provided for such enforcement, electors can, apparently, announce an independent attitude and follow it. The nature of the political system precludes resort to this right except in rare cases.

Objections to the Electoral College System. Despite this adaptation of the electors' role to the requirements of a party system, the electoral college has had few publicly announced friends. Beginning with the first congressional proposal for change in 1797, just ten years after the system was written into the Constitution, rarely has a session of Congress adjourned without at least one suggested amendment changing or abolishing this machinery. It is difficult to track down all of the charges against the college, but it is simple to point out the essence of them.

(1) The entire paraphernalia strikes some people as inherently indefensible, not only for its essential falseness but also for its implied limitations on the individual voter, who cannot vote directly for President and Vice-President. This theoretical deprivation of the voter alone would be enough to motivate some reform, especially when the electoral-college system is erroneously considered to have been conceived entirely as a scheme against the people's right of suffrage.[28]

(2) The use of electoral votes, especially with election of electors at large in every state, is opposed because the effect is to magnify or minify the popular vote cast. Presidential candidates do not receive a number of electoral votes proportional to their popular votes, and voters who cast ballots for the losing slate of electors in each state are disregarded in the final result.[29]

---

[27] *Ray* v. *Blair*, 343 U. S. 214 (1952). The constitutional argument by the recalcitrant Alabama elector was that the Twelfth Amendment limits an elector to voting for no more than one candidate from the same state as himself and that additional limitations were unconstitutional. This contention the Supreme Court specifically disagreed with.

[28] See Wilmerding, *op. cit.*, pp. 14-15, and above, pp. 154-155.

[29] For examples of disparities between popular and electoral votes, see Cortez A. M. Ewing, *Presidential Elections* (Norman: University of Oklahoma Press, 1940) pp. 136 ff.; Hearings on Nomination and Election, p. 52.

(3) Disproportions are built into the system by the fact that the electoral college favors the small states by giving them more weight than their population is entitled to and favors the largest states, which are unduly catered to in elections. The first objection is meaningful philosophically in a nation in which elections and voting are high in the scale of values. The second objection has little if any practical meaning, for it does not rest on the contention that the actual winner is not the just winner. The third objection goes to the heart of part of the political arrangement among the states hammered out in the Constitutional Convention of 1787.

(4) A special complaint against the electoral college is one of the most familiar and is raised freely by both those who would abolish it and those who would just reform it. Elections by electoral votes frequently result in "minority Presidents," i.e., Presidents who have a minority of the popular vote. Whether this situation is alleged to occur frequently or not, the allegation itself is constantly made. Different observers point out different elections as examples of the evil, but invariably they mention the elections of 1876 and 1888. These two years are the prize exhibits, inasmuch as only the two major-party candidates received electoral votes. In all of the other examples, the electoral votes were split among three or four candidates, and it is no reflection on the electoral college system that the winning candidate in a three- or four-cornered race received less than a majority of the popular votes; at least in these cases, the winner had a plurality of the popular votes, except in 1824.[30]

The years 1876 and 1888 are unique, and upon them the case against "minority Presidents" rests. Actually, the case rests unqualifiedly only upon 1888, when Grover Cleveland (Democrat, New York) had a plurality of popular votes, but Benjamin Harrison (Republican, Indiana) had a majority of electoral votes. This election is the classic operation of an

---

[30] Since 1824, when popular votes were first recorded, thirteen presidents have been elected with less than a majority of the popular vote:

| | | % of votes: | |
Year	President	Elec.	Pop.
1824	Adams	31.8	29.8
1844	Polk	61.8	49.3
1848	Taylor	56.2	47.3
1856	Buchanan	58.7	45.3
1860	Lincoln	59.4	39.9
1876	Hayes	50.1	47.9
1880	Garfield	57.9	48.3
1884	Cleveland	54.6	48.8
1888	Harrison	58.1	47.8
1892	Cleveland	62.4	46.0
1912	Wilson	81.9	41.8
1916	Wilson	52.1	49.3
1948	Truman	57.1	49.5

electoral-college victory based on slim pluralities and majorities in large states and large losses in smaller states. While endless hypothetical cases can be conjured up, at least once the real case occurred.[31] The difficulty with the election of 1876 is that it was too confused to prove much of anything at all. Because of frauds by both parties the returns from three states were officially in doubt, and returns from other states can properly be questioned. No official popular vote was certified, and each party announced its own total. The practice is to accept the count issued by the Democrats, but no one can have full confidence in it.[32]

A reversal of the criticism of "minority Presidents" is the objection to the requirement that a candidate must get a majority of the electoral votes or the House of Representatives chooses the President. The only actual example illustrating this point is the election of 1824, when Andrew Jackson had a plurality of both the popular and electoral votes but J. Q. Adams was chosen by the House. In this way, it is pointed out, a minority candidate with a plurality was passed over in favor of the candidate with an even smaller minority who was the runner-up in the balloting.[33] The Twelfth Amendment provides that the House shall choose from among the three highest candidates if none has a majority in the electoral college. Judging from 1824, this provision can result in the election of a candidate with the smallest or an intermediate number of electoral votes. Inadvertently the majority-vote requirement can result in the defeat of a plurality candidate. A separate objection to choice by the House is that balloting is done by states and not by individual members.

Hypothetical Shifting of Votes. An incidental or indirect criticism of the use of electoral votes is the quadrennial sport after every presidential election of showing how the result could have been changed by shifting a few thousand votes in a few selected states from one candidate to the other. Or conversely, by shifting some strategic votes to the other side, a close election could have been a rout. These exercises demonstrate that either a close vote or a landslide in a state produces the same result in the electoral college when the state elects all electors at large. These exercises

---

31 Cleveland carried all of the states of the former Confederacy with comfortable to overwhelming majorities except Virginia, where he had a plurality. In the six other states he carried, his majority was thin in Delaware, Maryland, Missouri, and West Virginia; in Connecticut and New Jersey he had only a plurality. The only state with a large electoral vote that Harrison carried handily was Pennsylvania. Cleveland won 33 electoral votes from states where he had a plurality; Harrison, 101, which was half the number needed to be elected.

32 Edward Stanwood, *A History of the Presidency from 1788 to 1897* (Boston: Houghton Mifflin Company, 1898) Chap. 25; Ewing, *op. cit.*, pp. 21–22, 137; Ruth C. Silva, "The Lodge-Gosset Resolution: A Critical Analysis," *American Political Science Review*, Vol. 44 (1950) pp. 90–92.

33 See House of Representatives, Report No. 1199 from the Judiciary Committee to accompany H. J. Res. 19, 82d Cong., 1st sess., p. 18 (hereafter cited as House Report). Silva, *op. cit.*, pp. 90–91 answers the objection regarding 1824.

are, of course, fruitless in any sense, although they serve to remind us that "the result in a single State cannot be disassociated from the result in other States. . . . It is ordinarily the case at every election that some precincts, districts, counties, or States are carried . . . by narrow margins; and it is those which make the difference between victory and defeat. That the same thing is true of our Presidential elections is not a good ground for criticism of the electoral system." [34]

Abolish the Electoral Votes Entirely. The most pertinent complaints about the results of the electoral college can be itemized as follows:

(1) The distortions of the popular vote by its translation into electoral votes which, in addition, misrepresent the states' populations.
(2) The possibility of duplicating the unusual circumstances of 1888.
(3) The undemocratic feature of not permitting people to vote directly for presidential and vice-presidential candidates.
(4) The requirement that the House of Representatives, voting by states, settle unresolved elections.

These features are required by provisions of the United States Constitution except for the at-large (general-ticket) method of election, which is a constitutional usage. It is significant that the feature which is most responsible for the distortions in the electoral college is the voluntarily adopted method of election at large.

Growing out of these complaints, the proposals for reform turn first to the direct corrective of abolishing the electoral college outright.[35]

Putting the issue so bluntly brings into immediate focus the continuing justification for assigning unit votes, in the form of electoral votes, to each state.[36] Essentially, the reasons are still the same as they were in

---

[34] Stanwood, *op. cit.*, pp. 18, 19. These various objections are discussed in: House Report; Berdahl, *op. cit.*, pp. 25-28; Dayton David McKean, *Party and Pressure Politics* (Boston: Houghton Mifflin Company, 1949) p. 641, adds a few more objections, such as, preserving sectionalism; "enhancing the power of pressure groups; driving the two major parties toward meaningless similarity; and discouraging minor parties and parties with coherent programs."

[35] One of the most inveterate proponents of abolishing the college was the late Senator George W. Norris (Republican and Independent, Nebraska). He finally brought the issue to a vote in the Senate and was defeated. See Joseph E. Kallenbach, "Recent Proposals to Reform the Electoral College System," *American Political Science Review*, Vol. 30 (1936) pp. 924, 928-929. The cudgels were then taken up by the late Senator William Langer (Republican, North Dakota) who continued to introduce the Norris proposal session after session. See Hearings on Nomination and Election, pp. 61-73 and 116 ff. Supreme Court Justices Robert H. Jackson and William O. Douglas, in dissenting in the 1952 Alabama case described above, note 27, departed from the issues involved by urging the abolition of the electoral college as a gain for "simplicity and integrity."——*New York Times*, April 16, 1952.

[36] The justification is much weaker or nonexistent in the case of the county-unit system. See above, pp. 150-152.

1787 when the Constitution was written. To elect wholly by popular vote is to reflect not only the relative differences in population among states but also the variation in the voting turnout. The electoral college system was adopted as a method for protecting the small states against the large states by giving the former the same equality in the college that they have in the United States Senate. It was also a method for protecting any state where the vote happened to be below normal in one given election, because a state's weight in the electoral college is not predicated upon the number of voters going to the polls, but upon a dual formula reflecting both equality of the states and their population.[37] While this reasoning was understandable enough in the 1780's, it is now hardened and ingrained by practice. Political vested interests of the smaller states are too directly involved for anyone to expect their leaders to give up their advantage without great effort and a tremendous change in political evaluations.

That this logic of the electoral college, supported by what is now immemorial usage, is highly persuasive if not impregnable has been shown repeatedly by most of those who want to make changes. When challenged to go the limit in their proposals for reform, they respond that outright abolition is impossible to achieve, politically speaking. Even if a two-thirds majority can be mustered in Congress, far less than three-fourths of the state legislatures can be expected to cooperate.

(1) Nine states have over half the population of the country. These have eighteen Senators and eighteen electoral votes for those Senators. Thirty-nine states have the other half of the population, with seventy-eight Senators and seventy-eight electoral votes for those Senators. This represents the compromise by which the Constitution was adopted.

(2) In the election of 1932 each elector chosen represented a national average of 231,000 voters. In twenty states, however, the electors were chosen by a local voting average of 10 per cent and more below the national average. If their votes were made part of a national pool and so counted, without first translating them into electors, these states would lose 10 per cent and more of their power to determine the national result. . . .

(3) But this 'evil,' implicit in the Constitution, is minimized by the fact that the twenty states are scattered over the map of the Union. They are in every section. Since most bitter political controversies in this country have been sectional, this distribution forecloses the probability that all would support one candidate.

(4) Under the Constitution there is no universal law of suffrage. Each state has the power to determine the qualifications of its voters, and no amendment withdrawing that power could be approved. The result is that a much larger percentage of voting eligibles exists in one state than another. Hence the influence on a national election of states

---

[37] Hearings on Nomination and Election, pp. 152–153. The most acute problem in 1787 as far as voting turnout was concerned involved the South, where slaves were disfranchised.

with stronger limits on the privilege of suffrage would be greatly reduced if the units of electors are done away with and choice made directly by an over-all popular plurality. . . .[38]

Abolish the College and Proportion the Votes. The answer to these very real obstacles to electoral-college reform is a method which corrects the weaknesses without abolishing electoral votes. This objective can be realized only by abolishing the at-large method of election. One frequent proposal has been to divide a state's electoral votes among candidates in the same proportion as the state's popular votes are divided.[39] If a presidential candidate were to receive 50% of a state's popular vote, he would also receive 50% of its electoral vote. Since percentages would not come out evenly, the proposals generally require that the vote for each candidate in each state be computed to three decimal places only, unless carrying it further would change the result. Plans have varied regarding the specific plurality required for election. After the Senate in 1950 insisted upon at least 40% of the electoral vote as necessary for election, plans have varied on this point from requiring an outright majority to requiring a plurality of 35%. Previously the Lodge-Gossett Amendment would have given the victory to the candidate with a plurality, no matter how small, and would have settled the unlikely case of a tie by awarding the office to the candidate with more popular votes. Usually the authors of these plans have retained the feature of congressional settlement in case of a tie or of no one getting a minimum plurality. Election would be either by the House, voting by individuals, or by a joint session of Congress, voting as individuals. All of these same provisions would apply to the choosing of a Vice-President.

The proponents of this particular type of change point to a number of *advantages to be achieved.*[40]

(1) The problem of getting the states to agree to such an amendment is not so great because each state retains its electoral vote, and therefore its individual weight and separate identity, in presidential voting.

(2) The all-or-none system of at-large elections is wiped out.

(3) By adopting a plurality requirement in the electoral votes, situations like that of 1888 cannot be repeated.

(4) By eliminating presidential electors the hazard of their voting independently is removed and voters can be sure that their intentions will be executed in the casting of the electoral votes.

---

[38] Arthur Krock in the *New York Times*, November 21, 1948.

[39] Although this kind of proposal drew attention in the years from the 1930's to the 1950's and reached its height of popularity under the sponsorship of Senator Henry Cabot Lodge, Jr. (Republican, Massachusetts) and Representative Ed Gossett (Democrat, Texas), it was first presented to Congress in 1848.—Kallenbach, *op. cit.*, p. 925.

[40] House Report, pp. 9–10, 14–30.

(5) The power of small, strategic pressure groups in key states will be reduced, for their votes will count no more than the votes of the same number of people elsewhere in that state.

(6) The landslides under the at-large system, "which grossly magnifies the victory of the winner and exaggerates the defeat of the loser," would be replaced by a system affording "a more accurate yardstick whereby 'mandates' can be measured." [41]

(7) One of the most controversial claims on behalf of proportionally alloting the electoral votes is its effects upon the two-party system. The one-party states, the proponents allege, will become more bipartisan because the minority party will be credited in the electoral voting with whatever popular votes it receives. For this reason Republicans will be motivated in the South and Democrats in the northern and central states. At the same time the whole concept of key states will be overthrown because the popular vote of such a state, if close, will benefit neither party. One result of this change will be to widen the area of availability in presidential nominations. A resident of a large, doubtful state will no longer be the only serious contender, since candidates from smaller states, if they have nation-wide appeal, would also be "available." Once the dominance of a few key states is broken, a presidential campaign will no longer be concentrated in them, but will be truly national in scope.

Most of *these claims are countered* by advocates of election by popular votes or by the district system as well as by those who want no change.

(1) One of the main points in rebuttal is that the proportional system can defeat a candidate with a plurality of popular votes just as easily as the at-large system. Hypothetical cases to support this charge have been made,[42] just as hypothetical cases have been drawn upon to attack the at-large system. While it is true, Professor Silva pointed out, that the pro-

---

41 *Ibid.*, p. 20. Applying the proportional system to the 1948 election, Truman would have received 258 instead of 303 electoral votes, and Dewey would have received 221.4 instead of 189.——*Ibid.*, p. 27. There are discrepancies in the computations for 1948; compare these figures with those prepared by the Legislative Reference Service, Library of Congress, *New York Times*, February 9, 1950.

42 Wilmerding, *op. cit.*, p. 1, poses a case of two states, each with 24 electoral votes, in which the popular and electoral votes are distributed:

	DEMOCRATS' VOTES		REPUBLICANS' VOTES	
	Popular	*Electoral*	*Popular*	*Electoral*
First state	1,000,000	6	3,000,000	18
Second state	2,100,000	21	300,000	3
Total:	3,100,000	27	3,300,000	21

"The proportional voting system *may* therefore reflect the nationwide popular vote even less accurately than the currently used general ticket (winner-take-all) system, under which in the given case the two candidates would be credited with 24 electoral votes apiece."——P. 2, italics in the original.

portional system would have elected Cleveland instead of Harrison in 1888 (assuming that "its operation had not altered American's voting habits"), in other elections it "would have defeated the candidate with the popular plurality" (e.g., Garfield in 1880) or would have raised a question of who won.[43] The best illustration of the difference in earned electoral votes depending upon their concentration in a few states or dispersal over many states, is furnished by the minor-party votes in 1948 for J. Strom Thurmond (States Rights, South Carolina) and Henry A. Wallace (Progressive, New York). The difference in popular vote between them was a mere 12,212: Thurmond 1,169,312, and Wallace 1,157,100. With the at-large system, Thurmond received 38 electoral votes from the four states he carried; Wallace carried no states, so he received no electoral votes. On a proportionate basis Thurmond would have had 38.6 and Wallace only 9.4 electoral votes.[44]

(2) The effect of a proportional vote on the two-party system occasions the sharpest controversy. Proponents insist that the two-party vote would be encouraged, but opponents are doubtful. The partisan implications of the reform have always been openly discussed. Former Senator Lodge insisted the change would aid the Republicans greatly in the South while the late Senator Robert A. Taft (Republican, Ohio) insisted that the Republicans would lose more in the North than they could possibly gain in the South, and would be unable to win elections. By the same token many Southern Democrats evidenced interest in the change, hoping that a proportional vote would increase the importance of the Southern states, where a heavily concentrated vote would have greater relative weight than under the at-large system. Many Northern Democrats, apparently fearing the same result, seemed less enthusiastic. Eventually the proportional system was denounced frontally as a scheme promising everything to everybody.[45] If the results in the one-party states are problematical, neither party can risk a concentrated popular vote for the other in large states. As a result, each party would be forced to campaign furiously in these key states in order to at least get an approximately even split in the key-state vote. The effect upon minor parties is speculative, but their

---

43 Silva, *op. cit.*, p. 92. In 1900, apparently, McKinley would have had a lead of .1 electoral vote despite 861,759 more popular votes than Bryan. It was contended by others that Bryan would have defeated McKinley in 1900. See the *New York Times*, February 2, 1950; Hearings on Nomination and Election, p. 65 and Tables, pp. 211–225. In 1896 McKinley with 50.9% of the popular vote would have won by only six electoral votes although Bryan had only 46.8% of the popular vote.

44 See House Report, p. 27. Actually, Thurmond received one additional electoral vote from Tennessee, but this was not normal under the at-large system since he ran third in that state.

45 Silva, *op. cit.*, pp. 97–99; *New York Times*, February 27, 1950, and Arthur Krock's column, March 12, 1950. Statement by Joseph W. Martin, Jr. (Republican. Massachusetts) in the House, reported *ibid.*, July 18, 1950.

assurance of getting some electoral votes may encourage them, whether the effect would be to threaten the two-party system or not.[46] Regardless of the value of landslides to the major parties, the question can be asked, Why go to the trouble of changing the Constitution if the new system would not change the results?

(3) The issue of proportional representation arises again, and the arguments against it reappear. It was noted that to introduce proportional distribution of electoral votes would, if carried to its logical conclusion,

> require the creation of a plural executive . . . in order that the several parties might share in it in proportion to their numbers. The reasoning is simple. If it is 'unfair' for a candidate who has received 54 per cent of the nation-wide popular vote to receive 84 per cent of the nation-wide electoral vote, why is it not even more unfair for him to receive 100 per cent of the prize?
>
> It is, to be sure, unlikely that the adoption of the Lodge amendment would actually lead to the creation of a plural executive. There is more danger that it might give countenance to a move for some form of proportional representation in our legislative bodies, national, state and local. If the electoral vote of a state should be divided between the several parties in the same proportions as its popular vote, why not its representation in Congress also? . . .[47]

Advocates have replied:

> No phase of proportional representation is included in this proposal. Proportional representation exists only in cases where two or more officials are to be elected to one office and jointly share its responsibility. . . .
>
> The translation of popular votes into electoral votes has nothing to do with proportional representation. It is simply a means of translating the popular votes of the State into electoral votes as a measure of each State's voting power. The suggestions that such a plan might lead to the adoption of a proportionate system in other elections is too visionary to require practical concern.[48]

In summing up the proportional system, one opponent noted that it

---

[46] *Ibid.*, February 23, 1949; March 21, 1949; January 30, 1950; February 1, 1950. Specific proposals such as the Lodge–Gossett Amendment were objected to because they would permit the election of a President from one party and a Vice-President from the other party. Professor Silva also believed that the system would increase contested elections where the results were close.——*Op. cit.*, pp. 91, 92, note 16.

[47] Wilmerding, *op. cit.*, p. 7. Walter Lippmann, seeing the same possibility of extending PR to Congress, concluded that it would be preferable, as an alternative, to keep "the obnoxious general ticket system which we now have."——Syndicated column reprinted in hearings on Nomination and Election, p. 191; Letter of Professor Edward S. Corwin in the *New York Times*, February 5, 1950.

[48] House Report, p. 20. The authors of this defense also argued that proportioning the electoral votes would overcome the general tendency of the at-large system to be "ruthless in its mistreatment of minorities" even though "minor groups" can exercise power in close states disproportionate to their numbers (p. 15). This statement is a classic of PR sentiment and implies that a nongeographical constituency is the aim.

corrected only one of the causes for existing disparities between electoral and popular votes, i.e., election of electors at large. Two other causes were untouched: allocation of electoral votes on the basis of congressional representation and without regard to the size of the popular vote.[49]

Revert to the District System. In order to obviate the weaknesses previously noted, a third proposal has been made, to amend the Constitution to require the election of presidential electors from districts within the states—the method, apparently, that many of the men who wrote the Constitution had expected would be used. Proposals of this nature go back to Senator Thomas Hart Benton (Democrat, Missouri) in 1823 and to Senator Oliver P. Morton (Republican, Indiana) in the post-Civil War period. Although a number of states during the first thirty-five years of our history used this method, they could not compete with the general ticket of other states. Proposed amendments in the 1950's adopt the plan of two electoral votes per state at large and the remainder from congressional districts, but they differ in other respects. A 40% electoral vote plurality or choice by majority of a joint session of Congress is found in one plan while another requires either a majority in the electoral college or a plurality of a joint session. Usually there is a provision authorizing Congress to district a state if the legislature fails to do so following the decennial census.

Proponents of the district system, despite keeping two electors at large in every state, are in agreement with other reformers in disliking the all-or-none casting of electoral votes. They disagree to the extent that they consider the electoral votes inherently useful and would, according to most of their plans, keep the presidential electors themselves. Recognizing that they cannot vary the number of electoral votes according to the number of popular votes cast, and not wishing to disturb the equal distribution of electoral votes to the states so far as United States senators are concerned, the proponents adopt a concept at complete variance with the proportional concept.

(1) The district system is based on the recognition of the right of representation by those living within defined geographic boundaries. Different partisans in each state can have some representation in the electoral college, if not a mathematically proportional representation. This position is based on the judgment

> that each equal mass of persons (comprising voters and non-voters alike) is entitled to an equal voice in the choice of a president. If the qualifica-

---

[49] Silva, *op. cit.*, pp. 89-90. With reference to the last point Senator Harley M. Kilgore (Democrat, West Virginia) observed that in his state "we will cast twice as many votes in the general election as the State of Virginia next door; yet they have 12 electoral votes and we have 8."——Hearings on Nomination and Election, p. 25.

tions requisite for voting are higher in one mass than in another; if, in order to express their disapproval of their party's policy, the voters in one mass stay away from the polls while those in another cast their ballots for opposition candidates; if local issues vary the proportions of the electorate voting in different masses; if stormy weather keeps more voters at home in rural areas than in urban areas—none of these is a valid reason for reducing the weight of the masses casting the fewer votes. The electoral vote may reflect the will of the people—of all the people not merely of the active voters—more correctly than the popular vote.[50]

(2) The motivations for the district system and the kind of opposition it is likely to encounter if brought to a vote are made clear by understanding the partisan effect that the system is intended to have. To put the point bluntly, the district system is seen as curbing those groups concentrated in metropolitan areas which have been more closely associated with the Democrats, notably since the inception of the New Deal.[51] The logic of the plan was shown succinctly by pointing out that in New York, with its forty-five presidential electors, a voter "packs fifteen times the power of every voter in Delaware" with its three electoral votes. If every voter could vote for just three electors (the one from his district and the two from his state) this power would be equalized.[52] Still, the Democrats are not likely to warm up to the plan when they examine figures on past elections showing that election by districts would generally have been more favorable to the Republicans than the proportional system.[53]

Additional values claimed for the district system are sometimes the same as those claimed for the proportional system and sometimes different.[54] Again, the potency of key states is seen declining, although the reasons for supposing that this result would be true here or in the proportional system rest entirely upon inferences. The claim that the district system would open up one-party states has merit to the extent that congressional districts in those states are dominated by the minority party, the actual

---

50 Wilmerding, *op. cit.*, pp. 2–3.

51 The most indefatigable supporter of the district system in Congress has been Representative Frederic R. Coudert (Republican, New York). The district system would possibly offset the influence of the combined AFL-CIO labor union.——Arthur Krock, *New York Times*, February 24, 1955; Hearings on Nomination and Election, statement of J. Harvie Williams, pp. 178–179.

52 Speech of Senator Karl E. Mundt (Republican, South Dakota) February 22, 1954, at the annual Washington Day dinner of the American Good Government Society. Senator Mundt has been only relatively less active than Representative Coudert.

53 Hearings on Nomination and Election, Tables pp. 211–225. Professor Silva concluded that the district system "would probably make it possible for a party to win the Presidency without carrying the metropolitan areas—especially if the State legislatures continue to gerrymander the States against these metropolitan areas"; "would tend to favor the party which failed to carry the State"; and "would make Presidential elections closer contests by enlarging the electoral vote of the defeated candidate."——*Ibid.*, p. 235.

54 *Ibid.*, pp. 93–95. For a detailed comparison of these two systems with the at-large system, see pp. 81–85.

situation in some Southern states. It is plausible that the President and a majority of the House of Representatives will more likely be of the same party by carrying the same districts, although with split-ticket voting this result is far from assured.

Those who have reached *negative conclusions regarding the district system* have evaluated it as proponents either of an unqualified popular election or of the proportional system. The latter, particularly, have noted objections.[55] By retaining the presidential electors, the people are still deprived of a direct vote. The district system is a "crude substitute" for proportioning votes, because minorities within a district would not be represented. The fact that the district system was long ago abandoned is proof that it is discredited and inferior. (This point is contrary to the facts.) The major and most telling count is that the gerrymandering practices of state legislatures or their failure to keep districts reasonably even in population (whether gerrymandered or not) would so distort the result that at-large election would be preferable. In elaboration, it is maintained that states would still be likely to cast a solid electoral vote for one party or the other. Even though Congress be given the power to redistrict a state if the state legislature fails to do so, there is doubt that the Congress would act. Its failure to prevent gerrymandering or wide discrepancies in district populations for the election of members of the House is not a reassuring precedent. If the district system were adopted, Congress may create districts in a state for electing presidential electors different from the districts from which members of the House were elected. In any event, no matter who was responsible for the districting, complaints could be made that favoritism or discrimination was shown in one way or another and that the results were not fair and just to this or that group. Pressure on Congress or state legislatures to redistrict or not to redistrict could become terrific.[56]

The question is a choice of conceivably undesirable results as between the proportional and district systems. There is the possibility in the former of a candidate being elected under a plurality rule who is not the choice of a majority of the voters. In the latter there is the possibility of a candidate being elected who is wanted by the second largest group of voters instead of the largest group.

Merely Abolish the Presidential Electors. A final possibility in reforming the electoral college is the less drastic act of just abolishing the college itself and keeping the electoral votes, a possibility first alluded to, apparently, in 1801.[57] This change can be made whether the votes are cast as a

---

[55] *Ibid.*, pp. 150-152 and House Report, p. 5, where the lists of drawbacks in each case include not only the same points but are stated alike almost word for word.

[56] Wilmerding, *op. cit.*, p. 13, concedes these difficulties, but notes that if both kinds of districts were gerrymandered the same way, the President and majority of the House would be fellow partisans.

[57] *Ibid.*, pp. 13-14.

unit or allotted one to a district and two at large. Each state's electoral votes would be cast in accordance with its popular vote by the state official charged with the responsibility of compiling the total votes, and he would then certify the returns to the President of the United States Senate, as the presidential electors do under the present system. Considering the perfunctory nature of the electors' duties, the case for having them at all appears weak.

If electors were abolished: (1) The voters would not be voting for intermediate officials but voting directly. (2) A voter could write in the names of candidates for President and Vice-President, whereas with electors he would be required to write in names of electors who he had reason to believe would vote for the candidates he favored. (3) The human and political elements would be removed, for the state official would have no discretion in casting the votes. The possibility of a rebel among the victorious presidential electors refusing or ignoring a commitment to vote for his party's candidates would be removed completely. (4) Every state would be guaranteed against the loss of any of its electoral votes from the death of an elector between the November election and the assembling of the college in December. States would also be protected against the inadvertent nomination and election of people who are federal officials and therefore disqualified to act as electors.[58]

Potential Value of Electors. At last the question arises, What can be said for keeping presidential electors and the quadrennial operation of the college? Since these individuals normally do nothing unique or even distinctive, their genuine value, if any, is potential rather than actual. If electors are chained by party discipline, the election of both a President and a Vice-President of the same party is insured. If the electors are to be abolished, candidates for the two offices should run as a team to insure the continuation of this result. Two other values are potential or remote. (1) Occasionally an election presents sufficient confusion that electors need to know the nation-wide outcome before being sure how they should vote, e.g., some Roosevelt electors in 1912 would have voted for Taft if the election had lain between him and Wilson, with Roosevelt eliminated.[59] (2) A different kind of problem could arise where a majority of the electors, though divided among two or more candidates, may prefer to vote for one candidate to defeat a plurality candidate unwanted by a majority

---

[58] Such a situation occurred in Virginia in 1948, but fortunately was discovered in time to replace the ineligible persons.

[59] The same situation might have arisen in 1948 among some Democratic electors in the South if Truman had not been clearly elected. If one vote would have made any difference in the outcome, a second Tennessee elector would probably not have voted for Truman.

of the people. In these potential cases, obviously, more than two genuine candidates would be involved in the final outcome.[60]

Objectives in Electoral-College Reform. The real problem in deciding what to do about the electoral college and electoral votes lies not in the detached study of alternate proposals, weighing one alternative against another as though one were an apothecary filling a prescription, but in the prior decision of what a presidential election system should be and should do. What objectives are important in choosing a President?

Do we want to elect by a majority-vote or a plurality-vote rule? If the latter, do we want a specified plurality or just any plurality? The advocates of plurality elections have strong ground to stand on, for majorities are seldom required in general elections for offices other than President and Vice-President.[61] Yet the predominant expectation is that candidates for all offices—local, state, and federal—will receive a majority anyway. Plurality elections are uncommon anywhere in the country. Election by a majority, on the contrary, is asserted to be a traditional value in American government and the "foundation" of the two-party system. "Of necessity the parties must reach out for wide support. A lesser objective than an electoral majority cannot have the cohesive force necessary to maintain a two-party system and would permit the continued existence of third and fourth parties because of their balance-of-power positions." [62]

Two allied considerations are suggested by this difference of opinion. The first is whether choosing a President is sufficiently different from choosing a sheriff, a governor, or a member of Congress to justify a majority-vote requirement. Are the risks of intrigue, of being saddled with a candidate strongly opposed by a majority, of fragmenting the vote to the point that no majority will is evidenced—are these risks greater in the

---

[60] Wilmerding, *op. cit.*, pp. 16-17.

[61] The requirement of a majority has seldom been made in this country. Connecticut, Georgia, Massachusetts, New Jersey, New York, and South Carolina were the only colonies which required a majority. See Cortlandt F. Bishop, *History of Elections in the American Colonies,* Columbia University Studies in History, Economics and Public Law, 1893, Vol. 3, pp. 178-179. Majorities are required, one, in the election of governors in Georgia, Maine, Mississippi, and Vermont (failing which the legislature in Georgia an Vermont and the lower house in Maine and Mississippi elect); two, in the Democratic direct primaries in most Southern states; and, three, in municipal nonpartisan elections. Cortez A. M. Ewing, *Congressional Elections, 1896-1944* (Norman: University of Oklahoma Press, 1947) p. 72, pointed out that approximately 9% of the contests during the years he covered were decided by pluralities, not majorities.

[62] Statement of J. Harvie Williams in Hearings on Nomination and Election, pp. 168-169; see also pp. 104, 154. The advocates of the proportional system make a case for the rights of minorities within states, those who are said to be "disfranchised" by the plurality election of presidential electors at large. If a plurality in the state is evil, why is not also evil in the nation? The only answer is that most thinking so far has not moved beyond this concern for intrastate minorities, but fears that it will move beyond instill opposition to the proportional plan.

nation than in a state or district or county? Apparently, some of them are greater because of the stakes involved and the extent of the geographical and ideological areas where schemes can be hatched.

The second consideration is the alternative effects on the two-party system of a majority or plurality requirement. The problem of securing a majority does not arise from two-party competition but from minor-party competition with major parties.[63] To encourage minority groups is one of the objectives of some of the reforms, but whether they would be more likely to work within major parties or as minor parties is a matter for speculation. If the electorate is compartmentalized by states on the at-large or the proportional plans or by states and by districts, the campaign effort must reach to enough of the compartments to offer some assurance of a victory. In either of the first two plans, the influence of minority groups or parties can be felt if they cast a sufficiently large vote in the largest states. The district plan alone promises to reduce the effect of minority parties or groups, unless they have both widespread and strong support. In any plan, with or without the electoral votes, the abandonment of majority rule, when there are more than two genuine candidates, will reward the efforts being made to influence the outcome of presidential elections by the alliances or accidental coincidences of minority voting.[64]

Do we want a supplementary method for choosing Presidents? Whenever a majority is required, whether by popular or electoral votes, the public balloting may fail to elect a candidate. A desire to avoid these inconclusive situations of deadlock and to have the electorate settle the issue is advanced as an argument against a majority requirement. The dilemma of the majority-versus-plurality question is theoretically as great if a particular-sized plurality is required. A plurality set at 40% will less likely result in an inconclusive vote, since only one President (Lincoln, 1860) was put into the White House by the voters and one President (Adams, 1824) was put there by the House, with a smaller percentage. Nevertheless, whether a candidate must receive 51% or 40% or 35% or some other number, the mere requirement itself must be accompanied by provision for a supplementary election method to cover the exceptional case when the primary method fails to produce a winner.

A great deal of resentment is shown for the present supplementary method of election by the House, voting by states. However, this undue weight given to small states in the resolving of deadlocks counterbalances the weight of the large states in the electoral college. If the large states lose their advantage, leaders in the small states may be willing to give up their advantage and agree to voting in the House by individuals. How the small-state leaders can be assured on this point is not entirely clear, but

63 Wilmerding, *op. cit.*, pp. 19–21.
64 See above pp. 33–34.

an alternative method of supplementary election at a joint session of Congress—each senator and representative casting one vote—would alleviate two difficulties: The small states could keep their advantage, and the possibility in the present method of the House choosing a President and the Senate choosing a Vice-President of different parties, would be removed.

What other methods for a supplemental election, besides the Congress, are available? Little consideration can be given to reconvening the electors in a second meeting to break the deadlock. A more familiar method is the runoff between the two highest candidates, although its results are incalculable (inasmuch as the existing models for comparison in cities and in Southern Democratic primaries may or may not be reliable guides). Runoff machinery would also have to be considered in connection with reformed methods of nominating, particularly if the runoff were introduced into a national direct primary system. If both were possible, the citizens could conceivably be called upon to go to the polls four times in one year to nominate and elect a President.[65]

Do we want a relocation of political power? Inasmuch as the existing machinery of presidential elections is built up around the vested political interests of major-party leaders in states and sections, fundamental changes in the machinery will undoubtedly disturb these traditional power relations and will shift power to other leaders operating from different bases. If these changes are inevitable, there is nothing gained in discussing them. If they are not inevitable and if there are choices in the kinds and amounts of reform to be adopted, it is pertinent to evaluate the proposals in the light of what power relations one wants to encourage and to discourage.

The choice is not between having centers of power or not having them. The choice is between one or another kind of power, exercised from one or another source, oriented toward one or another set of interests. These choices cannot be dictated, for they spring from people's sense of values and interests. Unquestionably, the traditional centers of political power and the characteristics of the political system are interdependent. Whether or not lodging power in state and sectional leaders is *a* cause or *the* cause of bipartisanism, the kind of bipartisanism we have had is featured by such location of power. To change the centers of a system's power will certainly produce commensurate changes in the system.[66] This cause and effect will occur despite the motives of those urging the changes. While dangers can

---

[65] *Ibid.*, pp. 21-22. McKean, *op. cit.*, p. 642, also suggests the use of preferential voting, an even more remote possibility.

[66] This likelihood was well appreciated by various groups, such as the United Automobile Workers and the National Association for the Advancement of Colored People, as well as members of Congress, in 1956 when they opposed S. J. Res. 31, 84th Cong., 2d sess., a proposed amendment requiring the states to adopt either the proportional system of casting electoral votes or the district system of electing presidential electors. The Senate rejected the proposal. *New York Times*, March 16, 1956 to March 28, 1956 and *Congressional Record*, United States Senate, 84th Cong., 2d sess., for the same period.

be located in plans to encourage more splintering and fragmentation, dangers also lurk in proposals directed entirely to current trends and dominated by supposed partisan advantages. The immediate picture we see may change completely in the near or distant future.

This third question, the desirability of changing the location of political power, raises, in turn, the much larger and more important subject of the efficacy and future course of the American party system. This subject is taken up in the next chapter.

Selected Bibliography

A Study of the Presidential Primary. Carson City, Nevada: Legislative Counsel Bureau, Bulletin No. 32, December, 1958.

David, Paul T., *et al.* (eds.), *Presidential Nominating Politics in 1952.* Baltimore: The Johns Hopkins Press, 1954. Especially Vol. 1.

Judah, Charles B., *The Presidential Primary.* Division of Research, Department of Government, University of New Mexico, 1953.

Overacker, Louise, *The Presidential Primary.* New York: The Macmillan Company, 1926.

Silva, Ruth C., "The Lodge-Gossett Resolution: A Critical Analysis," *American Political Science Review,* Vol. 44 (1950) pp. 86–99.

Stanwood, Edward, *A History of the Presidency from 1788–1897.* Boston: Houghton Mifflin Company, 1898. See especially the early chapters.

Wilmerding, Lucius, Jr., *The Electoral College.* New Brunswick: Rutgers University Press, 1958.

Much applicable material is constantly available in newspapers and periodicals, particularly during a presidential-election year. Check indexes such as the *Readers Guide to Periodical Literature.* The renewed interest in these subjects has been reflected in a number of congressional hearings which can be obtained through the Government Printing Office, Washington, D. C.

CHAPTER TWENTY-FIVE

Can and Should We Make Over the Party System?

In the panorama of the American party system, views range far and wide in every direction. From the one extreme of labeling politics as sin and calling upon the hosts of benighted citizens to repent and reform while there is time for political salvation, intervening positions have been noted bearing upon the existing dynamics of widespread nonvoting and of denying ideological minorities a mathematical representation. Next, the whole machinery of presidential politics was examined in the light of proposals for reviving popular control and repressing suspected leadership. Now comes the other extreme in the analysis of our system, that of reformers who not only accept permanent party organization and the need for continuing leadership but also wish to broaden and formally institutionalize them in order that the maximum responsibility of party government be established.

This last area of discussion of reforms touches directly and purposefully upon machinery and overtly probes into the dynamics of the system as well. The effect of these reforms upon machinery is the more pronounced; but basically they raise questions which involve mainly dynamics. Truly, the consideration of party responsibility and centralization is a synthesizing process which brings together all knowledge and understanding about how the party system works and all of the most mature evaluations about how it should work.

THE ACTUAL STATUS OF PARTIES

Assessment of the Existing System. In the final analysis of the two-party system, it is always pertinent to ask if we know actually what it is, how it works, and what its real characteristics are. The possibilities for inquiry are so many and so dispersed that the task of simply surveying the raw materials is onerous. Limiting the survey to "purely political" topics does little more than cut off some segments of the potential total area.

> It is evident that the roots of partisanship extend far below the surface of political campaigns and are deeply embedded in the traditional interests and inveterate habits of the men and women throughout the land who compose the national electorate. An adequate understanding of the bipartisan system in national politics calls for more than analysis of the characters of the candidates and inquiry into the circumstances of the campaigns. It is necessary also to investigate the character of the

factions which constitute the major parties and the conditions which make for durability in their relations with one another. A satisfactory explanation of the bipartisan system should throw light on the permanent causes of the existing alignment of parties and on the outlook for a partisan realignment which would be more pleasing to voters seeking a rational basis for partisanship. Above all, it should throw light on the conditions which govern the formation of electoral majorities and on the validity of Madison's theory of the natural limits to partisan power.[1]

INDICTMENT OF THE SYSTEM

Originally a Lack of Plan. The creation of the party organization was carefully designed for its maximum popular appeal and was carried forward on that basis, but this development was taken without much regard for the "logical" formation of so important an institution. Materials were taken where they were found and no questions asked, as long as the improvised techniques served the pragmatic purpose of organizing followers and winning elections. This oversight or unconcern was not universal among politicians at the transition from the eighteenth to the nineteenth century. The Federalists, as a party of aristocracy, had looked upon organization as beneath contempt, as a pandering to the masses; but even the Federalists saw a new light when they were swept from office in 1800. Alexander Hamilton, the energetic coordinator of the scattered patches of Federalist sentiment and power, finally turned his mind to the subject of party organization as the alternative to the demise of the Federalist heritage.

Hamilton's Plan. He concluded that the opposition's victory had resulted from their successful appeal to the voters' "passions," while "the Federalists seem not to have attended to the fact sufficiently, and that they erred in relying so much upon the rectitude of their measures, as to have neglected the cultivation of popular favor by fair and justifiable expedients." He justified a future Federalist appeal to the people, even though "we renounce our principles and objects," because "we must consider whether it be possible for us to succeed, without in some degree, employing the weapons which have been employed against us." Characteristically, both for him personally and for his colleagues, he thought in terms of a centralized structure with power retained at the pinnacle and supported by the rank and file at the pyramid's base. He suggested, first, a council with a president and twelve members; second, a subdirecting council in each state with a vice-president and twelve members; third, "as many societies in each State as local circumstances may permit to be formed by the subdirecting council." Each state council would send representatives

---

[1] Arthur N. Holcombe, *Our More Perfect Union* (Cambridge: Harvard University Press, 1950) pp. 108–109.

to Washington, D.C., to nominate presidential and vice-presidential candidates. Information would spread horizontally through this machinery by the practice of weekly meetings of local clubs and of continuous correspondence between different societies and vertically by the centralized organization being constantly informed by its local organizations of public sentiment throughout the country.[2]

Nature of the Problem of Reform. The Hamiltonian type of model has inspired efforts to work reforms of the parties' organization, but the starting point of later discussions is quite different. While Hamilton was concerned with generating enthusiasm and support for policies, the problem has become how to devise programs and policies which can be carried through after the popular appeal has succeeded. Political speeches filled with assurances that promises seriously made will be seriously redeemed are interspersed with insistence that the party members join together in implementing the policies the party officially has announced.

> No one would deny that there should be full and free expression and an opportunity for independence of action within the party. There is no salvation in a narrow and bigoted partisanship. But if there is to be responsible party government, the party label must be something more than a mere device for securing office. Unless those who are elected under the same party designation are willing to assume sufficient responsibility and exhibit sufficient loyalty and coherence, so that they can cooperate with each other in the support of the broad general principles of the party platform, the election is merely a mockery, no decision is made at the polls, and there is no representation of the popular will. Common honesty and good faith with the people who support a party at the polls require that party, when it enters office, to assume the control of that portion of the Government to which it has been elected. Any other course is bad faith and a violation of the party pledges.[3]

These words state both the proposition and the dilemma. How to avoid "narrow and bigoted partisanship" while having "full and free expression and an opportunity for independence of action" and at the same time keep faith with the pledges given during the campaign.

Wilson's Experience. A unique individual in the movement to accomplish these results was Woodrow Wilson, who as a scholar expounded and as a politician continued to believe in the superiority of British govern-

---

[2] *Hamilton's Works* (New York: G. P. Putnam's Sons, 1885, Lodge ed.) Vol. 6, pp. 540, 544; Vol. 7, p. 462; Vol. 8, pp. 596–599. See George P. Luetscher, *Early Political Machinery in the United States* (Philadelphia: University of Pennsylvania, 1903) pp. 151–153. Incidentally, Hamilton wanted to recruit new members by creating societies for the relief of immigrants.

[3] From the Inaugural Address of President Calvin Coolidge, March 4, 1925. *Inaugural Addresses of the Presidents of the United States from George Washington 1789 to Harry S. Truman 1949*, House Doc. No. 540, 82d Cong., 2d sess., p. 209.

ment forms in making parties responsible.[4] The record Wilson made as President is some basis for evaluating the success of the application of his theories. During his first term the results were promising, but in these years he was operating in conformance with the American system. When the days of trouble broke upon him and he attempted to operate in conformance with the British system, the results were not promising. His management of the Democratic Party eventually contributed to its being swept from office in 1920. The Wilson record, finally, cannot be considered a success. His adaptation of parliamentary responsibility to the American Presidency was incompatible with the American political system. His party colleagues could not adapt even when they understood.[5]

Obstacles to Reform. Nevertheless, the desire for reform of parties has not abated. The obstacles to a new kind of operation of the party system are widely recognized as existing in the governmental system of separation of powers and federalism, which have fostered and reflected a decentralized power structure and a localism in sentiment. Operating this kind of government, party leaders have been preoccupied with patronage and not with policies.[6] Others, who see the United States Government becoming ever more responsible for operating the economic system and are concerned with the adjustment of institutions to the rapid and profound changes overtaking the nation, are struck with the failure of the party system to provide the necessary coordination which the government structure itself fails to provide.[7]

---

4 See Austin Ranney, *The Doctrine of Responsible Party Government* (Illinois Studies in the Social Sciences, Vol. 34, No. 3, 1954) Chap. 3.

5 Wilson's concept of party government, growing out of the peace settlement of World War I, was "to go to the country" in the manner of British elections. When the Senate failed to consent to the Treaty of Versailles in the form he wanted, he declared the 1920 elections would be a "solemn referendum" on the League of Nations issue. This type of decision is not possible in an American election since so many issues intrude upon the campaign. Wilson, of course, knew this and even thought up a different solution: In January 1920 he prepared a statement to the country which was never issued but was preserved among his papers. He listed all of the Republican senators who had voted against him on the League and called upon them to resign and run for re-election at a special election in their states. Wilson promised, if a majority of them were re-elected, to invite one of them to become Secretary of State and he and the Vice-President would resign.——Thomas A. Bailey, *Woodrow Wilson and the Great Betrayal* (New York: The Macmillan Company, 1945) pp. 214-215. "He had gone far politically but had wrecked the party. . . . Wilson, like Lincoln, was in many respects one of the best politicians, who felt that he had great capacity to read the minds of his fellows, and to understand and anticipate the popular drift, just as he knew he had great powers to sway and manipulate masses of men. His was not party leadership but part dictatorship. When he got ready he made a complete reversal of policy, without any thought of its effect on the party's fortunes."——James Kerney, *The Political Education of Woodrow Wilson* (New York: The Century Company, 1926) p. 450.

6 E. Allen Helms, "The President and Party Politics," *Journal of Politics*, Vol. 11 (1949) pp. 42 ff.

7 Merle Fainsod, "Consolidating Party Control," *American Political Science Review*, Vol. 42 (1948) pp. 317-321.

Schattschneider's Indictment. The indictment of the existing party system has nowhere been more sweepingly or cogently stated than by Professor E. E. Schattschneider.[8] As a firm advocate of party responsibility, he concluded that the present state of irresponsibility is due to two particular conditions.

(1) The organization of the parties is decentralized; i.e., local leaders have control over nominations because they control the machinery. The result is that men and women are nominated and elected to state legislatures and Congress who are beholden to the local organizations back home. A party program must first clear the hurdle of local interests in spoils to which legislators, of necessity, must give priority. This traditional mode of operation has been that local and state leaders are in control of the machinery and dominate both state and national governments through spoils politics.

(2) Legislators are forsaken by the organization leaders when pressure groups come into the picture. If the organization has been taken care of, its leaders are either unconcerned with the results beyond that point or are themselves solicitous of the pressure groups in their own bailiwick. Legislators are exposed to the pressures of selfish groups and have no way to defend themselves except by their own devices. No party program can be developed and no responsibility of parties can be realized under this system. The solution is to centralize the party organization and deprive the local leaders of their control, for a centralized leadership will be concerned with policy and will see that its program is protected from the onslaughts of pressure groups. This position, like many similar ones, is also based on the premise that times are changing and that parties must keep step. Professor Schattschneider notes that sectionalism is a concomitant of decentralized parties, while class interests are a concomitant of centralized parties.[9]

Response of the A.P.S.A. Committee. The next logical step is to get down to cases and lay out the specifications for the reorganized party machinery. The outstanding effort of this nature was the *Report* of the Committee on Political Parties of the American Political Science Association.[10] The *Report* is by no means the only plan for changing party machinery, for various writers have been making similar suggestions over

---

8 Schattschneider, *Party Government* (New York: Farrar & Rinehart, Inc., 1942), *The Struggle for Party Government* (College Park: University of Maryland Press, 1948), and various articles and reviews; see "Pressure Groups Versus Political Parties," *Annals of the American Academy of Political and Social Science,* Vol. 259 (1948) pp. 16–23.

9 Schattschneider, *Party Government,* p. 118.

10 "Toward a More Responsible Two-Party System," *American Political Science Review,* Supplement, Vol. 44, No. 3, Part 2 (1950). Hereafter cited as *Report.*

the years.[11] What distinguishes the *Report* is the joint efforts of a number
of specialists in bringing together an inclusive plan specifically designed to
be capable of adoption in the foreseeable future.

A PLAN FOR PARTY REORGANIZATION

The *Report's* plan for changing the operation of parties follows
Hamilton-type thinking and ignores as far as possible Jefferson-type
practice.

Party organization begins with the *national convention,* which is
considered to be too unwieldy in its present form—a traditional piece of
machinery that probably cannot be abolished, but can be made useful.
Its membership would be reduced in size to five or six hundred members
chosen as follows:

1. Some 300 to 350 delegates elected directly by party voters
2. About 150 ex-officio members, including the national committee, state chairmen, and congressional leaders
3. About 25 members constituting selected leaders outside of the
   party organization

The national convention would function as the principal representative
and deliberative organ of a party, meeting regularly every two years and
at special times in between as needed. It should meet for longer periods
than it does now in order to permit real discussions. It will continue to
nominate presidential and vice-presidential candidates, or if the presidential primary is adopted, will merely declare the results of the primary.
It will "adopt and approve" the party platform, "adopt rules and regulations governing the party," and "act as the supreme organ of the party." [12]

The *national committee* would also be retained, but its capacity becomes somewhat dubious. While its composition would apparently remain
the same, its voting power should reflect the party's voting strength in the
respective states—a practice followed by some state committees. It should
be selected by the national convention in a substantive sense, not in the
perfunctory manner in which it is chosen. Its members should be loyal
to the policies and the candidates of the party.[13]

---

[11] See, *e.g.,* Charles E. Merriam and Harold F. Gosnell, *The American Party System*
(New York: The Macmillan Company, 1949, 4th ed.) pp. 356–358. Dayton D. McKean,
Party and Pressure Politics (Boston: Houghton Mifflin Company, 1949) pp. 640–643, goes
far beyond any other proposals by boldly calling for the parliamentary system of government, the strengthening of the Presidency since this is the only office accountable to the
whole electorate, a national system of PR, the barring from nomination of candidates guilty
of party disloyalty.

[12] *Report,* pp. 37–38.

[13] *Ibid.,* pp. 38–39.

The key unit of organization would be a completely new agency, the *party council,* composed of fifty members as follows:

1. Five from the national committee
2. Five from each house of the Congress
3. Ten from state committees chosen by regional groups or by the national convention
4. Five governors chosen by them
5. Twenty from other groups such as the Young [Republicans or Democrats] and the party rank and file; these to be chosen by the groups themselves or by the national convention
6. Ex-officio members in the persons of the President and Vice-President (for the "ins") or the nominees for these offices, Cabinet members designated by the President, and the highest national party officials

The functions of the council are to settle the larger problems of management as determined by the national convention; to propose a preliminary draft of a platform to the national convention every two years; to "interpret the platform in relation to current problems"; to choose twenty-five leaders to the national convention; to make recommendations regarding congressional candidates for both houses in all states; to make recommendations regarding departures from general party decisions by state and local organizations. The council would also be a place for discussing presidential candidates and "screening" them in a "preliminary way." [14]

In addition, the *Report* suggests a *party cabinet* composed of the highest party officials, i.e., permanent chairman of the national convention, the chairman of the national committee, the chairman of the party council, the floor leaders in each house of Congress, the Speaker and the Vice-President. This cabinet would function within the council and act as an adviser to the President or to the presidential nominee.[15]

State and local organizations should be reappraised in line with the new centralized authority and control over policy, and regional organizations should be further encouraged.[16] Discussion groups should be held frequently at local party meetings, with reports and recommendations sent to the council to "make clear the views of the rank and file, and aid in discovering and bringing out good candidates for party and public office." [17] From these discussions, local party groups would be organized, composed of people who have an interest in party policies with emphasis upon national questions and seeing local issues in their national context.

14 *Ibid.,* pp. 39–44.
15 *Ibid.,* p. 44.
16 *Ibid.,* pp. 44–47.
17 *Loc. cit.*

Policy would be developed out of the "raw ideas" generated at these grass-roots meetings. The "two-way communication" between these local groups and the council would be promoted by a publicity and research program under the council's direction. This new system and relationship between the base and the pinnacle of the party pyramid would compel "the traditional local party unit . . . to come to terms. . . . The outcome may be far different from the familiar conditions of the past." [18]

The Council would enforce loyalty on the basis of its interpretation of the platform in the light of current developments; and its interpretations would be "generally binding." The national platform would be supreme on general principles and national issues; and to avoid conflicts, state platforms should be written after the national platform is adopted. The basis for acceptance of the platform would be its reflection of existing party sentiment, not its character as a lure for votes.[19] The reorientation of parties into policy instruments would bring like-minded people into a party organization and would partly solve the problem of determining party membership, although there should be no "mindless discipline enforced from above." [20]

Congressional organization would be reformed in keeping with the new regime, so that party leadership can be exercised through the caucus. Recalcitrant members would not be rewarded with high committee posts, and the seniority rule would be scrapped in favor of a system of selection by the caucus in line with party policy.[21]

THE EXTENT OF REFORM

This making over of the whole party structure leaves no doubt about the completely reformed parties which would emerge. The immediate question which can be asked is whether the parties are accurately described by these reformers. Are parties so ambivalent, so decentralized, so irresponsible, so lacking in unity?

Contradiction Between Source of Power and Its Motivation. Within the analysis of parties two strains have run parallel. Both take as their beginning the dissatisfying aspects of parties revealed in iron rule by local and state leaders and the sometimes resultant corruption in politics. The more orthodox view has been that the decentralized organization and preoccupation with local affairs to the exclusion of national questions are the culprits in the picture. The other view takes note of another characteristic, namely, that the principal preoccupation of political leaders all along the

18 *Ibid.*, pp. 66–69.
19 *Ibid.*, pp. 48, 52, 53, 54.
20 *Ibid.*, pp. 69-70.
21 *Ibid.*, pp. 56–65.

line has been with national politics although not necessarily with national policy matters. Ostrogorski's case against oligarchy in the parties was based partly on his observation that the "anxiety for the spoils of presidential patronage . . . has subordinated all the elections, from those of the township up, to the presidential election." [22] At about the same time Ostrogorski was writing, Professor Macy, a more friendly student of the American party system, noted virtually the same condition.

> Yet thus far party names have stood almost wholly for Federal policies. Local issues and policies have been ignored. State and local committees have thus been made to feel that their sole reason for existence as party officials was the fulfillment of the behests of those near the source of authority. From the very nature of its professed object the party has been controlled by the President, the members of Congress, and the national committees.[23]

Another writer almost ten years later came to substantially the same conclusion that Professor Macy had reached:

> Today the domination of the national party is nearly complete; there are no state parties which look after state issues and which are distinct from the parties and the policies that are of continental dimensions. In every step taken in ward or township, in every nomination made for local office, there is deference to the interests of the great national organization; local interests are nearly submerged. . . . When this system is complete, it means nothing more nor less than the disappearance of local self-government.
> . . . Time and time again a party which had disgraced itself in state management, which was under the influence of a corrupt machine, and which was even acting in neglect of the most obvious interests of the commonwealth, has been retained in power, lest its defeat injure the party at large. . . . The simple, unadorned truth is that, because of the stupendous organization of national parties in a so-called federal republic, federalism in its more desirable aspects has largely disappeared.[24]

We are faced with a contradiction which makes the analysis of the party system even more complicated. The party organization is decentralized in that the power is located within states, but a party is also centralized by the universal concern for national affairs. While the local leaders are not policy leaders taking the lead in drives to adopt some

---

22 M. Ostrogorski, *Democracy and the Party System in the United States* (New York: The Macmillan Company, 1910) p. 379.

23 Jesse Macy, *Party Organization and Machinery* (New York: The Macmillan Company, 1905) pp. 9–10. Interestingly enough, Professor Macy concluded that this nationalizing of interest and issues would be largely corrected if United States senators were directly elected instead of being chosen by state legislatures. This change in senators' election method was made after 1913—with what accompanying changes in the national orientation of parties it would be difficult to say.

24 A. C. McLaughlin, *The Courts, The Constitution and Parties: Studies in Constitutional History and Politics* (Chicago: University of Chicago Press, 1912) pp. 136, 141.

particular program, they are representatives of the national interests of the party in their states and localities. Both sides of this controversy can find substantiation for their points of view, for both have some part of the truth.

Existing Disciplinary Powers. The disciplinary function of the projected party council contained in the *Report* would not be a radical departure, but, if genuinely used and seriously enforced, would be an innovation. The power already exists if the leaders can agree on its use. Following the 1948 presidential election, the Democratic National Committee refused to seat five Southern members who had supported the State Rights ticket. A man and woman, chosen by the loyalist faction in Mississippi, were seated in the committee although it was made clear that their acceptance was on the basis of appointment of the national chairman. The Louisiana Democratic State Central Committee removed the national committeeman in 1958 because of his moderate views on segregation, but the National Committee continued to seat him, contending he was subject to removal only for violation of its rules, and refused to recognize that the state could change its representative.[25]

Differences Between the Parties. The degree of satisfaction with the choices offered by the parties to the voters depends upon which and how many choices one thinks the parties should offer. There is no doubt, despite the assertions to the contrary, that the parties do offer differences in their party platforms, in the positions taken by most of the party leaders in Washington, D. C., on numerous policies, and in the record of the parties in office. The subjects of taxation and labor-management relations have at most times been a bone of contention between Republicans and Democrats. Public-versus-private-power policies have likewise divided the major factions within each party from each other. The interesting fact about platforms is that they differ more than is commonly supposed, although some of the differences are difficult to detect because of the way the planks are worded. If the existing differences are not enough, it can only be concluded that they should be both greater in number and more specifically stated; but when it comes to carrying this sort of thing beyond present practices, this

would impose a burden which politicians in a republican system could not be expected to bear. If the platforms were to point out clearly all

25 *New York Times*, August 14, 24, 25, 1949; October 9, 1958 and December 6, 1958. See *American Political Science Review*, Vol. 50 (1956) pp. 553-568 for attempts of the Democrats to solve the loyalty question at national conventions as well as among national committee members.

differences between parties, then each party would be forced to reveal not only its assets but also its liabilities. . . . Such political naiveté is not characteristic even in countries with highly disciplined parties, and would not be countenanced by American politicians, however reformed.[26]

Congressional Party Cleavages. Professor Turner's study of voting records in selected sessions of Congress between 1921 and 1944 produced the conclusion that party is more important in accounting for the votes "than any other discernible factor." Sharp and consistent party cleavage was found on the issues of tariff, government action, social welfare, labor, and agriculture; moderate cleavage on government regulation, Negroes and immigration; sharp but inconsistent cleavage on patronage, specific public works, and the bureaucracy; moderate but inconsistent cleavage on state rights, general public works, armaments, foreign affairs, the executive, and Congress; little apparent cleavage on veterans claims, women's rights, the government of Washington, D. C., prohibition, and civil service.[27] When he carried his studies on into subsequent sessions of Congress, the general conclusion remained the same. Of the total of eight sessions shown since 1921, "party behavior could be scientifically distinguished on 407 of the 455 roll calls recorded in the House," or an average for all of the sessions of 89.5%. Less than 4% in the House and 7.4% in the Senate bolted their parties on a majority of the votes.[28]

State Legislatures. One of the difficulties in making studies of state legislatures is the tendency for so many to be predominantly one-party so that factions rather than parties offer the real choices. Two legislatures (Nebraska and Minnesota) are elected without party designations of the candidates. Examining party differences in state legislative voting is facilitated by the fact that roll calls are frequently required on every measure. However, a difference of opinion can result from the treatment of all of these roll calls. A large number of them are either unanimous or so one-sided as to present no contest. If these roll calls are included in tabulations, the result creates the appearance of a high degree of interparty unity. If only roll calls involving party divisions are considered, the result may

---

26 Julius Turner, "Responsible Parties: A Dissent from the Floor," *American Political Science Review*, Vol. 45 (1951) pp. 144–145.

27 Julius Turner, "Party and Constituency: Pressures on Congress," *The Johns Hopkins University Studies in Historical and Political Science*, Series 69, No. 1, 1951, p. 34 and Chap. 3.

28 Turner, *"Responsible Parties,"* pp. 145–147. A different conclusion from different data is found in Clarence A. Berdahl, "Some Notes on Party Membership in Congress," *American Political Science Review*, Vol. 43 (1949) pp. 311–321, 492–508, 721–732. These articles sketch the history of congressional party regularity in both the present-day Republican and Democratic parties and in the Whig Party. The emphasis is upon the character of ambivalence in enforcing party doctrine or regularity among members. Voting on roll calls is not included in the analysis.

obscure the amount of party agreement while more carefully identifying the extent of party divisions.

Studies have produced contradictory conclusions about the role of legislative parties in determining public policy and the degree of party cleavage over policies. Professor Lowell, using nineteenth-century data, found that parties were relatively insignificant except in New York.[29] The same general finding has been made subsequently by others.[30] Party leadership was found to be unimportant or less important than in Congress in the case of two states.[31] On the other hand, studies of Connecticut and New Jersey led to conclusions that parties do control legislative proceedings and that party leaders are more important than committee leaders.[32] An examination of eight states led to the discovery that those most highly urban are more likely to produce partisan social and economic issues resulting from the urban-rural clashes—Democrats identified with large metropolitan areas and Republicans with smaller cities and rural areas. Party voting was not necessarily found where the parties competed sharply in state elections. The influence of the governor and the degree of party unity in legislative voting vary from state to state.[33] Many policy decisions in the states and in Congress are made on a nonpartisan basis, whether by voice vote or unanimity on a roll call. However, in both national and state bodies there emerges the pattern of party divisions over such issues as taxation, labor relations, and social policies.

These phenomena give some credibility to the observation of Ostrogorski that opposition in the parliamentary sense had disappeared in Con-

---

[29] A. Lawrence Lowell, "The Influence of Party Upon Legislation in England and America," *Annual Report of the American Historical Association*, 1901, I, pp. 321–543.

[30] O. Douglas Weeks, "Politics in the Legislatures," *National Municipal Review*, Vol. 41 (1952) pp. 80–86.

[31] William J. Keefe, "Party Government and Lawmaking in the Illinois General Assembly," *Northwestern University Law Review*, Vol. 47 (1952) pp. 55–71. Keefe, "Parties, Partisanship, and Public Policy in the Pennsylvania Legislature," *American Political Science Review*, Vol. 48 (1954) pp. 450–464. In the session covered by this last article, a majority of Republicans opposed a majority of Democrats on only 6.3% of the roll calls in the Senate and 13.2% in the House; unanimous roll calls were 81.6% and 69.7%, respectively.

[32] W. Duane Lockard, "Legislative Politics in Connecticut," *Ibid.*, Vol. 48 (1954) pp. 166–173; Dayton D. McKean, "A State Legislature and Group Pressures," *The Annals*, Vol. 179 (1935) pp. 124–130.

[33] Malcolm E. Jewell, "Party Voting in American State Legislatures," *American Political Science Review*, Vol. 49 (1955) pp. 773–791. In a questionnaire survey, it was reported that party spirit and cohesion were strong in seventeen states, occasionally or moderately strong in eleven states, and weak or nonexistent in twenty states; that pressure politics was more important than party politics in twenty-four states, about equal in fourteen states and less important in seven states.——Belle Zeller (ed.), *American State Legislatures, Report of the Committee on American Legislatures of the American Political Science Association* (New York: Thomas Y. Crowell Company, 1954) pp. 192–194; in general Chap. 12.

gress [34] and to Edmund Burke's qualification of his own definition of a party: The need for agreement was not

> blindly to follow the opinions of your party, when in direct opposition to your own clear ideas; a degree of servitude that no worthy man could bear the thought of submitting to; and such as, I believe, no connexions [parties] . . . ever could be so senselessly tyrannical as to impose. Men thinking freely, will, in particular instances, think differently. But still as the greater part of the measures which arise in the course of publick business are related to, or dependent on, some great *leading general principles in government*, a man must be peculiarly unfortunate in the choice of his political company if he does not agree with them at least nine times in ten. If he does not concur in these general principles upon which the party is founded, and which necessarily draw on a concurrence in their application, he ought from the beginning to have chosen some other, more conformable to his opinions.[35]

Choices in Election Campaigns. Candidates in campaigns present their respective party's positions on issues to some extent at least. Exceptions occur where a candidate appeals to constituents more strongly inclined to the other party's position and can hope to win only by repudiating his own party's position. The assertion that voters are bilked because a victorious party does not carry out its promises is sometimes based on extreme cases. In presidential elections, promises have been made either in or outside of platforms to strategically placed groups in key states when the party as a whole was not committed to any such promises and the promiser knew it was not. His means of keeping the support of the pressure groups was to continue to talk as if his party was committed and was failing in its duties in not redeeming his promises.[36] The electoral-college system supports this kind of operation by forcing "candidates to place great weight on votes received in large, marginal states, whose voters may not necessarily agree with the rest of the country. Members of Congress may, therefore,

---

34 *Op. cit.*, p. 385.

35 *The Works of the Right Honourable Edmund Burke* (Boston: Wells and Lilly, 1826) I, pp. 428–429.

36 The celebrated illustration of this situation which undoubtedly was foremost in the minds of the Committee on Political Parties was the election of Harry S. Truman in 1948 with a platform and campaign appealing to such groups. However, the majority of the Democrats in Congress, living outside of these key states, made it clear that they were not running on some of these promises. There was no more repudiation after the election than there had been before. The machinery described in the *Report* would have had to be used to support President Truman or would have wobbled on the issues and in effect failed to function as the *Report* envisions. "While there is no end of despair in the United States about the irresponsibility of parties and especially of members of Congress, there is a lack of appreciation of Presidential irresponsibility. The parliamentary system corrects this tendency; a Prime Minister cannot afford the rebuffs that a President blissfully absorbs; a Prime Minister cannot appeal for votes making vicarious promises that apparently cannot be carried out."—William Goodman, "How Much Political Party Centralization Do We Want? *Journal of Politics*, Vol. 13 (1951) p. 548.

furnish a better index of public opinion than the President, although congressmen, too, are unrepresentative to the extent that districts are gerrymandered and voters are uninformed." [37]

POSSIBILITY OF THE REFORMS

Possibility Accepted. The first question which is likely to arise is the possibility of these reforms of the party system being realized. No one fails to take a serious view of this question. The *Report* was most particularly designed to find "readjustments" which "will not require legislation or any other process of formal enactment. Rather, if they are to come at all, they must result from the growth of supporting opinion." In any event, "party responsibility cannot be legislated into being." [38] The Committee did think that the statement of a new kind of party organization could and, it hoped, would help to widen the area of agreement which heretofore has been "limited" when "specific questions are raised" about the kind of party system needed.[39] Although the Committee agreed that parties had remained virtually unchanged since the Civil War,[40] parties can be changed by proposing the kind which people will recognize and accept as better suited to the exigencies of their own day.

Traditional Influences. The reasons for the parties being what they are can be briefly reviewed. The *governmental forms* of federalism and separation of powers are almost always pointed to as causes, but they are also results. Why were they adopted in the first place? One reason is that in the eighteenth century the national impulse was comparatively weak. There was no concept of the national character of parties because there was no necessity for such a concept. Decentralization in the operation of the electoral college and in the selection of United States senators by state legislatures failed to give elections a national character.[41] Parties developed when the local emphasis in government still prevailed; when the suspicion of government naturally attached to parties; when the purpose of political institutions, according to one editor, was purely to protect liberty.

> All governments are more or less combinations against the people; they are states of violence against individual liberty, originating from man's imperfections and vices, and as rulers have no more virtue than the

---

[37] Turner, "Responsible Parties," p. 148.

[38] *Report*, pp. 85, 35.

[39] *Ibid.*, p. 17.

[40] *Ibid.*, p. 25.

[41] "We vote at stated intervals for the President of the United States. In this voting there is evidence of patterns of political behavior, formerly geographic in character but now determined by class interests. There is, however, no evidence in the vote by counties of a so-called 'national' vote. Very few of the men who devote their lives to the practice of politics in the nation ever think of it as a national vote."——E. E. Robinson, *They Voted for Roosevelt* (Stanford: Stanford University Press, 1947) p. 9.

ruled, the equilibrium between them can only be preserved by proper attentions and association; for the power of government can only be kept within the constitutional limits by the display of a power equal to itself, the collected sentiment of the people. Solitary opinions have little weight with men whose views are unfair, but the voice of many strikes them with awe.[42]

The *spirit and tradition of localism* were created and fostered both by the doctrine of democracy and by the growing size of the country and the expansion of its people across the continent during the nineteenth century. It is no wonder that the local-residence rule took hold and was cultivated by local political leaders.

The attitude toward politics generally and toward parties specifically can be characterized in two different ways.

(1) There has been the *tradition of political independence* among both voters and politicians, the latter often posing as unencumbered and taking dictation from no one including the party "bosses." The independence movement has blossomed forth from time to time in citizens' refusals to register as party members. This resistance to requiring party oaths or other tests of regularity and membership is more often than not sympathetically received by people who do not have a strong sense of party identification. Even bolters or recalcitrants within the party organization invariably try to justify themselves to their constituents by making a virtue of not being controlled, particularly if they can make their case in terms of some issue or issues which are designed to place them on the popular side.[43]

(2) The second attitude toward politics and parties is more meaningful because of its relation to independence. This attitude is a composite of *suspicion* and a *materialistic or practical view of politics*. The suspicions

---

[42] *American Daily Advertiser*, December 29, 1794, quoted in George P. Luetscher, *Early Political Machinery in the United States* (Philadelphia: University of Pennsylvania, Ph.D. dissertation, 1903).

[43] Some classic examples of this kind of appeal are found in the statements of Senator Wayne Morse of Oregon in his interview in *U.S. News and World Report*, November 19, 1954, pp. 68 ff. A few are chosen at random: Political parties did not exist when the Constitution was written and were an "afterthought. They were never devised to determine policy" (p. 68). "You see the term 'party loyalty' itself is an emotional sanction. What do you mean 'party loyalty?' The only loyalty you owe is to the constituents" (p. 69). "I think that all your party machinery is, or should be, is a matter of party housekeeping and the doing of chore work, not of policy formation. If you're going to have the party determine the policy which the individual Senator is to follow, then you enslave him" (p. 70). "What is it about organization that is separate and distinct from a legislative issue? If you're going to look at party organization . . . as a dictator for carrying out legislative policy on issues, then you make a shibboleth . . . out of party organization. Then you make a man bow down and kneel to a political party-organization concept. He then loses his freedom of action in behalf of his State and nation. He's got to be free" (p. 70). "I'm never moved by such emotional concepts as 'party loyalty.' I'm concerned only by what I think is right or wrong. I think you should vote for what you think is right or wrong, and that is the highest type of party loyalty" (p. 70).

have been evidenced not only in denouncing politicians but also in trying to eliminate them as much as possible. Probably no one single shot at the party system has had more effect than the nonpartisan movement in city government. "Politics," in the peculiar sense it is often used in this country, was acquiesced in for the nation and even for the state and county; on those levels we had to put up with controversies and divisive issues presented by parties. In cities, it was proclaimed, the kinds of issues were entirely different and the parties had no place. Instead of campaign oratory of politicians, city problems would respond to discussion by civic-minded men who would offer themselves for office if they did not have to put up with the graft and "bossism" of parties. The permanent party organization was discarded in favor of an *ad hoc* organization for each candidate in each election. If this antiparty suspicion is carried far enough, what will be the effect upon the party system?

> The idea that neither of the major parties is any good has been culti-
> vated by extremists . . . and echoed by unthinking persons who somehow
> believe they are expressing a new kind of political independence. Actually
> they are contributing toward a breakdown of the two-party system and the
> development of splinter parties and blocs.[44]

This result is not inevitable unless enough people accept the negative view of parties, but the general attitude is probably nearer to this extreme than to that propounded by the *Report* of the Committee.

The practicality of American thinking about politics is borne out by evidence that the game is played for what there is in it. The materialistic rewards are to a limited extent patronage; but they include much more: direct benefits in the form of pensions, contracts, appropriations, and exemptions. As long as government policies are directed to "priming the pump"—whether by large-scale construction, foreign aid, or domestic relief —neither party's leadership dares to strike out in a new direction which would endanger any of the built-in securities or vested rights won by political negotiation and by conditioned responses at the polls.

Politics most of the time has been no center of ideological conflict but has been a *center of conflict for office and perquisites* in which segments of the public would join from time to time as they became involved. Aside from the materialistic objectives, most people could adopt an attitude of indulgent benevolence or of disinterest or of disdain toward the party battle and let the politicians fight out their troubles among themselves.

While the proponents of reform would insist that past conduct is not a reliable guide to future conduct if parties were changed into vehicles for policy formation and execution, this metamorphosis of the voters cannot be projected without taking into account their past and present responses. The carpings commonly heard about the parties being "crooked"

---

[44] David Lawrence, syndicated column, February 12, 1954.

and standing for nothing are not necessarily to be taken too seriously. Some of them are likely to be rationalizations for not taking part in political processes. The inherent desire to criticize and look down upon those above comes out in protestations about "what is being done" and assertions that the average citizen could do much better. To make proposals for different kinds of parties will not by itself change people's attitudes toward parties.

Party membership tests are now meager enough, getting down in most cases to taking the word of the voter that his party is the one he says it is.[45] Unless one votes in a direct primary or takes part in other party activities, he is under no compulsion to do even this much by way of declaration. The incidence of split-ticket voting in general elections appears to be on the increase, an independence based in many cases upon personalities of candidates, not particularly upon policy differences among them. The discrepancy between formal party enrolment and voting behavior reflects voters' tendency to continue registering in the same party because of loyalty to a party name even when they vote against some or all of its candidates.[46] This kind of voter activity is not designed to make candidates hold vigorously to a party policy if some other position has greater promise of voter appeal.

Attempts at Policy Formation. Various proposals of the *Report* can be examined in the light of traditional party operations. Varying amounts of dissatisfaction with existing policy leadership can be found. Both parties in the West have organized associations because the members thought the national leadership was not doing enough in the way of particular programs.[47] An attempt was made to draft a Republican platform for the 1950 congressional elections on behalf of the National Committee and the state committees, but the actual statement that was issued was prepared by Republican members of Congress, not all of whom concurred.[48] When the Republican national chairman tried to consolidate some of the functions of the congressional and senatorial campaign committees in the National Committee, he was beaten in a meeting of the party's finance committee by members of Congress.[49] When the situation was reversed in the attempts of some Western Republicans to organize all state chairmen into a national organization, it was the National Committee leaders who blocked the move.[50]

---

[45] The resistance of South Dakota voters to a law requiring them to declare party membership was so strong that the law was changed.——Clarence Berdahl, "Party Membership in the United States," *American Political Science Review,* Vol. 36 (1942) p. 31.

[46] *Ibid.,* pp. 256-259.

[47] Hugh A. Bone, "New Party Associations in the West," *ibid.,* Vol. 45 (1951) pp. 1115-1125.

[48] *New York Times,* August 5, 1949; November 30, 1949; February 7, 1950.

[49] *Ibid.,* January 26, 1951.

[50] *Ibid.,* February 5, 1952.

The most far-reaching development of this nature has been the Democratic Advisory Committee established by the Northern faction to formulate party policy, following the Party's defeat in the 1956 presidential election. The national chairman was a leader in the movement, and the National Committee, by a vote of 65 to 26 in May, 1957, upheld the authority of the Advisory Committee to issue policy declarations between national conventions. The members, appointed by the national chairman, represent the entire party, at least in theory. Some are designated "at large," such as Adlai Stevenson and former President Harry S. Truman; others are governors, mayors, and former office holders. Only two members of Congress accepted appointment (Senators Humphrey and Kefauver). The antagonistic attitude of the Democratic leaders of Congress has made it clear that they intend to fight to hold their preeminence in making party policy. The result has been a sharp factional fight periodically brought to public attention.[51]

Handling Insurgents. The *Report* refers to disciplinary powers through the projected Council, but the *Report* never comes to grips with a situation in which the top leadership of a party disagrees. The assumption is that the leaders in the new organization will be able to compose their differences and still present a program sharply different as between the parties. How to handle the powerful insurgents who refused to leave the party voluntarily is not explained.[52] The late Senator George W. Norris while a Republican openly supported Franklin D. Roosevelt for President in 1932 and 1936; finally, Senator Norris left the Republican Party and declared himself an independent. What would a party council do if it read an announcement such as the late Senator Robert M. La Follette, Sr., issued in 1912?

> I shall remain in the Republican party at this time. I shall continue
> to denounce its representatives when they betray public interest. I shall
> refuse to be bound by its action whenever it fails in its duty to the coun-
> try, and I shall do all in my power to restore it to the high place in the
> service and confidence and affection of the American people, which it held
> when it was the party of Abraham Lincoln.[53]

---

[51] *Ibid.*, December 6, 1956, lists the original appointees. Subsequent articles have appeared in the press chronicling successive developments, including the policy statements issued by the Advisory Committee. For a general review and appraisal, see *ibid.*, February 9, 1958, p. 4E.

[52] There was no need for the *Report* to deal with bolters after their retirement from active politics, *e.g.*, the Democrats' 1928 presidential candidate, Alfred E. Smith, supporting Alfred M. Landon (Republican) in 1936 or the Democrats' 1924 candidate, John W. Davis, supporting Dwight D. Eisenhower (Republican) in 1952.

[53] Robert M. La Follette, *Autobiography* (Madison: Robert M. La Follette Company, 1913, 5th ed.) p. 758.

Far from disciplining such members, party leaders have almost without exception been loath to exclude the bolter, whether from party primaries, conventions, or Congress. Party regularity is proved by supporting all of the candidates of the party in the general election, no matter how the leadership opposed them in the direct primary or nominating convention. James Farley stated the orthodoxy in these matters when he declared that contests for the nomination were a good thing for the party by putting the various factions to the test of the ballot. Following the nominations,

> the vendetta must end . . . . Party loyalty is requisite for party success. Discipline is as necessary in the ranks of a political organization as in the files of an army. As your national chairman, I have announced with all sincerity and without reservations that the national committee is behind every Democratic nominee. That has to be the guiding tenet of every honest Democrat if we are to continue in power in state and nation.[54]

Direct Primaries and Party Responsibility. The *Report's* handling of the nomination process deserves special mention. Probably because the direct primary is an accomplished fact and opposition would be fruitless, the *Report* raises no question of its use, but does hold out for the closed primary. The preprimary endorsement by the parties' councils is also recommended, by implication, for members of Congress and for presidential candidates as long as challengers are free to enter the contests.[55] What remains to be clarified is how party leaders can run a coherent and responsible party if they cannot control the nomination of candidates. A preprimary convention for designating organization candidates may have the practical effect of vindicating the leaders if the endorsed candidates are nominated. If the organization candidates are beaten, the leaders can truthfully say that they have no responsibility, although they will do their best to elect the candidates. A maverick, an outsider who beat the organization in a primary, may feel that his independence is an asset, while not being truculent, he may not be amenable.

The answer probably is that if the people accepted the new parties and swung into the spirit of the movement, they would not nominate an insurgent. Under any circumstances, some voters will not be genuine party members and some who are may want to cross party lines on occasion. The new parties can hardly function properly unless there are at least minimum tests for membership which are enforceable. The point is not that voters can never change affiliation, but that a change should be well considered

---

54 Quoted in Berdahl, *op. cit.*, No. 1, p. 18; also pp. 31–35.

55 *Report*, pp. 71–74. Not all of the thinking is uniform on the primary, or at any event, on the presidential primary. Professor E. Allen Helms suggested in effect the return to the congressional caucus.——*Op. cit.*, pp. 63–64. Key, *op. cit.*, pp. 16–25, advanced the hypothesis that statewide direct primaries may have been responsible for the decline of local party organizations.

and not be a fickle response to a particular campaign. The amount of missionary work required in the open-primary states to convert them to closed primaries and in closed-primary states to secure enforcement will be great, as nearly as one can tell. Special case work and persuasive techniques will certainly be required in Washington to get rid of the wide-open primary.[56]

Increased Use of National Conventions. Whether or not presidential nominations are made at national conventions, the suggestion for more frequent conventions means that these gatherings will be deliberative and not full of the enthusiasm and color which go with the nomination function. Proposals for mid-term conventions in both parties have been overcome by objections from congressional leaders who insisted that in these years their respective parties should run on their congressional records. No complete meeting of minds is found in deciding when such conventions should be held. Some favor a time after the state direct primaries in order to avoid the wrangling that would go on if contending candidates were present. If the convention prepared a platform for the candidates to run on, logic would dictate its being written before their nominations. Otherwise, candidates may run on mutually contradictory commitments during their campaigns and would be unable to reverse positions which subsequently conflicted with the national platform. Justification for a mid-term convention has been found in the opportunity to size up the major areas of disagreement and to perfect organization in advance of the presidential year.[57]

It is a good question how deliberative a body of five or six hundred members can be. The House of Representatives, with 435 members meeting for several months at a time, is unwieldy and operates only by the rigid exercise of leadership using rules for keeping members in line and eliminating dilatory tactics. The existence of a party council furnishes a clue to the nature of the leadership which would dominate the convention, and the rules of the House would be an inevitable model for the parliamentary procedure. Discussion on the convention floor would be far more important than it now is; like members of Congress, delegates would be speaking for the record and would be trying to advance whatever cause or candidacy they were supporting. Debate time would be limited and something like the five-minute rule might be necessary. One cannot help agreeing with

---

[56] Purely as a speculation, one wonders what would happen if, upon the strict application of party-membership tests, the vote at the direct primary began falling below its present low levels. Would there be a corresponding outcry about nonvoting, and what would be the remedy? To relax the requirements would undermine the party system.

[57] See the *New York Times,* May 4, 1952; July 19, 1952; April 2, 1953; April 29, 1953; and May 18, 1953.

the judgment of one of the most persistent opponents of the national nominating conventions, who wrote that once they were "stripped of their role in nominating candidates, they would have lost their vitality."[58]

Effect of Clear-cut Issues on Candidates. If the formation of a platform in mid-term years would complicate the task of harmonizing the party and endanger the position of some of its legislative candidates, what would party leaders do to compensate? The most crucial contests are likely to be found in mixed urban-rural districts where the clash of opposing interests is potentially greater. If the parties split cleanly on the important issues of the day, their candidates could hope to do no better than appeal to that portion of the constituency which would respond favorably to the respective party's program. Instead of trying to compose differences in order to win—what is often called "fence straddling"—the cleavage would be widened and deepened. The only hope of each candidate would be to mobilize as nearly 100% of his party's supporters as possible. Incidentally, this situation may help alleviate the problem of nonvoting, but at the cost of unalleviated peace and quiet of the constituency. In those districts where one interest predominates, the effect would be to create more of a monopoly for the party which more nearly satisfied that interest.[59]

Motivations of the System. When studying parties in a practical sense, it is necessary to be clear about the motivations of the system. The ostensible motivation is to be elected to office, and in the past this objective has been desirable because of the spoils nature of the system, the opportunity for rewards if one held the power and authority. A reading of the *Report* implies that the new motivation for holding office will be the coordination of the government machinery in the interest of advancing a program of public policies. It is possible to state this motivation differently. In the transition from spoils politics to all-pervading-government politics, the motivation for winning may be to exercise the sheer weight of power that goes with victory, both for the sake of the power itself and for fear of the other side exercising it. The leaders of either party will not be seeking to hold back any policy they want advanced and they no doubt will have policy objectives. Whatever the motivation for gaining office, it cannot be indulged until the office is held. At this point, the *Report* is most likely to unravel, for no party leaders or candidates are going to adhere to a program just for the sake of being logical if the result is to endanger their election.

---

58 Senator Estes Kefauver, "Indictment of the Political Convention," *New York Times Magazine*, March 16, 1952. Nevertheless the Senator was agreeable to the various reforms of the convention and to holding conventions more frequently.

59 Malcolm Moos, *Politics, Presidents and Coattails* (Baltimore: The Johns Hopkins University Press, 1952) pp. 144, 166–167.

Position of the "Out" Party. The *Report* does not adequately treat the means for the "out" party to control its own machinery. It was natural that the Committee on Political Parties would deal most directly with the operation of the party holding the White House. With a leader provided in the person of the President, a party would have an easier task of coordination and the outlines of its action can be more easily seen. The chaotic conditions usually found in the other party can only be placed within the plan of the *Report* with difficulty. The Committee could not have been expected to reorganize chaos, but the omission, while completely understandable, figures in the question of possibility. A defeated presidential candidate is, in a sterile sort of way, the leader of his party. He is leader in name only as a rule, because his defeat justifies his colleagues' repudiating him. When ambitious competitors within his party begin working for their own nomination, the defeated candidate can no more establish himself personally than he can lay down a program for the party to follow. Perhaps no one summed up this equivocal situation better than Thomas E. Dewey after his second defeat.

> I find that I have been re-elected for a second straight term to that somewhat mythical office known as titular head of the Republican party. It is an ancient and honorable office that carries with it the theoretical right to speak for the party but no guarantee whatsoever that anybody will listen to you.[60]

A party council can screen, in a preliminary way, presidential candidates if it has the power of the White House behind it. The council of the "out" party would have no such supporting backdrop. If it was controlled by one of the prospective candidates, his competitors would be very unlikely to accept council decisions or trust its power as projected into the national convention.

Meaning of Responsibility. At this point a great deal of argument can arise because the *Report* itself is not sufficiently specific. The difficulty arises in two consecutive paragraphs:

> It is here not suggested, of course, that the parties should disagree about everything. Parties do not, and need not, take a position on all questions that allow for controversy. The proper function of the parties is to develop and define policy alternatives on matters likely to be of interest to the whole country, on issues related to the responsibility of the parties for the conduct of either the government or the opposition.
>
> *Needed clarification of party policy* in itself *will not cause the parties to differ more fundamentally or more sharply than they have in the past.* The contrary is much more likely to be the case. The clarification of

---

[60] Text of address delivered in Washington, D.C., *New York Times*, February 9, 1949. In his series of four lectures at the Woodrow Wilson School of Public and International Affairs in February and April, 1950, Dewey sought to lay down the program he would have had the Republican Party adopt.

party policy may be expected to produce a more reasonable discussion of public affairs, more closely related to the political performance of the parties in their actions rather than their words. *Nor is it to be assumed that increasing concern with their programs will cause the parties to erect between themselves an ideological wall.* There is no real ideological division in the American electorate, and hence programs of action presented by responsible parties for the voter's support could hardly be expected to reflect or strive toward such division.[61]

These words, taken in the context of the entire *Report,* raise serious questions of interpretation and intent. Further pursuit of the elusive thread leads only to more puzzlement. If the words be taken purely at face value, they would seem to mean that the differences between the parties would be only little more in the future than in the past. In this case the problems of winning elections would be the same as they are now, and the only overhaul of the party would be in its machinery. Yet this meaning seems scarcely tenable in view of the sweeping condemnations elsewhere in the *Report* and the ambitious preparations for policy enforcement all along the line.

The fathoming of this final question of possibility of the plan must await clarification of terminology. What is meant, more exactly, by "party responsibility"?[62] What kinds and numbers of differences constitute effective parties for the age of atomic energy and movements into outer space? How much difference, without ideological division, must and can there be in order for us to be able to tell a Democrat from a Republican?

DESIRABILITY OF THE REFORMS

In many respects the second major question to be asked about plans for reorganizing parties is more important than the first. The possibility of sweeping changes becoming adoptable and acceptable is always highly speculative because of the difficulty of foreseeing the new situation which must precede the changes. The possibilities for realization of the reforms contained in the *Report* cannot be assessed with as much accuracy as one would like because of the questions the *Report* leaves unanswered. What does emerge clearly from the *Report* is a reorganization plan, and superficially this part can be declared possible of accomplishment. What remains is the question of the desirability of the reorganization, quite apart from the intentions of the Committee as to how it will operate. Because of the nearly two centuries of experience with political organization as a nation, we can evaluate the results of the projected plan, asking if it would be desirable on the assumption that it is possible.

---

[61] *Report,* pp. 20–21; italics in the original.

[62] See J. Roland Pennock, "Responsiveness, Responsibility and Majority Rule," *American Political Science Review,* Vol. 46 (1952) pp. 796–797, for an inquiry into the meanings of responsibility.

INTERNAL PARTY CONTROL

Who Constitutes the Party? The *Report* emphasizes "intraparty democracy" as a control or guide for the policy positions of the party.[63] The inference is that the party members in the grass-roots discussion groups will have a real influence on the council and will be a firm bulwark for the council in its decisions on policy matters and in disciplinary cases. If it is to be democracy, the new party will function as a myriad of town meetings from which some consensus will emerge. Otherwise, the word "democratic" would be misused and the references to "internal responsibility" of the parties would be meaningless. In fact, intra-party democracy and accountability are declared to be necessary in developing party responsibility to the nation at large.[64] Who are the party leaders to be responsible to within the party? Who within a party are to participate in the development of the party's program through the network of local discussion groups?

The *Report* directly and indirectly answers these questions by saying the people to be included are those who vote the party ticket. To adopt this concept of party membership is itself to work considerable revolution in the party system, for it means "internal responsibility" to all those who, at the last election, cast their ballots for the party candidates. The national electorate of the parties in 1952 was 33,000,000 plus for the Republicans and 27,000,000 plus for the Democrats. The *Report* seems to be saying that these many millions must be both organized in some way for discussion and must be consulted in the development of programs. Of course, this kind of "democracy" is impossible or it would not be necessary for us to have a representative governmental form, and the *Report* obviously does not mean to say it is possible. The membership for the purpose of influencing policy through discussion groups would be composed of those who are active in party affairs and by virtue of their participation have a right to be heard.[65]

Location of Control. The party system in the past has produced "bosses," not because the organization is decentralized, but because of the inherent nature of organizations. The control in the *Report's* organization would be exercised locally by those who were active and in harmony with the national leaders. Control in the nation would lie with those party leaders who dominated the council. If the party cabinet is established, the final touch would be given. The council will be the wheel within the

---

63 *Report,* pp. 65–70.

64 *Ibid.,* p. 23.

65 Ranney, *op. cit.,* pp. 155–157. Also Ranney, "Toward a More Responsible Two-Party System: A Commentary," *American Political Science Review,* Vol. 45 (1951) pp. 488–492. See above, p. 4.

convention, dominating its activities and determining its consideration of subjects by controlling its procedure and time schedule. The party cabinet will be the wheel within the council. This situation would make for rule by a minority of the electorate even if it were a majority of the majority within a party.[66]

Dominance by the President. For the purposes of the "in" party, this machinery would be well adapted to make of the President and his advisors in Congress and within the executive branch the group that runs the "in" party. What will happen within the "out" party is more questionable, but if the council actually functions there, the titular leader in the person of the last defeated nominee for the Presidency will play the part that the President plays for the "in" party. The *Report* expresses a fear of over-extending the powers of the President; if a party does not become a well-organized agency with a coherent program, its members will flock around a President's program for want of any other.[67] Unfortunately, the organization of council and cabinet for the "in" party promises to establish the President as the unquestioned strong man, for he would have the machinery for enforcing the policies he and his advisors formulate. Under this new machinery, if it is to work as intended, factionalism must be ended at the council and cabinet levels in order to establish unity. Otherwise, the result would be in no way different from past practice and the council and cabinet would become merely additional pieces of machinery in which factions carry on their quest for objectives and negotiate compromises among themselves.

Factional Supremacy. To take the view that the reforms can be carried through without the dominance of one faction being established is to ignore what happens to the minority who will not, eventually, agree "to go along." To fail to foresee this situation is to assume that dissent in the presence of extended discussion will in time melt away like ice in the sun.[68] If discussion by itself would solve the problem of insurgency, the problem would already be solved, for discussion goes on constantly among the leaders of factions. Under the existing arrangements, discussion leads to composing differences among equals, but the result is often a hodgepodge of equivocation.

---

[66] Pennock, *op. cit.,* pp. 799 ff.

[67] *Ibid.,* pp. 89, 93–95. That there is an already existing party difference in reliance upon the President has been frequently noted. Professor Holcombe, *op. cit.,* p. 133, more nearly pinpointed the reason. "The greater proportion of mixed districts in the Republican Party and the greater concentration of its support in the North make for greater solidarity in its congressional representation. . . . These characteristic differences between the two major parties make the Democrats, when in control of the Congress, more dependent on vigorous executive leadership than is necessary for Republicans."

[68] Ranney, *The Doctrine of Responsible Party Government,* p. 161.

REALIGNMENT

The organizational ability to control and discipline dissenters who ultimately refuse to accept policy can be used to make parties not necessarily more responsible, but more oligarchical. If one faction of a party is established in control of the machinery, the possibility for setting a program and carrying it out becomes much greater, whether the program of one party would in this way materially differ from that of the other party or not. What needs to be considered now is the desirability of party reorganization in the light of the various open and subtle invitations to party realignment which have been in the political air as an aftermath of the New Deal, just as proposals for realignment have sporadically appeared throughout our history.

Dissatisfaction with Present Alignment. The realignment forces are found in the factions of both parties, among those who take the most decided "policy attitudes." The impetus is not alone from those who prefer a symmetrical system with every ideology neatly in place, but more strongly from those who want to be gathered together with their own ideological colleagues in order to oppose all of those who disagree with them. Some of the more extreme factions of the Northern Democrats have publicly toyed with the possibility for making their party into a farmer-labor vehicle or even forming a labor party.[69] Among those who consider themselves on the other side, with a conservative bent, efforts have been made to convince one faction of the Republicans and the Southern Democrats that they should join forces.

Opponents of the traditional alignment see the parties as essentially divided into two major factions and are positive that each faction in each party is more compatible with a particular faction in the other party. References are made to the "four-party system," followed by suggestions that the factional disunity be reorganized into compatible party compartments.[70] A Committee to Explore Political Realignment hoped for a segregation of the "Constitutionalists and Socialists" into opposing parties in the interest of continuing the two-party system and of clarifying the

---

[69] Compare these words of Louis Hollander, President of the New York CIO: "I believe we can force the reactionaries of both old parties to form their own third party. Then labor can sit down and rebuild one of the two remaining parties, supporting the liberals who stay on."

"There can be no political party of labor unless we first have a united labor movement. There is no room for short cuts. Others have tried but ended up in the ditch."

If, in the next ten years, a united labor movement could organize 15,000,000 to 20,000,000 more people, "there will be no need for a labor party" because "every politician will come to you and ask you to join his party."——Quoted in the *New York Times*, February 15, 1955.

[70] See, *e.g.*, David Lawrence, editorial in *U.S. News and World Report*, March 12, 1954, p. 128.

issues of "excessive centralization" as against "a properly balanced and defined dual system of State and Federal government." [71] In some way, all of these dissatisfied observers agree, national harmony and the parties' strength and responsibility will emerge from dichotomizing the ideological struggle; whereas with the struggle present in both parties, the result will continue to be discord and meaningless parties. These expressions amount to a plea for transferring the function of composing differences away from the parties and placing it entirely on the government level. This is a characteristic of the multiparty system. How it can be made a characteristic of the American two-party system is never made clear.[72]

Contribution of the Report. The Committee *Report* seems not to enter this realm of realignment at all, but the crux of realignment is how to handle diverse interests within the two-party system, and the crux of the plan for responsible parties is how to handle pressure groups which operate in both parties. The *Report* furnishes a simplified guide to the study and classification of pressure groups. There are two types. One is the *"highly organized special interests with small or no direct voting power"* which finds its "main stock in trade in the bad features of the present situation." The second is the "large membership" organizations in labor, agriculture, and business which are watched by the public whether they like it or not. The first can be expected to oppose the plan for reorganizing the parties because they prefer that officials be *"kept defenseless in the face of their special pressure."* The second make demands upon the parties which "at least appear justifiable to large numbers of voters. . . . the scope of its success in the political arena is being explained to its members by each large-membership organization in terms of the need for compromise with other interests indicated by the party program." [73]

The second type, it is expected, *"with wise leadership will generally support the turn toward more responisble parties."* This support will be likely to result in either of two circumstances: when the organization identifies itself with one of the parties or when it is willing to compromise with other groups having different interests. There is little doubt in the concluding words of the *Report* on this subject but that the first circumstance is more likely to be the reason for supporting the new party organization, since a large group identified with a party will be more interested in the party's having a dependable program which the group can support and which its members will insist upon.

---

[71] *Final Summary of Survey*, pamphlet issued January 1, 1952, p. 4. The reason for the two-party system is "historic," developing out of the battle over ratification of the Constitution in the state conventions of 1787 and 1788. The two-party system has continued as a split over centralized and decentralized government not, fundamentally, over sectional and economic cleavages.——Pp. 1-4.

[72] A different kind of realignment is the long-term change in voting behavior. V. O. Key, Jr., "Secular Realignment and the Party System," *Journal of Politics*, Vol. 21 (1959) pp. 198-210.

[73] *Report*, pp. 85-86; italics in the original.

Parties and Large Groups Identified. What all of this amounts to saying is that the parties will succeed with their organization of centralization by depending upon the mobilization of large-membership groups and orienting the party program toward those groups. The result could be a labor-farmer party versus a farmer-business party or some other combination whereby large groups with significant voting power are put together. No one can doubt that in this lining up of sides among basic interest groups, the fullest desires of the "liberal-conservative" realignment forces will be fulfilled. This proposal further encourages grass-roots political activity of large groups by making them, through the discussion groups, the local party organs. Parties' programs would be commitments because the interest groups concerned will be part of the local party leadership. How responsive such leadership would be to new challenges or to new ideas is problematical, but it has been suggested that the *Report* is going in the wrong direction, in this respect, by keeping parties' leaders resistant to "new blood." "The party is in great need of insurgents. The Committee might consequently devote its attention to the promotion of insurgency within the party rather than to reforms which will cement present groups in power." [74]

Enforcement of Choices. Another factor not considered in this new situation is the citizen who is not a member of or directly influenced by the large-membership groups. In time, with the growth of organizations, everyone may be at least nominal members of such groups, and this encouragement of party and group identification should help to speed the day. However, the day has not yet arrived. This realignment poses a problem for those who may wish to dissent in some manner that the two parties do not permit. The formalizing of pressure-group interests into the party divisions may make for greater responsibility but for a more restricted range of choices in discovering a candidate to vote for.

Self-government demands a free circulation of individuals' impulses. This calls for a varied network throughout the social structure. Disciplined parties, clearly differentiated, result in a hardening of these arteries. The affliction would not be so severe as the atrophy of the individuals' political strength caused by a one-party system, but to urge government

---

74 Turner, "Responsible Parties" p. 152.

75 Pendleton Herring, *The Politics of Democracy* (New York: Rinehart & Company, Inc., 1940) p. 110. "There are many also in whom the opposing instincts are so well balanced or so undeveloped that they are easily led to the opposite side in conscious or unconscious protests against the errors or misfortunes or mere dominance of the party in power. These are they who make party government so insecure for the party, and, perhaps, so safe for the nation."——Robert M. MacIver, *The Modern State* (London: Oxford University Press, 1950) p. 407.

by two such parties is to ignore the inevitable rigidity of organization necessary if their programs are to be realized. Any such dichotomy is an oversimplification of our social and economic pattern.[75]

Implications for the Two-Party System. No one has satisfactorily explained how parties, realigned and identified with great interest groups, can continue as two major parties. There is much testimony to the effect that two parties cannot operate this way. "In modern states no party can become a great party save by winning recruits from those who never accept its principles." [76] "In the nature of things national parties must be leagues of local factions as well as organizations in which the influence of wealth is combined with the influence of numbers." [77] If these are not valid generalizations for all nations, they are valid conclusions based on American experience. Two parties or not, the question is one of practicability and usefulness of parties for citizens of the United States.

> This talk about dividing the country into two political camps—one progressive and the other conservative—is all so much stuff. There will always be agitation of this realignment, but in my considered judgment, it will never come. If it did you'd find you'd have a radical and a reactionary party and neither of these could serve the nation. Each of the two parties is in a sense a coalition. Any party to serve the country must be a party of all sorts of views, and through a reconciliation and adjustment of these views you get harmony and a program for good legislation and good administration. The country is neither radical nor reactionary. A party has got to strike a balance.[78]

WHAT KIND OF A SYSTEM DO WE WANT?

Relation of Parties and Government. The question of making over the parties comes back to the question of why we have a two-party system. Both questions are matters of value judgments. The reforms discussed in this chapter involve a change in all of the existing characteristics of parties, directly or indirectly, and are tantamount to proposals for reorganizing the government itself. Professor Schattschneider himself concluded that the parties we have were meant to accompany the kind of governmental system

---

[76] Anson D. Morse, *Parties and Party Leaders* (Boston: Marshall Jones Company, 1923) p. 17.

[77] Holcombe, *op. cit.*, p. 400.

[78] John N. Garner, quoted in Bascom N. Timmons, *Garner of Texas* (New York: Harper & Brothers, 1948) p. 236. This expression by a Democrat was echoed by a Republican who was glad that the parties' "policies are inextricably entwined. . . . Probably the strength of the two-party system lies in this fact. They are administrative rivals rather than political rivals. Either is in position to take over from the other without involving a complete and predestined change in the foreign and domestic policies of the nation. . . . We 'splinter' inside the party. We do not have to run off and form a new party when the necessity for splintering appears urgent."——Ralph E. Flanders, "The Future of the Republican Party," *Virginia Quarterly Review*, Vol. 28, (1955) pp. 177, 178.

we have.[79] Decisions about the kind of government we want cannot be divorced from forms and organization. The overhauling of party machinery will not revolutionize either the parties or the government unless the reformers are correct in their assumption that the people want what *they* want. "No purely organizational approach can magically dissolve the resistances to centralization of party power. The problem of consolidating control cannot be solved at the center alone." [80]

If the intention is to adopt the parliamentary form of government, abolishing separation of powers, and to centralize the government, cutting off the last vestige of federalism, the picture takes on a different hue. To centralize the parties can hardly have any other effect upon the government. The real questions are the possibility and the desirability of introducing parliamentary and unitary government, where the former is certainly a stranger and where the already accentuated power of the President would be joined with the complementary powers of a prime minister.[81] The establishment of a theoretical legislative supremacy in Congress would be no real check upon the executive, since even in British parliamentary practice the direction of the control has been toward the Cabinet.[82]. The only reliable checking function left in these reorganization plans is that which one party exercises upon the other, for no checks would be left within the government system itself.

> To say that the people can cast aside the domination of the national party regime is, however, to disregard the control of a powerful organization, a part of whose strength comes from the very multiplicity of local interests; to disregard the influence of prejudice and pride and party allegiance; to fail to reckon with the imagination to which national party leaders and party contests strongly appeal; and, above all, not to estimate correctly the force of inertia and the sheer difficulty of maintaining state or local organizations distinct from the national party system.[83]

---

[79] See Schattschneider, *Party Government*, pp. 123–128. Carl J. Friedrich, *Constitutional Government and Democracy* (Boston: Ginn & Company, 1950, rev. ed.) pp. 419–420, pointed out the fallacy of seeking reform of party government while presuming that the government structure will remain unchanged. The "party system, precisely because it is directed toward the control of the government, will closely resemble the government's pattern. If the government is divided federally and functionally, the effort to control it will be similarly dispersed."

[80] Fainsod, *op. cit.*, p. 326.

[81] In combining the role of head of the state and of the prime minister into the presidential office of the United States, proposals for the parliamentary system become "an attempt to reform American government by grafting upon the Presidential system selected characteristics of the parliamentary system without the protections of the latter and by discarding the protective features of the former."——Goodman, *op. cit.*, p. 548.

[82] Holcombe, *op. cit.*, pp. 410, 411. If the observation that the power to dissolve the Government in Britain is equivalent to the power of patronage in the United States, the legislature has waned in both countries.——Walter Bagehot, *The English Constitution* (New York: D. Appleton & Company, 1892, rev. ed.) p. 210. See Maurice Duverger, *Political Parties: Their Organization and Activity in the Modern State* (New York: John Wiley & Sons, Inc., 1954) pp. 393–407.

[83] McLaughlin, *op. cit.*, p. 143.

Relation of Citizens to Parties. There are two ways of thinking and acting regarding the parties. Either they supply candidates and perform internal functions in conformance with the views of active partisans, or it is the public's business—to the extent that people make it so—to select the candidates from whom they will choose in the general election and to decide what policies will be encouraged. If parties are wholly electoral and patronage organizations, their leaders are relieved of and indeed denied a large amount of responsibility. This relation of the parties and the public seems to be the one most citizens prefer and is illustrated in Diagram I.

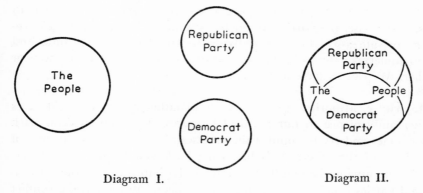

Diagram I.   Diagram II.

If the parties are considered part of and indistinguishable from the people, the relation can be illustrated as in Diagram II.

In Diagram I the citizen who does not take an active part in party affairs looks upon a party decision as one from which he is excluded. He can claim that this condition is undemocratic and destructive of the ends of the Republic. The corrective is to admit "the people" to party processes; if those processes are not adaptable to the widest participation, the processes should be changed. The direct primary was adopted largely for this reason, and the same reason has become the main force behind proposals for a presidential primary and for modification or abolition of the electoral college. When people demand that they make the decisions, they usually think of themselves as standing in the relation shown in the first diagram. Even activities conceded to a party agency, like a committee hearing at a national convention, must be broadcast and televised in order that people can know what decisions affecting them are being made. In this climate it is impossible to have the kind of party system where the party leaders assume all the responsibility for what they do or propose. They are not free agents, but must contend both with specific pressures for consideration and with the general suspicion of the public when it is excluded from what it considers to be its business. Party leaders must contend with the opinions of all people who are politically interested and informed, not just with that indefinite body of supporters of the leaders' own party. Even Democrats and Republicans are not so self-conscious that they watch only their own party, and politically active independents are, of course, watching both.

Either of the above diagrams poses a possible danger. If parties and people are indistinguishable, as in Diagram II, the evils of oligarchy and lack of responsiveness to the public may develop. If parties and people are separate as in Diagram I, the evils are the accentuation of multiple hierarchies in numerous groups (concerned with candidates, issues, and factional fights) both competing with parties and exercising pressure upon party leaders. Democratization of politics is the multiplication of organized interests, complementing party organizations while operating within both parties. Otherwise, the parties would be permitted to operate the government as private associations of individuals who have the aptitude and drive to undertake the task. We can have the system either one way or the other. We cannot have it both ways.

Majority v. Minority. Refusal to accept either system outright gives a further ambivalence to our political practices. We tend to draw back from extremes and try to counter the excesses of one system with some of the qualities of the other. This balancing back and forth is usually acclaimed as occupying the middle of the road. Its imprint upon our government and parties comes from our refusal, in theory, to resolve the conflict involved in the choice between majority rule and minority rights. We say we seek both, but carried to their logical conclusion they reach an impasse. It can be argued forever which of the two is the more democratic, but when the impasse is reached and a decision has to be made, it is minority rights that have won the day, starting at least with the Constitutional Convention of 1787. While neither extreme is palatable and we try to steer a middle course by saying Yes and No to each side of the question, minority rights outweigh majority rule. Our government and party systems reflect this judgment, which in turn has produced one of the outstanding characteristics of American parties—that they have more unity and discipline in campaigning than they have after winning an election, because in our government system a victorious party does not come into the full governmental power.[84]

By the same token, as long as this judgment about majority rule and minority rights exists, the centralizing reforms of the party organization will not strike a responsive chord [85] any more than those reforms on the

---

[84] Ranney, *The Doctrine of Responsible Party Government*, p. 21.

[85] *Ibid.*, pp. 158–159, and "Toward a More Responsible Two-Party System," pp. 495–499.

other extreme—to destroy party organization—have been anything more than academic discussions.

There is another dimension of this same choice between the kinds of parties and between majorities and minorities. Not all people are concerned with or cognizant of the party system and its significance, much less with the great issues of the day or the developments and implications of current events. Only those who are aware and involved are likely to be influential in the decisions. Our system, whether intentionally or not, protects those who are unaware and inactive by placing checks on those who are aware and active. To discard these checks would leave the inactive exposed to and threatened with rapid exploitation by the active. More people may become active and organized, but in the increasing tension of the battle they may simply make the casualty rate higher. The inevitable oligarchical tendency of organizations can be checked to protect both those who know and see and those who do not. The reason for the two-party system may lie deeper than has been generally suspected. It certainly goes beyond economic interests, for it includes the phenomena of people voting against their apparent economic interests because of loyalty, tradition, or some other "irrational" reason. Exhibiting the genius necessary for operating the system, political leaders have looked for durable bases of support in economic interests, which appeared to be stable and basic, without overlooking other influences when they have been pertinent.

Is politics to continue to be played as a game or is it to become a deadly business? As a game it involves the distribution of the good things of life and the resolving of conflicts by give and take. As long as the good things of life exist, this kind of operation is possible. If misfortune befalls the United States and the sources of materialistic rewards become more limited, then politics will become a much grimmer business, and party responsibility may become an attribute of political survival. While the game can still be played, we are offered the prospects for making politics into a deadly business voluntarily, and this is the question to be decided as far as the making over of the parties is concerned. Is it so important whether we can tell a Republican from a Democrat? Whether this makes a difference is itself a basic difference.

A theoretical system has to give way before a functioning, practical system. It is an extremism of some sort to denounce practice because it does not conform with the way one postulates that practice should be.

The moving finger writes. And while we often fail to understand what it is writing, we can hardly fail to see what it wrote.

Selected Bibliography

Bailey, Stephen K., *The Condition of Our National Political Parties,* The Fund for the Republic, 1959.

Herring, E. Pendleton, *The Politics of Democracy.* New York: Rinehart & Company, Inc., 1940.

Holcombe, Arthur N., *Our More Perfect Union.* Cambridge: Harvard University Press, 1950.

McLaughlin, Andrew C., *The Courts, The Constitution and Parties.* Chicago: University of Chicago Press, 1912. Chap. 3.

Ranney, Austin, *The Doctrine of Responsible Party Government.* Urbana: University of Illinois Press, 1954. Illinois Studies in the Social Sciences, Vol. 34, No. 3.

Report of the Committee on Political Parties, "Toward a More Responsible Two-Party System," *American Political Science Review,* Vol. 44 (1950) Supplement.

Schattschneider, E. E., *Party Government.* New York: Farrar & Rinehart, Inc., 1942.

—— *The Struggle for Party Government.* College Park: University of Maryland Press, 1948.

Index

Abbott, W. C.: 6, 8
Abel, Hazel H.: 373
Abraham, Henry J.: 592
Accidental presidents: 248, 365
Adams, Abigail: 337
Adams, James T.: 535
Adams, John: 70, 155–156, 157, 158, 182, 224, 226, 259, 262, 337
  on Caucus Club: 58
  on party differences: 35, 57
  and patronage: 101
  on Vice-Presidency: 181
Adams, John Q.: 101, 162, 167, 226, 262, 405, 499, 512, 611, 612, 624
Adams men: 262, 263
Adams-Clay men: 168
Agar, Herbert: 601, 605
Agriculture, discontent in: 346–347
  organizations in: 331–333
  ownership concentration in: 345
  parity in: 347, 348–349
  partisanship: 348–349
  political power: 259, 261, 263–265, 266, 267, 270, 325–326
  surpluses: 347–348
Almond, Gabriel A.: 391
Allinsmith, Wesley and Beverly: 370
Allport, Gordon W.: 534
American Association of University Women: 338
American Council of Christian Churches: 337
American Council for Judaism: 337
American Dairy Association: 322
American Farm Bureau Federation: 332–333, 334, 348, 381
American Federation of Labor: 327, 334, 335, 341, 355
AFL-CIO: 329, 335, 346, 356, 381
American Heritage Foundation: 578
American Labor Party: 42–43, 341
American Legion: 327, 335–336, 337

American Medical Association: 329, 384
American Political Science Association, Committee on American Legislatures: 638
  Committee on Political Parties: 631–632
  Committee on Servicemen Voting: 434–435
American Vegetarian Union, Inc.: 342
American Veterans Committee: 336
American Veterans of World War II: 336, 337, 357
Americans as "joiners": 321–322
Anti-Federalists: 255–257, 258–259
Anti-Masonic Party: 168
Anti-Saloon League: 327, 342, 381
Applegate, Albert A.: 456
Aron, Raymond: 306
Ashurst, Henry F.: 514
Asseff, Emmett: 80
Attitude groups: 389
Attlee, Clement R.: 364
Australian ballot: 138, 438–439, 440
Automatic Voting Machine Corporation: 439, 442–444
Availability (in choosing Presidents): 158, 223–232, 298, 616

Bagehot, Walter: 590, 592, 656
Bailey, Stephen K.: 391, 660
Bailey, Sydney D.: 7, 8, 9, 13
Bailey, Thomas A.: 476, 630
Bain, Henry M., Jr.: 446
Bain, Richard C.: 214
Baker, Ray S.: 319
Ballots, length: 446–448
  marking and counting: 454–455
  office-block: 440–441, 445
  order of names: 445–446
  paper: 436, 437–438, 439, 440
  party-column: 440, 441, 445
  preparation: 452–453

Ballots *(cont.)*
  sample: 164–165, 197–200, 447, 453–454
Baltimore as national-convention city: 187, 189
Band-wagon psychology: 237, 243, 476, 502, 527
Bank of the United States: 258, 259, 261, 263, 264, 298, 476
Barkley, Alben W.: 181, 182, 227, 493
Barnard, Harry: 118
Barnhart, John D.: 394
Bayard, James A.: 260
Bean, Louis H.: 299, 311, 320, 370, 397, 398, 402, 404, 406, 408, 413, 503, 537
Beard, Charles A.: 5, 35, 36, 52, 62, 100, 155, 252, 254, 256, 257, 258, 273, 274, 277, 303, 320, 369, 510
Beasley, Norman: 221
Becker, Carl L.: 57, 58, 63, 64, 71, 212, 436, 525
Benedict, Ruth: 362, 390
Bennett, Charles E.: 600
Bennett, Edward: 373
Benton, Thomas H.: 619
Berdahl, Clarence A.: 131, 144, 237, 543, 572
Berelson, Bernard R.: 281, 286, 287, 293, 370, 472, 537, 578
Bernard, Bertram M.: 450, 457
Beveridge, Albert J.: 11, 13
Bingham, Alfred M.: 306, 309
Binkley, Wilfred E.: 57, 71, 277
Bipartisanism—*See* Two-party system
Bishop, Cortlandt F.: 58, 60, 61, 63, 71, 129, 422, 436, 437, 449, 450, 457, 504, 582, 623
Bishop, Joseph B.: 71, 211, 214, 232, 242, 529, 540
Black, Theodore M.: 503, 525, 528, 540
"Black and Tan": 366
Blaine, James G.: 221, 230, 247, 267, 409, 519, 536
Blair, George S.: 586
Blumberg, Nathan B.: 522
Bolingbroke, Henry S., Viscount: 9
Bone, Hugh A.: 43, 76, 103, 119, 148, 183, 588, 590, 591, 643
Borah, William E.: 177
Boswell, James: 9
Bowen, Croswell: 85
Bower, Robert: 473

Boyd, James P.: 155
Breckenridge, Adam C.: 148
Breckenridge, John C.: 226
Brogan, D. W.: 363, 369, 390
Bromage, Arthur W.: 508
Brown, Guy L.: 356
Brown, Walter: 497
Brownell, Herbert: 500
Brownson, Orestes A.: 322
Bruner, Dick: 356
Bryan, William J.: 226, 269, 274, 299, 395, 403, 409, 512, 519, 555, 556, 560, 608, 617
  nomination in 1896: 243
Bryce, James: 36, 45, 53, 116, 232, 569
Buchanan, James: 210, 226, 267, 530, 611
Buchanan, William: 43, 288
Buck, Solon J.: 331, 389
Buley, R. Carlyle: 106, 119
Bullitt, Stimson: 540
Bulmer-Thomas, Ivor: 13
Burdette, Franklin L.: 573
Burke, Edmund: 1, 10, 639
Burns, James M.: 607
Burr, Aaron: 156, 158, 159, 261
Bush, Chilton: 540
Business, campaign contributions: 544, 554–556
  and government regulation: 351–352
  leadership: 114–115, 255, 259, 264
  monopoly in: 345–346, 349
  opinion measurement: 469–470, 471
  organizations in: 333–334
  political activity and partisanship: 326, 352–353
  and tariffs: 349–351
  and taxes: 351
Businessmen, and national-convention delegates: 241
  as members of national committees: 219
Byrd, Harry F.: 215

Calhoun, John C.: 167
California, cross-filing in: 148
California Republican Assembly: 148
Camelon, David: 376
Cameron, J. D.: 176
Campaign appeals: 513–515
Campaign committees, *ad hoc*: 182
Campaign expenditures, concern for: 548, 558–559

Campaign expenditures (*cont.*)
  in direct primary: 145–146
  effectiveness: 548–549
  election-day: 506, 545–546
  federal regulation: 552–558
  government contributions for: 560–563
  government spending as: 549
  growth and extent: 545–548
  party differences in: 549, 555
  regulation of: 559–560
  sources of funds: 175, 180, 542–545
  state regulation: 550, 558
Campaign techniques, adaptability and variety: 483, 515–516
  alternatives in: 539–540
  answering opponent: 528–530
  coattail influence as: 531–532
  effectiveness: 537–539
  partisan attacks as: 533
  presidential: 512, 530–531
  publicity in: 517, 525, 526, 533
  rumors as: 534–535, 536
  sense of timing: 525–527
  slogans: 535–536
  strategy of attack: 527
  television: 524–525, 531
  vote-getting names as: 518–519
Campaigns, advantage of "outs": 512–513
  continuity in: 511, 538
  corrupt practices in: 504–507
  cycles: 394, 526
  newspaper influence in: 521–524
  organization for: 503–504
  taboos in: 511–512
Campbell, Angus: 281, 286, 289, 290, 292, 293, 309, 410, 471, 537, 578, 579
Campbell, Douglas: 437
Candidates, analyses of constituents by: 513
  dependence upon organization: 18, 139–142, 508–511
  individual differences: 516–517, 527
  newspaper relations: 519–521
Cannon, Clarence: 173, 201
Cantrill, Hadlay: 472, 484
Caraway, Hattie: 373
Carleton, William G.: 231
Carney, Francis: 119
Case, Francis: 376

Cater, Douglass: 521
"Catholic vote": 369–370
Catholic War Veterans of the United States: 336
Catholics: 337, 591
Catt, Carrie Chapman: 338
Caucus: 64, 67, 68, 123
  See also Legislative Caucus; Nominations by Congressional Caucus
Centers, Richard: 308, 320
Chamber of Commerce: 333, 334, 381
Chamberlin, Edward H.: 379
Chandler, Zachariah: 170, 174
Charlesworth, James C.: 4, 31, 35, 37, 39
Chase, Stuart: 474
Chicago as national-convention city: 187
Childs, Harwood L.: 459
Childs, Richard S.: 600
Choctaw Club: 95
Civil rights: 255, 273
  lobbying as: 377
  voting related to: 418
Clapper, Raymond: 458
Clark, Champ: 210
Class(es), definitions and distinctions: 305–309
  and partisan politics: 318–320
  and sectionalism: 310–318
Clay, Henry: 161, 162, 166, 167, 168, 224, 247, 262, 383, 409, 512, 534
  and election of 1844: 223
  as party leader: 265
  unavailability of: 231
Cleveland, Grover: 224, 230, 267, 268, 358, 396, 555, 611, 612, 617
Clinton, DeWitt: 168
Clinton, George: 99, 156, 161
Clopton, John: 436
Closed primary—*See* Direct primary
Clubs, political: 95
Coattail influence in elections: 397–399, 531–532
Collins, Edward H.: 406, 458
Committee, on Credentials: 184–185, 202, 203, 205
  on Permanent Organization: 185, 205, 206
  on Platform and Resolutions: 186, 205, 206–207
  on Rules and Order of Business: 185, 205, 206

Committee on Economic Development: 390

Committee on Political Education (COPE): 356

Committees—*See* Political party committees

Committees of Correspondence: 58

Communication media: 480, 516, 519–525, 545, 559, 560–561

Communications: 245, 464–467, 478–479

Communist Party: 6

Compromise, in British party system: 24
  in French party system: 24–25
  in operating government: 23
  in tyrannical government: 25–26

Compulsory voting: 418, 580, 582

Condon, George A.: 151

Congress of Industrial Organizations: 334, 335, 355, 367, 386, 556–557

Congressional caucus—*See* Nominations by congressional caucus

Congressional-district conventions—*See* Nominations by congressional-district conventions

Conkling, Roscoe: 105, 242

Constitution, adoption related to party controversy: 61–62

Constitutional Convention, economic conflict in: 255–257

Constitutional interpretation, of Democrats: 263–264
  of Federalists: 259
  of Jeffersonian Republicans: 259, 261, 262
  related to two-party system: 35–36

Conventions—*See* Nominations by conventions

Converse, Philip E.: 288

Coolidge, Calvin: 182, 224, 228, 233, 271, 273, 395, 396, 508, 511, 530, 536, 629
  Vice-Presidential nomination: 248

Coombs, L. C.: 319

Corrupt practices: 138, 423, 425, 430, 432, 440, 449, 455–456, 457, 504–507, 542, 552–554

Corwin, Edward S.: 618

Coudert, Frederic R.: 620

Coughlin, Father Charles E.: 482

County chairmen: 77, 84

County conventions—*See* Nominations by county conventions

County unit system: 150–152

Court and country parties: 57–58

Courthouse ring: 123

Cox, James M.: 244, 498, 500

Crane, Frank: 569

Crawford, William C.: 162, 226

"Crawford County system": 129

Croly, Herbert: 569

Crossman, R. H. S.: 460

Crump, Edward H.: 123, 141, 215

Cumulative voting in Illinois: 31, 585–586

Curley, James M.: 85

Cycles, in elections: 393–400, 410–411, 412–413
  in group influence: 380–381

Dahlgren, Harold F.: 281

Daley, Arthur: 401

Dallinger, Frederick W.: 64, 65, 67, 68, 71, 73, 123, 126, 128, 152, 158, 161, 167, 169, 182, 189, 212

Dangerfield, George: 261

Daniels, Josephus: 221, 488

Dark horse candidates: 232, 234, 243, 246–247

Daughters of the American Revolution: 338

Dauer, Manning J.: 198

Davenport, Walter: 52, 86, 88, 119, 122, 128, 527

David, Henry: 390

David Paul T.: 43, 198, 214, 597, 598, 606, 626

Davis, John W.: 210, 608, 644

Dawes, Charles G.: 182

Dearing, Mary R.: 335, 391

Debs, Eugene V.: 341

DeGrazia, Alfred: 324

Delaware, rise of party committees in: 69–70

Delegates—*See* National convention delegates

Democratic Advisory Committee: 644

Democratic Digest: 522

Democratic National Congressional Committee: 174, 175–176

Democratic Party, administrations and policies: 263–264, 270, 271–273, 348, 350, 351
  alignments and factionalism: 263–264, 270, 271, 272–273, 274–275

Democratic Party (*cont.*)
beginning, with Jackson: 262–263
labor unions in: 355–356
merger with Populists: 268–269
national-convention rules: 189, 191, 201, 211–212
Negroes in: 367
in New York City: 42
and presidential elections: 311–315
urban strength: 303
veterans in: 358
Democratic-Republican Party: 73, 168, 259, 266
Democratic Senatorial Campaign Committee: 174–176
Democratic societies: 62–63
Derber, Milton: 390
De Salle, Michael: 239
De Sapio, Carmine G.: 118
Designating petitions: 139
De Voto, Bernard: 480
Dewey, Thomas E.: 118, 163, 215, 226, 234, 242, 243, 244, 285, 399, 409, 463, 473, 500, 521, 616, 648
Dickerson, John J.: 115
Dieterich, William H.: 181
Dimock, Marshall E.: 390
Direct primary: 130–146
beginning of: 129
caliber of candidates: 144–145
candidate procedures: 139
candidates' expense: 145
candidates and party organization: 139–141, 645–646
changing parties in: 132–133
closed primary: 131–132
competition: 141–143
crossing-over: 136–137
effect upon issues: 492–493
evaluation: 143–146
federal regulation: 430, 431
majority requirement: 138
minor parties: 138–139
minority nominations: 143–144
modifications of: 146–148
motives for: 128–129
national, proposals for: 601–605
open primary: 132–133
party platforms with: 146
permanence: 148–149
public expense: 144
"raiding": 133, 136, 603

Direct primary (*cont.*)
runoff in: 138, 150
in South: 136
statutory regulations: 137–138
tests of party membership: 130–133, 144, 453
voting turnout in: 143, 144
"wide-open" (blanket): 133
Dirksen, Everett: 243
Disabled American Veterans: 336
Dixon, George: 481, 519
Doob, Leonard W.: 459, 474, 479, 480, 484
Doty, Robert C.: 39
Douglas, Paul H.: 571, 600, 605
Douglas, Stephen A.: 210, 224, 384, 512, 518
Douglas, William O.: 613
Driscoll, Alfred E.: 115
Duffield, Marcus: 336, 391
Dulles, John F.: 493
Duverger, Maurice: 4, 13, 15, 28, 37, 53, 591, 656

Ebersole, Luke E.: 321, 337, 376, 391
Economics and politics: 252–277, 297, 402–407
Edison, Thomas A.: 439
Edmonds, Helen G.: 366, 390
Ehrmann, Henry W.: 391
Eisenhower, Dwight D.: 108, 181, 183, 202, 203, 204, 214, 222, 224, 227, 244, 274, 275, 276, 286, 348, 368, 370, 383, 395, 396, 397, 405, 408, 499, 500, 519, 522, 523, 529, 532, 535, 571, 573, 603, 644
Eldersveld, Samuel J.: 289, 291, 293, 294, 303, 317, 319, 320, 330, 376, 456, 537
Election Day, development of national: 448–450
as holiday: 450–451
official preparations for: 451–453
Election procedures, criticism of: 455–456
organization of: 451–455
reform of: 456–457
before Revolutionary War: 58
Elections, acquiescence in outcome: 29
betting odds: 502
business conditions and: 52, 268, 270–271, 402–407

Elections (*cont.*)
  as civil-service examinations: 111
  congressional control over: 420
  contested (1876–1877): 34, 612
  dissatisfactions and outcome: 409–410,
    513
  distortions in outcome: 30, 411–412,
    589–590
  fixed dates: 393–394
  left-right cycles: 399–400
  majority requirement: 623
  need for information to win: 501–502
  opinion formation in: 417–418
  organized groups in: 378
  personalities and outcome: 408–409
  public opinion polls and: 469, 470,
    472–473, 502
  purpose: 16–17, 417–418
  reward to friends in: 63
  runoff: 32, 623
  uncontested: 41
  in U. S. colonies: 58
  upheavals: 401–410, 412–413
  use of county courthouses and towns:
    60–61
  weather and: 394
  See also Nonpartisan elections
Electoral-college system, abolition: 613–
  615
  changed by Twelfth Amendment:
    158–159
  evolution: 154–157, 162–163, 166
  as explanation of two-party system:
    33–34
  majority requirement: 33–34, 623–624
  objections to: 610–613
  reasons for creating: 154–155, 614–615
  reform of: 615–625
  Vice-Presidency and: 159
  See also Presidential electors; Electoral
  votes
Electoral votes, counting: 436
  proportioning: 615–619
  twelve largest states': 304
Engelman, Frederick C.: 4, 15, 28
Epstein, Leon D.: 43
Equality, concept of: 309
Eriksson, Eric M.: 99, 102, 103, 119, 499
Erpf, Armand G.: 353
Eulau, Heinz: 309
Everett, Edward: 107

Ewing, Cortez A. M.: 42, 49, 143, 152,
  398, 413, 576, 585, 589, 591

Factionalism, fluidity of: 81
  in national committees: 219–222
  in national conventions: 239, 243
  sources of: 81
Fainsod, Merle: 630, 656
Farley, James A.: 85, 87, 88, 117, 119,
  127, 152, 181, 232, 235, 239, 489,
  494, 498, 501, 502, 509, 534, 540,
  606, 645
  and patronage: 102, 106, 110
Farm Bloc: 348
Farmer-Labor Party: 340
Favorite-son candidates: 234, 237, 243,
  598–599
Federalism in U. S. government, decline
  of: 385–386
  value of: 253
Federalist Party: 17, 35, 44–45, 155–159,
  273
  administrations and policies: 257–259
  party organization: 69, 70–71, 167–
    168, 628
  patronage: 100–101
Federalists and ratification of the Con-
  stitution: 255–257
Federalists and secession: 12
Ferguson, Ma: 373
Fine, Nathan: 390
Finer, S. E.: 382
Fish, C. R.: 99, 101, 102, 104, 105, 106,
  119
Fisher, Marguerite J.: 373
Fite, Warner: 460
Flanders, Ralph E.: 655
Flynn, Edward J.: 82, 87, 88, 94, 96, 103,
  115, 119, 127, 140, 152, 214, 235,
  488, 540, 546, 570, 572
  and patronage: 109–110
Follett, M. P.: 569, 570, 593
Force Bill: 267
Ford, Henry, II: 350
Ford, Henry J.: 9, 36, 53, 57
Forthal, Sonya: 76, 87, 548
Franklin, Jay: 220
Frary, Donald P.: 418, 437, 451, 457, 506
Free Soil Party: 266
French Revolution: 62–63
Frenkel-Brunswik, Else: 470
Friedman, Robert S.: 152

Friedrich, Carl J.: 4, 6, 13, 38, 39, 55, 656
"Front porch" campaigning: 530–531
Fuchs, Lawrence H.: 325, 370, 371, 388, 390

Gable, Richard: 334
Gallup, George: 286, 287, 292, 294, 300, 303, 307, 470, 473, 474, 484, 502, 570
Garceau, Oliver: 391
Garfield, James A.: 105, 107, 210, 224, 246, 395, 396, 512, 611, 617
   nomination in 1880: 242–243
Garner, John N.: 244, 272, 655
   on Vice-Presidency: 181–182
General Federation of Women's Clubs: 338
General Welfare: 253, 254, 381–382
Georgia, county unit system in: 150–151
Gerrymandering: 412, 590, 620, 621
Ghost writers: 492
Gill, N. N.: 411
Gillam, Bernhard: 403
Glaser, William A.: 579
Glass, Carter: 272
Gobbledygook: 481
Goetz, Rachel M.: 541
Goldberg, Arthur J.: 390
Goldenweiser, E. A.: 458
Goldman, Ralph M.: 214, 578
Gompers, Samuel: 63, 327, 341
Goodman, William: 80, 141, 639, 656
Goodwin, Harriet M.: 373
Gore, Albert: 536
Gorman, Arthur P.: 170
Gosnell, Cullen B.: 150
Gosnell, Harold F.: 86, 92, 103, 119, 295, 411, 579, 593, 632
Gosset, Ed: 615
Government, and belief in authority: 468–469
   increasing power: 179, 359, 385–386
   inspection and regulation by: 112
   legislative and executive branches: 113
   taxation: 112
Government employees, political restrictions on: 542, 553–554
Governors, as presidential candidates: 224, 226
Gower, Sir Ernest A.: 484
Grand Army of the Republic: 335, 358
Grandfather clause: 429–430

Granger, Walter: 245
Grant, Ulysses S.: 212, 221, 222, 224, 227, 242, 395, 396
Grass-roots politics: 76
Gray, Justin: 336
Guysenir, Maurice B.: 370

Hague, Frank: 88, 95, 112, 141, 172, 179, 215
Halifax, Charles M., Lord: 9
Hallett, George H. (and C. G. Hoag): 588, 590, 591, 593
Hallinan, Walter S.: 203–204
Hallowell, John H.: 460
Hamilton, Alexander: 11, 36, 154, 155, 156, 157, 158, 258, 260, 273, 510, 628–629
Hamiltonianism: 35–36
Hanna, Marcus A.: 215, 218, 248, 497, 501, 554
Harder, Marvin A.: 152
Hardin, Charles M.: 328, 332, 348, 389
Harding, Warren G.: 182, 224, 230, 246, 367, 395, 396, 530
Hardman, J. B. S.: 390
Hare, Thomas: 587
Harris, Herbert: 390
Harris, Joseph P.: 152, 422, 425, 456, 457
Harris, Louis: 286, 305, 391
Harrison, Benjamin: 268, 396, 611, 612, 617
Harrison, Pat: 181
Harrison, William H.: 106, 394, 395, 512, 533, 535
   nomination in 1836: 169, 265
Hart, Hornell: 406
Hastings, Philip K.: 293
Hathorn, Guy B.: 548
Havemann, Ernest (and Patricia Salter West): 281, 286, 289, 290, 293, 294
Hayes, Isabella M.: 563
Hayes, Rutherford B.: 105, 267, 396, 611
Heady, Ferrel: 554
Heard, Alexander: 42, 43, 53, 151, 390, 563
Hecock, Donald S.: 446
Hein, Clarence J.: 152, 577
Helms, E. Allen: 4, 9, 14, 30, 33, 219, 226, 392, 630, 645
Hermens, Ferdinand A.: 590, 593
Herring, E. Pendleton: 28, 53, 96, 127, 351, 360, 386, 388, 391, 654, 660

Hesseltine, William B.: 53, 75, 318, 340, 341

Hexter, J. H.: 13

Hicks, John D.: 268, 331, 366, 389

Higham, John: 391

Hill, Isaac: 168

Hillman, Sidney: 557

Hitler, Adolf: 273, 459

Hoar, George F.: 221

Holcombe, Arthur N.: 5, 12, 33, 46, 47, 51, 53, 254, 255, 256, 265, 269, 277, 303, 309, 311, 317, 318, 319, 320, 340, 341, 384, 401, 539, 628, 651, 655, 656, 660
  sectional analyses: 298–299, 300–302

Holland, Lynwood M.: 150

Hollander, Herbert S.: 119

Hollander, Louis: 652

Holmes, Jack E.: 16

Holtman, Robert B.: 415, 459, 484

Homestead Act: 266

Hoover, Herbert: 218, 224, 226, 227, 228, 233, 241, 270, 319, 367, 383, 396, 402, 497, 519

Hoover, I. H.: 233

Hopkins, Harry: 245, 272

House, Edward M.: 497

Howe, Louis M.: 235

Howe, Quincy: 524, 540

Hughes, Charles E.: 149, 226, 228, 270

Humphrey, Hubert H.: 644

Hundred, as political subdivision: 61

Huntington, Samuel P.: 305, 316, 317

Hutchinson, William T.: 85

Hyman, Sidney: 606

Hyneman, Charles S.: 360, 391

Independent Socialist League: 341

Independents: 118, 286
  and direct primary: 132–139
  See Voting, independent

Index of political predisposition: 288–289, 293, 472

Indiana, party organization in: 80, 84

Indiana ballot: 441

Indirect primary: 128, 130

Ingalls, John J.: 571

Irion, Frederick C.: 321, 476, 477

Issues, agricultural: 346–348
  business: 349–352
  conflict of, in 1940: 408
  delegated powers as source of: 254–255

Issues (cont.)
  in Democratic National Convention (1924): 25
  in Democratic-Whig period: 263–265
  development of: 490–495
  durable: 254–255
  embarrassment of: 18, 528–530
  in Federalist-Republican period: 257–262
  of government bureaucracy: 359–361
  inconsistency on: 476, 491, 514
  labor: 353–354
  monopoly: 344–346
  of Negro status: 365
  and organized interest groups: 344
  proposals for treating: 647
  public knowledge of: 379–380, 492–493
  and public opinion polls: 473–474
  race and nationality as: 362–363
  in Republican-Democratic period: 266–275
  religious: 368–369
  scarcity of: 18, 515
  selection of: 490–491
  in U. S. colonies: 57–58
  war: 254, 408, 476

Jackson, Andrew: 70, 162, 167, 168, 169, 262–263, 264, 265, 274, 370, 405, 446, 476, 488, 519, 612
  elective offices during Presidency: 58, 446
  and patronage: 99, 102–103

Jackson, Robert H.: 492, 613

Jackson County Democratic Club: 95

Jackson men: 262

Jacksonians: 44–45

Janowitz, Morris: 288, 289, 537

Jay, John: 99, 156

"Jaybird primary": 432

Jefferson, Thomas: 36, 65, 100, 161, 162, 166, 224, 226, 254, 258, 262, 263, 266, 274, 326, 370, 384, 488, 530, 535
  administration: 260–261
  election to the Presidency: 158–159, 259
  as opposition leader: 12, 156, 157–158, 259, 260
  and patronage: 101, 104

Jefferson-Jackson Day: 543

Jeffersonian Republican Party: 35, 44–45
  administrations and policies: 259–262
  and Democratic societies: 62–63
  development of Congressional Caucus
    by: 159–160, 161
  development of party committes by:
    68–70
  factionalism: 161
  and patronage: 101–102, 104
  realignment: 262
Jeffersonianism: 35–36
Jewell, Malcolm E.: 638
Jewish Veterans of the U.S.A.: 336
"Jewish vote": 370–371
Jews: 337, 591
Johnson, Andrew: 174, 512
Johnson, Hiram: 137, 247
Johnson, Samuel: 9
Jones, Richard S.: 336, 391
Judah, Charles B.: 16, 625
Justus, Roy: 216

Kallenbach, Joseph E.: 613, 615
Karson, Marc: 390
Katz, Daniel: 370, 459, 484
Keefe, William J.: 638
Kefauver, Estes: 522, 602, 644, 647
Kelland, Clarence B.: 220
Kelley, Oliver H.: 331
Kelley, Stanley, Jr.: 525, 540
Kelly, Edward: 181
Kendall, Amos: 102, 168
Kendall, Willmoore: 40
Kennedy, Gerald H.: 344
Kennedy, John F.: 370
Kenny, John V.: 115, 179
Kent, Frank R.: 76, 82, 83, 85, 87, 88,
    89, 90, 95, 98, 103, 106, 110, 113,
    115, 120, 140, 152, 215, 227, 236,
    402, 486, 488, 489, 491, 501, 506,
    508, 510, 511, 517, 518, 523, 529,
    533, 540, 542, 546, 547, 549, 570,
    572, 580
Kerney, James: 88, 486, 630
Kesselman, Louis C.: 390
Key states: 236–237
Key, V. O., Jr.: 40, 42, 53, 127, 130, 142,
    143, 146, 152, 367, 390, 576, 579,
    645, 653
Kile, Orville M.: 332, 389
Kilgore, Harley M.: 619
King, Rufus: 224

Kingsley, J. Donald: 358
Kitchen Cabinet: 168
Klain, Maurice: 31
Kleeberg, Gordon S. P.: 170, 175, 182,
    212
Knowland, William E.: 137
Knowles, Clayton: 595
Krajewski, Henry: 341
Krock, Arthur: 47, 182, 240, 406, 521,
    524, 532, 537, 544, 559, 615, 617,
    620
Kurtzman, David H.: 60, 82, 88, 91, 92,
    103, 112, 115, 120, 127, 152, 505,
    507, 541

Labor-management relations: 275
Labor party, hindrances of: 341
Labor-union leadership: 305
  and minor parties: 340–341
Labor unions: 272, 273
  campaign contributions and spending:
    544, 556–558
  merger of: 335, 620
  monopoly in: 346
  issues involving: 353–354
  organizations of: 334–335
  political power and partisanship: 326–
    327, 355–356
La Follette, Robert M., Jr.: 340–341
La Follette, Robert M., Sr.: 86, 128, 146,
    190, 280, 340, 341, 355, 596, 644
Landon, Alfred M.: 228, 644
Lane, Robert E.: 390
Langer, William: 613
La Palombara, Joseph G.: 22
Larrabee, Eric: 580, 583, 608
Lasswell, Harold D.: 389, 461, 470, 484
Latham, Earl: 43, 80, 120, 152, 333, 376,
    387, 390
Lausche, Frank: 118
Lavine, Harold: 479
Lawrence, David: 88, 571, 642, 652
Lazarsfeld, Paul F.: 281, 294, 471, 537,
    579
  Erie County study: 288
League of Nations: 630
League of Women Voters: 338
Lee, Alfred M. (and Elizabeth B.): 482
Legislative caucus: 67–68
  presidential nominations by: 167
  See also Caucus; Nominations by con-
    gressional caucus

Legislators, state: 66–67, 74
Lehman, Herbert H.: 235
Leiserson, Avery: 386, 391
Levine, Mickey: 337
Levinson, R. B.: 460
Lewis, John L.: 334, 335, 356
Lewis, R. Cragin: 380
Lewis, William B.: 168
Libby, Orin G.: 257, 277
Liberal Party in New York: 42
Library of Congress: 491
"Lily Whites": 367
Lincoln, Abraham: 273, 274, 384, 395,
    401, 518, 519, 528, 530, 542, 546,
    611, 624, 630, 644
  administration: 266–267
  availability: 230, 231–232
  nomination in 1860: 242
Lincoln Day: 543
Lincoln-Douglas debates: 518
Lippmann, Walter: 411, 459, 484, 591,
    618
Lipson, Leslie: 8, 31, 38
Lobbying: 375–380
  federal regulation of: 377–378
Lockard, W. Duane: 152, 638
Lodge-Gossett Amendment: 615, 618
Lodge, Henry C., Jr.: 615, 617
Lodge, Henry C., Sr.: 86
Long ballot: 602
Long, Huey: 40
Lorant, Stefan: 181, 466, 541
Lorwin, Lewis L.: 334, 390
Louisiana, party organization in: 79–80
Lowell, A. Lawrence: 283–284, 484, 638
Lowell, James R.: 12
Lubell, Samuel: 37, 47, 53, 283, 285, 287,
    289, 293, 294, 303, 304, 305, 306,
    307, 309, 318, 319, 320, 363, 364, 391
Luetscher, George P.: 59, 60, 65, 67, 68,
    72, 129
Lure of politics: 486–487
Lyford, Joseph P.: 152

McAdoo, William G.: 210, 233, 244,
    608
MacArthur, Douglas: 180, 204
Macaulay, Thomas B.: 13
McCally, Sarah P.: 28
McCamy, James L.: 360, 541, 549
McClellan, George B.: 222
McCloskey, Herbert: 281

McCombs, William F.: 86
McConnell, Grant: 321, 326, 331, 332,
    333, 347, 390
McCune, Wesley: 390
MacDougall, Curtis D.: 459
McGovney, Dudley O.: 419, 426, 457,
    593
Machiavelli, Niccolo: 496, 537, 541
MacIver, Robert M.: 3, 7, 13, 45, 285,
    309, 468, 478, 495, 654
McKean, Dayton D.: 85, 86, 88, 103, 112,
    115, 120, 141, 376, 506, 541, 542,
    613, 632, 638
McKeller, Kenneth D.: 536
McKenzie, R. T.: 28
McKinley, William: 215, 230, 248, 269,
    270, 273, 395, 396, 403, 497, 530,
    532, 554, 617
McLaughlin, Andrew C.: 635, 656, 660
Macmahon, Arthur: 32, 35, 38
McTaggart-Cowan, Patrick D.: 481
Macy, Jesse: 73, 79, 80, 95, 120, 170, 174,
    175, 182, 394, 635
Madison Avenue: 525
Madison, James: 156, 159, 160, 161, 162,
    166, 226, 254, 261, 262, 320
  on economic basis of politics: 252–253
  on federalism: 384–385
  on power struggle: 11–12, 16
Maine, Sir Henry: 45
Maitland, Frederick W.: 8
Managers, administrative skill: 498, 503–
    504
  anonymity: 497
  attitudes toward: 496
  background: 497–498
  campaign strategies: 501–504
  and corrupt practices: 504–507
  function: 495–496
  government employment: 498–499
  as organization leaders: 497–498
  relations with candidates: 499–501
Mao Tse-tung: 459
Marshall, John: 13, 436
Martin, Joseph W.: 617
Marx, Karl: 306, 307
Maryland, county-unit system in: 151
Mass meetings: 64–65, 167
Massachusetts, party organization in: 80
Massachusetts ballot: 441
Massachusetts Bay Colony: 63
Meany, George: 356

Members of Congress, party voting among: 638
as presidential candidates: 223–226
Members of Congress (Representatives), campaigns and elections: 62, 66, 74, 173–176, 503, 531–532, 642
cycles in election: 397–399
nomination contests: 142–143
sectionalism in election: 298, 315–316
Members of Congress (Senators), campaigns and elections: 174–176, 531–532
methods of election: 66–67, 174, 420, 635
Menez, Joseph F.: 183
Merit system: 107–109
Merriam, Charles E.: 12, 14, 85, 107, 120, 127, 130, 143, 146, 149, 152, 295, 411, 571, 579, 593, 632
Merriam, Robert E.: 541
Merritt, LeRoy C.: 541, 549
Meyers, (Mrs.) Beryl: 172
Meyner, Robert B.: 606
Michelson, Charles: 541
Midwest Federation of Consumers Cooperative Association: 333
Milbrath, Lester W.: 378
Mill, John S.: 437, 438
Miller, Warren E.: 281, 288, 289, 399, 537, 579
Milligan, Maurice M.: 83, 85, 86, 88, 115, 120, 123, 506, 507, 541, 554, 571
Mills, C. Wright: 390
Minor offices, voting for: 399
Minor parties, character of: 50
and direct primary: 138–139
as factions of major parties: 50–51
influence on elections: 51
legal status: 74–75
v. major parties: 50
and organized groups: 339–343
strategy: 342
weakness: 49–51, 590, 591
Minority party, monopoly of opposition by: 30
"Minority Presidents": 611–612
Mitchell, Stephen A.: 117
Moley, Raymond: 487, 493, 497, 501, 541
Monroe, James: 104, 160, 161, 162, 226
Montgomery, Ruth: 517
Moon, Henry Lee: 367, 368, 391

Moos, Malcolm: 42, 303, 398, 399, 413, 503, 576, 607, 647
Morlan, Robert L.: 76, 391
Morris, Gouverneur: 154, 159
Morrow, Dwight W.: 3
Morse, Anson D.: 3, 4, 17, 45, 655
Morse, Wayne: 641
Morton, Oliver P.: 619
Moscow, Warren: 53, 88, 94, 120, 141, 399, 495, 502, 521, 541, 554, 558, 591
Mosher, William E.: 358
Mosteller, Frederick: 473, 484
Multiparty system, in France: 30–31, 38–39
in New York City: 42
value judgments of: 21–22
Mundt, Karl E.: 620
Murdock, John S.: 168
Murphy, Charles F.: 89, 95, 118, 127
Murray, William ("Alfalfa Bill"): 211
Myers, Gustavus: 59, 95, 120
Myers, Robert C.: 582
Myers, W. I.: 404–406, 413

Napoleon: 415, 459
Nash, Howard P., Jr.: 391
Nast, Thomas: 466
National American Woman Suffrage Association: 338
National Association for the Advancement of Colored People: 327, 365, 625
National Association of Manufacturers: 329, 333, 334
(National) Business and Professional Women's Clubs: 338, 439
National Civil Service League: 108
National committee chairmen: 215, 636
chosen by presidential nominee: 170, 220, 221
open national conventions: 203
powers and duties of: 219
National committees, arrangements for national convention: 171, 184, 219–222, 238
composition: 169, 170, 171–172, 219
and congressional campaigning: 173–175
economic interests in: 219
factionalism in: 219–222
headquarters: 173, 218
history: 169–171

National committees (*cont.*)
 importance: 218–220
 method of electing: 170, 172, 213
 organization: 172–173
 power: 170, 186, 218, 636
 reform of: 632
 role in delegate contests: 201–202
 selection of convention officers by: 203
 weaknesses: 218
National committeewoman, creation of
  office: 171
National convention delegates, alternates for: 200
 apportionment and accrediting: 188–
  191
 candidates' influences on: 236–237,
  239–240
 commitment to presidential candidates: 194, 195, 198, 200, 239, 598–
  599
 influence of party leaders on: 240–241,
  597
 methods of selection: 191, 192–200,
  596–598, 600
 pressure group influence on: 241
 seating contests: 200–203
 uncommitted: 239–240, 598
National conventions, activity of leaders
  in: 217, 239–240
 basis of representation in: 189–191
 bipartisan arrangements: 188
 choice of cities: 187–188
 color and lore: 238–239
 committees: 184–186, 203, 205–207
 deadlocks: 210, 244–245, 246–247
 defensive tactics: 245
 delegate behavior: 188, 238–248
 demonstrations in: 185, 186, 209, 241–
  242
 dissatisfaction with: 594–596, 605
 effect of speeches in: 186, 214, 242–243
 emotionalism: 204, 208–209
 housing delegates: 188
 Jackson's use: 168–169
 keynote speeches: 186, 204–205, 206
 majority voting: 185, 210
 management: 184–185, 245–247
 methods of calling: 168–169, 170, 186–
  187
 as national organization: 215–217
 officers of: 203, 204, 206
 order of business: 203–207, 213–214

National conventions (*cont.*)
 organization of delegations: 185
 origin: 166, 167–169
 party preparations: 217–222
 permanent chairmen: 170, 206, 245
 platforms: 206–207
 preconvention procedures: 186–203,
  217–238
 problems in Republican: 189–190
 reform: 596–601
 roll of delegates: 185–203
 rules: 204, 206
 seating delegates: 185, 188, 608–609
 sessions: 203–214
 stampeding: 241–242, 243–245
 state representation: 189–191
 televising: 595, 609
 transition to: 157–169, 594
 two-thirds rule: 210–212, 244
 unit rule: 211–212
 U. S. territories in: 185, 188, 191, 200
 value: 594, 606–608
 voting procedures: 185–186, 207–208,
  210–212, 243–247
 without nominating function: 603,
  604, 646–647
National Council of the Churches of
  Christ in the U.S.A.: 337
National Council of Farmers' Cooperative Marketing Associations: 333
National Democratic Club: 95
National Farmers Union: 331–332, 348
National Grange (Patrons of Hus-
  bandry): 331, 333, 348
National Republican Congressional
  Committee: 174, 175–176
National Republican Party: 168, 262–
  263
National Republican Senatorial Com-
  mittee: 174–176
Nationality: 362–364
National Temperance League, Inc.: 381
National Women's Party: 338, 372
Nebraska, party organization in: 80
Negro voting: 267, 420
 in the South: 428–432
Negroes: 363, 364–368
Neufeld, M. F.: 390
Neumann, Sigmund: 28
New Deal: 271–272, 273, 274, 275, 284,
  285, 286, 293, 549, 620, 652

New Hampshire, rise of party committees in: 68–69
New Jersey, rise of party committees in: 69
Newspapers: 519–524, 559
New York, literacy test: 426–427
  party organization: 58, 84, 93–94
Nixon, Richard M.: 522, 544
  and Vice-Presidency: 183, 214
Nominations, balanced ticket in: 127
  controversial nature of: 146
  and county leaders: 77
  dependence of candidates upon party for: 18
  dissatisfaction of leaders with: 128
  and independent candidates: 138–139
  for local offices: 64–66
  and party organization: 121–123
  and representative government: 129
  and state-wide offices: 66–68
  in U. S. colonies: 63, 64, 129
Nominations by congressional caucus, advantages and disadvantages: 160–162
  development: 157, 159–160
  See also Caucus; Legislative caucus
Nominations by congressional-district conventions: 65, 124, 166
Nominations by conventions, absentee voting in: 125
  basis of authority: 65
  beginnings: 63
  choosing candidates: 126–128
  coercion in: 126, 128
  confusion in: 125
  control of: 124–127
  degeneration: 128–129
  evolution from mass meetings: 65
  for local offices: 123–124
  selection of delegates for: 123–125, 192
  theory of: 123
Nominations by county conventions: 65–66, 123–124
Nominations by petitions: 138–139
Nominations by self-announcement: 63–64, 65
Nominations by special-district conventions: 123–124
Nonpartisan elections, ballot forms: 445
  in U. S. cities: 32, 117, 623
  See also Elections
Non-Partisan League: 340

Nonvoting: 49, 574–585
  causes of: 577–579
  degrees of: 399, 448, 574–577
  remedies: 579–584
  significance: 584–585
Norris, George W.: 613, 644
Nourse, Edwin G.: 330, 391

O'Brien, John C.: 373
Odegard, Peter H.: 4, 9, 14, 30, 33, 219, 339, 391
Ogburn, William F.: 319
Ogden, Frederic D.: 366, 429, 457
Ogg, Frederick A.: 25, 27, 39
Ogle, Marbury B., Jr.: 459, 465, 473, 479
Ogul, Morris S.: 577
"One-party press": 522–524
One-party system: 40–43, 366
Open primary: See Direct primary
Opinion measurement: 469–478
  limitations: 470, 471, 472, 474–478
  objectives: 473–474
  techniques: 470–472
Opinions, and beliefs: 467–469
  and communication: 464–467
  compulsion to have: 461
  v. consensus: 467–468
  and individuals: 462–464
  intensity: 462, 477
  simulated: 462, 475
  and social values: 463
Order of the Cincinnati: 335
Organized interest groups, attitudes toward: 325–327
  checking function: 384–388
  and civil rights: 377
  classification of: 324
  and development of issues: 344–345
  differences among: 653
  dual representation through: 323
  and general welfare: 381–384
  government bureaucracy as: 359–361
  identification of: 323–325
  influence: 380–381
  influence on members by: 287–288, 461
  influence on national-convention delegates: 241
  internal organization and operation: 329–330
  issues developed by: 379–380
  leaders and members: 329–330

Organized interest groups (*cont.*)
 membership in: 327–328
 middle class: 388
 nonpartisanism: 322–323, 378
 number of: 321–322
 partisan differences in: 287, 326, 327, 348–349, 352–353, 355–356, 364, 366–368
 promotional efforts: 322–323
 public relations: 380
 as reform movements: 339, 342, 343
 relations with parties: 342–343
 religions as: 337
 responsibility for governing: 386
 techniques of: 375–380
 types of: 330–339
 veterans as: 335–337
 women as: 337–338, 371–372
Ostrogorski, M.: 58, 67, 72, 85, 159, 160, 162, 169, 182, 211, 569, 593, 635, 638
Overacker, Louise: 127, 130, 143, 146, 149, 152, 214, 542, 543, 547, 548, 555, 556, 561, 563, 596, 597, 602, 626

Packard, Vance: 525, 541
Padgett, L. Vincent: 28
Page, Walter H.: 544
Parker, Alton B.: 226, 409, 608
Parker, John J.: 367
Partisanship, by age: 285
 difficulty of explaining: 290–291, 401, 411–412
 in doubtful areas: 502–503
 by economic and social status: 286–288
 by education: 286, 288–289
 enduring features of: 251–252, 279–283, 411, 502–503
 intensity of: 289
 issue attitudes in: 289–290
 minorities': 287
 national influences on: 279–280
 nationalities': 364
 Negroes': 366–368
 parental influence in: 280–281
 and religion: 287, 288, 369–370
 and sex: 286
 and tradition: 281–282
 and residence: 288, 311, 316–318, 401
Parton, Mildred: 484
Party cabinet: 633, 651
Party council: 633, 634, 648, 651
Party regularity: 19–20, 645

Patriotism, appeal of: 359
Patronage: 84, 656
 background: 99–103
 decline of: 107–109
 defense of: 100, 109–111
 degeneration: 105–106
 and rotation in office: 99
 and employment of politicians: 487, 488, 498–499
 functions: 103
 growth: 106
 power of Congress in: 104–105
 and Presidents: 103–104, 178–179
 private business as: 114
 state and local: 77, 103–105
Pearson-Myers formula: 404–406
Pendergast, Thomas J.: 85, 140, 215
Pendergast organization: 123
Penniman, Howard R.: 6, 14, 38, 45, 46
Pennock, J. Roland: 349, 649, 651
Pennsylvania, rise of party committees in: 69
Penrose, Boies: 52, 86, 88, 122, 527
Pickering, Timothy: 100
Pinckney, Charles C.: 158, 512
Pinckney, Thomas: 157, 158
Piquet, Howard S.: 350
Platt, Thomas C.: 105, 118
Plumer, William: 163
Plunkitt, George W.: 89, 106, 117
Poe, Edgar A.: 80
Poinier, Arthur B.: 403
Political parties, as alternative to tyranny: 7
 brokerage services of: 18, 48
 characteristics: 4–6
 compromise function: 23–26
 conflict in: 15
 and democratic philosophy: 3
 discipline by: 5, 20, 636
 and elections: 16–20
 electoral function: 19, 20
 extralegal status: 4
 as factions: 10, 11–12
 and ideological choices: 21–22
 inevitability: 6–7
 issues developed by: 18
 loyalty to: 5, 19–20
 and nation-state: 3, 15
 as nationalizing force: 27–28
 as organizations: 5
 patriotic nature of: 5–6

Political parties (*cont.*)
  role in power struggle: 15–16
  and size of electorate: 17
  and supplying candidates: 17–18
  symbols and insignia: 19–20, 466
  as voluntary associations: 4
Political parties in England: 7–9
Political parties in the U. S., antecedents: 7–10
  definition: 3, 6, 74–75
  regulation: 74–75
Political party centralization: 627, 631, 635, 654, 657–659
Political party committees, autonomy in: 83–84
  in cities: 76
  in congressional districts: 77
  and conventions: 73
  in counties: 76–77
  development: 68–70
  in districts: 77
  election of: 90–92
  executive: 93
  hierarchy: 82–84
  leaders' control through: 73
  rise: 68–70
  in states: 77–78
  use in selecting delegates: 192
Political party leaders, background: 85–86
  characteristics: 85–89
  and direct primary: 139–142
  evolution of: 117–118
  influence in national conventions: 239–241, 243–247
  information concerning: 86, 88
  motivations: 86–87
  as national leaders: 215
  objectives: 88, 122–123
  relations among: 89–90
Political party membership, in direct primary: 131–137
  taboos against: 641, 643
  tests of: 131
  what constitutes: 4, 650
Political party names: 262–263
Political party organization, acceptance of: 571
  antecedents and forerunners: 57–63
  arrangements for women: 78
  autocratic operation: 85, 634–635, 658
  changing nature of: 116–119

Political party organization (*cont.*)
  characteristics: 70–71
  condemnation of: 11–12, 568–571
  control of: 83, 88–97, 122–123
  and controversy: 57–58, 61–63
  decentralization in: 71, 631, 635
  description of: 77–80
  and direct primary: 143, 146
  and elective offices: 66–67, 121
  executive branch of government as: 179–181
  factionalism: 81–82
  and French Revolution: 62–63
  Hamilton's plan for: 628–629
  national: 153–182, 215–217
  and national conventions: 217–222
  and nominations: 121–123
  opposition to: 116–117
  and population size and make-up: 59–60, 94–95
  public participation: 80–81, 98, 571–572
  reorganization proposals: 632–634
  service function: 113–114
  sources of rules for: 74
  techniques: 94–96
  terminology: 93
  and Vice-President: 182
Political party realignment: 275, 652–655
Political party responsibility: 26–27, 627, 648–649
Political party system (U. S.), aristocratic tradition in: 58, 61–63, 64, 71, 511–512, 628
  assessment of: 627–628, 631
  attitudes toward: 11–13, 47–48, 577–579, 641–643
  compromise function: 25, 599, 653
  discipline: 636
  dissent: 654–655
  factionalism: 651, 652–653
  and government: 98–99, 179–180, 628, 630, 640–641, 655–656
  location of power in: 625
  majority v. minority: 658–659
  winning elections: 647
Politicians, attitudes toward: 485, 489, 494, 568
  as candidates for office: 485–495, 508, 536

Politicians (*cont.*)
  desire to operate government: 22–23
  as managers: 184–185, 236–238, 243–247, 495–507
  v. statesmen: 85, 494
Polk, James K.: 210, 224, 246, 611
Poll tax, *See* Voting qualifications
Pollard, James E.: 521, 541
Polling places, development: 60–61
  definition: 75–76
  location: 451, 453
Pollock, James K.: 152, 542, 543, 545, 546, 547, 550, 555, 558, 561, 563, 589
Poor, Henry V.: 548
Popper, K. R.: 460
Populism: 268–269, 366, 394
Porter, Kirk H.: 59, 72, 418, 419, 420, 457
Postman, Leo: 534
Postprimary convention: 144
Powell, A. L.: 80
Preferential voting: 144, 586–587, 625
Preprimary convention: 143, 147–149
President, office of: 153–154, 176–181, 519
Presidential elections, bellwether counties in: 503
  cycles: 394–397
  party percentages: 311–315
  and state elections: 412, 602–603
  states' rank in: 299
  supplementary methods: 261, 612, 624–625
Presidential Electors, abolition of: 621–622
  at-large election: 34, 74, 163, 610, 613, 616, 623
  ballot listing: 166
  direct election: 162–163
  district election: 162, 619–621
  independence: 157, 163
  meeting day: 436
  nomination: 162–166
  party control of: 163
  value of: 622–623
  voting: 435–436
  See also Electoral-college system; Electoral votes
Presidential nominations, acceptance speeches: 213–214
  ambition in: 222–223
  appeals to delegates in: 236

Presidential nominations (*cont.*)
  availability in: 223–232
  candidates' background for: 222
  dependence upon leaders: 235
  difficulty of achieving: 232–233
  factionalism: 234, 237
  key states in: 227–228, 247–248
  managers in: 236–238, 243–245
  money in: 235–237, 240, 602
  and preconvention campaigns: 166, 167, 220–238
  and publicity: 235–236
  and sectionalism: 298–299
  and strategy: 203, 206–213, 238–248
  and types of candidates: 233–234
Presidential preference primary: 194–200, 595, 596, 599–601
Presidential short ballot: 166
Presidents, alternatives in election methods of: 154
  identity with the times: 230
  party leadership: 177, 220
  patronage power: 178–179, 181
  policy leadership: 176–178, 180
  political background: 395–397
  popular leadership: 176
  power over national committees: 181, 220–221
  pressures on Congress: 181
  relations with Cabinet: 179
Pressure groups, odium of: 9
  See also Organized interest groups
Price, Hugh D.: 42, 391, 432, 457
Progressive Party: 50, 270, 340, 341, 561
Prohibition Party: 49–50, 341, 342
Propaganda, audiences: 479–481
  as campaign techniques: 483–484
  censorship in: 482
  deception in: 479, 482
  definition: 478–479
  predictability: 483
  techniques: 479–482
Property interests: 253–255, 258
Proportional representation: 31–32, 587–592
"Protestant vote": 370
Protestants: 337, 344, 369, 591
Prothro, James W.: 287
Public opinion, definition: 459–461
  group objectives through: 379–380
  and individuals' demands: 463–464
  role of: 458–459

Public opinion polls and surveys, and availability: 231
and election predictions: 472–473
and measurement of opinions: 469–478
partisan measurements in: 286–291

Quay, Matthew: 170, 215

Race: 362–368
Rae, Saul F.: 307, 474, 502
Rankin, Jeannette: 373
Ranney, Austin: 40, 569, 630, 650, 651, 658, 660
Raskob, John J.: 497
Rayburn, Sam: 245
Reforms: 455–457, 559–563, 567
differing attitudes toward: 284–285
Registration, See Voting qualifications
Religion: 337
and availability: 229
membership: 328
and partisanship: 287, 288, 369–371
symbols in: 467
Repeating, definition of: 141
Representation, reform of: 585–592
Representative government, limits: 253, 323
Representatives, U. S.—See Members of Congress (Representatives)
Republican-Democrat alignment, enduring nature of: 265–266
Republican Party, administrations and policies: 266, 267–271, 348, 350–351, 355
advisory committee: 173
alignments and factionalism: 266, 269, 270, 271, 274–275
formation: 169–170, 266
national convention rules: 189–190, 201–202, 212
Negroes in: 366–367
in New England: 282, 299
in New York City: 42
and presidential elections: 311–315
selection of Southern delegates: 192, 194, 201
in the South: 40, 275, 280, 281, 366–367, 601
urban strength: 308
veterans in: 358
Reston, James: 523

Reuther, Walter P.: 355
Reynolds, George M.: 83, 88, 95, 106, 110, 115, 120, 127, 140, 502, 511, 546
Richards, Allan P.: 386
Riesman, David: 110, 584
Riordan, William L.: 89, 106, 120
Roach, Hannah G.: 316
Roach, William N.: 171
Roady, Elston E.: 550
Robinson, E. E.: 5, 47, 77, 269, 271, 277, 300, 302, 311, 320, 413, 640
Robinson, James A.: 142
Rockefeller, Nelson: 118
Rogers, Lindsay: 472, 474, 476, 477, 481, 484
Rogers, Will: 211
Roosevelt, F. D., Sr.: 42, 127, 177, 181, 206, 222, 236, 244, 248, 271, 272–273, 274, 275, 280, 303, 319, 367, 395, 396, 398, 399, 408, 445, 487, 498, 519, 522, 524, 528, 529, 530, 532, 533, 549, 556, 644
acceptance speeches: 213
availability: 230
nomination (1932): 235
and third term: 233
Roosevelt, Theodore: 85, 181, 202, 220, 224, 226, 248, 270, 395, 396, 405, 409, 511, 512, 519, 560, 622
Root, Elihu: 7, 18, 36, 37, 54
Roper, Elmo: 286, 470, 472
Rose, Arnold: 365
Roseboom, Eugene H.: 278
Ross, Nellie: 373
Rosten, Leo C.: 541
Rubaiyat of Omar Khayyam: 565
Ruml, Beardsley: 324, 390
Rustow, Dankwart A.: 28

Sait, E. H.: 38, 460
Salter, J. T.: 86, 88, 113, 115, 120, 218, 402, 490, 507, 541
Sarasohn, Stephen B. and Vera A.: 110, 355
Sayre, Wallace S.: 219
Scammon, Richard M.: 304, 368, 574
Schattschneider, E. E.: 4, 5, 7, 14, 17, 18, 30, 54, 93, 218, 299, 300, 310, 320, 376, 390, 631, 655, 656, 660
Schlesinger, Arthur M., Sr.: 322, 381, 399, 400, 413
Schlesinger, Joseph A.: 40

Schmidt, M. J.: 411
Scott, Winfield: 512
Sectionalism, agricultural: 348
  and bipartisanism: 264, 267, 268, 269,
    270, 271, 272, 273, 274–275, 280,
    281–283, 298–305, 310–318
  and Constitutional period: 265–267
  economic: 295, 297, 298–299
  and federalism: 299–300, 310–311
  metropolitan: 304–305, 317
  noneconomic: 295–296, 297
  rural v. urban: 303–304, 316–317
Sections, identification and classification:
    255–259, 263–264, 266, 271, 296–303,
    311, 314, 316–317, 412, 426, 590,
    616–617
Segregation: 365
Senatorial courtesy: 104–105
Senators, U. S.—See Members of Con-
    gress (Senators)
Sergeant, John: 168
Seward, William H.: 232, 242
Seymour, Charles: 418, 437, 451, 457, 506
Shannon, David A.: 392
Sheldon, Horace E.: 353
Sherman, John: 243
Sherman, William T.: 233
Shoup Voting Machine Company: 439,
    442–444
Shull, Charles W.: 590
Silva, Ruth C.: 166, 612, 616, 617, 618,
    619, 620, 626
Sindler, Allan P.: 120
Single-member district system, as ex-
    planation of two-party system:
    30–32
  attacks upon: 585, 589–590
Slavery: 263, 264, 265, 266
Slogans, in campaigns: 535–536
  in national conventions: 242
  printed on ballots: 560
Smith, Alfred E.: 188, 209, 210, 218, 229,
    235, 303, 318, 367, 370, 467, 497,
    508, 519, 555, 608, 644
Smith, F. E.: 9
Smith, Frank L.: 552
Smith, Henry Nash: 325
Smith, Margaret Chase: 373
Smith, Rixey: 221
Smith, Rhoten A.: 152
"Smoke-filled room": 127, 246
Socialist Labor Party: 341

Socialist Party: 49, 50, 341, 342
Socialist Workers Party: 341
Sokolsky, George: 595
Somit, Albert: 358
Sorauf, Frank J.: 109, 118, 381
Soth, Laurin: 348, 390
South, direct primary in: 136–137, 139,
    623
  lack of elective offices: 66
  literacy laws: 427–428
  Negro voting: 428–432
  nominations: 63–64
  nonvoting: 576, 579
  party organization: 73, 79
  political revolt: 273
  poll tax: 428–429
  as support of Democratic Party: 270,
    271, 274–275, 280, 281, 296, 299
  in Vice-Presidential nominations: 227
Sparkman, John: 227
Spoils system, bipartisan operation of:
    115–116
  description of: 98
  influence on elections: 122–123
Spring, Samuel: 580
Stahl, O. Glenn: 358
Stalin, Josef: 459
Standing, William H.: 142
Stanton, Elizabeth C.: 338
Stanwood, Edward: 155, 156, 158, 159,
    160, 161, 166, 167, 168, 182, 189,
    211, 214, 450, 535, 570, 612, 613, 626
Starr, J. R.: 75, 124, 139
Stasiology: 15
Stassen, Harold: 236, 244
State conventions—See Nominations by
    conventions
State legislatures, party voting in: 637–
    638
State Rights Party: 50
Stedman, Murray S., Jr. (and Susan W.):
    54, 75, 118, 309, 340, 379, 392, 404,
    413
Stein, Charles W.: 221
Stengel, Casey: 401
Stevenson, Adlai: 214, 220, 229, 238, 245,
    246, 355, 395, 397, 401, 503, 517,
    522, 544, 606, 644
Stimpson, George: 67, 106, 120, 169, 182,
    439, 450, 457, 466, 512, 534, 541
Stokes, Donald E.: 288
Stokes, Thomas L.: 241, 595

Stouffer, Samuel A.: 474
Strayer, Martha: 339, 392
Strong, Donald S.: 43, 151, 427, 432, 457
Suffrage—*See* Voting
Summerfield, Arthur E.: 499
Swift, Jonathan: 9
Sydnor, Charles S.: 60, 410, 419, 436, 449, 450, 451, 457, 490, 504, 505, 512, 535, 541, 582
Symbols: 19–20, 464–467, 478, 533

Taft, Robert A.: 202, 203, 234–235, 245, 247, 283, 481, 523, 535, 617
Taft, William H.: 190, 202, 224, 226, 228, 270, 396, 409, 514, 622
Talmadge, Eugene: 40
Tammany Hall: 59, 73, 89, 95, 96
Tanenhaus, Joseph: 358, 556, 557
Tatum, Elbert Lee: 368, 391
Taylor, John (of Caroline): 326
Taylor, Zachary: 222, 224, 227, 395, 519, 611
Teapot Dome oil scandal: 548
"Telethon": 524, 525
Temperance League of America: 381
Texas, party organization: 79, 80, 93
  white primary: 431–432
Thomas, Norman: 342
Thompson, Charles A. H.: 214, 541
Thurmond, J. Strom: 446, 617
Tibbetts, Clark: 406
Tilden, Samuel J.: 366, 555
Timmons, Bascom N.: 182, 655
Titus, Charles H.: 19, 88, 89, 120, 330, 413, 465, 496, 541
  presidential cycles: 395–396
Tocqueville, Alexis de: 322
Townsend Clubs: 342
Trial balloons: 177
Truman, David B.: 294, 329, 342, 376, 392
Truman, Harry S.: 179, 180, 181, 182, 220, 227, 244, 248, 273, 274, 275, 283, 285, 367, 382, 395, 396, 397, 401, 405, 409, 413, 473, 512, 532, 573, 595, 605, 611, 616, 622, 639, 644
Tumulty, Joseph P.: 221, 532
Turner, Frederick J.: 263, 295, 298, 310, 320
Turner, Henry A.: 110, 376, 380

Turner, Julius: 27, 42, 142, 316, 320, 637, 640, 642, 654
Two-party system, superiority of: 28
  and value judgments: 21–22
Two-party system (Britain): 38
Two-party system (U. S.), and Anglo-Saxons: 37–39
  beginning of genuine: 265
  characteristics: 44–51
  citizens' relation with: 657–658
  economic basis: 252–275
  economic conflict in: 273–277
  explanations: 29–39
  and government organization: 27–28
  and ideological function: 44–45
  implications of nationalizing: 44, 656
  as "ins" v. "outs": 51, 53, 221, 265, 402, 404–410, 512–513, 648, 651
  lack of competition: 52
  as liberal and conservative: 282–285, 652–655
  moderation in: 46, 319–320, 583–584
  and organized groups: 48, 654–655, 658
  party differences in: 45–48, 275–277, 569, 636–638, 648–649, 651
  problems of alignments: 274–275
  and proportional representation: 31–32, 591, 592
  symbols of elephant and donkey: 20, 466
  voters in: 417
Tyler, John: 265, 536
Tyler, L. G.: 98, 101

Union League Club: 95
United Automobile Workers: 355, 625
United Daughters of the Confederacy: 338
United Mine Workers: 334, 356, 556
Unit rule: 211–212, 237

Van Buren, Martin: 104, 167, 169, 210, 226, 403, 536
Van Deusen, G. G.: 534
Van Doren, John: 563
Van Riper, Paul P.: 120
Vare, William S.: 91, 127, 552
Vegetarian Party: 49–50, 342
Vermont, poll tax in: 429
Veteran: 357–358
Veterans of Foreign Wars: 336

Vice-President, office of, dissatisfaction with: 182
  evolution: 182–183
  nomination of candidates for: 213, 247–248, 604–605
  status: 181–182
Voters, objection to revealing party: 132, 641
  right to have vote counted: 431
  time of decision by: 537–539
Voting, absentee: 433, 434
  in city elections: 576–577
  in congressional elections: 315–316, 575, 576
  hardships in: 60, 61
  hours of: 450
  independent: 251–252, 291–293, 399, 441, 445
  negative motives in: 223, 402, 407, 409–410
  in presidential elections: 574–576
  proxy: 436
  public: 436–438
  reasons for: 417–418
  secret: 436, 437–440
  split-ticket: 299, 412, 441
  in standard metropolitan areas: 304–305, 317
  straight-ticket: 441
  time off for: 450–451
Voting machines: 438–440, 442–444, 453, 454, 456
Voting procedures: 453–454
Voting qualifications, age: 421, 573
  in Armed Forces: 423, 433–435
  citizenship: 421
  economic: 59
  evolution in U. S.: 59–60
  exclusions in: 425–426, 577–578
  federal provisions: 419–420, 435
  and grandfather clause: 429–430
  literacy: 426–428, 434
  poll tax: 428–429, 433, 434, 453
  and race: 420
  registration: 421–425
  religion as: 59–60
  residence: 421, 577, 578
  sex: 420
  state control over: 419, 435
  standards for: 418–419
  in U. S. colonies: 59–60, 419
  white primary: 430–432

Voting turnout, dissatisfaction and tensions: 407–408
  and partisanship: 289

Wakefield, Dan: 427
Wallace, Henry A.: 248, 272, 341, 617
Wallas, Graham: 484
Walpole, Sir Robert: 8
Warren, Earl: 118
Washington (State of), party organization in: 79
Washington, George: 11–12, 62, 70, 160, 224, 383, 510, 535, 568
  administration of: 62, 156, 157, 257–259
  election to Presidency: 155–159
  and patronage: 100, 101
"Wasted" votes: 585, 592
Watson, Richard A.: 351
Weaver, James B.: 268
Weaver, Leon: 87, 92, 103
Webster, Daniel: 247, 273, 409, 544
  on parties: 12
  on patronage: 107
  on politics and economics: 254
  unavailability of: 231, 232
Wechsler, James: 479
Weed, Thurlow: 231–232
Weeks, O. Douglas: 40, 42, 43, 432, 638
Wells, Gideon: 542
Whig Party: 169, 274, 366, 637
  administrations and policies: 263, 264
  breakup: 265
  name: 262–263, 264
  national-convention rules: 212
  and patronage: 102
  and rise of bipartisanism: 265
  weaknesses: 45, 264
Whiskey Rebellion: 63, 258
White Citizens Council: 365
White, George: 498
White, Hugh L.: 167
White, Leonard D.: 100, 101, 102, 104, 105, 107, 120
White, William A.: 88
White primary: 430–432
Whitebrook, Lloyd G.: 525
Whitehead, Betty: 373
Whyte, W. F.: 88
Wiener, Norbert: 478
Wild, John: 460
Wilder, Philip, Jr.: 108

Wilkinson, Thomas: 406
Williams, G. Mennen: 355
Williams, J. Harvie: 620, 623
Williamson, Hugh: 154
Willkie, Wendell L.: 214, 222, 226, 228, 240, 246, 527, 528
nomination in 1940: 241–242
Wilmerding, Lucius, Jr.: 609, 610, 616, 618, 620, 621, 623, 624, 626
Wilson, Francis G.: 585
Wilson, James: 154
Wilson, Woodrow: 210, 220, 224, 270, 271, 319, 325, 396, 486, 497, 519, 532, 536, 611, 622
and party responsibility: 629–630
Winspear, A. D.: 460
Wirt, William: 168
Wirth, Louis: 481
Wittke, Carl: 392
Woman suffrage: 337–338, 372

Women, and equal rights: 372
in politics: 372–374
as presidential candidates: 230–231
Women's Christian Temperance Union: 339, 342
Woodward, C. Vann: 366
Woodward, Julian L.: 543, 572
World Veterans Federation: 337
Write-in candidates: 446
Wuerthner, J. J., Jr.: 353

Young, Edwin: 390
Young, Milton R.: 376–377

Zeller, Belle: 375, 376, 377, 392, 588, 590, 591, 638
Zero presidents: 394–395
Zink, Harold: 25, 27, 39, 85, 86, 88, 103, 120
Zionist movement: 337, 354